The Essential Agus

THE
ESSENTIAL
AGUS

THE WRITINGS
OF JACOB B. AGUS

Edited by Steven T. Katz

NEW YORK UNIVERSITY PRESS

New York and London

NEW YORK UNIVERSITY PRESS
New York and London

Library of Congress Cataloging-in-Publication Data
Agus, Jacob B. (Jacob Bernard), 1911–1986.
[Selections.   1996]
The essential Agus : the writings of Jacob B. Agus / edited by
Steven T. Katz.
p.   cm.
"Bibliography of the works of Jacob B. Agus": p.
Includes bibliographical references.
ISBN 0-8147-4692-6
1. Judaism.   2. Philosophy, Jewish.   3. Agus, Jacob B. (Jacob
Bernard), 1911–1986.   I. Katz, Steven T., 1944–   .   II. Title.
BM45.A3932   1996   96-46040
296.3—dc20   CIP

New York University Press books are printed on acid-free paper,
and their binding materials are chosen for strength and durability.

Manufactured in the United States of America

10 9 8 7 6 5 4 3 2 1

031298-4400T

CONTENTS

Contents

PREFACE
Steven T. Katz

The present anthology, culled from the voluminous writings of Rabbi Jacob B. Agus, is intended to make available in one easily accessible work a sampling of Rabbi Agus' large and important corpus of published and unpublished material. In addition, it serves as a compilation of primary materials that complements and runs parallel to a new set of original essays on the thought of Rabbi Agus published by New York University Press in 1996 under the title *American Rabbi: The Life and Thought of Jacob B. Agus* and edited by Steven T. Katz.

The selections of Agusana reprinted here were made by the distinguished contributors to the parallel volume of original papers. In each case the selector chose material that he felt would illuminate the particular subject matter of his contribution to *American Rabbi*. Thus the two publications are closely interconnected and readers will benefit from consulting both, though each stands on its own resources. A full table of contents for the second collection can be found at the end of this Preface.

AMERICAN RABBI: THE LIFE AND THOUGHT OF JACOB B. AGUS

ix

SELECTORS

DAVID R. BLUMENTHAL is Jay and Leslie Cohen Professor of Judaic Studies at Emory University, Atlanta, Georgia.

ELLIOT N. DORFF is professor of philosophy at the University of Judaism, Los Angeles, California.

EUGENE J. FISHER is director of the Secretariat for Ecumenical and Interreligious Affairs of the National Conference of Bishops, Washington, D.C.

NEIL GILLMAN is Aaron Rabinowitz and Simon H. Rifkind Associate Professor of Jewish philosophy at the Jewish Theological Seminary of America, New York City, New York.

STEVEN T. KATZ is director of the Center for Jewish Studies and professor of religion at Boston University.

WILLIAM E. KAUFMAN is rabbi of Temple Beth-El, Fall River, Massachusetts.

MILTON R. KONVITZ is professor emeritus at Cornell University, Ithaca, New York.

MARK LOEB is rabbi of Congregation Beth El, Baltimore, Maryland.

DAVID NOVAK is Professor of Jewish Studies at the University of Toronto and Vice President of the Union for Traditional Judaism.

MORDECAI WAXMAN is rabbi of Temple Israel, Great Neck, New York.

The Essential Agus

I

JACOB B. AGUS—AN
INTRODUCTORY OVERVIEW

Steven T. Katz

LIFE

JACOB AGUS (Agushewitz) was born into a distinguished rabbinical family in the month of Heshvan 5671—corresponding to November 2, 1911—in the shtetl of Sislevitch (Swislocz), situated in the Grodno Dubornik region of Poland. Descended through both parents from distinguished rabbinical lines (his mother being a member of the Katznellenbogen family), the young Agus, one of a family of seven children—four boys and three girls—early on showed signs of intellectual and religious precocity. After receiving tutoring at home and in the local heder, he joined his older brothers, Irving and Haim, as a student at the Mizrachi-linked Tachnemoni yeshiva in Bialystock. Here he continued his intensive talmudic and classical studies, winning high praise as an *illui* (a genius) from the faculty of the yeshiva, and also began to be exposed to the wide variety of Jewish lifestyles and intellectual positions—ranging from secularist and bundist to Hasidic—that existed among Eastern European Jews. Raised in an almost totally Jewish environment, he knew little Polish and had limited relations with the non-Jewish world.

In the mid-1920s, as economic and political conditions worsened in Poland, many members of the Jewish community of Sislevitch emigrated to Palestine. This migratory wave also included the Agushewitzes, who arrived in Palestine in 1925. Unfortunately, the economic conditions and the religious life of the *Yishuv,* the emerging Jewish community in the land of Israel, were not favorable, and the Agushewitz family, including Jacob, now sixteen, moved again in 1927. This time they traveled to America, where Jacob's father, R. Yehuda Leib, had relocated one year earlier to fill the position of rabbi in an East Side New York synagogue. R. Yehuda Leib later became a *schochet* (ritual slaughterer).

The family settled in Boro Park (Brooklyn), and Jacob, who already was able to read and write in English at a high school level, attended the high school connected with Yeshiva University. This marked a turning point in his personal life, for in this American yeshiva not only did students pursue a talmudic curriculum but—on the ideological presumption that all true human knowledge, the whole of creation, reflected God's wondrous ways—they were also exposed to a wide variety of secular and scientific subjects. For the remainder of his life, Jacob Agus would adhere to this religious–philosophical model.

After completing high school, Jacob attended the recently established Yeshiva University, where he continued both his rabbinical and secular studies, distinguishing himself in the secular realm in the areas of mathematics and science. He was so good at chemistry that he was encouraged to attend courses in this subject at Columbia University, which he did. He even briefly flirted with the idea of graduate work in chemistry. However, his deepest, commitment was to Jewish studies and to the Jewish people, and he therefore chose a rabbinical career. A favorite of the founder and president of Yeshiva University, R. Bernard Revel, and the outstanding student of R. Moshe Soloveitchik, the head of the rabbinical school, Agus received his rabbinical ordination *(smicha)* in 1933. After two further years of intensive rabbinical study, Agus received the traditional "Yadin Yadin" *smicha* in 1935, an ordination intended to place Agus on the same level as those rabbinical students who graduated from the European yeshivas and to enable him to act as a *Poseik* (halakic, or legal, decision maker).

While still at Yeshiva University, Agus also served as an assistant to R. Leo Jung, a distinguished member of the American Orthodox rabbinate. In this role, at R. Jung's request, he researched the basis for requiring a *mechitza* (a partition between men and women) in the synagogue and concluded that there was no firm biblical or rabbinical basis for this halakic requirement—an early sign of important decisions to come.

After graduation from Yeshiva University in 1935, Agus took his first full-time rabbinical position in Norfolk, Virginia. Here he began to learn the trade of an active pulpit rabbi while continuing his Jewish education. Foremost among his educational pursuits at this time was an intensive study of midrash (the rabbinic commentaries on the Bible), guided, via the mail, by Professor Louis Ginsberg of the (Conservative) Jewish Theological Seminary of America, the great authority on midrash.

Having satisfied himself that with this control of the vast midrashic material, along with his talmudic erudition, he had reached a sufficiently well-rounded knowledge of classical Jewish materials, Agus began to pursue further secular studies in a serious and concentrated way. Convinced that these pursuits required a more intensive academic environment, he left Norfolk in 1936 for Harvard University, where he enrolled in the graduate program in philosophy. At Harvard his two main teachers were Professor Harry A. Wolfson, a master student of the history of Jewish philosophy, and Professor Ernest Hocking, a metaphysician of distinction.

While in the Boston area, Agus paid his way by taking on a rabbinical position in Cambridge and continued his rabbinical learning with R. Joseph Soloveitchik, the son of his Yeshiva University mentor, with whom he quickly formed a close friendship. For several years, Agus and the younger Soloveitchik met weekly to study Maimonides' philosophical and rabbinical works, as well as to discuss a host of more contemporary theological and halakic issues.

It was also in Boston that Agus met his future wife, Miriam Shore, the daughter of Bernard Shore, a Lithuanian Jew who had immigrated to America and become a Boston businessman. The Aguses married in 1940, with R. Joseph Soloveitchik officiating.

Harvard, however, was not all joy. In this great center of learning Agus for the first time in his life encountered serious, even intense, criticism of traditional Judaism. In response, he decided to devote a good deal of his energy for the remainder of his life to explicating, disseminating, and defending the ethical and humanistic values embodied in the Jewish tradition, particularly as these values were interpreted by its intellectual and philosophical elites, beginning with the Prophets and running through Philo, Saadya, Maimonides; and such modern intellectual giants as Hermann Cohen and R. Abraham Isaac Kook. Agus' first step on this path was his doctoral dissertation, published in 1940 under the title *Modern Philosophies of Judaism,* which critically examined the thought of the influential German triumvirate of Hermann Cohen, Franz Rosenzweig, and Martin Buber, as well as the work of Mordecai Kaplan, who in 1934 had published the classic *Judaism as a Civilization* that established his reputation as the leading American Jewish thinker.

After receiving his doctorate from Harvard, and with the encouragement of R. Revel, who wished to strengthen the foundations of modern Orthodoxy in the Midwest, Agus accepted the post of rabbi at the Agudas Achim Congregation in Chicago. Though the congregation permitted mixed seating, it was still considered an Orthodox synagogue. In this freer midwestern environment, removed from the yeshiva world of his student days, the orthodoxy of Yeshiva University, and the intensity of Jewish Boston, Agus began to have doubts about the intellectual claims and dogmatic premises of Orthodox Judaism. In particular, he began to redefine the meaning of halakah and its relationship to reason and independent ethical norms. Encouraged in this direction by Chicago's leading Conservative rabbi, Solomon Goldman, and by the radical reconstructionism of Mordecai Kaplan, Agus had initiated the process of philosophical and theological reconceptualization that would define his increasingly revisionist and non-Orthodox thought.

In 1943, disenchanted with his Chicago pulpit, Agus accepted a call to Dayton, Ohio, where three small synagogues merged to form a liberal Orthodox congregation that became a Conservative congregation during his tenure. Given the proximity of Dayton to Cincinnati, he began an ongoing and cordial dialogue with the faculty and students of the Reform movement's Hebrew Union College (HUC). In particular, Agus became a colleague of R. Abraham Joshua Heschel, who had fled war-torn Europe and taken up a position at HUC. Like Agus, Heschel was the heir of a great rabbinical family and a master of all branches of classical Jewish and rabbinical learning, with a special affinity for the thought of Maimonides. Alienated from the "tone" of classical Reform, which still dominated HUC, Heschel became a regular visitor at the Agus home on Sabbaths and holidays, and Agus and Heschel formed a lifelong intellectual and personal collaboration that later manifested itself in joint efforts to alter the curriculum and character of the Jewish Theological Seminary, whose faculty Heschel joined in 1945, and in common undertakings on behalf of Jewish–Christian dialogue and various political causes.

Because of this intensive rethinking of modern Jewish thought—and perhaps also as a consequence of his engagement with Heschel—Agus turned his attention to the thought of R. Abraham Isaac Kook, the remarkable mystical personality who had served as the first chief rabbi of modern Palestine after World War I. (Kook died in 1935.) The result was Agus' *Banner of Jerusalem,* published in 1946, which sought to explore Kook's neocabalistic, panentheistic notion of holiness *(kedusha),* that is, the doctrine that God's presence was suffused throughout creation and incarnated most concretely in the Jewish people, the land of Israel, and the Torah. Deeply impressed by Kook's intense spirituality and authentic mystical vision, Agus yearned to invigorate American Orthodoxy with something of the same visionary passion. Yet at the same time, his deep engagement with Kook's traditional cabalistic *Weltanschauung* persuaded Agus that this essentially medieval worldview was one he did not, and could not, share. Modern Judaism had need of much that Kook had to teach, but it required that Kook's lessons be made available through a different vehicle, in a form more suitable to the modern temperament.

At this point Agus still hoped he could achieve his goal of effecting meaningful religious and structural change within the parameters of the Orthodox community. Like Mordecai Kaplan, he now advocated the creation of a reconstituted, metadenominational Sanhedrin (supreme Jewish religious legislative body) that would possess the power to alter— to modernize—Jewish religious life and practice. Though several important members of the Orthodox rabbinate, including R. Leo Jung and R. Joseph Lookstein, apparently were sympathetic to this call in private, none, including R. Joseph Soloveitchik, would support it openly. This lack of support, as well as Agus' own increasingly expansive and universalist spiritual and intellectual odyssey—one that was ever more appreciative of Western, non-Jewish culture and ever more critical of what Agus took to be certain forms of Jewish parochialism and chauvinism—led him, after his failure to gather support for an agenda of change and halakic reform at the Orthodox Rabbinical Council of America (RCA) convention in 1944 and 1945, to break decisively with the organized Orthodox community and its institutions.

This repercussive decision also reflected his personal experience as a community rabbi in a relatively small midwestern town like Dayton; for here Agus faced several new challenges. First, he had to be the force behind the restructuring of three congregations into one new, cohesive synagogue. Second, he had to respond to the personal needs of a religiously diverse group of Jews. Third, in the face of the unfolding catastrophe that engulfed the Jews of Europe, he had to offer Jews of limited learning who were attracted by the seductive options of assimilated life in America a Judaism that was intellectually and spiritually meaningful. Moreover, to his surprise he had discovered that he derived great satisfaction from his duties as a congregational rabbi. He enjoyed presenting sermons and lectures to his congregants—tasks at which he became very proficient, having hired a voice teacher to help him refine his oral delivery—meeting their pastoral needs, and even being active in the day-to-day affairs of the synagogue management; for example, he was very involved in the architectural design of the new sanctuary.

Disaffected from the Orthodox rabbinical community, Agus officially broke with the RCA in 1946–1947 and joined the Conservative movement's Rabbinical Assembly. In this new context, by virtue of his rabbinical erudition, his Orthodox *smicha,* and the force of his personality, he became a powerful presence and an agent of change. Over against the conservative force exerted by Chancellor Louis Finkelstein and the great Talmudist Saul Leiberman, who between them controlled the faculty of the Jewish Theological Seminary, which in turn dominated the procedural processes of the Conservative movement, Agus, in consort with like-minded Conservative rabbis such as Solomon Goldman, Robert Gordis, Morris Adler, Milton Steinberg, Ben Zion Bokser, and Theodore Friedman, argued for a more open and dynamic halakic process within the movement.

As a first major step in this direction, Agus proposed that the Law Committee of the Conservative movement be restructured into the Committee on Jewish Law and Standards (CJLS)—a change in more than name, the rationale for which is explained in his essays in *Guideposts in Modern Judaism.* He was, in turn, appointed to this committee (and to others) and remained a member of it for nearly forty years, until his death.

One of the earliest and best examples of his view on how the halakah should be interpreted is reflected in the important "Responsum on the Sabbath" that was issued by the Committee on Jewish Law and Standards in 1950. This responsum stated that the use of electricity was permitted on the Sabbath and that riding to and from the synagogue on the Sabbath was also permitted. The first decision was arrived at by use of the traditional halakic process, with one major exception, and the second was justified as a *takkanah* (a rabbinic enactment) responding to the "needs of the hour." Both instantiated Agus' view that a reverent and reasoned approach to change and the admission of where the halakah was lacking were required to revitalize Judaism in the contemporary world.

It should also be remembered that these decisions were embedded in a lengthy report that placed central emphasis on a proposed program to "revitalize sabbath observance"; this was not merely a call for radical change and a capitulation to modernity. The program was to consist of standards to be promulgated for all United Synagogue member synagogues to lift the levels of observance. In the late 1940s and early 1950s observance by laypeople was extremely lax—few attended services, many worked, few had Friday-evening dinners, and many Jewish communal organizations held events that violated the Sabbath and at which nonkosher food was served.

R. Agus, impelled by a drive for honesty and integrity, held it wrong to encourage people to attend the synagogue on the Sabbath, with the knowledge that many individuals would have to drive there, and then to insist that driving was an *averah* (a sin). In general, he thought that in keeping with modern sensibilities and the intellectual levels of congregants, the primary emphasis should be placed on encouraging mitzvot and not on alleging *averot*. The doing of each mitzvah was a good in itself and would lead to the doing of other mitzvot. This positive view, stressing the appropriate performance of mitzvot, is expressed in *Guideposts* and was an underlying principle of Agus' halakic decisions.

As a recognized halakist, Agus was also asked by the United Synagogue to defend the principle of mixed seating in two secular court cases—one in New Orleans and one in Cincinnati—both of which occurred in the early 1950s. In both cases a deceased person had left funds in his will to his synagogue on condition that the synagogue remain "traditional." At the time of the deaths, both synagogues had separate seating for men and women, but they did not have a halakically acceptable *mechitza*. In fact, by 1950 both congregations wanted to introduce mixed seating, a move that prompted a minority group of congregants to sue for the retention of separate seating on the grounds that mixed seating was a violation of the tradition.

In response, Agus pointed out that neither synagogue had a *mechitza* and yet each had been considered traditional in the eyes of the now-deceased donor. Therefore, one could argue that mixed seating was no less traditional than separate seating. He also explained the lack of any clear halakic basis for separate seating and the nature of change within the tradition.

To the Orthodox members of the Agudas ha-Rabbonim, the organization of European-trained rabbis, this was wholly unacceptable. They were engaged at the time in an effort to force all Orthodox synagogues to maintain a *mechitza* as a way of drawing a distinction between Orthodox and Conservative synagogues. In the early 1950s, under the aegis of R. Joseph Soloveitchik's Halachah Committee, the Rabbinical Council of America issued a statement that *mechitzas* were required.

The Agudas ha-Rabbonim went further and issued a ruling that prayer within a synagogue without a kosher *mechitza* was not permitted and would not fulfill a person's religious obligations. In the same ruling, they placed R. Agus in *herem* (excommunication) for teaching false ideas. Intermarriage with R. Agus and his immediate family was prohibited. It should be noted, however, that two of the *gedolai ha-dor* (recognized halakic authorities), R. Aharon Kitler and R. Moshe Feinstein, who were friends of R. Yehuda Leib A. Agushewitz, denied knowledge of and repudiated this action. Three other rabbis— Eisenstein, Groubard, and Greenfield—were also specifically placed in *herem*. However, several years later the leaders of the Agudas repudiated this document and claimed that it had never been properly executed.

In 1950, R. Agus accepted the position of rabbi at the newly formed Conservative congregation Beth El in Baltimore. A small congregation of some fifty families when he arrived, it grew over his three decades as its rabbi into a major congregation—so popular, in fact, that it had to restrict new memberships—and one of the premier Conservative synagogues in the United States.

In his role as community rabbi, Agus attended the daily morning minyan (prayer quorum), taught Mishnah or Talmud for ten to fifteen minutes to those who came, and always returned for the evening daily service as well. He visited the sick weekly, paid shivah (week-of-mourning) calls, attended committee meetings in the evenings, and met congregants at all hours. He gave serious forty-minute lectures to the men's club each week, and hundreds of men attended on a regular basis. He did oral book reviews for the sisterhood. Agus also started adult education institutes for the whole community, attended by thousands. He planned the curriculum for the Beth El schools and taught the post–bar mitzvah class. He produced a siddur (prayer book) for everyday use that allowed services to be of a moderate length. He also changed the content of the services for late Friday night, Saturday morning, and holidays in ways that retained the traditional core of the liturgy but made the services more aesthetically pleasing, intellectually challenging, and time-efficient. His approach to services included intellectual sermons and beautiful congregational singing—all in a two-hour package. Congregants came on time and participated.

As a consequence of all this effort, Beth El moved to new suburban surroundings in 1960, reopened its membership rolls, and grew to a congregation of more than fifteen hundred families. It was typical of Agus that in the construction of the new building he worked closely with the architects and designers to ensure that it would be both aesthetic and Jewishly pleasing.

Here a word needs to be said about Agus' view on the role of women in the synagogue. Consistent with his more general theological position, he felt that artificial barriers to the full participation of women should be eliminated. However, he cautioned that societal change must occur at a pace and in a manner that allowed people's sensibilities to evolve and new means of order and value-teaching to develop. He was very concerned that the family be strengthened, not weakened, and feared that a radical transformation rather than measured progress on the role of women would disrupt the family and social order. In line with this understanding, he established a bas mitzvah ceremony on Friday nights because the issue of a woman's receiving an *aliyah* (call to the Torah) had not yet been addressed by the Rabbinical Assembly. Once it was, and once the assembly's CJLS approved *aliyot* for women—with Agus' active support as a member of the committee—he instituted the practice at Beth El. Likewise, when the counting of women in the minyan was approved by the CJLS with Agus' endorsement, Beth El followed suit.

The issue of female rabbis proved more complex. Agus felt that the CJLS should address the subissues of women as judges, witnesses, and *shlichit tzibbur* (leaders of public prayer) before that of rabbi. For political reasons, the Jewish Theological Seminary addressed the issue by setting up a commission, whose report attempted to skirt these halakic issues. R. Agus was upset at the process—he thought the report was deliberately disingenuous in not addressing the other issues of status, since everyone knew that once ordained, female rabbis would perform all of the functions not addressed. Though he agreed with the result, he disagreed with the process. Therefore, in a move that surprised both the left and the right, he led a group of Rabbinical Assembly members in rejecting the report's recommendation.

During the 1950s, despite his congregational responsibilities, Agus continued his scholarly work. He was a regular contributor to a variety of Jewish periodicals, such as the *Menorah Journal, Judaism, Midstream,* and *The Reconstructionist,* and he served on several of their editorial boards. He also published on occasion in Hebrew journals. At the same time, he began to teach at Johns Hopkins University in an adjunct capacity, lecture at Bnai Brith institutes, and speak at colleges and seminaries around the country. In 1959 he published his well-known study *The Evolution of Jewish Thought,* an outgrowth of his lectures.

During this period, Agus also took an active interest in national and international affairs. A firm supporter of Franklin D. Roosevelt during the 1930s and 1940s and a supporter of the creation of the United Nations, he distrusted socialism and hated communism. However, he believed in the necessity of moderate dialogue with the Soviet Union and supported public figures such as Adlai Stevenson who advocated a less belligerent relationship with the USSR. He was a significant opponent of Senator Joseph McCarthy and openly fought McCarthyism, testifying on behalf of individuals who were under suspicion, and he invited Professor Owen Lattimore of Johns Hopkins University to lecture at Beth El. Agus fought for the limitation of nuclear weapons, even for nuclear disarmament. He even disregarded a federal requirement that Beth El build a nuclear shelter, arguing that such an action legitimated the idea of nuclear war. He supported the Civil Rights movement and efforts to desegregate Baltimore, though he opposed affirmative action programs as unfair and had a visceral fear of black inner-city violence, which threatened many Jewish shopkeepers. He was an early and consistent opponent of the Vietnam War and supported the antiwar political positions of Senators Eugene McCarthy and George McGovern. In the 1970s, Agus was an active participant in an interfaith group started by Sargent Shriver to discuss the intersection of religion and politics.

Beginning in 1968, Agus, while continuing his rabbinical duties in Baltimore, accepted a joint appointment as professor of Rabbinic Civilization at the new Reconstructionist Rabbinical College (RRC) in Philadelphia and at Temple University. Though not a reconstructionist, Agus had a long-standing relationship with Mordecai Kaplan, the founder of the reconstructionist movement, and he respected what promised to be a serious and innovative rabbinical training program. Agus taught in this capacity until the end of the academic year in 1970, when he resigned from the RRC in a dispute over the curriculum and the amount of Talmud students should be required to learn. The faculty wanted to reduce the hours devoted to talmudic study, while Agus wanted to increase them. However, he retained his professorship at Temple University and continued to teach graduate courses at that institution until 1980, when he resigned and accepted an adjunct appointment at Dropsie College in Philadelphia. He held this position until 1985, when his health would no longer permit the heavy schedule of travel that professorship entailed. Agus also had served as visiting professor in 1966 at the Rabbinical Seminary in Buenos Aires, affiliated with the Jewish Theological Seminary of America.

In addition to formal teaching, R. Agus taught the members of the local rabbinate on numerous occasions over the years. When he first came to Baltimore, he assisted local Conservative and Reform rabbis on an informal basis. In later years he gave seminars to rabbis in the Baltimore-Washington area on a bimonthly basis. Agus came to be known as the "rabbi of the rabbis" in the Baltimore-Washington area, because rabbis from all denominations of Judaism came to him not only to learn but also for advice on both personal and halakic issues. While his teaching was well known, the personal contacts were in confidence. The rabbis did invite him to speak before their congregations on a regular basis; for example, for a number of years he was invited to give a series of four lectures a year as part of the Sunday Scholar Series at Washington (Reform) Hebrew Congregation. Also, over the years students at the Ner Israel ultra-Orthodox yeshiva in Baltimore would come to see Agus at his house late at night to study Talmud. This study was kept secret because if it had become known, it would have resulted in the students' expulsion from Ner Israel.

Another environment in which Agus taught was Christian seminaries. He lectured at Woodstock (Jesuit), Union Theological in New York City, and St. Mary's Seminary in Baltimore. St. Mary's is the largest school for Catholic priests in the United States and is under the direct supervision of the Vatican. R. Agus was the first nonpriest, let alone Jew, officially authorized by the Vatican to teach Catholic seminarians. He lectured on the Jewish background and content of the Gospels for over ten years on a regular basis.

During the 1960s and 1970s, Agus was also active in projects that cut across the lines of Jewish organizational life. For example, he became involved in the recently founded organization of Jewish academic scholars and helped to establish a Jewish Philosophical Society. He worked with the American Jewish Committee at both the local and the national level on various communal issues, with the Synagogue Council of America on Jewish-Christian issues, and with a host of Jewish communal agencies.

In 1979–1980, Agus became part of a group of fifteen rabbis—five Orthodox, five Conservative, and five Reform—that was put together by the leaders of the Rabbinical Council of America (Orthodox), the Rabbinical Assembly (Conservative), and the Central Committee of American Rabbis (Reform) and that met in secret for a number of years to explore issues of theology and practice. Much of the early work of this group was based on papers prepared by Agus. He was very interested in and excited by this undertaking, as it brought him back into contact with people from Yeshiva University, including R. Joseph Lookstein, an old mentor. He found significant areas of commonality among the movements and even harbored some optimism that his quest to create a viable, religiously based Judaism for America would begin to move forward. Unfortunately, his illnesses and other factors aborted this effort.

From the 1950s, Agus likewise was active in the Jewish-Christian dialogue, in the hope of reducing anti-Semitism and helping to restructure the Christian understanding of Jews and Judaism. He worked closely with the American Jewish Committee in developing interfaith programs and was directly involved in relationships with Cardinal Bea that bore fruit in Vatican II. He worked with the National Council of Christians and Jews and actively participated in interfaith conversations, programs, and education at the local and state levels.

R. Agus became rabbi emeritus at Beth El in 1980. From 1980 to 1986, despite poor health, he continued his academic work, publishing his last book, *The Jewish Quest,* in 1983. He died on the twenty-third day of Elul, September 26, 1986.

THOUGHT

Despite all his rabbinical teaching and public roles, Jacob Agus is best known as an important Jewish thinker and student of Jewish thought.

This scholarly activity, which spanned nearly half a century—beginning with his Harvard doctoral dissertation, which became his first book, *Modern Philosophies of Judaism* (1941)—covers an enormous historical and conceptual range, stretching from the biblical to the modern era. Nothing Jewish was alien to Agus, and his research and reflections involved talmudic, philosophical, and cabalistic sources, though quite clearly the philosophical material had pride of place.

In *Modern Philosophies of Judaism*, Agus undertook the task of explicating and criticizing the work of the great German Jewish thinkers Hermann Cohen, Franz Rosenzweig, and Martin Buber—Cohen and Rosenzweig being little known in America at the time—as well as the radical theology of Mordecai Kaplan. Among this group of seminal thinkers, Agus was attracted most especially to the work of Franz Rosenzweig: "The spirit which permeates his work perforce escapes analysis. And that spirit is great and bright, glowing with the fire of God" (209). In particular, Agus was drawn to Rosenzweig's nonliteral, nonpropositional theory of revelation, which, he argued, "will be found to accord with an enlightened view of tradition and with the ways of thinking of the earnestly critical modern mind" (350). Cohen he found too abstract, his conception of God too distant from "the pattern of religious emotion" (126). Buber, whom Agus saw as a mystic, according to the criteria of mystical experience set out by William James,[1] is criticized for his subjectivism—"Devotion uncontrolled by reason is a greater danger to society than selfishness, history proves abundantly. We find this truth scrawled all over the story of mankind, in letters of fire and blood" (276)—and for his rejection of rational, objective criteria in religious and ethical matters:

> Those of us, however, who are constrained to judge the value of these "inner calls" by external standards, may well feel uneasy at the total absence of the rational element in the decision advocated by Buber. If only we were certain that the call came from God! But, what if Satan should intervene instead! How are we to tell the voice of the "Eternal Thou" from that of the "demonic Thou?" (Is not Hitler, too, a mystic?)

Alternatively, Kaplan, though described as a rationalist and a pragmatist, is found wanting because of internal contradictions within the structure of his thought, the inability "to develop [his] own conception of God to the point where it could serve as the basis of a life of religion" (315), and an excessive nationalism that, if not carefully counterpoised by "a deep conviction in the reality of the universal value of ethics" (322), could lead to disastrous consequences.

But interestingly, beyond the systematic differences among his four subjects and his individual criticisms of their work, Agus found a common core in all of them. As distinctively Jewish thinkers, all were said to recognize that

> the moral law appears in consciousness as an absolute command, spurning all selfish and unworthy motives. It can only be understood on its own face value, as an objective law of action, deriving from the structure of reality. An essential part of ethical experience is the feeling that there is an outside source to our judgments of right and wrong, that the stamp of validity attaches to our apprehensions of the rightness and wrongness of things.
>
> This conviction is not only common to the philosophers discussed in this book; it constitutes the main vantage point of their respective philosophies. While they express this fluid intuition in radically different ways, they agree in founding their systems of thought upon it. (330)

This conviction was also Agus:

> The intuition of the objective validity of ethical values must be taken into consideration. In moments of intense moral fervor, we feel that rightness and wrongness are eternally fixed in the scheme of things; that it is not our own personal dictates and impulses that are the source of ethical feeling; that the sense of authority attaching to our ethical judgment is not derived either from the opinions of other men or from the unconscious influence of society; that the things we call "good" and "bad" are similarly designated by the Eternal One, Who stands outside of us and yet dwells within us, speaking through our mouths in moments of great, ethical exaltation.
>
> This intuition is the basis of my philosophy and religion. I believe it, not only because on many occasions it has come to me with dazzling clarity, but, far more because this insight has been shared by the great thinkers of humanity, in particular, by the religious geniuses of Israel. (340–41)

All his later philosophical reflections are predicated on this religio-ethical premise.

Agus' second book, *Banner of Jerusalem: The Life, Times and Thought of Abraham Isaac Kuk* (1946), intended as a complement to *Modern Philosophies of Judaism,* on its face dealt with a surprising subject for Agus, given his modernizing sympathies, his reservations about nationalism—including certain formulations of Zionism—and his often severe criticisms of cabala; for Rav Kook (Kuk) (b. 1865; d. 1935), the first Ashkenazi chief rabbi of modern Palestine (1919–1935), was, vis-à-vis halakah, a traditional rabbinical figure, an ardent religious Zionist, and the most original and creative cabalist of the twentieth century. Yet Agus, who shared much in the way of biography with R. Kook, was drawn to Kook's profound spirituality, his intense religious passion, his concern for all Jews, his support of the rebirth of all types of Jewish life in the renewed land of Israel, his unwaveringly religious Zionism, his mystical embrace of all things as part of the divine life, his respect for the religious potential of all men. Kook, for example, had written that

> it was indeed proper that the whole content of holiness should have reference to humanity in general, for the perception of holiness is universal and the content of holiness, the bond between man and God, is independent of any nationality. This universal content would, in that event, have appeared for Jews in a special Jewish garment, but the wave of moral perversion that set in later in world history caused the elements of holiness to be forgotten among all men. And a new creation was made in Israel. . . . Nevertheless, there are still titans of the spirit who find the cosmic element in the root of Adam's soul, which still throbs in the heart of mankind generally.[2]

Agus also was drawn to Kook's intense effort "to meet the manifold challenges of modernism thru *[sic]* the deepening of piety and the inclusion therein of the new and aggressive values" (Banner, 20) and to what Agus described in the "Preface to the Second Edition" of *Banner of Jerusalem* (retitled *High Priest of Rebirth*) as Kook's "generous, outgoing humanism" (*High Priest,* ix):

> The ritual of Judaism is designed to replenish the mystical springs of idealism in human society. Loyalty to Israel, [Kook] taught, was wholly in accord with unalloyed faithfulness to humanism, since Israel was "the ideal essence of humanity." With all his intense nationalism, he never allowed himself to forget that the ultimate justification of nationalism

consisted in the good that it might bring to the whole race of mankind. (*High Priest,* 240)

It is also most probable that Agus was drawn to R. Kook because he saw in various of R. Kook's halakic enactments a prototype for his own halakic reforms. Thus, for example, one feels the passion in Agus' reprise of Kook's creative stand on the question of the observance of *sh'mittah* (the biblical law that in the seventh year the land should not be cultivated or worked) in the fledgling agricultural settlements of the renewed Jewish community in Palestine. R. Kook, developing an earlier ruling, allowed for sale of the land to a gentile as a way of circumventing the strict rule that agricultural work cease during the "sabbatical year of the land." Despite intense opposition from many in the Orthodox community, Kook held firm, and his ruling was adopted by most of the religious agricultural settlements. Here is R. Agus' description of R. Kook's moral courage during and after this religious crisis:

Aware of the undeserved abuse heaped upon him by many who sought to make partisan, political capital out of the affair, but, certain of the rightness of his position, he did not permit even a drop of rancor to enter his mind. As soon as the storm of controversy subsided, the Jewish world in Palestine and abroad recognized in him, not only a great Talmudic scholar, but one of the gentle saints in Israel. Almost despite himself, he became a central figure in world Jewry, the symbol of brave and adventurous leadership in Orthodox Judaism and the hero for thousands of young *yeshivah* students in every part of the globe. Those who maintained that Orthodox Judaism was not rigid and petrified, hopelessly caught in the paralyzing grip of ancient law and doctrine, were able to point to the rabbi of Jaffa as proof of the pliancy, adaptability and courage of genuine Orthodox leadership. (*High Priest,* 83)

For Agus, this type of religious leadership was required more generally within the Orthodox world; and in certain real ways he worked to effect, as he saw it, similar halakic transformations within the orbit of American Jewry. What Agus said of R. Kook might also be taken as the theme of Agus' own life's work:

He transformed Orthodoxy by reviving the components of humanism and secular culture in the Jewish tradition. And he appealed to the secularists to appreciate and reverence the depths of mystery, out of which spring man's genuine values. He lived "on the boundary" between the sacred and the secular, between the mystique of particularism and the outreach of universalism. And it is to this boundary that we must find our way in every generation. (*High Priest,* xiii)

In 1954, R. Agus continued his significant publishing activity with a collection of essays titled *Guideposts in Modern Judaism.* In the opening essay, "The Impact of American Culture," Agus expressed his admiration for American liberalism, his strong (correct) belief that Zionism cannot be a substitute religion for American Jews—though critical of this vicarious Zionism and various political forms of Zionism, he was a Zionist and defended the basic concept of a Jewish state in the land of Israel—his (correct) view that anti-Semitism is receding as an important issue in forming Jewish identity in America, his (correct) view that ethnicity is declining as a factor in Jewish identity in America, and his judgment that religion in America is distinctively pragmatic in tone and value. The second, quite provocative essay is an extended review and critique of various trends in the modern branches of Judaism. Agus is, not surprisingly, a keen critic of all the various conceptual efforts that have been advanced to explain, justify, or alter Judaism in the modern period. His critical comments on the philosophy of halakah of his former close friend, Rav Joseph Soloveitchik, are notable (37–44), while his own sympathy for the Conservative movement is clear in his analysis of that movement's handling of halakic matters (133–37).

The third essay in *Guideposts,* "The Jewish Community," revolves around the seminal issue of nationalism, that is, how and in what sense Judaism is Zionism. In particular, the essay is critical of Ahad Ha'Am's and Mordecai Kaplan's cultural form of Zionism and of the classical Zionist doctrine, espoused by David Ben-Gurion, among others, of "the negation of the diaspora" *(shelilat ha-golah).* (Agus was critical of all purely secular forms of Zionism, all forms of Zionism that called for the "normalization" of the Jewish people, and all efforts to deny the legitimacy of the *golah*—Jewish life outside the land of Israel.) In America, Judaism must dominate the Jewish agenda as religion, not nationalism. The fourth essay, "Ends and Means of Jewish Life in America," originally published in the *Menorah Journal* in 1949, argues the same point but advances the argument by introducing an idea that henceforth would be central to Agus' general position on Jewish matters: what he calls the "meta-myth" and defines as "that indeterminate but all-too-real *plus* in the consciousness of Jewish difference, as it is reflected in the minds of both Jews and Gentiles" (*Guideposts,* 181). For non-Jews, this meta-myth manifests itself in the belief that

> the Jew is different in some mysterious manner. In the imagination of the untutored he may appear to be now partaking of divine qualities, now bordering on the diabolical, now superhuman in his tenacity, now subhuman in his spiteful determination to survive; but always, in some dim sense, the traditional stereotype of the Jew held by the Gentiles includes the apprehension of deep cosmic distinction from the rest of humanity.
>
> This feeling has been reflected in the mythological substructure of antisemitism from its very origins. (*Guideposts,* 181)

Both positive and negative aspects of Jewish-Gentile relationships over time—and here Agus includes both anti-Semitism and Zionism—have been directed, affected, and shaped by this belief. But Agus opposes this myth in all its forms. Instead, he again argues for optimism about the status of the Jew in America and for the centrality of the religious dimension in American Jewish life. Agus' moral idealism, his unceasing universalism, never wavers:

> The true Jewish way is to rise above the hatred by recognizing it as a universal evil, found in ourselves as well as in others, and to labor for its cure both within ourselves and in the total society of which we are a part.
>
> By cleaving to the spiritual interpretation of Jewish experience we provide a means for the non-religious among us to progress in the realm of the spirit through their Jewish identification. To be sure, we have now shown how the gulf in many men's minds between adherence to spiritual values and the convictions of religion may be bridged. There is in fact a plus of conviction in religious faith, with regard to the roots in eternity of spiritual values, which cannot be obtained by the cultivation of a humanist attitude alone. Spiritually minded people will still find congregational life the best means of continuing their own spiritual progress, through self-identification with Jewish experience in the religious interpretation, and by promoting its values in the social grouping of which they are a part. (*Guideposts,* 201)

This cardinal theme is further developed in "Building Our Future in America." While continuing to criticize the notion of a Jewish "mission," Agus here advocates what he calls "the concept of a 'creative minority,'" by which he means that the American Jewish community should emphasize "autonomy, on creativeness, [which] will cherish and foster whatever cultural and spiritual values are generated by every individual interpretation, every aspiration, within the community" (*Guideposts,* 213). That is to say:

> A "creative minority" is, first, a minority that senses its underlying and essential unity with the general population, even as it is conscious of its own distinguishing attributes. We are not as a lonely island, battered by the endless waves of the encircling ocean, but one of a chain of islands which form a solid continuous range beneath the raging, restless surface. Distinctive as our history and tradition are, they yet constitute a vital part of the realm of ideas and experience upon which American civilization is based. Thus we are part of Christian culture, though apart from it; and, even as we cherish and cultivate our own specific heritage, we must not ignore the massive historical reality, the "Judeo-Christian tradition," which forms the spiritual substratum of Western civilization.
>
> Secondly, a "creative minority" evolves new values for the general community, of which it is a part, out of the peculiar circumstances which set it apart. While not officiously seeking to lead or teach or preach, it expands the cultural horizons of the whole community by developing the implications of its unique position. In this sense the Jewish community, by faithfully tracing out the inner logic of its traditions and developing the implicit truths of its peculiar status, might unfold fresh insights for the guidance of the entire American nation.
>
> Thirdly, a "creative minority" is value-centered and oriented to the future. Neither exhausted by the elemental struggle for bare survival nor overcome by the great glory of the past, its face is turned toward the sunlight of spiritual growth. It refuses either to chafe vainly against the boundaries that enclose it or to look above them with Olympian detachment as if they did not exist. (*Guideposts,* 214–15)

The Jewish community will and should remain in America and can flourish here, if it works to maintain and enhance its religio-spiritual identity.

The remaining essays in *Guideposts* are more directly theological in nature, beginning with a two-part essay titled "A Reasoned Faith" and subtitled "The Idea of God." The first half of this essay tries, with considerable success, to establish the conceptual basis for a knowledge of God; the second half deals with God as known through our experience. Here Agus argues for the intuitionist position: "When we are face to face with a striking truth, an act of triumphant goodness or an event of surpassing beauty, we recognize the quality of time-transcending reality, as an immediate, direct experience, and we thrill to it as a fact, not merely a reasoned argument" (*Guideposts,* 257). The most important theological claim advanced in this essay, however, is that God is to be conceived of in personal rather than impersonal terms:

> Shall we think of Him in physical-philosophical terms such as Principle, Power, Absolute, Form or Cause, or shall we employ the personalistic-biblical terms of Father, the Merciful One, the Living God? Manifestly, the only concept which, in our experience constitutes the polar opposite to the concept of mechanical causation. Yet, God is not the Self or Soul of the universe, but, as the Kabbalists correctly pointed out, He is the Soul of the Soul, etc. of the universe. And we have no way of knowing how many links there be found in the spiritual chain of being. (*Guideposts,* 268)

The second theological paper deals with the absolutely essential and Jewishly unavoidable issue of "Torah Mi-Sinai," that is, the nature and claims of revelation. Rejecting the rejection of faith while affirming the authenticity of revelation, yet aware of the philosophical problems that the traditional, literalist notion of revelation has engendered in the modern world, Agus attempts to steer a middle ground that argues for the reality of nonpropositional revelation. God speaks to us in our ethical intuition, in our religious feeling (piety), and in moments of inspiration—our ethical intuitions being the most "objective" category (*Guideposts,* 288)—rather than in the literal legal and historical formulations of the Bible:

> Since revelation occurs between man and God, it is obviously unscientific and therefore untruthful to assume that the human or particular element is not felt in the content of revelation. Inevitably, the "Torah speaks the language of men," in all its finiteness, limitation and particularity. Thus, objectively, God's speech is not verbal expression; God's com-

mand is not a specific precept; God's behest is not the fire, clamor and whirlwind of dogmatic rivalries. (*Guideposts*, 291–92)

What makes Judaism distinctive—what makes Judaism, Judaism—is that it translates this encounter with God into legal categories—"the command of God," (296), the halakah:

> Halachah is for us the way in which God's word is progressively being shaped into ways of life. This view is in perfect harmony with our historical knowledge of the evolution of Halachah. The laws of Halachah were not only consciously ordained for the purpose of fostering the "normative" consciousness; they were also in part subconsciously evolved out of the inner religious drive, to translate "feeling" into "law." In this way, the regimen of Halachah made the observant Jew feel that the whole world was encompassed by the sway of Divine Law. (*Guideposts*, 297)

However, the halakah is, like all products of revelation, an admixture of human and divine elements:

> We must make it clear from the objective viewpoint that the revealed character of Jewish legislation refers to the general subconscious spritual drive which underlies the whole body of Halachah, not to the details of the Law. The vital fluid of the Torah-tree derives from the numinous soil of the Divine, but the actual contours of the branches and the leaves are the product of a variety of climatic and accidental causes. It is of the very essence of the reasoning process to recognize that the particular is accidental and contingent. . . . All that we can and do affirm is the Divine character of the principle of Halachah. From the viewpoint of history, we know that the Shulchan Aruch did not spring fullblown from the mind of Moses. It is the product of gradual evolution, in which diverse social and economic factors were conjoined with those of a purely religious character. (*Guideposts*, 298–99)

And the outcome of this complex, evolutionary, historical process, according to Agus' criteria, allows for change, modification, and innovation in the halakah—but not for the rejection of the Law itself, that is, a full denial of the category of halakah per se.

Agus then applies this understanding of the halakah in the next three essays, which are devoted, respectively, to (1) "Law in Conservative

Judaism"; (2) "Laws as Standards"; and (3) "Pluralism in Law." He rightly recognizes the fundamental difference between his understanding of halakah (also that of the Conservative movement) and that of the Orthodox tradition. With honesty he acknowledges, "Manifestly, then, the Conservative movement cannot be described as falling within the limits of 'Halachah'—true Judaism. On the other hand, it does not reject 'Halachah' in the slightest in theory and it does not accept Halachah very largely in practice" (*Guideposts,* 310–11). Alternatively, he contends that, for the Conservative movement, "the present is more determinative than the past" (312); and therefore the movement must depend on the legitimacy of its own considered *takkanot* (rabbinical enactments), in order to modernize the halakah as it deems necessary. To aid in this process, Agus supported the creation of a modern Sanhedrin, empowered to make halakic change as necessary:

> I would therefore suggest the creation of a Synhedrin-Academy to consist of Jewish scholars and leaders in every field of culture and achievement, chosen from among the world-wide community of Israel. Meeting annually, this convocation of the best representatives of the spirit of Judaism would deal with the moral and spiritual problems of the land of Israel, of the Jewish people, and of humanity. Its discussions and decisions would, of course, not be binding upon the government of Israel, though it would no doubt take up for review and critical appraisal the moral issues involved in the debates and proceedings of the Kenesset.
>
> The discussions of the Synhedrin-Academy, constituting as they would a running commentary upon the varied problems of the Jew in particular and of man in general, would in time perhaps come to form a new Talmud, expressive of the best thought of our time. World Jewry, through its leading representatives, would be given the opportunity to think together, and to unfold the implications of Jewish tradition for the understanding of the crises of our own day and age. (*Guideposts,* 376–77)

Guideposts' collection of essays ends with two critical book reviews: the first of Mordecai Kaplan's *The Future of the American Jew* (New York, 1948), the second of *The Theology of Paul Tillich,* volume 1 in the Library of Living Theology (New York, 1953).

R. Agus' fourth major publication was *Evolution of Jewish Thought* (1959). Growing out of a variety of teaching contexts, this study sets out to provide an educated review of the main historical stages of Jewish thought. It opens with chapters on the Bible and the Rabbinic period—including, interestingly, a chapter on "The Secession of Christianity" (chapter 4)—and then moves through "The Rise of Jewish Rationalism" (chapter 6), "The Decline of Rationalism" (chapter 7), cabala (chapter 9), Hasidism (chapter 10), and "The Age of Reason." This last chapter analyzes the work of Baruch Spinoza and Moses Mendelssohn and the repercussive intellectual and political issues that arose from the debate over Jewish emancipation after the French Revolution. The specific character and the academic strengths and weaknesses of individual aspects of this long and fascinating history, as retold by Agus, are treated at length in several of the original essays in the companion volume to the present anthology. For my part, I would call attention not only to Agus' wide erudition and mastery of the entire range of rabbinical philosophical, and cabalistic materials but, more importantly, to his methodological insight:

> In this volume, we propose to show that Judaism in nearly every age resembled an Oriental tapestry in the plenitude of colors and shades it embraced and unified. The comparative unity of law and custom concealed the great diversity of thought and sentiment. Within the authentic field of Jewish consciousness we recognize an unending struggle between the self-exaltation of romantic nationalism and the self-dedication of prophetism; between the austere appeal of ruthless rationality and the beguiling seduction of self-flattering sentiments; between the gentle charm of moralistic and pietistic devotions and the popular preference for routinized rites and doubt-proof dogmas. The mighty tensions within the soul of contemporary Western man were reflected faithfully and clearly in the currents and cross-currents of the historic stream of Judaism. (*Evolution,* 6)

In contradistinction to older, monolithic renderings of the Jewish past, Agus here expresses the most important insight generated by the best modern Jewish scholarship, namely, that Judaism is a "rich spectrum of colors ranging from the twilight moods of mysticism to the stark clarity of rationalism, from the lofty heights of universal idealism to the dark depths of collective 'sacred egoism' " (400).

Yet despite this diversity, this absence of a central authority, this tolerance of various intellectual approaches and understandings, there was an abiding "unity of the Jewish tradition." This lay in the text, the context and the emphasis of all schools in Judaism. The unity of a river consists of the bedrock and banks of the channels through which it flows, the intermingling of the tributaries in the course of its flow and the impetus of direction shared by its waters. In Judaism, the unity of source is the chain of sacred literature, the unity of source is the chain of sacred literature, the unity of bedrock is the social structure of Jewish life and the unity of impetus is the quest for the realization of the Godlike qualities of the human personality. The text is the series of sacred documents, the Pentateuch, Bible and Talmud, and all the varied books of the classical tradition. All interpreters of Judaism, as far as their ideas may range, return for inspiration and guidance to the same sacred books. There exists also the unifying code of conduct regulating worship, home ritual and everyday life. (*Evolution*, 413)

Despite Agus' desire to "modernize" central aspects of classical Judaism, he was too rooted in the rabbinical tradition to fail to understand (and to want that) some residue of vital meaning and authority remain in the canonical texts of the tradition and in the ongoing Jewish community.

However, with regard to the Jewish people, Judaism, and the Jewish community, Agus is quick to add—sensitive to the criticism regularly directed at Jews and Judaism, that they are "narrow-minded" and paro-chial in their interests and concerns—that Jews and Judaism need be neither of these things. In particular, he reinterprets the doctrine of Israel's chosenness, of the Jews as the "chosen people," in this way:

Is it the intention of this concept that the people ought to be dedicated to the ideals of God, or does it mean that the life of the people is supremely important because the ideals of God are attached to it? The two alternatives do not appear to be mutually exclusive. Yet there is a real choice between the two attitudes in every concrete situation. In the one case the community acts as a "prophet-people," gauging its policies by means of universal, ethical principles and sacrificing its own temporal welfare for the sake of its ideals. In the other case the welfare of the nation itself is ranked as the supreme value and embraced with the wholeheartedness and totality of devotion that is characteristic of genuine piety. In effect the second alternative turns nationalism itself into a zealous religion and all universal ideals are accorded only secondary significance. The posture of a "prophet-people" is still assumed, but the ideals of prophecy are no longer the goal of the nation's existence and the measuring rod of its actions, only so much guise and disguise. (*Evolution*, 419–20)

Ever sensitive to the universal ethical implications of religious dogmas, Agus here once again deciphers the tradition in broad, humanistic, and nonexclusivist terms.

Agus' next major publication was his two-volume *The Meaning of Jewish History* (1963). This can fairly be described as an ideological history of the Jewish people from biblical times to the present. The concern of the narrative is to show the breadth and diversity of Jewish historical experience, its plural spiritual and political forms, while de-mythologizing its essential character. In the course of his exposition, Agus continually throws light on the dialectic between ethnic and universal loyalties in this history, arguing against the ethnic, mystical, romantic, and chauvinistic and for the ecumenical, rational, philosophi-cal, and broadly humane elements within the tradition. The latter values and principles are to be our model and guide into the Jewish future.

Two historical cases discussed at some length are especially notable. The first, "The Jewish-Christian Schism," is of unusual interest because of Agus' long and profound involvement in Jewish-Christian dialogue. According to Agus, the missionizing success of Christianity was the result of two phenomena. One was the specific Christian resolution of the tension within Judaism between the Jewish people and others:

First, the tension between the Jewish people and humanity. It is not true that the Christians were more universalist than the Jews, opening up the boon of salvation to all men, while the Jews sought to keep the Promise all to themselves. But it is true that Christianity was less *nation-centered* than Judaism. The fact is that within Pharisaic Judaism there was a powerful, liberal trend that aimed to disseminate the faith among the nations and that taught "the pious of the nations have a share in the world to come." There was also a tendency to take account of the monotheistic currents of piety, flowing beneath the surface trends of paganism. On the other hand, in the first two centuries, Christian thought was distinctly illiberal, discountenancing the belief that God reveals Himself in different ways to different peoples. Did not the Fathers consign the vast majority of mankind to perdition and open the gates of paradise only to those who accepted their dogmas?

Yet the Christian community was far better disposed for the winning of converts than the Jewish people, precisely because it was a church, not a historical-sociological group. The essential difference lay in the fact that the Christian community consisted of *individuals,* who gained or lost their own title to salvation. Anyone could enter and anyone could leave this "Israel of the spirit." The promise of salvation and the warning of damnation were directed to the individual. In Judaism, the individual could dissipate or enlarge his heritage, but the faith was still his heritage, as a member of "the people."

In Christianity, the balance between the individual and the historic community was shattered by the rejection of "the people" as the focus of Divine concern. Any number of individual Jews could enter the Christian community, but "the people" as such was repudiated. (*Meaning,* 1:167–68)

The other phenomenon was the way in which the Church shattered the tension, inherent in Judaism, between prophecy and priesthood:

The evolution of events was paradoxical. For in the beginning, it was the renewal of the mystical-ecstatic phase of prophecy that served as a substitute for the priestly concern with ritual. To become a Christian was to be baptized by the "Holy Spirit." (*Meaning,* 1:168)

The second case concerns the development of the Talmud. As a true *talmid chacham,* Agus knew his Talmud, and therefore his reflections on its creation, organization, and meaning—in light of his liberal philosophy of halakah—are full of theological interest. He does not disguise the narrow aspects of talmudic teaching—for example, regarding the difference between Israel and the nations—but he is at pains to indicate that the opposite tendencies are to be found in the Talmud as well. And he leaves no doubt as to where his preferences lie:

Within the Talmud, the tension between humanism and ethnicism was continuous and unresolved. It was possible for Talmud-trained people to effect their own resolution of these conflicting trends, some magnifying the one aspect of the tradition and some emphasizing the other aspect. As we have noted previously, the masses of the people probably inclined toward the pole of ethnic pride and prejudice, while the saintly few thought in universal and humanistic terms. (*Meaning,* 1:222)

In the second volume of *The Meaning of Jewish History*, Agus takes his narrative forward into the medieval and modern eras. Of the two chapters on the medieval period, the first is a rather long essay on what might be called Jewish social history. It intelligently, and with considerable historical learning, seeks to explore the perplexing issue of Jewish survival in this hostile epoch. Agus rightly stresses that Jews were subjects, as well as objects, who took responsibility for their circumstances and acted to defend their interests and assure their collective survival. And Agus pays special attention to the role of messianism in this historical context (*Meaning*, 2:269–80). The second essay deals critically with what Agus calls "The Triumph of Subjectivism: Qabbalah." Agus is fundamentally unsympathetic to this tradition of esoteric speculation, which he describes in this way:

> While philosophy seeks to explain life in terms of the categories of *spirit*—logic, ethics, and esthetic harmony—Qabbalah aims to take account of man's existence, especially the destiny of the Jew, in terms of the categories of *life*—the rhythms of the Divine Being and the various emanations deriving from it. To the philosopher, all human history is ultimately reducible to mechanical forces and mathematical formulae. To the Qabbalist, all explanations are ultimately the narration of a series of events in the *Divine Pleroma* (the Emanations and Sefiroth), which stands between God and man. Yet Qabbalah is not altogether a reversion to pagan mythology, since the impetus of monotheism is still contained within it. The Qabbalist strains with all the powers of personality toward the dark, comforting shadows of insulated piety, but there is a desperate tension in his soul for he has been driven from the paradise of naivete by the subtle serpent of speculation.
>
> It is important to take a good look at the bizarre pattern of Qabbalistic speculations, for Qabbalah was not merely a temporary aberration of Medieval Jews. As a matter of fact, Qabbalah captured the Jewish mind at the end of the fifteenth century, at the very time when the diverse movements of Renaissance, Reformation, and Counter-Reformation were struggling for supremacy. Steadily through the sixteenth and eighteenth centuries, it dominated the minds of Jewish thinkers. (*Meaning*, 2:287–88)

Agus attributes the power and attraction of cabalistic thought to the oppressive situation in which Jews found themselves in the late medieval and early modern eras. Amid the brutality and persecution, cabala provided a "pious fantasy" that consoled the Jewish people while they waited "supinely for the Messiah" (2:289). Agus' understanding of cabala is not flattering, and there is more to be said about the nature of cabalistic teachings than Agus says, but he is certainly correct in his historical judgment that

> Qabbalah . . . aided the Jew in his struggle for survival under adverse conditions, but it also separated him from any intellectual-ethical communion with the emerging society of mankind. It provided an exciting mythology, elevating every Jewish custom and every nuance of the liturgy to the rank of a world-saving enterprise. At the same time, the speculative notions and the debris of ancient philosophical systems contained within its volumes offered substitute satisfactions to the insistent quest of the intellectuals. But these services of Qabbalah were purchased at the high price of deepening the isolation of the Jew. The ritual barriers were raised higher. Even more important, the division between Jew and Gentile was now univerally assumed to be one of metaphysical substance and origin. It was no longer a matter of belief that separated the Jew from "the nations," but the fact that the Jewish souls were derived from the Divine Being, while the souls of the nations were sparks from the satanic *Pleroma* of shells, the so called "other side" (*Sitra Ahra*). On this basis, there could not possibly be any kind of intellectual contact between Jews and Gentiles. (*Meaning,* 2:295)

In his treatment of the modern period, Agus begins by tracing the influence of cabala in Sabbatianism (seventeenth century) and Hasidism (eighteenth century). He then turns to the process of emancipation in Western Europe and retells the familiar tale of Spinoza; Mendelssohn; the Haskalah; the "Jewish Question" before, during, and after the French Revolution; early Zionism; bundism; Napoleon; romanticism; Reform Judaism; Dubnow's "autonomism"; and the rise of modern anti-Semitism. Agus has read widely on all these matters, makes sober judgments (whether or not one agrees with all of them), and is, in general, a reliable guide to this complex historical development. What make the exercise interesting are Agus "opinionated" views on nearly every subject reviewed. He knows who the "good guys" and the "bad guys" are—and he has thought through the merits of the various ideological positions reported on.

In the "Epilogue," Agus discusses the rebirth of the State of Israel and the state of Jewish life in America. One must remark that the thirty-odd years since the publication of the *The Meaning of Jewish History* have shown Agus to be about half right in his view for the future of Arab–Israeli relations and of American Jewry—half right on the former because, while his insistence that peace was achievable has been proven true in the peace with Egypt, Jordan, and the accord with the Palestine Liberation Organization, his idealism that caused him to counsel:

> At this writing, we cannot foretell the course of Israel's development, nor can we outline a specific policy for immediate implementation. But this can be said with certainty, the moral health and the very life of Israel depend upon its finding ways to win over the Arabs. The task is not one of concluding pacts with the neighboring governments, but of achieving true *bonds of fraternity* with the Arab people. To this end, the Arabs within Israel's borders and those encamped on its periphery must be converted into a bridge of friendship between the two ancient peoples. By working for them and with them, smoldering hates can be transmuted into a new blaze of amity and unity. (*Meaning*, 2:466)

still seems out of touch with the harsh mass situation on the ground.

Likewise, Agus' optimism vis-à-vis America was largely correct. The United States has proven to be a "golden land" of unlimited opportunities for Jews, especially in the last thirty years. Yet the corresponding erosion in commitment to the identity and precepts of Judaism—indicated most clearly by the rate of intermarriage—within the American Jewish community is unprecedented and threatens the very shape and enduring vitality of the community.

In 1966, Agus published his mature views on Jewish ethics in *The Vision and the Way*. Polarity again dominates his thought. Ethics is born of two sources, the intellect and feeling. Jewish ethics is notable, commendable, by virtue of the fact that it manages to hold these two "pillars" in creative tension. In consequence, the transrational vision which asserts that God is the source of all goodness and beyond human judgment is balanced by "the Way of 'justice and righteousness,'" that is, a rational, universal ethic which requires that ethical norms be subject to human investigation and judgment: "To believe in God, Who is beyond Nature and *unlike* all things, and, at the same time, to insist that the moral-rational Way, as it is manifest in the light of reason, is a revelation of His Will—this dual conviction establishes the central polarity in biblical religion" (*Vision and Way*, 33).

Agus traces this fruitful polarity through the main ethical categories of Jewish thought and life. He draws a rich picture of Jewish ethics from the talmudic texts that provide an image of an "Ideal Society"—with its concern for social justice, the poor, and the oppressed; its "massive philanthropic enterprises" (*Vision and Way*, 63); and its hope for messianic perfection, brought on by human deeds, at which time evil will be finally eradicated and the good vindicated—and an "Ideal Personality" (chapter 4) in which the moral "hero is the incarnation of the ideal(s)" (73), an heir of the prophets, a person who blends priestliness and the virtues of the "Disciple of the Wise" (78):

> Unlike the saint, he never forgets the claims of humanity—of family, of work, of innocent delights. He is aware of the "Evil Desire" and of the many ways in which it corrupts man's best intentions, but like the philosopher, he reveres the regenerative and intellectual qualities of human nature. (*Vision and Way*, 79)

In addition, Agus deciphers "The Virtue of Obedience," "The Infinite Dimension of Purity," "The Ethics of Self-Realization," and "Freedom and Determinism." For each topic, he presents the tradition in its variety, its strengths and limits. In sum, the book is, through his extensive quotation of primary materials, mainly an anthology of rabbinical doctrines on the good life, compiled by a master anthologizer.

In regard to the contemporary situation in comparative historical perspective, Agus makes the important observation that

> looking at the total spectrum of Jewish ethics, one sees that the popular notion, that the Law governs every question in Judaism, is a fallacy. As has been pointed out, there were indeed times when nearly all creative principles were locked into the rigid categories of an all-embracing law that was presumed to be God-given. But *pan-halachism* is more characteristic of extremist Orthodoxy in the modern period than of the premodern tradition. In the Talmud the cast-iron logic of legalism was balanced by several factors—the projection of an ethical domain "beyond the law" *(lifnim mishurat hadin)*, the recognition of the validity of the mores and morals of civilized humanity *(derech eretz)*, and by the mystical or philosophical notions that were cultivated in esoteric circles.

As late as the sixteenth century, when the Shulhan Aruch was codified, the realm of Perfection beyond the Law was cultivated in pietistic and mystical literature. (*Vision and Way*, 321)

He goes on to argue:

An analysis of the inner dynamics of Jewish ethics does not reveal a monolithic philosophy of life. It is possible to resolve the tension between the Vision and the Way by choosing any one of many positions within the ethical–religious polarity. Tolerance of differences is a marked characteristic of rabbinic discussions — "these and these are the words of the Living God." A broad consensus on any one issue may emerge at any one time, but we can hardly dignify any one synthesis as being the Jewish, or the "normative" one. (*Vision and Way*, 324)

Once again, Agus calls for a rational, nonracial, non-"in-group" ethic. Such an inclusive ethic includes a concern for the world order, the search for international justice, disarmament, the end of nuclear weapons, and support for the United Nations so as to mitigate conflict and prevent new crimes against humanity.

Tradition and Dialogue, published in 1971, continued Agus' reflections on a variety of contemporary issues. Here the essays concern the Jewish–Christian dialogue; Agus' ongoing dialogue with Arnold Toynbee over the continuing vitality of Judaism (for Toynbee's change of opinion regarding Judaism, due to Agus' influence, see volume 12 of Toynbee's *A Study of History: Reconsiderations,* which includes two essays by Agus published as an appendix); his response to the "God is Dead" movement, in two sympathetic but critical essays collected under the heading "Dialogue with the New Atheists"; a variety of issues identified as "Dialogue with Secular Ideologies"; and last, ten essays on internal Jewish matters ranging from "The Prophet in Modern Hebrew Literature" to "The Concept of Israel" and "Assimilation, Integration, Segregation: The Road to the Future."

What strikes one in reading these diverse pieces is the breadth of Agus' Jewish learning. Not only are biblical, talmudic, medieval, and modern sources critically evaluated, but Hebrew poets such as Hayim Nahum Bialik and the modern Hebrew authors Saul Tchernichovsky, J. H. Brenner, and Uri Zvi Greenberg are engaged in a serious and informed way.

In 1978, Agus published his next to last book, *Jewish Identity in an Age of Ideologies*. This is a sustained effort both to situate the Jew and Judaism vis-à-vis the most important European ideologies of the past two hundred years and to view these ideologies from a Jewish perspective. He begins with Mendelssohn and the issue of Jewish-Christian relations in the age of Enlightenment. He then reviews Immanuel Kant's hostility toward Judaism and the efforts by Jewish Kantians such as Moritz Lazarus, Hermann Cohen, and Leo Baeck to bring about some rapprochement between Kantianism and Judaism. He considers the attitude of the German romantics toward religion, Judaism, and religious reform, including a critique of Jewish "romantics," that is, those who deprecate the role of reason in the religious life, such as Samuel David Luzzatto (1800–1865) and, in Agus' controversial view, Samson Raphael Hirsch (1808–1888). In chapter 4, titled "Are the Jews 'Ahistorical'?" Agus takes up a critical dialogue with G.W.F. Hegel's historicism and three Jewish responses thereto by, respectively, Samuel Hirsch (1815–1889), Solomon Formstecher (1808–1889), and Nahman Krochmal (1785–1840). Hirsch and Formstecher tried to meet Hegel's criticism of Judaism by calling for the internal reform of Judaism. Krochmal, a far deeper thinker, tried to respond to Hegel by denying the applicability of the Hegelian system to Judaism; that is, he argued, in contradistinction to Hegel's systemic claims, that Judaism is *not* subject to the normal laws of national development and decay that govern other nations. Other schools and movements dealt with by Agus are nationalism; socialism in its various forms, namely, bundism and Marxism; Zionism; racism in its myriad forms; Bergsonian vitalism; Jewish existentialism (Buber and Rosenzweig); biblical criticism; Barthianism (Karl Barth [1886–1968]); and Toynbeeism (Arnold Toynbee). In every instance Agus is a serious and respectful critic; in every dialogue he makes the case for a liberal, humanistic, nonromantic Judaism, shorn of the meta-myth of Jewish being. Though one can differ with Agus' various judgments, one can never ignore or dismiss them. In the end, he has accomplished what he set out to achieve in this work: to view Judaism from both within and without as it struggles with modernity.

Agus' last work, a collection of theological essays, was published in 1983 under the title *The Jewish Quest*. "The Jewish Quest," he tells us, "is to make oneself and the world fit for the indwelling of the Divine Presence; theologically speaking, it is a yearning for the 'kingdom of heaven' " (vii). Here familiar themes are taken up, clarified, and deepened: America and the Jewish people, Jewish self-definition, classicism and romanticism, the meta-myth, Zionism, holism, nonliteral revelation, Jewish ethics, Judaism and the world community, Maimonides' philosophical rationalism, the defense of Conservative Judaism, the foundations for a modern revision of the halakah anti-Semitism, and various aspects of the Jewish-Christian dialogue. To the end Agus was sober, cautious, yet hopeful; opposed to fanaticism of all sorts; an enemy of Jewish "self-mythification," of "biblical claims of singularity and uniqueness," of "the seductive fantasies of self-glorification" (*Jewish Quest,* 10); suspicious of messianic and self-serving metaphysical claims; and intensely committed to a demanding ethical vision that united all peoples.

Agus' philosophical and theological corpus can, in summation, be seen as extensive, consequential, and provocative. Perhaps best characterized as a neo-Maimonidean, Agus belongs to the long chain of Jewish rationalists that includes Philo, Saadya, Maimonides, and Mendelssohn, and which has been more recently represented so brilliantly by Hermann Cohen. Like Cohen, of whom he wrote admiringly, Agus held firm to the conviction that Judaism was explicable and defensible in universal rational and ethical terms. Possessing their own deep spiritual integrity, the classical sources of Judaism embodied a profoundly humane moral vision that was both philosophically compelling and metaphysically attractive. Those who, out of religious frustration or a failure of philosophical nerve, seek to turn away from rational analysis and criteria in their deconstruction of Judaism and its God do a serious disservice to the intellectual and spiritual tradition they seek to excavate and defend. Here is the ground of Agus' sharp disagreement with Buber's dialogical philosophy and his reservations about the work of Abraham Joshua Heschel and other contemporary religious existentialists. Agus admired their religious intentions but faulted their method and logic.

Agus was not a stranger to religious feelings or deep traditional religious commitments; but he held that these necessary aspects of the religious life must be regulated by constraints that only reason could supply. Thus, for example, though a longtime colleague of Mordecai Kaplan, he was critical of Kaplan's reconstructionist views, not only because they lacked grounding in the traditional halakic and intellectual sources of Judaism but also because Kaplan's systematic revision of Judaism along functionalist anthropological and sociological lines was spiritually impoverished and impoverishing. God, for Agus, had to be more than "the power that makes for salvation"; Jewish behavior had to be more than sociologically defined "sancta," and the obligations of Torah and halakah more than pragmatic initiatives and psychological panaceas. Indeed, it was this tension, this firmly held belief in the necessity of holding onto a more traditional spirituality, that led Agus to admire the genuine mystical personality of Rav Kook, even though he was profoundly critical of the cabalistic *Weltanschauung* that defined Kook's entire thought world. Kook's spirituality, his sense of the presence of the Living God, attracted Agus—not least because he shared the same openness to the numinous.

Agus' rationalism also separated him from all forms of romanticism, the most important modern Jewish manifestations of this inclination being found in certain versions of Zionism. While he defined himself as a supporter and defender of the Jewish right to a national state, Agus' outspoken criticism of aspects of American Zionism—that is, nationalism as a substitute for authentic religious commitment—made him many enemies. In arguing for this position, he manifested an attitude close to the intellectual-spiritual stance that had been struck by Franz Rosenzweig, though Rosenzweig was writing in the 1920s, before the Shoah and the creation of the modern State of Israel. Like Rosenzweig, and unlike Buber, Agus was suspicious of all forms of nationalism, including Jewish nationalism. I believe his stance vis-à-vis the State of Israel was too critical and that he was too optimistic with regard to both the future of Jewish life in the diaspora, especially in America, and Israeli-Arab relations, but he was certainly right to warn of the pseudomessianic temptations that the creation of a renewed Jewish state, and especially Jewish victory in 1967, has spawned. The State of Israel need not be the messianic state for it to be Jewishly necessary, legitimate, and worthy of our unwavering, though not uncritical, support.

If Agus had serious reservations about the systematic work of other nineteenth- or twentieth-century Jewish thinkers and movements, he shared, in a broad sense, their call for halakic revision. This he did on ethical and rational grounds—and here especially he becomes a "modern" thinker among the pantheon of modern thinkers, stretching from the early reformers to certain contemporary feminists. However, even in this area of fundamental concern, his approach was distinctive. As a true *talmid chacham,* he demanded that the halakic changes he supported be undertaken in a way consistent with the spirit of the halakic process as he understood it. In consequence, he was considered too conservative and traditional for many of his Conservative rabbinical (and other) contemporaries, while for the Orthodox (and certain members of the Jewish Theological Seminary hierarchy) he was too radical.

Agus was also distinctively modern in his openness to interreligious dialogue. Almost all major Jewish thinkers of the twentieth century—for example, Baeck, Rosenzweig, Buber, and Heschel—have significantly involved themselves in reevaluating the relationship of Judaism and Christianity. Jacob Agus did likewise. Given his universal ethical norms and broad humanistic concerns, this is in no way surprising. Agus assumed that all people shared certain basic values, which were then individually expressed in the world's differing religious traditions. It was this dialectic between the universal and the particular that lay at the base of his deep, personal engagement in this area and that energized his theological conversation with such dialogue partners as Arnold Toynbee, Cardinal Bea, and Baltimore's Catholic hierarchy. Then too, like many Jewish thinkers before him—Philo, Maimonides, Mendelssohn, Cohen, and Rosenzweig—his participation in ecumenical dialogue was not free of apologetic concerns; that is, he sought to defend Judaism against its detractors and to share its spiritual and intellectual resources with others on the assumption that non-Jews could benefit from its distinctive wisdom.

Taken altogether, Agus pursued his own unique, quite American modernizing vision, which ardently sought to remain in touch with the wellsprings of the rabbinical tradition while being open to the intellectual and moral currents of his own time.

CONCLUSION

The selections from R. Agus' writings in this volume and the selectors' original essays in the new companion volume titled *American Rabbi: The Life and Thought of Jacob B. Agus* (New York, 1996) consider the main aspects of Agus' life and work in more detail. They flesh out the broad and repercussive themes adumbrated in a schematic way in this Introduction. And taken as a whole, they present a broad and substantial picture of a remarkable American rabbi and scholar. One does not have to agree with all of Agus' views—I, for one, disagree with aspects of his writings on Zionism, nonpropositional revelation, the Torah, the vitality and future of Conservative Judaism, and the basis for revising (or not revising) the halakah in our time—but one has to admire his commitment to the Jewish people everywhere, his profound and unwavering spirituality, his continual reminders of the very real dangers of pseudomessianism and misplaced romantic zeal, his devotion to "Talmud Torah" in all of its guises, his personal piety, his willingness to take politically and religiously unpopular stands, his defense of such men as Owen Lattimore and Arnold Toynbee, his consistent faith in reason, his erudition in Western philosophy, and his tenacious ethical humanism, which knew no ethnic or racial boundaries. In sum, much of the best of Jewish and Western tradition was incarnated in a *yeshiva bocher* from Sislevitch. May his memory be for a blessing.

NOTES

1. William James, *Varieties of Religious Experience* (New York, 1958), 292–93.
2. Jacob B. Agus, *High Priest of Rebirth* (New York, 1972), 154–55; hereafter cited as *High Priest*. This book is the retitled second edition of *Banner of Jerusalem*.

SELECTIONS
Steven T. Katz

THE FOLLOWING SELECTIONS have been chosen by Steven T. Katz and are taken from *The Vision and the Way* (New York, 1966), 73–93 and 321–60; and from *The Jewish Quest* (New York, 1983), 171–94.

2

THE IDEAL PERSONALITY

THE ÉLAN of a religious culture is frequently symbolized in the one or more hero-images that it produces. The hero is the incarnation of the ideal. Greater than life-size, he represents in perfect measure that which others must try to emulate in whole or in part. The saint and the knight are the two chief hero-images of medieval Europe, as the philosopher and the warrior were of the Greco-Roman age, the monk and the missionary of early Christendom, the many-sided artist of the Renaissance, the gentleman of Victorian England, and the captain of industry of the rapidly expanding American republic.

In Holy Scriptures, we recognize a deliberate design to avoid the exclusive adoration of one hero-image. Moses is by far the outstanding personality, but, we are told, he was ineffective by himself. He needed the help of Aaron and the support of the seventy-two elders. "Man of God" though he was, he was still liable to sin and to punishment. None of the beloved patriarchs, prophets, kings, or priests was either sinless or infallible, though they were "chosen" by the Lord as His elect. Actually, God alone is the hero, and all that man can achieve is to attempt "to walk in His ways." But, God cannot serve as a hero-image, for man is not allowed to imitate Him in all ways; man may not be "jealous," for instance, though the Lord is jealous, for in Him this quality derives from His uniqueness and His absoluteness. And only the Lord is Absolute.

Several hero-images reflect the diverse ideals of the Bible. To the end of the biblical period the priest remains a most revered authority.

Abraham offers tithes to Melchizedek, "the priest of God Most High."[1] And Malachi, the last of the prophets, describes the priest in these glowing terms:

> The Torah of truth was in his mouth, and no wrong was found on his lips. He walked with me in peace and uprightness, and he turned many from iniquity. For the lips of a priest should guard knowledge, and men should seek instruction from his mouth, for he is the messenger of the Lord of hosts.[2]

A priest is universally the guardian of the tradition. He performs the ritual in the ancient, wonted ways, without question and without deviation. His life is hedged about with special ordinances, which keep him undefiled. In Israel, only those born in priestly families, possessing authenticated pedigrees, could officiate. The priests formed a caste of their own, with secrets that were jealously kept from the eyes of the general public. In terms of religious needs, the priest responds to the emotional-mystical phases of piety. To the worshipper, the priest is the surrogate of the Deity. The ritual is mysteriously, magically effective— but only when the priest performs it. The more archaic and irrational the ritual is, the more it symbolizes and dramatizes the mystery of life itself. The priest ministers to the *feelings* of religion—anxiety, guilt, the need for lustration, the desire to express gratitude and to seek forgiveness. To priests, worshippers come, seeking solace and comfort, the blessing of sharing in the redemptive Grace that flows from above. And if they seek instruction, it is the hallowed precepts of tradition they look for, not original words of wisdom.

The priestly hero-image was included in the Bible, but it was also transcended. Moses announces his intention of founding a "Kingdom of priests and holy nation."[3] Every Jew is to share in the glory of priesthood, shunning "the unclean" and periodically cleansing himself from "all their defilements." While the priestly prophet Ezekiel seems to say that the priest alone must not eat unclean and improperly slaughtered meat *(nevelah uterefah)*,[4] the Torah ordains this law for all Jews.

The prophet is probably the most distinctive hero-image of the biblical period. While all religious cultures have priests of one kind or another, we do not know of exact parallels to the classical prophets. The institution of prophecy was, of course, common in the Near East. But while the Canaanite prophets, like the Hebrew "prophetizers," were primarily ecstatics, the Hebrew prophets were philosophers as well as rhapsodists, statesmen as well as enthusiasts, religious innovators rather than temple functionaries. The prophet's source of authority is not the tradition, but the living Word, which is like a "burning fire" in his bones. He articulates a personal inspiration, which, he feels, *ought* to be convincing to others as it is convincing to him.

The prophet is a mediator between the voice of reason and conscience, on the one hand, and the feelings of mystical reverence, on the other.[5] He revitalizes the tradition precisely because it is transformed in his consciousness, by the white fire of religious ecstasy. The prophet sees the heavenly Vision of Perfection, as if it were concrete reality here on earth, but he interprets its meaning in the rational terms of everyday life—the Way of Wisdom.

A renowned biblical scholar pointed to the tension between prophet and priest, as forming the perennial source of self-renewal in the West:

The Judeo-Christian religious continuum is historically a synthesis of two main factors. First, we have a developing pattern of Covenants between God and early Israel, governing faith, ethics and cult. Second, we see the interaction of two distinct elements in periodic tension; an institutionalized hierarchy of religious functionaries and an upsurge of charismatic spiritual leaders. Because of this ever-renewed tension between hierarchy and charisma, the Judeo-Christian continuum has always been capable of periodic self-criticism—a process to which Western conscience owes its persistent revivals of sensitivity.[6]

The Sage is the third hero-image of the Bible. He is the teacher of practical wisdom, which is concerned with the attainment of success and happiness here on earth. The precepts of wisdom were more or less international in character. Such books as Job, Proverbs, and Ecclesiastes deal with human problems in a context that is not specifically Jewish. Since the biblical canon includes the writings of the Sages as well as those of the priests and prophets, it tempers the fiery lava of prophetic revelation with the cool stream of gnomic wisdom that is both practical and universal. The Sage appeals to reason, human experience, or the common mind of man. The tripartite structure of the Hebrew Bible suggests that the wisdom of the Sages derives from God, as much as the prophet's revelation and the priest's tradition. Wisdom asserts, "The Lord created me at the beginning of His work, the first of His acts of old."[7] Thus wisdom antedated the Torah in the mind of God. The prophet Jeremiah was inclined to equate the three components of the sacred tradition: "For there shall not be lost the Torah of the priest, the word of the prophet, and the counsel of the Sage."[8] Following is Philo's description of the stature of Moses as prophet, priest, and philosopher:

> We have now fully treated of two sides of the life of Moses, the royal and the legislative. We must proceed to give account of the third, which concerns his priesthood.[9]
> . . . The chief and most essential quality required by a priest is piety, and this he practiced in a very high degree, and at the same time made use of his great natural gifts. In these, philosophy found a good soil, which she improved still further by the admirable truths which she brought before his eyes, nor did she cease until the fruits of virtue shown in word and deed were brought to perfection. Thus he came to love God and be loved by Him, as have been few others. A heaven-sent rapture inspired him, so markedly did he honor the Ruler of the All and was honored in return by Him. . . .
> But first he had to be clean, as in soul so also in body, to have no dealings with any passion, purifying himself from all the calls of mortal nature, food and drink and intercourse with women. This last he had disdained for many a day, almost from the time when, possessed by the spirit, he entered on his work as a prophet, since he held it fitting to hold himself always in readiness to receive the oracular messages. As for eating and drinking, he had no thought of them for forty successive days, doubtless because he had the better food of contemplation. . . .[10]
> . . . Afterwards the time came when he had to make his pilgrimage from earth to heaven, and leave this mortal life for immortality, summoned thither by the Father Who resolved his twofold nature of soul and body into a single unity, transforming his whole being into mind, pure as the sunlight.[11]

In the post-biblical period, the three biblical hero-images were blended into a new heroic image, that of the Disciple of the Wise *(talmid hacham).* This popular ideal emerged slowly, after a number of experiments. The early pietists *(hassidim horishonim)* of the second century, before the common era, formed probably the basic society of spiritual athletes, out of which there diverged in later years the Essenes, the Theraputae of Philo, the sectarians of the recently found Dead Sea Scrolls, and the Pharisees. In their turn, the Pharisees were pulled apart by the tensions between a militant activism and a submissive quietism, between zealous exclusiveness and a missionary universalism, between the passion for individual excellence and the ideal of serving the entire community, between the puritanical ambition to control every aspect of life and a human recognition of the virtues of diversity.

After the destruction of the Temple, the ideal of the *talmid hacham* began to preempt the collective energies of the people. The Sages of the Mishnah and the Talmud were called *hachamim,* Wise Men, by the people, but they referred to themselves by the less pretentious designation, Disciples of the Wise. This hero-image, the *talmid hacham,* was modified in subtle and diverse ways in the various lands of the Diaspora. Yet, its basic lineaments may be discerned in life and literature down to our own day.

The Disciple of the Wise is a blend of priest, prophet, and sage. Like the priest, his life is hedged about with numerous rituals, from the moment he awakens to the reading of the *Shema* in bed. He eats "his secular food in accordance with the priestly requirements of purity." [12] The law envelops his life as an Oriental woman is wrapped in garments, from head to toe. He delights in obedience, shunning the very thought of deviation. Rabbi Akiva, incarcerated in jail, was given only a small cup of water, which he could use either to wash his hands, in keeping with the injunction of the rabbis, or drink. He preferred to wash his hands, saying, "I'd rather die than transgress the words of my colleagues." [13]

Yet, the Disciple of the Wise is a prophet, as well as a priest. In matters of thought, he is restless. Disdaining to force his mind into the rutted grooves of a hallowed tradition, he questions and assays the ancient answers. He seeks to understand "the reasons of the Commandments"; he confronts the realities of the market place and battles for the amelioration of the ills of society; he is cognizant of the ethical dimension, beyond the line of the Law; as an athlete of the spirit, he endeavors to reach beyond the goals of moral perfection to that mystical consummation of *Ruah hakodesh,* when the Spirit of Holiness lends a Divine resonance to every utterance. His piety is activist, even if not militant, full-bodied and community-minded, even when it plumbs the depths of the soul and aims at the salvation of the individual. In addition, he is also an heir of the Sages, willing "to learn from all men," keeping his mind open to the varied challenges of the environment, and continuing the tradition of coining brief, memorable precepts for instruction in the ways of the good life. He is a lifelong student, refusing to decide an issue "in the presence of his master," but he is also a dedicated teacher, who offers instruction freely to all who will listen, even as God confers wisdom freely upon all who listen with heart and soul.

Like the philosopher, the Disciple of the Wise ranks the pleasure of learning as his chiefest delight. His vision of heaven is a gathering of "saints sitting with their crowns upon their heads, enjoying the radiance of the Shechinah." [14] But, in this world, the Disciple of the Wise must resist the temptation to withdraw from the community and to contemplate Divine truths in splendid isolation. For, like Moses, he is a "servant of the Lord," entrusted with His work. It is his task to build up the philanthropic and educational institutions of the community and to supervise their operation. Wherever he settles, "the problems of the city become his problems." [15] Like the prophet, he knows that his task is in this world, here and now. "More beautiful is one hour of Torah and good deeds in this world than all the delights of the world to come." [16] But like the pietist, he conceives of Perfection as subsisting beyond the boundaries of "this world": "Better is one hour in the World to Come than all the glories of this world." [17] Like the philosopher, the Disciple of the Wise seeks to achieve a harmony and an equilibrium in which no endeavor is carried to excess. But, like the saint, he dares to scale the heights and storm the heavens, seeking the "nearness of the Lord," with all his heart, all his soul, and all his might. Yet, he knows that to love God is "to be occupied in the upbuilding of the world," not to nurture in serene isolation a glowing ember in the soul, but to labor in the community so that the Name shall be beloved by all. [18]

Unlike the saint, he never forgets the claims of humanity—of family, of work, of innocent delights. He is aware of the "Evil Desire" and of the many ways in which it corrupts man's best intentions, but, like the philosopher, he reveres the regenerative and intellectual qualities of human nature. "I have created the Evil Desire, but man need not be enslaved by it, if he will be guided by Torah." [19] The good life is possible, virtue is attainable, "the Lord created man straight" and "the soul which Thou hast given me is pure"; [20] "a person commits a sin only when the spirit of folly enters in to him." [21] The varied pleasures in life are not evil in themselves, but only when they are abused. Happiness is not only possible, it is mandatory: "And thou shalt rejoice before the Lord thy God in all that thou puttest thy hand unto." [22] The

Shechinah rests upon a man only when he is joyous, and a person will have to render an account for the pleasures that came his way, and he did not enjoy.[23]

The ideal, we recall, is not of an intellectual elite, but of all the people: "Every person should try to imitate the ways of a Disciple of the Wise."[24] In practice, only a few will qualify for this distinction: "Who is a Disciple of the Wise?—He who is worthy of being nominated as a leader of the community."[25]

Aristotle speaks of the high-minded man "who is first of all a good citizen," and "who can rule and be ruled." The Romans enlarged the virtue of citizenship into the ideal of patriotism. Cicero wrote: "But, when with a rational spirit you have surveyed the whole field, there is no social relation among them all more close, none more dear than that which links each one of us with our country. Parents are dear; dear are children, relatives, friends; but one native land embraces all our loves."[26]

Since the Sages did not belong to the governing elite of an independent state, the ideal of citizenship or patriotism assumed among them a different aspect—that of voluntary leadership in behalf of communal needs. They acknowledged the validity of the laws of the imperial government—at least, the later Babylonian rabbis did—"the Law of the government is Law."[27] But they shied away from any close association with the political and military authorities.[28] Their patriotism took the form of organizing philanthropic organizations, primarily for the Jews, but by extension also to the entire community.

We are to feed the Gentile poor along with the Jewish poor, to visit the Gentiles who are sick along with the Jewish sick, to bury their dead together with the dead Israelites—in order to multiply the ways of peace.[29]

As an heir of the prophets, the true disciple is likely to be the storm-center of society. With the vision of Perfection glowing in his mind, he will not be content to submit tamely to entrenched evils: "A Disciple of the Wise who is liked by *all* the people of the community—it can only be because he does not rebuke them in respect of their duties toward heaven."[30]

While humility is the highest virtue, the leader must be proud of his work and aware of the high worth of his task; hence, in a way, also proud. "A Disciple of the Wise must have one-eighth of one-eighth of pride."[31]

The Disciples of the Wise supported themselves by their own labors, in order to be independent and unbiased: "Rabban Gamaliel, the son of Rabbi Judah the Prince, used to say: 'It is good to combine the learning of Torah with the acquisition of worldly skills, for sin is overcome when one labors in both directions. Torah without a craft leads to frustration and sin.' "[32] They were to combine the refinement of feeling, the training of the intellect, and the rigors of practical leadership.

Rabbi Hanina, the son of Dosa, used to say: "He whose fear of sin is prior to his wisdom, his wisdom will endure. But if his wisdom is prior to his fear of sin, his wisdom will not endure.

"If his deeds are more than his wisdom, his wisdom will endure, but if his wisdom exceeds his deeds, his wisdom will not endure.

"If one is liked by his fellow men, he is liked by the All-Present; if one is disliked by his fellow men, he is disliked by the All-Present."[33]

Following are some of the guidelines of the ideal disciple.

Ben Zoma used to say:
"Who is the Wise Man?—He who learns from all ... Who is the wealthy man?—He who rejoices with his portion ... Who is the mighty man?—He who conquers his own desire ... Who is the truly honored man?—He who honors his fellow men. . . ."[34]

Rabbi Zadok used to say:
"Do not separate yourself from the community and do not make yourself into a pleader of private causes, and do not make your learning a crown in which to glory or an axe with which to dig." So too Hillel would say, "He who utilizes the garment of a scholar for private purposes is doomed." Hence, you learn that he who makes personal profit from the words of Torah takes his life from the world.[35]

Yehudah ben Tema used to say:
"Be fierce as a tiger, light as an eagle, swift as a deer and heroic like a lion to do the will of your father in heaven.

Those who are bold-faced will go to hell, those who are shamefaced will go to heaven." [36]

This is the way of Torah—eat bread with salt and drink water by measure. Sleep on the ground and endure the hardships of life, while you labor in the Torah. If you do this, you will find happiness and goodness—you will be happy in this life and attain goodness in the world to come. [37]

This is the way of a Disciple of the Wise:

"He is humble and lowly of spirit, alert and world-wise, beloved by people and not domineering toward the people of his own household. While he is ever critical of himself [fearing sin], he judges other people according to their deeds. He says—'all the things of this world, I do not really care for.' He willingly covers himself with dust by sitting at the feet of the wise. No man can see evil in him. He presents his questions logically, and he replies correctly.

"Be as an open vessel, which does not shut out fresh air, and as a deeply plowed field which keeps its waters, like a waxed can which keeps its wine, but also as a sponge which absorbs all things.

"Do not be as a large opening which makes the room drafty, but also not as a tiny opening, in order to avoid staleness and stagnation. . . .

"Let all your ways be for the sake of heaven. Love heaven, but also fear it. Tremble over the Commandments, but also rejoice in them." [38]

A Disciple of the Wise must be modest in the way he eats, drinks, washes and oils himself, dresses and carries himself, in his manners and in his deeds. . . . He does not speak in the presence of one greater than he, does not interrupt the words of a colleague; he thinks before he replies; he orders his words, and if he does not know, he admits the fact; he always consents to the truth.

He is in perpetual pursuit of truth, as against falsehood, of faithfulness as against robbery, of modesty as against vulgarity, of peace as against war, of the counsels of elders as against those of youth, of courage as against lust. [39]

At times the Sages described the path of the Disciple as an endless upward climb, consisting of the mastery of level after level of virtue.

Greater is Torah than priesthood or royalty, for royalty is acquired by thirty rungs, priesthood by twenty-four and Torah by forty-eight—namely:

Learning, training one's ear, disciplining one's lips, the understanding of the heart; by awe and reverence, by humility, joy and purity; by serving the wise, clinging to friends, by discussion, reflection on Scripture and Mishnah; by lessening one's preoccupation with business, the ways of the world, pleasure, sleep, conversation and laughter; by patience, a good heart, trusting the wise and accepting anguish cheerfully; by recognizing one's place, rejoicing in one's lot, hedging his words and avoiding self-righteousness; by being beloved, loving the All-Present, loving people, loving justice, good deeds and rebuke; by shunning honors, pride and authority; by sharing the burden of colleagues; helping them toward the scale of merit and leading them toward truth and peace; reflecting on his learning, adding to what he has learned by the dialectic of questions and answers; learning for the sake of teaching and doing; sharpening the wisdom of his teacher and giving right direction to the tradition that he has heard. . . .[40]

This is how a Disciple of the Wise takes care of his health and his appearance:

Hillel the Elder used to walk part of the way with his pupils, after they left the House of Study. Said his pupils to him—

"Our teacher, where do you go?" Said he, "To do a *mizvah.*" "And what is that *mizvah?*" said they. He replied, "To wash in the bath-house." Said they, "What kind of *mizvah* is this?"

He explained, "The pictures and statues of Kings are washed and cleaned by men who are especially designated for this task. It is considered a high honor. But, I, being created in the Divine Image, must surely deem it a privilege to take good care of His image."[41]

A Disciple of the Wise is deserving of death, if a blemish is found on his garment.[42]

THE MODESTY OF THE HILLELITES

For three years, the houses of Shammai and Hillel debated—each faction maintaining that the law was in accord with its position. Then a Divine echo announced—"These views and these views are the words of the Living God, but the law is in accord with the words of the House of Hillel." But if both opinions are the words of the Living God, why is the law according to the words of the Hillelites?—Because they were modest and well-mannered. They teach the doctrines of the Shammaites as well as their own; furthermore, they state their opponent's position first, and only then do they give their own opinion.

Hence, we learn that whoever humbles himself, the Holy One uplifts him, and whoever exalts himself, the Holy One humbles him.[43]

THE DIALECTIC OF TORAH-STUDY

When Rav Kahana came up to the land of Israel [from Babylonia, at the beginning of the third century], Rav advised him, "Don't question the decisions of Rabbi Yohanan for seven years."

He found Resh Lakish, repeating the daily lesson to the pupils. Rav Kahana inquired, "Where is Resh Lakish?" And they said, "Why do you ask?" He answered—"One may pose ever so many questions [in regard to the lesson] and give so many answers." Then Resh Lakish came to Rabbi Yohanan and said, "A lion came up out of Babylonia."

On the following day, Rav Kahana was placed in the first row in front of Rabbi Yohanan. The latter stated one law. Rav Kahana did not question it; then, a second law was proposed; still, Rav Kahana did not question. He was then demoted seven rows, till he came to the last row. Said Rabbi Yohanan to Resh Lakish, "The lion you spoke of turned out to be a fox."

Said Rav Kahana, "May these seven rows count for the seven years that Rav asked me to abstain." He stood on his feet and asked Rabbi Yohanan to repeat the lesson from the beginning. When Rabbi Yohanan stated the first law, Rav Kahana confronted him with one question, then another, so that he was returned to the first row.

Rabbi Yohanan was sitting on seven pillows, and he would remove one pillow for every question that he could not answer. In the end, all the pillows were removed and he sat on the ground.[44]

Rabbi Yohanan was deeply grieved [over the death of Resh Lakish]. Said the Sages, "Who will undertake to comfort him?"—Let Rabbi Elazar Ben Padat go, for his lessons are very keen. He came and sat before Rabbi Yohanan. Whatever Rabbi Yohanan would say, Rabbi Elazar would support with additional evidence.

Then Rabbi Yohanan cried out, "Are you like Resh Lakish?" Whenever I would state a law, he would put to me twenty-four objections, then from the questions and answers, the matter would be clarified. But you only say—"let me show you how right you are." "Do I need you to tell me I am right?"

He then stood up and tore his clothes, crying, "Where are you Resh Lakish? Where are you Resh Lakish?"[45]

THE MYSTICAL POWER OF TORAH-LEARNING

The Disciples of the Wise were heirs of the prophets. "From the day when the Temple was destroyed, prophecy was taken from the prophets and given to the wise."[46]

The ideal Disciple of the Wise was, therefore, somewhat of a mystic. His learning was more than an accumulation of knowledge—it was also the attainment of a high degree of holiness. The Divine Presence *(Shechinah)* was in attendance whenever the Disciples debated the Law.

"From the day when the Holy Temple was destroyed, the Holy One, blessed be He, possesses in His world only the four ells of Halacha."[47] In the Talmudic period, the Disciples of the Wise were believed to experience mystical visions and to possess miraculous powers. While this phase of their personality was not always elaborated by way of tales of wonder, mystical potency forms part of the ideal. The Disciple of the Wise is more than a scholar; he is a pneumatic personality, a spiritual athlete, forever striving to approach the Divine Presence and, on extreme occasions, disposing of superhuman powers.

VICARIOUS ATONEMENT

Said Rabbi Yose, son of Abin: "All these years that Rabbi Judah the Prince suffered from toothaches, there was not one miscarriage in the land of Israel and no woman suffered the agonies of childbirth."[48]

Many legends circulated about the friendly relations between Rabbi Judah the Prince and a Roman Emperor. In one of them, the Emperor exclaims: "I know that even the least one of your disciples is capable of reviving the dead."[49]

On the day when Rabbi Judah the Prince died, a Divine Echo *(bath-kol)* came out from heaven and announced: "Whoever was present at the time when he died is invited to the life of the world to come."

"Ever since he died, there was no longer humility and the fear of sin." [50]

THE GIFT OF THE HOLY SPIRIT

When Haggai, Zechariah and Malachi, the last of the prophets died, the Holy Spirit was removed from Israel. Nevertheless, they were able to make use of the Divine Echo *(bath-kol)*. One day, the disciples were sitting in the garret of Guriah at Jericho, when they heard a heavenly Divine Echo announce:

"There is one here who is worthy of the Shechinah resting upon him even as it descended on Moses our teacher, but his generation is not worthy of this honor!"

Then the Sages directed their eyes to Hillel the Elder, and when he died, they said of him — "Oh, the saint, oh, the humble man, a disciple of Ezra." [51]

They said of Rabbi Jonathan, son of Uziel, — At the time when he would sit down to learn Torah, every bird that flew above him would immediately be burned. [52]

The story is told of Rabbi Yohanan ben Zakkai [died c. 80 C.E.] that he was riding upon a donkey, with his disciple Rabbi Elazar ben Arach holding the reins. Said Elazar, "My Master, teach me a chapter concerning the Divine Chariot."

Said the Rabbi, "Did I not tell you that one may not teach about the Divine Chariot save to one person at a time — and he must be one who understands by himself?"

"May I then present to you some teaching that I derived from you?" asked Elazar, and Rabbi Yohanan consented. He descended from his donkey, wrapped his coat around him and sat under an olive tree. "Why did you get off the donkey?" asked Elazar, and his teacher replied:

"Can it be that you will speak of the Divine Chariot, and the Shechinah is with us, and the ministering angels follow after us, and I shall be riding upon a donkey?"

Then Rabbi Elazar, son of Arach, began to preach of the intricacies of the Divine Chariot, and a fire came down from heaven and irradiated the trees of the field, which began to sing their praises to God . . . And an angel cried out of the fire — "This, surely, is the right account of the Divine Chariot." [53]

MIRACLES AND MARTYRDOM

Said Rav Papa to Abaye [early fourth-century Babylonian scholars]: "Why were miracles performed for the early scholars, but none seem to happen to us? Is it on account of Torah? In the days of Rav Yehuda, they would learn only the Order of Torts, while we learn all six Orders. Yet, the moment Rav Yehuda would remove his shoe [to begin a fast-day] the rains would come down, while we cry and torment ourselves—yet no one minds us?"

Rav Papa replied:

"The early scholars used to give their lives for the holiness of the Name, but we no longer give our lives for the sanctification of His Name."[54]

CHARITY AND COMPASSION FOR ALL

The Disciples of the Wise were to beware of an excess of piety and zeal. Elijah the Prophet was punished for "demanding honor for the Father, but ignoring the honor of the son (Israel or mankind)." They were expected to concern themselves with the institution of charity and to be charitable to all.

Rabbi Shimeon and his son, Rabbi Eliezar [second-century rabbis], lived twelve years in a cave. Then Elijah came, and standing at the entrance, called out, "Who will tell Rabbi Shimeon that the Emperor had died and that his decree is nullified?" [Rabbi Shimeon was suspected of sympathy with Jewish rebels.]

Then, they came out of the cave and saw people going about their work, plowing and sowing. They cried out, "What? These people neglect the life of eternity and concern themselves with the life of the hour?" Wherever they focused their vision, that place would immediately burn down. Then a Divine Echo *(bath-kol)* was heard to say:

"Did you come out to destroy my world?—Return to your cave."[55]

Rabbi Judah the Prince opened his granaries in a year of famine and said,

"You are welcome to enter, if you have mastered the Pentateuch or the Mishnah or the Talmud, or the Law, or the legends—but those who are totally ignorant may not enter."

Then, Jonathan, son of Amram [a disciple] pushed himself to the front of the line, crying, "Rabbi, feed me."

Said he, "Did you learn Torah?" and Jonathan replied, "No."

"Did you learn Mishnah?"

— "No."

— "By what merit should I feed you?"

— "Feed me, as one feeds a dog and raven."

He was given a portion of grain. When he came out, Rabbi Judah was aggrieved—"Woe is me, I gave my bread to an ignoramus."

Said his disciples, "Perhaps, it was Jonathan who refused to derive an advantage from his knowledge of Torah."

Then, Rabbi Judah realized his mistake. Thereafter, he would say: "Let all enter to be fed."[56]

Whoever shuts his eyes to the needs of charity, it is as if he worshipped idols.[57]

Rabbi Eliezar would give a coin to the poor, and only then would he say his prayers.[58]

The Disciple of the Wise remained the central hero-image of Jewish life down to the present day, but different aspects of this ideal were emphasized in the different periods of Jewish life and among the several schools of thought within Judaism.

The rationalists would stress the philosophical ideal of universality and harmony—*Ha-adam hasholem,* the complete or perfect man, who is at home in all the domains of wisdom. He studies philosophy, follows the progress of science, reads poetry, even as he faithfully pursues the ways of Jewish piety in prayer, Torah-study and communal responsibility. His guidelines are reasonableness and moderation.

The romanticists would stress the superiority of Jewish over secular studies, and of faith and tradition over reason and the general consensus of mankind. They would minimize the importance of a sense of balance and harmony, while they would rhapsodize over the wonder and mystery of the transrational treasure in Judaism and the transnatural vision of the world to come. They would glorify all that is specifically Jewish, and restrict their philanthropic enterprises to their own people. They would still study "external categories of wisdom," but largely for the purpose of recognizing the "vanity" of non-Jewish learning and of all worldly goods. In the minds of the romanticists, the Vision of eternal life and the World to come triumphed over the concerns of this world and the life of reason.

The great legalists of the Orthodox tradition were frequently neither rationalists nor romanticists, in the philosophic sense. They considered all speculation to be a danger-filled area, bordering on the forbidden. The Law encompassed the whole of life, and meditation upon its intricacies was the noblest task of the Jew. The Disciple of the Wise of this school was a legalist and a pragmatist, satisfying his romantic-mystical interests in private prayer, public worship, and the most scrupulous observance of the rituals.

But, even the dry legalistic Torah-scholar was not a stranger to the occult nuances of mysticism. It was essential to his own self-image. Here are excerpts from a recent book by the master of a Lithuanian, non-Hassidic Yeshiva:

> ... and in pursuing the dialectic of the law you feel how you are uplifted. Your soul unites itself with the spiritual currents, holy and pure, that flow from above, and you exult in sacred delight. You begin to feel the sacred and exalted joy for which there is no comparison in all the pleasures of this world ... You then begin to feel the motivations and arguments of the Law in all the parts of your soul, and the right thought comes to you by itself, and this is a kind of holy inspiration *(meain Ruah Haokodesh),* like the Holy Spirit. . . .
>
> He used to say that he would hear and feel a kind of ring above, whenever he would render a difficult decision in matters of law, a ring, which he was certain confirmed and endorsed the truth.[59]

The mystics and the Qabbalists concentrated on the single goal of achieving direct immediate contact with the Divine. They would, as a rule, spend the first half of their life in mystical studies and exercises, returning to public activity after they had attained certain "levels of holiness." They would then be honored as "holy men," whose prayers could work wonders. The Zaddikim of the Hassidic movement in the eighteenth century belonged to this school.

NOTES

1. Genesis 14:18.
2. Malachi 2:8–10.
3. Exodus 19:6.

4. Ezekiel 44:31.

5. "The Prophet in Modern Hebrew Literature," *HUC Annual,* 1957.

6. Wm. F. Albright, *Samuel and the Beginnings of the Prophetic Movement* (Cincinnati, 1961), p. 19.

7. Proverbs 8:22.

8. Jeremiah 18:18.

9. Philo, *Life of Moses, Loeb Classics* (Cambridge, Ma. 1930), II, 66.

10. *Ibid.,* p. 88.

11. *Ibid.,* VI.

12. Hagigah 18b.

13. Airuvin 21b.

14. Berochot 172.

15. Moed Katan 6a.

16. Abot 4:8.

17. *Ibid.*

18. Sifri; Deuteronomy 6:5.

19. Kiddushin 30b.

20. Ecclesiastes and standard Prayer Book.

21. Sota 3a.

22. Deuteronomy 12:18.

23. Shabbat 30b; Yerushalmi, end of Kiddushin.

24. Berochot 17b.

25. Taanit 10b.

26. Cicero, *De officiis.*

27. Gittin 10b.

28. Aboth 2:3.

29. Gittin 61a.

30. Kethubot 105a.

31. Sota 5a.

32. Aboth 2:2.

33. *Ibid.,* 3:11–13.

34. *Ibid.,* 4:1.

35. *Ibid.,* 4:7.

36. *Ibid.,* 5:23.

37. *Ibid.,* 6:4.

38. Derech Eretz Zutta.

39. *Ibid.*

40. *Ethics of the Fathers,* VI, 6.

41. Leviticus Rabba 34.

42. Shabbat 114a.

43. Airuvin 13.

44. Baba Kama 117.

45. Baba Mezia 84a.
46. Baba Bathra 12a.
47. Berochot 46.
48. Genesis Rabba 33.
49. Aboda Zara 10a.
50. Kethubot 113a.
51. Sanhedrin 11a.
52. Sukka 28a.
53. Hagigah 14a.
54. Berochot 20a.
55. Genesis Rabba 79.
56. Baba Bathra 8a.
57. *Ibid.*
58. *Ibid.*
59. R. Yosef Yehuda Bloch, *Sheurai Daat* (New York, 1949), pp. 18, 22.

3

CONTEMPORARY ISSUES

LOOKING at the total spectrum of Jewish ethics, one sees that the popular notion, that the Law governs every question in Judaism, is a fallacy. There were indeed times when nearly all creative principles were locked into the rigid categories of an all-embracing law that was presumed to be God-given. But *pan-halachism* is more characteristic of extremist Orthodoxy in the modern period than of the premodern tradition. In the Talmud the cast-iron logic of legalism was balanced by several factors—the projection of an ethical domain "beyond the law" *(lifnim mishurat hadin),* the recognition of the validity of the mores and morals of civilized humanity *(derech eretz),* and by the mystical or philosophical notions that were cultivated in esoteric circles. As late as the sixteenth century, when the Shulhan Aruch was codified, the realm of Perfection beyond the Law was cultivated in pietistic and mystical literature.

Throughout the medieval period, the inner tensions within the Jewish community did not disrupt the façade of unity. There were recurrent struggles in the thirteenth century between those who favored the rationalism of Maimonides and those who insisted on unquestioning faith. Later, the Qabbalah impressed its theosophic and mystery-mongering seal upon the piety of some localities, while other regions rejected it in part, if not entirely. However, prior to the upsurge of Hassidism, the popular mystical movement of the eighteenth century, these disputes did not split the communal organization. After the first two generations, even the Hassidic-rationalist controversy was largely resolved.

The centripetal force that prevented the fragmentation of the scattered community was the authority of the Talmudic law, which remained unchallenged until the nineteenth century. The Qaraite rebellion against the Talmud and against the Gaonic-Exilarchate hierarchy hardly touched the Jews of Christian Europe, and in the Near East it declined steadily. The law of the Talmud was loose-jointed, allowing for considerable flexibility and adjustment to local conditions. In Western and Central Europe, there was no concrete social focus to attract the rebellious, since there was no self-perpetuating hierarchy. And the rabbinate was not so closely allied with political power as to be corrupted by it. In addition, the persistent pressure of a hostile environment served to cement the beleaguered community and to restrain the divisive forces within it.

With the dawn of the emancipation, Jewish people plunged avidly into the streams of secular thought. In a short time, the incisive criticism of modern philosophy and the scientific approach to the study of religions made their impact upon the Jewish community. Today the Reform Jews no longer regard the Law as divinely revealed and eternally valid. They accept the dynamic moral-religious impetus behind the façade of the Law—not the details of its prescriptions. The Conservatives accept some ritual laws and negate others, on the ground that the living community must be the judge as well as the custodian of the heritage from the past. Even those sections of the Law that they accept, the Conservatives regard as divinely inspired in essence, not in detail. The entire tradition bears the contingent marks of its human, historical formulations. For the Conservatives, the legal pattern of rituals is a series of regulations, which the historic "congregation of Israel" accepted, as if it were ordained by God. This pious rhetoric reflects a twofold truth: first, all that is done "for the sake of His Name in love" is "revealed," or "inspired," since our love derives from Him and leads to Him; second, the dedicated community of Israel is a vehicle of the Divine Presence *(Shechinah),* and its authorized spokesmen reflect the unity of God, Israel, and Torah. Rabbinic ordinances and interpretations were therefore considered to be authoritative only when the people accepted them.

For the Orthodox today then, Jewish ethics tends to merge into the accepted code of laws *(Shulhan Arukh).* However, Orthodoxy too cannot be of one mind, since the Law is part of a more complex tradition. The various parties within Orthodoxy derive their inspiration from the diverse streams within that tradition.

The ultra-Orthodox, led by the Grand Rabbi Joel Taitelbaum, are most uncompromising. They regard the State of Israel as the product of a sinful rebellion against the injunction to wait for the Messiah.[1] Less intransigent but still uncompromising are the pietists of the *Agudat Yisroel,* who conduct an independent school system in the State of Israel. The Mizrachi in Israel and the "modern Orthodox" in America seek to effect a "synthesis" between the modern realm of ideas and the Talmudic ways of thought. Naturally, they too are in agreement only on basic issues.

In view of the wide divergence of basic beliefs among Jews, the façade of unity that communal organizations present from time to time is utterly misleading. For example, there are basic differences about such issues as the saying of nondenominational prayers in public schools, the question of federal support for Church-related educational institutions, the morality of artificial birth-control methods, etc. The semblance of unity on these social questions is imposed by "interdenominational" councils within the Jewish community; these organizations were, as a rule, set up originally in order to combat anti-Semitism. In regard to the question of nondenominational prayers in public schools, Rabbi Shnaiurson, head of the Liubavich Hassidic dynasty, was more "liberal" than the "nondenominational" public-relations experts, who are frequently Jewish only in a marginal, ethnic sense. He based his position favoring prayer-assemblies in the school upon the ancient principle of the "Seven Noachide Commandments," which makes the acknowledgement of a Supreme Being mandatory for people of all creeds.

An analysis of the inner dynamics of Jewish ethics does not reveal a monolithic philosophy of life. It is possible to resolve the tension between the Vision and the Way by choosing any one of many positions within the ethical-religious polarity. Tolerance of differences is a marked characteristic of rabbinic discussions—"these and these are the words of the Living God."[2] A broad consensus on any one issue may emerge at any one time, but we can hardly dignify any one synthesis as being the Jewish, or the "normative" one.

However, some sort of equilibrium between the Vision and the Way is inescapable; the moment the tension is broken altogether, and moral energy is drained into one of the two polarities, then the characteristic dynamics of Judaism cease to be operative. Thus, the portrayal of Orthodoxy as sheer dry legalism, or as unrestrained mysticism, would be a caricature. There is no law in Judaism, either in the relation of man to man or in the relation of man to God, that is not complemented by the surge of creative love, for man as well as for God. By the same token, there is no constructive and enduring love that is not restrained by the laws that emerge out of the structuring of society, and out of earlier crystallizations of Divine Word. Apart from the context of religious tradition, the moral tension is between empathy, or love, and an objective view of the good society; philosophically, the polarity is between the subjective quest of Utopia and the rational laws of right and wrong; socially, there must be tension at any one time between the existing pattern of the community and the Vision of Perfection. And truth is in the tension, or rather in the process whereby personal and social growth is maintained.

BEYOND IDEOLOGIES

In the perspective of Jewish ethics, we develop an immunity to ideologies. Soon after the peoples of Western culture stopped butchering one another on account of their different theologies, they started to use ideologies as fig leaves with which to conceal their collective aggressions. The term "ideology" implies an attempt to focus all the values of life upon one idea or ideal. Manifestly, that one ideal is elevated so high that all other human concerns appear to be inconsequential. The Absolute is transferred from metaphysics and religion to social life and politics; the fragmentary light of one ideal is substituted for the life of the All. This absolutization of politics is essentially a contemporary phenomenom. While liberalism and romantic nationalism competed for the loyalty of European men throughout the nineteenth century, it was only toward the end of that century that the competing ideologies became impassioned and all-embracing. In the twentieth century, this trend was continued with socialism turning into Bolshevism, nationalism into totalitarian fascism, or into nihilistic Nazism, and the ethics of self-realization into individualism, cynicism, or "Social Darwinism."

For each, the goal was to "transvalue all values," to restructure the whole of society in terms of a scale of values that is self-contained, hence, absolutely right. In the communist mentality, there is a solid logical structure that begins with a few axioms, explains all history, accounts for all deviations, and leads to the one party line. Its categories are part of a closed system of discourse that is impervious to the facts and arguments of the outside world. In the case of fascism and Nazism, the primitive values of "blood and soil," power and glory, hierarchy and order, are foisted upon the natural feelings of ethnic kinship. The result is an attempt to imbue the technocratic Utopia of the engineer with the savage pathos of a primitive war of conquest. Modernistic science is placed at the service of an ethic that barely rises above the level of primitive times, when barbarian hordes burst out of the steppe to enslave or to exterminate a native population and to usurp its land. Social Darwinism, glorifying the free individual in his "struggle for existence," is the secret ideology of most people in the democracies, though it is rarely espoused on public occasions.

Both communism and fascism arose out of the miasma of disillusionment and despair. Philosophy, or man's search for truth, was to the communists, as to the fascists, an unreal self-delusion, because to the former there were only class-truths, and to the latter, there were only the myths of the "collective unconscious." Similarly, religion, man's quest for reality, holiness, and true values, was for the ideologists of both camps a panoply of propaganda, to fool the naive. The Way of Reason had turned into a shambles and the light of Religious Vision had failed. This was the sad experience of millions in the aftermath of the First World War. "God is dead," Nietzsche announced. Spengler declared that the West was dying, and that only in the blind worship of force can the foundation be laid for the civilization of the future. To G. Sorel, the teacher of Mussolini, violence was the secret of creativity. Camus summed it all up when he spoke of the "cult of the absurd." In our post-Christian world, Pilate's question "What is truth?" is on the lips of millions.

Yet, the two ideologies contain a mock-image of the religious philosophy of the West. They substitute an immanent law of history for Providence, a predestination that operates with inexorable force, regardless of "good and evil," in place of the free individual, and a Utopia in place of the "Kingdom of God" as the goal of all history. They assume that the course of history is driven by a *transrational* force, which can be sensed truly only by those who have been "converted," or by those who were "chosen" for salvation. Between the "elect" and the "damned" there is an unbridgeable abyss. People are either absolutely right or absolutely wrong. They recognize only one satanic force, capitalism, or non-Aryanism, or individualism. This "monosatanism" is a caricature of the Judeo-Christian monotheism against which they rebel.

The communist-fascist ideologies may be considered as "heresies" in terms of the faith of Western man. The rebellion they incite is directed against the dignity of the individual, in both his historical facets, the Hellenic and the Hebraic. In the Hellenic world, the individual asserted himself as a philosopher, a man of reason, and, in the Hebraic world, man was given his charter of worth as the "image of God." The dehumanization of man, which seems to be the inevitable by-product of the ideologies of the twentieth century, may be traced to the ongoing scientific revolution of our time. Yet, science in itself is neutral, and the humanity of man, his unique worth in the scheme of things, is basically a matter of faith. One aspect of that faith is philosophy, in its original and essential meaning, the quest of wisdom for its own sake. And the other aspect is the assertion of a sense of kinship between man, the Seeker, and God, the Creator.

Does one climb out of the abyss of nihilism by the ladder of reason or with the aid of religion? Both procedures are commonly followed as if they were independent of one another. Actually, there can be no vibrant humanism without the ardor of faith in the unique values of the human personality. Nor can a reassertion of faith be meaningful and relevant in our world today, if it does not accord validity to the rational, ethical, and esthetic ideals of man. We maintain that faith and reason are two phases of the rhythmic beat of life. For all meaning is in essence circular, the relation of a part to the whole and the whole to a part. The core-experience of religion is at once the search for and the assurance of meaning for the individual. It is therefore truth and trust blended together.

In our analysis, philosophy and religion are not antagonistic disciplines, but the two aspects of one endeavor. Religious experience is essentially paradoxical in that it is at one and the same time a feeling of possession and of privation. In relating ourselves to God, we sense our unreality, our unworthiness, our frailty, our nothingness. But, as this feeling deepens, we begin to sense our belonging to a high, overarching realm of meaning; we find that we are embraced by a structure of value and truth; it is in Him, the Absolute, that we live and move and have our being.

Thus, religion can only affirm the supreme worth of man's spirit—

the quest of truth, goodness, reality, and harmony, but it cannot articulate its insight without succumbing to human limitations and errors, failings which reflect the pressures, privations, and prejudices of the particular place or time. "The Torah spoke in the language of man."[3] Our living faith can only assert that God *exists,* not *what* He is; that His Will is akin to man's, when man is most loving and self-giving, but it cannot give detailed specifications; that man *is* potentially Divine, not *what* he can do to attain this end. We have to recognize the distinction between the psychological kind of faith and its social manifestations.

Unfortunately, the spokesmen of religion have frequently arrogated to their rites and doctrines the seal of absolute certainty. They have elaborated the aspect of self-assurance into intricate theologies and ignored the corrective feelings of privation, at least insofar as the collective tradition was concerned. Hence, the bifurcation between Faith and Reason in the nineteenth century. The quest for truth was left to the philosophers, while the religionists contented themselves with religious feelings and the rhetoric of symbolism. Philosophers became professional "no-sayers," to the riddles of existence, and religionists, "yes-sayers"; while the disaffected and the disillusioned reverted to the crass idolatries of primitive man.

In three ways, the creative tension in the human soul rebels against the modern idolatry of ideologies. First, it removes the Absolute from the realm of mundane affairs. Only God is Absolute, and all our human plans, designs, and programs are of relative worth and adulterated truth. Hence, it might serve to prevent the ideological mass stampede that is the perpetual danger in a society dominated by the agencies of mass communication. The conservative role of religion is probably more needed in our restless, revolutionary age than the dynamic role, just as on a crowded highway, good brakes are more important than good accelerators. Second, this dynamic equilibrium returns us to the source of all creative activity, the individual, for the image of God is revealed in him, not in the state or in any social class, nor in any institution. Third, it calls upon us to recognize the inner unity of religious faith and the rational quest. In substance it points to the dynamic progressive character of all that is human. We must never be content to stand still, as if perfection were already here. At any one time, the human advance is a slow and pedestrian affair, a walking along a way, while the Vision of Perfection lures man onward. "Seek Me, and live, saith the Lord."[4]

Essentially, the ethic of religious humanism is a blend of two forces, the one symbolized by Socrates, the other by Amos. Both were path-breakers. They were alike, in a profound sense, though the father of classical philosophy represented the voice of reason, while the founder of literary prophecy spoke in the name of faith. Both Titans of the spirit conveyed to their contemporaries the psychic syndrome of doubt, a higher faith, and a continuous quest.

Socrates questioned the certainties of the teachers of his day—the dogmas of the traditionalists and the nihilism of the Sophists. Yet he "knew" that the quest of truth and goodness was not an illusion. He defended the faith that somehow goodness, truth, and beauty belong to the structure of reality. And he gave his life to prove the supreme worth of the quest of truth, for, as Plato put it, "The unexamined life is not worth living."

Amos too exemplified a similar, threefold approach—doubt in the efficacy of the priestly ritual, faith in the justice of God, and the ineluctable duty to "seek" God, in order to live. To be sure, the pathos of prophecy is at the opposite pole from the serenity of the philosopher. So, to the prophet, the voice of God was as the terrifying roar of a lion, while to Socrates, the intimation of Divine guidance was conveyed by a "daemon," the faint echo of a distant call.

A PERSONAL PHILOSOPHY OF LIFE

In the development of a philosophy of life for the individual, the tension between the Vision and the Way provides the general perspective. The Way for us today in the Western World is to be found in the accumulated wisdom in our common heritage. While our philosophy and literature have become infinitely more complex than those of the Greek world, the essential outlines of human wisdom have not been greatly altered. The counsels of the ancient Sages are still valid—the avoidance of extremes, the "golden mean," the sense of balance, the endeavor to "give all men their due," to be a good citizen, and to know ourselves. Above all, it is to order one's personality and one's work so as to permit the serene joy of contemplation.

We might describe this classical view as the attempt to see life in its wholeness, and to order all things accordingly.

Within our own personality, the sense of the whole guards us against the medieval nightmare of dualism and the modern disease of alienation. In the ages of faith, the body and all its impulses were assumed to be evil, corrupted by "original sin" and subject to the wiles of Satan. Accordingly, man was to be forever embroiled in a battle against his lower nature. While Judaism did not surrender to the spell of this dismal doctrine as completely as medieval Christianity, it did feel the effects of this philosophy, and its lingering after-effects are recognizable even today.

The sense of the whole leads us to accord to every impulse its due place. Man is urged to cultivate all the facets of his personality, to esteem beauty as much as truth, the health of the body as well as the soundness of the mind, the competition in the arena as much as the dialogues in the forum. The goal is to become *Headam Hashalem,* the Perfect or the Complete Man.

This ideal appears to be self-centered in an age of mass-conformity. Is it not sinful to lavish one's energy on one's own self? But if we do not concern ourselves with the improvement of our understanding and the refinement of our sensibilities—old-fashioned as these goals may appear—we shall not acquire a firm base for our social ideals. The river cannot rise above its source. So, there cannot be in the mass that which is not in the individuals composing it. To love one's neighbor as oneself makes sense only when one does love oneself—intelligently. Without a reasoned self-love, social idealism is certain to deteriorate into some kind of technocratic Utopia, where the wheels of society as a whole hum most efficiently, but where the individual is no more than a bolt or a nut.

The sense of alienation that our literary artists have been describing for half a century is essentially the inhospitality of our society to the life of the soul. Those who strive to polish the mirror of their soul, the better to reflect the Divine, are bound to feel alien among people who are content to be mirror-images of one another. In the "lonely crowd" of "other-centered" people, the mass is all and the individual is nothing. There is then no unforgivable sin, save that of straying too far from the Gallup-poll. But, if the faceless mob should become aware of its power and shake off the reins of restraint, it will gallop to destruction. Hence, the need of keeping alive the classical ideal of wisdom—the man who is as well-governed and motivated as the ideal republic. Said Plato in *The Laws:* "If you ask what is the good in general of education, the answer is easy; education produces good men and good men act nobly. . . ."

For the Greeks, the individual was incomplete apart from the state.

Man is by nature a political being, Aristotle insisted; hence, he is complete only when he fulfills his role as a citizen: "In addition to the full development of his personality, a person should train himself to serve the state. . . ." The citizen should be molded to suit the form of government under which he lives.[5]

In Judaism, man is made complete, not so much by loyalty to the state, as by the love of God. The Divine mystery is within the individual, as well as between him and his neighbor. Man is fully himself only when he detaches himself from the mass so as to reflect in his being "the image of God." "Complete ye shall be," says the Torah, "with the Lord your God."[6] The polarity that Judaism established is between man and God, with the love of neighbor as a corollary of the love of God. "Thou shalt love him as thyself, I am the Lord thy God."[7]

The love of God presents to man the vision of an infinite task. To love God is not to wallow in sentimentality, but "to make His Name beloved in the world."[8] It is, therefore, to be loyal to an ideal kingdom that can never be fully realized in this mundane world. This loyalty serves as a check upon the web of political loyalties, in which we are involved.

In this view, the state is ideally not an all-consuming Leviathan; nor is it simply the supreme focus of loyalties; rather it is the social context within which we are to fulfill our obligations to our neighbors and to the Kingdom of God. Thus, religious humanism rejects all concepts of the state, which are based either upon the analogy of a biological organism or that of a machine. The ideal is to have a minimum of force and maximum of persuasion—a society of individuals responding voluntarily to calls of duty and compassion. The individual is the enduring focus of all values, while the community of which he is a part continues to change. At one time, it was the clan, then the tribe, then the nation.

To the Greeks of old, the *Polis* was the center and circumference of all laws and all duties. It is difficult for us today to realize that states and nations too are transitory phenomena, like the *Polis* in the classical world. An Atlantic community may arise in our day, superseding the nation-states. The ideal society is always in the future. We must recognize the tension between the empirical state, within which we belong and by the laws of which we are bound, and that vision of humanity which looms as a potential reality on the horizon.

NATURAL LAW AND THE LIFE OF THE FAMILY

What role does the Law of the Torah play today in the life of the non-Orthodox Jew? It no longer controls his daily life, and the rituals which it prescribes are observed spottily and sporadically by most people. In the absence of universally recognized synods and councils, a tacit consensus allows some sections of the Law to become inoperative and obsolete, except for the ultra-Orthodox. Yet, even today the Law, insofar as it is studied or followed, serves as a symbolic reminder of the duty of obedience to the positive law of the community and of reverence for the moral-spiritual Law of God. In Judaism, the law of the land is sacred, if it is enacted on the basis of equality for all citizens — "The law of the government is law." [9] At the same time, we are called upon to be more than law-abiding and to go "beyond the line of the law," in the quest of that "which is good and right in the eyes of the Lord." The Absolute Law of right and mercy is not merely a distant ideal; it is a living reality, as firmly fixed in the nature of things as are the physical laws of the universe.

Do we then reaffirm the ancient doctrine of "natural law"? — Yes and no. Yes, insofar as the nature of the spirit in itself is concerned; no, insofar as our total comprehension of these laws is concerned. It is significant that the "Seven Precepts of Noah," reflecting the universal imperatives of God, were never spelled out in detail.

All the expressions of the human spirit are structured in terms of laws — descriptive and narrative. These are most exact in the domain of knowledge, especially of inanimate matter. Our categories become less accurate in the sciences of life. In the realm of esthetics, we cannot speak of rigid laws, only of norms of design and harmony. There is also a general consensus, if not universal agreement, in some areas of ethical conduct.

Yet, these norms and categories do not encompass the depths of the human situation, which is constantly changing. Even in the case of physical matter, we encounter fresh riddles the moment one or another mystery is solved. The laws that summarize our knowledge are being steadily and subtly transformed by the growth of our understanding. We know that the essence of reality eludes our grasp, even while we employ methods of research which presuppose the iron inexorability of the laws of nature.

We think of God as the source of personality as well as the creator of the cosmos. The affirmation of Divine unity in the "Shema" affirms precisely this mysterious identity of Person and Law in the Divine Being. Every person is a blend of character and freedom, a reliable structure of patterns of feelings, coupled with an unpredictable spontaneity. In the Supreme Being, that we encounter in the glow of love as in the regularities of our existence, spontaneity and invariant law coexist in a mysterious unity.

So, the Will of God is revealed for us in the texture of moral-spiritual laws, as well as in the free and creative flow of empathy, the love of God and man. The two forms of revelation, love and law, must be balanced against each other, with love losing some of its infinite freedom, and the law advancing in its slow and shambling manner toward the new perspectives opened up by the eyes of love.

In the domain of sex and love, we recognize the mystery of Divine creation. We affirm the validity of the command not to abuse God's greatest gift to us. Our fundamental conviction is that sex belongs preeminently to the whole of our personality; hence, without love and the fullness of self-giving implied in love, it is a travesty and a mockery of our own inmost being. In love, we accord supreme value to the mysterious essence of the person who is the object of our affection. But love is also free and unpredictable; proverbially "blind," it can be easily abused and delusive. Hence, sex must be fitted within a context defined by law, which safeguards its mystique, its sanctity, fostering the feelings of mutual reverence in the two persons concerned. Also, since the community is affected by the consequence of sex, no two people can do what they please without affecting society as a whole. The discoveries of modern psychoanalysis have brought fresh evidence to support the belief that the sexual instinct affects the whole of our mental makeup. So, sex cannot be left to the momentary impulse of the individuals concerned, as exponents of the "new morality" may assert. Too much of the individual and too much of society are involved for any feelings of the moment to be decisive.

But, while the regulation of love belongs within the moral law of God as well as the positive law of the community, the exact specifications of such laws cannot be fixed with finality for all time. Allowance must be made for the changing patterns of social life as well as for the ebb and flow of human sentiments. We find in Scripture a deep awareness of the horror of sexual sins and deviations, but we cannot maintain that the penalties for adultery and sodomy, prescribed in the Bible, are valid today. Yet these are certainly sins; so too, are all extramarital relations—they furtively taint man's highest expressions with fraud and self-deceit.

In the case of birth-control, we do not concur that "natural law" prohibits the use of contraceptive devices. Here is an example of the failure of man's imagination to keep pace with the growing complexities of our global problems. We repudiate the notion that the sole function of the sexual act is to produce children. As we interpret the account of man's creation, the woman was designed to be man's companion. While it is a Divine injunction "to be fruitful and to multiply," this command is properly fulfilled, according to the Talmud, when a family possesses two children, according to some, and four children, according to others.

In the Talmud and the Codes, birth-control practices are limited to only a few special cases, those in which the life of the mother might be endangered by pregnancy, or when a community suffers from famine. However, Conservative and Reform Jews have held that a supreme reverence for human life dictates the proper spacing of children. It requires that emphasis be placed on the quality of the mother's life and on the right atmosphere for the rearing of children. The mere multiplication of human beings is not an end in itself. Society, then, has a positive obligation to further the promotion of birth-control knowledge and the dissemination of whatever aids are available.[10]

As to abortion, both Philo and Josephus express the sense of horror felt by Jews at such a flagrant attempt "to destroy God's structure and His Work."[11] On the other hand, the unborn foetus is regarded as simply a part of the mother's body, until it has emerged out of the birth-canal. Therapeutic abortion was generally allowed, with the life of the mother taking precedence over that of the unborn child.[12]

With our present knowledge of the slow growth of the embryo, we do not esteem the unborn foetus, especially in the early stages, to be a human being. Hence, there is room for the positive law of the community to determine the cases when abortion be permitted. Since the foetus is part of the mother, she and her husband should have the right to determine whether an abortion should be performed. But, the moment a child is born, it acquires the status and dignity of a human being. For many centuries Judaism protested against the pagan practice of abandoning or killing unwanted children.

PRINCIPLES OF SOCIAL ETHICS

In the domain of social and economic life, we recall that the Jewish religion was born in a recoil of the soul from the horror of enslavement. In the first of the Ten Commandments, the Lord is identified as the author of freedom. The Sabbath is ordained for two reasons—one to emphasize man's kinship with the Supreme Being, Who contemplates serenely the work of His hands; the other, to afford all servants and even animals the opportunity to rest one day a week. Man was designed to be free, to be like God, in His creative labor and His calm reflection.

At the same time, the leaders of society were urged to ordain laws that would mitigate the hardships resulting from human inequality and the caprices of fortune. The Jubilee year, the returning of fields to their original owners and the liberating of the slaves, is an example of Pentateuchal legislation in this area. So, too, is the cancellation of debts in the seventh year and the prohibition of usury.

However, even in ancient times, these laws were insufficient to control the blight of poverty. Hence, the injunction to establish charitable enterprises in behalf of the poor. "The Holy One, blessed be He, loves the poor."[13]

In Talmudic law, artisans were permitted to band into guilds in order to establish standards for their trade and to fix prices. Merchants were allowed to use various gimmicks to attract customers to their stores. But there were also certain definite limits upon these rights. The resident scholar and the representative heads of the community had to approve the regulations of the guilds. The merchants were not allowed to charge more than the right price, even when the demand far exceeded the supply. Workers could band together to strike against an employer. Even a single worker had the right to discontinue working at any time, "even in the middle of the day."[14] However, a strike was justified only if its purpose was to compel the employer to submit to arbitration in accordance with the Torah *(din Torah)*.

What are the basic, inalienable rights of man? They are the circumstances that are needed for the realization of his humanity, the "image of God" within him. In the course of history, different "rights" and "freedoms" become essential, if men are not to be "dehumanized." Stalin in his constitution for the U.S.S.R., and Pope John XXIII in the encyclical "Pacem in Terris," have written of the "right to work." Certainly, governments are obligated to provide a minimum subsistence for all who, for one reason or another, cannot fit into the normal spaces of the economic system. Already, the Book of Deuteronomy makes the elders of a city responsible for the life of all who enter its boundaries.[15]

Justice Brandeis maintained that every person should have the right to choose between staying in his own native land and emigrating to another country. Pope John XXIII expressed a similar view. In Judaism, this right appears to be fundamental, for we belong to God first and only secondarily to a particular nation or state. Thus, the first Divine command to Abraham was to go forth from his native land. And the first of the Ten Commandments introduces the Lord as the One "who took thee out of the land of Egypt, out of the house of bondage." The ceremony of *pidy on haben,* the redemption of the firstborn, in the course of which the father "buys" his son from a priest, dramatizes the principle that a child belongs to God, not to the state, nor the tribe, nor even the family.

In general, Judaism does not insist on one or another economic system, but it asserts the inadequacy of all systems. In a society where free enterprise is the rule, Judaism asserts the constant need to combat poverty and to safeguard the freedom and dignity of the individual. In a socialistic society, it would stress the sanctity of the human person and the inviolability of his basic rights. Whatever the existing structure of society, the Vision of Perfection looms above it, as a goal and as a standard of judgment.

The Messianic ardor of Judaism is directed toward the building of a just, even a perfect society, here on earth. But this massive force is balanced by the built-in caution against the belief that any concrete plan or any visible structure is indeed Messianic. Jewish history is as dramatic a warning against pseudo-Messianism, as Jewish idealism is a persistent source of Messianic longing. In the non-Orthodox realm of discourse, the Messiah is a symbol of the attainment of perfection, in the life of the individual as in society generally. But, so paradoxical is human nature, that actual perfection is almost a contradiction in terms. The Messianic ideal can only loom on the horizon as a many-splendored vision, urging mankind to advance along the diverse pathways of the spiritual life, but it cannot be fully realized. If the Messiah claims to exist here and now, he is a false Messiah.

The dominating motif of Jewish social ethics is therefore melioristic, rather than Messianic—that is, we are bidden to improve our society, not to impose a perfect plan upon it. The Talmud asserts that we are not permitted to force the coming of the Messiah, only to hasten his arrival by deeds of charity and repentance.[16] We are therefore enjoined to be active builders of the "Kingdom of God," but also to know that our efforts cannot but be fragmentary and more often than not contradictory. As we noted earlier, the religious spirit is at once conservative and reforming.

THE VIRTUE OF WISDOM

Perhaps the most significant insight of Jewish ethics is its stress on the supreme value of learning and thought. Our entire literature bears the impress of this ideal. The prophets reproached the people for their lack of "the knowledge of God."[17] In the *Ethics of the Fathers,* the pillar of Torah is put before those of worship and deeds of charity.[18] Hillel went so far as to assert "that he who does not learn is deserving of death."[19] The "houses" of Hillel and Shammai debated for several years as to whether learning is more important than good deeds.[20] They concluded that learning is indeed more important, for, in addition to its own worth, it ultimately leads to all kinds of good deeds.

In rabbinic literature, learning was not simply the totality of human wisdom, but the specific lore of Judaism—Torah, Talmud, and Commentaries. However, as a basic ideal, the pursuit of truth was implicit in the ardor of Torah-learning. The Torah was to be studied "for its own sake." In the activity of the intellect we enter the company of the Divine, as it were.

Can we recapture this insight in behalf of our own age?

We seem to be living in an age of exploding education. The colleges are bursting with eager students, and the Federal Government is preparing to enter this field on an unprecedented scale. Still, the emphasis is utilitarian. Education is essential to prepare people for good jobs and to make it possible for them to learn new skills when their old jobs are no longer available. It is also a prerequisite for a healthy democracy. Accordingly, the emphasis is now placed on mass education and, in the universities, on the sciences.

But we need to realize that religion itself is expressed in part through the quest of truth and the acquisition of wisdom for its own sake. Learning must be understood as a high purpose of life, not merely as a way to improve one's earning power. As Rabbi Zadok put it, we must not turn wisdom into "a spade with which to dig."[21]

This emphasis would, in the course of time, change the prevailing spirit in our academic campuses. Students would not be driven to equate learning with grades, and professors would not be pressed to "publish or perish." Learning would be esteemed as a way of life, noble in its own right. Whatever professions we may choose, we need to acquire the zest for wisdom as the supreme value of the good life.

The new age of automation is likely to provide many people with leisure hours that they could well utilize in a continuous program of self-education. But education requires emotional, hence religious motivation: "the beginning of wisdom is the fear of the Lord." [22]

In the Western World, the marks of a religious life have been identified almost exclusively with the virtues of faith, hope, and charity. Noble as these qualities are, they can be easily suborned and put to the service of fanatics and benighted crusaders. Does not history afford a thousand illustrations of this melancholy fact? Indeed, the virtue of self-criticism is as essential to faith, personal or collective, as a steering wheel is to a car. The task of *aggiornamento* is a divine imperative for every generation and for every faith. It is the Word of God in action—"The soul of man is a candle of the Lord, searching his inmost parts." [23]

The practice of self-criticism is our only safeguard against the tyranny of the mob, which, as Plato warned us, is the peculiar disease of democracy. Mass education made possible the kind of totalitarian thought-control that even the medieval world did not know. The soft virtues of faith, hope, and charity are of little help in resisting totalitarian idolatry. Propagandists do not dispute the maxim "love your neighbor"; they merely distort the image of the neighbor into that of a monstrous fiend. And distortions of this type exert a peculiar appeal to the "pooled pride" of the people. Bloody crusades are far more likely to be initiated by calls addressed to man's noblest instincts than by appeals to his selfishness. This is particularly true in our day, when nuclear war could only result in the total impoverishment, if not the annihilation, of mankind.

It would seem that only madness could drive the world to a nuclear holocaust. Yet, such madness will surely wear the mask of the Messiah—it will inaugurate the "Reich of a thousand years," it will establish the "classless" society, it will "make the world safe for democracy." Only the readiness of people to accept the scalpel of criticism as the cutting edge of faith is likely to protect us against a resurgence of the seductive delusions of pseudo-Messianism.

THE ETHICS OF RACE AND GROUP RELATIONS

It is now generally accepted that national boundaries do not constitute the limits of our ethical obligation. So, the Torah begins the teaching of Judaism with the narrative telling of the creation of mankind.

In addition to our duties as American citizens, we owe certain obligations to those who share our faith and our historic heritage; we possess a certain kinship with those who share our culture and our freedoms; we are obligated to serve the entire society of mankind. There is no neat way in which these duties can be meshed together. In the perspective of the Way and Vision polarity, we recognize that a dynamic transition from one social pattern of loyalties to another is the rule rather than the exception.

First, within the boundaries of America. As a "nation of nations," creating one community out of diverse ethnic strains and religious traditions, America cannot but strive for a unity of sentiment and fellowship as well as of multifarious strands of law. While we begin with the law affording equal justice to all, without any distinctions of race or creed, we cannot be content with the bare bones of legal justice, but must supplement it with the sentiments and aspirations of a common fellowship. If the French nation, emerging suddenly into the air of freedom, found it necessary to aim at fraternity, as well as liberty and equality, we cannot set a lesser goal for America. The inner logic of patriotism does not permit us to stop short of this consummation. Hence, the need of supplementing the legal structure of the nation by positive acts of philanthropy and concern, interethnic and all-American in scope, that will have the effect of creating a true American brotherhood, not merely a congeries of competing groups.

It follows that we need to combat the divisive spirit of racism, whether it arises among "white supremacists" or "black nationalists." Upon all of us, there rests the duty to help those who for historical reasons were late in enjoying the benefits of American society. We have to complete the laws of equality by charitable concern for those who stand in the doorway of our society, partly in and partly out, either in a social, or in an economic, or in a cultural sense.

However, in our drive for national unity, we must not ignore either the claims of individuals or the values that are inherent in the subcultures of our society. It was the specious siren call for unity that in our time served the fascist dictators so well. The Vision of Unity that we seek must not be a doctrinaire mold, imposed from without, but an organic reality growing out of the American Way; integrating its values, not crushing them into the monolithic gray of conformity. The image of the "melting pot" suggests the ultimate homogenization of society, its turning into a viscous soup, without any lumps. In the realm of ideals and sentiments, the abstractionism of radicals may be as vicious as the prejudice of reactionaries; with due attention to the existing patterns as well as the looming vision, we can only aim at the growth of fellowship and mutual regard, not the obliteration of differences.

In the integration of the Negro, the Mexican, and other races, our guiding policy must be to guard the rights of the individual and to administer even-handed justice to all. Our governing principle is equality of opportunity, rather than egalitarianism, the attempt to impose an artificial level of equality upon all groups. We know from the sad annals of our history that such attempts create discord and stifle the creative talents of those who have most to give to society. In the interests of the nation as a whole, we cannot allow the organization of ethnic groups on a quasi-political basis, groups that would fight each other for the spoils of the national economy. The bitter rivalry of racist pressure-groups is a corrosive poison that our society can ill afford.

An economy that is open to all individuals on the basis of merit will be supplemented by a cultural atmosphere that is receptive to all ideas and values, allowing the diverse ethnic subcultures and religious faiths to make their respective contributions to American culture. While it is true that some Americans have no subculture or religious faith to enrich their lives, we must insist that only an inverted sense of justice would require that all social-cultural enclaves be erased in order to make all "equal."

TENSIONS BETWEEN NATIONAL AND TRANSNATIONAL VALUES

To what extent should ethnic and religious subgroups maintain their bonds of unity with their coreligionists or their respective national homelands? On the one hand, the subgroups should recognize the rightfulness of the overriding loyalties of the American nation. This is the context into which, as individuals, we assume our rights and obligations. On the other hand, all cultural values, feelings of kinships, and sentiments of philanthropy are worth-while in themselves; hence, their claim upon us is that of moral values, which, if possible, ought to be incorporated into our life.

In the event of a conflict between these parochial values and the interests or ideals of the American nation, the latter take precedence. Such is the implication of the moral-legal context of our day.

The emphasis on the sanctity of the individual in our tradition implies that it is for the individual to resolve such matters of cultural conflict as do not concern the nation as a whole. In turn, the choice by the individual is to be made on the basis of his moral obligation to sustain as many as possible of the positive values impinging upon his personality. On the one hand, he should familiarize himself with the constellation of values in his heritage, so that his choice will not be determined by ignorance; on the other, he should recognize that all historic clusters of ideas and sentiments are creations of contingent circumstances. Born in time past, inevitably they must change or be changed with the passage of time. The only enduring sources of value are living individuals and universal ideals.

As a general rule, we may distinguish between the political legal context, in which there cannot be room for "nations within nations," and the spiritual domain, containing religious values, historical associations, and philanthropic activities, where diversity of loyalties is creative rather than competitive. The more a man learns of other cultures, the more is he conditioned to appreciate his own; the more a person concerns himself with the needs of his own ethnic group, the more he is likely to be sensitive to the needs of his fellow citizens. Yet, these generalizations must be tested in practice, for we know only too well that ethnic loyalties can become constrictive and self-centered.

In this area, the world-wide experience of the Jewish people demonstrates the dangers as well as the potentialities of ethnic enclaves within a nation. On the whole, we can say that modern Jews have learned to effect a viable synthesis between their loyalties to the Jewish people as a whole and their bonds of unity with the respective nations among whom they have lived. They have confined their Jewish loyalties to the areas of religion, antidefamation, and philanthropy, while they have reserved their national loyalties for their respective states. This solution has been upset only in periods of extreme turbulence.

Now that the State of Israel is ready and willing to accept those who wish to be part of the Jewish national homeland, those who opt to remain in their native lands can return in good conscience to the normative pattern of adjustment in the Diaspora. To be sure, a twilight area of uncertainty remains—the host-nation might become narrowly zealous, succumbing to the "know-nothing" mentality which takes offense at the slightest resistance to full homogenization. Also, the Jewish group might so interpret its religious-ethnic heritage as to pre-empt the whole spectrum of national feelings, leaving only the outer shell of the overall legal-political context. Cultural subgroups might become so exclusively concerned with their own specific ethnic interests as to introduce the sword of ethnocentric warfare into the vitals of the nation. Needless to say, an ethnic group so minded and so constituted can hardly contribute to the promotion of those feelings of fraternity that every nation strives to attain.

If Jewish history teaches us anything at all, it is the need of actively cultivating feelings of fraternity with the host-nations, and the dire disasters that are sure to follow the failure to attain this consummation. This failure may derive from a narrowing of the vision of the host-nation, and it may also be due to the rigidity of the ethnic minorities. In any case, the ethical problem of an ethnic minority is affirmatively to develop its philanthropic activities in such a manner as to embrace the entire nation, thereby contributing to the creation of a fraternal society. As the Talmud teaches, "We are obligated to feed the poor of other nations along with the poor of Israel, in order to improve the ways of peace."[24] On the other hand, the host-nation must raise the sights of national unity to the plane of cultural-moral values, so that its resident minorities may be embraced by its cultural and social dimensions, as well as by its political boundaries. Both groups must recognize that they are in a transitional context, between the existing pattern and the vision of the future.

Within the Jewish community, the debate on this issue is still being formulated in terms of the choice between survivalism and assimilation. The proponents of both alternatives seek to impose a vision of their own upon the protean reality. In the actual situation, the living community at any one time can hardly do more than take a few steps in either direction. It cannot envision all contingencies and it cannot pretend to "guarantee" the end that it seeks. Inevitably the debate degenerates into a contest between competing pseudo-Messianic frenzies.

In the perspective of our analysis, the actual issue is on the plane of the contemporary Way, rather than on the futuristic plane of the Vision.

Naturally, the cherished Vision, either of the perpetual endurance of the Jewish identity or of its total dissipation, exerts its proper pull upon the complex of values in the present. But we must not presume to play the part of God, who alone knows the End. In the contemporary situation, we face the issue of incorporating as many creative values as possible in our life and in the lives of our children. We focus attention on the living individuals, here and now; it is their happiness and their moral growth that should determine our decision. There will be no unanimity on this score either, but then the alternatives are clear and concrete. As to the future, it will grow out of our actions and the actions of our successors; hence we are called upon to act so as to hasten the Messiah's advent, but not "to force the end." Thus, the Midrash comments on the verse, "Don't touch my messiahs—these are the children of our schools." [25]

The Golden Rule applies to social groupings as to individuals. While every group is entitled to preserve its own integrity, it must keep itself "open" to the ideals, values, and individuals that impinge upon it. A "closed" society, barring its gates either against the coursing currents of doctrine or against people who might want to become part of it, is in standing violation of the elementary principles of good manners. "Good fences make good neighbors," is an old adage; yet, as Robert Frost pointed out, the barriers must not be raised too high, and only where they are absolutely necessary.

PEACE AND THE INTERNATIONAL ORDER

The Hebrew prophets projected the vision of a united society of mankind, in which all "the families of the earth" will join together to eliminate the scourges of war, injustice, and poverty. Yet, in the Jewish tradition, pacifism finds little support, for we must not imagine at any one time that the millennium is already here. We are called upon to strive for the realization of the dream of human perfection—as if it could be achieved tomorrow. But we must begin with the existing patterns of international relations and work from there, taking a step at a time.

Nevertheless, individual Jews may incline to one edge of the spectrum and become "conscientious objectors." They may draw their convictions from the mystical stream in the Jewish heritage, which asserts that all is in the hands of God. All that man can do is to refrain from evil. Or they may come to feel that, as Jews, they stand outside history; they have been assigned a unique task and consigned to the realm of eternity. Hence, they must not immerse themselves in the power struggles of the nations. While in our judgment such views may seem "extremist," we have to recognize that in the dynamic polarity of Judaism, some small groups will cling to either one of the two poles. Such people should be allowed to serve the nation in ways that accord with their religious convictions.

With our emphasis on justice as well as on love, we can advance toward the Ideal Society in two ways: by helping to build an international network of institutions of justice, and by engaging in various international projects of benevolence. The first task is largely a governmental effort. A reign of law among nations may be established by degrees, through the extension of international law and the promotion of international institutions. The United Nations organization should be encouraged to build up an international civil service and a panel of judicial administrators who, perhaps, would be required to give up their individual citizenships and become world citizens, an affiliation that would entitle them to live anywhere and to be protected by a special covenant. From such a panel, the men and women who administer the various U.N. projects could well be drawn. Ultimately, this panel might include renowned judges, who would be selected to arbitrate any and all international disputes. We cannot expect that an order of law will be established overnight, but neither can we delay indefinitely the beginning of such an order.

The second task is largely personal, the extension of a helping hand to those in need, regardless of existing barriers. The Peace Corps project of President Kennedy and the vast Foreign Aid Program are particular expressions of this activity. In this field, there is ample room for the initiative of private individuals.

The Jewish people, recalling the evils of national zealotry, are likely to bring to this effort the impetus of their historic tradition. Also, the wide dispersal of Jews throughout the globe makes them aware of the need of stretching the bonds of fellowship across national boundaries. A residue of the sense of alienation, however weak and muted, remains in the minds of Jewish people, and this feeling serves to immunize them against the temptation to lay down rigid lines either for the character of the nation or for its destiny. Jews are the natural "protestants" against national idolatries and the outcroppings of chauvinism in all ethnic groups.

The young State of Israel has already launched a far-flung foreign aid program, with the object of extending technical assistance to the underdeveloped nations. This program is still in its infancy; yet, already it serves more than fifty nations.

WAR IN THE NUCLEAR AGE

The invention of the A and H bombs poses the question whether there are any contingencies in which a nuclear catastrophe may be ethically justified. It is now fairly certain that nuclear weapons have not been put by the major powers in the category of poison gases, that by common consent were not to be used in the event of war, save possibly in isolated cases. Atomic weapons are now so thoroughly integrated into the armament of the regular forces that a major war, in which both sides would refrain from using atomic weapons, is now scarcely conceivable.

Diplomacy is in part at least the art of using the threat of war as a way of preventing it. For nuclear weapons to serve as a "deterrent," their employment under certain conditions must be "credible." If we assume that a full-scale war would result in the obliteration of all human life on earth, can we still conceive a contingency when a nation might be justified in launching that ultimate catastrophe?

The logic of our entire analysis negates any attempt to introduce the Absolute into the ethical equation. No alternative can be so utterly evil as to justify the total destruction of humanity. Suppose Hitler had obtained complete control of the entire globe, and suppose he had proceeded to annihilate the Jews, to decimate other races, and to set up a universal slave system. Even then, he would have died one day, and his followers would have regained by degrees their human sanity and dignity. No evil can be so total or so eternal as to justify the total annihilation of civilized mankind.

Long ago, the rabbis laid it down as a governing principle, "All sins a person may commit if the alternative is the loss of his life, excepting these three—idolatry, sexual immorality, and murder."[26] In other words, a person does not have the right to cause the death of an innocent individual in order to save his own life. By way of explanation, the Talmud adds, "Why should you think that your blood is redder than that of another?"

In the case of nuclear warfare, the victims would be millions of innocent bystanders. Thus, even if we could feel that our own life would be saved, we have no right to take the lives of noncombatants. Moreover, the Talmud recognizes the rights of generations yet unborn. A witness was urged to reflect that his testimony, if false, would bring upon him the guilt of "the blood of the innocent man's unborn children and descendants to the end of all generations." [27]

In the case of atomic warfare, the genetic damage to future generations is itself sufficient cause to bar use of the bomb to "protect" any interest of the nation whatever, not excepting its independence.

As we have pointed out, national independence and even the survival of a nation's collective identity are not absolute values. Only God is Absolute, and His image in man is the source and focus of all values.

An ethical principle, such as reverence for the lives of the innocent, should rank higher in our scale of values than our own lives. So the Talmud declared, "If a group of people is told—give us one from among you, and we shall kill him; if not, we shall kill you'—let them all be killed, but they should not yield a person for execution. However, if that one person is specified, like Sheva ben Bichri,[28] then they should surrender him, that they might not all be killed. Said Resh Lakish—'Only when that person is deserving of death, like Sheva ben Bichri.' Rabbi Yohanan said—'even if he is not deserving of death.'" [29]

Occasions may arise when a nation might have to swallow its pride and surrender its independence in order to save the lives of its people and preserve their ideals. Jeremiah counseled the people of Jerusalem to lay down their arms and to go into exile in Babylonia, to guard the purity of their faith while bowing to the yoke of national slavery. The reason that resistance to idolatry was ranked so high in rabbinic ethics as to require martyrdom is the perennial tendency of men to deify their collective image. In the Roman Empire, the emperors and the geniuses of Rome were worshipped as if they were Divine. We today are too sophisticated to make use of the old naive terms, but the spirit of national apotheosis is more rampant than in any previous age. In fact, the greatest service religion can render in our day is to keep peoples from absolutizing their temporary selves. The Vision is always ahead of us—not here, not now, not within our grasp.

From a strictly ethical viewpoint, we cannot escape the logic of *Absolute Nuclear Pacifism*—that is, the non-use of the Bomb, even as retaliation for a direct attack. However, the existing patterns of society would make such a policy illusory and self-defeating. It would be impossible to secure an enforceable and verifiable ban on the production and the possession of nuclear weapons. In the present circumstances, "the balance of terror," deriving from the possession of such weapons by both sides in the world struggle, is serving more effectively than the balance of power in the past.

In Judaism, we are cautioned to examine ethical questions in the light of their consequences, not merely in terms of their inherent ethical quality. Living in this mundane world, we must not assume that we can suddenly plunge into the perfect world of the future, or act as if we were there already. In the present context of international affairs, the cause of peace would not be served by a unilateral renunciation of all nuclear weapons on the part of the United States or the NATO powers. On the other hand, to live in awareness of the tension between the Vision and the Way, means to refuse to stand still, but to be ever-straining toward the ideal. Whatever the necessities of the moment may be, we dare not accept them as the unyielding verdicts of history, but we must move toward the vision of our hearts, a few steps at a time, even if no comparable concessions from our opponents are immediately forthcoming. We must accept the principle of nuclear retaliation for nuclear attacks, refraining from escalating the struggle as much as possible. At the same time, we must inaugurate a race for peace, by seeking out diverse ways in which we can act to reduce the heat of the struggle and provide a fitting example for our opponents.

But the greatest contribution that religious groups can make toward the building of a permanent peace is to remove the aura of the Absolute from the social-political issues of the day. No war is likely to break out in our day, without a prior explosion of the apocalyptic frenzy, which sees the ultimate struggle as the battle between the Children of Light and the Children of Darkness. In the light of the glowing embers of our faith, we should recognize our own shortcomings and the transitory nature of our economic and social patterns. We, too, live under Divine Judgment, and it is not for us to play the role of God, all over the world.

At the same time, our faith should keep us from the sin of distorting the image of our opponents. It is so natural and so seductively easy to portray the opponent in lurid colors, that it might be well for religious groups to concentrate their moral forces on the front of public information. The communists, by their controlled press and their bars against migration, have been the chief offenders on this score. But, on our side, too, there have been failures at communication. We bar our correspondents from visiting China. And the pseudo-patriotism of our editors leads them voluntarily to distort the image of our opponents, as communist editors are persuaded to do, by fear of censorship.

The religious groups in our free society should lavish their resources on the cultivation of the vision of humanity, in the full knowledge that the interests of the state will be fully taken care of by its secular agencies. In this endeavor, our major task will be to maintain a counterbalancing endeavor against the perversion of our nation's image and the distortion of our antagonist's image resulting from the natural feelings of ethnocentric arrogance and "collective thought."

MONOSATANISM, SUBVERSION, AND INTERVENTION

In the world view of monotheism, the creative forces in the universe are believed to derive from one source. God is Truth and Love and Peace. But, the diverse evils of human life are due to many unrelated factors. There is not in opposition to God, an Ahriman, an all-encompassing Principle of Evil that rivals Him in unity of purpose and concentration of power. Satan in the Bible is also an obedient servant. *Mastema* of the Book of Jubilees and *Ashmedai,* the prince of the devils, belong to popular religion. For the populace finds it easier to believe in the unity of satanic forces than in the unity of the Divine. Monosatanism is more common than monotheism.

The assumption that all the unrest in our world is due to communism corresponds to the equally fatuous dogma of the communists that all the evil in the world is due to capitalism. Both axioms are examples of contemporary monosatanism in the secular domain, the one area of life which modern man takes seriously. Actually, social unrest is more often the rule, in human affairs, than the exception. Thucydides tells us that the Greek cities of his day were divided, each in two cities. The battles between the popular and the aristocratic factions were interrupted only occasionally by the rise of a ruthless tyrant. And each faction sought aid from the super-powers of the day—Athens or Sparta, Persia, Macedonia, or Rome.

If the United States and Russia were simply super-powers in a shrunken globe, the various factions in the infantile and adolescent areas of the world would still have aligned themselves with one or the other. They would have invented ideologies to justify their pleas for help, if such ideologies had not already existed.

However, in many areas of the world we have acted as if there were only one common enemy, as if we were confronted not by an ideology but by the conspiracy of a few masterminds to control the entire human race. Living in a country where the social struggles of the underprivileged never reached the boiling point of revolution, we find it difficult to imagine that in many areas of the world a genuine democracy is impossible. And it is precisely in those areas that communist subversion is going on. The choice there is not between democracy and dictatorship, but between the maintenance of one ruling group as against another.

We cannot maintain that it is right for us to intervene in an internecine struggle, such as is going on in South Vietnam or such as is likely to arise in Africa or Latin America, if the legal government invites us. For we know only too well that such governments have no real roots among the people. Should we transfer to all ruling cliques the ancient illusion of the Divine Right of Kings or Hegel's abstract idealization of the state? Such notions have done incalculable harm in the past.

By the same token, the communists have no right to help the so-called "liberation" movements. These struggles are actually latter-day imperial wars, led by governments that disavow imperialism and derive no selfish benefit from their enterprises. Yet those governments are equally guilty of imperialism, in the sense of extension of influence, hidden under the guise of an ideological crusade—freedom, in our case, "anticolonialism," in the case of the communists.

Crusades are perversions of religious idealism. If the moralistic fig leaf were torn away, these struggles, exposed in their naked brutality, would soon simmer down. In the hybrid union of idealism and national interests, the real interests of the nation are distorted by the pious patina of propaganda. On any basis of enlightened selfishness, crusading wars do not make sense. They are secularized versions of the medieval crusades, deriving from the distortions of the political faiths of the Western World.

A crusade is morally wrong, first, because it is likely to be based on false premises either initially or as it continues; second, because it is

based on the ineradicable sin of *hubris,* the endeavor to play the part of
God. To doubt our own wisdom or strength is the first implication of
humility. We cannot attempt to run the affairs of the whole world and
to arbitrate every dispute, because we must not assume that we alone
are worthy of the trust of all mankind. If the skepticism of the Age of
Reason ended the frenzy of the religious wars, a similar skepticism in
the domain of politics is likely to dampen the fervor of the embattled
secular ideologies. Religious skepticism was made possible by faith in
man; a healthy skepticism in regard to all global crusades derives from
faith in God.

Furthermore, in view of the world-wide competition between the
Free World and the communists, we have to assume that our opponents
will seek to counter every one of our moves to combat communism by
equal and opposite moves of their own. And we have to allow the moral
equivalence of their efforts, in many parts of the world, since the status
quo governments in former colonial areas were instituted in the first
place by their former masters.

Should we, then, do nothing to counter the deliberate attempt by
aggressive communist nations to destroy neighboring governments? Not
by ourselves, but we should assist the United Nations and its agencies
to stand guard over the legitimate rights of all peoples.

RELIGIONS IN A PLURALISTIC, SECULAR SOCIETY

The role of the historical religions in the pluralistic society of our day
cannot be delimited by a hard-and-fast rule—such as by the separation
of religion and government. The beginning of wisdom is to recognize
the interpenetration of all elements of culture and the restless dynamism
of society. As there is a democracy of people, so there is a corresponding
democracy of ideas, a certain range of freedom for ideas within an
existing context. At any one time, the prevailing pattern is a patchwork
of compromises, the product of historic contingencies. As situations
change, the compromises of the past need to be reviewed.

The Jewish attitude to the relations between the government and
religion consists of two antithetical principles—the one deriving from
the Bible and Talmud, the other emerging out of the recent centuries
of Jewish history. In the ancient tradition of Judaism, there was no
division between religion and public life whatever. As we have seen,
Moses Mendelssohn, living at the dawn of the Emancipation, con-

tended that the Mosaic unity of religion and state referred to a *unique* period; hence it was not normative for the future. In the reconstituted State of Israel in our day, there is still a firm integration of the Synagogue and the state. But, many of the non-Orthodox groups would like to separate the Synagogue and the rabbinate from the agencies of government.

In the past two centuries, Jewish people were impelled to associate themselves with the Liberal thesis that government on all levels must be free from any entanglement with religious bodies. The Jews drifted into the various Liberal camps, since their rights and their rootedness in the lands of the Diaspora depended entirely on the acceptance of the Liberal thesis. The Conservative parties and the clerical lobbies could not but resist the breakdown of the walls of the ghettos.

Armed with two mutually contradictory axioms, Jewish leaders cannot be unanimous on the issues of religion and government. The Orthodox groups, deriving their guidance from the sacred tradition rather than from the configurations of modern history, will be prone to build parochial schools and to seek government support for them. The non-Orthodox, particularly the secularists, may go so far as to demand a doctrinaire, total separation of all the institutions of faith from all the agencies of government. A synthesis of the opposing theses of Jewish faith and Jewish history is still a desideratum.

In our analysis, Judaism is a pattern of institutions and symbols plus an outreaching of ideals, sentiments, and hopes. A similar situation obtains not only in the other faiths of America, but in secular society as well. For the term "secular" does not necessarily imply a total divorce from the ideal content of religion. American society is secular in an institutional, not in an ideal sense. It still assumes that a certain philosophy of life, containing the ideals and values of the Judeo-Christian tradition, will be conveyed to its citizens, directly or indirectly. Every society must provide for the moral and psychological undergirding of its social-legal texture. A communist society has its commissars, a fascist its uniformed squads. In a democratic society, people are not "told," or "trained," but they must still be taught, guided, stimulated, and motivated.

It is in the ideal dimension of secular society that we have to find room for the ethical core of the religions of the Judeo-Christian tradition. This does not mean that we assume the existence of a unitary, easily defined and identified core of ethical principles. In each tradition, there is likely to be a spectrum of interpretations of its ethical substance. But every religious community possesses an obligation to contribute to the moral-spiritual elan of the nation as a whole, as well as to mold the character of its citizens.

The attempt of the New York Board of Regents to formulate a prayer, expressing the common core of American religions, was declared unconstitutional by the United States Supreme Court. It is not for the agencies of government to fix the outlines of the common core. Its meaning may be conveyed only indirectly, by teaching about the religions of the community, for instance. There is need in this area for experimentation and for the spirit of accommodation, since the alternative of a total "wall of separation" is unthinkable. It would drive both the Church and the Synagogue to the catacombs.

The religions of the Judeo-Christian tradition nurture a common vision of perfection for the individual and for society, but they articulate this vision in diverse ways. Within the context of a democratic society, they have a twofold obligation: to maintain the distinctiveness of their own heritage and to sensitize their people to the appreciation of other traditions. The first obligation has been generally recognized in our contemporary society. It is axiomatic for every religious community to seek to perpetuate its heritage in its own way. But the second duty is equally important. We have to teach our young to understand and to revere the religious ideas and the symbolic panoply of the faiths of our neighbors. In the past, we have acted as if diverse religions were antagonistic to each other as a matter of course. The differences are of course real, and they must not be blurred. But, there is also the common heritage of the Judeo-Christian tradition, the Holy Scriptures, and the grand evolution of the culture of the West. There is also the common task to combat the universal evils of "extremism" in spiritual life—fanaticism at one end, nihilism at the other.

Through our instruments of religious education we have now begun to guard against the building up of "negative stereotypes" of other faiths. A sincere effort is being made to refrain from identifying Jews as "deicides," to keep from stigmatizing Catholics as idolators, to guard against the misrepresentation of diverse Protestant groups. While this effort is only in its initial stages, we should look ahead to the positive task of teaching our followers to appreciate the depth and grandeur of other faiths. Does one religious group have the right, or even the duty, to seek converts from other groups? From the standpoint of Judaism, every religious community can find salvation by nurturing the core of religious idealism, "the Seven Commands of Noah." There is no need for conversion, except in the case of intermarriage. We recall the words of Micah, "Let each people walk in the name of its God, and we shall walk in the Name of the Lord, our God." [30]

Missionary propaganda can be offensive, even though it be motivated by a self-sacrificing idealism. We must revere the people of other faiths and admit the finitude of our own knowledge about the Infinite. In a democratic society, all religious groups should maintain an attitude of openness to each other. They can only profit by learning from one another and by laboring together for the needs of the community. It is only the "men of little faith" who can have any reason to fear any untoward consequences resulting from the interreligious dialogues that are becoming a permanent fixture in our society.

COMPARISON OF JEWISH AND CHRISTIAN ETHICS

It is extremely difficult to establish a fair basis for the comparison of Jewish and Christian philosophies of ethics. On the one hand, when the two traditions are taken as historic wholes, it is easy to see that the colors which are bright and strong in one faith are mixed and muted in the other. On the other hand, both traditions were deeply transmuted by the modern spirit. The patina of modernism overlies the two faiths, obscuring the differences of shade and nuance. Furthermore, the Jewish as well as the Christian traditions are now so deeply divided, in doctrine and in practice, that a philosophy of life purporting to be Jewish or Christian is more likely to reflect the personal opinion of the author and the temper of his time, than it is to represent the historical tradition.

Be it noted that the realm of ethics was not a battleground in the ancient and medieval disputations between Jews and Christians. The issue was the Messiahship of Jesus, the nature of the Promise in the Bible and the character of God—all else was incidental. Those Jews who accepted the Christian interpretation of the Messianic verses in the Bible had no difficulty in accepting the ethical injunctions of Jesus; the self-sacrificing pietists, Essenic, Pharisaic, or Hellenistic, who actually lived by the ethical precepts of Jesus, remained part of the Jewish community if they did not accept the dogma of his being an incarnation of God's Word.

To abstract an ethical issue out of the eschatological context of the first century is hardly instructive, though both Jewish and Christian authors have done so with gusto. On the Christian side, writers have asserted that Jewish ethics were at worst legalistic, at best a rigid insistence on the principle of justice, while Christian ethics were based on love. In this juxtaposition, the specific atmosphere of Jesus' life and teaching was forgotten. As Albert Schweitzer pointed out, the ethics of primitive Christianity was "interim-ethik," the thought and action of a community that expects daily the end of the world. Hence, their proto-communism, their total unconcern with the normal tasks of society. With the records of the Qumran sect available to us, we see how a similarly minded community, living in anticipation of Messianic redemption, retreated from the world and gave itself up completely to the service of the Lord.

We need hardly add that the Jewish tradition fostered the virtues of love, compassion, and faith as well as those of obedience to law, justice, and reasonableness. Jewish ethics have been presented as the field of tension between the Way and the Vision; the philosophic counsels of balance, fitness, and harmony, constituting the pattern of the Law at one pole, and the religious passion for supreme self-giving at the other. Leo Baeck, writing from the Jewish viewpoint, described the Christian ethic as romantic, the Jewish as classical. This distinction is justified only if we narrowly restrict our view of Christianity to certain specified periods. Thus, in the time of Jesus and in the Apostolic period, we see a "threshold-mentality," the mood of a people living on the verge of the End, giving all for love. Such moods were recreated at various times—by the "Montanists" in the second century, the Franciscan spiritualists, the Anabaptists at the time of the Reformation, the English Radicals of the seventeenth century. In terms of our analysis, we should say that in those periods the tension between the Way and the Vision was broken, with the Vision of the End becoming all in all.

But the Christians did not normally emulate the Montanists, who, we are told, would crowd into the Roman governor's chamber, pleading to be allowed to die. Paul's rejection of the Law and Jesus' injunction, "Judge not that ye be not judged," did not prevent the pious Emperor Justinian from promulgating his code.

Actually, Christianity reestablished the tension between the Way and the Vision when it set out to embrace the philosophic heritage of the Greeks and the legal principles of Roman Law. Only at rare intervals did the consuming fire of romanticism burst asunder the restraints of reason and law. To be sure, in Catholic Christianity, it would appear that two ethical codes are offered—one for the "religious," the other for secular society. Yet, Catholics would maintain that there is no break between the two classes, only a state of mutual challenge. For monks and nuns retreat from the world only in order to serve it better.

The idealization of celibacy is far more prevalent in Christianity than in Judaism. But it would be wrong in our day to impute to Christians, Catholic or Protestant, the view of St. Paul, that "it is better to marry than to burn." Marriage is a holy state of life; sanctity embraces the whole of man, not merely his soul.

In general, Christians and Jews come together closest in the realm of ethics. The rigidities of law and dogma in both camps yield progressively to the softening effects of the historic perspective that is common to both of them. The differences in the nuance of each ideal within the two traditions are fruitful and enriching for both. If love in the Christian tradition evokes the images of self-giving and self-denial, and if in Judaism it evokes primarily devotion to the building of the community, the two traditions gain in depth as they welcome each other's insights. In the infinite quest for perfection, people can only follow one pathway at a time, but by imaginative empathy they can feel the zest and grandeur of their confreres climbing by other paths toward the same broad summit.

NOTES

1. J. Taitelbaum, *Vayoel Moshe* (Brooklyn, N.Y., 1959).
2. Airuvin 13b.
3. Berochot 31b.
4. Amos 5:4.
5. *Politics.*
6. Deuteronomy 18:13.
7. Leviticus 19:34.
8. Yoma 86b.
9. Gittin 10b.
10. The Orthodox literature on this subject is summarized in I. Jakobovits. *Jewish Medical Ethics* (New York, 1962), pp. 167–69. The author concludes: "Some later authorities add that, when a pregnancy constitutes a permanent danger to life, X-ray or surgical contraceptive treatment is to be preferred to devices requiring constant use. But under no circumstances is the husband permitted to do anything to render his act ineffective. Nor are mere considera-

tions of health, as distinct from life, usually sufficient to warrant active precautions on the part of the wife. Already in the eighteenth century, it is true, a rabbi recognized that it might be advisable to space the arrival of children; but the recommended means to achieve this did not include recourse to contraception."

11. Zohar, Exodus, beginning.

12. See Philo, *De. Spec. Legibus*, III, 108–10; Josephus, *Contra Apionem*, II, 202; I. Jacobovitz, *Jewish Medical Ethics,* pp. 182–91.

13. Baba Bathra 10a.

14. Baba Mezia 10a.

15. Deuteronomy 21:1–9.

16. Sanhedrin 97a.

17. Hosea 4:1, 6; Isaiah 5:131.

18. *Ethics of the Fathers,* I, 2.

19. *Ibid.,* I, 13

20. Megillah 26a.

21. *Ethics of the Fathers,* IV, 11.

22. Proverbs 9:10.

23. *Ibid.,* 20:27.

24. Gittin 61a.

25. Midrash Tehillim, Psalm 105:15.

26. Sanhedrin 74a.

27. *Ibid.,* 37a.

28. Samuel 2:20.

29. Jerusalem Talmud, Terumot 8.

30. Micah 4:5.

4

NEO-MAIMONISM

THE TERM "Neo-Maimonism" is coined in the same manner and for the same reason as the well-known designations—Neo-Aristotelianism, Neo-Platonism, Neo-Thomism, Neo-Kantism and Neo-Hegelianism. Strictly speaking, we should speak of Neo-Maimonideanism, but we prefer the shorter form, for the sake of convenience.

There are only so many basic positions that a thinker can assume vis a vis the riddle of existence. And all serious scholars are aware of the historical roots of their thoughts. So, the ends of logical clarity and historical perspective are both advanced when a contemporary movement is described as a version of a well-known historical position.

In the case of Neo-Maimonism, this policy is all the more to be commended because the "Guide of the Perplexed" served as a touchstone of philosophic speculation ever since it appeared. To the religious liberals, it was the pillar of light, blazing a bold pathway through the arid wilderness of contending passions and superstitions. To the naive and the literalists, the philosophy of Maimonides was a snare and a delusion, even when they admitted that his Code was a most precious part of the sacred tradition. In a sense, the Maimonidean controversy continued unabated into our own time. While in the thirteenth century, the question for the literalists in regard to the "Guide" was "to burn, or not to burn," the subsequent centuries rephrased the alternatives, but they continued the debate. The rise of Kabbalah and its triumph, after the expulsion from Spain, did not succeed in suppressing completely the influence of Jewish rationalism. And every new wave of enlightenment was powerfully assisted by the momentum of the Maimonidean philosophy. If Hassidism generally scorned the "Guide," the *Maskilim* felt that it propelled them directly into the intellectual world of the end of the eighteenth century. Moses Mendessohn found that Maimonides prepared him to understand Spinoza, Descartes and Leibnitz. Solomon Maimon went directly from Maimonides to Kant. Several decades later, Nahman Krochmal and Samuel David Luzzatto defended opposing positions in regard to the place of Maimonides within authentic Judaism. In the past century and a half, when Jewish intellectuals were beguiled by the spirit of the times to move in different directions, drawn now to the nationalist-romanticist pole, now to the humanist-rationalist pole, it was the adequacy of the Maimonidean synthesis that they debated.

Our generation is called upon to undertake a basic reexamination of our convictions and goals. We are no longer driven by desperation to fight for sheer survival. In Israel and in the free world, we are sufficiently secure to face the ultimate questions and to take seriously Maimonides' admonition to let our ideas grow out of the facts rather than to tailor our convictions to suit our peculiar situation.

On the other hand, we cannot gainsay the obsoleteness of Maimonides' picture of the cosmos, with its basic categories of Matter and Form, its four earthly elements and the ethereal substance of the heavenly bodies, its many "spheres" and "intelligences," and its deference to Aristotle's authority in regard to all matters "below the moon." Also his knowledge of comparative religion and of history was inevitably minute by our standards, though he pioneered the exploration of these themes for the understanding of the *mizvot*. Again, we cannot assent to his aristocratic disdain for the common people. Yet, if we transpose the living core of his thought into the structure of nature and history, as they appear to us, we arrive at a philosophy of life that is balanced and harmonious. Neo-Maimonism also harks back to Maimonides in terms of the approaches he rejected—the personalistic voluntarism of Ibn Gabirol, the ethnic romanticism of Judah Halevi, the "reductionism" of those who confined all thought within "the four ells of Halachah," the imaginative exuberance of proto-Kabbalists and even the mild, superficial rationalism of Saadia. Each one of the rejected viewpoints has its counterpart in our time. Neo-Maimonism, therefore, is definable negatively, as well as affirmatively.

TENSION AT THE HEART OF REALITY

We begin with the pathways that Maimonides disdained to follow. He conceived his task to be the resolution of the perplexities troubling the educated Jew. On the one hand, such a person could not conceive of life without the guidance of Torah and the assurance of redemption contained in it. On the other hand, he was made uneasy by the literal meaning of many verses in the Torah, which described the actions of God in crass anthropomorphic terms. M.* prefaces his mighty effort with the confession that the contradictions in Torah cannot be understood with full clarity. The wisest can only get occasional, lightning-like flashes of the truth. ("More Nebuhim," Petiha; Pines' translation, *The Guide of the Perplexed* [Chicago, 1963], p. 7.) Only Moses can be said to have perceived the mysteries of creation and providence in the full light of day. But, Moses is more a dogmatic than a historical figure, with the beliefs concerning him falling into the category of "necessary truths," to be discussed presently.

At this point, we call attention to the modernity of M.'s position. The modern age in philosophy was opened by Descartes, who proceeded to subject all experiences to the acid-test of total doubt. When we face the ultimate mystery of existence, we sense the tension between the polar opposites of being within ourselves. The rational points beyond the rational; the immanent feelings of holiness intimate His transcendence; the traditional accounts of God speaking to His Chosen People are somehow right, yet also far too narrow, too particularistic; since God addresses Himself to all men. In rare moments of inspiration, God speaks to those who are properly qualified, but excepting Moses, His "speech" is filtered through the thick strands of imagination. We are torn between our awareness of creaturely dependence on Him, without whose "everlasting arms" we should instantly disappear, and our rational conviction that we cannot say of Him aught that is meaningful and affirmative. Nor can we ever outgrow this state of tension. All our attempts at a synthesis are but so many words strung together, waiting to be fused into flecting lights of meaning by bolts of lightning from above.

Is not this recognition of our human condition essentially compatible

---

*In this essay, we shall refer to Maimonides as M.

with the vision of reality in our time?—We no longer think of the flux of existence in terms of tiny billiard-balls in motion. Atoms, we know now, consist of many tiny particles, which can be described both as electromagnetic waves and as bits of matter. Modern physics operates in terms of fields of force, which are condensed into relatively stable structures of congealed energy. Every thing is in reality an event, a series of tremors, fixed in space, yet infinite in outreach. Should not, then, the human soul in its confrontation with the Infinite Whole of the cosmos be similarly caught in a ceaseless tension?

On a more popular plane, we recall Pascal's famous remark—"reason which is small enough for the mind is too small for the heart; if it is big enough for the heart, it is too big for the mind." Here, then, in simple language, is that cluster of contradictions, which we can resolve only in those moments when heart and mind join to lift us temporarily above ourselves. Yet, it is not knowledge that we glimpse in those moments, but the assurance that our inner quest for wholeness and consistency is right, in direction, if not in content. We must try again and again to understand in love and to love with understanding, for only the whole man can approach the Creator of the Whole. We are launched on an infinite road.

"SOVEREIGNTY OF REASON"

M. maintained that his "Guide" was the first effort to deal with the mysteries of Creation and Providence *(maasai bereshit* and *maasai merkava).* (Moreh, Petiha; Pines, p. 16.) He scorned the works of Saadia and Halevi, as being either superficial or fallacious. To him, a "philosopher" was an Aristotelian who recognized the sway of the unvarying laws of nature. Saadia associated himself with the Moslem school of Mutazila, and Halevi reflected al Ghazzali's critique of "the philosophers." (Moreh, I, 71; Pines, p. 176.)

In a larger sense, Saadia and Halevi represented the "short but long road" that popular theologians prefer in all generations. Saadia's way is that of superficial rationalism. He rejected the coarse anthropomorphism of literalists. In M.'s view, Mutazilites thought they removed materialization from their notion of God, but, they did not really, since they ascribed to Him, emotional and psychological factors. (Moreh, I, 53; Pines, p. 119.) All the references in the Torah and the Bible to physical appearances of God apply to His temporary theophanies, not to His own Being. So, there is a "created light" or divine effulgence, which the Lord employs as a manifestation of His Presence. This luminous body called *Kavod* or *Shechinah* was seen by Isaiah and Ezekiel, by "the elders of Israel," and by some of the Sages. Similarly, the Creator formed a "created voice," which spoke in so many words to the prophets and to Moses. In this way, Saadia managed to retain the literal significance of the anthropomorphic passages in Scripture and Talmud, without ascribing to God Himself any material qualities. But, this method is, after all, an invention of the imagination. If the "lights" and "voices" are not themselves divine, why should we assume that they attest to the truth of prophecy? What is to prevent us from rejecting them as merely visual and auditory hallucinations?—If they are not temporary and detached events but integral manifestations of the Supreme Being, His emanations or His "Garments," then we fall back into the trap of idolatry, where all kinds of images might be said to be His representations and "incarnations." Furthermore, truth can only be self-authenticating, an extrapolation of man's outreach, but not an alien intrusion from another realm—a communication which man can only accept in blind faith. As a matter of fact, the "created light" and the "created voice" of Saadia became the basis of the neo-anthropomorphic school of the Ashkenazi Hassidim. They conceived of the Divine manifestations as permanent "forms" of the Deity, allowing the fevered imagination of mystics to rhapsodize on their visions of the various parts of the Divine anatomy.

M. did not altogether reject the doctrine of "created lights." He granted that it was helpful to those whose minds were too unsophisticated to grasp the concept of an immaterial Deity. At least, this doctrine kept them from ascribing materiality to God Himself. Also, it is extremely difficult to interpret the Pentateuchal description of the gathering at Sinai, without those "lights" and "sounds."[1] Yet, M. aimed to raise his readers to a higher philosophical level, which demands inner coherence and rejects the possibility of self-contained islands of truth, breaking into man's consciousness.

In M.'s view, the sustained quest of man for truth, as seen for example in the works of Aristotle, is itself the product of revelation. When a person's rational faculties attain a pitch of perfection, while his intuitive and imaginative powers are not equally perfected, he becomes a speculative philosopher. The school of Saadia was, according to M., remiss in that they accepted uncritically the premises of the Moslem Mutazilites.

As a child of his age, M. believed that classical Greek philosophy was an integral part of the esoteric tradition of the biblical prophets and sages of the Mishnah.[2] M.'s historical knowledge was faulty, but not his reverence for the sovereignty, indeed the holiness of reason. To him, systematic and objective reasoning is the highway to truth, and God disdains those who forsake the manifest principles of truth for the sake of pleasing Him.[3] The anti-intellectualist mentality of a St. Paul, a Tertullian, a Luther, a Kierkegaard, with their subjective, or "existential" "truths" was to him an abomination.

Neo-Maimonism, too, asserts that rationality is of the essence of humanity. There is more to humanity than reason can comprehend, but the irrational and the subjective cannot serve as clues to the Image of God in man. To love God is to seek to know Him, and the greater our knowledge of Him, the greater our love of Him and of all who are created in His image.[4] And God's love of us is manifested in our love of Him and His Kingdom on earth.

REJECTION OF ETHNIC MYSTICISM

M. scorned the Halevian axiom that Jews and Jews alone are endowed with a special capacity for the "divine manifestation." To Halevi, Jewish people occupy an exalted level in the hierarchy of being, somewhere between the angels and the rest of mankind. All Jews inherit this unique intuition, which was given to them for the sake of humanity as a whole. As God has chosen the biblical prophets for the purpose of bringing His admonitions to the Jewish people, so too He has chosen the Jews from among the nations and endowed them with a unique capacity for things divine, and assigned to them the task of functioning as "the heart" of mankind. This "heart" will regain its vigor in the land of Israel, and then all mankind will be "saved" through Israel. However, even in the messianic future, ethnic Jews alone will serve as the channels of communication between God and mankind, for only ethnic Jews can function as prophets.

The Halevian approach has not lost its popularity even in our own day. Its plausibility derives, not alone from its seductive appeal to the hurt pride of a persecuted people, but also from the uniqueness of Jewish history. Here is a people that has been reduced to "dry bones," yet all the nations of the western world were brought to the service of God through its prophets. And the western world appeared to Europeans until recently to be synonymous with civilized humanity. If, then, in the past, Israel served as "a prophet unto the nations," why not in the future?—The fact that this self-image entailed the anguish of martyrdom and the aura of dedication to the service of all men kept this doctrine from turning narrowly chauvinistic and narcissistic. Furthermore, with the rise of romantic nationalism in the modern world, the Halevian approach was rendered the flattery of imitation by such popular "prophets" as Fichte, Mazzini, Mickiewicz, Danilevski and Dostoevski. Ethnic mysticism proved to be fantastically contagious.

Even the builders of classical Reform and cultural Zionism succumbed to the seduction of Halevian racism. Geiger, with all his rationalism, based his Jewish theology, especially his concept of Israel's "mission," on the axiom of an innate Jewish "genius" for religion. A'had Ha'am believed that "the national ethnic" and "the national soul" were all but atrophied when the people of Israel was uprooted and driven into exile and that with the return of Jews to their native land Israel's ancient genius would be revived and revitalized. Echoes of mystical racism abound in the works of Buber and Rosenzweig. As Christian theologians are perpetually tempted to transfer the mystery of the Divine Being to "the secular city," so Jewish theologians are equally prone to transfer the mystery of Divine oneness and uniqueness from God to the people of Israel, or to the land of Israel, or to both. "Sanctified egotism" is the demonic underside and shadow of traditional Judaism.

M. refused to indulge in collective self-sanctification. The quest of truth is not a national monopoly. It is man qua man that is the subject of all speculations about God. To limit "the divine manifestation" to Jews living in the land of Israel is as unworthy of Jews as it is destructive of the principle of human equality, which is affirmed in the *Mishna*. To be sure, in his letter to the Jews of Yemen, M. found it necessary to descend to the level of popular mythology and to argue that those who are descended from the men and women that stood at Sinai cannot possibly disbelieve in the promises of the Torah. However, in his "Guide," he does not restrict prophecy either to the land of Israel or to the people of Israel. The reason prophecy is not attained in the lands of exile is due to the wretchedness of life in those countries. (II, 36.) And in a famous chapter (III, 51) he ranks the philosophical saints of all nations ahead of "Talmudists" and *mizvah*-observers. Also, in the well known letter to R. Hisdai concerning people of other faiths, he avers, "God seeks the heart. . . ."[5]

Neo-Maimonism, too, disdains the mystique of racism and ethnic narcissism along with the assorted brands of anti-intellectualism. All who base their faith upon their existential identification with the historical career of the Jewish people, affirming that such existence is unique and *sui generis,* simply beg the question. The task of reflection is to analyze, to discover relationships, to demonstrate the universal components in all particular events. All individuals, all historic peoples, are unique. And the conviction of being chosen by a supreme deity for high ends is by no means unique, either in ancient or in modern times. To insist on the uniqueness of the Jewish people as an irreducible phenomenon, that can be understood only by reference to the meta-historical, the meta-philosophical and the metaphysical is as irrational in principle as it is vicious in actual, historical consequences. For a people that is lifted out of the common run of humanity and enveloped in the ghostly haze of mythology is far more likely to be demeaned by opponents as subhuman than to be exalted as superhuman. If the holocaust demonstrates anything at all, it is the vulnerability of Jewish people to the mystique of racism. Jews should be in the forefront of the fight against this social disease, not promote it. Haven't we been decimated by its ravages?—Yet, so strangely seductive is the temptation to mythicize our own being that the Jewish "meta-myth" is still a potent force in our midst and, owing to the mirror-image effect, among Christians.

THE QUEST OF SELF-TRANSCENDENCE

M. was a rationalist, but not in the flat sense of this term. Speculative reason, directed toward the ultimate mysteries of life, is far more than the sheer process of intellection. In fact, one must guard against the temptation to plunge prematurely into reflection on God and creation, before one has properly prepared himself for this arduous and perilous task. The preparatory disciplines are not only logic and mathematics, but ethics and esthetics. Also, one must be endowed from birth with a balanced disposition, which shuns all tendencies to excess and exaggeration. The prophet must be gifted in all the disciplines that are needed for the perfection and balance of the human personality. His imaginative and intuitive talents must be as excellently attuned to the reception of the Divine Influence as his intellectual faculties. The prophet shares in the talents of the statesman, whose spiritual antennae relate him to the needs of the community as a whole, so that he senses "the general will" of the nation, to use a Rousseauist phrase. The prophet is also a gifted poet, creating myths and metaphors that reverberate with powerful resonance all through the ages. So, while the man of intellect can only gain from the Divine Influence some philosophical reflections, and the man of intuition and imagination can only be inspired by the same divine source to devise some ordinances and works of literary art, the one who is gifted in all faculties of outreach can hope to attain moments of prophetic inspiration, that lead him to channel divine energy into the community of Israel and the society of mankind.[6]

It follows that man's pathway to God consists in the attainment of balanced perfection, or to put it differently, the quest of God is dependent on the attainment of wholeness and harmony, since God is the builder of wholes. This emphasis might be termed classical. It resists any endeavor to fragmentize the human personality and to set the ideals of the spirit over against the hungers of the flesh. To be sure, M. tended to downgrade sex as a "shameful" activity. (II, 36.) He described the Hebrew language as "holy," because it contained no words for the genital organs and employed "pure" euphemisms for the sexual act. In this respect, he was probably influenced as much by the feverish over-indulgence of the Moslem princes as he was by the teaching of Aristotle. But, his essential teaching was in keeping with the aims of the classicist. He regarded the health of the soul as paralleling the health of the body, rejecting the Augustinian claim that the love of self opposes and contradicts the love of God.[7]

Neo-Maimonist ethics is also a blend of the quest for balance of the classicist and the lyrical temper of the religionist. Along with M., we affirm the ancient principle of the Golden Mean. All virtues are happy syntheses of opposing tendencies. But, man's perennial quest for wholeness leads him again and again toward the brink of self-transcendence. M. supplements the classical ideal by the principle of *imitatio dei,* though in his view this principle could be asserted only in a metaphorical sense. To us, the urge for self-transcendence is a fact of human nature, for we cannot attain self-fulfillment without surrendering to a high ideal. The consequences of this hunger to be part of a greater whole are not always salutary. People are driven on occasion to serve idols and to reject the tensions of freedom. Here, again, is an illustration of the dangers inherent in the polar tension within the human soul. Self-surrender to a partial good may be socially destructive as much as the anarchical drive for self-assertion. In the childhood of the human race, the limited whole which becomes the surrogate of God, is the clan, the tribe or the city-state. It is rare individuals, philosophers, statesmen and above all prophets, who have opened up wider horizons for the psychic need of self-transcendence. Plato, Aristotle and Xenophon shattered the naive idolatry of the Greeks. Isocrates expanded the meaning of the term, "Hellene," to embrace those who acquire the culture of the Greeks. And, it was the long line of Hebrew prophets that most effectively contrasted the adoration of the One God with the sterile folly of worshipping any and all idols. The pathos of the prophets set its seal upon the deepest layers of the Jewish heritage. "Leave the Israelites alone—if they are not prophets, they are surely the sons of prophets." (Pesahim 66a.)

The rejection of idolatry is an ethical as well as a theological principle. It means that no ideal is more than a fragment of our total goal, more than a way-station on the road to personal and universal perfection. In every generation, the classical procedure of harmonizing conflicting interests and ideals issues in a consensus of what is reasonable and morally obligatory—a Way, which is then structured into laws and ordinances *(halachah)*. But, along with this legal pattern, there is also the beckoning ideal of greater perfection—a Vision of the sublime, which is only dimly reflected in articulate ideals. Beyond these ideals is the Nameless One, to whom alone our worship is directed. The concrete ideals of the age are all too readily transformed into idols, and the resounding No of prophetic monotheism, impels humanity to go beyond the "idols of the market-place" in quest of the receding horizon of perfection. "Without vision, a people is undone."

The religious Liberal, by virtue of his dynamic Vision, will be keenly conscious of the failures of the age and the limits of the regnant ideals. To him, the worship of the One God will result in an awareness of our human sinfulness. We ask forgiveness, not alone for the sins we have committed, but even more so for permitting some ideals to preempt our total loyalty, shutting all else from our view. Sin is the failure to heed the call of the whole—the whole of our self, the whole of society, the whole of the spectrum of ideals, that is the light of God.

There is an old pietistic comment on the claim of the Sages that in time to come, God will slaughter Satan. Why should Satan be punished? it is asked. Was it not his duty to mislead and seduce people?—The answer is—Satan will be punished for the *mizvot* he urged, not for the sins that he commended. How beautiful!—The perfect world will be attained only when the demonic is totally separated from the divine—a consummation which can hardly be reached in our mundane existence.

THE MEANING OF GOD

M.'s conception of God is the most misunderstood part of his system. It is taken to be "The Unmoved Mover," Who can only be described in negations. He is not this and not that. While we may think of Him as being One, Living, Almighty, All-knowing, we have to bear in mind that His unity is unlike that of all other forms of unity, that His Life, His Power and His Wisdom are totally unique, in no way comparable to the meaning that those adjectives normally convey. We seem to be left with a vacuous Naught. Since M. takes pains to hammer home the principle that "the end of our knowledge of God is to know that we don't know" (I, 59), many scholars in medieval and modern times have concluded that his God-idea was really devoid of religious content. At least one contemporary scholar even went so far as to infer that logically M. was a naturalist.

Actually, when the "Guide" is seen as a whole, the positive aspects of M.'s conception become clear. Existentially, M. confronted the Divine Being in times of meditation as the Ground of all being, the Purpose of all existence, the ultimate object of man's total devotion and affection. Intellectually, M. identifies the Divine with the marvelous wisdom that is apparent in living things, reserving the term, "nature," for the mechanical laws that prevail in the inanimate world. (I, 69; III, 19; III, 23.) In the designs of plants and animals, the reality of purposiveness is apparent. The whole is far more than the sum of its parts—one spirit dominates and controls the functioning of myriad components. Furthermore, certain species depend for their existence on other forms of living beings. A Wise, All-powerful Will is at work, over and above the unvarying mechanism of nature.[8]

This blend of Wisdom and Will is manifested on a still higher level in the creation of humanity. Even in its most primitive stages, mankind received inflows of Divine Power and Wisdom from God. (II, 40.) These upward thrusts led to the development of skills needed for survival and of social customs that provided a modicum of order and justice. Among the Greeks and other cultured peoples, there have arisen statesmen, scientists, inventors and poets, who have contributed mightily to the formation of a civilized society. Yet, the laws of the Greeks *(nomoi)* did not meet the spiritual needs of their people. The only perfect law is the Torah, which addresses itself to the ethical and religious concerns of the individual as well as the economic and political interests of society. "So, the Torah, which is not a natural product is led up to by natural developments." (Ibid.) The Torah was given to the Israelites, but in the course of time the "Torah of Truth" will govern the lives of all men and women. (Code, "Hilchot Melochim," end.) "For all of existence is like one living individual." (I, 72; Pines, p. 117.) The thrusts of God, manifested in the biblical prophets and less perfectly in statesmen, poets and philosophers will ultimately redeem all mankind.

Here, then, is a holistic and evolutionary conception of God's work in history. The vistas of the contemporary theory of evolution were of course not open to M. But, he conceived of God as being actively at work, creating the ideal human society of the future. Having postulated the doctrine of *creatio ex nihilo,* M. insisted that the Divine Flow from the sphere of Active Reason amounted to a series of additional creative acts, which transpired in the domain of history. While the material laws of nature have been fixed at creation, the spiritual horizons of mankind remained open, and the help of God is extended to the diverse builders of the ideal society of the future—to scientists, investors, statesmen, poets, but above all to those who prepare themselves in mind and heart for prophecy. The perfect God must have designed "the best of all possible worlds," but only as a potentiality, revealed to prophets. And He is working in the dimension of time along with the elite of Israel and the nations in order to achieve this goal.[9]

The revival of prophecy is an indispensable step on the road to messianic perfection. The Messiah of the House of David will inaugurate the glorious era, but it will continue to grow in perfection for a long time, as the Messiah and his successors proceed to convert all of mankind "to the religion of truth." The laws of physical nature will remain unchanged, but man's productivity and prosperity will increase marvelously, so that people will be able to devote most of their time to Torah and religious meditation. (M.'s Code, "Hilchot Melochim." Ch. XII.) In M.'s view, then, progress is many-sided, economic as well as spiritual, secular as well as religious. And the ultimate source of this ceaseless advance toward perfection in time is the Supreme Being, Who is also the Purpose of all purposiveness in nature and in history, and the Ground of all that exists.

The important thing to remember is that M. combined a rationalistic version of the biblical philosophy of history with his philosophic system. Thereby, he resolved the contradiction between the Perfect God, Who is the Cause of an imperfect but steadily improving world. To be sure, M. considered that goodness far outweighed all forms of evil in human life. The residual evil is due to the resistance of matter, and in the course of time, this resistance will be gradually overcome.

What is the contemporary religious import of this concept of God? — It does not allow us to think of God either as a loving Father or as a stern King, Who is placated by sacrifices, rituals and prayers. (III, 28.) It does not console us with the assurance that we can win His magical intervention, whereby the laws of nature will be changed in our behalf. Neither repentance, in the popular meaning of the word, nor the recitation of prescribed prayers, nor the distribution of our possessions for charity will change the course of events.[10] We can speak of God as Compassionate only in the sense that He ordered the world in such a way as to provide for the needs of every living species.[11] But the concerns of the majority of mankind are, after all, self-centered. The truly religious personality will love God, without presuming that God must love him in return, as Spinoza later put it. Furthermore, our awareness of the Divine Being generates supreme joy within our souls.[12] The more we learn of His majesty, the more we yearn in love for His Presence, and this love is itself joy unalloyed. Indeed, God's love and concern is directed toward us, to the extent to which we prepare ourselves to receive His overflowing, creative energy. Providence is proportional to the readiness of our personality to serve as His vessel in behalf of the uplift of mankind.[13]

In M.'s philosophy, the only true miracles are those of the human spirit, when it is touched by the Divine Power.[14] The miracles of Scripture were built into the structure of natural law at creation. (II, 29.) Thereafter, we can look forward to the inflow of fresh freedom-generating creative power into the minds and hearts of creative men and women. All inventions, all the mighty achievements of the human spirit in every field of endeavor are the products of divine inspiration. (II, 45.) Man is not a passive victim of blind fate. On the contrary, God permeates the world only through the cooperation of great men and cooperative societies. (II, 40.) He achieves human progress not by suddenly interrupting the chains of causality but by inspiring men to utilize the opportunities available to them. And the goal of this divine-human cooperation is certain to be the ever more perfect society of the future.

This concept of God is thoroughly in harmony with the modern spirit. We know the tremendous potential of the human spirit for the improvement of the living condition of mankind, where M. could only hope and trust. The parallels between M.'s philosophy, stripped of its medieval picture of the cosmos, and the views of such modernists as Bergson, Alexander and Whitehead are obvious. God is the unifying, integrating, perfecting Pole of the di-polar universe, but matter, the source of perpetual resistance and negation, is also His creation. The ultimate triumph of Freedom and Purpose is asserted in the doctrine of *creatio ex nihilo.*

M.'s philosophy could be described as panentheistic, in that God includes the world, but the world does not include God. While He is eternal, He works within time. God is both personal and non-personal, for personality is a blend of freedom with purposiveness, and God is at once the Purpose of all purposes in the cosmos and the Free Creator, "who renews the world daily by His goodness." He is immanent in the noblest momentary outreaches of the human spirit, but also transcendent, for we can affirm of Him only by negative attributes.

In sum, God is not only static perfection, but also a dynamic force, acting within history. Charles Hartshorne wrote, "Modern philosophy differs from most previous philosophy by the strength of its conviction that becoming in the more inclusive category [than, being]." (Ch. Hartshorne in "Philosophers speak about God," U. of Chicago Press, 1953, p. 9.) Also, reflecting the Kabbalistic tradition, A. J. Kook wrote of the two forms of perfection, attributable to God, though he hesitated to apply any potentiality to God in Himself.

"We say that Absolute Perfection is necessarily existent and there is nothing potential in it. The Absolute is all actual. But there is a kind of perfection which consists in the process of being perfected; this type of perfection cannot be applied to the Deity, since Infinite, Absolute Perfection leaves no room for any additional increments of perfection. In order that Being shall not be devoid of growth in perfection, there must be a Becoming, a process beginning from the lowest depths, the levels of absolute privation, and rising therefrom steadily toward the Absolute Height. Thus existence was so constituted that it could never cease from progressing upward. This is its infinite dynamics." ("Orot Hakodesh," (Jerusalem, 1938), p. 549; "Banner of Jerusalem," by J. B. Agus, p. 172.)

The Kabbalistic solution is to distinguish the Pure Being of God, as *En Sof,* from His Becoming in the Pleroma of Sefirot. Modern philosophers feel no such compulsion—"there is no law of logic against attributing contrasting predicates to the same individual, provided they apply to diverse aspects of this individual." (Hartshorne, op. cit., p. 15.)

MEANING OF FAITH

Can we prove the existence of God? M. demonstrates the existence of God by a variant of the cosmological proof—for every existent effect there is a cause; hence, an ultimate Cause, an Unmoved Mover. But when the issue of creation vs. eternity of the cosmos is raised, M. takes refuge in a theory of faith. The issue cannot be decided by the arguments of logic alone. An extra-logical factor must be brought into the equation. If the cosmos is created, "then the Torah is possible." Since the scales of logic are evenly balanced, we are free to put our weight on the scale of creation and Torah.

M.'s resort to the Jamesian "Will to believe" must not be understood in superficial, tactical terms. M. made clear that his choice was not dictated by the literal teaching of the first chapters of Genesis. "The gates of interpretation are not closed to us." (II, 25.) Nor did he opt for creation simply because of the possibility of including the miracles of Scripture in the primary act of creation. His argument moves on a deeper plane, so that it remains convincing in our contemporary universe of discourse. God does act in the world by relating Himself now to one person, now to another and by choosing a whole people as his instrument. (Ibid.)

Torah, in the sense of the harmonious unity of the supreme values of life, is itself a form of cognition. To love is to seek understanding, as M. put it.

Speculative reason is intimately one with the imperatives of ethics and the intuitive perceptions of "the imagination." It is our personality as a whole that confronts the mystery of the universe, and when the judgment of logic is neutralized, the associated forms of outreach within us impel us to choose that view of the world which is consonant with the ultimate reality of spiritual values. In a created world, where the free spirit of God is sovereign, the human spirit finds its validation.

It follows that faith is not an alien element to the quest of truth, or a separate faculty detached from or even opposed to reason. On the contrary, faith is an extension of the adventure of speculative reason. Faith is the total posture of man, as "in fear and love," he confronts the awesome majesty of the Supreme Being. God is "the soul of the soul" of the universe, the Ultimate Whole, Whose Wisdom proceeds from the whole to the parts, rather than the other way around. Hence, in our quest of His "nearness," we have to integrate the whole of our being— our imagination and intuition, our balanced ethical virtues and our quest of God, our hunger for aloneness with God in the ecstasy of meditation (III, 51), and our eagerness to redeem the world by deeds of justice and compassion. (III, 52–54.)

M.'s teaching in regard to the meaning of faith and its decisive role in the trans-logical realm is applied in Neo-Maimonism to the issue of God's existence, not merely the creation of the world. Defining God as the Perfect Personality, the ultimate Whole in an evolutionary holistic-mechanical cosmos, we cannot demonstrate with mathematical logic that God does indeed exist. We point to the marvelous ladders of evolution, in which wholes of ever greater complexity and range of freedom have come into being. The appearance of the human mind marked the emergence of a new phase of holism—conscious, deliberate, multi-dimensional, creative. In the geniuses of art, ethics, science, statecraft and religion, new phases of spirit are briefly glimpsed. All great achievements well up into the conscious mind of their own accord, as it were, like invasions from a sea of Super-Spirit, when the dikes are lowered, or like bolts of lightning, illuminating the dark night. The mysteries of life, mind and flashes of genius point toward the possibility of divine thrusts, impelling us toward perfection. Indeed, we perceive, however dimly, intimations of the supreme source of all values in our ethical deeds, esthetic apprehensions and experiences of holiness. But, we cannot prove that the theistic hypothesis is true.

Still, and here we touch bases with M., our inner aspirations for growth in the realms of the spirit impel us to choose that view of the cosmos, in which Spirit, Freedom and creative Growth triumph over the dead entropy of matter. Our faith in God is an extension of "the lines of growth" in our personality—our hunger for justice, our thirst for beauty, our longing for truth, our experience of holiness, when we sense the cosmic resonance of eternity. Faith is the fragmentary arc within our being, extrapolated into an invisible, eternal circle. It is the outward reach of our entire being; hence, it cannot be unreasoning, or immoral, or blind. It becomes demonic when it sets itself over against the moral, or the rational, pretending to go "beyond good and evil." It is the whole of our self orienting itself toward and seeking support from that all-embracing Self, of which our minds are but so many cells. And faith, as M. points out, is not a steady, static condition. It is rather a tremor of the soul, an assurance and an inquiry, at one and the same time.

REVELATION

While prophecy is the central theme of the "Guide," the novelty of M.'s contribution consists in his tri-partite division of revelation. He discusses first two pre-prophetic stages, along with other proto-prophetic phenomena; second, various stages of prophecy, the highest being that of Abraham; third, the super-prophetic quality of Mosaic revelation. In this way, the Torah of Moses is placed within the generally human context of inspired achievements and noble visions. The act of revelation is a quantum-extension of human perception, not the incursion of a totally foreign element.

Proto-prophetic are the diviners and the inventors, who discover new inventions intuitively, without any understanding of scientific and mathematical principles. (II, 38.) Their imagination and dedication are stimulated by the flow from Active Reason, enabling them to create instruments of human progress. Philosophers and scientists are also proto-prophetic, with their fresh visions of reality arising out of an inflow of Active Reason. However, in their case, the imaginative and intuitive faculties are short of perfection. (II, 37.) And the logic of the mind, however great it be, cannot suffice to reflect faithfully the total import of the divine thrust, which affects ideally man's entire personality.

The prophet is one whose imaginative, intuitive and rational faculties are all fully developed. Yet, even in his case, moments of genuine revelation occur infrequently. True, the good God is ever ready to grant His impulsions of goodness and wisdom. Though He is free to withhold

His gift, He, in His Goodness, is ever ready to uplift men. But, even the noblest prophet can rise to the requisite levels of perfection only on a few occasions. Moses was far superior to all other prophets; indeed, he was unique and incomparable. Still, Moses was incapable of reaching the heights of prophecy during 38 of the 40 years that the Israelites wandered in the wilderness. (II, 36.)

M. lists two pre-prophetic stages that great men may reach. Both are characterized by the influx of the Holy Spirit *(ruah hakodesh)*. (II, 45 & II, 41.) In the first case this influx is manifested in great deeds, accomplished by leaders who are fired with the determination to redeem an oppressed people or to advance the cause of mankind. In the second case, the Divine power is employed to compose great works of inspiration and wisdom—such as, the Writings *(kethubim)* of Holy Scriptures.

Taking the proto-prophetic and the pre-prophetic stages together, we have here a conception of revelation that embraces all that makes for the advancement of mankind, unifying religion with the several branches of culture. Revelation is a thrust toward higher levels of holiness, in the life of the individual and of society. And the culmination of this advance will be attained in the messianic era, when material prosperity will be conjoined with ethical maturity and religious truth.[15]

In these stages of *ruah hakodesh* we are given a theory of universal progress, since philosophers, poets and cultural heroes address themselves to all mankind. We recall that, in M.'s view, Aristotelian philosophy was itself an integral part of the esoteric wisdom of the prophets and sages. His interpretation of the Noachide principles as a body of "general revelation" fits into his scheme of an all-embracing philosophy of culture, consisting of artistic achievements and ethical principles intended for all men along with the Torah designed for the Jewish people.

If we now skip across the nine specific stages of prophecy and examine M.'s concept of the prophecy of Moses, we find that he takes pains to stress its radically dogmatic character. Everything said about other prophets and prophecy in general, he tells us, does not apply to Mosaic revelation. (II, 35; II, 39.) Since his original problem was to reconcile the Torah of Moses, not merely prophecy in general, with the dictates of philosophy, it is certainly paradoxical that he exempts Moses from the normal category of prophets. Evidently, another principle is here involved, and we shall discuss it presently.

At this point, we note that the biblical prophets occupied the middle ground between the "general revelation" of the pre- and proto-prophets and the post- or super-prophetic status of Moses. (II, 45.) While the prophets admonished the people to be loyal to the Torah of Moses, they dared to be extremely selective in their emphasis, as if they were authorized to weigh and measure the various *mizvot*. In regard to the sacrifices and the choice of Israel, they distinguished between the Primary Intention of God and His Secondary Intention. (III, 32.) Accordingly they chided the people for their ethnic zeal and their preoccupation with sacrifices, pointing out that the ultimate aims of God were the same as in "general revelations"—namely, the ethical virtues of personal life and the perfection of society. So, while the spectrum of revelation ranges from the general principles of faith to the specific ordinances of Torah, it is basically the same phenomenon.

Why, then, does M. put Mosaic prophecy in a category all its own? In the first place, he was compelled to follow the teaching of Bible and Talmud, on this point. In terms of his own philosophy of prophecy, Moses is unique because there was no admixture of imagination in his teaching. (II, 36.) But strangely enough, M. states it as a rule that the prophet is superior to the philosopher, precisely because the latter lacks the qualities of imagination and intuition. (II, 37.) Evidently, in terms of prophetic receptivity, the more the imagination is developed, the better, but in terms of the content of prophetic revelation, the less it is enveloped by the fancies of imagination, the better. The role of the prophet is to serve as the "channel," whereby the divine uplifting thrust is conveyed to mankind. To this end, imagination or intuition is essential, since the prophet, in distinction from the philosopher, addresses himself to an entire community, which is more likely to be affected by rites and symbols than by ideals and ideas. However, the inner content of revelation can be discovered only by penetrating through the poetic imagery of prophecy and isolating its rational content. The Primary Intention, say, of the sacrificial ritual, described in the Torah, is the purpose of the Divine Will. The Secondary Intention was the "cunning" of Providence in leading Israel and mankind by slow and devious steps from idolatry to true religion. (III, 32.) And the prophets, from Amos and Hosea to Haggai and Malachi, taught the Israelites to distinguish between the Primary Intention of God, reflecting His Purpose for mankind, and His Secondary Intention in providing the social institutions and rituals needed for the ultimate triumph of the Divine Will.

At this point, we note a most important distinction which M. draws between "True Beliefs" and "Necessary Beliefs"—the former are true in themselves, the latter, while strictly untrue, serve the cause of truth. (III, 28 & III, 32.) As an example of the latter, he cites the belief that God listens to the prayers of men, turning from the policy of Wrath to that of Compassion, and changing the course of events in response to the earnest petitions of people. (III, 28.) In the case of rituals, the elaborate ordinances regulating the sacrifices in the Temple were designed to wean the people away from dependence on animal offerings. Similarly, the laws regulating family life continued relics of barbarism which the contemporaries of Moses were not willing to abandon all at once. (III, 32 & III, 47.) So, too, in the case of ideas, the "Necessary Beliefs" were designed to establish a community dedicated to "True Beliefs." Some popular beliefs are essential to the formation of a community that would become the bearer of great, liberating truths. That the Torah of Moses can never be replaced by other prophets is one of those "Necessary Beliefs," that insure the continuity of the Jewish faith as against the claims of Christianity and Islam. In a larger sense, the entire dogmatic structure of Judaism, insofar as it reaches beyond the truths of philosophy, the impetus of prophecy and the messianic vision, belongs in this category of "Necessary Beliefs," particularly the teachings about hell and the resurrection of the dead.

What is the content of revelation, in M.'s scheme?

If we ignore for a moment the Torah of Moses, revelation is an energetic thrust, rather than a rational proposition. It is so protean that it assumes in different minds, forms as diverse as the speculations of the philosopher, the insights of an inventor, the visions of a poet, the arts of the statesman. In every case, the intent of the divine inflow is directed not alone to the prophetic personality but to the society of which he is part. And the nobler the level of prophecy, the more it is oriented toward the entire community and ultimately toward all of humanity. Revelation contains a rational core; indeed, the Divine inflow affects reason primarily and imagination secondarily; but it is more than sheer reason, since the ideal prophet's grasp exceeds the reach of the philosopher. What, then, is the plus of prophetic revelation?

To say, as does Franz Rosenzweig, that God reveals His own Being is beside the point. "The entire world reveals His Glory." And in a more direct sense, God does not reveal Himself. The prophet receives a call, a command together with an intimation of God's reality. To assert that

God reveals His love is true in a general sense, but this answer does not capture the special nuance of the Maimonidean philosophy, or the genius of Hebraic prophecy. The prophet loves his people, but he is also their severest critic. It would be more correct to characterize revelation as a thrust toward messianic perfection of the individual and of society. The two goals are one in essence, for the closer one comes to God the more he is dedicated to the promotion within society of "steadfast love" *(hesed),* "righteousness" *(zedakah)* and "justice" *(mishpat).* (III, 54.) An anticipation of the building of God's Kingdom on earth is implicit in the "inflow" from Active Reason, whether it occurs on the lowest, pre-civilization level, or on the highest, prophetic level. In each case, the recipient is impelled to bring some gift for the Kingdom; he is filled with "divine discontent," he must destroy as well as build, he is charged with a mission. All things are judged by Him in the light of the future kingdom. So, he is hopeful when others are despairing and embittered when others are celebrating. His sole standard is the "nearness of God" and His Word. So, Job, who was not a prophet, came to realize that the highest good, "the knowledge of God," is available to us, even when we are troubled in body and anguished in soul. (III, 23.)

In a word, revelation brings a dynamic unity of reassurance, discontent and the vision of the long road ahead; hence, it impels the prophets to bless even as they curse, to speak of the glories that are to come, even as they expose the moral failings of their contemporaries. Above all, revelation is a "quest," a demand for creative action of one kind or another.

In our day, this concept of revelation is completely tenable, though our view of the world does not consist of Spheres and Active Reason. If we accept the world-view of what Hartshorne calls the "convergent philosophy," we recognize that new creative energy may well enter into us. God is the Pole of whole-creation, but He also includes the Pole of resistance or raw matter, in His Being. He is eternal, but He also lives in time. He enters into human history, when hearts and minds are readied for Him. To paraphrase Matthew Arnold, "He is the Power, not ourselves, that makes for growth in Life, Mind and Spirit." Is not the course of evolution, as analyzed by Morgan, Bergson, Alexander and Teilhard de Chardin, a demonstration of the continuing creativity of the Divine Being? Can we not discern an advance toward the emergence of creatures with greater measures of freedom?—If God is the Pole of wholeness building in the cosmos, then a series of pulsations toward ever greater wholes is precisely what we should expect.

Neo-Maimonism, then, accepts the principle of revelation as an incursion of supra-human energy into the souls of creative individuals and into society. Along with M., we recognize the many-sidedness of revelation. It is by no means confined to the sphere of religion. It reinvigorates "the lines of growth" in the spirit of man. It is reflected in the realms of art, science, philosophy and statecraft. It ranges in power from everyday premonitions, that occur to most of us, to the creative ecstasies of geniuses.

Neo-Maimonism differs from the "life-philosophies" of Germany and the philosophy of Bergson, in the recognition that the fresh incursions of spiritual energy center on the expansion of the range of intelligence. The heart of reality is not the sheer impetus of a cosmic will, as in Schopenhauer and Nietzsche, nor is it a blind life-force, the *elan vital,* but spirit in the sense of the total outreach of man, including the disciplines of reason, ethics and esthetics. At the same time, Neo-Maimonism rejects the separation of religion from the other domains of culture. There is a goal and purpose to human history, and all efforts "to improve the world by the Kingdom of the Almighty" subserve that goal.

The essential characteristic of revelation is not the transmission of static information, but the confirmation of a direction. The recipient is powerfully oriented toward the achievement of "the nearness of God." The content of revelation is a hunger and a thirst for more and more of the things of God. As a dynamic phenomenon, revelation consists of three elements—an affirmation, a negation, a drive toward action.

As an affirmation, revelation is basically the reorientation of man's spirit toward the infinite goal of building God's Kingdom on earth. One comes to feel part of that wondrous company of great men and women who dared dream of the ideal society of mankind. One is reassured that this infinite quest will come closer and closer to realization. None of us comes to the experience of revelation totally alone and naked. On the contrary, we are sustained in our quest for God's "nearness," by the "sacred tradition" of our community. And in the experience of revelation, we find the values of the past confirmed and reinvigorated, in so far as their intent is separable from the external forms which they assumed in the various contingencies of history. God's

Word at any one time cannot be in contradiction with His Eternal Will, as revealed to all men and women of good-will.

Neo-Maimonism applauds the principle of M. that the main road to true revelation is that of critical, objective rationality. Moses is praised for not daring to engage in metaphysical speculation before he has prepared himself fully for that task by means of mathematical and logical studies. And when the influx of Divine energy comes, it inspires man's rational faculty primarily. We cannot attain the insights of revelation by means of emotional rhapsodies, or by withdrawing from the world. Kierkegaard's slogan, "subjectivity is truth," is only partially true, in the two senses—first, that the final fulcrum of truth is the mind of the individual; second, that all truth is inescapably filtered through the forms and limitations of our minds. Our formulation would be, "in all truth there is subjectivity," since it is the individual's hunger for truth and meaning that opens his mind to the influx of revelation. For this very reason, we are called to prepare ourselves for revelation by a critical analysis of the several ways in which we are subjectively structured. We are subjective, as individuals, as Jews, as Americans, as professionals. These varied influences increase our receptivity only when we have subjected them to critical analysis. The would-be prophet, even to the smallest extent, must emulate the prophets in the ardor of self-criticism.

So, we come to the second component of revelation—its negation. The prophet, knowing himself to be in the vanguard of mankind, condemns not merely the vices of his contemporaries but their virtues as well. His lips have been touched by the embers of eternity; he is impelled to surge beyond the landmarks of the past; he rails at the limitations and shortcomings of his contemporaries.

Above all, the divine-human encounter in Judaism must be translated into one action or another. In the first paragraph of the *Shema,* the love of God is carried out by way of teaching one's children, building one's home and spelling out its meaning in the market-places of the city.

In Neo-Maimonism, we have to recognize the role of "Necessary Beliefs"—that is, of ideas which are essential to the maintenance of the community. Without rituals and a common texture of ideas and sentiments, no community can live and serve as a bearer of truth. However, the "Necessary Beliefs" must be constantly subject to review and reexamination. Do they really, in our time, serve to provide a vehicle of truth and kingdom-building energy? Or is the opposite the case, with the rituals and "Necessary Beliefs" tying our people in knots and preventing them from facing up to the challenges of our time?

In general, the "sacred tradition" in its totality is our starting point. And this tradition is far from being monolithic. It is neither *Halachah* alone nor "ethical monotheism" alone, but the living texture of ideas and sentiments, ranging from the darkest hues of folk-mythology to the brightest ideals of humanity. We accept it with the greatest reverence as the deposit of revelations in the past, which is essential to the continuity of the Torah-community. But in the spirit of classical prophecy and philosophy, we accept it critically, distinguishing between the essence of faith and its external manifestations, at any one time or place. We recognize that what may have been a "necessary" belief at one time, may no longer be so today. We also affirm that a rite, devised by the "cunning of God" for a particular time, might well become counter-productive in our day. So, we of the Conservative movement no longer pray for the reestablishment of the sacrificial system in the Temple, drawing the consequences of M.'s reasoning, though in his own time he could not do so, without tearing the Jewish community apart.

NOTES

1. In his "Guide," M. makes use of "created lights" and "created voices," but only grudgingly, as a concession to the unsophisticated. See 1, 5, where M. concludes, "If an individual of insufficient capacity should not wish to reach the rank to which we desire him to ascend and should he consider that all the words [figuring in the Bible] [for seeing] concerning this subject are indicative of sensual perception of created lights—be they angels or something else— why, there is no harm in his thinking this." (Pines, *The Guide of the Perplexed,* Chicago, 1963, p. 31.) Still, in 1, 10, M. writes as if the "created light" was indeed there—that is, on Mount Sinai. Shem Tov on 1, 19, writes that "created lights" were indeed externally visible to the common people, but only the prophets apprehended the inner light. Generally, M. confines the hearing of God's voice to the dreams of prophets, save in the case of Moses, who heard Him in a vision. Afudi on 1, 37. In 1, 25, M. offers both interpretations of *Shechinah*—in the sense of "created light" and in the sense of Providence. We may assume confidently that the latter sense corresponds to his own belief. See also 11, 44.

2. "Guide," 1, 71.

3. "For the Lord, blessed be He, loves only truth and hates only falsehood." (11, 47.)

4. Second paragraph of first chapter of Sefer Hamada.

5. Whether M. believed that he had indeed attained the rank of prophecy is a question of semantics, for he refers more than once to quasi-prophetic insights that came to him. So, in the introduction to third part of the "Guide," he remarks, "No divine revelation (nevua elohit) has come to me to teach me . . . Now rightly guided reflection and divine aid in this matter have moved me (vehine orartani bo hamahshavah hameyusheret vehoezer hoelohi)." (Pines, p. 416.) In "Guide" III, 22, M. exclaims, "See how I succeeded as if by prophecy" (kidemut nevuah). Pines translates—"See how these notions came to me through something similar to prophetic revelation" (p 488.)

In our view, M. assimilates prophetic revelation to the many kinds and variations of inspiration that come to the great benefactors of mankind.

6. The role of courage and intuition (Koah Hameshaer) in prophecy is mentioned in 11, 38. The orientation of prophecy toward the greater society is stressed in 11, 39 See also 11, 37, "the nature of the intellect is such that it always overflows."

7. This thought is more clearly presented in M's "Eight Chapters."

8. The teleology of M. is discussed in detail in Z. Diesendruck's article, "Hatachlit Vehataarim betorat Horambam" in Tarbitz, II, (1930), pp 106–134 & pp. 27–73. Also in his "Die Teleogie bei Maimonides." H.U.C.A. vol. V (Cincinnati, 1929).

9. M's conception of the positive functions carried out by Christianity and Islam in preparing the way for the Messiah is stated explicitly in his Code. "Hilchot Melachim," Chapter XI, uncensored version.

"But it is beyond the human mind to fathom the designs of the Creator, for our ways are not His ways, neither are our thoughts His thoughts. All these matters relating to Jesus of Nazareth and the Ishmaelite (Mohammed) who came after him, only served to clear the way for King Messiah, to prepare the whole world to worship God with one accord, as it is written, 'For then I will turn to the peoples a pure language, that they may all call upon the name of the Lord to serve Him with one consent' (Zephaniah 3, 9). Thus, the Messianic hope, the Torah and the commandments have become familiar topics—topics of conversation (among the inhabitants) of the far isles and many peoples, uncircumcised of heart and flesh . . ." (transl. by I. Twersky, *Maimonides Reader* [New York, 1972], p. 226).

M. makes use here of the conception of "Divine Cunning" ("Guide" III, 32), whereby God achieves His purpose indirectly.

10. M. defines repentance as the actual transformation of the sinner's disposition, so that "He who knows all secrets can testify that were the sinner to be

presented with similar temptations he would not ever commit that sin." ("Hil-chot Teshuvah," II, 2).

11. (III, 12) "His compassion in His creation of guiding forces [i.e. instincts] for animals."

12. (II, 29) "For faith in God and the joy inherent in that faith are two matters which cannot change . . ."

13. (III, 17) "But I believe that providence is consequent upon the intellect and attached to it." (Pines, p. 474.)

14. In chapters III, 17 & 18, M. expatiates on the principle that divine providence is extended in proportion to a person's closeness to God. In opposition to the argument that a whole ship, containing hundreds of people, might sink through the action of wind and water, he responds that the decision to enter the ship was in every case, a personal one. Presumably, the saint who is close to God would have been warned by some intimation *(hearah)* not to enter that ship.

15. "Therefore I say that the Law, although it is not natural, enters into what is natural. It is a part of the wisdom of the Deity with regard to the permanence of this species . . . [i.e. humanity] . . ." (II, 40.)

PART ONE

JACOB B. AGUS AS A STUDENT OF MODERN JEWISH PHILOSOPHY

SELECTIONS AND
PREFATORY REMARKS
David Novak

FROM 1941, when he published his first book, *Modern Philosophies of Judaism* (originally his Harvard Ph.D. dissertation), until the end of his life, Jacob Agus continually wrestled with and reflected on modern Jewish thought in all its many variations.

The following selections, chosen to accompany David Novak's essay "Jacob B. Agus as a Student of Modern Jewish Philosophy" in *American Rabbi: The Life and Thought of Jacob B. Agus* (New York, 1996), are drawn from Jacob Agus' *Modern Philosophies of Judaism: A Study of Recent Jewish Philosophies of Religion* (New York, 1941), 325–51; and *High Priest of Rebirth: The Life, Times and Thought of Abraham Isaac Kuk* (New York, 1972), 129–55 and 227–34 (originally published in 1946 under the title *The Banner of Jerusalem*).

5

THE COMMON CORE OF
MODERN JEWISH PHILOSOPHY

HAVING SCRUTINIZED in detail the philosophies of Cohen, Rosenzweig, Buber and Kaplan, we turn now to the task of obtaining the necessary perspective in which they may be viewed as a whole. There is little direct influence that these four exponents of modern Jewish philosophy of religion exerted upon each other. Yet, there are certain basic ideas that are common to them all. These ideas are more important by far than the numerous points of difference between them.

Together, the four systems constitute the typical trends of modern Jewish philosophy of religion. Outside of the Orthodox and neo-Orthodox philosophies, there have not been produced other works on the Jewish religion that introduce any new element, or that contain a fundamentally new approach.[1]

Our search for the points of contact between the philosophies of Cohen, Buber, Rosenzweig and Kaplan resolves itself, therefore, into an attempt to establish whether there are any basic convictions, apart from Jewish ritual and ceremony, that are common to all great Jewish thinkers. Naturally, we cannot expect sameness or even similarity in the detailed exposition of their systems, since there is no accepted philosophical tradition in the modern world. In the Medieval era, there were many acrimonious conflicts over philosophical propositions, but in the background of those disputes, there was a body of principles, methods, terms and dogmas employed by all who ventured to explore the infinite sea of thought. In our own era, this situation no longer obtains. There is no "logic" acceptable to all, no unquestioned universally revered philosophical tradition, not even one set of technical terminology. Consequently, it is to be expected that modern Jewish theology will be discussed in the light of diverse philosophical viewpoints and that it will be radically reinterpreted to suit the opinions of the different trends of modern thought. Yet, if Jewish philosophy of religion is to be Jewish as well as philosophy, it must contain certain fundamental convictions, that are really derived from Jewish tradition, not merely artificially interpreted into it.

On the surface, it may appear that there is little, if any, common ground to the four philosophies. Cohen was an extreme rationalist, carrying faith in reason to unprecedented limits. He refused to take for granted any data, other than those of reason. At the base of his system, he placed the astounding assertion that reason is capable of producing its own ideas and developing its own concepts, without the aid of data derived from experience. To be sure, Cohen regarded reason as incapable of obtaining metaphysical knowledge. He insisted on a severe distinction between objective knowledge and metaphysics. But, at the same time, he thought of reason as a timeless world-process, entirely self-sufficient as an instrument of knowledge, containing the seeds of its own infinite development. He scornfully repudiated any form of intuition as a source of true knowledge and he had no patience with materialists and empiricists. The conclusions of "pure reason" alone are true knowledge. Everything else is sheer opinion, or as he put it, a task for knowledge.

Buber, on the other hand, is a neo-mystic. While he differs from the "grand mystics" in maintaining that no union with or absorption into the Divine Being is possible, he is a mystic in the sense that he seeks a direct contact with God. The speculations of reason, "pure" or not, are mere bubbles on the surging waves of reality. Disinterested thinking can only lead to an unreal artificial world of laws, principles and material elements—a world that is largely the product of our own mentality. The only way to approach reality is through the Thou relation. It is "blind" love, not the cold eye of reason that is capable of penetrating to the core of things.

Rosenzweig called himself an empiricist. He was a believer in experience, in the sense that his philosophy was founded upon an experience—the experience of revelation. This experienced intuition was employed by Rosenzweig to reverse the entire course of philosophy.

His refutation of that vast system of thought, which was unfolded by degrees from Thales to Hegel, was based upon our alleged dissatisfaction as individuals with the consolation of philosophy. The individual's fear of death, Rosenzweig asserted, is not allayed by the admonition of the philosophers to contemplate the Absolute. Evidently, he argued, there is something in the nature of man that escapes the net of the philosophy—a something, which reason can only regard as a Naught. Yet, it is a fruitful naught, the matrix of the true human self. Rosenzweig insisted, in substance, that the whole of man must be taken as the test of a philosophy, not his reason alone. Otherwise, he claimed, philosophy is but a half-truth. As contrasted with the German idealistic school, Rosenzweig may therefore be called an empiricist. It is hardly necessary to point out that there is no connection whatever between him and the English empirical school.

Kaplan is a pragmatist. His main interest throughout his writings is practical. Sharing the disdain of the American pragmatical school for the speculations of the metaphysicians, Kaplan is concerned only with establishing those beliefs that have a direct, practical bearing on life. The one belief of religion that really matters is the assertion that there is a Power—not ourselves, that makes for righteousness. This belief helps man to live a noble life; therefore, it is both good and true. A healthy man will accept it and build his life upon it. Apart from this belief, Kaplan regards all phases of human experience as equal in value. There is no Absolute Moral Law, nor any set scheme for approaching the Divine. Human happiness, or salvation, is the ultimate test of any belief or course of action. The bewildering flow of variegated human experience is the final reference and test of all truth.

Notwithstanding these basic differences, there is a core of belief that is common to all these philosophers and—what is more important, common as well to the long line of Jewish sages and prophets, from Moses down. This core of belief, it will appear upon analysis, is the main theme and the real starting-point of all these thinkers, forming the one cornerstone of their respective systems of thought.

We shall approach most conveniently this all-important common ground of Jewish philosophers through an examination of the following question, "what is the source of ethical value?"

As human beings we are prone to pass judgment on all things. We either approve or we disapprove of the millions of phenomena that enter within the range of our experience. In most cases, the reasons for our value-judgments are the very evident ones of self-interest. Adjectives such as pleasant, painful, enjoyable, boring, promising, ominous, reassuring, menacing, etc. are obviously conferred on things because of our concern with our own welfare.

Now, the question arises whether the judgments, good and bad, right and wrong, ethical and unethical, are similarly based on subjective considerations, or whether they are derived from our apprehension of the existence of some objective standards. Why do we uncompromisingly approve of charitable deeds and disapprove of acts of robbery, disloyalty and duplicity? Our own personal interest is, in many cases, unaffected by the deeds that we so warmly applaud or by those that we so heartily condemn. Since self-interest is not the source of these judgments and since, furthermore, they are characterized by the quality of objectivity, are we justified in assuming the awareness, on the part of men, of an impersonal moral law in accordance with which the judgments of right and wrong are made?

This question as to the source of ethical valuation is, of course, a very ancient one. It would take us far beyond the limits of our subject, if we attempted even a bare outline of its history. Suffice it to say that a large and respectable group of thinkers, headed by Aristotle, have maintained that all human judgments could be understood as variations of self-interest. Various ingenious explanations have been offered for the apparent objectivity and earnestness of "the voice of conscience." Generally speaking, these theories may be classified as either materialistic or humanistic. In the former category belong all the explanations which "explain" morality away in the process of trying to understand it. The best known modern representative of this group is Friedrich Nietsche, whose apology for unbridled brutalitarianism was based upon his purported discovery of the origin of traditional morality in the thwarted will to power of the slave-peoples, primarily, the Jewish nation.[2] In the latter category belong those doctrines which maintain that the ethical insight of human beings is somehow valid, though that insight is really a development of the instinct for self-preservation. The humanists take the civilized conscience of man as their standard of reference. All human interests are good and the ethical strivings of man are of essentially the same value or authority as other human desires and aspirations.

Cohen, Buber, Rosenzweig and Kaplan—all agree in rejecting both materialism and humanism. They concur in maintaining that there is something about our experience of the moral law, which cannot be reduced to self-interest. You cannot analyze the voice of conscience in terms of selfish or indifferent impulses, without proving false to it. The moral law appears in consciousness as an absolute command, spurning all selfish and unworthy motives. It can only be understood on its own face value, as an objective law of action, deriving from the structure of reality. An essential part of ethical experience is the feeling that there is an outside source to our judgments of right and wrong, that the stamp of validity attaches to our apprehensions of the rightness and wrongness of things.

This conviction is not only common to the philosophers discussed; it constitutes the main vantage point of their respective philosophies. While they express this fluid intuition in radically different ways, they agree in founding their systems of thought upon it.

Cohen begins his system with the "basic law of truth" (Grundgesetz der Wahrheit). Truth, he then goes on to say, is the recognition that the two directions of spirit, logic and ethics, must be "pure." The requirement concerning the "purity" of ethics in turn implies the assertion that the judgments of ethics are intrinsically valid and authoritative. We must not attempt to find the origin of morality in the consciousness of social pressure or in the sublimation and rationalization of some unworthy motive; the "basic law of truth" directs us to treat ethics as an independently authoritative and valid science.

If we should now inquire for the reasons that lead Cohen to accept his so-called "law of truth," we shall be confronted with the answer that truth is its own final authority. In other words, Cohen's philosophy of life is based upon an original insight into the objective validity of ethical judgments. To be sure, Cohen insisted that philosophy must not start with anything "given" by experience or intuition. But, then, that insistence was an impossibility, to begin with. Cohen's initial axiom, the requirement that logic and ethics should be "pure," must itself be assumed. In the final analysis, then, Cohen's system is based upon the conviction that our ethical experience contains the seal of objective validity. The concept of God, which logically belongs at the beginning of Cohen's system, further supports this observation that the intuition of the authoritativeness of the moral law and of its ultimate vindication is the starting point of his thought.

Buber's "Thou-relation" may also be classified as an ethical experience. As we have seen before, this relation is the concentration of the individual in the feeling of love. Whenever this relation appears, communion with the Deity, to a limited extent, is established. "The extended lines of relations meet in the eternal Thou; by means of every particular thou, the primary word addresses the eternal Thou." It is through love, then, that man reaches out toward the Deity. Without doubt the impulse of non-sexual love should be regarded as ethical in character. Many thinkers viewed the feeling of love as the highest culmination of ethical experience. Buber's claim that reality can only be attained through the Thou-relation, involves, therefore, the conviction that the road of ethics alone leads to God. Ethical thought and life are the response of man to the call of God. "Dialogue-living" is real, valid and authoritative.

The sense of the omnipresence of God, breaking through the "It-world" with overwhelming suddenness and power, is, to Buber, a valid intuition of reality. Yet, this mystical apprehension of God's presence is attained only through the long sustained practice of concentrating and directing our entire fund of devotion upon the needs of our fellow-men. The Thou-relation is at once, and essentially both, ethical and religious. It is religious not only in the superficial sense of being com-manded by God, but in the deeper and more intimate sense of a direct communion with God.

The philosophies of Cohen and Buber appear to be so contrasting in character that it is difficult to realize that they derive from similar intuitions concerning the objective validity of ethical experience. The assurance of objective reality in the feeling of rightness may be expressed in two ways. It may be construed as arising from our awareness of the reign of a cosmic law or a series of laws, according to which the right acts and attitudes in every conceivable situation are determined with inflexible definiteness. Or, the source of validity of ethics may be identified as the Will of God, and the answer in every situation is accordingly sought through a fresh orientation to the Being of God.

The systems of Buber and Cohen represent extreme developments of these two alternatives, respectively. Cohen began with the recognition of the "lawfulness" of ethical judgments. He noted the similarity in development of both logic and ethics and, in his "Grundgesetz der Wahrheit," he set forth the requirement of "purity" for both these directions of spirit. "Purity" is, clearly, a technical designation for abso-lutely perfect and self-sufficient lawfulness. While in his "Ethics," Co-hen stressed this aspect of the ethical will, in his later writings, he came to recognize more and more the importance of the reference to God, which is vaguely implied in the apprehension of ethical values. Buber, on the other hand, chooses to ignore the element of rational lawfulness in ethical experience altogether. The validity of ethical insight is not due to any agreement with a cosmic law, but to the call of the Divine Voice. The reference to God, implied in the Thou-relation, is the one essential element of the ethical, or, as he would say, of the real life.

Cohen's interest is essentially that of cognition. Hence, in dealing with the meaning of the ethical values, he expressed the intuition of their validity, from the viewpoint of knowing, as "truth." In his later writings, Cohen conceived of this basic certainty as the guarantee of God. It cannot be emphasized too often that the concept of God is the most central idea in Cohen's philosophy. Though God is an "idea" and a "methodological concept," He is nevertheless a real Being, unique and transcendent. We must not be deceived by the language of Cohen. Writing from the standpoint of epistemology, he naturally wrote only of ideas and concepts. Still, in his view, God partakes of the processes of both will and thought and is the ultimate Reality. Thus, the apprehension of the validity of ethics contains, with Cohen, a direct reference to God, as the Source of ethics.

Buber's interest is practical. Scanning the wide field of ethical experience, he concludes that the life of ethics cannot be expressed either in cold principles, or in bare maxims. Ethics is neither thought, nor will, nor feeling, but life, the fulness of life, which is all-inclusive. Wherever self-less love is expressed, there Buber finds the perception of ultimate reality and a reference to God, as the final focus of all earthly Thous— the eternal Thou.

The common elements in the basic insights of both Cohen and Buber are, first, the state of mind in which both the good and the true are sought as one. They start with the feeling that these two goals are somehow one, that there is a common core, accessible to the heart of man, which is at once valid and right. In the "Thou" relation, the will to serve God and the will to know God are merged. Similarly, the "law of truth" stands at the borderlines and unites the processes of thought and will. Secondly, there is a sense of the "reality" of the ethical life— that is, the feeling that the good life is in accord with the eternal structure of things. To Buber, the "dialogue" life is the only "real" life and the reward of morality is the knowledge of being real. Cohen, too, sees no sanction to ethics. The good man has the satisfaction of knowing that his life is steered in the direction of the three "pure" processes of Being. Thirdly, both believe that the ultimate validity of ethical motivation is due to the Will of God. Buber's thought is expressed in the belief that all love is love of God; every Thou-relation is an address to the eternal Thou. Cohen's belief takes the form of the principle that the validity of the direction of pure will and its eternity are guaranteed by the God of truth.[3]

Rosenzweig's basic intuition is similar to those of Cohen and Buber. It will be remembered that Rosenzweig's philosophy is based upon the experience of revelation. The love of God streams into the heart of man, who is, thereupon, constrained to reply with love to his fellow-man. Rosenzweig believes that human love is derived from the love of God and that the love of man to his fellow-man is an integral link in the eternal triangle of creation, revelation and redemption. Clearly, then, there is no essential difference between Buber's and Rosenzweig's versions of the nature of the ethical-religious experience.

Kaplan's one belief is, as we have seen, the affirmation that ethical rightness and wrongness are rooted in the ultimate structure of reality. God is the Being, Who assures the final triumph of the ideals of mankind. Kaplan does not describe the line of demarcation between the consciousness of ethical and non-ethical ideals, nor does he indicate how God functions in the world. Obviously, if ethical values are to be accorded supreme ontological status in the scheme of existence, they must be conceived as endowed with distinguishing characteristics, which mark them off decisively from the stream of ordinary phenomena. Nevertheless, in spite of his failure to draw such a line of demarcation, Kaplan, in his own way, bases his religion upon the assertion that our awareness of ethical values includes a perception of their objective validity and a reference to God as their Guarantor.

Thus, we see that the four greatest and most typical exponents of recent Jewish thought agree in basing religion upon the perception of ethical values. Though they represent widely differing philosophical movements, these thinkers agree that, at bottom, religion and ethics are one and that the voice of conscience is somehow also the voice of God. In this belief, modern Jewish philosophers continue to cultivate the original insight of their ancestral faith.

Jewish monotheism was derived from the impulses and longings of ethics, not from reasoned speculations concerning the cosmos. For this reason, there was always an impassable gulf between the monotheism of the Greeks, especially of Aristotle, which was based upon the recognition of the metaphysical unity of the world, and the monotheism of the Hebrew prophets, which was so powerfully epitomised in Abraham's query, "Can it be that the Judge of the whole world will not do justice?" God as the "Righteous Ruler of the Universe" and God as the Source of "Order" in the world are the two conceptions, stemming from Judaism and from Greek philosophy respectively, which theologians, since Philo, have sought to harmonize.[4] Modern Jewish philosophy continues, in the main, to be derived from a heightened sense of ethical values. In all its diverse ramifications, modern exponents of Judaism remain true to the deep insight of Elijah that God is not to be found through the contemplation of the fire and wind of the physical universe, but that the "still, small voice" of conscience is indeed the voice of God.

I have endeavored to present a strictly objective account of modern Jewish philosophy. However, I am conscious of the fact that a completely impartial history of philosophy cannot possibly be written. The essence of philosophy is the description and explanation of things from certain viewpoints and you cannot chart the map of viewpoints without revealing the coordinates of your own thought. For this reason, many philosophers began the exposition of their own systems of philosophy with histories of philosophy, believing that their views of the development of thought were clear illustrations of their own basic ideas.

In order to enable the reader to judge this work for himself, it is necessary that I set forth here the basic principles of my own thought, insofar as they are relevant to the construction of a philosophy of religion.

    1. From a logical standpoint, complete skepticism is possible. We may sit down in an easy chair, pass all the data of our mind in review and demand incontrovertible proof from them that they are not all part of one grand illusion. To an aggressively skeptical state of mind, all "proofs" must be further substantiated through "proofs of proofs" and so on, ad infinitum. In the pale light of skepticism, all facts and values assume of necessity the ghostly aspect of unreality. Thought itself is powerless to arrest this process of total dissolution, through militant disbelief, whereby the world and its contents are turned into an ephemeral nightmare. But no such power is required by thought, since the pressure of life itself soon puts an end to the unearthly speculations of the skeptic. Away from

the easy chair and within the seething cauldron of life's actual problems, no one but the insane will question the reality of the existence of the world or of man. Our "animal faith," to employ a celebrated phrase of Santayanna, brushes aside with supreme unconcern and ease the vast array of logic so torturously assembled by the philosophical skeptic.

When we pose to ourselves the question of the ultimate foundation and purpose of existence, we are similarly able in strict logic to adopt an agnostic attitude. Perhaps, there is no eternal Reality behind the flux of phenomena, we may say, or if there be such a Reality, it is to us totally incomprehensible. The best we can do, it may be argued, is to designate that Reality as the Unknowable. This attitude, too, is refuted, not by any rational means, but by the fact that *human* life and *human* ideals continue to demand that we orient our lives to some valid goals. As skepticism in regard to the existence of the physical universe is overcome by the pressure of animal impulses, so is agnosticism in regard to the ultimate nature of reality surmounted by the spirit of man which impels us never to give up the search for God, for truth and goodness. Complacent agnosticism is itself a sin against the human spirit. In spite of past failures, it is our spiritual duty to employ our best lights in the attempt, at once human and divine, to know the Unknowable. From this sacred endeavor, we may not fall back in weak despair without losing our title to the crown of human dignity. "For the righteous man falleth seven times and riseth up again." [5]

If, then, we spurn the deathly refuge of the skeptic, we can only answer the basic question of philosophy, "what is the essence of all things?" by postulating frankly a reasonable assumption or by referring to an intuition of reality. This fact becomes evident through an examination of the nature of logical thought. Deductive logic proceeds from the general proposition to the particular instance. Possessing the major premise, we are enabled, through deductive logic, to note the appropriate minor premises and to draw the correct conclusions. But, the final major premise, how can it be obtained? Here is where thought ends and intuition begins. Inductive logic proceeds from the particular to the universal. Major premises are built up through the consideration of a number of relevant individual cases. Strictly speaking, inductive logic requires the verification of all the instances that are comprised within the major premise. Otherwise, the major premise must still be regarded as unproved. In the case of the question before us, inductive logic is obviously inapplicable. Clearly, then, our views on the essence of things will be based on an intuition. There is room for reason in the criticism of alternative answers, of course. Thus, I agree with the idealistic criticism of the materialistic position on the ground that the concepts of matter, force, energy, etc. are not valid metaphysical concepts. I further believe that the progress of science has rendered materialism totally untenable. But, when we come to the presentation of a positive answer concerning the essence of things, we are compelled to fall back upon our own deepest convictions.

There is no way of evading this choice of an intuition. Cohen dared to reject all "given" elements in the construction of his system. So long as he was occupied with the problems of logic, he managed to retain this position. But, we have seen, that when he came to construct a philosophy of life, he found it necessary to begin with the "law of truth." A similar examination of all great philosophers will show, I believe, that no one can build the palace of metaphysics who does not himself provide the cornerstone.

2. The principle which we have to lay down at the base of metaphysics cannot be an arbitrary assumption. The recognition of the dependence of a rational philosophy upon a basic intuition does not grant a general license for all manner of irrational and unproved beliefs. In the history of thought, disappointment in the power of reason led all too often to the silly excesses of romantic subjectivism, which, in its turn, sooner or later, culminated in a neo-obscurantism. No intuition deserves to be taken account of which is not shared by the generality of mankind.

The difference between an intuitional truth and a rational axiom is that an axiom retains the quality of certainty at all times, so that we are never able to doubt its validity. The metaphysical intuitions, on the contrary, appear to us as overwhelmingly and incontestably true only at certain moments. Thus, Bergson's intuition of the élan vital, Schopenhauer's intuition of the cosmic Will, Jacobi's intuition of freedom— all these insights, we are told, come only at rare moments of intense concentration.[6] In other words, the claim of the intuitionists is that knowledge concerning the ultimate structure of the universe can be reached by us, only when we *are* in certain states of mind. We must assume a certain "existential" attitude, as the German thinkers put it, before we can glimpse reality. At the base of reason, it is what you—the whole of you—are that counts.

3. In seeking to solve the riddle of existence, we face the choice of beginning either with the lowest or with the highest concepts. In the first case, we assume simple elements—Democritean atoms, or electrons, or some general form of matter in motion, or a series of "neutral"

essences. From these elements, we then proceed to explain the emergence of the more complex organisms, through the operation of some simple mechanical rules. In the second case, we begin with an all-inclusive concept, the Absolute, Self, or Reason, or the Infinite, or Personality, and then attempt to reason down to earthly things.

It obviously makes a big difference in the final result, as to whether we begin with the simplest or the most complex concepts. If everything is, at bottom, particles of matter in motion, then the distinguishing traits of mankind appear to be accidental phenomena, mere temporary freaks of existence. We are higher than the universe and rightfully look down upon it. If, on the contrary, we begin with the highest concept, then man's spirit is more akin to reality than his body. Man looks up to the universe and is the more at home in it the higher he rises to the loftiest spiritual levels of which he is capable. From a strictly logical viewpoint, both assumptions are equally admissible. The final decision must come from an extra-logical source, from the depths of our own being.

4. At this point, the intuition of the objective validity of ethical values must be taken into consideration. In moments of intense moral fervor, we feel that rightness and wrongness are eternally fixed in the scheme of things; that it is not our own personal dictates and impulses that are the source of ethical feeling; that the sense of authority attaching to our ethical judgment is not derived either from the opinions of other men or from the unconscious influence of society; that the things we call "good" and "bad" are similarly designated by the Eternal One, Who stands outside of us and yet dwells within us, speaking through our mouths in moments of great, ethical exaltation.

This intuition is the basis of my philosophy and religion. I believe it, not only because on many occasions it has come to me with dazzling clarity, but, far more because this insight has been shared by the great thinkers of humanity, in particular, by the religious geniuses of Israel. To be sure, an intuition is a fluid state of mind, which cannot as a whole be imprisoned in some hard formula. Every statement in which this intuition has traditionally been phrased necessarily reflected the philosophical background and particular bias of those who have experienced it. We have seen before how beneath the apparently opposed philosophies of Judaism of our generation, there is hidden one group of insights, pointing to the divine origin of ethical values. By seizing upon different aspects of this intuition, philosophers may evolve widely varying world-views, the common source of which it is difficult to discern.

We are concerned with discovering whether there is indeed vouchsafed to man, albeit admittedly at rare moments only, an intuition of the eternal validity and of the extra-human source of ethical values. In advocating an affirmative answer to this query, I point to that long line of Hebrew prophets, who taught that God, the Creator of the world, to Whom alone true Being can be imputed, is also the Source of morality. It is the opinion of nearly all scholars that the Jewish teachers have arrived at their monotheistic faith through their intense moral enthusiasm. Their religion arose and developed out of their intuition of the absolute authority of the moral law. Among the Greeks, it was Plato who gave to the world the classic formulation of this belief, in the thought that the Good, the True and the Beautiful are One. Kant, in modern times, attempted to formulate in rigid terminology the dictates of the "practical reason," which he conceived to be a divine and eternal law, akin to the timeless principles of logic.

There are many scholars who maintain that the objectivity of ethical values is due to the unconscious pressure of society. Thus, Durkheim wrote, "If religion has given birth to all that is essential in society, it is because the idea of society is the soul of religion."[7] I do not believe that consciousness of society is the source of the highest ethical experiences. The greatest advances in ethical feeling were consummated in the hearts of those few who dared to oppose the mass-mind. The mob is always stolid and blind, motivated most powerfully by the least common denominator of moral feeling. Durkheim's "idea of society" does not, therefore, refer to any consciousness of the opinions or wishes of the actual human society in which we live, but to some vague abstraction. Furthermore, the conviction, that ethical validity derives from sociological forces, if actually believed in, is likely to dispel belief in ethical validity altogether. For it is of the essence of the highest ethical experience to feel that the source of its authority stands outside and above the shifting sands of popular approval.

We do not always apprehend in consciousness the objective validity of ethical values. It is possible for us to view moral action from an indifferent, non-moral standpoint. In that event, we see nothing peculiar in the life of morality, nothing, that is, which cannot be explained on the basis of ordinary, human impulses and drives. But there are moments in life, when, no longer skeptical and indifferent, we feel the values of morality to be supremely real, more real even than our own lives. At such moments we cannot but regard the materialistic explanations of morality as utterly false and irrelevant. Most of us, in the ordinary run of things, take moral values for granted and are not much concerned over them.

When, however, we are suddenly confronted with an outrageous crime, we realize, through the violence of our indignation, that the springs of morality are very deep indeed, streaming forth from some mysterious, divine source.

5. The intuition of objective ethical validity leads directly to the conclusion that there is a Divine Will, operating behind the veil of phenomena. Ethical values are obligatory for us, because they are willed by a Supreme Will. They could not appear to us as objective, if they did not exist apart from human minds. But values can have no existence apart from a Mind which envisages them and a Will, which, in willing them, confers upon them the status of values.

This conclusion may be drawn, no matter in what form the intuition of the validity of ethical values is conceived. In a general way, we may say that intuitional ethics may be divided into two classifications, under the headings, "justice" and "love." In the former category, ethics is conceived as a system of eternal laws, to which men on earth ought to conform. In the second category, the moralist stresses a feeling of attraction toward an elusive goal. The two different ways of construing the meaning of the ethical experience are illustrated in the philosophies of Buber and Cohen. In either case, the idea of God is found to be implied, in one way or another, in the basic insight of the moral life.

6. On the basis of this argument, I believe that metaphysics should start with the highest concept available to man, that of Personality. We are unable to give a full account of what is meant by God as Personality, any more than we can tell all about our own persons. The term "personality" is the most inclusive in our vocabulary. It includes the elements of matter, spirit, will, caprice, character, emotion, mind and the mysterious unity in which they are all fused together. By thinking of God as Personality, we indicate that from His Nature, all the multiple and diverse phenomena of existence are somehow to be explained.

For a long time, it was believed that philosophers could only believe in a "negative theology." God had to be defined in negative terms only and every adjective referring to His real positive action could only be taken in a symbolic sense. I believe with Rosenzweig that God is to be conceived as a Living Person, containing within His Being the contradictions of necessity and freedom, eternity and timeliness, matter and spirit, lawfulness and creativity, "midas hadin" and "midas horahmin." Is not the human self a similar unity of diverse elements? I do not believe that we can possibly hope to improve over the conceptions of the God of Israel in Talmudic literature, where He is pictured as at once "Our

Father," "Our King," "Lord of the Universe" and "God of Israel," "the Place" and "the Merciful." "Wherever you find the greatness of God, there too you find His humility," we read in the prayer-book. God as the metaphysical principle of unity and God as the source of ethical values are one or, as the Rabbi Levi Isaac of Berdichev was wont to phrase this truth, "God as the Far and God as the Near is One."[8]

A conception of God, reached through the process of progressive abstraction, can only be of the most general sort. Hence, it cannot possibly permit such warm attributes of His Nature as the language of true piety and genuine prayer requires. But a monotheism which derives from an intuition of ethical validity leads naturally to that view of God, which does justice to His relations with man and the world. There are in the ethical experience elements of both generality and particularity— the apprehension of a universal law of justice as well as a call to love. There is no reason, then, to decree that God cannot think of or love the individual. I see Rosenzweig's great contribution to the philosophy of religion in his contention that God does indeed love the individual.

Against the concept of God as Self or Personality, the argument is often advanced that we have no knowledge of any self. The term "self" or "person" is based upon the absence of analysis, it is pointed out. Thus, Hume and more recently Bradley have shown that we have no perception of self. They searched their minds and found nothing which endured through time, apart from the changing flux of mental representations. It was this criticism of Hume, which, more than anything else, led to the abandonment of the concept of a "personal" God, since there appeared to be no real meaning vested in that term. Yet, the argument of Hume is nothing but a quibble; I cannot imagine how, with his procedure of eliminating particular mental data, any other result was possible. McTaggart has shown that we do possess an awareness of self.[9] I feel that, little as we may know concerning the inner unity of personality, the term itself is one of the least equivocal in human parlance.

In any event, it is only as Personality that God can be worshipped. In recent years, the tendency has arisen to think of God as a Process, or a Force, or a Principle. John Stuart Mill suggested that God be worshipped as a power within reality, working steadily for the good, omnipresent, but not all-powerful. This God-force manifests itself especially in the endeavors of mankind to subdue nature and to improve the structure of society. Mill's reversion to neo-animism was motivated by the apparent insolubility of the problem of evil on the basis of traditional theology. A similar attitude prevails among some of the "Reconstructionists." Thus,

Eugene Kohn writes, "a God who is the source of evil no less than of good and who is conceived as having the power to save mankind but not using it, cannot command the reverence due to a God."[10] In this disdainful manner, he brushes aside three millenia of monotheistic piety, offering us instead the view of a God who is only an "aspect of reality." It is not my purpose to examine in detail views, which have not yet been fully developed. Here, I wish only to indicate that the conception of God as "personality" is alone capable of affording a rational solution of theological problems, while retaining the capacity of evoking the spirit of worship. It is of the essence of personality to unify and to integrate, to make room for the ideal, while yet the real continues to exist.

All so-called "contradictions" in the traditional concept of God revolve round the apparent conflict between the Will of God and His work. Yet, if we are not to be guided by the law of the jungle, this distinction must never be lost sight of. On the other hand, any doctrine which implies a complete severance between these two phases of the activity of God must end eventually in the reduction of the stature of God to that of man.

The solution of the problem of evil, which Cohen proposes, in which suffering is interpreted as "yissurim shel a'havah," "afflictions of love," appeals to me most. The point to remember is that the concept of God as the ideal personality presents many aspects, contradictions if you will, sublimed into a higher unity in the Consciousness of God. We may remonstrate with Him even as Jeremiah, complain and protest even as Job, praise and extol even as David. But it is to Him, to Him Who is mysteriously one in all His many-sidedness, that, in our moments of humble piety, we always return.

Conceptions of God as a "power" or as a "process" are altogether worthless for religion. The concept of "power" is derived from the science of physics, where it is employed to designate a potential force. Clearly, then, this term cannot be applied to God, since He must be an actual Being. If God is an actual "force" for the good interacting with the ethically neutral forces, then we should identify the effective causes of everything that is good with God—an obvious absurdity. The term "process" is one of relation, possessing no inherent meaning of its own. It becomes significant only when it is indicated what kind of process is meant.

God, as the Supreme Personality, remains an inscrutable Being. This means for religion, that we approach Him in humble supplication, conscious of our human limitations. In philosophy, this concept of God presents innumerable problems, which it is our task as thinkers to resolve. At the base of human thought, lies the feeling of humble reverence. We cannot, as living beings, see the Face of the Lord. Moses, through his humility, came closest to God. There can be no cocksureness in matters of religion, then. Often the restless agnostic comes nearer to genuine piety than the professional religionist. For piety is, at bottom, a seeking and a quest.

7. We have seen before that the awareness of the validity of ethical values comes to us in rare moments, but it is upon the insights gained in those moments that the entire moral structure of mankind is perilously reared. Every generation inherits a certain fund of moral idealism from the accumulated experience of its predecessors. But, the genuinely moral sentiments in our heritage are bound to wane, unless they are periodically strengthened through renewed devotion to the Source of ethical motivation. If worship is neglected and disdained, then, in the course of time, morality loses its distinguishing fervor. It is inevitable that it should then be classed along with other human impulses as merely a form of subtle selfishness, required by "common sense."

The highest ethical experience is a reply to a Thou as well as an awareness of the eternal "rightness" of ethical life. It is this double nature of the ethical experience, which accounts for the ancient controversy, as to the relative merits of the concepts of "justice" and "love" in expressing the essence of the moral life—a controversy, which Achad Ha'Am and many others thought was the main issue between Judaism and Christianity. Really, the religious element which enters into the highest forms of ethical awareness can only be described as love, whereas the ethical motives in ordinary life are better subsumed under the term of "justice." Without this saving grace of devotion to a Person, the element of lawfulness in ethics steadily loses its appeal, wilting away like an uprooted tree. During the first stage of irreligion, the Kantian stage, the moral law appears to be suspended in mid-air. Then, it gradually falls to earth, either as materialism or as humanism—no longer distinctly itself.

Worship is the exercise whereby the attempt is made to keep moral fervor at a high level. In reminding ourselves of our relation to the Supreme Being, we strengthen the ties of ethics which are common to man and to God. Through worship we endeavor to reach that high state of spiritual exaltation, when the reality of the good is experienced most poignantly. To be sure, worship does not always accomplish this result, but, if it achieves this purpose once in a lifetime, it is more than justified as a regular practice.

The intimate relationship between religion and ethics serves to explain why public worship is often so much more inspiring than private prayer. We must unlimber our bonds of oneness with each other, before we can feel the ties that bind us to our Father in heaven. Here, too, we find a major reason for loyalty to the inherited forms of particular religious groups, for people of a like education and background acquire more easily the feeling of unity and brotherhood. Thus, public worship is an ethical duty, for it is our obligation to strive always to be better than we are.

But worship is more than a spiritual exercise for the ends of ethics. It is one of the follies of our time, that support for religion is sought in the fields of sociology and political science with the claim that "social justice" and "democracy" are secure only on the basis of a strong religious faith. Whatever truth is to be found in those claims may be sufficient to justify public support for religion; it cannot serve as a good incentive for religion itself. However, the truly religious require no extraneous motivation. Witness the joy of the Psalmists in their communion with God. Those who have once experienced the pure earnestness and the deep sense of devotion which floods the whole of one's being, submerging, if only for the moment, all that is petty and unworthy, will not require special reasons for religious worship. They will feel it both a duty and a privilege to pray, even as they feel it a duty and a privilege to do good and to shun evil, for the root of religion and ethics is one.

Is worship a form of communion with the Deity or is it primarily a dedication of oneself to the Will of God? Students of the history of religions know that in the lower forms of religion, worship is an element of secondary importance in the sacrificial ritual. The value of worship is thought to lie in its efficacy as a means of bringing down the Grace of God, in one form or another, to the suppliant. The fact that religious worship has so often been the prelude to bigoted hatreds of all sorts is doubtless due to the circumstance that the element of dedication to a life of ethics, as the Will of God, has been ignored and worship was thought of in non-ethical, ritualistic terms. When religion is not guided to its goal through the voice of conscience, it is liable to sink to the level of black magic and become a vehicle for mass-fanaticism and blindness. On the other hand, the voice of conscience should be recognized as hailing from beyond ourselves, being indeed a faint echo of the mighty call of God to man. Worship, then, is primarily self-dedication and secondarily, communion with the Will of God.

8. The above outline of the philosophy of religion agrees, I feel, with

the innermost essence of Judaism. It remains to point out the obvious truth that there are values to the entire body of Jewish life, over and beyond the truths contained in this exposition. Judaism is a revealed religion. The meaning of this term can only be understood against the background of the long and glorious role which the Jewish religion played in world history. If we believe that the course of human events is directed by the Providence of God, we must look upon our role in the cosmic drama as a Divine command. Rosenzweig's theory of revelation, expounded at length before, will be found to accord with an enlightened view of tradition and with the ways of thinking of the earnestly critical modern mind.

In recent years, the question has been hotly debated, is Judaism primarily a religion or a civilization? This question is generally so phrased as to preclude a definite answer in favor of either alternative. Judaism is, of course, more than a national civilization. On the other hand, religion is not just a philosophy of life; it is that plus a regimen of conduct intended to saturate all phases of life with the spirit of faith. Thus Judaism is the central, all-pervasive and all-absorbing element of the civilization of the Jewish people.

Judaism may be described as a civilization in the sense of being the treasure of a definite historical group. It is the duty of every group to keep alive for humanity the ideals of its peculiar heritage. Group effort is needed to maintain group-values, especially the values of religion, which are inaccessible to the naked eye—much less, to the naked heart. Not one of the finer treasures of the culture of a group—neither its better music nor its noblest literature, nor its greatest works of art, nor the basic faith underlying its form of government—could be transmitted from one generation to the succeeding one without some form of social organization and common endeavor. For the flesh is weak and the upward climbing of the human spirit requires constant prodding.

To ask whether Judaism be a religion or a civilization is not so much a question of definition and historical study, as it is one of motivation. Its real meaning is, which motive for the maintenance of Jewish life shall we stress, the nationalistic or the religious one? In other words, what is involved is a change of valuation and emphasis. I am opposed to this change for many reasons, principally because I believe that the motive of nationalism is productive of good only when it is kept in the background, as subordinate to the universal ideals of ethics and religion.[11]

To close with a word of exhortation, I feel that it is impossible to over-estimate the role which a genuine renaissance of the Jewish religion could play in protecting the Achilles heel of Western civilization, its gradual loss of a religio-moral basis. Our people in this country and in many other lands are favored with a high degree of culture, and we are very much in the public eye. If we could win our people back to real piety, not merely to passive observance of certain rituals or to weak panderings to popular taste, we shall have unleashed intellectual forces which cannot fail to influence powerfully the entire trend of current events. In the past, our people performed this function for the world. Somehow, the lines of history follow ancient grooves. This, then, is still our task and this our destiny—to labor for the revival of genuine piety among our people, so that we may bring nearer the promised day, when "the knowledge of God will cover the earth as the waters cover the sea."

NOTES

1. Leo Baeck's "Essence of Judaism" (New York, 1948) is an excellent and balanced work but it is eclectical in nature. Schechter's "Aspects of Rabbinic Theology" (New York, 1961) is primarily a historical study. Montefiere's little book on his philosophy of religion is written in a superficial and practical vein. D. Neumark's philosophy expressed in his extended criticisms of Cohen in the "Hatorem" have not been presented in a systematic manner in any of his published works. Felix Adler's ethical philosophy of life does not belong since Adler saw no value in Judaism. For the same reason we did not include the views of those Jewish thinkers who wrote on philosophy and religion in general, without any direct reference to Judaism.

2. F. Nietzsche, "Genealogy of Morals" (New York, 1930), p. 24.

3. Franz Rosenzweig's in his "Einleitung" finds the common ground of both Buber and Cohen in the concept of correlation. We noted that point in our discussion of Cohen's concept of God, but, in our view, the similarity is more verbal than actual.

4. See Josiah Royce's article on "Monotheism" is the *Encyclopedia of Ethics and Religion* (New York, 1920), Vol. VIII, p. 819.

5. Proverbs 24, 16.

6. Already Maimonides in his introduction to the "Guide" speaks of the elusiveness of truth, which flashes lightning-like upon the mind of man, only to give way to total darkness with equal suddenness.

7. E. Durkheim, *Elementary Forms of the Religious Life* (New York, 1915), p. 419.

8. K'dushath Levi, "Mishpatim." See also Leo Baeck in "The Essence of Judaism," who enunciated this principle at great length.

9. David Hume—"Treatise of Human Nature." F. H. Bradley—"Appear-

ance and Reality." McTaggart—article on "Personality" in Encyclopedia of Religion and Ethics.

10. *Reconstructionist,* Vol. 7, No. 2, March 7, 1941.

11. See my article, "Judaism as a Civilization—A Critique," in the "Opinion," June, 1934.

6

THE NEARNESS OF GOD

CHIEF RABBI KUK was essentially a mystic. His claim that "man is by nature a mystic"[1] may or may not be applicable to the generality of mankind, but it was certainly an accurate reflection of his own state of mind. His posthumous works, in particular, reveal him as a mystic of rare profundity and scope. All the facets of his fascinating personality become understandable only when they are related to the mystical experiences that were the central events in his psychic life. His bold metaphysical speculations and his radical reinterpretations of Kabbalistic concepts derive their significance and value from the facts of his own life. Daring as some of his ideas appear to be, they never break out of the charmed circle of mystical experience and contemplation. The stormy waves of doubt that assailed him from time to time and threatened to topple the structure of his convictions were not allayed by rational or even by the traditional arguments so much as by a resurgence of that strange and overwhelming spiritual phenomenon, whose glories he never tired of singing. The many volumes of published and unpublished writings that he left behind are but a series of symphonic variations on the basic melody of his life—his yearning for and discovery of the "nearness of God."

How does he describe this central fact in his spiritual life? In common with nearly all other great mystics, he insists that the mystical experience is unique and ineffable, so radically different from the nor-

144

mal course of events as not to be expressible in the medium of common speech. Silence alone does justice to the sacred intensity of mystical ecstasy. Thus, he writes,

> And life is so joyous, so sacred, so filled with the majesty of the Name of the Lord. You long to express His name, to interpret the exalted light. You are filled with an intense thirst, pleasing in the extreme, to fill your mouth with the praise of the God of gods. And out of the abundance of pure fear, the intensity of holy trembling, you return to silence.[2]

But, incommunicable though the fulness of mystical ecstasy be, he returns again and again to the attempt to capture in human language some of its fleeting aspects. In poetic, winged words he rhapsodizes on the majesty of the mystic's inner life, its cosmic effects and significance, and the spiritual "certainties" that it leaves behind.

> Expanses, expanses
> Expanses divine, my soul doth crave.
> Enclose me not in cages,
> Of matter or mind.
> Thru heavenly vastness my soul doth soar
> Unfenced by walls of heart
> Or walls of deed—
> Of ethics, logic or mores—
> Above all these it soars and flies,
> Above the expressible and nameable,
> Above delight and beauty.
> Exalted and ethereal.
> Lovesick am I—
> I pant, I pant for my Lord,
> As a deer for river banks,
> Oh, who can my anguish relate?
> Who lyre be, to sing my agony,
> To voice my bitterness,
> The endless pain of expression?
> I thirst for truth, not concepts of truth.
> Lo, I ride above the heavens,
> Wholly absorbed within the truth
> Wholly pained by travail of expression;

How can I the great truth articulate
Which my heart overfills?
Who can to multitudes uncover,
To nations and individuals
The total fulness that is creation,
The sparks of light and warmth
Which my soul doth contain.
I see those flames arising,
Bursting thru all firmaments.
Who perceives them?
Who of their vigor can relate?
I am not one of God's elected heroes,
That found all worlds within them
And did not care if others
Their riches knew or not.
These herds of sheep that walk erect,
Will it matter if they know the height of man?
Is then aught harmed by ignorance?
But, I am to this world enchained.
The living, they are my friends.
My soul with them is intertwined;
How then illumination share with them?
For all that I relate
Doth only hide my radiance,
Becloud my inner light.
Thus, great is my pain and anguish.
My God, be Thou my help in trouble!
Grant me the gifts of articulation,
Expression, the mind's translation—
That I might of Thy truths narrate,
Thy Truth, Oh, my God.[3]

Strangely enough, there are no exceptions in nature, and the unique psychical experiences of the Chief Rabbi exhibit the same general characteristics that are found in the records of all so-called "grand mystics." The following stages on the way of mysticism are abundantly illustrated in his writings, though they are nowhere clearly schematized or systematized.

CONFLICT AND THE INWARD PATH

The first stage on the path of mysticism is marked by an uneasy apprehension of inner conflict and contradiction. The seeker tires of the "fragmentariness" of conceptual knowledge, and he undertakes in utter sincerity the task of discovering his own soul and the substance of the universe. He realizes that the surface phenomena, both of his own soul and of the outside world, present a pluralistic panorama, a multitude of diverse data and feelings, without any inherent principle of unity. Turning his gaze inward, he finds numerous mental images, a restless current of ideas and emotions, but no underlying, unifying principle, no subject corresponding to the pronoun, "I." Projecting his glance into the outer world, he finds similarly unrelated events, bits of knowledge "that cast shadows upon one another." Kuk believed that the multitudinous, chaotic appearance of the external world was merely a reflection of the loss of the sense of unity and personality in one's own soul. "Because of the narrow receptive faculty of man," he writes, "one datum contradicts the other datum; one feeling combats the other feeling, and one image pushes out the other; but, in truth, one datum fortifies the other datum, different feelings vitalize each other, and the several images in one's mind complete each other. The more a man is uplifted, the wider his faculties expand, until he comes to find within himself the satisfying fulness of inner peace and the consequent consistency between all data, feelings and images."[4] In one of his poems, he wrote,

> How great is my inner battle!
> My heart is filled with yearning, spiritual, multi-directional,
> I beg for sweetness, divine, to permeate me. . . .
> I long without cessation,
> Cry out in my inward essence,
> in loud voice:
> "The light of God give me. . . ."[5]

The first step, then, consists in a deep revulsion against the multiplicity of external knowledge and in a determination to discover the principles of truth and unity within the deeper layers of the soul. Reality cannot be apprehended by the senses in one all-encompassing vision. Consciousness is like a narrow gleam of light cast into the vast mysterious darkness of the outer world bringing only one object at a time within the range of our mental perception. It follows that the view of the total pattern of existence is forever excluded from the reach of those who pursue only the path of external knowledge. "The thoughts which derive from the externality of the world mislead all men, even the best of them. A kind of inner intoxication is dissolved in them. And the vast majority of mankind readily succumbs to this intoxication."[6]

To break the spell cast by the material world upon one's mind, it is necessary to make a gigantic effort to achieve the feeling of inner unity. Thus we seek to discover reality by finding ourselves. The deeper we descend to the recesses of our own soul, the closer we come to the inwardness and essence of all things. Nature surrenders the key of her being to the one who has discovered the key to his own personality.

UNITY

The quest for truth, then, must begin with the endeavor to achieve inner unity. This goal is unfortunately too often taken for granted. Living from hand to mouth spiritually, we are seldom sufficiently critical of ourselves to notice the conflicting tides of emotion and currents of thought within us. It is essential, to begin with, to recognize the truth that inner unity is an ideal that may be reached for fleeting moments only and is never permanently an accomplished fact. Thus, Kuk is reported to have said,

> Whoever said concerning me that my soul is torn apart, was quite right. Of course it is torn. We cannot picture in our intellect a man whose soul is not torn. Only inanimate objects are complete. But man consists of contrary aspirations, so that there is always an inner battle within him and his task is to overcome the contradictions in his soul thru an all-embracing principle, in the universality of which everything is included and brought to perfect harmony. Naturally, no human being can ever completely attain this ideal for which we strive; but, thru our efforts, we can approach it more and more. And this is what the Kabbalists call "unification."[7]

Kuk's predilection for the ideal of harmony and his method of reinterpretation of Kabbalistic concepts is here illustrated with striking clarity. The practice of *Yichudim* among the masters of Kabbalah con-

sisted in the repetition of certain names and formulae, by which "unification" was believed to be achieved in the mysterious upper worlds of
the *sefiroth*. As a result of this "unification," the flow of "light" and
grace from heaven to earth was supposed to be eased, with the soul of
the saint receiving a major increment of it. Kuk applies the term in this
passage to the unification of the personality of the mystic, though in
other passages he continues to employ the same term in its classic
significance.

The basic need, then, is a recognition of the divisiveness of our being.
The next step is an attempt to overcome the dichotomies within us and
to attain a measure of unity. It must be understood that the mystic is
not in search of an abstract principle of unity, but of the psychic feeling
of unification that overcomes at one stroke all the inner and outer lines
of demarcation. Kuk does not offer a rational principle that is capable
of precise formulation. He can merely point to his own experience, in
which there was revealed to him an intuition of the organic unity "of
all the world." He relates that on many an occasion he would become
keenly aware, in fear and trembling, of the supreme majesty of the
Divine power that dwells within every particle of the universe.

> The gates are opened, the King of glory enters. . . . The worlds are
> united, the hidden and the revealed are commingled, body and soul are
> merged, the "lights" and the "vessels" are linked together. And an
> exquisite sweetness, an inner, intense and highly exalted pleasure is
> uncovered in the source of the rejoicing soul. Then power and light from
> above appear unto thee with all the ornamentation of their many lights.
> Thou wilt recognize thy power and the intensity of thy exaltation; wilt
> know thy humbleness and thy unworthiness, the unworthiness of all
> creatures. . . .[8]

It is apparent from this description that Kuk's vision of unity is not
the result of an arbitrary fiat on his part, but is rather due to a sudden
invasion of the normal consciousness by a current of feeling from the
mysterious realm of the unconscious. Inner and outer unity is achieved
simultaneously in a wondrous blaze of glory. "God enters" and all things
become one in and thru Him, for in essence all creatures are but sparks
of the invisible radiance of God. This does not mean, that, according to
Kuk, the pluralistic universe is unreal or that, at bottom, the universe is

an undifferentiated and unvaried manifestation of the Divine. On the contrary, the principle of differentiation is directly implied in the process of revelation, as will be shown in the sequel. Thus, even in the glow of mystical ecstasy, the separateness of things does not disappear. In Kuk's vision, unity is an added, transforming quality, not a sea of identity. A new dimension comes into view, so to speak, which uncovers the merging roots of all things. "The distinguishing mark of the spiritual intuition is the view of all things together."[9]

This togetherness is not horizontal in character, but vertical. Things arrange themselves in accordance with their nearness to the source of life, so that the whole universe takes on the appearance of a multitude of "ladders of Jacob," which are "set up on the earth and the top of them reaches to heaven." Kuk describes this hierarchy in the inner structure of things with infectious enthusiasm: "But the thing which causes us to think, to reflect, to sing and to believe is the foundation of the worlds. And this foundation includes links of one great chain, long and ordered, in which every link is attached to the next one, in a natural arrangement of sanctity."[10] In this mystical chain of being, all the objects of creation and all human deeds and thoughts find their proper and respective places. There is no leveling of value in the inner world. All things are not equal, but there are bonds of fellowship between the highest and the lowest. In the all-inclusive chain of creation, there are neither irrevocable breaks, nor missing links. There is no unbridgeable gulf between the sacred and the secular or between the spiritual and the material or between the good and the bad. As Kuk puts it, "The heavens and the heavens of heavens together with the depths of the earth constitute one unit, one world, one being."[11]

In another connection, he describes the hierarchy of Being in intellectualistic terms, as graded particularizations of the one Great Thought. Thus, he writes, "What do we see in the vision? We see the Supreme Thought *(HaMachshavah HaElyona),* the Thought which embraces all things, the Thought which contains the power and the fulness of the Whole. We see that all the great rivers flow from it, and streams issue from the rivers, and brooks from the streams, and the brooks divide into many channels and the channels divide into many thousands, indeed an infinity of little canals, which pour forth the bounty *(shifoth)* of will, life and thought."[12]

FEAR AND TREMBLING

The sudden incursion into normal consciousness of the Divine current of light and life is sometimes preceded or followed by a keen feeling of fear and awe. A physical shudder, without apparent cause, shakes the mystic to the depths of his being. At the very threshold of delighted ecstasy, he is seized by a mysterious anxiety, which gradually deepens into a sense of nameless, inexplicable terror. In keeping with his Kabbalistic background, Kuk interprets this phase of the mystical experience as being a vague, subconscious memory of the cosmic catastrophe of the "destruction of the vessels." Thus, he writes, "The first step, which derives from the ancient event of destruction, arouses that shudder in the soul *(zi-azu-a)* which is to pure fear, as the shell is to the seed." [13] According to Lurianic Kabbalah, the first ten *sefiroth*, also called vessels, were shattered because they could not contain the flow of God's grace, when it was poured into them for the purpose of creating the world. This cosmic catastrophe is conceived in Kabbalah not as an event of the dead past but as an integral phase of the eternal riddle of the universe and of the human soul. In the case of Adam and Eve and millennia later when the Israelites stood at Sinai, the same drama was reenacted, the "vessels" proving too weak for the transcendent power of the Almighty. The creature is always liable to "break" when it comes into direct relation with the overflowing boundless energy of the Creator which impels it to levels of being for which it is not prepared. Therefore, when the soul of the mystic becomes aware of the imminent influx of the Divine current of grace, it recalls vaguely the tragedy of ancestral experience and it trembles in fearful anticipation of being unable to bear the blinding radiance that might ensue.

The shudder of mystical ecstasy has its counterpart, according to Kuk, in the peculiar spiritual travail that is the special burden of all original creators. "Great are the agonies of creation," he writes. "They remove man from the troubled world in which the material forces of life are so deeply rooted, to the realm of Divine emanation and purity in which the human soul is a rightful citizen, exercising its powers in freedom." [14] The more profoundly original a new creation is, the more it is accompanied by "the agonies of creation reminiscent of the destruction of the worlds." [15] Since all genuine creativeness is mystical in character deriving from an inflow of Divine energy into the soul of the artist, there can be no real artistic productivity without the sting of spiritual tension and pain. "Superficial artists dream of creativeness, while they indulge in satiety, in lightheartedness, in a life of eating and drinking and promenading. They regard the pain and bitterness in which the royal crown of the spirit is hidden as a kind of sweat which is reserved for second rate artists. But this is a bitter mistake. . . . "[16]

FREEDOM

An essential phase of Kuk's religious experience is a unique awareness of freedom. The iron laws of causation which hold all creation in thrall seem to break and fade away for the mystic in his moments of exaltation. The normal human sense of freedom of choice seems to increase in intensity a hundred-fold as the mystic becomes more keenly conscious of the springs of power in his own soul. So characteristic is the experience of freedom in Kuk's pattern of piety that he consistently refers to the spiritual world of mystical intuition as the "world of freedom" *(Olam HaCheruth)*. This realm of freedom is closer to ultimate reality than the physical world of sounds, shapes and colors. Glimpses of it come to every man whenever he opposes the free dictates of his own conscience to the temptations of the world. Kuk employs Kant's terminology when he designates every moral act as a free act, but he parts company with the great German philosopher when he declares our human standards of justice, including the Golden Rule and the Categorical Imperative, to be merely rough crystallizations of the fluid spiritual current of freedom that derives from the Creator. In other words, God is above morality, and whenever we ascend nearer to Him, we glimpse the reality of freedom, of which the principles of human ethics are but rough approximations.[17]

From a psychological point of view, the basic meaning of freedom is the absence of limitation on one's power. Thus Kuk writes,

> Mystical apprehension is founded on the inner conviction of almightiness, the absence of limitation on the possibilities of infinite power. Objective cognition is, on the other hand, built on the knowledge of the limitation of power in accordance with the circumstances in which power manifests itself in this world. In each sphere, the form of one or the other cognition enjoys absolute sovereignty. There is no limit to one's power in the inner world; there is no freedom in the outer physical world.

But, freedom is not only a negative feeling, denoting the absence of foreign, limiting forces; it contains also a positive phase, the feeling of being true to the nature of one's own inner life. Kuk portrays the interior life of the spirit as a living wellspring of ceaseless creativity, that is normally hemmed in and held in check by the pressure of outside distractions. The surface processes of the human mind can only register impressions, arrange them in their proper classifications and rearrange them according to need. Even the power of reasoning is superficial in character, suited for practical calculations, for the critical appraisal of new creations, for finding faults and adjudging merits. The real source of creativity lies in the deeper recesses of the human soul, where it is in contact with the Divine current of creativity. Thus as soon as one's consciousness is liberated from the bewitching power of the outer world, his soul becomes aware of the tremendous stores of creative power within it.

> In every second, in the smallest instant of time, we create, consciously and unconsciously, an endless multitude of creations; if we can only learn to perceive them, bring them within the borders of clear cognition, accustom ourselves to include them within the framework of expression suitable for them, then their splendor and majesty will be revealed and their power in all the phases of life will become visible.[18]

This creativity of the inner soul is not always understood, because it is too vibrant with the intensity of life to be captured in cold, conceptual terms, but, then, Kuk declares emphatically that whatever is genuinely creative derives from it. "It is only the free soul that creates."[19]

In common with Maimonides, Kuk describes the process of creation in the inner realm of freedom as being neither smooth nor constant, but as consisting of intermittent, fleeting flashes of insight, very much like the flashes of lightning in a dark sky. Even if their real import is not realized at the moment, the residue of "spiritual fulness and grace" that they deposit in the soul develops in the course of time into works of art.[20]

> For in them the secret of the higher life is revealed; all rational labor, all systematic work, all laws and judgments, religious precepts and verdicts, profound conceptions and maxims of logic derive the spirit of their life

only from the shadows of the shadows of the radiance of these great flashes.[21]

PRINCIPLE OF ALTERNATION

In the writings of Kuk, the thought is frequently reiterated that the path of mystical enlightenment is not one of continuous ascent, but that, in accordance with the law of rhythm that governs all phenomena of life, the highest experiences of piety contain phases of depression as well as exaltation. In fact, these ups and downs in the inner life of the spirit are as intimately related as the crest of an ocean wave and its trough. Every upward step into the joy of ecstasy and freedom is followed by a downward plunge into the depths of darkness and despair. The glorious lightning-like vision of the organic unity of the universe is succeeded by a gradual relaxation of inner tension, which slowly deepens into a feeling of gloom and frustration. "Hours of this kind," he writes, "are most bitter to the possessors of a higher soul. Then they groan and moan in spiritual travail; then the world and its pains cannot measure up to the intensity of their agony. Then their souls cry unto God out of their terrible anguish, out of the fathomless deep, and the Lord turns unto them and bestows more of His Light unto them."[22] Kuk returns again and again to this fascinating theme of the alternation of light and darkness, joy and pain, exaltation and depression, in the great spiritual adventure of the mystic. The profound melancholy of the mystic's "dark night" is a kind of psychical recoil from the dizzy height to which his soul had leaped. It is the "morning after" feeling of returning, with eyes dazed by the glory they beheld, to the drab routine of ordinary existence. The riddle of the universe is felt to be agonizing in its obdurate opaqueness, because of the unforgettable memory of the brief glimpse into its solution that was afforded to him. As Kuk phrases it,

> Thereupon, there follows the recognition, how everything is dark and devoid of any value in comparison with the light of the Infinite; how the endless depths which separate the Creator from the created render seemingly impossible any kind of relation between them. Then everything is dried up and emptied of meaning.
>
> And out of this travail of the soul and out of this deep insight into the nothingness of all things and the majestic fulness of their Source and the power of the exalted existence of the Supreme Light, its positive phases

and its brightness begin to fill all the chambers of his soul. . . . And he begins to ascend, the confidence of his soul and the sense of the eternity of his life is intensified and he is uplifted to higher spheres, until he recognizes his frustration and wretchedness, and, with a broken spirit, he succumbs to despair; thereupon, the spirit returns to shine for him. It comes and goes like flashes of lightning.[23]

Thus, there was an ebb and flow of spiritual insight and exaltation in the inner life of Kuk, as in the case of most mystics, his spirit oscillating between feelings of ecstasy and moments of deepest despair.[24]

CONTENT OF THE MYSTICAL EXPERIENCE

We have already sketched some of the characteristics of Kuk's mystical experience, the sense of unity, the experience of freedom and the resolution of conflicts. These are qualities of the psychical phenomenon of mysticism. But what does the mystic himself "see" in his highest moments? What is the substance of the reality that is revealed to him? What is the nature of the message that he receives from the Divine?

In common with other great mystics, Kuk affirms that the "what" of the mystical experience remains nebulous even in the lucid moments of ecstasy. But, there is the ineluctable certainty "that" one is listening to a call from above and that this call derives from a transcendent source. A profound feeling of consecration to high ends takes hold of the mystic, abiding with him as a dynamic urge to discover the significance of these ends and to attempt their realization in the circumstances of his actual life. Generally, he need not wait long before the nature of the duties to which his life must now be dedicated is manifested to him.

Though we do not perceive articulate letters and distinct words, we regard our secular and Torah studies as intended solely for the purpose of obtaining as much as possible the clarity of words out of the exalted sound which beats constantly in our inner ear, that we may present them to ourselves and to others in a form that leads to action and to properly ordered and systematized reflection.[25]

Kuk frequently refers to the "call" that wordlessly transmits a message to the mystic. Thus he defines the basic attitude of the mystic as being that of absorbed, whole-souled listening.

The higher waves beat upon our soul increasingly. The inner movements of our spirit are products of the notes which the violin of our soul sounds, in its rapt exaltation. Though we cannot know what it is all about, nor express it in any detail, nor give a rational summary of it, nor define the topics of the higher sounds, nevertheless we listen with a total listening. The voice of words do we hear. . . .[26]

Again, he speaks of the "call" as a paradoxical combination of light and sound, as in this passage,

When all the parts of man, the physical and the spiritual, are readied and purified, and the lust for the holiness of the exalted Nature of God . . . breaks for itself a path, then, to the extent that this is done, the walls of limitation are removed and a straight light and a straight sound reaches us, suffused with the riches of life and the wisdom of truth.[27]

Weaker echoes of this mystical "call" seem to have been almost daily occurrences in the life of Kuk. Thus he frequently writes of the "song of the soul" as an ever present, never silent, inner melody, an expression of the ceaseless yearning of the creature for its Creator. All religious life and thought is simply an attempt to grasp and to express this melody of faith.

Faith is the song of life, the song of Being. And a song is the most penetrating perception, more inward by far in its conceptual essence than any prosaic conception can be. . . . Woe to him who wishes to denude life of the splendor of its poetry; he loses all the inwardness and truth of life.[28]

The profound religious experience of Kuk transformed for him the entire sordid panorama of mundane existence into one infinite expanse of radiant beauty. Consequently, the dark pessimism of the modern man is totally alien to his spirit. In one of his poems, he wrote,

> Radiant is the soul of the world,
> Beautiful and resplendent,
> Soul-wealth, overflowing,
> Holy Spirit, abounding,

Fountains of fortitude,
Majesty and beatitude.
Proudly I am unlifted,
Raised to the world's elan,
Loftiest peak of its soul.
How gorgeous the vision!
Come all, partake, enjoy,
Take in this delight,
This heavenly bliss.
Taste and see that God is good.[29]

DYNAMISM

The world of reality as revealed in mystical intuition is not an empty placid Nirvana, but a dynamic current of vitality, full of vigor and verve and creativity. Far from being an escape from life, the path of mysticism takes one to the very source of life, "the life of life" in Kabbalistic terminology. The discovery of the mystic consists in the claim that at bottom the world is not a dark dead machine, running down to total stillness, like an unwound spring. The real world is, on the contrary, full of life and light and overflowing energy, seeking to express itself in ever new forms. To the interior vision, "everything flows on and on, trembles and aspires."[30] There is a nisus in the substance of the world, which breaks forth in new creations, from time to time, bringing a chunk of recalcitrant matter one step nearer to God. "The strong will to become part of the body of the King, to return to the high, pure, free and strong Source of existence, the Source of Infinite Light, is imbedded in all living creatures, in the whole of creation. And this is the fundamental force that drives the whirling wheel of all existence, the force of development."[31] We must bear in mind that this account of the elan of the universe is not a statement of dogma, but a description of that momentary glimpse of reality, which flashes across the mind of the mystic at the apex of his ecstatic experience. Thus, he writes of the "experienced process of development"[32] and of "the phenomenon which comes to man, whereby he senses all creation, not as a thing that was done and completed, but as a thing which is always becoming, uplifted, developed and exalted. . . ."[33]

Mystical ecstasy, then, is basically an intensification of the feeling of being alive in the midst of a vibrant world. Kuk refers very frequently to this feeling of the restless drive and upward surge of the current of life in his poetic descriptions of his spiritual experiences. Note this gem of religious poetry:

> All being whispers a secret to me: I have life, take, please take—if you have a heart and in the heart there is blood, that the poison of despair has not sullied;
> But, if thy heart be uncircumsized and my beauty holds no charm for you—Being whispers to me—away, away from me, forbidden am I to thee!
> If every gentle twitter, every flash of beauty, not the splendor of holy song but the stream of foreign fire in thee arouse—away, away from me, forbidden am I to thee.

> And a living generation will arise
> That will sing to beauty and life;
> And youth without end
> From the dew of heaven will derive.

> And a living people will attend to the flow of the secrets of being from the splendors of Karmel and the Sharon, and out of the tenderness of song and the beauty of life—the light of holiness will rise to overflowing; And all being will murmur to him, My chosen one, I am for thee intended![34]

UNIO MYSTICA

Does the mystic, at the height of his ecstatic experience, know himself to be at one with God? This question stands at the vague and shifting borderline between the actual experience of mysticism and its philosophical interpretation. Among Christian writers, the prevailing opinion is that *unio mystica* is the goal toward which the long and tortuous path of mysticism ultimately leads. In Jewish mystical literature, on the other hand, the possibility of actual union with the Supreme Being is ruled out in advance. Martin Buber, who sensed the true pulse of Jewish mysticism, insists in his little work, *I and Thou,* that the apex of religious experience is a dialogue with God, not a union with Him. The Jewish pattern of piety has no room for the ideal of *unio mystica,* based as it is upon the profound consciousness of the absolute distinction between the Creator and His creatures.

Kuk sometimes employs language which suggests the attainment of complete unity in the mystical experience. Thus he writes of the psychical level of sanctity, "when man becomes one with the body of the King, and there is no longer any separation between him and his God."[35] In another connection, he asserts that when man reaches the state of moral excellence in which the exercise of his own free will is identified with the categorical demands of absolute justice, he becomes part of "the body of the King."

These passages, however, are not to be taken literally. The "body of the King" is a Kabbalistic designation for the *Sefiroh* of *malchuth*, the last of the ten stages in the descent of the "Grace" of God to earth. Kuk identifies this *Sefiroh* with the free moral order of the Universe, of which man becomes aware in moments of grave ethical decision. To be a part of the "body of the King" is therefore merely a euphemistic expression for the attainment of that degree of ethical perfection, in which man becomes fully responsive to every shade and nuance of the spiritual life.

His inner life was so stirring and exulting that he could not help feeling that his soul had attained some sort of contact with its "Source" in God. As to the manner of this contact, he was understandably silent, since it is beyond the human ken.

> The first, He pulled me, as by a rope,
> To His palatial dwelling place,
> And thru the strings of His holy violin,
> My soul doth listen to His song.[36]

INTERPRETATION

Even in the case of normal, routine experience, the line of demarcation between fact and interpretation cannot be drawn with certainty. How much more is this true in the case of the mystic who strives constantly for the complete integration of his personality round the central core of his ecstatic insights! Mystical literature proves abundantly that the whole training of the mystic, the ideas derived from books and the subtle influence of the environment, enters into the very texture of the mystical experience. Fact and interpretation get to be so intimately commingled as to be completely indistinguishable from each other. The mystic is rarely a devotee of religion in general. As Schleiermacher pointed out, the mystical *Gefühl* is an amorphous, albeit exalted sensation, which is molded into definite shape by the subjective character and background of the mystic.

This observation applies with particular force and pertinence to the religious consciousness of Kuk, which was peculiarly synthetic and many-sided. Passages describing the ideals of mystical piety are to be found side by side with rhapsodies on the occult virtues of the Hebrew alphabet. Descriptions of the mystical current of creativity, *à la* Bergson, alternate with paeans of praise about the cosmic effects of the study of the secrets of Kabbalah. Kuk was an Orthodox mystic, in the exact sense of the term; his orthodoxy and his mysticism were as closely related as body and soul. The heritage of his past was turned into living, vibrating reality for him by the fire of his ecstatic piety.

The two basic concepts, in the light of which Kuk interpreted his mystical experience, were grace *(shefa)* and holiness *(k'dushah)*.

Kuk's doctrine of grace stands in the direct line of the evolution of Jewish religious thought. It is a tribute to the originality and uniqueness of his thinking that his writings which read at times as thoroughly Bergsonian in spirit and modern in temper are really the expression of a deeply traditionalist mind. The dried bones of Jewish tradition took on new life in the mind of Kuk, because he had actually experienced the profound and ennobling feelings of genuine piety. In the insights vouchsafed to him in the hours of his mystical ecstasy Kuk found a bridge between the ancient, esoteric world of Kabbalah and the modern world of science and bold philosophical speculation. He virtually identified the Kabbalistic doctrine of the flow of grace with the elan vital of Bergsonism, which is the cosmic dynamic urge behind the process of evolution and the progress of mankind. By the same token, he ranked the scientific achievements of the modern era on a par with the mystical "improvements" of Lurianic Kabbalah. Thru this reinterpretation of Kabbalistic thought, Kuk arrived at a philosophy of religion that is ultra-modern and ultra-traditionalistic at one and the same time.

In numerous passages, he emphasizes the many-sided influence of the Divine flow of grace which affects every aspect of existence. It generates life and strength, which interpenetrate the entire world.[37] Every part of the universe is filled with the overflow of blessing which breaks into the souls of the saints.[38]

The souls of all creatures and all the worlds are filled with pleasure. Nations are blessed, scholars and writers are crowned with thoughts of peace and blessing. Every spirit is endowed with sweet hope. Trust in God . . . fills all. . . . The splendid determination to be uplifted above all epochs of time in order to cleave unto the value and splendor of eternity suffuses all things. . . . The plants of the earth rise to be blessed . . . the love of life becomes refined . . . who can properly glorify the preciousness of these exalted hours which ebb and flow with their light! The light of the Torah is their source. . . .

The effects of religious inspiration are to be found in every phase of social progress. Human society as a whole is the ultimate beneficiary of Divine grace. Oftentimes, the recipients of mystical inspiration are temperamentally unsuited for the study of the detailed sciences. "The two capacities contradict each other subjectively, as they are united objectively."[39] As a rule, "geniuses of piety" lack the talent and inclination for experimental research and the run of the mill scientists are insensitive to the mystical "yearning for God." Nevertheless, there is a direct chain of causation between these two fields of endeavor. The creative power which invades the consciousness of the ecstatic mystic is the real source of the selfless devotion to truth that constitutes the core of the scientific attitude, and it is also the ultimate origin of those intuitive insights into the structure of the universe, those bold leaps in the dark, which periodically raise the sciences to ever higher levels.

If men had not waited until the revelation of the "rootlight," no wisdom would have developed, no forward step in ethics, public law and practical progress would have prevailed.[40]

But the influence of man upon the physical universe is not confined to the techniques of science and industry. Thru the mastery of mystical knowledge and practice, man affects the "essence of the world," refining it and rendering it more subservient to the needs of humanity.[41] Thus the saints, who never descend from the high pinnacle of "attachment to God," induce progress and achievement in every field of human activity, "for the great light of their life fills the entire universe with 'improvement' and light."[42] Kuk does not even find it difficult to believe that the fruits of the soil are perfected by the "Divine overflow" that courses thru the soul of the mystical saint.[43] For the world in essence is constituted of the same substance as is the flow of Divine illumination. All things are part of one living organism—a deathless, ever growing "tree of life." There are no solitary souls, no isolated events in the universe. The coarsest clod of matter is joined in its root to the source of all life and thought. "To the great soul, characterized by the qualities of absolute freedom, unity and rightness, everything is united."[44]

The supreme importance of mystical inspiration places the personality of the *tzaddik* in the very center of the cosmic drama of redemption.

Pathways these men of rectitude are, for the purpose of disseminating light and life for every creature. Instruments they are for the irradiation of the light of eternal life—the servants of the Lord and the executors of His Word; His faithful messengers, to give life to the dying, to fortify the weak, to awaken the dormant. . . . And they call in the name of the Eternal, Lord of the Universe, Who speaks thus unto every creature, "Live and rejoice in all that is good! Rise and be uplifted ever higher, higher!"[45]

Though they seem to have no visible part in fashioning the course of history, the saints are in reality the focal points of progress.

And these individuals (the saints), from the heights of their spiritual elevation, uplift the world from its low state, thru their existence alone, not thru their recognizeable influence. The inner secrets they do not reveal and cannot reveal. But, that which the great light causes to come into being thru the scattering of its sparks over that which is revealed, over the glance of an eye, over every conversation and gesture, over the essence of will, the purpose of life—in all these ways they act, encourage, strengthen and sanctify the All.[46]

The mystical effectiveness of the saints is in direct proportion to the intensity of the ties of affection and love by which they are united to the larger circles of society.

This great event begins with drops that come one by one. But as one continues to ascend, the Divine Power, in the height of its sacred purity being fortified by the good desires of men, of the individual and the group, shatters the walls which dam its flow; the drops begin to come more frequently, to coalesce and turn into streams; the streams in turn become mighty rivers, a "multitude of many waters," the echo of a multitude of men, like the voice of the Lord when He speaks.[47]

The saint is aided in his efforts to attain the highest state of mystical ecstasy by "the good desires of men," the sea of good will and piety that fills his social environment. Unseen channels bind all men into one living entity. The ideals and aspirations of diverse individuals, each seeking a pathway to God in the isolation of his chamber, are mutually reinforced and integrated in the soul of the saint, where they contribute to the attainment of the noblest pinnacle of man's spiritual life, the illumination of the Holy Spirit. In turn, the "Divine Overflow" that is granted to the saint is communicated first to the social group of which he is the focal center, and then, by degrees to ever larger groups, spreading out in concentric waves until it reaches the whole of humanity.

The bond between all the souls in Israel is such that many channels pour the radiance of life one into the other, and in the higher levels of spiritual existence there is complete unity in the knot of the roots of their life. Thus it is that the ascent of one soul into the light is felt thru radiation, as it were, by all the souls, whether they sense this spiritual increment or not. Naturally, the personal bonds of love, trust, respect and mutual attachment in practical matters . . . open the spiritual channels more and more and fortify even more powerfully the knot of the roots of the soul. . . . And the inner light shines at the image of God in mankind generally.[48]

The apparent separateness of individuals is itself due to the spell of the physical veil of reality. The deeper we probe into the inner depths of our souls in order to reach the roots of things, the closer do the discrete souls of humanity merge into the one great Self of Man.

HOLINESS

Out of his soul-shaking mystical experience and his original doctrine of Divine grace, Kuk evolved a new and striking interpretation of the feeling of holiness that lies at the root of all religion.

The distinction between the holy and the secular is exceedingly deep and thorough-going in Judaism, affecting not only a few occasional, sacramental rites, but the whole regimen of life of the pious Jew. However, this distinction was most often conceived not as an intrinsic quality, but as an external fact, resulting from the arbitrary, inscrutable will of God, Who determines what is unclean, permitted or sacred. In Kabbalistic thought, on the other hand, every *mitzvah* was related to some cosmic event, so that its scrupulous performance entailed automatically a triumph of holiness, in the inner structure of the universe. The Chassidic movement laid particular stress on the attitude of the worshipper, declaring that the realm of holiness is approachable only by the qualities of the "fear and love" of God.

Kuk goes one step further, citing the testimony of his own inner life for the claim that the feeling of the holy is a datum of human experience. He tells us not only what man ought to feel in the presence of his Maker, but what he does in fact feel. Piety was to him neither an ethereal abstraction nor a gloomy retreat from life, but an indubitable, thrilling and exalting event.

The outstanding characteristic of his conception of holiness is its life-affirming quality. In accord with the basic tendencies of Judaism and the disposition of the modern temper, Kuk considers the basic attitude of religion to be the endeavor to live life more fully, not to escape from it. Accordingly, he describes the feeling of the holy as a heightened sensitivity to the pulsating current of vital power in the inner substance of being. The holy is not a static quality, but a dynamic, vitalizing stream that is apprehended by the deeply pious person as a mighty current of becoming. "The good and the holy pass in a powerful current."[49] A sense of increased power, deriving from the felt accession of energy in the ecstatic revelation of the Holy Spirit, is an essential part of the feeling of the Holy. "Great and overflowing streams of power rise, thru the mighty intensification of pure intellectual concentration, that is revealed in the light of the Holy Spirit."[50]

Far from implying the existence of any dichotomy between the physical and the spiritual phases of life, Kuk declares repeatedly that holiness is an intensified form of vitality, dependent for its very existence upon the exuberant health of the physical organism.[51] Commenting upon the striking verse in Ecclesiastes, "Better than wisdom, than honor, is a little folly," he asserts that the dumb, restless strivings of men resulting from an abundance of natural energy, is the necessary substratum for the Holy Spirit.[52] In the life of the nation as of the individual, the same relationship obtains between physical health and the current of spiritual life. "The exalted powers of holiness, in the spirit of the nation and in the light of its soul, are concealed in its vital forces. . . ."[53]

The feeling of the holy includes an apprehension of its transcendental character that is certain and unmistakable. Thru a lifelong habituation in the disciplines of piety and thru the sustained study of Kabbalah, "there is created in man a special sense whereby he can distinguish the taste of a thought that is charged with holiness from a merely profane thought."[54] This feeling of the numinous is experienced not only in sacred ritual or in the ecstasy of revelation, but also in every good and selfless act that bears the mark of consecration to a high cause . . . "every good inclination, every good quality, every work, every act of holiness, every commandment, every deed of righteousness—it can be felt that they come to us from a strong and exalted world. . . . The living world comes to us with the fulness of love and we kiss it in overflowing affection. . . ."

In his all-encompassing love of life, Kuk recognized the seal of holiness in many and diverse fields of activity. "And everything that is beautiful and wonderful is a phenomenon of revelation, in which the life of all life dwells in one form or another."[55] There is indeed no limit to the extensive ramifications of the stream of holiness, "for there is in truth nothing in the universe that is absolutely secular."[56] The triumph of mysticism will prove "that there is exalted greatness in everything that is small."[57] While it is the height of destructive folly to disregard the line of demarcation between the holy and the secular, it is nevertheless clear that the distinction is one of degree, for the underlying current of reality drives on unceasingly toward the goal of sanctifying all the spheres of existence.[58]

The term "holiness" thus has a general universal significance, in addition to its particular significance which is conceived strictly along the lines of orthodox Kabbalism. The "lights of holiness" emanate from the study of the Torah, the observance of the *mitzvoth,* the contemplation of the truths of Kabbalah and the practice of "unifications." Uncompromising insistence on these principles of Orthodoxy does not negate the universal denotation of holiness, that is defined in generally psychological and philosophical terminology. In this latter sense, the holy is a simple quality that is native to the human mind and that is perceptible even by children.[59] Its appearance of unreality is due to a peculiar illusion of the human imagination, that turns things upside down and makes the real seem unreal and the unreal seem real.[60] In reality, nothing is simpler to the human mind than holiness, for "the higher a truth is, the more simple it is . . ."[61]

Kuk was too deeply a *homo religiosus* to be insensible to the universal aspects of holiness, and too rigidly loyal to tradition to concede any validity or authority to non-Jewish forms of religious experience. He was therefore led to arrive at the following synthesis of the universal and particular types of holiness:

> It was indeed proper that the whole content of holiness should have reference to humanity in general, for the perception of holiness is universal and the content of holiness, the bond between man and God, is independent of any nationality. This universal content would, in that event, have appeared for Jews in a special Jewish garment, but the wave of moral perversion that set in later in world history caused the elements of holiness to be forgotten among all men. And a new creation was made in Israel. . . . Nevertheless, there are still titans of the spirit who find the cosmic element in the root of Adam's soul, which still throbs in the heart of mankind generally. . . .[62]

These "titans of the spirit," or saints, are peculiarly sensitive to the feeling of holiness which is the sum and substance of their lives. Their whole personality becomes a living incarnation of holiness.

> The light of holiness extends first to the power of speech which wells up out of the living source of holiness . . . then, too, the sense of hearing is ennobled, so that all that is heard is added up to a great, pure and holy light, which expands further to reach the sense of sight. Thus, all that strikes the eye is sanctified and uplifted and the final account of the world appears to be pellucid and transparent . . . and then every movement, every feeling and tremor become full of favor and high glory. . . .[63]

We have here an excellent account of what the students of mysticism designate as the "state of illumination." The confusion of metaphors, bounding from sight to sound and back again, the extreme vagueness of terminology and the lyricism of the style, are all expressions of the attitude which they expound. A kind of euphoria intoxicates the senses, as if they had been vouchsafed a momentary perception of the indwelling glory of the universe. "Kissed with love," the saints yearn to bestow love upon their fellowmen, to serve and unite in spirit with all mankind and to forge ever more powerful bonds of unity among men.[64]

NOTES

1. *HaMachshavah HaYisrealith* (Jerusalem, 1920), edited by Alexander Zisskind Rabinovitz, p. 26.
2. *Oroth HaKodesh* (Jerusalem, 1938), p. 79.
3. *Zikkaron* (Jerusalem, 1945), p. 17.
4. Kovetz Maamorai Horav Kuk (Jerusalem, N.A), p. 16.
5. Zikkaron, p. 16.
6. *Oroth HaKodesh*, pp. 11, 98.
7. *HaMachshavah HaYisrealith*, p. 13.
8. *Oroth HaKodesh*, p. 32.
9. *Ibid.*, p. 41.
10. *Ibid.*, p. 144.
11. *Ibid.*, p. 144.
12. *Ibid.*, p. 460.
13. *Ibid.*, p. 59.
14. *Ibid.*, p. 197.
15. *Ibid.*, p. 196.
16. *Ibid.*, p. 196.
17. *Ibid.*, pp. 69–74.
18. *Ibid.*, p. 173.
19. *Ibid.*, p. 193.
20. *Ibid.*, p. 187; Maimonides, *Guide,* introduction.
21. *Ibid.*, p. 187.
22. *Ibid.*, p. 126.
23. *Ibid.*, p. 345.
24. For parallels in general mystical literature, see chapter on "The Dark Night" in Evelyn Underhill's *Mysticism* and chapter on "The Principle of Alternation" in William Hocking's *Meaning of God in Human Experience* (New Haven, 1928).
25. *Ibid.*, p. 346.
26. *Ibid.*, p. 346.
27. *Ibid.*, p. 176.
28. *HaMachshavah HaYisrealith*, p. 23.
29. *Zikkaron*, p. 15.
30. *Oroth HaKodesh*, p. 386.
31. *Ibid.*, p. 388.
32. *Ibid.*, p. 540.
33. *Ibid.*, p. 535.
34. *HaTarbuth HaYisrealith* (Jerusalem, 1923).
35. *Oroth HaKodesh*, p. 409.
36. *Zikkaron*, p. 21.

37. *Oroth HaKodesh,* p. 85.
38. *Ibid.,* p. 343.
39. *Ibid.,* p. 47.
40. *Ibid.,* p. 93.
41. *Ibid.,* p. 351.
42. *Ibid.,* p. 354.
43. *Ibid.,* p. 343.
44. *Ibid.,* p. 433.
45. *Ibid.,* p. 85.
46. *Ibid.,* p. 86.
47. *Ibid.,* p. 138.
48. *Ibid.,* p. 139.
49. *Ibid.,* p. 433.
50. *Ibid.,* p. 90.
51. *Ibid.,* p. 64.
52. *Ibid.,* p. 77.
53. *Ibid.,* p. 149.
54. *Ibid.,* p. 93.
55. *Ibid.,* p. 103.
56. *Ibid.,* p. 143.
57. *Ibid.,* p. 106.
58. *Ibid.,* p. 322.
59. *Ibid.,* p. 333.
60. *Ibid.,* p. 320.
61. *Ibid.,* p. 4.
62. *Ibid.,* p. 30.
63. *Ibid.,* p. 311.
64. *Ibid.,* p. 457.

7

RAV KUK, AN APPRECIATION

IT IS STILL too early to essay an estimate of Kuk's place in the history of Jewish life and thought. As these lines are being written, ten years after his death, some of his manuscript material is still unpublished and the full impact of his thought is just beginning to be felt. The influence which his personality exerted on the minds of numerous friends and disciples has not yet crystallized into definite literary creations. Certain it is that he belonged to the class of men whose stature grows with the passage of the years. Nevertheless, it is high time that an effort be made to evaluate the significance of Kuk's thought for the solution of the problems of Judaism in our time and place. The extraordinary religious consciousness that is revealed in his writings should prove to be a salutary influence in the confused and amorphous state of American Jewish theology. While it is certain that his philosophy as a whole cannot pass muster in the light of modern criticism, there are elements in his thought that deserve to be included in any healthy system of Jewish theology. This much is indisputable: the Jewish theologian of the future will not be able to ignore the work of Kuk, the mystic, or Kuk, the defender of the Orthodox faith.

THE MYSTIC

Many a reader will in all probability conclude that Kuk's ideas and feelings moved within an ethereal and esoteric realm of its own, a realm that is removed from the affairs of this world and is therefore wholly irrelevant and meaningless to the mental habits of rational humanity. Kuk was a mystic and the basic currents of his thought were mystical in origin and conception. But is not mysticism something that is occult and mysterious, a wondrous and bizarre discipline that is not of this world? Those who hesitate to condemn it outright as an abnormal delusion of tormented souls incline generally to the view that it is an exclusive doctrine, of consequence only to so-called "mystics," and quite unintelligible to non-mystics who constitute the whole tribe of normal humanity. Indeed, if mysticism is itself the peculiar treasure of peculiar people, how can it help in the solution of the religious problems of the common man? The mystic's report of his ecstatic vision can be accepted by the average man only as a matter of faith. How, then, can mysticism afford support to the tottering pillars of faith in our time?

The answer is that the mystical experience is really an intensification of a form of experience that is common to the generality of mankind. While in its full extent and grandeur it is granted only to rare souls, weaker echoes of it belong to the common experience of humanity. For mysticism is nothing but an overwhelming concentration of religious feeling, and, in accordance with the logic of feeling, mystical literature and contemplation is certain to arouse and stimulate the emotions of piety. There is a strange fascination in the mystical adventure that appeals to all who seek the nearness of the Lord. The genuinely pious cannot but feel that the mystic may err in details but that the general direction of his efforts is true to the Divine scheme of things.

In recent studies of the psychology of religion, much is made of the so-called "feeling of the holy." While the investigators of this subject may not be entirely agreed as to the exact description of all the various phases of the emotional complex of holiness, there is no question of its widespread prevalence. There is scarcely a sensitive human being who has not been overcome by this feeling at one time or another in his life. Some may experience it in worship, others may find it invades their souls in moments of profound crisis, fundamental spiritual decision or earnest rededication. In every case, it appears in a characteristic pattern of its own, with all its phases discernible thru the telescope of analysis. Rudolf Otto, in his classic study of this subject, describes it as a *tremendum mysterium* consisting of the "moments" of awe, bigness, fear, reverence, trust, inscrutability, a feeling of the numinous, etc. This feeling, it will easily be recognized, is but a weaker example of mystical ecstasy.

The relation of the mystic to non-mystical humanity is therefore very much like that of a musical composer to the average person. The latter dimly feels the rightness of the sequence of notes, approving of it in his heart, though he himself could not have composed it. This was in fact the analogy with which Kuk generally operated. He conceived of the joys of mysticism as being outbursts of the pent up inner song of the soul. The melody of man's psychic life, he felt, was unheard and un-heeded in the tumultuous hubbub of superficial consciousness. But when thru a magnificent effort the noise of routine existence is silenced, the inner music of mystical yearning breaks forth. All who listen to it will, if they make the necessary effort, recognize it as the voice of their own deepest consciousness.

Kuk's works on mysticism were written in the style of personal "confessions." The author made no effort to convince by logical argu-mentation, to prove a point by meticulous analysis, or even to persuade thru the medium of stirring eloquence. He wrote for himself, as it were, jotting down the reports of his own experiences and ideas and challenging the reader to rediscover the same events in the recesses of his own soul. Well did he realize that the spirit of religion may be awakened but not communicated, and he firmly believed that in chart-ing the events of his own psychic life, he was rendering an account of the deepest realities in human nature generally, since, in their roots, the souls of all men and women are one.

He was quite aware of the occasional obscurities in his writings and of the abrupt mystical "leaps" which abounded in his style. As he wrote to a friend:

I wish to call your attention to the general circumstance that in spiritual matters we are always related to the mystical element which is the deepest truth in our consciousness. Therefore, it should not occasion surprise if in the midst of a usual and factual exposition we suddenly encounter expressions which lift us out of the realm of the normal, the sensible and the logical. For the most part, it is just then that we resume to speak with simple naivete, the naivete of childhood, as was said, "out of the mouths of children and babes hast Thou founded strength." These ob-scure passages are inevitably to be found in the words of those who speak out of the depths of their soul—and it is thru them that the radiance of inner truth is revealed. It seems to me that this observation is a faithful key to the understanding of the difficult sections in my works and the works of those who write in this style, both of past generations and of the present time.[1]

We shall regard his estimate of the mystical experience with greater sympathy and understanding if we bear in mind the undoubted fact that, philosophically speaking, mysticism is possible. There is very little that all philosophers worthy of the name are agreed upon. Nevertheless, it may be stated with little danger of contradiction that the whole point of philosophy is an attempt to expose the naivete of common sense humanity, that is inclined to take the world simply as it appears to the naked eye. Philosophers may and do differ regarding everything under the sun, but on this they are agreed, that "there are more things in heaven and earth than are dreamed of" in the philosophy of non-analytical common sense. The so-called "naturalistic" school of philosophy seeks to approximate the common sense picture of the universe, but there is all the difference in the world between a post-critical philosophy of Force and Energy and the naive views of non-philosophical humanity.

The grand course of the evolution of philosophical thought was begun when thinkers became aware of the distinction between primary and secondary qualities of objects. Sound, color, odor, taste and the tactile appearance of an object were obviously the product of interaction between the object in itself and the senses. This was even more obviously true in the case of such qualities as beauty and harmony or repulsiveness and awkwardness. On the other hand, certain qualities, like mass or size, or shape, seem to belong directly to the object, being independent of the vagaries of the perceiver. Further reflection reveals that all objects are subject to change and mutation, capable of assuming a multitude of diverse forms and shapes. Evidently there is a substance that is common to all objects of existence and that underlies the current of change. This much is elementary observation and deduction. Philosophical thought began with speculation concerning the nature of this underlying substance. Was it water, air, the four elements, the Indeterminate, Mind, Fire, Unchanging Being, Numbers, Ideal Forms, Substance? These were the questions that occupied the ancient Greek philosophers and basically, the character of the essence of all things is still the fundamental question of philosophy.

In our scientific age, this line of reasoning has become common knowledge. We know now that sound is the movement of waves of certain lengths and that sight is due to the excitation of the optic nerve by a different type of wave. Behind the facade of the physical universe, as it appears to our senses, there is the "real" world of atoms and molecules, electrons and neutrons. More recent scientific studies prove that the electrons are not simply tiny particles whirling about their fixed orbits in perpetual motion, but that they too are multi-dimensional waves of some sort in an ether that does not really exist. At this point, the human imagination gives up and abstract mathematics take over. Einstein's search for an all-embracing mathematical formula that would express the underlying substance or energy of the universe is really the attempt of a mathematician or scientist to encroach upon the domain of philosophy and capture the key to its riddles. The atomic bomb which demolished Hiroshima also dealt a body blow to the mechanistic conception of the universe, for it demonstrated that matter is not the basic unit of existence. If matter is congealed energy and energy in turn is defined as that which sets matter in motion, then how shall we picture ultimate reality? Theoretical physics endeavors to penetrate the mystery of existence, veil by veil; no sooner is one veil torn apart by the genius of research than there is displayed another and more baffling one. The progress of scientific research and reflection tends to confirm the intuition of the great minds of all ages, that behind the simplest grain of matter there lie hidden oceans of mystery.

But, do we only think of the world and its contents? Do we not also live in the world, and is it not possible for us to reflect upon the current of life in our own being and thereby to attain a glimpse of the real nature of existence? Is it not true that unbeknown to our conscious selves we carry the secret of life within our breast and that if we could only probe ourselves deeply enough, we should solve at one stroke the riddle of our Self and of the Universe? Logically, there is no reason whatsoever to deny the validity of this method of introspection. Historically, mystics have been among the most fastidious and thoroughgoing logicians.

Metaphysical intuition has long been a respectable doctrine in philosophy. There is scarcely a great system of thought that does not include or leave room for an intuitive grasp of reality. The whole vast range of philosophical speculation may, as a matter of fact, be divided into two categories—those that are frankly based upon an intuition and those that presume to be wholly objective or scientific. In the former category, we should include names like those of Plato, Plotinus, Fichte, Nietsche, Schopenhauer, Bergson and S. Alexander. The latter category includes all the incorrigible Aristotelians who know quite definitely that there is nothing mental or physical that can elude the rigid methods of the test tube. Now, intuition is essentially an attempt to pursue the path of mysticism, albeit to a limited degree. Bergson, the outstanding exponent of intuition in our day, identified it in his last book, *Two Sources of Morality and Religion,* with the doctrines of mysticism.

As a mystic, Kuk was exceedingly healthy, sober, optimistic and many-sided. Many a thinker or pietist who sought to find God thru the *pardes* of mysticism could not endure the emotional strain and became in one way or another "peculiar." The annals of mysticism are filled with such perversions—a considerable part of which are of an erotic character. Kuk was happily free of any such distortions. His mystical experiences were uniformly of the healthy-minded variety, lending fresh wings to his creative faculties and endowing him with an enormous capacity for sheer drudgery.

The essential content of Kuk's mysticism is also free of any trace of asceticism, acomism, or any form of "sick-minded" escapism. The terms that occur most often in his description of the mystical state are "light," "life," "love" and "creativity." In his mysticism, a happy combination of the loftiest faculties of normal consciousness is brought to the highest pitch of efficiency. Kuk's persistent emphasis on the current of vitality perceived in the mystical state is especially worthy of note. It would be most difficult to find any parallels to this phase of Kuk's piety in the vast range of Christian or Buddhist mysticism. In this respect, both Kuk and Bergson are true to the life-affirming character of Jewish piety, in which holiness is not a thing "other than life," but an intensified form of life itself, transmuting and sanctifying all that is coarse and earthy.

Kuk's mysticism is of particular importance in the history of Jewish philosophy because he was practically the first Jewish literary mystic. As a state of mind, mysticism was naturally never completely absent from the Jewish scene, but the fact is that introspective mysticism of the kind that is so common among Christians, detailing all the steps of emotional refinement on the way to mystical ecstasy, is almost completely lacking in the enormous literature of Jewish piety. Prof. G. Scholem attributes this fact to a certain bashful reticence on the part of Jewish mystics. However, this reticence itself needs to be explained. Whatever the explanation, the fact is that Kuk blazed a new path in Jewish thought.

When we bear in mind the fact that modern philosophy of religion is for the most part founded upon the theory and practice of mysticism, we are enabled to see Kuk's contribution in the proper perspective. Theology was not always tied to mysticism. In the Middle Ages and in the early period of modern philosophy, theology could afford to be thoroughly rational. Philosophy was then still the handmaiden of theology, proving in four different ways the existence of God. After Kant's devastating criticism of this rational approach, religious thinkers almost uniformly found themselves compelled to resort to the realm of feeling and ethical will for the foundation of their faith. Mysticism and religious experience generally then came into their own. As a matter of experience, religion could meet the challenge of modern criticism without difficulty since the test of experience is the touchstone of truth for the modern mind. The renewed interest in mystical literature, however, could find only indifferent material in Jewish sources. Whether because of "voluntary censorship" or because it did not seem to fit into the established molds of Jewish piety, the fact itself is incontestable, that only rare and vague instances of genuine mysticism can be discovered in Jewish sources. Kuk's writings fill in this gap with unique distinction, adding fresh potentialities and nuances to the future growth of Jewish religious thought.

NOTE

1. *Igroth Hor'iyah* (Jerusalem, 1934), p. 131.

PART TWO

JACOB B. AGUS AS A STUDENT OF MEDIEVAL JEWISH PHILOSOPHY AND MYSTICISM

SELECTIONS AND
PREFATORY REMARKS
David R. Blumenthal

RABBI AGUS was a lifelong and informed student of medieval Jewish thought in both its philosophical and mystical modes. Though an ardent admirer of the former and a severe critic of the latter, he wrote intelligently on both.

The following selections, chosen to accompany David R. Blumenthal's essay "Jacob B. Agus as a Student of Medieval Jewish Philosophy and Mysticism" in *American Rabbi: The Life and Thought of Jacob B. Agus* (New York, 1996), are drawn from Jacob Agus' *Evolution of Jewish Thought* (New York, 1959), 193–203 and 276–90.

8

THE RISE OF JEWISH
RATIONALISM

HAVING ESTABLISHED the validity of the general belief in prophecy, Maimonides proceeded to reassert the Orthodox dogma that only
the Torah of Moses could be regarded as true revelation. Many Jewish
sectarians, including the Qaraites, had accepted the belief that both
Jesus and Mohammed were "true prophets." Unwilling to risk the
dangers of complete tolerance, Maimonides insisted that Christianity
was only one step above idolatry, and Mohammed was just "insane."
How could one pretend to be a prophet who has not even learned to
despise the pleasures of the senses? "Holiness is the repudiation of sexual
relations."[1]

Nevertheless, both Christianity and Islam were, according to Maimonides, divinely ordained "preparations" for the ultimate establishment of the kingdom of God. In other words, they tended to lead
mankind toward the truths of monotheism, though they were not
absolutely true in themselves.

Just as it is impossible to assign a valid purpose to every phenomenon
in life, though the existence of inner purposiveness within living things
is obvious, so too we can find the radiance of purpose in many portions
of the Torah, though not in every verse and every detail. However, we
cannot but affirm that there is a general purpose for the precepts of the
Torah and that this fundamental purpose is "the improvement of the
body and the soul" of men. Rationality is the noblest quality of human
beings. Could God be conceived then as less rational than men? With-

out attempting to account for every detail of the law, we must discover God's purpose at least in the most important precepts and *mizvoth*.

Maimonides divided the *mizvoth* of the Torah into fourteen categories, assigning some rational motivation for each of them. In general, he declared, rituals and ceremonies are related to ideals and sentiments in several diverse ways—as practical guidance is to good intentions, as a concrete illustration is to an abstract doctrine, as a shell is to a kernel, as the body is to the soul. "For ideas without deeds which affirm and fortify them cannot continue to be effective among the people."[2]

The attainment of perfection in piety is dependent upon the establishment of ideal physical conditions for the individual and a just order in society. Spiritual perfection is intellectual greatness superimposed upon ideal moral qualities, which are in their turn dependent on a just and equitable order in society. Consequently we arrive at a threefold goal as the ultimate purpose of the Torah:

> Our final conclusion emerging out of all these postulates is that every commandment, be it positive or negative, has as its purpose to correct injustice or to instill such ethical qualities as are needed for the good of society; or to teach opinions that are true or ideas that are needed for the prevention of evil, or the training in good virtues . . .[3]

It is interesting to note that Maimonides referred to two classes of beliefs, those that were true in themselves and those that needed to be affirmed as true for the sake of an ideal, stable society. Like Plato in *The Republic,* he was keenly conscious of the need for cementing a society by means of affirmations that were not strictly true, but were suited to the needs of that particular society. Like Aristotle, he frequently affirmed that "man is by nature a political being." It is impossible for great men to attain their full spiritual stature in isolation. A just and perfectly ordered society is needed as the matrix, for the emergence of a small number of chosen souls who will attain the perfection of "cleaving unto the Active Reason." This select group of saintly philosophers will understand and continually contemplate the abstract conception of the Deity. But the large masses of the people cannot be expected either to comprehend so subtle a concept or to rest content with a God idea that is completely stripped of all the elements that they associate with personality. A façade of opinions or dogmas is needed, Maimonides believed, in order to provide a foundation of ideological unity for the Jewish community. For this reason the Torah enjoined the belief in certain humanlike qualities of the Deity, such as His hearing and seeing, His pitying, loving, and avenging. These qualities are not true, in the strict sense of the word, but they must be affirmed *as if* they were true, since they are "necessary" for the maintenance of the community of Israel. These "necessary" ideas, considered strictly as social instruments and armored with the unyielding rigidity of dogma, do not conflict with the logical truths of philosophy; on the contrary, the dogmas of the Torah-community provide a moral atmosphere and a congenial social environment for the emergence and growth of philosophical and saintly souls. At the same time, these "necessary" ideas do not violate the philosopher's passion for truth, since for his own meditations he will know how to interpret them in accord with the axioms of reason.

> Understand what we said in regard to beliefs: at times the commandment contains a true belief, which is true in itself, not in its relation to some other purpose, like the belief in the unity of God, His eternity and incorporeality. But at times a belief is enjoined which is necessary for the removal of iniquity or for the acquisition of good qualities, like the belief that the Lord, may He be exalted, becomes angry at the one who robs, as it is written, "And my wrath shall be kindled and I shall kill," or the belief that He, may He be exalted, will hear the cry of those that are wronged and oppressed and will save them, as it is written, "And it shall be, when he will cry unto me, I shall hear, for I am merciful. . . ."[4]

Some beliefs tend to authenticate themselves by the actions that they inspire:

> It is clear that the belief in the possibility of a sinner's return belongs in the category of the beliefs which are indispensable for the existence of the Torah-community, for it is impossible for man not to err or sin . . . and if he believes that he will never be able to atone for his sin, he will continue in his error, possibly even intensifying his rebelliousness to the point of becoming irretrievable. But thanks to this belief in repentance, he will mend his ways and return to the practice of good virtues, becoming possibly even more perfect than before his sin. . . .[5]

In another connection, Maimonides defines repentance as the attainment of that psychical level which in the judgment of God would make the erstwhile sinner reject the temptation to sin, if the identical opportunity were again presented to him. In other words, repentance is not success in winning an act of pardon from the Almighty, but the mending of one's character, by dint of persistent effort. But to people generally who are beset with the feelings of guilt and helplessness the practices of prayer and repentance must be represented not as so many exercises in self-purification, but as petitions for the grace and favor of the Almighty King and compassionate Father. The belief in divine forgiveness is the example of a "necessary" idea that becomes true if accepted in all sincerity.

This twofold meaning of the same act, one for the philosopher and one for the masses, is not self-contradictory, since every society is inevitably an organic whole. The ultimate purpose of the Torah is fulfilled in the lives of the few philosophical saints, but these giants of the spirit can thrive only in a concrete, many-sided community and for its sake. As one commentator put it:[6]

And it is necessary that the mass-man should believe that God is moved by human petitions and rituals of propitiation. Though this belief is false, strictly speaking, it is necessary for the existence of society. Therefore these beliefs are called necessary, not true. The wise man will understand that these beliefs are said in accord with the maxim, "The Torah spoke in the language of men. . . ."[7]

Along with ideas true and "necessary" the Torah enjoined the observance of many commandments, which were designed for the purpose of maintaining an ideal, justly ordered society. This overarching purpose was the central motivation of all the laws regulating relations "between man and man."

As to ritual observances, Maimonides noted that the Torah was given in the midst of certain historical circumstances and that the significance of each rite can be seen only when it is viewed against the background of the prevailing pagan practices in the time of Moses.

The complex laws, regulating the sacrifices in the sanctuary and temple, were designed for the purpose of weaning the people away from the worship of pagan deities. In the days of Moses the people were not yet ready for more elevated forms of worship. They could not conceive of serving the Almighty in any other way than by bringing offerings into the temple. Hence, it was necessary for Moses to adapt his teaching to the primitive habits of his contemporaries.

Moses' predicament may be compared to the appearance of a prophet in our day who would call to the service of God in the following manner: "The Lord commanded you not to pray to Him and not to fast and not to seek His help in time of trouble, but to let your service consist in thought only, without deeds."[8]

Such a message would be in keeping with the inner truth of faith, but it would hardly be accepted by the people of our day. In the same way, Moses was compelled to take account of the habits, rites and ideas which prevailed in his generation. He could not antagonize the people by rejecting ways of thinking and acting that were dear to them. He could only regulate and spiritualize their customs, so as to lead them by degrees in the right direction, and he had to begin at the people's actual point of spiritual development.

Maimonides was familiar with some pagan practices from quotations and descriptions which he found in contemporary Moslem literature. Though he was clearly aware of the paucity and inaccuracy of the information available to him concerning the rituals of the heathen, he felt justified in propounding the general rule that Judaism evolved in the course of an arduous struggle against the follies and rites of the pagan world. All the quasi-magical rites in Judaism were ultimately due to the strategy employed by Moses and his successors in their relentless efforts to combat the inroads of the pagan mentality. Many a time the architects of the Jewish faith had to stoop in order to conquer.

The essence of paganism is the worship of the creature, rather than of the Creator; i.e., the attribution of independent dominion to stars, mountains, rivers, names of angels, etc. For this reason Maimonides considered astrology and the juggling of mysterious "names" by the proto-Qabbalists of his day to be at once sheer stupidity and unalloyed paganism. Judaism is, in essence, a continual protest against the pagan worship of the creature and against magical reliance on the manipulation of occult forces. It is at the point where magic and naïve superstition end that Judaism begins.

The knowledge of these [pagan] ideas and rites is a very important gateway leading to the comprehension of the reasons for the commandments, for the root of our entire Torah and the axis upon which it turns is the determination to erase these ideas from the hearts of men and to eliminate them from the world . . . it is the primary, general intention of the whole Torah. . . .[9]

With the limited information of the history of religions at his disposal, Maimonides endeavored stoutly to explain the rites of Judaism as being primarily so many acts of symbolic repudiation of the ways of heathendom. Occasionally, too, a magical practice had to be included within the Torah, as an unavoidable concession to the ingrained primitive habits of the people of Israel at the time of Moses. For, as Maimonides put it, "It is impossible for human nature to go suddenly from one extreme to the other."[10]

The Torah, for example, prohibited the eating of the fruit of a tree in its first three years of growth *(Arla)*. This prohibition was a silent protest against the policy of the pagans to dedicate such fruit to the use of their temples. The Torah ordained the bringing of the fruit of the fourth year to the Holy Temple; the purpose of this commandment was to make certain that the people will not bring the fruit to the pagan altars. It will be noted that Maimonides was not dismayed by the fact that two opposing strategies were employed by the Torah to counteract the same pagan custom. Maimonides also pointed out that the bringing of fruits to pagan temples was occasionally accompanied by immoral and orgiastic fertility rites which were intended to hasten the growth of the trees. After four years, there was no longer any danger of such practices.

The Torah prohibited the practice of grafting the branch of one tree upon the stem of another because the pagans would indulge in unnatural sexual acts in connection with this work *(Kilaim)*. Similarly, the planting of grains in a vineyard was prohibited so that the Israelites would be removed as far as possible from the temptation to indulge in the immoral, magical rites that were frequently performed in connection with these practices. The prohibition of interweaving threads of flax and wool *(Shatnez)* is based on similar reasoning; namely, the fact that pagan priests made it a point to wear garments made from cloth that was woven in this manner.[11]

In the Holy Temple, the tablets of the law were placed in the Ark, within the Holy of Holies, not because there was any holiness or divinity in the tablets themselves, but simply to indicate that the words of the prophets constituted the basis of the covenant between God and Israel. Since prophets derived their inspiration from angels (the Active Reason), the belief in angels had to be reinforced by the representation of the cherubim. The rite of burning incense in the Holy Temple was designed for the purpose of eliminating the noxious odors resulting from the burning of the sacrifices on the altars, not to offer a pleasing fragrance to the Almighty. The sacrifices offered in the temple consisted of cattle, goats and sheep, for these were sacred "totem" animals to many of the pagan nations, and in slaughtering them the Jews demonstrated their disbelief in the sanctities of the pagan world. The pagans would bring leavened and sweetened offerings to their gods, but not salt. This is why the opposite practice was enjoined in the Torah; i.e., leavened and sweetened foods were prohibited, but salt was to be sprinkled on all offerings upon the altar.[12]

The drinking of blood was prohibited "for blood was very unclean in the eyes of the Sabeans [Near Eastern pagans], who nevertheless would drink it on special occasions, believing blood to be the peculiar drink of the demons, so that when they partook of it, they thought they entered into partnership with the demons and learned the future from them."[13] It is for a similar reason that the eating of meat was prohibited altogether, so long as the Israelites dwelled in the desert of Sinai, for the worship of demons is very widespread in the desert. Later, when they entered into the land of Israel, where such practices were almost unknown, the prohibition on meat was rescinded.

In the Torah we find a detailed description of sacrifices that were to be brought daily, on the Sabbath or in honor of the new moon. The new moon sacrifices are of special interest to us, since they appear to be the residue of moon worship. Manifestly, the sacrifices described in the Torah were in effect long before the Torah was accepted by the Israelites. The Torah simply allowed the established practice to continue since the Israelites were powerfully addicted to it, specifying, however, that the offerings were to be brought to God, not to the moon. In this manner the danger of moon worship was averted. But as to "the offering of wine," Maimonides wrote, "I am disturbed about it up to this day. Why should it be commanded, seeing the pagans also offered wine to their gods?"[14] For that matter, Maimonides also confessed his inability to find a good reason for the table in the sanctuary and the showbreads that were placed upon it.[15]

As to the laws of ritual uncleanliness, which seem so cumbersome and unnecessary, Moses' general aim was to soften the harsh and complicated regulations of the pagan nations, but he could not shock the sensibilities of the people and defy their ingrained prejudice. "For this Torah of God . . . came to lighten the burden of existing rites, and if some of them appear to you to involve a great deal of trouble and annoyance, it is so only because you do not know the customs and ideas which prevailed at that time . . ."[16]

Thus the laws of ritual defilement were designed in part for the purpose of discouraging people from coming into the Holy Temple too frequently. Insofar as the masses are concerned, familiarity breeds contempt. The more the common people were kept away from the Holy Temple, the more they were likely to revere it. Accordingly, the laws of defilement were so designed that, at any one time, "you will find very few people that are clean." Another motive for these precepts is to induce people to stay away from that which is ugly or disgusting. Third, "The Torah had to accommodate itself to the accepted customs of the time, for the Sabeans lavished a great deal of energy upon such matters as ritual uncleanliness."[17]

A good illustration of the primitive obsession with rites of purification is the law governing the periodic "uncleanliness" of women and the complex ritual of lustration in specially designed baths *(mikvah).* Among some primitive people, "the menstruating woman had to be locked in a house all by herself, the places upon which she walked were burned and whoever spoke to her became unclean. . . ." If you compare these stringencies with the comparative mildness of the regulations in the Torah, Maimonides concluded, you will note the spirit of moderation that governed the laws of Moses.

As to the dietary laws, most of the requirements of Judaism are simply sanitary regulations. "The best part of the meat is permitted for us." The flesh of the pig was prohibited because of the unclean habits of this particular animal. "And if the eating of pork were permitted, the streets and the houses would be as dirty as latrines, even as are the countries of the Franks [Europeans] in our day." This is what the famed physician of Egypt thought of the Christian lands of Europe. *Mutatis mutandis!*

Blood and *trefa* (non-kosher) meat are bad for digestion. As to the mixing of meat with milk, "it appears probable to me that there was about it an odor of pagan worship. It is possible that they boiled meat with milk in the course of one or another of their celebrations."[18]

The laws of marriage and divorce constitute the basis of a justly ordered society. The law concerning the "bitter waters" to be given to the woman suspected of adultery, establishing an ordeal for the discovery of sexual sins, was designed to discourage marital infidelity by scaring the superstitious women and embarrassing the understanding ones.[19]

The law of levirate marriage existed long before the covenant at Sinai. Since the people could not be weaned away from this primitive custom all at once, the Torah modified the law by the introduction of the ceremony of *Halitza*.[20]

The law of circumcision established a sign which is common to all Jewish people. At the same time,

> One of the reasons for circumcision, to my mind, is to lessen the enjoyment of sexual intercourse and to weaken this organ as much as possible. . . . That circumcision lessens this organ's capacity for conjugal relations and sometimes removes the pleasure associated with it, I have no doubt.[21]

The major portion of the Torah was devoted to the ordering of an ideal society, so designed as to encourage at least some people to devote themselves to the cultivation of the noble qualities of the soul. As to the *lex talionis*, the principle of "an eye for an eye," it was, to Maimonides, simply an application of the principle of absolute justice.

> And he who lost a limb through the actions of an assailant, then the same limb should be removed from the assailant, "as he put a blemish in a man, so a blemish shall be put in him." Though we today substitute money for this punishment, do not be disturbed, for our intention is here to explain the reasons of the verses in Scripture, not the words of the Talmud.[22]

Sufficient illustrations have been cited to indicate the rigorous and even ruthless logic which Maimonides brought to the analysis of the Jewish faith. The essence of Judaism is the belief in the one incorporeal Deity and the determination to cleave unto Him. But the Jewish faith developed in distinct historical circumstances; therefore, it adopted and preserved in its passage through history some irrational rites, vestiges of the ancient struggle against paganism. For the most part, these rituals possess no intrinsic significance, save insofar as they are needed for the maintenance of the Torah-community.

Maimonides himself did not draw any conclusion as to the superfluity or obsolescence of the rituals, but his system of thought was bound to lead to this consideration. And, in spite of his silence, he did not doubt for a moment the rightness of following the inner logic of his ideas to its ultimate conclusions. For, as he saw it, reason is virtually identical with the will of God. Indeed, it is the one quality which derives directly from God, being the inherent law of His being. Scriptural language at times attributed all natural phenomena to the Deity, since He was the source of all power and the laws of nature were designed and fixed by Him.[23] But while the forces of nature were established by God, they did not represent. His will in the same sense as the light of reason, deriving automatically from God, through the agency of the Active Intellect. Sin and failure are due to matter; the direct action of the Deity is reason. And reason is at all times good.

"For through the knowledge of truth, all hatred and quarrels are eliminated, and people cease to injure one another."[24] We must not compromise with the strict dictates of the intellect in interpreting the Torah, "for only the truth is acceptable to Him, and only falsehood does He hate."[25]

NOTES

1. *Moreh Nebukhim,* 3:33.
2. *Ibid.,* 2:31.
3. *Ibid.,* 3:28.
4. *Ibid.,* 3:28.
5. *Ibid.,* 3:36.
6. *Ibid.,* 3:34.
7. *Ibid.,* 3:28, commentary of Shem Tov *ad locum.*
8. *Ibid.,* 3:32.
9. *Ibid.,* 3:29.
10. *Ibid.,* 3:32.
11. *Ibid.,* 3:37.
12. Leviticus 2:11, 13.
13. *Moreh Nebukhim,* 3:46.
14. *Ibid.,* 3:46.
15. *Ibid.,* 3:45.
16. *Ibid.,* 3:47.
17. *Ibid.,* 3:47.
18. *Ibid.,* 3:48.
19. Numbers 5:18.

20. Deuteronomy 25:9.
21. *Moreh Nebukhim, 3:49.*
22. *Ibid.*, 3:41.
23. *Ibid.*, 2:48.
24. *Ibid.*, 3:11.
25. *Ibid.*, 2:47.

9

THE QABBALAH

IT WAS in the eighties of the thirteenth century that the classic text of Qabbalistic literature, the *Zohar,* appeared. The scholar, Rabbi Moses de Leon, is now presumed to have written the major portion of the *Zohar,* which is not really one systematic work, but a collection of many books and brochures, varying in clarity and emphasis and held together by an inner unity of theme and ideology. This vast compendium of esoteric lore is a pseudo-epigraphic composition, attributed by its editor to Rabbi Simon Bar Yohai and a coterie of his "illuminated" disciples. This second-century Palestinian rabbi was believed to have spent thirteen years in a cave, studying the hidden mysteries of Torah, with the direct aid of the "spirit of holiness." What more natural than to ascribe to him the authorship of a book which is replete with visions and revelations!

Soon after its appearance, the authenticity of the *Zohar* was questioned, by mystics no less than by their opponents. Rabbi Isaac of Akko reported the testimony of de Leon's widow to the effect that her husband was the ghost writer of the *Zohar,* in all its complex subdivisions. But this testimony was ignored and later controverted with the utmost vehemence. So congruous was the comforting message of the *Zohar* with the overriding needs of the contemporary Jewish consciousness that all critical objections were set aside. Fundamentally, the Zoharic mentality was "true" to the increasing impetus of the dogmatic and romantic phases of contemporary Judaism; ergo, it had to be an authentic revelation. For two centuries, the rise of the *Zohar* in popular acceptance was slow and steady. Then, when the travail of Spanish Jewry reached its climax in the fateful expulsion of 1492, the *Zohar* was catapulted to canonical holiness, attaining a degree of authority that was third only to the Bible and the Talmud.[1]

While the *Zohar* is the central text of Qabbalah, there was a great body of esoteric lore antedating it, which was incorporated in the Talmud, the *Midrashim*, and in a number of Qabbalistic works of which the *Sefer Yezira (The Book of Creation)*, attributed to the patriarch Abraham, was the best known and most revered. Altogether, the term "Qabbalah" comprises today a vast literature, containing more than three thousand volumes. While some of the classic works contain elaborate metaphysical systems, most of these volumes spin the ancient threads in endless variations, with the view of uncovering the "inner secrets" of the Torah or proposing a quasi-magical formula of "holy names" for the propitiation of angels and the banishment of demons. Yet, in all its vast variety, Qabbalah contains certain basic intellectual principles and concepts, which its devotees employ with virtual unanimity.

While some rationalistic students of Jewish thought regard the Qabbalah as a temporary aberration, born of ignorance and despair, which could rightfully be excluded from the history of Judaism, we cannot overlook the fact that, for many centuries, the Qabbalah constituted the regnant philosophy of the Jewish faith. From Crescas to Mendelssohn, no Jew dared venture into the field of metaphysical speculation without treading the approved pathways of Qabbalah. Nor can it be said that Orthodox Judaism in our day has repudiated the organic complex of Qabbalistic ideas, for so authoritative a religious personality as the late chief rabbi of Palestine, Abraham Isaac Kuk, framed his ideas in the molds of Qabbalah. And the Hasidic movement of the eighteenth century was essentially a reassertion of Qabbalistic thought. Hasidism converted the esoteric lore of Qabbalah into a mass movement, preaching its doctrines in public and applying them in practice.

The degree of authority and prestige enjoyed by the Qabbalah may be gauged by the circumstance that Rabbi Joseph Karo, author of the *Shulhan Arukh,* was not only a devotee but also a living "channel" of Qabbalistic revelation. *Maggidim,* or holy souls from heaven, would visit him when he was in a trance and bring him tidings from "the world of

truth." Rav Hai Gaon believed in the authenticity of the mystical
visions of his contemporaries, the *yordai hamerkabah,* who were precursors of the Qabbalah. Nahmanides, whose commentary on the Torah
was widely read and whose influence on Spanish Jewry was unsurpas-
sed, was one of the master builders of Qabbalah. Rabbi Joel Sirkis,
author of the classic halachic work, *Baith Hodosh,* asserted flatly that "he
who denies the truth of the wisdom of Qabbalah is called a heretic."[2]
Rabbi Moses Isserles, the greatest halachic authority of Polish Jewry,
allowed himself considerable latitude in the interpretation of Qabbalistic
doctrines and deplored the tendency of improperly trained scholars to
venture into the dangerous domain of the "wisdom of the hidden." Yet
he too agreed that Qabbalah was authentic tradition, received by Moses
at Sinai and "transmitted from mouth to mouth."[3] The Gaon of Vilna
and his disciples were staunch believers in the revelations of Qabbalah,
insisting only on the relative independence of the realm of *Halachah.*[4]

On the other hand, a few bold voices even in medieval times dared
to challenge the pretensions of Qabbalah. Rabbi Isaac ben Sheshet
Barfat took issue with the Qabbalistic method of directing different
prayers through different channels or *sefiroth,* insisting that childlike
naïveté is the best attitude for prayer.[5] The sixteenth-century Italian
rabbi, Leo de Modena, condemned the whole Qabbalistic theosophy as
spurious, identifying it as pagan in origin.[6]

The eighteenth-century rabbi, Jacob Emden, accepted the general
texture of Qabbalistic ideas in his introduction to the prayer book; yet,
worried by the possible misuse of Qabbalah by sectarians, he asserted
that the text of the *Zohar* was corrupted, so that it can only be used
with the greatest of caution.[7]

From all the above, it would appear that although the Qabbalah
dominated Jewish thought for several centuries, there was never a time
when its authority was entirely unchallenged.

The term "Qabbalah" means "tradition." Unlike the discipline of philosophy, the Qabbalah is founded upon the testimony of revelation, not
the axioms of reason or the wisdom of experience. The Qabbalists
maintained that their "hidden wisdom" was charged with cosmic potency and given over to the safekeeping of chosen individuals. The basic
books of Qabbalah were alleged to be written by ancient revered sages,
or by heavenly beings such as "Raziel, the angel."

Enthusiastic adherents of the "wisdom of truth" maintained that

Elijah the prophet revealed the principles of Qabbalah to Rabbi David of Provence, who was the father of Rabbi Abraham (RabD), famed as the bitter critic of Maimonides. The son was also privileged to behold Elijah in his visions. His disciple Rabbi Yizhak was similarly blessed, transmitting his lore to Ezra and Azriel, "who were the fourth generation, receiving direct information from Elijah."[8] Another Qabbalist maintained that a certain Rabbi Keshisha Gaon brought this secret lore from the ancient academies of Babylonia to Rabbi Yehudah he-hassid of Germany.[9]

Rabbi Jonathan Eibshitz, one of the leading rabbinical figures of the eighteenth century, declared categorically that "the Qabbalists received their doctrines directly from the prophets."[10]

Modern scholars encounter no difficulty in finding parallels between the central concepts of Qabbalah and the Gnostic systems of the ancient world, which in turn were compounded in diverse combinations out of the floating debris of pagan mythology and Judeo-Christian elements. But the building blocks of philosophic systems are not as significant as the cement of thought and inspiration that holds them together. At its noblest reaches, Qabbalistic thought is rich in profound insights and noble sentiments, though it is never entirely free from the clinging "shells" of superstition. So thoughtful an author as Rabbi Joseph Irgash did not disdain pragmatic "proofs" for the truths of Qabbalah. Proceeding on the principle that truth is that which works, he challenged the philosophers with this clinching argument: "Which philosopher ever created a calf, as the Talmudic sage, Rovo, is reputed to have done?"[11] The classic Qabbalists believed in the possibility of the miracle, but scorned the employment of lofty principles for such lowly tasks, contending that only a "calf" would bother to make a calf. This was the aspect of Qabbalah which Maimonides particularly resented as rank stupidity and madness.[12] The Qabbalists retorted in time by inventing a letter in which the aged philosopher is said to have repented of his errors.

In its essential motivation, Qabbalah sought to re-establish the validity of the Jewish ritual against the challenge of rationalistic philosophy. It represents, therefore, a reflective formulation of the principles of naïve faith, a blend of the philosophic passion for analysis and systematic consistency with the religious yearning for the assurance of divine favor, humanly won and securely held. This mighty effort to provide solid intellectual scaffolding for the tender tremors of naïve piety underlies all of Qabbalah. And this effort was directed through several channels, for, as we have seen, the rational philosophy of the Middle Ages emasculated the sinews of piety and assigned to religious ritual a subordinate role in the attainment of intellectual perfection, exalting the virtue of philosophic reflection above that of strict ritual observance. Compelled to live in perpetual readiness for martyrdom, Jewish people could ill afford the corrosive effects of rational criticism.

A mild but ever-present undercurrent in Qabbalistic writings reflects the hurt pride of the Jew. How could Maimonides possibly be right in his description of the "alien" wisdom of the Greeks as the essence of Jewish teaching? If profound essences are hidden in the Torah, they would be revealed to great Jews, not Gentiles. Are loyal, observant Jews to be compared to those who wander about the palace, while the Greek philosophers were safely inside?

> Rationalistic wisdom is not at all peculiar to Israel, but is the portion of all nations, reflecting as it does human efforts. Thus, the other nations had among them greater philosophers than we, even when our people were seduced by this wisdom. But the wisdom of Israel is inward, divine, received from the Almighty and not shared by the other nations.
>
> Jewish reason is different from the reason of the other nations, even as the Jew is different in the possession of a different soul, as is known to the wise, and Jewish reason is perfected through the study of Torah, its mysteries and secrets and through the dialectics of the true wisdom, which is far above the wisdom that is derived from experience. This level the philosophers did not attain and did not merit.[13]

To be sure, we are bidden to make use of our speculative and reasoning faculties, but the Qabbalists agreed with Halevi that every rational system starts out with a number of unproved axioms or assumptions. We may make use of our powers of reasoning only when the "tools" of basic intuitions are made available to us by revelation. All philosophers base their speculative systems upon one or more "first principles," and these "first principles" are extra-rational, deriving either from the illusions of human imagination or the truths of God. "For Torah and wisdom were both derived from the divine reason, and are substantially one, complementing each other, and the believer requires both for his perfection. But the first principles upon which the philosophers build their systems are not derived from the divine reason. Hence, all their conclusions are false, incapable of providing salvation."[14]

On a deeper level, the Qabbalists were concerned with the task of reconciling the personal philosophy of Jewish monotheism with the implicit mechanistic naturalism of Greek philosophy.

In Judaism, the fundamental analogy for the bonds between God and man in all their variation and complexity is the relationship between two personalities. There is God, the Master, the Father or the King who commands, instructs, pleads, demands, promises or punishes. None of the seductive impulses of the flesh affect Him, for He is spirit, and none of the forces of nature prevail against Him, for He is the creator of the totality of existence out of the naught. Still, in all His omnipotence and omniscience, God is a person. The Talmudic sages shied away from attributing material qualities to Him, but they did not envisage Him without the temperamental and psychical qualities of a human being. It is significant that Rabbi Abraham of Posquieres, who opposed the Maimonidean conception of an abstract Deity, arguing that material qualities are applicable to the nature of God, was deemed to be one of the inspired fathers of the Qabbalah.[15]

But even those who shunned the coarse attributes of the flesh conceived of God as the ideal saint, who learns, prays, judges and administers His domain, so that His every action might serve as a model for human action.

Upon this basic insight, the entire world view of Judaism was founded. The tortuous and uncertain course of the human adventure in history is explained as the result of the perpetual tension between God and men. There is no fundamental force that is arrayed against the Deity, even Satan serving His purpose in some way, but from time to time the free human will sets itself in direct opposition to the divine will. The consequences of this human rebellion are not automatic or necessitous, for the Lord may, according to His Wisdom, elect to act in accord with the "policy of mercy" or the "policy of law." Typical of the personal concept in Judaism is the rejection of the pagan-magical view of guilt as an intangible slimy substance clinging to a person as well as the philosophical view of punishment as being causally related to its corresponding crime. The concept of *teshuvah,* repentance and reconciliation, reflects the genuine nonmechanistic impetus of Jewish genius—the causal chain is set aside by God, who forgives the sinner out of His goodness and His love for His creatures.

In Jewish monotheism, nature was not conceived as operating in accord with laws that were forever fixed in its very being. All the forces of nature are His "servants," with the sun "rejoicing" to do His bidding and the stars being "counted" upon their disappearance from the sky. The heavens are His "chair" and the earth His "footstool"; still, He speaks to man "out of the hair on His head," and "looks upon the poor and those that are contrite in spirit."

It is through speech that He reveals Himself to man, for speech is the fundamental form of communication between two rational beings. While God cannot be seen, He can be heard, with all the Israelites hearing His words at Sinai; later, His words were restricted to the prophets and still later the sages heard the "echo" of His voice *(Bath Kol)*. In all these relationships, there was no basic difficulty for the religious imagination, since God was conceived as the epitome of a free spirit, able to move about wherever He pleased.

It was Aristotle's concept of a natural law operating in the whole of nature that provided the basic antithesis to the personal concept of Judaism. Man's relation to the universe about him could now be conceived in terms of the necessitous laws of cause and effect, which, once postulated, could not be terminated at any arbitrary point. The inner bond between the logical process and the concept of causality opened up a way of reasoning which sought to find necessitous connections between all events. Even the world exists by necessity, and if man is to rise above the destiny of the animal kingdom, he must achieve his goal by using the laws of necessity to his advantage, avoiding the downward pull of the material and the fever of desire in favor of the truly human exercise of philosophical contemplation. The principles of necessity and of will are polar opposites; each is capable of being stretched so far as to account for the whole of existence, and the two philosophies so generated are perpetually in conflict. The Jewish concept exalts freedom and God as the source of all life, seeing nature as a pale reflection of His dynamic will; the Aristotelian allows necessity and nature to absorb God, as it were, leaving the whole of existence in the iron grip of an inexorable machine.

While Maimonides sensed the ominous implications of this fundamental conflict, nevertheless he yielded to the Aristotelian conception of mechanism and necessity. He concurred in the description of the Deity as "alive, powerful, wise and purposive," but he emptied these adjectives of any real content by declaring that they were only to be taken as negations of negations; i.e., God is not not-alive, not not-wise, etc. To Maimonides, the way to reach God is to declare concerning all things: "They do not apply to the Deity." Accordingly, the relation between man and God, so simple and natural in prephilosophical monotheism, becomes an insuperable problem. "How then can one conceive the relation between Him and that which is outside of Him, thus postulating a dimension of existence including them both?"[16]

Man's rise in the scale of being occurs in accord with the necessitous laws of nature. As his mind grows into unison with the Active Reason of the universe, man achieves a kind of "nearness" to the divine being and a measure of liberation from the swirling currents of passion and the universal sway of death. But it is man himself who thus achieves the ascent, so that at the level of prophecy, a direct intervention of the Deity is required in order to prevent prophecy. Philosophical contemplation is, in this view, the crown of the good life, with the laws of morality and the regulations of piety serving only as the necessary preparation and context for the art of contemplation.

The *mizvoth* of the Torah are interpreted as fulfilling their function in a necessitous manner, by affecting the mind of the worshiper or the social pattern of society. The inner mechanical logic of Aristotle reigns supreme within the Maimonidean conception of Judaism. The dynamic concept of personality, in which fundamental reality is in continuous tension between the human qualities of love and domination, justice and mercy, wrath and forgiveness, is replaced by the static concept of a self-perpetuating machine in which no change ever occurs. The prophetic declaration, "I, the Lord, did not change," was intended only to describe the reliability of His character, asserting that God does not forget His promises. But when the rational spirit came to prevail within the "tent of Shem," this verse was interpreted as referring to the rigid inflexibility and unchangeability of the divine nature; hence, it meant also that God was not moved by prayers, petitions or penitence.[17]

To many saintly souls, the austere and heroic synthesis of philosophical Judaism could only appear disastrous. As a Qabbalist of the eighteenth century put it, "This concept is in truth desolation and death; whoever accepts it should be separated from the community that is in exile, and he should not bother with *mizvoth*."[18]

This tension between freedom and necessity, personality and mechanism, is overcome in Qabbalah by the assumption of an infinite chain of being, in which personality constitutes the one direction and necessity the other. It is the progressive diminution of the "grace," emanating from the source of divine personality, that permits reality to freeze into a rigid system of inexorable "laws." There are no dichotomies or absolute divisions in existence, with the total character of the universe shading off progressively from the source of all meaning that is God to the Satanic naught.

If reality is infinite, then all that is finite partakes of unreality and every line of demarcation is only relatively true. Hence, we are led to the conclusion that all separable categories are not really separate, but united by some mediating categories. "Between every two categories there is always a middle category," and "It is of the nature of existence to have a mediating entity between two opposites."[19] The principle of continuity furnishes us with the master key for the understanding of the universe, which bears in all its ultimate constituents the double seal of both freedom and necessity, spirit and matter, personality and mechanism. This duality, the *Zohar* points out, is reflected in the divine name, *Elohim,* which frequently stands for the Deity as reflected in nature, the numerical equivalents of its letters being equal to those of the Hebrew word for nature *(teva)*. This name consists of two words, *aile* and *mi,* standing respectively for the "many" of existence and the "who" of personality. The inference that is drawn from this quaint juggling is that nature consists of a continuous flux of phenomena, moving between these poles of being.[20]

In all likelihood, this organic concept was derived from the contemplation of the human personality, which is spiritual in essence and physical in appearance; free in its own consciousness, yet subject to the operation of a multitude of mechanical laws. "For man is a microcosm, therefore it is right and proper to take him as an analogy and archetype of all the worlds."[21]

While the Qabbalists derived their teaching from many sources which were not always mutually consistent, they rarely dispensed with the principles of continuity and polarity. In respect of the doctrine of God, they envisaged the Deity in the most "negative" terms, referring to Him as *Ain Sof* ("Endless"), and denying to Him any physical attributes whatsoever. "For the single Master, called *Ain Sof,* cannot be said to possess will or desire, intention or thought, speech or action."[22]

At the same time, they envisaged the *Ain Sof* as identified in some way with primal man *(Adam Kadmon),* which is the spiritual archetype of personality, and it was considered rank heresy to separate these elements in thought. As will appear in the sequel, they also conceived the primal man, in his lower representations, as functioning in automatic response to the performance of *mizvoth* on earth. Mechanism leads into personality and beyond—on to the inscrutable and the incomprehensible. The primal man consists in his turn of ten *sefiroth,* which were conceived as being both God and not-God. "For that which is infinite and boundless could not make that which is finite and definite; therefore, it was necessary to postulate ten *sefiroth* in the middle, which are both finite and infinite." [23]

Similarly, the human soul was regarded at its lowest as quasi-material, ascending thence by degrees to higher levels which receive "light" from its "roots" in primal man. Whatever man does on earth strikes echoes in the upper reaches of his soul, reverberating in the "upper worlds," bringing about either the "hardening" or the "sweetening" of the "laws."

Fundamentally, the religious content of the principle of continuity is best seen in the practical inference of the supreme importance of every human action. Qabbalistic symbols, which are generally coarse and frequently intricate in detail, were not intended to be merely symbols, but to be taken as the lowest links in the chain of being, which when moved "below" effect changes "above." Nothing that man does is unimportant, for he was designed to be the custodian of the vast palace; that is, the universe, "constricting" or "expanding" the channels of grace by his obedience to the law or his rebellion against it. "The Lord is thy shadow" was interpreted to mean that the Deity reacts in automatic fashion to the actions of men. (While we employ the term "man" in this connection, we must remember that for most Qabbalists only an Israelite deserved this designation. The souls of other nations were not connected by "channels of light" to the upper worlds and were therefore incapable of affecting the operation of the sefirotic world by their deeds or misdeeds.[24]

Thus, the absolute dichotomy between matter and spirit, between this earthly world and the divine being, was overcome in Qabbalah by the assumption of a host of mediating and connecting entities. The metaphysical difficulties posed by philosophical analysis were solved by the bland denial of the logic of contradiction and the law of the excluded middle. The world is one; hence, all opposites are dynamically related by entities that were at once of one category and of its opposite.

For our abstractions are not metaphysically ultimate. "They reach and do not reach" *(mo-to v'lo moti).*

The problem of a change having occurred in the eternally changeless nature of the Infinite, when the universe was created by His will, is resolved by the assumption that creation took place at levels that were far removed from the inner being of God, with the extent of volition required diminishing as the current of Divine influence is traced back to its ultimate source, so that virtually no effort was needed at the end of the infinite chain of causation: ". . . so that when we come to the ultimate Emanator, we find that no change occurred in Him, because of the chain of will leading to will. . . . At the source, we find that which is midway between potential and actual functioning."[25]

In the same manner, the Qabbalists solved the paradox of God's spirituality and mercy leading to the materiality, harshness and satanic uncleanliness of this world. In the endless chain of being, things get "coarser" and more evil in proportion to their "remoteness" from the source and in direct relation to the number of "garments" in which the holy spark is hidden. "Just as all the laws are love in their source, so the unclean are clean, and everything is rooted in the will of wills."[26]

The Qabbalistic logic of continuity obliterated all distinctions between intellectual concepts and the physical world, by the assumption of intermediate essences, with the result that seemingly naïve primitive ways of thinking were reinstated by the supreme subtleties of their dialectics. The term "spirit" for instance, which originally meant breath, came to be reidentified with the breath of the spoken word, especially the spoken Hebrew words of prayer.

> For, behold, the letter is a palace and fortress for the spirituality to which it points, and when a man mentions or moves one of the letters, that spirituality is necessarily aroused. Also, holy forms come to be made out of the breath of the mouth which are uplifted and bound together in their roots within the domain of Emanation. Not only this, but in their physical existence; that is, in their writing, spirituality rests upon the letters. This, indeed, is the reason for the holiness of the Scroll of the Law.[27]

By the same token, the ethereal realms of spirituality were conceived to be fashioned in forms corresponding to the Hebrew letters, the alphabet being elevated to the rank of a cosmic, eternal pattern.

They said that the higher intelligences are precious lights, of the utmost purity, fashioned in the form of letters. This association applies to all forms of light, for even physical light consists of letters, as the masters of the wisdom of magic testify, for when they make fire they see letters, by means of which they comprehend diverse branches of knowledge and are enabled to foretell the future. And if this be true in the case of physical fire, how much more is this applicable to the case of the higher lights, which contain the forms of letters and *sefiroth*, with little letters subsisting within big letters. . . .[28]

This concept enabled the Qabbalists to interpret the actual Torah as an earthly embodiment of a corresponding "spiritual" Torah, consisting of divine "lights," functioning as the key to the upper realms of grace.

"The verse, 'Torah is light,' is to be interpreted as meaning real light, not illumination in the sense of analogy, and not wisdom only but actual light, for this is the form of its existence above." [29]

It follows that the earthly domain of time and matter was bound by a chain of mediating essences unto the spiritual realm of eternity and spirit. The *sefiroth* were at once God and not-God, spatial and nonspatial, temporal and eternal.

We say that it is true that the realm of Emanation is not body and not matter, but that from it body and material issue. Thus, the masters of Qabbalah believed that the four elements are "pointed to" in the *sefiroth*. . . . Not that the actual elements are to be found in them, heaven forbid, but the roots of the elements out of which they issue: even so, with the dimensions and concepts of body. That is why we are justified in saying, length, width and depth, for we mean the power whence length issues, the power of width and the power of depth.[30]

From all the foregoing, the net religious substance of the Qabbalistic world view becomes clear. The observant Jew was assured that his every action was charged with endless "cosmic" ramifications. Upon him and his fellow Jews, the cosmic order in all its vastness and complexity hung breathless. Every *mizvah* he performed helped to effect an "improvement" in the upper spheres, while, at the same time, it provided an additional "thread of light," out of which he would eventually accumulate those "garments of light," in which his soul might be clothed when it dwells in the "lower paradise." By the same token, every *avera* (sin) constituted a "blemish" in the higher "realms of purity," which redounded ultimately to the injury of the entire world, besides daubing his soul with a diabolical stain, which would have to be removed by pain and repentance, before the soul could ascend back to its source. This ascent was conceived as an infinite adventure, continuing in the various domains of paradise in the hereafter, until the soul attains a higher degree of beatitude than it had before creation. And all these effects are virtually automatic, with the "above" domain of the spiritual responding mechanically to the actions of the Jewish people here "below." To the believers, the psychological motivations for the utmost exertions of piety were manifestly all embracing. They labored at the salvation of their own souls, yes, but at the same time they fulfilled the most crucial function in the total economy of the universe. Their prayers were for the sake of "the world above" and for the well-being of mankind generally. Their piety partook of universal, even cosmic, idealism and of the urge to sacrifice one's own comforts in behalf of the salvation of all men.

The Qabbalistic mentality was saved from the danger of sinking to the level of theosophic juggling by constant emphasis on the psychological attitude of the worshiper. The old virtue of humility was conceived to be the master key to every forward step in the domain of Qabbalah. In all their fantastic flights to the upper realms, the Qabbalists did not forget to extol the simple and fundamental virtues of Jewish piety, guarding against the insidious sins of pride and complacency. As they strove for the powers "above" they did not neglect the moral struggle of men here "below."

Furthermore, their concept of the cosmic "mission" of the Jewish people was so exalted that they were kept from indulging in the cultivation of their own individual piety. While individual "saints" are capable of moving the worlds, the Jewish people as a whole constituted the major link between the upper and lower worlds. Though every nation possesses a governing "genius," the Jewish people represent an earthly embodiment of the *Shechinah,* which is the tenth *sefirah,* and is called *malkhuth,* or dominion. Not humanity, but Jewry in its totality, is the center of the cosmic drama, and it is for Israel to bring about by its actions the "union of the worlds," the return of the fallen *sefirah* back to its source. The individual Jew was thus bidden to unite himself in thought and sentiment with the totality of the Jewish people, performing every *mizvah* for the sake of "the unification of the Holy One, blessed be He, and His *Shechinah,* in the name of all Israel, through Him who is hidden and inconceivable."

The particularistic loyalties of the Jew were exalted in the most superlative terms. While philosophic Judaism labored to widen the common intellectual and moral ground of all faiths and peoples, the Qabbalah sought to isolate Israel from the culture of "the other nations," which is derived "from the worlds of uncleanliness." By its general doctrine of things in this world "pointing to" essences in the higher worlds, the Qabbalah was able to assign supreme importance to every Jewish custom and practice, and to give added impetus to the growth of fanaticism and ethnic self-exaltation. Rabbi Shalom Sharabi, author of a "holy" Qabbalistic prayer book, which is still used by pictists in Jerusalem, boasted in his introduction that he had never looked at any book which was not written by the great Qabbalists, Isaac Luria and Hayim Vital and their authentic disciples; i.e., the "purity" of his vision was not dimmed, God forfend, by the "shells" of "impurity" dwelling on unholy letters.[31] Thus did those who aimed so high, seeking to encompass the daring of philosophy along with the depth of piety, occasionally sink so low in fanaticism and self-aggrandizing dogmatism. The Qabbalists tapped new wells of enthusiasm and devotion in behalf of the Jewish faith, raising the pitch of piety to feverish heights and strengthening the resistance of the Jew during the dismal, torment-filled centuries of the later medieval and the early modern period. But this good was purchased at a price, a price which all but extinguished the sweet rationality and even-tempered humanity of Judaism at its best.

NOTES

1. See introduction to T. Tishbi, *Mishnath Hazoar* (Jerusalem 1971).
2. *Teshuvoth HaBah Hayshonoth,* 5.
3. *Torath Haolah,* III, 4.
4. *Nefesh HaHayim,* IV; see also the introduction of Rabbi Hayim Volozhin to the commentary of Rabbi Elijah of Vilna to the *Safro Dizniuta.* Printed in *Shiveath Hameoroth* (Vilna, 1913).
5. *Teshuvoth Ha-Rivosh,* 157.
6. *Ari Noem,* 15.
7. J. Yavetz, *Mitpahath Seforim.*
8. Rabbi Meir Ibn Gabbai, *Avodath HaKodesh,* III, 18.

9. R. Shem Tov ben Shem Tov, *Sefer Hoemunoth*, IV, 14.

10. J. Eibeshutz, *Shem Olam* (Vienna, 1891), p. 11.

11. *Shomair Emunim*, I—Dispute. See also beginning of *Sefer HaPeliah*, where a human being is created by a combination of letters and then restored by reversing the formula.

12. *Guide to the Perplexed*, I, 62.

13. *Avodath HaKodesh*, III, 17.

14. *Ibid.*

15. See reference above to chain of authority; also, *Meirath Ainim*, Beshalach; commentary of *Rikanati on Torah*, Nasso.

16. *Guide to the Perplexed*, I, 53.

17. *Ibid.*, III, 28:36:32.

18. Basila, *Emunath Hakhamim*, Chap. 13.

19. Commentary of RabD to *Sefer Yezirah*, p. 54; also R. Hayim Vital in beginning of *Aitz Hayim*.

20. See *Zohar*, Hakdomo.

21. *Shomair Emunim*, p. 27.

22. Quoted in the name of Rabbi Isaac the Blind in *Shem Olam*, p. 77; see also commentary of RabD to *Sefer Yezirah*.

23. *Shem Olam*, p. 41.

24. See *Shefa Tal*, Chap. 13; *Tanya*, Chap. 6; *Nefesh HaHayim*, I. 4. On the other hand, note the opposing view of R. Elijah Ginazina: "But know that the other nations can also effect some improvements in the channels, when they observe the seven Noachide *mizvoth*, but their improvements are not as perfect as those of the 613 *mizvoth*." (*Iggeret Hamudoth*, p. 37.)

25. *Alima Rabati*, ain Kol Tamar, I, 15.

26. *Ibid.*, II, 6–18.

27. *Pardes Rimonim*, shaar haotiot, II.

28. *Shem Olam*.

29. R. M. Ch. Lazzato. *Kelach Pithhai Hokhmo*, introduction.

30. *Pardes Rimonim*, shaar taam hoaziluth. Some Qabbalists referred to the *sefiroth* as quasi-spatial entities. See *Kelach Pithhai Hokhomo*, 29: "But, before space came into being, it was impossible for anything to exist; only after space came to be, the *sefiroth* emerged in accordance with the nature of space." Of particular interest is the manner in which the category of space is derived by some writers from the ten *sefiroth*. As the infinitesimal point "expands" out of the naught, it asserts itself along three dimensions, each of which possesses a beginning, middle and end, thus reflecting the number ten. This derivation has its philosophic parallel in the "critical" philosophy of Hermann Cohen, particularly his *Category of the Source*.

31. *Nahar Shalom*, in introduction.

PART THREE

JACOB B. AGUS AND JEWISH-CHRISTIAN DIALOGUE: A VIEW FROM THE CHRISTIAN SIDE

SELECTIONS AND
PREFATORY REMARKS
Eugene J. Fisher

DEEPLY SENSITIVE to the inseparable historical and theological connections between Judaism and Christianity, and well aware of the evils that Christian anti-Semitism had legitimated, Rabbi Agus was an unwavering advocate of Jewish-Christian dialogue.

The following selections, chosen to accompany Eugene J. Fisher's essay "Jacob B. Agus and Jewish-Christian Dialogue: A View from the Christian Side" in *American Rabbi: The Life and Thought of Jacob B. Agus* (New York, 1996), are drawn from Jacob Agus, *The Jewish Quest* (New York, 1983), 205–22 and 239–48; and *Jewish Identity in an Age of Ideologies* (New York, 1978), 1–36.

10

JUDAISM AND THE NEW TESTAMENT

FATHER FLOROVSKY summed up the challenge of an interfaith dialogue in these well-chosen words—"It is delicate and painful, but not hopeless." The subject of this paper illustrates the aptness of his judgment. The long centuries of historic hostility demonstrate the anguish, yet the essence of both testaments, as Paul understood it, was precisely hope (Acts 28:20; Eph. 2:12).

Judaism and Christianity meet theologically on the following common ground: the Hebrew Bible, reverence for Wisdom, and the genius of prophetic inspiration. Beginning with the last element, we note that rabbinic Judaism maintained that biblical prophecy had come to an end. Yet, it also asserted that the Holy Spirit guided the deliberations of the sages. Hillel attributed this blessing to all pious Israelites—"You may rely upon the Israelites, the Holy Spirit is upon them. If they are not prophets, they are sons of prophets." [1] The deliberations of the sages were aided by a divine echo. [2] The medieval philosopher, Judah Halevi, expressed the general belief when he asserted that the Mishnah and Talmud were composed with divine assistance (*The Kuzari* 3:73).

The concept of prophetic inspiration consisted in attempting to penetrate the deeper meaning of Torah and the concomitant belief that God works through history, generating ever greater understanding of God's revelation. So, in the rabbinic tradition a prophet could not set aside a *halachah*, or establish a new *halachah*, but could decide which *halachot* were to be applied in his day. [3] Divine inspiration in the interpretation of a biblical book was claimed by the writers of the Dead Sea Scrolls.[4]

A parallel development of the operation of the Holy Spirit lies at the very heart of Christianity. Whether the view prevailed that the Holy Spirit worked through the community as a whole or through the bishops or through the papacy or through the mystics, the obligation of penetrating to the deeper meaning of the Bible was incumbent upon every generation. And Jesus illustrated this obligation by the comment on divorce, sifting the divine intent from "the hardness of the heart," which conditioned an earlier saying.[5] We dare say that in every faith deriving from the Bible a renaissance took place whenever theologians returned to a fresh study of Holy Writ. The reinterpretation of Scripture, in the light of the prophetic emphasis on justice, compassion, and love, is the common task of Jews and Christians.

In our day, we bring to the study of the Scriptures in particular, and the past generally, certain tools and insights that were scarcely available in previous generations—which brings us to the second component of theological common ground, the element of wisdom. The obligation to pursue the quest of wisdom in order to understand the implications of faith is of the essence of biblical religion, since the books of wisdom formed part of Holy Writ. The sages formulated the matter succinctly—"If there is no wisdom, there is no piety; if there is no piety, there is no wisdom" (Abot 3:14). Similarly in Christianity wisdom was extolled, and Greek philosophy preoccupied the attention of the Fathers of the Church beginning with Clement of Alexandria.

Wisdom today has the added dimension of history-mindedness in all its facets—a recognition of the context in which every event must be viewed, a critical and comparative approach to all documents, an understanding of the fluidity of meaning, and its determination by psychological and sociological factors.

The duty to study history in order to understand the meaning of providence is already stated in Deut. 32:7. But while history was in the past the handmaiden of theology, it now asserts its own independent validity, compelling theology to take account of its data. History-mindedness need not degenerate into an all-questioning historicism; on the contrary, by deepening our awareness of our human limitations, as individuals and as heirs of a specific tradition, it heightens our appreciation of the third part of the prophet Micah's admonition, "to do justice, to love mercy, and to walk humbly with the Lord, thy God" (6:8).

When we speak of Judaism in relation to the New Testament, we have to make clear that we view Judaism as a river which contains many trends and flows on several levels. Modern Judaism contains a broad range of views, from a tenuous attachment of those who are primarily ethnicists to a whole-souled, mystical absorption in Torah as the embodiment of the divine will. We speak of three main branches of the Jewish faith—Orthodox, Conservative, and Reform. But, in actuality, each of these divisions is a loose grouping of diverse views. On the whole, there is greater emphasis today on the historical-cultural matrix of faith, hence a willingness to include within the tradition sects, trends, and opinions that were previously excluded. We include the Karaites, for instance, and appreciate the boldness of their founder's slogan— "Search well in the Torah, and do not rely on my opinions." These audacious rebels against the rule of the Talmud articulated a Jewish ideal, although their maxim proved to be impractical. By the same token, we look upon the spectrum of Jewish groups in New Testament times without identifying ourselves completely with any one of them.

The discovery of the Dead Sea Scrolls expanded further our awareness of the immense fermentation in the spiritual life of ancient Israel. The Qumran sectarians drew a sharp line between "the children of light and the children of darkness," but in modern Israel their writings are ensconced in a special building, *Bet Hasefer,* as a great national treasure. Each sectarian group considered itself to be "the true Israel," as did the Pharisees, who spoke of their teachers as *hachmai Yisroel,* the sages of Israel; the Sadducees who stigmatized their opponents as Pharisees, or separatists; the Zealots; the Essenes; the Samaritans; and the Apostolic Jewish-Christian community in Jerusalem.[6] The Pharisees captured the loyalty of the masses of the people even before the Great Revolt and, following that disaster, the Hillelite school of Pharisaic thought came to predominate. Because of a series of catastrophes, the treasures of Hellenistic Judaism were neglected. The sages of Yavneh were compelled to limit the range of Scripture, eliminating the apocryphal and pseudo-epigraphic works.[7] They acted in order to lower the fever of messianic speculation and provide a protective shield against the inroads of Gnostic sectarians.

Ever since the opening of the modern era, Jewish scholars endeavored to reclaim the works of Philo, the books of the Maccabees, and the entire library of intertestamentary literature. Judah Maccabee, unmentioned in rabbinic literature, was reclaimed as an exemplary hero. It is now evident that the apocalyptic writers formed circles or schools within either the Pharisaic or the Essenic movements. And Philo's thought is now regarded as essentially and authentically Jewish.[8] As we see it, the tannaitic sages of the Hillelite school did not approve all that the Pharisaic order represented, either in fact or in popular fancy.[9] As to the high priestly hierarchy, it consisted largely of Sadducees, and the Talmud contains ample evidence of the resentment they aroused among the people (Pesahim 57a, Yoma 18b, Kiddushin 66a). Considerable latitude was allowed for differences of opinion among the tannaitic rabbis, heirs of the Pharisees. It was considered a blessing that "disputes for the sake of heaven" would endure (Abot 5:20).

In the historical interpretation of Judaism, which was begun in the nineteenth century, we take it as our task to acknowledge the dark shadows as well as the bright glories of the Pharisaic movement. We are also aware of the distortions and perversions that crept into the two Talmuds by reason of the fact that they were not edited, with the result that unworthy and unhistorical references to Jesus and Christianity found their way into the Talmud and Midrashim. We regard such passages as the debris of folk-myths, rather than as teachings of the faith. Modern Jewish scholars can find ample justification for this attitude in the authoritative works of the rabbinic tradition.[10]

From all the above, it is clear that the theological spectrum of historic Judaism is far bigger and more diverse than either Bousset's concentration on the Apocrypha or Moore's concept of "normative Judaism" would suggest. Schechter's stress on rabbinic Judaism and Moore's classic description of the ideas implied in rabbinic literature were needed correctives of the previously prevailing views, especially among German scholars, which described first-century Judaism largely in terms of the Apocrypha. On the other hand, it is equally one-sided to ignore Philonic and intertestamentary literature.

The great historian, F. Baer, has proposed the thesis that a synthesis of Judaism and classical Hellenism was effected by the sages of the fourth and third pre-Christian centuries, when the ideal of a *Hassid* emerged as a blend of the Greek philosopher and the prophetic disciple. There was born the concept of an earthly society of ascetics, striving heroically for spiritual perfection and for the establishment of a perfect society here on earth, mirroring the harmony prevailing in the cosmos. Even if Baer's theory is not accepted in its totality, we cannot doubt that for generations Greek philosophers and Jewish sages recognized one another as kindred in spirit.[11]

Philo, then, was not an exceptional figure who undertook an impossible task, but the heir of a long tradition to which, as a matter of fact, he refers from time to time. The Alexandrian school of Jewish thought helps us to see the roots of the New Testament in the teachings of diaspora synagogues. There is, for instance, the distinction in Philo between God who is unknowable, and God's manifest powers, chief of which was the Logos.[12] Whether the origin of the "heavenly man" be sought in Persia or in Greece, this concept was employed by Philo in his description of the creation of Adam and Eve (Philo, *Legum Allegoria,* I, XII, 31, Ed. Loeb Classics).

The Alexandrian Jews and Christian historians were convinced that Plato and Aristotle were disciples of the biblical prophets.[13] A bold, universalistic outreach to all people informs the entire range of Hellenistic-Jewish literature—from Philo to the author of the Testaments of the Twelve Patriarchs.[14] Philo interprets "the reasons of the commandments" in purely human terms, as sign-posts for the human soul in its struggle to attain perfection. Even the name "Israel" is for him a title, rather than an ethnic designation—the mark of one who has attained the vision of God.[15] Philo's use of the allegorical method to discover the inner meaning of Torah is today no longer regarded as an alien importation into Judaism. The authors of the Dead Sea Scrolls employed a similar method. Furthermore, Hillel or his teachers did not scruple to adopt the methods of Alexandrian grammarians in the interpretation of the written law.[16]

Philo's description of the Theraputae, Josephus' description of the Essenes, and the Dead Sea Scrolls allow us glimpses of the variety of schools within first-century Judaism. We now recognize the tremendous polarity between a gentle, all-embracing humanism and a fanatical dogmatism seeking to limit the circles of the "elect." In the Babylonian Talmud itself we encounter the two contrasting attitudes—the constricting one, limiting the rewards of heaven to the few pietists, and the outreaching one, opening its blessings to all "who direct their hearts to heaven."[17]

From the standpoint of historical Judaism, the documents of the New Testament acquire a special importance. They reflect the process whereby the central concepts of the Jewish religion were transferred to the great non-Jewish world. Yet this transfer was carried out in a way which cast the Jewish people in the role of the dark, satanic force. This double effect—an acceptance of the Jewish message in essence, and a rejection of the Jewish messenger in fact—has determined the character and destiny of Jewish history. Hence, there is a renewed interest in the study of the New Testament and its ancillary literature on the part of Jewish scholars.

For a long time, Jewish scholars studied the New Testament only for the purpose of holding their own in debates with Christian counterparts. Such disputations centered on the meaning of certain proof-tests or, as Nahmanides and Albo pointed out, on the logical tenability of certain Christian dogmas.[18] By far, the vast majority of medieval rabbis ignored the New Testament and shunned interfaith discussions for fear of being accused of blasphemy. Even in our day, some rabbis maintain that, while Christianity must take account of Judaism, the latter does not have to evaluate the import and truth of the former. While for Christianity, Judaism is the foundation, they say, for Judaism, Christianity is simply a development outside its own walls.

Indeed, the Orthodox, who are comfortable with dogmatic walls, frequently take this view. But, if our self-awareness as Jews is determined by our overview of Jewish history, we cannot but regard the emergence of the Christian branch out of the Jewish stem as the most momentous event in our millennial experience. The Jewish self-image is largely affected by this development, as well as the image of the Jew among the nations. The "big idea" of our heritage was demonstrated in this phenomenon, in that "the God of Israel" triumphed over the pagan deities and all their works. But also the "big burden" of Jewish life was here heaped upon our shoulders, since the Jew was in effect compelled to wear the sign of Cain. While in actuality the Jewish spirit achieved a magnificent triumph, this process was associated with a systematic denigration, even the demonization, of the Jew.

Hence, the thoughtful Jew who desires to follow the ancient counsel, "know thyself," must grapple with the many riddles posed by a study of the New Testament. To begin with, the Jew knows that the entire New Testament was composed by Jews. Luke was probably a convert to Judaism before he joined the Christian community. Yet, the Jew also knows that the various documents constituting the New Testament were edited by Christians at a time when the church consisted largely of Gentiles and was engaged in bitter fights against Jews. The two communities broke apart in the generation following the destruction of the Holy Temple (70 A.D.), amidst bitter curses and implacable hatred.[19] We cannot tell whether the *birchat Haminim* of the Jews preceded or followed the anathemas of the Christians. In any case, neutrality appeared impossible to both sides. The historical approach makes it possible for us to rediscover our kinship with one another, while repudiating the seeds of malice that the duststorms of history have scattered over the pages of sacred Scripture.

The central theses that emerge from the study of the New Testament in the context of Jewish rabbinic literature include:

First, that the teaching of Jesus did not imply the repudiation either of Judaism or of the Jewish people.

Second, that the closer we come to the Apostolic community centered in Jerusalem, the less we encounter any suggestion of the "rejection" of Israel.

Third, that the New Testament passages implying the "rejection" of the Jewish people, as a reversal of their having previously been chosen, were superimposed upon the earlier traditions of the church after the fall of Jerusalem; that the essence of Christian teaching, according to medieval interpreters, consisted in the repudiation of Judaism.

Fourth, that all such anti-Judaism and anti-Jewish passages resulted in part from the gradual transference of the Gospel tradition from the Jewish to the Hellenistic culture sphere, during the seventy-year period, 65–135 A.D., and in part from the impassioned bitterness of the second and third centuries when the New Testament canon attained its present form.

Fifth, that it is incumbent upon Christian scholars, as seekers of truth in love and love in truth, to eliminate anti-Jewish and anti-Judaism inferences from their interpretation of the New Testament.

Sixth, that it is incumbent upon Jewish scholars to reclaim the New Testament as an integral part of their domain of study and to develop the implications of the teaching that Christianity is an "ecclesia for the sake of heaven," employed by God as an instrument whereby humanity is being prepared for "the kingdom of heaven," *malchut shomayim.*

1. The first thesis has been established for several generations among Jewish scholars. Jesus was a supremely original personality, and his views did not coincide completely with those of any of the movements that existed in his day, but the building blocks of his spiritual edifice were

taken from the Jewish world of that day. Jesus stood closest to the Pharisees, in that he believed in the resurrection, in angels, in the worship of the synagogue, and in the role of providence within the life of the individual and within Israel; but he was also close to the Essenes, as is evident in his ethics, in his relation to John the Baptist, in his closeness to the apocalyptic circles, and in the life of the Apostolic community of Jerusalem.

But Jesus differed with *some* of the Pharisaic leaders. After all, James the Elder testifies that many Pharisees had joined the early Christian community without giving up their zeal for the Law (Acts 21:20). Jesus' arguments with the Pharisees referred to specific issues of the oral law, which were probably topics of disputation in the schools. His critique of the high priests reflected popular sentiments that are also echoed in the Talmud (Pesahim 57a). Jesus' chief complaint was the non-recognition on the part of most Pharisaic leaders of his claim to be the apocalyptic Messiah.[20] As we learn from occasional references in the Talmud, some apocalyptic circles taught that the Messiah would bring down the Holy Temple from heaven and put it in the place of the earthly one.[21]

2. The second thesis is proved by scholars through the comparative textual analysis of the Gospels. Paul Winter, in his book *On the Trial of Jesus* (Berlin, 1961), puts side by side the various references to the enemies of Jesus. He takes the passion chapters of Mark to be the most ancient portion, and he concludes his analysis as follows (p. 124):

The oldest synoptic tradition (however restyled it may have become in the process of literary formulation) does not include the Pharisees among the enemies of Jesus at all; there is not a single instance in which Pharisaic hostility towards Jesus finds mention.

A similar view was already put forward by the famous scholar, Daniel Chwolson, who suggested that the second-century editors changed in many places the word "scribes" for the word "Pharisees," since in their day there were no longer Sadducee scribes.[22] Joseph Klausner pointed out that Jesus debated as a member of the Pharisaic movement. Paul Winter argues similarly: "Yet in historical reality, Jesus was a Pharisee . . . when an eschatological emphasis may have pervaded Pharisaic thought more strongly than in the tannaitic age" (p. 133).

The viewpoint of Jewish scholars was summarized in the old *Jewish Encyclopedia,* published in the first decade of the twentieth century (article on the New Testament):

... that the older and the more genuine the records, written or unwritten, of the doings and teachings of Jesus, the more they betray close kinship with and friendly relations to Jews and Judaism; but that the more remote they are from the time and activity of Jesus, the more they show of hostility to the Jewish people and of antagonism to the Mosaic Law.

The gulf between the Jews and Christians was deepened by the lynching of Stephen, and the persecutions directed by the Sadducee high priest were opposed by Rabban Gamaliel the Elder. Agrippa probably followed the counsel of the Sadducees. The Pharisees still resented the execution of James the Elder, but with the approach of the Great Revolt (65–70 A.D.) tempers were inflamed throughout the Jewish world. In some places, Jewish leaders sought to remove the protective mantle of Judaism, as a *religio licita,* from the proliferating Christian churches. Thus, the soil was prepared for Nero's persecutions. With the outbreak of the Revolt, which was spurred by intense messianic expectations, and punctuated by outbreaks of pogroms throughout Syria, the Christians left Jerusalem, according to a tradition recorded by Eusebius.

With the disappearance of the mother church in Jerusalem, leadership fell into the hands of Gentile Christians. The remnant of Jewish Christians were beset by pressures from both Jews and Christians. The Jewish curse formulated by Rabban Gamaliel the Second and the Christian anathema combined to crush the middle position. In addition, when the Roman Empire imposed a special tax upon Jews, the Christians were exempt; and when Marcus Aurelius Antonius was friendly to Jews, he was implacably hostile to Christians. The course of history raised a high barrier of hostility between the two communities just at the time when their respective traditions were taking firm shape. But it was the rise of Gnosticism that contributed most effectively to the introduction of mythological Antisemitism in Christianity.

3. The third thesis points to the most persistent anti-Jewish animus that is inculcated almost unconsciously by the New Testament. To illustrate its dark impetus, I will cite a recent popular scientific commentary on Matthew, edited by the late Professor Albright, who yielded to no one in his stout defense of Judaism and the Jewish people. Yet, in commenting on Matt. 9:17 (*Matthew,* Garden City, N.Y., 1971), he wrote (p. 108):

Romans IX–XI is evidence of the great concern felt about the precise relationship of the Messianic Community to Judaism. On the view that vss. 16–17 are to be regarded as Jesus' teaching on the relationship of his Community to Judaism, then the final clause *"and both are preserved"* is either editorial comment, or a misplaced saying from another context in an attempt to deal with the question.

But this must be regarded as unsatisfactory. The whole tenor of Jesus' teaching, in all four gospels, makes it hardly possible to suppose that he looked to a continuance of his Messianic Community and Judaism side by side.

So, even Albright assumes that the establishment of the Messianic community implied the rejection of those who did not join it. But, is not this attitude a retrojection of later attitudes? If Paul could not reconcile himself to such a rejection, could Jesus, whose Jewish roots were far deeper, adopt such a judgment? Whether or not we adopt Schweitzer's interpretation of Jesus' eschatological attitude, we cannot deny that Jesus' central concern was to preach "the good news" to his own people. And his few acts of benevolence toward Gentiles were entirely in keeping with the teaching of Jewish ethics, certainly not a repudiation of his people. But the pervasive feeling to which Albright calls attention embodies an impetus, deep and strong. What is its source? The answer uncovers a fundamental struggle which continues to the present.

The canonization of the New Testament was brought about through the partial rejection and the partial acceptance of two contending philosophies — Judaism and Gnosticism. Marcion formed the first canon, and he excluded the Old Testament altogether, consigning the God of Israel and God's Law to the sinister role of demiurge, the creator of this world and its numberless evils. Jesus was the Son and Messenger of the good, transworldly realm, whose followers, by repudiating this world and all its works, would inherit that glorious realm. Marcion was repudiated by the emergent Catholic Church, but Gnosticism was too insidious and too deep-rooted to be altogether eliminated. The Church looked for the middle way between Judaism and Gnosticism.

What were the essential differences between these two poles of the spirit? We take Gnosticism to be the opposite of classical Hellenism as well as of prophetic Judaism. While the stars were "gods" to the Hellenes and noble creations of God, or angels, to Jews, they were part of the evil order of reality to the Gnostics.[23] The essence of Gnosticism is the myth of catastrophe, describing how Sophia, or the heavenly one, or supernal light was imprisoned by Satanic forces, and the belief that the way of redemption depends on a special knowledge deriving from beyond this world, whereby the soul reverses its path and ascends to heaven. Hence, the polarity is threefold—whether or not truth is co-extensive with natural human powers of reason; whether or not goodness is that of human effort and conscience; and whether or not certain people are provided from birth with a pneumatic soul, rendering them capable of redemption. Gnosticism asserts the *discontinuity* of human wisdom and redemptive knowledge, of sanctification through deeds and intentions, or through an inner spirit and Divine Grace. Similarly it asserts the dichotomy of the human race between ordinary people and pneumatics.[24]

Paul wavered between Judaism and Gnosticism, inclining sufficiently to the latter pole to provide a handle to Marcion. Some portions of John contain the reverberations of Gnostic rhetoric. Generally, the Gnostics were bitterly anti-Judaistic and anti-Jewish. Within Christianity the Gnostic orientation, identifying the divine with the discontinuous, the transcendental, and the ascetic, triumphed especially in heretical movements. But, it frequently generated a powerful undertow, even within the official forms of the faith. And whenever Gnostic anti-Judaism prevailed, anti-Jewishness was always the result.

The Gnostic theory of pneumatics is easily translatable into mystical racism. Fichte, prophet of modern German nationalism, demonstrated the perennial appeal of Gnosticism in his philosophy of history, stigmatizing the Jews as the children of worldly cleverness, *Verstand,* and elevating the Teutons to the rank of people of *Vernunft.*[25] A great deal of modern biblical study expatiated on the contrasts between Jewish "good deeds" and Christian grace; between Jewish intellectualism, which is presumably barren, and the noble intuition of Teutons, or Nordics, or Aryans; between the Jewish ideal of equality before the Law and the arbitrary "election" of the Gentiles.[26] Naturally, in German Gnosticism, the Slavs and the Greeks are condemned equally with the Jews, though a special hell on earth was reserved for those who were "chosen" by the evil Creator. Ideas are "carried over" from religion to politics and back again. Gnostic, that is non-Hellenic and non-Jewish, was the asserted discontinuity between the Old Testament and the New Testament, between the Old Covenant and the New, between the old Israel and the New, between the Old Morality and the New, between Jew and Gentile. It is time to allay this metaphysical mythology, wherever it appears—in Christian as in Jewish thought.

4. The fourth thesis purports to explain how what was originally a

fervently Jewish faith became so bitterly anti-Jewish. In part, the answer is simply the transference of the same rhetoric from a Jewish to a Gentile popular base. When an Isaiah or a Jeremiah castigates his people, he does not infer that they are indeed degenerate and God-forsaken. The prophet demands so much because he trusts the essential nobility of his people, and his words are preserved by the people as expressions of their own conscience. But, when the same words are taken out of context by external enemies, they add up to a verdict of condemnation.

A contemporary Jesuit scholar summarizes the import of the biblical prophets as follows:

Ancient Israel was played out and had to go. . . . This new Israel could, however, only be born of the downfall of the old. . . . The salvation of the new people of God was the reverse of the divine judgment passed on the ancient people of God.[27]

Yet, note that the same words which convey this meaning to the Catholic scholar were cherished by Jews as "the hope of Israel."

So, the occasional bitter outcries of Jesus or Paul or Matthew or John were spoken in the revered vein of prophetic admonition, but their Gentile editors, living in a different milieu, edited them in keeping with their own lights. Following the fall of Jerusalem, the mother church fell apart, and the branches in the Gentile world had to establish their legitimacy on their own grounds, despite the fact that they were worshipping one who was condemned and executed by Rome. Modifications and qualifications that existed in the original document, describing various personalities within the Jewish community, were all generalized into the term which made sense only in the new social environment— i.e., the term "Jews" was substituted for "witnesses" or "crowds" or "opponents" or "skeptics."[28]

In part, this editorial policy was a reflection of the bitter animosity between Jews and Gentiles during the Civil Wars of 65 to 135 A.D. By the middle of the second century the Jewish Christians were reduced to a marginal minority. How could the hatred of Jews coexist with the love of so much of the Jewish literary and spiritual heritage? The sad truths of human nature provide the answer, and history corroborates the insights of psychology. Josephus tells us that in Damascus the Syrian women were "God-fearers," attending the synagogues on the Sabbath, while many of their husbands were Jew-haters, planning physical massacres of their Jewish neighbors.[29]

5. The fifth thesis is an appeal to Christian conscience and truthfulness. There is absolutely no reason to interpret the documents of the New Testament in such a way as to teach that the Jews are condemned or accursed or rejected, much less that they are eternally guilty of deicide. The Catholic Church is to be heartily commended for its decisiveness in confronting this issue. I can say without fear of contradiction that no passage in the New Testament gives aid or comfort to Antisemitism, if it is seen in the light of the social-cultural context of contemporary Jewish life.

The disputations with Pharisaic leaders are instructive examples of the arguments that went on in the schools. Their general import is an emphasis on inwardness and principle that is indeed laudable and by no means rare in Jewish tradition. The numerous parables, so rich in meaning, are all-human, not Jewish-Gentile in reference. Always the concept of Israel included an all-human dimension in hope and faith. And the narration of Jesus' life and death, read in context, is free of any anti-Jewish animus.

By way of example, the sentence of Matthew 27:25 which served as the foundation for the myth of deicide can be easily understood in its Jewish context. As it reads it is utterly incomprehensible. "All the people" could only refer to the crowd actually present. Why should people voluntarily take guilt upon their children as well as upon themselves? The medieval mind understood this action as the work of Satan, but medieval myths have a way of persisting beneath modern rationalizations.

If we see the crucifixion in the light of the practices then prevailing, then we know that witnesses were indeed warned, prior to the execution of the defendant, that the guilt for that death and the death of any potential descendants down to the end of time would rest upon them. In turn, the witnesses would reassert their testimony and say they are so sure that they are willing to assume this blame.[30] Now, Jesus was condemned on the basis of the presumed testimony of witnesses, or of those present in the house of Caiaphas. The followers of the high priest, then, stated their willingness to be judged in heaven for the blood of Jesus and his potential descendants. When this incident was transferred to the milieu of a different culture, "his children" seemed blasphemous, if Jesus was God, and the term "witnesses" was simply generalized to the phrase "all the people"; as in most other cases, the specific term was generalized to the all-inclusive category, "Jews."

A similar example may be taken from John 8:44, wherein the devil is said to be the father of the Jews. We have here a sermon, given presumably in a synagogue, with Jesus addressing "those Jews who had believed him" (8:31). The author dramatized the tension between belief and unbelief within the soul of Jewish people. When this inner dialogue is transferred into a Gentile-Christian universe of discourse, the inner voice of admonition is transformed into an external verdict of condemnation.[31]

6. The first part of the sixth thesis deals with the reclamation of the New Testament. It is part of Jewish history as literature and life, but with respect to the sacred heritage it marks the boundary between Judaism and Christianity. Frequently, we can see how the same words acquired different meaning as they were transferred from the Jewish to the Hellenistic context.

So the name "son of God" was applied to Jewish people generally, to righteous men, to the kings of the house of David, and by implication, also to the Messiah.[32] But, within the ideological context of Judaism, the concept of divine unity precluded any notion of a "son of God" in any essential sense. Precisely because Jews lived in a society where Caesar was proclaimed son of God and *Kyrios,* Jewish opposition to this notion was firmly established. Philo could speak of God being three in appearance — i.e., God's sovereignty, benevolence, and unknowable being—but he added that, to the thoughtful, God is One.[33] So, the same series of titles of "Messiah," "son of Man," "Son of God," and "Kyrios" could by degrees acquire totally different meaning as the Jewish culture-context was replaced by the Hellenistic.[34]

Similarly, the concepts of redemption, faith, the Law and its inner meaning, the ideal congregation of Israel, the salvation of Gentiles, the replacement of the sacrificial ritual by deeds of "steadfast love" — all these and many more—are observed in the process of transformation.

In one century, the nascent Christian community underwent several transformations, brought about by a series of "scandals." The first "scandal" was felt within the Apostolic community, which was almost entirely Jewish—the Messiah came unto his own people, and "they" rejected him. "They," in this case, meant the leaders and teachers, the Pharisaic masters "who sit in Moses' seat." In the light of this "scandal," the differences between Jesus and the Pharisaic teachers were magnified, but the belief prevailed that this resistance of Jewish leaders and their followers was provisional and temporary. The second "scandal" was felt on the boundary between Jewry and the Hellenistic world as a result of the progressive transference of biblical and rabbinic ideas to the Hellenistic realm of thought. What was "unthinkable" in Judaism became the mark of a transcendent wisdom, the sign of a fresh upsurge of the Holy Spirit in the churches which continued to develop the ideas of Paul and John, particularly after the church became entirely Hellenistic. While Philo represented the synthesis of Judaism and Hellenic philosophy, the Pauline churches represented the blend of Judaism and Hellenistic religion. The third "scandal" was felt by the Gentile converts, following the fall of Jerusalem. How could they adore one who was convicted and executed by Roman authority? Gradually, the notion prevailed that Jesus was condemned by the Jews, while Pontius Pilate was the passive reluctant agent of Jewish, or demonic, fury.

In the modern world, all of us are bidden to live in two universes of discourse—within our traditions and in spirit, in an all-embracing universe of discourse. *On the Boundary* is the title of Paul Tillich's autobiography. And to live "on the boundary" is part of our universal experience.

The second portion of the sixth thesis might be called a Jewish theology of Christianity. This task will be carried out in diverse ways by the theologians of present and future generations if the contemporary irenic orientation within the Christian and Jewish worlds is maintained and deepened. It takes time for old ideas to fade away totally. Who can tell whether the old demons will arise from their graves and once again point to Jewry as anti-Christ, whose sin is the free intellect or a conscience geared into universal law or piety ossified in ritual? If the ecumenical movement endures, we can expect a deepening of the sentiment of community in the family of God's children. Let me outline some of the sign-posts of a Jewish theology of Christianity:

a. God judges individuals, one by one, as well as groups as a whole. A rabbi who lived through the siege of Jerusalem taught "that the pious among the nations share in the World to Come," even if they are not converted. According to their personal merit, the Holy Spirit rests upon them. Pious Gentiles are described in the Talmud as examples for Jews.[35]

b. Christianity, in all its variations, was declared by the Tossafists to be a monotheistic faith. Gentiles were allowed to associate other divine beings with God in their worship *(shittuf),* though this practice was not permitted to Jews. The "curse of heretics" *(birkhal haminim)* was not included in the prayers of European Jews, since the close of the Babylonian Talmud.[36]

c. Occasional hints of a still more affirmative relation to Christianity should now be developed systematically and in depth. Such an orientation is contained *in nuce* in the rabbinic characterization of the church as an "ecclesia for the sake of heaven" that God causes to endure and expand through the vicissitudes of history.[37] This estimation of the church as a divine instrument by no means implies the ending of Israel's role. The high purposes of God require many instruments for their "fulfillment." So, we return to the view of Rabban Gamaliel the Elder, as recorded in Acts 5:33, and to the opinion of James, "the brother of Jesus" (Acts 15:13–21). Highly significant is the imagery of the twelfth-century philosopher, Judah Halevi, who spoke of Israel as "the heart"; other faiths, like other internal organs, are equally necessary for life. He also employed the figure of a tree with three branches, growing out of the same seed (*The Kuzari* 4:23).

d. While Jews cannot accept the dogmatic framework of the New Testament, they can and do recognize its sublime teachings. Many scholars, including preeminently Martin Buber, saw in the revivals of Jewish pietism at various times, and particularly in Polish-Russian Hassidism, a similar efflorescence of religious genius—an emphasis on inwardness, an aspiration for "the nearness of God," an anticipation in the present of the glories of the blessed future. Some modern Jewish philosophers regarded Christianity as the outstretched arm of the Jewish faith, seeking to redeem humankind.[38]

Above all, the historical approach with its strong dash of relativism orients our thinking along the lines of pragmatism. Truth *is* as truth *works.* Does any proposed idea really motivate people to sow the seeds of justice and truth, of faith, hope, and love? Indeed, Jesus anticipated this mode of thinking in the maxim. "By their fruits shall ye know them" (Mt. 7:16).

In the pragmatic orientation we focus our attention on the task that faces us, the task of regaining for the living Word of God a society which is so largely atheistic, materialistic, and bitterly cynical. It is an overwhelming task, far more "delicate and painful" than the interfaith dialogue, but by no means "hopeless."

All of us are called upon to share in the covenant of the spirit which transcends all ritualistic and historical differences. It is in this way that we see the contemporary meaning of Jeremiah's *"berit Hadashah,"* which underlies the term "New Testament" (Jer. 31:30). Neither the old ritual nor the new is in itself decisive. What is decisive is the spirit in which rites are performed and the consequences that flow from them (Lk. 22:20; I Cor. 11:25). To the extent that any of us individually or collectively achieves the prophetic ideal, we share in an enterprise that is eternal. Whether we derive our inspiration through the rabbinic tradition, which in turn is linked to the Hebrew Bible, or through the Christian tradition and the New Testament, which are also linked to the same sacred Scriptures, our ultimate quest is the same — *malchut shomayim,* the Reign of heaven in our hearts and in society.

NOTES

1. Tosefta, Pesahim 4, 13. Jer. Talmud 6, 1. The version of the Babylonian Talmud, Pesahim 66b, does not mention the Holy Spirit.

2. The reference to Hillel in Tosefta Sota 13,3. Pesikta Rabbati, Ch. 35. The relation of Halachah to prophecy is examined in detail by A. Urbach in *Tarbitz,* 1947.

3. B. T. Shabbat 104a. He could revive a law that was forgotten. The term used here is "Tsofim," which means mystical visionaries. In this sense, the sages were considered to be the heirs of the prophets. [B. T. Baba Bathra 12a, where the strange comment is given—"A Sage is better than a prophet." A prophet's authority did not extend to concessions to idolatry, even as a temporary expedient (Sanhedrin 90a).]

4. "The Habakkuk Commentary," *Pesher Habakkuk,* is a case in point. Note particularly this sentence. "And as for what it says, *that he may run who reads it,* this means the teacher of righteousness, to whom God made known all the mysteries of the words of his servants, the prophets" [Millar Burrows, ed., *The Dead Sea Scrolls* (New York, 1955), p. 368]. The ideal of the prophet has continued in Judaism, down to our own day. See my essay, "The Prophet in Modern Hebrew Literature," in *Dialogue and Tradition,* p. 385.

5. Mt. 19:8. A similar view is stated in the Talmud, Kiddushim 21b, in reference to the law described in Deut. 21:10–14.

6. The Pharisees, it had been noted long ago, do not refer to themselves under that title. On the time and the issues that brought about the split between the Pharisees and Sadducees, see S. Zeitlin, *The Rise and Fall of the Judean State* (Philadelphia, 1968), vol. 1 Prolegomena. L. Finkelstein, "Haperushim Keneset Hagedolah" (New York, 1950), p. 81, note 243.

7. Rabbi Akiba favored proclaiming the exclusion from *Olam Haba* of those who read "external books" (Sanhedrin 100b), but there is considerable uncertainty as to the meaning of "external books." The only example offered in both the Palestinian and Babylonian Talmud is the work of Sirach, or Ben Sira, yet Sirach was quoted in the Talmuds. It seems that Rabbi Akiba's maxim was his own private opinion. In the Midrashim, echoes of apocalyptic writings are heard. Even the books of Enoch, so close to New Testament thought, are

praised in Zoharic writings, which contain echoes of the ideas of Pharisaic circles in the first century. It is noteworthy that the Tossafot assert that in some areas we follow the teaching of "the external books," as against the Talmuds (Berochot 18a, Zohar, Bereshit 72b, 37b, Shemot 55a, Vayikra 10b. See also the Jerusalem Targum on Gen. 5:24.).

8. See Harry A. Wolfson's *Philo,* in two volumes (Cambridge, Mass., 1948).

9. The description of "Pharisaic Plagues" in the Babylonian Talmud is already undecipherable (Sota 22a). Clearly, the condemnation referred to external acts of piety which were contrasted with "the Pharisee out of love," who follows the example of Abraham.

10. That some raw passages were inserted by "immature disciples" was already acknowledged by Judah Halevi (1085–1140) in *The Kuzari,* III, 73. Maimonides in the Introduction to the "Guide of the Perplexed," and in First Part, Chapter 59. Nahman Krochmal devoted chapter 14 of his classic work to this problem, *Moreh Nebuchai Hazeman.* In regard to the Pharisees, he stressed that they represented normative tradition only in a general way, not insofar as they defended their own sectarian interests (ibid., ch. 10, Edition Lemberg, 1863, p. 51).

11. F. Baer's studies appeared in the Hebrew magazine, *Zion,* vol. 27–28 (1952–1953), and vol. 37 (1962); in *Molad* (1964); and in his small book, summarizing his position, *Yisroel Bo-amim* (Jerusalem, 1956).

12. Harry A. Wolfson points out that God's "unknowability" was Philo's contribution to religious philosophy. While Plato considered that the human mind was closest to the Logos, Philo insisted that our mind is not self-activating, but that it reflects divine power and initiative. See *Legum Allegoria,* II, 69. Harry A. Wolfson, *Philo,* II, p. 110.

13. Josephus, "Contra Apionen," 1, 22. Eusebius, Praep. Evangelica XIII, 12.

14. The universalist note in the Testaments of the Twelve Patriarchs is particularly striking. Test. of Benjamin, IX, 2; Test of Naphtali, II, 5; Test of Levi XIV, 4.

15. *De Spec. Leg.* 1, 58. "Quod Deus sit Immort.," 30, 144. Good and holy men of all nations are called by him, "Sons of God," *De Spec. Leg.* 1, 318.

16. Saul Lieberman, *Hellenism in Jewish Palestine* (New York, 1950), chapter on "Rabbinic Interpretation of Scripture." David Daube, "Rabbinic Methods of Interpretation and Hellenic Rhetoric," *Hebrew Union College Annual,* 22 (1949): 239ff.

17. Berachot 18b: ". . . for I run, and they run. I run to the life of World to Come, and they run to the pit of destruction." Berachot 17a: ". . . The Sages of Yavne used to say, 'I am a creature and my colleagues (who do not study Torah) are creatures . . . Lest you say, 'I do more and he does less,' we have

learned. Alike are those who do more and those who do less, for all depends on the directing of one's heart to heaven. . . ."

18. Joseph Albo, "The Book of Principles," allows that two religions may coexist at one time and be equally divine. However, he disputes the validity of Catholic doctrine in his time, the beginning of the fifteenth century, on the ground of its logical impossibility. See I. Husik's edition, published by the J.P.S., volume III, chap. 25. Nahmanides argued at Barcelona, in 1263, as follows:

> The core of the true dispute among us is not the concept of the Messiah . . . but the crux of the issue and the reason for the argument between Jews and Christians is the fact that you impute to the Deity things which are exceedingly repugnant. . . . For what you state, and this is the essence of your faith, reason cannot accept, nature does not permit, and the prophets never implied . . . (*Sefer Havikuah Leboramban*, 12).

19. In a series of books, S. G. F. Brandon sought to uncover the implications of the catastrophic fall of Jerusalem on the formation and crystallization of the New Testament. His major works are *The Fall of Jerusalem and the Christian Church, Jesus and the Zealots,* and *The Trial of Jesus of Nazareth.* The disappearance of the mother church of Jerusalem is, in his judgment, the crucial fact.

20. Yehezkel Kaufman elaborates this view in his monumental study. *Goleh Venoichar,* vol. I (Tel Aviv, 1929), chap. 8.

21. "Jerusalem that is above" in II Enoch 55, 2. The heavenly Temple in B. T. Hagigah 12b. Jer. T. Berochot 4, 5. B. T. Sukkah 41a. Rashi's Commentary.

22. *Das letzte Passamahl Christs u. der Tag seines Todes* (1892, 1908), p. 118. Jesus' condemnation of evil Pharisees (in Talmud, "Pharisaic plagues," Mishin Sota 3,4) was generalized by later copyists. This was also the view of M. Friedlander, *Die religiösen Bewegungen innerhalb des Judentums in Zeitalter Jesu* (1905).

23. One blesses God, "The Creator of the beginnings," on seeing the stars (Berachot 59b). While the stars were occasionally made responsible for a person's fate *(mazal),* this dependence did not apply to Israel (Shabbat 156a).

24. Jaroslav Pelian, *The Christian Tradition* (Chicago, 1971), vol. I, p. 85. The ascription of marriage to Satan by the Encratites was the clearest expression of their unworldliness. The supposition of a third mediating kind of human being was a compromise to give substance to conversion. Wilhelm Bousset, *Kyrios Christos* (New York, 1970), p. 266.

25. F. G. Fichte, *Characteristics of the Present Age* (1849).

26. It has long been noted that the prophets of Teutonism were also exponents of "cultural despair." Such men as Ludwig Jahn, Julius Langbehn, Paul de

Lagarde, Richard Wagner, Eugen Dühring, and Oswald Spengler were agreed that the values of the democratic West were all degenerate. They looked for the awakening of a dark, slumbering soul, a peculiar racial psyche.

27. Henry Renckens, *The Religion of Israel* (New York, 1966), p. 238–239.

28. The Gospel of Mark was believed to have been written in Rome after 70 A. D. It includes older Aramaic logia and personal reminiscences, but it was composed with the aim of separating the Christian community from the odium that was then attached to Jewish people.

29. Josephus, *Wars of the Jews,* II, 20,2.

30. B. T. Sanhedrin 37a and 44b. There was no independent rabbinic tradition regarding the crucifixion, else there would have been some consistency at least in regard to the time or the place of execution. But the time is supposed to be roughly a hundred years before, and the place Lydda, instead of Jerusalem (Sanhedrin 43a: 107b).

31. Raymond E. Brown, in his introduction to his commentary on the Gospel of John, *Anchor Bible,* vol. 29, p. LXXI, writes as follows:

> . . . there is one stratum of Johanine material, particularly evident in XI–XII, where the term, Jews, simply refers to Judeans . . . the Fourth Gospel uses "the Jews" as almost a technical title *for the religious authorities, particularly those in Jerusalem, who are hostile to Jesus.*

32. The messianic interpretations of Psalms 2 and 110 occur in the late Midrash Tehillim, ed. Bober, but with the qualification that "sonship" is metaphorical, "as when a Master says to his slave, 'you are my son' " (Ps. 2:54). Midrash Tehillim, ed. Bober, 110,14. The Yalkut on Tehillim, 110,869, speaks of the Messiah sitting to the right of God, with Abraham sitting at God's left.

33. Referring to Abraham's vision of the three angels, Philo writes:

> Rather, as anyone who has approached nearest to the truth would say, the central place is held by the Father of the Universe, Who in the sacred scriptures is called 'He that is,' as His proper name, while on either side of Him are the senior potencies, the nearest to Him, the creative and the kingly. . . .
>
> . . . presents to the mind which has vision the appearance sometime of one sometimes of three (Philo, *De Abrahamo* (New York, 1962), XXIV, 121, 122).

34. W. D. Davies, in *Christian Origins and Judaism* and *Paul and Rabbinic Judaism* demonstrates that Paul's ideas were rooted in Judaism, though they were transformed in later years into concepts that could no longer be fitted within a Jewish ideological context.

35. Tosefta, Sanhedrin, 13. Rabbi Joshua ben Hanania's opinion. The twelfth-century authors of *Tossafot* on the B. T. Avoda Zara, 2a, declare that Christianity does not fall under the category of idolatry. The contrary opinion of Maimonides in his Code is mitigated by his letter to R. Hisdai Halevi, in which he points out that "God seeks the heart." Of Gentiles as examples, Jerusalem, Peah 1, 1. B. T. Kiddushin 31a.

36. Avoda Zara 2a. The Palestinian version of *"birchat baminum,"* which specifically includes Christians, was unknown to the Jews of Europe prior to its discovery by S. Schechter in the Cairo *Genizah.*

37. This application of a maxim in the *Ethics of the Fathers* (IV, 14) is offered by the eighteenth-century sage, Rabbi Jacob Emden, in his commentary, "Aitz Avot."

38. See the original edition of Martin Buber's *Reden.* Solomon Formstecher in the nineteenth century and Franz Rosenzweig in the twentieth century used the image of the sun and its rays as symbolizing the respective roles of Judaism and Christianity.

11

PERSPECTIVES FOR THE STUDY

OF THE BOOK OF ACTS

THE FAITH and career of Paul are generally regarded as marking the tragic break between Judaism and Christianity. While many Jewish scholars maintain that Jesus lived and taught within the ambience of Judaism, they argue that Paul was responsible for the separation of the two faiths and their mutual hostility. So, Joseph Klausner can find in the case of Jesus only the "seed" of denationalized piety. Kaufmann and Buber include Jesus completely within the sphere of Judaism.

But as to Paul, Klausner blames his alienation on the fact that he was a Jew from the Diaspora, hence inauthentic and anguished by contradictions. Montefiore similarly asserts that Paul could not help but experience the serene piety of the Pharisees, had he lived in the land of Israel. Raised in an alien environment, Paul was troubled by foreign influences and familiar only with the unlovely exterior of Jewish observances. Paul seems especially ignorant of the central ideas of Pharisaic Judaism—namely, repentance and forgiveness.

In sum, it is said by Jewish scholars that while the religion *of* Jesus was part of Judaism, the religion *about* Jesus, inaugurated by Paul, broke radically and completely with the Jewish faith.

Christian scholars find in the life of Paul additional confirmation of the thesis that the Jews, as a people, were "rejected," if not placed under a curse, and then replaced by the Gentiles.

Johannes Munck, in the *Anchor Bible* volume of Acts, commenting on Acts 28:17–28, says: "Israel's unbelief became the cause of his preaching the Gospel to the Gentiles." The same author comments on Acts 21:20, where James speaks of tens of thousands who joined the Christian community, while remaining "faithful to the law": "There could not be so many Jewish-Christians, since Jesus complained that his message was rejected."

The axiom of a mutual rejection that was immediate and total distorts the teaching of the New Testament generally. Paul would have preached to Gentiles, whether or not all or most Jews had accepted his message. After all, Peter had also preached to Gentiles. Here, we are concerned with the Book of Acts.

May I suggest the following perspectives for the interpretation of this book:

First, the concept of monotheism, as it emerged in Judaism, *included a set of polarities that were reconciled only in the Will of God.* Judaism is what it is, and it is what it will be. Its being is also its vision of the future.

God was absolutely transcendent, beyond the grasp of man's senses or man's imagination or man's intelligence. Already, Philo speaks of God as being unknowable. At the same time, God was revealed at Sinai, to the prophets, dimly also to the Sages. Mediating divine entities were conceived, such as "The Word," the *Shekhinah*, Primal Man, Metatron, "whose name is the same as that of his Master." In the interpretation of biblical oracles, God's help was granted from time to time, through these entities.

The Torah, too, was bi-polar. Given at Sinai to Moses, it contained specific commands, whose purpose was "pedagogical," "to refine human nature," and inner principles, which corresponded to the structure of the cosmos.

The Temple in Jerusalem was believed to correspond to a heavenly Temple.[1] God dwells in heaven and in the human heart, as well as symbolically in His earthly Temple; the Archangel Michael or Metatron functioned as the heavenly high priest offering the souls of the righteous, or "lambs of fire," by way of atonement for the sins of Israel.

Israel, too, was bi-polar. It refers to the empirical Jewish people, but also to "the pious among the nations of the world." "Whoever denies idolatry is called a Jew," says the Talmud. The so-called God-fearers of the New Testament were in this category.

This bi-polarity was evident in all the relations between God, Torah, and Israel—God deals in terms of law, but He also extends His mercy freely; man is free, yet all is determined; God forgives, yet man must earn forgiveness by sacrifices as well as by repentance; Israel was chosen, by the fiat of divine love, yet only individuals are so chosen; Israel will be vindicated in time to come, yet all of redeemed mankind will constitute the Israel of the future, while not all Israelites will be redeemed. Characteristic is the language of the Mishnah: "All Israel have a share in the World to Come, but the following classes of people, do not . . ." (*Sanhedrin* 10:1).

This bi-polarity in every aspect of the Jewish faith is inescapable in a living faith, based on monotheism, that seeks to do justice to the fullness of human aspirations. It grows out of the realities of human existence, on the one hand, and the nobility of man's ideals, on the other hand.

Now, in the Jewish vision of the future, the Messianic Era shading off into the World to Come, the gentler, bolder, more dreamlike pole of hopes and ideals was expected to predominate—God will be more present to His worshippers, His Holy Spirit being "poured out" in abundance; the inner light of Torah will be revealed; Israel will become the redeemed nucleus of humanity; forgiveness will be offered freely, conditioned only on one's willingness to accept; Jerusalem and the Temple that is Above will take the place of the concrete Temple in the earthly Jerusalem; the policy of Compassion, or love, will prevail over that of Law: redeemed mankind will be liberated from the body of flesh and join the company of angels, in whose company they truly belong.

Now, "the Time to Come" *(leatid lavo)* will begin with the days of the Messiah, eventuate in a cosmic Day of Judgment, and culminate in the revelation of the "World to Come" *(olam haba),* when the "Saints will sit with crowns on their heads delighting in the radiance of the Presence [*Shechinah*]."

Had the aeon of the Time to Come dawned already? At this point, the Christians diverged from the rest of the Jewish community.

Jesus and his disciples believed that the new aeon had begun. The religion *of* Jesus contained a firm belief *about* Jesus. Paul believed the culmination of the new aeon would come in his own generation. He was living in the Eschatological Age. It was incumbent upon him to be the instrument of saving those that were predestined for salvation. Otherwise, their "blood would be upon his head."

All of Paul's teaching is to be seen in the context of the appearance of the new aeon—hence, an Immanent Divine Presence, a Messianic

Torah, a new Israel, the redeemed nucleus of humanity, the assurance of the Holy Spirit, and the belief of the speedy coming of the Parousia.

Hence, the crux of the argument between Paul and the Jews, who did not accept his message, was whether or not the Messianic Age was truly begun and the World to Come would appear soon. All other differences were derived from this basic issue. Most un-Jewish as Paul's career seems to Jewish scholars today, he was utterly sincere when he claimed: "I have committed no offense either against Jewish Law or the Temple or Caesar" (Acts 25:8).

The exclusivism of the Apostolic community is understandable in this context: "Neither is there salvation in any other; for there is none other name under heaven given among men, whereby we must be saved" (Acts 4:12). In the End of Days, we are told, "the Lord will be one and His Name One" (Zech. 14:9).

Understandable also is the revelation concerning the Covenant, the Law, the formation of a new Israel, the concept of a high priest in heaven, and the idea of the Messiah "sitting on the right hand of God." The last notion, frequently described as blasphemous, is attributed to Rabbi Akiba (d. 135 C.E.) (*Hagigah* 14a).

In brief, the first perspective I would urge is that Paul be understood as far as possible within the context of his Jewish upbringing, though unconsciously he might well have absorbed the teachings of the "mystery" religions.

As the second perspective, I urge that neither the New Testament in general nor Paul in particular teaches that the Jews were "rejected" and the Gentiles were chosen in their place. Where such references occur, the meaning is that Judaism as such will no longer suffice in the coming Day of Judgment, inaugurating the World to Come.

Jews, on this view, are like the rest of mankind, that is "guilty" of the sin of Adam. Living under the Law, they were more conscious of their sinfulness. Indeed, a common motif in the High Holiday liturgy is "we and our fathers have sinned."

According to Luke in Acts, the nonacceptance of Jesus as the Messiah makes one "guilty" of human sinfulness and of the blood of Jesus. So, Stephen, addressing himself to a Jewish crowd, speaks of the murderers of Jesus in the third-person plural, "they," and to his audience directly as facing the possibility of becoming guilty: "They killed those who foretold the coming of the Righteous One, and you now living have become his betrayers and murderers . . ." (Acts 7:52).

The "rejection," if any, will occur in the Parousia, in the Day of Judgment.

For this reason, Paul says to Jews who did not believe: "Your blood be upon your own heads; I am clean; from henceforth I will go to the Gentiles" (Acts 18:6). But then he goes to the Jews in the very next town. And at the end of the book, he is still speaking to the Jews of Rome.

The third perspective is a recognition that the issue between Paul and his Jewish opponents was not universalism or humanism vs. Jewish particularism or ethnicism, but whether the Law remained valid in the new eschatological age, prior to the Second Coming.

It was not universalism as such, because the Jews accepted the "fearers of the Lord" in the fellowship of the synagogue and as candidates of the World to Come. Also, the acceptance of Gentiles in the Christian dispensation was qualified. So, at Pisidian Antioch (Acts 13:42–52), Luke writes: "As many as were destined for eternal life believed." Later he reports James as saying: "For the Gentiles to take out of them a people for his name" (Acts 15:14). Also, the Exodus of the Israelites from Egypt provided a paradigmatic image of redemption, and Israel then included a mixture of many peoples (Exod. 12:38).

The Apostles were surprised to find that the Holy Spirit fell upon Gentiles also, though they had not accepted the Law.

The issue was not admittance into the *national* community of Israel, but into the Covenant. The rabbinic expression for entering into the Covenant was "to come under the wings of the divine Presence."

Luke's writing is understandable from the standpoint of the second generation, which was impressed by the preponderance of Gentiles in the Christian churches. So, we read of Jewish "jealousy" (Acts 13:45), and we get the general feeling that somehow, by a fresh divine fiat, the Gentiles were substituted for the Jews as the newly chosen people. The very word *Gentiles* is meaningful only in a Jewish context. Out of the Jewish context, the word *Gentile* places the Jews apart from the rest of humanity, as if they were metaphysically superhuman or subhuman, not like other people.

The Apostles and Jesus and the classical prophets, speaking to their own people, demanded more from them—hence, the tone of bitterness and frustration. But this intra-Jewish family feeling must not be perverted by removing it from its historical context.

The couplet "Jews rejected, Gentiles accepted" must be put in its historical context. Paul finds the nucleus of his adherents in every city among Jews and their associates, the "God-fearers," *sebomenoi, yirai Adonai*. They were prepared by the synagogue for the understanding of the Gospel. When Paul preaches to a Roman like Festus, the Roman governor in Caesarea, the latter exclaims: "Paul, thou art beside thyself; too much learning doth make thee mad" (Acts 26:24).

Agrippa is not converted, but, as Jew, he understands what Paul is saying.

The number of Jews in the Roman Empire was between 5 and 10 percent of the total population. Suppose the Christian church obtained twice as large a percentage of converts among Jews as among Gentiles; the percentage of Jews within the churches would vary from 10 to 20 percent.

To illustrate the devious reasoning of some scholars—eager to maintain the simplistic couplet "Jews rejected, Gentiles accepted"—may I refer you again to Johannes Munck's comment in the *Anchor Bible* on Acts 11:1–18: "This Pauline view, which may suitably be named 'representative universalism,' represented a Semitic outlook. Where a part had accepted the Gospel, then, the whole, that is the nation concerned, had accepted it, and where a part had rejected it, the nation as a whole had rejected it."

Translated it means that the Jews rejected it, because a part did so; *the* Gentiles accepted it, not *some* Gentiles, because the part equals the whole. How even-handed! How Semitic!

The fourth perspective that is frequently ignored by Jewish as well as Christian scholars is that Pauline Christianity grew out of opposition to Temple Judaism, not the modified post-Temple Judaism that is reflected in the Mishnah and Talmud.

The theology of Paul and of the Letter to the Hebrews operates with the notion of forgiveness of sin through the supreme sacrifice of the "Son of God." Post-Temple Judaism maintains in practice the sufficiency of repentance, on the part of man, and forgiveness, on the part of God. However, in theory it cherished the hope of a reinstitution of the Temple and its sacrifices. Also, it speculated that in the heavenly Temple, "not built by human hands," the sacrifices of the righteous are even now being offered in the shape of "lambs of fire" and the officiating priest is either Michael or Metatron (*Hagigah* 12b, *Menahot* 110a).

The latter speculation was never raised to the rank of a dogma. Interesting is a *baraitha* which reflects the gulf between Temple Judaism and that of the rabbinic period: "A sinner, what is his punishment?— They asked this question of Wisdom. It responded, 'a sinner, he shall die'; they asked it of prophecy, it responded, 'evil pursues the sinner'; they asked it of Torah, it responded, 'let him bring a sacrifice and his sin will be forgiven'; they asked it of God, He answered, 'let him repent and all will be forgiven.' "[2]

Here, then, is a policy, representing the true intent of God, which is superior to the Divine Will, as it is found in the Torah.

A similar thought is presented in the name of Rabban Yohanan ben Zakkai, who assumed the leadership of Judaism after the destruction of the Temple (*Abot di R. Nathan* IV). He said to his disciple who wept over the destruction of the Temple: "We have an atonement of equal efficacy, deeds of lovingkindness."

Now we know that many pietists were embittered by the administrators of the Temple.

The Talmud notes the popular resentment of the high priests and their aides.[3] The Samaritans were implacable in their hostility, and Stephen may have been a Samaritan. The Samaritans referred to themselves as Hebrews, and the Epistle by this name may have been written to Samaritans.

More to the point, the Qumran community shows us a group of ardent pietists who disdained the high priests of the Temple as usurpers, since they did not belong to the family of Zadok. The Qumran *Hassidim* were organized by their Righteous Teacher, *Moreh Zedek,* as a holy community, in which God dwelt, a living sanctuary that could serve as a substitute for the Holy Temple. This community, or its governing council, *azat hayahad,* was "the true Israel." Their sacred meals were probably modeled after those in the Temple. They looked forward to the descent of the heavenly Temple, the one not built with human hands. (As Bertil Gärtner comments: "We have seen that the Qumran texts contain a consistent Temple symbolism, in which the community is represented as the new Temple, and in which the true sacrifice is seen as being spiritual in character, offered in the holy and pure lives, the praise and prayer of the members of the community.")[4]

The Temple symbolism of Paul in I Corinthians 3:16 and I Timothy

3:15 and of the author of Hebrews is paralleled by similar symbolism in the Qumran community and by rabbinic speculations concerning the heavenly Temple.

The frustrations of many Jews with the Temple ritual are reflected in Paul's and Luke's criticism of the Law and its supposed inefficiency. A large portion of the Law dealt with the Temple and the laws of "purity," which related to it.

The complaints that the Law could not be observed fully cut to the heart of many Jews—mostly in the Diaspora, but also in Galilee. The offering of *olah* was to be brought for "meditations of the heart."[5] How often could a Jew from the Diaspora go up to Jerusalem? The bringer of a sin-offering or a burnt-offering had to lean with both hands on the animal, prior to its sacrifice *(semikhah)*.[6] The laws of "purity" placed all Diaspora Jews in the category of the "impure," requiring a week of purification. Also, the commercialism of the priestly families and the legitimacy of the high priest were frequently questioned.

Apparently, before R. Akiba's time, the assumption was that anyone who did not observe *all* of the precepts of the Law was doomed. R. Akiba maintained that the observance of even one *mizvah* was sufficient to secure a share in the World to Come *(Makkot* 24a).

In brief, in Temple Judaism, many believed that "there is no forgiveness save in blood" *(Yoma* 5a). For the Apostolic community, the blood of Jesus has taken the place of the blood of lambs: "Him hath God exalted with His right hand to be a Prince and a Savior, for to give repentance to Israel, and forgiveness of sins" (Acts 5:31). Rabbinic Judaism asserted that both repentance and forgiveness required no sacrificial intermediary.

The greatest sin in Temple Judaism was *pigul,* to entertain idle thoughts while the sacrifice was being offered. Hence, Paul in I Corinthians (11:27) warns of punishment for thoughtless participation in the eucharist. It was the reenactment of a sacrifice.

The author of Hebrews argues that any sin committed after conversion cannot be forgiven: "For if we sin willfully after that we have received the knowledge of truth, there remaineth no more sacrifice for sins" (Heb. 10:26).

Temple Judaism was not identical with the Sadducee mentality, but the two attitudes were certainly very close. So, the Sadducees, especially the Temple functionaries, persecuted the early Christians, while the Pharisees defend Peter and John: "But if it be of God, ye cannot overthrow it . . ."(Acts 5:39). Paul too was defended by the Pharisees: "We find no evil in this man; but if a spirit or an angel hath spoken to him, let us not fight against God" (Acts 23:9).

Fifth, the perspective of universal history. If we look at the course of human history, as it unfolds in the succession of centuries, it is clear that some form of ethical monotheism, embracing the insights of Hebrew prophecy and Hellenic philosophy, was due to emerge in the Roman Empire. Paganism was spiritually bankrupt. Judaism appealed powerfully to the pagan population, but it was, after all, the religion of an ethnic community that was emotionally withdrawn, socially insulated, and politically subjugated.

The logic of spiritual development was directed decisively toward an integrated cosmos, governed by One God, Who is revealed in man's heart and mind. As Greek philosophy superseded previous speculations, so Jewish biblical thought advanced inexorably within the Roman Empire. Variations of Persian dualism and Chaldaic Gnosticism captured for brief moments the fancy of the populace, but they could not deflect the main current which aimed at the harmonization of all the demands of man's spirit.

A new synthesis was needed that included the impact of Judaism, with its antiquity and prestige, and yet was a new revelation, which non-Jews could enter on the ground floor.

As Toynbee pointed out, the external proletariat tends to embrace the culture of the nuclear people in some heretical form, which reflects their ambivalence of both admiration and contempt.

So, the Samaritans embraced Judaism, but with a difference; the Germanic tribes took up the Arian form of Christianity; the Persians, the Shiya form of Islam; the Russians, their own variation on Byzantine Orthodoxy. Religiously speaking, Judaism was the nuclear community. The time was ripe for a form of Jewish monotheism that would embrace its living core and at the same time dispute its legitimacy.

This historic role was carried out by Christianity, with Paul laying down the two basic lines of acceptance and rejection toward the mother faith. In Romans 9–11, he acknowledged in his own way that the nonacceptance of Christ by the Jews was providential. The ambivalent love-hate relationship between Judaism and Christianity was itself dynamic and restless, with the Gnostics stressing the anti-Judaic side and the second-century apologists emphasizing the pro-Jewish elements.

The rapid spread of Christianity in the pagan world was due to its serving as the vehicle of the biblical faith. In the case of the Jewish people, no such historical function existed, for they had experienced this development in the biblical period. Hence, the appeal of Christianity to Jews was comparatively modest. Its anti-Temple mood was neutralized by rabbinic Judaism, which in practice substituted prayer and good deeds for the sacrifices of the Temple but maintained the hope of the restoration of the Temple.

The sixth and final perspective that I urge is the personal attempt of Paul and other Apostles to overcome the isolation of the Jew and to eliminate the scourge of antisemitism. Paul's complex personality contained a keen feeling for the broad sweep of history along with a deep concern for the destiny of his own people. He spared no effort to bring salvation to all men, but he loved the Jewish people with a passion.

Paul was a theologian, and all his actions had to be consciously systematized and related to his central conviction of "Christ crucified." He was also a great Jewish personality, who was deeply concerned with the endemic hostility between Jews and Greeks in the Eastern Mediterranean, especially in Syria and Egypt. Doubtless, he felt deeply the anguish of his fellow Jews when Caius Caligula ordered that his picture be worshipped in the Temple (39 C.E.) The anti-Jewish riots in Alexandria, Egypt (38–40 C.E.), and the anti-pagan riots in Jamnia, Palestine, provoked outbreaks in many parts of the empire. Antisemitism had become a murderous mass-phenomenon (Josephus, *Wars of the Jews* II:18).

It was inevitable that Paul, a native of the Hellenistic Jewish Diaspora, would be deeply concerned with the need of bridging the tragic rift between the Jews and the Greeks. His conviction that the Eschatological Age had already dawned reenforced his determination to hasten the day when all ethnic rivalries and hatreds would be overcome. With fierce resolve, he battled against the notion of retaining the line of demarcation between Jews and Greeks within the Christian community. He would not allow the Law to enforce Jewish insularity within the community that was already living in spirit in the Messianic Age. Hellenistic Jews were keenly conscious of the social consequences of the Law, which surrounded them with an "iron curtain," as it were (*Aristeas to Philocrates,* ed. Moises Hadas, [New York, 1951], 139). They bore its restrictions with amazing courage, so long as its educational function was necessary. But in the time of fulfillment, the prophetic vision of the fraternity of peoples could no longer be postponed.

Paul felt called upon to prepare the way for the coming with power of the Messiah—hence, to insist that in Christ all divisions shall no longer be tolerated. "There is neither Jew nor Greek, there is neither bond nor free, there is neither male nor female; for ye are all one in Christ Jesus" (Gal. 3:28).

In sum, the perspectives that emerge out of Jewish scholarship are:

1. The bi-polarity and dynamism of the Jewish faith would be raised to the breaking point when the Eschaton was at hand.
2. The Day of Judgment was impending, but no "rejection" of the Jewish people had already taken place.
3. The core of the argument between Paul and the loyal Jews was not ideological but factual—had the Messiah arrived or not?—It was not universalism vs. particularism.
4. Temple Judaism was the stem out of which Pauline Christianity and Pharisaism diverged.
5. The macroscopic view of world-history, in which Paul's career is to be seen.
6. The microscopic view of Paul's complex personality and his dedication to the unity of the community of the newly "chosen people."

NOTES

1. Jer. *Yoma* 1, "Why did the priests serve in white garments?—As the service is above, so it is below."

2. Jer. *Makkot* 2.

3. *Yoma* 71a, *Pesachim* 57a.

4. *The Temple and the Community in Qumran and the New Testament* (Cambridge University Press, 1965), p. 47.

5. *Taanit* 26a, "How can a person's sacrifice be offered when he is not present?"

6. "Always an *olah* is brought only for meditation of the heart" (*Lev. Rabba* 7:3). (We can understand Paul's predicament in Romans 7.)

12

A NEW KIND OF CHRISTIAN-
JEWISH DISPUTATION

EVER SINCE Christianity was born, a dialogue has been under way between its followers and the defenders of Judaism. Since both Jews and Christians interpreted every aspect of life in terms of their respective central beliefs, this dialogue expanded in time to include nearly every phase of culture. In essence, the same arguments have been repeated, as if every generation were called upon to justify its position anew. But there were always fresh nuances, reflecting the particular bias of the age. Most of the time the antagonists were not present in the flesh, only in the imagination of the disputant. Yet a debate of some sort, even against the ghost of a contestant, has been going on since the Christian branch grew out of the ancient stem of Judaism.

For Christians this dialogue is inescapable, since it is enshrined in the New Testament. Jesus is represented in the Gospels as debating either with Pharisees or with "Jews." In the Synoptic Gospels he speaks as a Jewish teacher, not only when he agrees with his interlocutors, but also when he condemns with impassioned intensity the Pharisaic leaders of the people. At times he speaks in the style of the biblical prophets, hurling his rebuke at the people in thunderbolts of holy wrath. At times he poses a challenge or responds to a question in the style of the rabbis themselves. In the Gospel of John, the debate turns into a cosmic duel between the source of light and the children of darkness. There the argument on earth is conceived as a shadowy replica of the metaphysical struggle in the heavens. Every affirmation of the Christian faith is stated by God Himself, through His Son.

By the same token, Jewish opposition appears to be only the tip of the iceberg of Jewish depravity. The disputants do not speak to each other; they shout and declaim or rather, sing out their convictions.

To be sure, even in the darkest ages of history there were occasional glimpses of humanity and rational piety. May it not be that God employs diverse instruments to establish His Kingdom on earth? Thus, Rabban Gamaliel the Elder tells his colleagues in the Sanhedrin that the Christian community may well be "of God," playing its role in the divine scheme of redemption (Acts 23:9). And James, head of the mother church in Jerusalem, allows that there may be two communities of the faithful—a Jewish one consisting of "those who are zealous for the Law" and a Gentile one consisting of those who abide only by the Noachian commandments (Acts 15:1–29).

In the course of history, however, the mediating positions between the loyal Jews and the Gentile Christians were destroyed. The fall of Jerusalem was, perhaps, the decisive event in this polarization. Increasingly, the Jewish image in the Christian tradition was demonized. No longer was the Jew a human antagonist, but a minion of Satan, rejected and accursed. The Hebrew Bible was not an expression of Jewish life, but a record of the Jewish fall from grace, to be read as a warning for future generations. The prophets and psalmists had been "Christians before Christ," forever fighting against the pernicious spirit of Judaism. Jews studied the Torah and the prophets with all the passion of their souls, but a veil was draped over their minds and hearts that they might not grasp its true meaning. From beginning to end, the Old Testament was a tissue of myths, oracles, and metaphors, foreshadowing the career of Christ on earth. The true meaning was plain to all, save accursed heretics and Jews.

In Catholic Europe, heretics were ruthlessly persecuted and condemned to death. However, Jews, the worst heretics of all, were generally permitted to live albeit under severe restrictions. They were regarded by the Church as a special case, a paradoxical mystery, at once divine and demonic, since "they were beloved for the fathers' sakes" (Romans 11:28) and at the same time minions of Satan. Accordingly they were allowed to occupy a marginal position in society, a precarious one of degradation and humiliation, in which they might atone throughout historic time for the infinite sin of "deicide."

This medieval image of the Jew, in all its fantastic imagery, persists in the minds of millions down to our day. It is deeply imbedded in the folk imagery of most European nations. And it is capable of being infinitely varied by subtle minds. Its one invariant feature is the metaphysical uniqueness of the Jew; he is different from all other human beings in a cosmic, existential sense. His history and his destiny must be understood not in human terms but in the light of his special status in the divine scheme of things. It took the genius of Shakespeare in his "Merchant of Venice" to call attention to the basic dehumanization in the Christian image of the Jew.

Into the modern age the Christian-Jewish disputation has continued but in more diverse and subtler forms. A portion of the population continues to live in spirit within the mythological world of medievalism, and even enlightened people move uneasily between the poles of rationality and fantasy. All too often the underworld of ancient myths can be easily detected beneath the facade of contemporary rhetoric. In the modern world, individual Jews have come to play so central and powerful a role that no intellectual movement could afford to ignore them. As in Greek legends ancient ghosts acquired fresh life when they were given libations of blood, so the myths of antiquity have been reborn in modern times through interaction with contemporary conflicts. At times, the underpinning of medieval mythology is banished to the limbo of the unconscious; at times belief in it is passionately denied, and sincerely so, yet its impetus endures even in movements that are consciously anti-Christian. The Holocaust perpetrated by the Nazis was consciously anti-Christian and nihilistic; yet it was made possible by the massive momentum of medieval folk-antisemitism and by the fantastic mythology that grew for centuries under the aegis of the Church.

The Jew, for his part, has not always responded overtly and publicly to the challenge of Christians. Rabbinic literature contains only rare and scattered replies to the arguments of contemporary Christians. Ever since the banishment of Jewish Christians from the synagogues in the last decade of the first century, the rabbinic tradition virtually ignored the spectacular expansion of the Church. Talmudic literature attained its final form in Babylonia, where there were very few Christians. The Palestinian *Midrashim* were composed in the fifth and sixth centuries, when Jewish preachers could refer only indirectly and by the way of parables to the dominant Christian faith in the Byzantine Empire. In addition, the inner exposition of the Jewish faith did not require that account be taken of the emergence of Christianity. While the Church defined itself by reference to the Synagogue, the Synagogue did not feel called upon to define itself by any references to the Church.

Yet it would be wrong to conclude that the Jews of the medieval world ignored the challenge of Christianity. How could they fail to think about it? Believing that the hand of God was seen in history, they could not but assign some role to the Church in the divine plan for redemption. Maimonides stated explicitly that both Islam and Christianity are instruments employed by God to spread His teaching and prepare the world for redemption. Some French rabbis taught that Christians do not belong in the category of idolators that the Talmud describes, but in that of the Noachian semi-converts. Certainly whenever Jews pondered their destiny they could not help wondering at the uniqueness of their fate — on the one hand, their message was accepted, at least in part, by Christians to the north and by Moslems to the south; on the other hand, they, the bearers of the message, were scorned and persecuted. Their faith in their heritage, however, was reinforced by the steadily mounting evidence of its universal appeal, and their determination to survive, despite all detractors, was strengthened by the doctrinal and practical faults they found in the religions of their neighbors.

So, although genuine face to face dialogues rarely took place in the ancient and medieval worlds, Jews and Christians could not but agonize over their relations to one another.

BETWEEN TRADITIONALISTS AND PHILOSOPHERS

The public life of Moses Mendelssohn, 1729–86, was a living demonstration of the Jewish-Christian dialogue. He was an outstanding philosopher, read and admired by the intellectuals of Germany. Residing in Berlin, the capital of Prussia, he was generally regarded as the leading Jew of his day. As such, he was challenged by believing Christians, on the one hand, and by enlightened philosophers, on the other hand. The first challenge was directed at him by Johann Caspar Lavater, 1741–1801, a Swiss pastor and popular author, who had translated a work by the French historian, Bonnet, detailing the evidences of Christianity. Lavater sent a copy of that book to Mendelssohn, with a letter asking that he either refute the "proofs" offered by Bonnet or consent to their validity and convert to Christianity. Presumably, Jews had not been convinced in the past of the truth of Christianity because they had

willfully closed their minds to its message. As "children of the devil,"
(John 8:44) they would not listen to the truth. But Mendelssohn, as a
philosopher, was trained to be open-minded. Hence, the challenge.

Here the traditional position of the Christian protagonist is clearly
revealed. First, he does not put his own faith on the line. Like Au-
gustine, he affirms his belief *ab initio* and then proceeds to find justifica-
tions for it. He believed in order to understand. His faith does not grow
out of his own efforts to comprehend the mysteries of existence. So,
the Catholic catechism defines faith as follows: "Faith is a gift of God
infused into our souls, by which we firmly believe all those things
which God has revealed to us."

Lavater and his colleagues did not ask, if faith is God's gift transcending our understanding, may not God in His Wisdom devise different patterns of belief for different people? If faith is not founded on
rational proofs, why marshal those proofs? To the "enlightened" Jews of
Berlin, miracles reported in the Gospels do not prove that Jesus was a
divine being, any more than the miracles told of Hasidic saints. Mendelssohn repeated an idea that is emphasized in medieval Jewish philosophy. The Jews believed in Moses not because they were impressed by
his miracles, but because they were persuaded by the cogency of his
teachings. The belief that God could offer to men only one pathway of
salvation is itself non-rational. As Mendelssohn pointed out again and
again, the doctrine of religious exclusiveness is the one irrefutable proof
of the falsehood of a faith, for it imputes frank injustice to God.

Second, eagerness to convert, or missionary zeal, is characteristic of
the Christian protagonist's position. In itself, this zeal is laudable. People
should share their treasures with others. But this eagerness is combined
with a stigmatization of the faith of the non-Christian, judging it to be
inferior, or inadequate for salvation, or false. During the Enlightenment, when the intellectuals came to realize the folly and futility of the
wars of religion, any such denigration of a historic faith was manifestly
contrary to the spirit of the times. After the Protestant Reformation
called into question some of the central institutions of the medieval
faith, how could they in turn wield the sword of exclusiveness against
Jews?

Third, to men of enlightenment, be they Jews or Christians, it is the
turning of one's heart and mind to God that counts, not the rituals, or
ceremonies, whereby devotion is expressed. In this light, there is need
for all of us to be converted to a deeper spirituality. The *mizvot* of the

heart are infinite in number and in degrees of outreach, as Bahya Ibn Pakuda reminds us. Hence, conversion, in Jewish hope, is conceived as an inner transformation, a keener grasp of truth, a deeper love, a more determined consecration to "deeds of loving kindness." The spiritual convert may continue to practice the rites of his ancestral faith, while the essence of the true faith lives within him. So the messianic future includes the hope for a universal conversion, in this spiritual sense, while diverse faiths and peoples will continue to cherish their own individual identities.

In this sense, a true dialogue is indeed a call for conversion, but it is neither one-sided nor concerned with externals. Along these lines, Mendelssohn replied to Lavater both directly and through his active correspondence with many friends. "The internal religion of the Jews contains no other precepts than those of the Religion of Nature." As to the external expressions of faith, they are inevitably entangled with the history of a particular group—hence, they cannot be purely rational. "But, this I know, that no external religion can be universal." [1]

Lavater shared the widespread prejudice among Christians that Jews practice some form of desecration of the image of Jesus and that they continually abuse his name. How surprised was he to encounter in Moses Mendelssohn "a beautiful person," wise and tolerant, who extolled Jesus as a great teacher and a moral personality. Mendelssohn had to disabuse Lavater and his confreres of the notions that Jews curse the name of Jesus or that they reject his ethical teachings:

"It is an ingrained prejudice of your coreligionists that the Jews, all of them, incessantly slander the religion of the Christians and its founder, and thereby a great many things are conveniently explained in dogmatics, and much that is both irreligious and unrational is thereby justified in ordinary life." [2]

As to the distinction that Jews make between the ethical teachings of Jesus and the dogmas concerning his divinity. Mendelssohn wrote:

I also know many a Jew, who, like me, go a step further, and basing themselves upon the statements of Christian testimonies (for, I repeat, we have no reliable Jewish ones) acknowledge the innocence and moral goodness of that founder's character, yet do so on the clear condition

(1) that he never meant to regard himself as equal with the Father,
(2) that he never proclaimed himself as a person of divinity,

(3) that he never presumptiously claimed the honor of worship,
(4) that he did not intend to subvert the religion of his fathers.[3]

The concept of the Religion of Nature suggests the influence of Rousseau, whose description of the Vicar of Savoy was then extremely popular. Rousseau's *profession de foi*, in his book *Emile*, describes true religion as a synthesis of feeling, conscience, and intelligence. "God has given us conscience to love the good, reason to know it, freedom to choose it." Rousseau's famous hymn to conscience anticipated the moral philosophy of Kant.

Conscience! Conscience! divine instinct, immortal and celestial guide of an ignorant and limited, but intelligent and free being; infallible judge of good and evil, that makes man like unto God: It is you who make the excellence of his nature and the morality of his actions; without you I feel nothing in me that lifts me above the beasts except the sad privilege of straying from error to error with the help of an understanding without rule and a reason without principle.

The manifold evils of society were man-made, not inevitable products of our natural endowment. "Man is born free, yet, he is everywhere in chains."

It is important to note that Rousseau, unlike Voltaire and other contemporary philosophers, excoriated the Christian authorities for their oppression of Jews.[4]

Mendelssohn's claim that the Religion of Nature was identical with the central teachings of Judaism was challenged in an anonymous pamphlet. "Does not the Torah of Moses ordain the punishment of death for any number of offenses against the prescribed rituals? Does Mendelssohn, then, consider himself to depart from the laws of Judaism, or does he view religion as an evolving phenomenon, constantly continued, altered and improved?"[5]

Actually, Mendelssohn had ample justification within the Jewish tradition for the notion of a Religion of Nature and for the distinction between "internal" and "external" religion. The notion of "spiritual converts," that is, Gentiles who accept the central principles of monotheistic faith and ethics, without adopting the Jewish "external" ritual, goes back to the pre-Christian period of Judaism. "Spiritual converts," participating in Synagogal worship, were numerous in the far-flung

Jewish Diaspora in the Roman Empire.[6] Maimonides maintained that the divine mandate to convert the pagans to "the true faith" is fulfilled when they accept "the seven Noachian laws." Furthermore, Maimonides distinguished between laws of "first intention," such as the injunction to love God and to practice compassion, and laws of "second intention," such as the regimen of sacrifices in the Holy Temple.[7] Laws of "second intention" were instituted in order to meet certain specific historical needs. Maimonides distinguished also between ideas that are true in themselves and "necessary ideas," that is, ideas that serve to bind the community together, providing a viable organism for the maintenance and dissemination of the true faith.[8]

To be sure, Maimonides maintained that pagans are obliged to accept these Noachian principles on the ground that they are contained in the revelation granted to Moses.

> Whoever accepts the seven *mizvot* and observes them conscientiously belongs in the category of the "pious among the nations of the world" and shares in *olam haba,* the world to come. This is true, however, only if he accepts them and observes them because the Lord commanded them in the Torah, informing us through Moses, our teacher, that all the descendants of Noah were so commanded previously. But if he observes them because of his own reasoning, he is not a *ger toshav.* And he is not counted among "the pious of the nations," and not among their sages.[9]

In another version, the last phrase reads "but among their sages."[10] Spinoza quoted this passage from Maimonides, attributing it to "the Jews" generally.[11]

Mendelssohn pointed out that Maimonides had no textual justification in the Talmud for his qualification. Therefore, Mendelssohn concluded, Maimonides's position was only a personal opinion, not an integral part of Jewish teaching.

Possibly, Maimonides was impelled to adopt his formally dogmatic position because he saw the entire Judeo-Christian-Moslem world of thought set against a pagan world that he knew only from literature. Christians as well as Moslems were, in his view, disseminators of the scriptural world view.[12] Without the impulse deriving from the Torah, we cannot decide whether the world is created or not. This basic doctrine "should be accepted without proof because of prophecy."[13] His reference to Christians as idolators[14] was purely legalistic, having to do with the difference between reverencing and worshiping icons. For the law in question to apply, it was sufficient if someone *might* overstep the subtle boundary line. Maimonides's deeper view is expressed in the famous Responsum concerning a would-be Christian convert, in which he asserts that "God looks to the Heart."

The fifteenth-century Jewish philosopher, Joseph Albo, developed the concept of a God-given faith still further, allowing that several true, divinely revealed faiths may coexist at any one time. While the historic forms of true religion are many and diverse, adapted to the varying cultural contexts of their adherents, its essential core is one and the same. It consists of faith in the One God. His revelation of the laws of morality, and His Providence.[15]

To be sure Joseph Albo did not agree that the medieval, Inquisition-ridden Christianity of his day was consonant with the principles of a true faith. For that matter, did not the philosophers of the Enlightenment similarly condemn the horrendous perversion of the teaching of Jesus by their contemporary narrow-minded minions of the Church? In the modern world of his time, Mendelssohn argued, both Judaism and Christianity needed to divest themselves of the ugly rags and tatters of superstition and return to the pristine purity of their God-given faiths. Indeed, Christianity and Judaism today may be compared to "two pyramids of which the apices are exactly alike, but from then downward they vary in a great many respects."[16] Each apex is founded on its own traditional pyramid, and the lower one descends from the intellectual elite to the masses and from reason to emotion, the more the pyramids diverge in pattern and structure.

As a son of the Enlightenment, Mendelssohn thought in terms of individuals rather than groups. As "thinking reeds," human beings are expected to make use of their rational faculties in order to seek and find salvation. God, Who is just, did not fail to endow every individual with the gifts of intelligence and conscience, sufficient to lead him to salvation. Religion means literally that which binds, the bond between man and God, and, in essence, that bond is the capacity to reason and to judge. So Mendelssohn was bitterly opposed to any suggestion for the preservation or the reconstitution of Jewish autonomy. He took strong exception to the recommendation of his own friend, Christian Dohm, who authored an epochal work calling for the improvement of the civil status of Jews, that the Jewish community be given the right to impose discipline within its own ranks and to expel recalcitrant members. As an advocate of the Jewish cause, Dohm argued that "they may be allowed to bind their members amongst themselves by a voluntary covenant, to have their disputes judged and decided by their own laws."[17]

Through the centuries, Jewish people had insisted on the right to judge their own members in any agreement that they made with the rulers of the land. Generally, they had been taxed as a unit, and the burden of taxes had then been distributed by a committee of lay and rabbinic leaders. Internal discipline in religious as in communal matters had been maintained by means of the *herem*.[18] Spinoza was the most famous of all who fell under the interdiction of the *herem* because of his heretical views.

To Mendelssohn, the very thought of renewing the *herem* was an abomination. Religion must not resort to coercion. "True divine religion arrogates no dominion over thought and opinion, it knows no other force than that of winning by argument."[19] Since a religious community does not possess coercive powers by nature, a voluntary covenant cannot create such rights, "any more than cultivation can create a flower, where there was no natural seed."[20] Civil and criminal law should be applied without any regard to the religion of the litigants.

It is in this eagerness to eliminate the vestiges of communal self-government that Mendelssohn definitely and defiantly broke with the organic tradition of Judaism. The medieval ghettoes preserved intact the historical traditions of Judaism. The Talmud and the Codes of Jewish law embrace the whole of life in the fine meshes of the selfsame law, making no distinction between ritual and civil ordinances. In the Yeshivot, the scholars argued from the same premises in cases of civil litigations, of family purity, of Nazarite abstention, and of the scapegoat sent into the wilderness on Yom Kippur. Rabbis were generally preoccupied with the problems of commercial law rather than with any other phase of the tradition, and it was considered an act of treachery for businessmen to bring their litigations to non-Jewish courts. Looking ahead to the new order of freedom, Mendelssohn argued that a unitary society cannot permit separate, self-segregating enclaves. On the altar of freedom, he was eager to sacrifice the entire edifice of Jewish civil and criminal law as well as every other remnant of autonomy.

In contrast, Maimonides had been acutely conscious of the organic nature of the Jewish community. To him the purpose of the *mizvot* was communal as well as personal—that is, designed to maintain the kind of community that is suitable for the emergence of saintly philosophers.[21] True, the philosopher pursues his own path to God; he distinguishes between the *mizvot* of primary significance and the true ideas, on the one hand, and the communal disciplines and inevitable popular beliefs, on the other hand; he meditates in solitude on the love of God, pursuing the *via negativa,* determining what is not God, and the *via eminentia,* contemplating the marks of His excellence in creation and in Torah. In the end, he attains a state of religious ecstasy, when Divine Providence envelops him like a protective cloud. But this ecstatic union is only a stage in the life of the saintly philosopher. He must go beyond this state and reinvolve himself in the mundane concerns of the community.[22]

To Maimonides, the nature and content of the Jewish community was fixed and immutable. The children of Abraham, Isaac, and Jacob pledged themselves at Sinai to accept the covenant. Individuals from among the Gentiles joined them in the course of time. Such individuals should be welcomed at all times with open arms, for while Israelites are children of Abraham, the righteous proselytes are "children of God." Saintly and philosophical individuals may also emerge in the non-Jewish world and attain the highest levels of ethical and religious perfection. But Maimonides did not doubt that there was but one divinely ordained community and that this community was destined to regain its own land, eliminate all idolatry from it, and then proceed to impose the "true religion," at least in its internal sense, on all men. Characteristically, the order of redemption, as Maimonides saw it, is for the Jewish people to regain its land first, rebuild the Holy Temple, and bring back the dispersed from among the nations. Only when these national goals have been fulfilled will the redeemed people of Israel proceed to redeem the rest of mankind. To be sure, this sequence of events was presented by Maimonides with two reservations—first, that no one really knows how the process of messianic redemption will unfold; second, that this process will not be a sudden, supernatural manifestation, but that it will take place within the context of the laws of nature as they have been fixed in the six days of creation. Thus Maimonides prepared the way for an evolutionary and naturalistic interpretation of the messianic hope.[23]

Mendelssohn built on the Maimonidean vision, but with a radical reordering of priorities—the free, universal society, based on the rights of the individual, may well emerge in the early stages of redemption. A new community of the "enlightened" will shake itself loose from the grip of ancient hatreds. The historic faiths will be purified from all that is unworthy of a Religion of Nature. Jews as individuals will share in building this universal society. Ultimately, the land of Israel will once again become the possession of the people of Israel. The messianic hope, then, will be fulfilled first in its universalist-ethical dimension. The beginning of redemption for Jews is "but simply a period when they will be more humanely treated in the lands in which they dwell and put on an equality with the rest of the inhabitants." Then, with the advance of international amity, "the Israelites will gradually retrieve their rank as a nation."[24]

Thus Mendelssohn anticipated the approach that was subsequently adopted by Jewish liberals and socialists: the establishment of the universal, free society must come first: the complete fulfillment of Israel's national hopes, if they are still tenable at that time, will follow as a matter of course, as a natural consequence of the age of perfection. And this universal society must be built by a coalition of enlightened, emancipated individuals who constitute in effect a new, all-embracing brotherhood.

Yet Mendelssohn, in contrast to later liberals and socialists, was a thoroughly observant Jew. Did he then depart from the tradition in his vision of redemption? Did the Torah impose "walls of iron" around the children of the Covenant, which prevent them from joining with others in building the great society?[25] To be sure, there were various ordinances calculated to impede the natural process of social intercourse between Jews and their neighbors. And there was the mental attitude of the chosen people, insofar as this attitude was constantly nurtured by the biblical imagery of "a nation that dwells alone, and is not counted among the peoples" (Numbers 23:9).

Mendelssohn countered the first challenge by the claim, which was attested to by his own achievements, that it is possible to be loyal to the Law in every respect and yet be part of the emergent society of the enlightened. Furthermore, he maintained, the forbidding ramparts of the Law are gradually lowered in practice, if not in theory. Such prohibitions as the use of Gentile wine, for instance, are now obsolete.[26] As to cultural differences, modern Jews progressively divest themselves of the peculiarities of speech, dress, and economic specialization. Whatever is incompatible with the dawning sense of universal brotherhood will gradually wither and fade away. These observances were historic accretions, by no means part of the essential structure of the Covenant, which was designed to promote the love of God and the love of man.

As to the second challenge, Mendelssohn argued that the notion of belonging to the chosen people implies neither arrogance nor exclusiveness, but simply the spirit of obedience to a divinely imposed body of laws. In his German writings, he addressed himself to a society that accepted the Holy Bible as the basis of its own ideological structure. But while Christians were aware of their own emergence from the Dark Ages and of standing on the threshold of a new era, they persisted in seeing the Jews of their own day as a strange, petrified relic of the ancient people of the Old Testament. Christians must realize that even as they are no longer identical with the apostolic community of Jerusalem, Jews are no longer identical with the ancient biblical community, save that they continue to be obligated by the same basic Torah-law. This law was revealed at Sinai to the community as a whole in a unique manner so dramatic that it cannot be revoked except by God, and by Him only, in a similar, dramatic, and absolute fashion. Every Jew adds to his consciousness of humanity the remembrance of the revealed Sinaitic legislation, to which he remains subject, as an individual, so long as that legislation has not been superseded.

Mendelssohn refuted the Christian claim that this law had been annulled by the birth of Christianity. He pointed out that even the Synoptic Gospels fail to sustain this claim. Jesus lived and preached as a Jew (Matthew 23:2, 3; 5:17; 7:24–27; Mark 1:44).[27] But, whether or not loyalty to the law runs counter to Christian dogmatics, it certainly is fully in accord with the universal Religion of Reason. For the Jew does not substitute the precepts of the law for the demands of reason, but he *adds* these precepts to the principles of a Religion of Reason. Furthermore, there is an organic relationship between the *mizvot* and the rational essence of religion. The practical precepts articulate the theory of faith, just as speaking and writing give expression to our thoughts. The entire body of Jewish observances is a form of writing through deeds, articulating and reinforcing the essential principles of monotheism. Thus the purpose of the *mizvot* is to make the monotheistic faith a living reality in the hearts and minds of the children of the Covenant. And there is nothing irrational in the observance of these external precepts, though they are *non-rational,* having been dictated by God to Moses. As to why God did not impose similar obligations on

Gentiles, Mendelssohn pointed out that Providence employs diverse ways in guiding the historical evolution of different nations. So long as He provided for all people what they needed for salvation, through the gifts of conscience and reason, we cannot complain about the plurality of cultural and ceremonial devices with which He supplemented His essential revelation. In the case of the Jewish people, this supplemental revelation was the revealed law. Christians cannot question that this revelation had taken place, since their own faith is ultimately founded on the Old Testament. If the foundation of a building is shaky, one does not run for safety to the upper stories.

Like Spinoza, Mendelssohn insisted that the revelation at Sinai consisted not of doctrines but of laws that were meant to establish the Jewish polity. But while Spinoza inferred from this circumstance that the laws became invalid when the Jewish polity was destroyed,[28] Mendelssohn distinguished between the communal and the personal precepts. The communal precepts were indeed no longer valid, since the biblical constitution in which religion and government were merged together was a unique, divinely instituted experiment. Its singularity is affirmed in Scripture. After the breakup of the biblical polity, religion and government were intended to go their separate ways—religion directing its efforts to man's inner nature and employing only instruments of persuasion, and government directing its attention to the external actions of people and employing methods of coercion. Mendelssohn concurred with Spinoza that a free society should separate religion from the state, but unlike Spinoza, he insisted that the personal precepts of the revealed law remained the special obligation of Jewish people. Thus the Jew is bidden to share in the building of a universal culture while remaining subject to a special body of divine legislation.

In view of his living in a Christian society, however, among people who are dedicated to a culture and a philosophy that are intimately associated with a religious heritage of their own, why cannot the Jew accept the practical rites of Christianity as a supplement to his philosophical faith? It is at this point that the impact of Mendelssohn's interpretation becomes clear. Practical precepts are indeed consonant with a Religion of Reason, but dogmatic injunctions, ordering the mind to accept as true this or that irrational belief, are utterly incongruent with a rational faith. The central rites of Christianity are inseparable from their roots in a body of dogmas, which must be accepted on faith. On the other hand, in the entire Torah, Mendelssohn pointed out, there is no commandment imposing any beliefs on the Israelites. The dignity of man consists in his freedom to seek truth and to distinguish between good and evil. Man cannot surrender his intelligence and his conscience without ceasing to be human. Man's freedom is "the image of God" within him. Even God does not intrude into the inner sanctuary of man's soul. According to the Talmud, "everything is in the power of heaven, save the fear of heaven" (Berochot 33b). How could He, Who is the Source of Wisdom and Goodness, restrict and frustrate the faculties of the human personality by making salvation dependent on quasi-magical formulae?[29]

It follows that although Judaism adds *non-rational* ceremonies to the Religion of Reason, these "external" *mizvot* are not indispensable for salvation. Christianity, or Christian theology, in all its orthodox forms is essentially *irrational*. It may still serve as a Religion of Reason for its own constituents, who, as they become philosophers, modify its dogmas privately in order to preserve its essential, ethical-spiritual impetus. But official Christianity, glorying in its paradoxes, cannot serve in the same capacity, openly and universally—that is, in the Germany of Mendelssohn's day—so long as it remains unreconstructed, weighted down by dogmas that the free mind of man utterly repudiates. To be sure, man's reason points to its own limitations. Hence, "the fear of God is the beginning of wisdom" (Ps. 3; 10). But although man acknowledges a transrational mystery, he cannot succumb to irrationalism without surrendering his freedom, his essential, human, and divine dignity.

Mendelssohn's assertion that Judaism does not require the acceptance of beliefs was repeated throughout the nineteenth century by detractors as well as by defenders of the Jewish faith. The defenders pointed to Judaism's essential rationality, while the detractors asserted that Judaism was not a religion at all, since it did not aim to achieve a mystical communion between God and Man, requiring only the rote performance of certain deeds.

We need to take account of the special context in which Mendelssohn's argument was made. First, the Religion of Nature, to Mendelssohn, was a warm, full-blooded theism, in which the sentiments of the Psalmists acquired fresh and vibrant meaning—it is significant that Mendelssohn completed a sensitive translation of the Book of Psalms. Reason, to him, included that tissue of rational and moral arguments that leads to a firm assurance of the Divine Presence, of man's immortality, of the role of Providence and the freedom of will. Spinoza's pantheism, which denies human freedom, was to him an aberration. And the deism of the French Voltairians was a cynical abomination. He admired Rousseau's description of the faith of the Vicar of Savoyard. In his innocent age, people could hardly conceive of the enormities that were perpetrated a decade or so after his death in the name of the Goddess of Reason. Thus Mendelssohn included an existential "fear of God" and an impassioned love of Him within the Religion of Nature that he deemed to be purely rational. His religion included faith in the sense of trust in God's faithfulness, a trust that was common to both Judaism and Christianity. What he rejected was the blind, dogmatic beliefs that were blatantly irrational.[30]

In his recent *Jewish Philosophy in Modern Times,* Nathan Rothenstreich contends that "by subsuming religion under law and ethics Mendelssohn reduced Judaism to dimensions that satisfy the moral mind but not the religious temper."[31] But as we have noted, Jewish law, to Mendelssohn, was God-given—hence, charged with a special aura. Also, he was doubtless familiar with Leibnitz's distinction between the three stages of law—preventive of wrongdoing, affirming positive obligations for the common good, and instilling piety. Mendelssohn regarded Jewish law, in its particularistic areas, as falling within the second and third stages. And as to "the religious temper," no one can read the *Morgenstuden* without feeling the resonance of Mendelssohn's vibrant piety.

Second, Mendelssohn did not reject belief in those theses that are inferred by human reason. He was after all a disciple of Maimonides, who formulated the Thirteen Principles of Faith, beginning each one with the phrase "I believe with perfect faith." His disciples in the next generation did not hesitate to include these principles in their manuals and catechisms. For all but one of the Thirteen Principles of Faith are inferences of reason, affirming the existence of God and His Providence and the truth of the Sinaitic revelation, which was attested by the collective experience of the Jewish people. The only irrational Principle of Faith is the one affirming the resurrection of the dead, which many Maimonidean disciples interpreted in the sense of immortality of the soul.[32]

Third, every historical faith implies belief in a sacred tradition of interpretation, and Judaism was no exception. The character and extent of the authoritative tradition, however, might be disputed. In the first century, debate centered on the validity of the Pharisaic Oral Law; the authority of the Talmud was questioned by the Karaites, a sect founded at the beginning of the eighth century. To Maimonides, the authoritative chain of tradition continued down to the compilation of the Babylonian Talmud by Rabina and Rav Ashi (ca. A.D. 500). He rejected, therefore, the claims of the Babylonian Geonim (589–1038 c.e.) to speak as heads of "the great Sanhedrin and the small one." Among the authoritative Geonim between the Talmud and his own day he mentions those of Spain and France, along with those of Babylonia.[33]

The prevailing belief in the Yeshivot of Central Europe affirmed the continuity of the Holy Spirit down to the authors of the *Shulhan Arukh,* in the sixteenth century. The Kabbalists added a whole series of fresh revelations, including those of Rabbi Simon bar Yohai of the second century, the presumed author of the Zohar, and Rabbi Isaac Luria, of the sixteenth century, whose disciples instituted a number of new rites in the practice of the faith.[34] In the lifetime of Moses Mendelssohn, there raged a bitter debate between the Hasidim and the Mithnagdim of Poland and Lithuania, concerning the range and authority of the Holy Spirit in their day. Both sides accepted the authority of the revelations accorded to Rabbi Isaac Luria.[35]

We can hardly doubt that Mendelssohn wanted to introduce some basic reforms in Jewish life in order to further the process of integration, and that he consciously aimed to minimize the area of rabbinic authority. Living in a Protestant country, he found it natural to appeal to the authority of Scripture rather than to that of a living tradition. In regard to biblical exegesis, he found ample justification in Jewish commentaries for a non-literal, non-fundamentalist approach. In this area, as in so many others, Maimonides had shown the way by laying down the rule "The gates of interpretation are not closed to us" ("Guide" II, 25).

In sum Mendelssohn was called on to justify his Jewish loyalties by believing Christians and by the philosophers in his circle. He accepted the philosophers as brothers in spirit, asserting that the principles of modern theism coincided with the essential teachings of Judaism. As against the Christian challenge, he responded with the weapons of philosophy—the rejection of any theory of exclusive salvation as unworthy of a just God, and the repudiation of any shackles on the human mind in the shape of irrational dogmas, rejecting the charge of deicide directed against the Jews as an utter absurdity, and opposing the involvement of the external trappings of religion in the realm of political affairs as a grave fallacy. In the process of enlarging the scope of philosophy within Jewish life and in the policy of governments, Mendelssohn became the champion of a new humanism. He could uphold the Jewish side of the debate because of his achievements as a philosopher and as a humanist. In turn, the spirit of humanism could not but lead to new esthetic and ethical norms for the modification and transformation of Jewish life in the emerging, free society.

Two consequences of Mendelssohn's position are particularly worth noting. First, the repudiation of the corporate status of the Jewish community. In the debates on Jewish emancipation, following the French Revolution, the prevailing position of both Jews and Gentiles called for the enfranchisement of Jews as individuals, not as a closed corporation or caste. Jewish spokesmen willingly surrendered any claims for communal autonomy and submitted in all but purely religious matters to the civil authorities of the state. In the Assembly of Notables and in the Paris Sanhedrin, the Jewish representatives affirmed their eagerness to conclude a covenant with Gentiles, joining in the "fraternity" of the emerging nations of Europe. For generations, and in spite of recurring setbacks. Jews considered modern humanism as the common ground on which they and the "enlightened" Gentiles could build together.[36]

The other historic consequence of the Mendelssohnian position was to impoverish the rich complex of Jewish loyalties and to transform it into a commitment to intellectual liberalism. The closest disciple of Mendelssohn. David Friedländer (1750–1834), wrote a letter to Pastor Teller, a leading Protestant clergyman in Berlin, offering to bring a number of Jewish families into his church providing they would not be required to accept the Christian dogmas. Friedländer acknowledged that the severe restrictions to which Jews were then subject in Prussia accounted in part for this decision to join the prevailing faith. But, then, no financial or social blandishments have in the past induced Jewish people to give up their faith. To Friedländer, however, the sole obstacle to a Jewish-Christian fusion was the irritational dogmatism of the Church. And these dogmas could be allegorized, in theory at least. As to the obligations of Jewish law, many laymen had begun to disregard them.

In fact, it was the widespread violation of Jewish dietary and Sabbath regulations that induced the mid-nineteenth-century Reform leaders to base Jewish loyalty on the truth and relevance of the central ideas of Judaism rather than on the particular precepts of Jewish law. To be sure, they were still operating, in the synagogues at least, with the traditional pattern of symbols and rituals, but they could no longer assume that the prescriptions of rabbinic law governing personal life were indeed observed by their laymen. In contrast to the age of Mendelssohn, they had to contend against philosophers and historians, as well as believing Christians, in order to make room for the vital ideas of Judaism.

In German Jewry, it was the emergence of the nineteenth-century Conservative movement of Zechariah Frankel and Heinrich Graetz that led to a renewed appreciation of Jewish law as the historic embodiment of the Jewish spirit. In the middle of the nineteenth century the ideas of Savigny and other legal historians had prepared the way for an understanding of legal institutions as the distinctive expressions of a nation's soul, marking the evolution of its historic character.

In nineteenth-century France, Joseph Salvador (1796–1873) called attention to the social idealism that was embodied in the legislation of the Torah. If the liberals in Europe had to contend frequently against the Church in order to extend the horizons of liberty, equality, and fraternity, these ideals formed the living nucleus of Pentateuchal legislation. In Salvador's view, the mission of Judaism consisted not in the "purity" of its monotheistic ideals, but in the historic impetus of its ethical-social laws. The Jewish faith poses a continuing challenge to all Christian denominations, reminding them of the common task in every generation to hasten the establishment of a just and all-embracing society here on earth.

Mendelssohn was sustained in his intellectual position by the German Enlightenment *(Aufklärung),* which was basically religious and reverent toward the heritage of the past. His *Phaedo,* a demonstration of the immortality of the soul, was received with acclaim by the German public, which was well disposed to a Platonic line of reasoning. His lifelong friend, Gotthold Ephraim Lessing, was a brave champion of rationality in religion, but unlike Voltaire, he was not iconoclast, On the contrary, he cautioned his followers to treat the old faith with humility and reverence.

Take care, more capable individual, when you paw the ground and are aglow on reaching the last page of the first primer (the Jewish-Christian revelation!). Take care not to let your weaker school-fellows feel what you are sensing or already beginning to see. Until these weaker school-fellows have caught up with you, turn back the pages of this primer again, and find out whether what you take to be the result of mere expressions of method, makeshifts of the teaching system, is not perhaps something more.[37]

This reverence for tradition characterized Mendelssohn as well. He never forgot the third element in Micah's summation of the essence of piety, "to walk humbly with the Lord." Thus he wrote: ". . . our reasonings can never free us from the strict obedience we owe to the law."[38]

Lessing agreed with Mendelssohn that "natural religion" is the substance and "revealed religion" cannot add more than methods, instruments, or mnemonic devices to the basic core of the Religion of Nature: "The best positive or revealed religion is the one containing the fewest conventional additions to natural religion and least limits the good effects of natural religion."[39]

Lessing was more inclined than Mendelssohn to believe in the inevitable development of mankind toward a higher, universal faith. But the two friends were equally dedicated to the belief that the reasoning faculty of the human mind is itself the supreme expression of the Divine Will. Therefore, God cannot possibly demand dogmatic faith in a non-rational proposition, much less an irrational one. It is the very endeavor to seek truth that is divine. These famous words of Lessing's reflect Mendelssohn's basic approach as well:

> If God were holding all the truth that exists in his right hand and in his left just the one ever-active urge to find the truth, even if attached to it were the condition that I should always and forever be going astray, and said to me, "Choose!" I should humbly fall upon his left hand and say, "Father, give! Pure truth is surely only for Thee alone."[40]

Mendelssohn was profoundly disturbed and angered by the charge of F. H. Jacobi that Lessing was really a Spinozist. Jacobi himself had come to champion the position that reason was a weak reed, which was incapable of sustaining a theistic and ethical world view. Religion and morality must be based on faith. Those who lack faith are bound to drift toward the abyss of materialism or pantheistic naturalism. Jacobi challenged Mendelssohn directly. And Mendelssohn felt that Jacobi's message was only a sophisticated way of restating Lavater's original challenge. Blind faith is certain to lead men back to medievalism. If faith, not reason, be indeed the one foundation of both ethics and religion, how can we avoid the horrors of religious fanaticism?

Several decades after the death of Mendelssohn, even non-orthodox Jewish thinkers such as S. L. Steinheim could embrace the Halevian position and argue in behalf of revelation as a non-rational source of faith and morals. But Mendelssohn was extremely wary of "enthusiasm" and fanaticism. In his *Morgenstunden* and in his posthumous missive to the friends of Lessing, he maintained first that Spinozism could be interpreted in a theistic sense. He wrote of a "purified Spinozism." Did not Spinoza himself lay down core principles of faith, which express the essence of an enlightened faith? Spinoza's rejection of Judaism was based on non-philosophic grounds.[41] Secondly, Mendelssohn argued that pure reason needs to be "oriented" by moral feeling if it is to serve as the foundation of a theistic faith. He called for the aid of *sensum communis,* or common sense. Perhaps Mendelssohn had in mind the Maimonidean tradition in the "Guide"—that training in moral principles and in the life of piety were prerequisites to the use of reason in the realm of pure speculation. Perhaps he recalled Maimonides's principle in the opening of his "Code"—that the love of God is one with the quest for the understanding of God. In any case, he insisted on fidelity to "pure, authentic reason." And the fervor of his insistence was due in no small measure to his intuitive conviction that an upsurge of romanticism would pose a deadly challenge to the Jewish people in particular, and to humanist values in general.[42]

In contrast to Lessing and the liberals, the Christian traditionalists maintained that the Jews were not ready for emancipation. Their corporate character prevented Jews from becoming integrated into the emergent states of Europe. In the Christian view, Judaism is an ethnic community, "of the seed of Abraham," in which sovereignty belongs to an earthly Messiah, or to a messianic pretender, since the "true Messiah of Israel" had already come. The Jews of their day were seen by the Christian traditionalists as petrified fossils of the Zealots and the Pharisees in the New Testament who contended against Jesus and his apostles. It was difficult enough for them to accept the changes occurring in their own faith communities, owing to the irresistible pressures of the modern mentality. All the more difficult was it for them to recognize the surge of vitality in the Jewish community, which was gradually transforming the ancient and medieval concepts of Jewish identity and messianic redemption.

On the threshold of emancipation, the ardor of Jewish messianism was unfocused and disoriented. It was poised and ready to move into several different channels. It could turn toward a humanistic goal, or toward the establishment of a Jewish state. It could be emptied of vital content. In isolated enclaves of tight Orthodoxy, it continued to retain its supernaturalistic and mystical dimensions, along with the feeling of an imminent Eschaton, expected tomorrow if not sooner. Actually each of these interpretations of messianism was embraced by diverse segments of the Jewish community in the modern world.

Insofar as the Christian image of the Jew is concerned, the old messianic hope loomed as a forbidding barrier to Jewish integration. This point was raised by the German historian, Michaelis, in his critique of Dohm's book, and by many others in Germany and France. Mendelssohn's reply was as follows:

> The hope to return to the land of Israel is irrelevant to the life of Jews as citizens of their respective countries. Human nature impels one to love the land in which he lives in freedom, and if his religious doctrines interpose any obstacles, he assigns to them a place in his worship and liturgy, without according them any real significance in his daily life.[43]

In other words, the messianic hope is likely to become vestigial, just as the dogma of the Second Advent became peripheral and inconsequential in the life of the vast majority of Christians. A similar reply was given by Comte de Mirabeau, who spent some time with Mendelssohn in Berlin.[44] It is interesting to observe that Mendelssohn, in keeping with his philosophical rationalism, followed the lead of Maimonides in stripping the messianic hope of all supernaturalism and stating it in a nationalistic version:

> I believe that the children of Abraham, Isaac, and Jacob will not always live outside the borders of their land and scattered among the nations, but that the Lord will raise for them in the time known to Him alone a prince Messiah from the House of David who will make them a free people as in ancient times and will reign over them in the land of their fathers.[45]

Mendelssohn's willingness to allow the supernatural aspects of the messianic hope to become a desiccated formula, or a metaphor for the blend of humanistic and nationalistic aspirations, was not shared by the Orthodox leaders of his day or of future generations. The Hasidic

movement, which exploded with elemental force in the southern provinces of Poland during his lifetime, was profoundly messianic in character. The Mithnagdim (opponents), led by the Gaon Elijah of Vilna,
were similarly persuaded that "the footsteps of the Messiah" had already
been heard. In the following generation, when many Jews acclaimed
the French Revolution and Napoleon as messianic deliverers, the Hasidic Zaddik of Lublin regarded Napoleon as a kind of anti-messiah, the
chief figure in the apocalyptic wars of God and Magog.[46]

The Talmud asserts "there is no session in the house of study without
some innovation." Similarly, we may assert that no genuine dialogue
occurs without some modification of the positions of the debaters.
Mendelssohn contested Maimonides's interpretation that the category
of "saints among the nations" requires an acceptance of the truth of
Mosaic revelation. While he respected the erudition and authority
of Rabbi Jacob Emden, he took issue with the latter's endorsement
of Maimonides's restriction. As Altmann put it: "The ideal Judaism to
which Mendelssohn aspired possessed a kind of Platonic reality for
him."[47] He was prepared to admit that the Talmud contained some ugly
distortions of the Torah.

Mendelssohn asserted, in his response to Lavater, that Judaism is not
interested in any missionary activity, that it is even inhibited by its laws
from disseminating its teaching among the nations. We can allow for
the fact that Mendelssohn was driven to this untrue position by the
persistent challenge of Christian missionary efforts. Nevertheless, his
argument is unhistorical and contrary to the traditional hope. The
Reform leaders, in the middle of the nineteenth century, rejected
Mendelssohn's thesis and proclaimed it to be the Jewish "mission" to
convert all men to the doctrines of "ethical monotheism." Mendelssohn's assertion that only the laws of Judaism were revealed, and that
these laws were intended for Jews only, did not elevate the value and
sanctity of the ritual *mizvot,* since a parochial revelation could not be of
the same rank as a universal one. Also the act of revelation at Sinai was
inevitably interpreted in the nineteenth century as a continuing process
of inspired legislation. It was therefore historicized and relativized.
This devaluation of the ritual as mere ceremonialism is inevitable in a
philosophical version of Judaism. It implies also a relativization of the
actual practice of the Jewish faith. It cannot be allowed the claim
of being exclusively true, or even uniquely significant. Mendelssohn
anticipated this development when he wrote, "The Jewish faith is best

for us, but it is not the best absolutely. Which is the best form of worship for other nations? Who knows? Perhaps the Lord gave them guidance through their understanding or by means of prophets."[48]

Mendelssohn, and several of his Christian friends, looked forward to a basic revision of Christian doctrine, whereby its exclusivistic ardor would be curbed and its irrationalism modified. It seemed to him that the Unitarians and some English Deists represented the "wave of the future." Of the Christian Unitarians, he wrote in a letter to Bonnet, "I must confess to you honestly that this religious party seems to me to belong more to Judaism than to the really dominant Christian faith." He could look forward to a closer approach of Judaism and Christianity in the future, perhaps even a convergence.[49]

NATIONALISTIC DISSENT

The response of Mendelssohn to the challenges of Christianity, philosophy, and the emergent nation-states of Europe was itself challenged not only by the builders of Reform Judaism and the ideologists of political Zionism, but also by the pre-Zionist nationalists, to whom Perez Smolenskin (1840–85) belonged. Smolenskin spoke for the Maskilim ("enlightened") of the Pale of Settlement in Russia, who lived in massive enclaves, spoke Yiddish, and wrote in Hebrew. He argued in behalf of radical modifications of the traditional way of life, especially the liturgy of the Synagogue and the curriculum of the elementary schools. He sought to break down the inner walls of the ghetto and to foster effective communication between the Jewish people and their neighbors. Yet his opposition to Mendelssohn was based on the latter's identification of the Jewish heritage as basically religious. Smolenskin considered Judaism to be the product of "the spirit of the nation." The Jewish people were a "people of the spirit" *(am horuah),* and it was their mission to demonstrate the validity and viability of national communities that are held together solely by cultural and spiritual bonds. Like the romantic nationalists of the nineteenth century, he considered religion to be a most important component of Jewish culture, but only a component. The overriding bond is that of national culture, and a viable culture requires a large measure of self-government or national autonomy. Hence the chief target of Smolenskin's critique of Mendelssohn was the latter's willingness to surrender the corporate status of limited self-government that Dohm was willing to grant to Jewish citizens.[50]

Indeed, in France and Holland, following the French Revolution, the Jewish liberals pressed for complete individual emancipation, while the Orthodox pleaded for the limited freedom of a recognized corporate status. Similarly, the Gentile liberals echoed the sentiments of the French politician, Clermont-Tonnerre: "To the Jews as individuals, everything; to the Jews as a nation, nothing." On the other hand, the reactionaries and antisemites resisted the plea for total emancipation and pressed for the continuation of the medieval corporate status of Jewry, with possibly a few economic concessions.[51]

Smolenskin's program was elaborated and deepened by the great Jewish historian Simon Dubnow (1860–1941). In theory, the concept of cultural nationalism was recognized in the Treaty of Versailles, which included the recognition of ethnic minority rights in the constitutions of the states of central Europe. In practice, these guarantees were largely disregarded. But even in theory, it is doubtful that modern Jews prefer to be self-governing in civil matters when they are offered equality and the chance to share the obligations and privileges of an open society. As they broke out of the medieval shell and began to participate more fully in the cultural life of the western world, they began to turn away from the ideal of communal self-government, especially if it included an element of cultural, religious, or philanthropic coercion. The so-called Jewish values—reverence for learning, patterns of worship, and works of charity—belong to the realm of freedom, in which individuals choose to participate in one or another activity, as they please and on their own terms.

From the experience of Jewish communities in the lands of freedom, we may conclude that Mendelssohn was more right than his critics—in spite of the pressures of central bureaucracies and nationalist ideologists, Jewish people do prefer individual freedom to a corporate, self-governing status. However, even in lands of freedom the sentiment for collective self-government and self-discipline attains at times a fairly high pitch. In response to external challenges, such as the plight of a segment of world Jewry or the danger to the survival of Israel, Jewish philanthropic agencies take on temporarily the appearance of governing bodies—but not for long. As soon as the danger passes, they revert to their voluntaristic character.

EXISTENTIALIST DISSENT

In our own day, Arthur A. Cohen articulated the resentment of an existentialist against the rationalistic position of Mendelssohn. Cohen sees Jewish history as the intersection between two curves—the supernatural and the natural. We sin against the God of history, he maintains, when we define the status of Jewry in terms of general European culture. The Jew is unique in a metaphysical sense, not merely in the sense that all historical communities are unique. His destiny must be understood in the light of messianism, as an immediate concern, a waiting and an acting, as if our age were poised on the razor's edge between the "fallen" world and "the Kingdom of God." The attitude of Cohen, irrational though it be, is actually a direct continuation of the pre-modern conviction of both Jews and Christians.[52] But what the ancients and the medievalists accepted in simple faith, Cohen affirms as "an existential dogma" (p. 5). It is "existential" because "without it there is nothing I consider *ultimately* relevant or meaningful to believe." And it is a "dogma" in the sense of an "evocation of meaning."

"Without the command to sustain one's supernatural vocation (that is, the belief that God has called the Jew to Himself) to call oneself a Jew is but a half-truth—a mere designation without meaning."

Cohen reflects an intellectual posture that is not uncommon in our distraught generation, shocked as we have been by the incredible agony of the holocaust on the one hand, and the exaltation of the rise of Israel on the other hand. The irrevocability of the Covenant has been established, as a historical fact—Jews were gassed by the modern Satan, whether or not they accepted their role as children of the God of Israel. The pre-moderns believed in God, Torah, and the special destiny of Israel, in this order of logical primacy. Some of the post-moderns believe in the mystery of Israel's destiny primarily, with commitment to Torah and faith in God as vague and tenuous implications. In Cohen's view, Mendelssohn, standing at the gate of the modern world begging for entrance, is the symbol of the modern Jew's fatal mistake. Thus he writes:

The modern Jew who succeeded the age of Mendelssohn was a European according to nature and history, and a Jew according to God. Henceforward one's culture was that of one's nation and language, and one's faith was directed toward a God no longer covenanted to a specific people. It is no surprise that the earliest reformers—Israel Jacobson, Jacob Herz Berr, Abraham Geiger, and Samuel Holdheim—should have rejected a personal messiah, denied the centrality of the Land of Israel, abandoned the Hebrew language, and transformed the historical mono-theism of tradition into ethical monotheism. The messianism of the classic Jew disappeared and the new European messianism—culture, emancipation and equality—were substituted. Mendelssohn made credi-ble to Europe the existence of a rational Judaism and the possibility of the de-Judaized Jew.[53]

As we have pointed out, Mendelssohn did not give up the messianic dream, but he assumed that the universal aspects of "the Kingdom of God" might well be realized prior to the fulfillment of Jewish ethnocen-tric ambitions. The traditional spectrum of the messianic vision in-cluded both national and all-human goals, as well as a truly super-human, transcendent radiance.

Mendelssohn was attacked in his lifetime by Sonnenfels (1732–1817), a Jewish convert to Roman Catholicism, a "de-Judaized Jew." In fact, Altmann concludes that "Mendelssohn wrote his *Jerusalem* in the mis-taken belief that he was replying to Sonnenfels."[54] Sonnenfels argued that Mendelssohn had virtually given up the Jewish faith when he rejected all kinds of religious compulsion. "If it be possible, without detriment to unalloyed Judaism, to abolish churchly privileges (i.e., the right of excommunication), which is based upon positive Mosaic laws, why should it be impossible to cancel, for the nation's benefit, mere rabbinic measures of late vintage, which create such detrimental barriers between Jews and Christians? One more step and you have become one of us."[55]

Mendelssohn was in favor of making many changes in Jewish obser-vance. He was optimistic on this score, just as he was generally confident that sound reason will triumph everywhere. But he was not willing to allow the Jewish individual to be subject to the coercion of the rabbis. Spinoza had written that one may not surrender his inner freedom without violating his humanity. Mendelssohn agreed. Generally, he cautioned his followers to be ever community minded. It is one thing, however, to respect prevailing opinion and to cooperate freely with the members of one's community; it is quite another to submit one's mind to the dictates of others. Judaism respects the freedom of the mind; hence, in Mendelssohn's view, the Torah never commands "Thou shalt believe." Judaism is "revealed legislation," but the laws are intended to safeguard freedom, not to crush it.

H. J. Schoeps, a scholar and an existentialist, maintains that Mendelssohn cut out "the heart of Judaism; *the living God,* who without consideration for reason and 'ability to gain agreement' (which *Morgenstunden* VII defines as the highest form of suitability), has acted in the history of this nation."[56] In other words, the core of Jewish consciousness is the awareness of God's direct action in Jewish history.

There is no doubt that Mendelssohn was a man of deep piety, a *homo religiosus,* for whom God was a powerful, living presence. If he avoided the historical argument, such as "He who took you out of the land of Egypt" (Genesis 32:4), it is precisely because historical events are not self-explanatory. Theology does not spring full-grown from the mouths of canons, or of mass graves. The opponents of Moses who interpreted the Exodus by crediting its wonders to the Golden Calf Philosophy must provide the standpoint and the standards for the interpretation of history, not vice versa. Mendelssohn had to contend every day against the presumption of Christians who infer the depravity of the Jews and the falsehood of their faith from the circumstance of their dispersion among the nations.

A TWENTIETH-CENTURY DISPUTATION

It was easy enough for narrow-minded Christians in Mendelssohn's day to beat the Jew with one hand, and with the other point to the moral "Behold, the witnesses of God." If today, following the holocaust and the rise of Israel, the "mystique" of Jewish history has been revived, it is instructive to note how this line of reasoning looked during World War I, when two most gifted friends took up the Jewish-Christian Argument in a famous correspondence.

The debate between the young Franz Rosenzweig and Eugen Rosenstock-Huessy may be studied as a counterpoint to the dialogues in which Mendelssohn was engaged. It was highly praised as most revealing. H. J. Schoeps extols it with the greatest enthusiasm: "This dialogistic correspondence may be put forward as the purest form of Judeo-Christian dialogue ever attained, perhaps even for ages to come."[57]

The debate took place in 1916, when both men served in the German army. Rosenstock-Huessy had been converted to Christianity at the age of sixteen. Rosenzweig had also contemplated conversion, but he determined to make this crucial decision as a Jew, not a pagan. Hence, his search for the full significance of being a Jew within the stream of European history. Both had arrived at the need of recognizing the transcendent in personal life and in history. Both had come to reject the liberal version of religion, be it Jewish or Christian. Leo Baeck's "The Essence of Judaism" was as unacceptable to them as Adolf Harnack's "The Essence of Christianity." Both had moved the Jewish-Christian dialogue from the rational sphere to the domain of the transrational, the course of revelation in history. As Rosenstock-Huessy phrased it, fifty years later:

> Franz and Eugen came to agree on the futility of the shilly-shallying academic shibboleths of their day—objectivity, humanism, and the so-called enlightenment. They agreed that real people can be Jews or Christians, but they may not play the roles of "Benjamin Franklin" or "Thomas Paine," at least not for long, since there can be no common sense—certainly no good sense shared in common—among men who are content to be ciphers, dealing in generalities and platitudes.[58]

The confrontation, a century and a half after the Mendelssohn-Lavater exchange, was based precisely on the rejection of the Religion of Nature of the Enlightenment. The young debaters explored an existential approach, based on personal experiences and on the mysterious course of history. Rosenstock-Huessy wrote of "speech-thinking" and the "I-Thou" event long before Buber and Rosenzweig did. As he saw it, God takes the initiative. "The soul must be called *Thou* before she can ever reply *I*, before she can ever speak of *us* and finally *it*. Through the four figures *Thou, I, We, It*, the Word walks through us. The Word must call our name first."[59]

From this vantage point, it is indeed amazing to note how the medieval Christian's stereotyped images of the Jew were insinuated into Rosenstock-Huessy's dialectic: (1) the Jews "always crucify again the one who came to make the word true"; (2) "With all the power of their being they set themselves against their own promises"; (3) "the image of Lucifer"; (4) Israel's "naive way of thinking that one has won inalienable rights in perpetuity against God"; (5) "you (Jews) have no aptitude for theology, for the search for truth, any more than for beauty"; (6) the Jew strives too hard just to live; (7) the "Jew dies for no country and no cause"; (8) the reliance of the individual Jew is "on the number of his children." To sum up, the Jew "is a paragraph of the Law. *C'est tout.*"[60]

These stereotypes come naturally to those who view the Jew in history from the Christian viewpoint. Rosenzweig, at that time groping for a way back to Judaism, saw virtually the same picture:

This practical way, in which the theological idea of the stubbornness of Jews works itself out, is *hatred of the Jews.* You know as well as I do that all its realistic arguments are only fashionable cloaks to hide the single true metaphysical ground: that we will not make common cause with the world-conquering fiction of Christian dogma . . . and putting it in a popular way that we have crucified Christ, and believe me, would do it again every time.[61]

Not content with providing a metaphysical root for antisemitism, the young Rosenzweig, with the boundless fervor of a neophyte, maintained that the "metaphysical basis" of the Jewish attitude to Christians consists of three articles: "(1) that we have the truth, (2) that we are at the goal and (3) that any and every Jew feels in the depths of his soul that the Christian relation to God, and so in a sense, their religion, is particularly and extremely pitiful, poverty-stricken, and ceremonious."[62]

With all this mutual contempt, "metaphysically grounded," Rosenzweig went on to say, the Jew still feels that his own fulfillment lies in goading the Christians to complete their task. The Jew bursts like a rude intruder into Christian assemblies, crying out "the *Eschaton* is not yet here." He works "as a ferment on Christianity and through it on the world."[63] The Jew is not intimidated by the price he must pay in isolation and suffering. Rosenzweig even echoed the Nazi stereotype of the Jew as a parasite. "For you may curse, you may swear, you may scratch yourself as much as you like, you won't get rid of us, we are the louse in your fur. We are the internal foe; don't mix us up with the external one!"

In his later writings, Franz Rosenzweig's philosophy of Judaism was ripened and mellowed. He must not be judged by the above quotations from his years of agonized searching. But the debate as it stands is a historic record of the shape the Jewish-Christian argument assumes when it departs from the common ground of reason and religious humanism. The alternative to the Mendelssohnian approach consists in a preference for unreason and for the seductive half-truths that appeal to a group's "pooled pride." It is formulated through the positioning of private "mysteries" against private "mysteries," barriers of contempt against towers of scorn, providing a metaphysical blanket of justification for ancient lies, and multiplying hatred in the world.

The young Rosenzweig's reference to Jewish contempt for Christianity was based in part on the literature of the Romantic rebellion against the Jewish emancipation at the beginning of the twentieth century. It certainly reflects neither the standard Orthodox view nor that of the modernists. Mendelssohn championed, all his life, not only tolerance of other faiths but also a deep appreciation of the wisdom of Providence in providing diverse historical embodiments of the same Religion of Nature. This is also the import of Lessing's drama *Nathan the Wise,* in which Nathan is modeled on Mendelssohn.

In turn, Mendelssohn derived his basic approach to the Jewish-Christian Dialogue from the elitist philosophy of Maimonides, in whose famous parable the saintly philosophers in all historical monotheistic communities come closer to "the throne of the king" than the naive Talmudists, who simply follow the law.[64] The philosopher, however, must not detach himself from his historic community and must supplement his solitary meditations by active concern for the problems of the community.[65]

Still, he knows that within each of the monotheistic communities the differences among individuals are far greater than those among the several historic forms of monotheism.

Rosenzweig was probably familiar with the rejection of the Mendelssohnian approach by the Jewish thinkers of the Reform period. In his later years, Abraham Geiger (1810–1874) had become convinced that Christianity, Protestant as well as Catholic, was inevitably reactionary.[66] Judaism, in his own interpretation of its dynamic essence, was allied with the unfolding spirit of the age, while Christianity was incurably antirationalist in philosophy, antiliberal in politics, and antiprogressive in social legislation. Salvador, living in France, had arrived at a similar conclusion. His book, *Paris, Rome, Jerusalem,* takes Paris to be the city of the French Revolution, announcing the credo of modern man. Catholic Rome symbolizes the counterrevolution, assigning the ideals "liberty, equality, and fraternity" to an ethereal, heavenly realm and thereby removing them effectively from the earthly domain of social and political struggle. Jerusalem represents the ideal synthesis of a this-worldly faith and the humanist vision of a free, utopian society.

Philosophically, Rosenzweig had become an existentialist rebel against the shallowness of rationalism. Eager to discover the roots of his own faith, he began to devour Judeo-German philosophical literature. Among the Romantics he found echoes of a supreme, impassioned pride. From the liberals, he absorbed resentment against the reactionary social policies of the Church.

Rosenzweig lived at a time when the impassioned chauvinism of the Teutons rejected any Jewish contribution to German literature and philosophy as being essentially "un-Germanic." It is enough to read the poignant autobiography of Jakob Wassermann (1873–1934) to recognize the depth of despair that tormented those Jewish intellectuals who shone as the brightest stars in the cultural sky of Germany.

> It is in vain to keep faith with them, be it as cofighters or as citizens. They say—he (the Jew) is a Proteus, he can do everything.
>
> It is in vain to help them knock off the chains of slavery from their bodies. They say—he will surely make profit out of the deal.
>
> It is in vain to counter any poison; they brew it afresh.
>
> It is vain to live for them and to die for them; they say—he is a Jew.[67]

In reaction against the swelling tide of inhuman hatred, the young Rosenzweig concurred in the antisemitic premise and agreed that he could only do "hack's work" in Christian Europe and that the Jewish share "in the life of the peoples can only be *clam, vi, precario* ("secret, perforce, precarious"—expressions in Roman law)"[68] Here, then, is a complete reversal of the Mendelssohnian position.

We need hardly state our disagreement with the manic rhetoric in this correspondence, which reflects the newly found passions of existentialism. For us the debate is paradigmatic of the perverse posturing that is all too often the alternative to a dialogue based on the liberal plane of religious humanism.

Between the Mendelssohn-Lavater and the Rosenzweig-Rosenstock-Huessy debates, there emerged several tides of "Teutonomania," rising on occasion to the verge of collective self-deification. Germanic nationalism was from its beginning, in the Romantic period, infected with a resolute disdain for other nations and religions. No dialogue could possibly be meaningful with men who appealed to the "voice of blood."

Saul Ascher (1767–1822), one of the early Reform ideologists, was compelled to react against what he termed *"Germanomanie."* A nationalist in the tradition of Mendelssohn, he defended the role of rationalist as a non-rational faculty of the individual in confrontation with the riddles of reality, but he drew the line against any kind of irrationalism. He opposed Mendelssohn's concept of "revealed legislation" and argued that the validity of ritual laws depends on their effectiveness in sensitizing the individual to the moral imperatives of society.

In his day, however, the argument shifted from religious dogmatics to racial narcissism. His book, *Germanomanie* (Leipzig, 1815), a critique of the excesses of Germanic nationalism, was burned at the Wartburg Festival of the *Deutsche Burschenschaft*. In his open letter to E. M. Arndt, he wrote: "So long as you build your constitution on Germanism, Christianity, and Original Language, treating as bastards humanity, cosmopolitanism, and the religion of reason, no reasoning world-citizen can react to you with faith and love."[69]

The organic unity of Germanic nationalism and the Protestant faith was stressed by a long line of ideologists from Schleiermacher to the Teutonic Christians of the Nazi era. In their search for the elusive qualities of the national soul, the Romanticists were impelled to distinguish between the genuine piety of their own "folk" and the faith of other nations. Indeed, Schleiermacher was "one of the first to show that the national character of any group of people was determined by all their customs, and that their version of the Christian faith was as much a national expression of the German people as their language or their folk-ways."[70]

Strangely, even Germanic atheists, who reduced Christian theology to a tissue of myths, could reconfirm their opposition to Judaism for its nonparticipation in the national mythology. David F. Strauss's *Leben Jesu*, which described the teaching of the Gospels as products of "the mythical consciouness" of the community, provided additional justification for the resentment of Jewish aloofness—they refused to dream in the same metaphors as their neighbors.

NOTES

1. Letter of Moses Mendelssohn to an unknown recipient, dated 1770, in M. Samuels, ed., *Jerusalem*, vol. 1, London, 1838.

2. Letter of Moses Mendelssohn to Lavater dated January 15, 1771. Quoted in A. Altmann, *Moses Mendelssohn*, University of Alabama Press, 1973, p. 261.

3. Quoted in A. Altmann, *Moses Mendelssohn,* p. 262.

4. *See the most recent study, Lester G. Crocker, Jean-Jacques Rousseau,* vol. 2, New York: Macmillan Co., 1973, p. 151.

5. Mendelssohn, *Jerusalem,* vol. 1, p. 130.

6. The sources are listed in: Emil Schürer, *A History of the Jewish People,* rev. ed., New York: Scribner's, 1891, vol. 2, p. 831; G. F. Moore, *Judaism,* Cambridge, 1946, vol. 1, p. 325; H. A. Wolfson, *Philo,* Cambridge, 1947, vol. 2, p. 369.

7. Maimonides, *Guide of the Perplexed,* III, 32.

8. Maimonides, *Guide of the Perplexed,* III, 28.

9. My translation.

10. *Hilchot Melochim* VIII, par. 11.

11. Quoted in Spinoza, *A Theologico-Political Treatise,* Elwes translation, New York: Dover, 1951, ch. 5, p. 79.

12. *Hilchot Melochim* X, 14 ed. Constantinople.

13. *Guide of the Perplexed,* II, 16. Pine's translation, Chicago, 1963, p. 294.

14. *Hilchot Akum* IX, 4.

15. Joseph Albo, *The Book of Principles,* translated I. Husik, Philadelphia: Jewish Publication Society (hereafter abbreviated as J.P.S.), 1929. In III, 25, Albo argues that an irrational, or an unjust faith cannot be divine. He was compelled to fortify the resolution of his coreligionists to persevere in their faith by pointing to the irrationalities and unethical conduct of the fanatical Inquisitors of his day.

16. Mendelssohn, *Jerusalem,* p. 213.

17. Mendelssohn, *Jerusalem,* p. 101.

18. The historian Simon Dubnow regarded the quest of autonomy as a characteristic of Jewish history. "In this way the people build for themselves in every place something like a kingdom in miniature." Quoted by Koppel S. Pinson, in *Nationalism and History,* Philadelphia: J.P.S., 1958, p 49.

On the *herem* as the means of law-enforcement, see Salo W. Baron, *The Jewish Community,* Philadelphia: J.P.S., 1942, pp. 228–36.

19. Mendelssohn, *Jerusalem,* p. 104.

20. Mendelssohn, *Jerusalem,* p. 106.

21. Maimonides, *Guide of the Perplexed,* III, 28.

22. The ultimate goals of life were summarized by Maimonides in *Guide of the Perplexed,* Part 3, chapters 51, 52–54. In chapter 51, he described the goal of ecstasy. In the last three chapters, he described the creative acts of the philosopher who has attained the highest knowledge.

23. This description of the course of messianic redemption was presented by Maimonides in the last chapter of his Code, *Hilchot Melochim 11, 10.* In his "Letter to the Jews of Yemen," however, published in *Iggeret Teman,* Philadel-

phia: J.P.S., 1950, he spoke of the overwhelming effect of the miracles that the Messiah will perform (p. 101). Nachmanides, in his commentary on Isaiah 53, described the Messiah as a more exalted being than the patriarchs, Moses, and the highest angles; he will convert all the nations and through his merit the sins of Israel will be forgiven. This commentary is printed in Chavel's *Kithvai Rabenu Moshe ben Nachman*, vol. 1, Jerusalem, 1963.

24. Mendelssohn, *Jerusalem*, pp. 200, 203.

25. The phrase "fenced us round with impregnable ramparts and walls of iron that we might not mingle at all with any of the other nations" occurs in *The Letter of Aristeas*, verse 139, ed. R. H. Charles, Oxford, 1913.

26. In the first edition of the *Responsa of Moses Isserles* (No. 124), reference is made to the neglect and virtual disappearance of this prohibition in some Bohemian and other provinces. In later editions, this remark was eliminated. *Ozar Yisroel*, vol. 5, New York, 1952, p. 135.

27. It is interesting to note that Spinoza, too, insisted that Jesus did not intend to abolish the law. "Christ, as I have said, was sent into the world not to preserve the state nor to lay down laws, but solely to teach the universal moral law, so we can easily understand that He wished in no wise to do away with the Law of Moses, inasmuch as He introduced no new laws of His own." *A Theologico-Political Treatise*, ch. 5, p. 70.

28. Spinoza, *A Theologico-Political Treatise*, ch. V, p. 68.

But with regard to the ceremonial observances which were ordained in the Old Testament for the Hebrews only, it is evident that they formed no part of the Divine Law, and had nothing to do with blessedness and virtue, but had reference only to the election of the Hebrews, that is (as I have shown in chapter 3) to their temporal bodily happiness and the tranquility of their Kingdom, and that therefore they were valid only while that Kingdom lasted.

29. Spinoza had argued similarly, in regard to political sovereignty, that man *qua* man cannot barter away the freedom of his mind: "No one can ever so utterly transfer to another his power and consequently his rights, as to cease to be a man." *A Theologico-Political Treatise*, ch. 17.

30. In his last work, *To Lessing's Friends*, Mendelssohn had written that Spinoza could be interpreted in a theistic way. "Besides, I knew that there was purified Spinozism, and [that this] purified Spinozism was quite compatible with Judaism in particular; that irrespective of his speculative doctrine, Spinoza could have remained an Orthodox Jew had he not contested authentic Judaism in other writings of his, and had he not thereby withdrawn from the law." Mendelssohn, *Gesammelte Schriften*, vol. 3, p. 5; A. Altmann, *Moses Mendelssohn*, p. 753.

31. Nathan Rotenstreich, *Jewish Philosophy in Modern Times* (New York: Holt, Rinehart and Winston, 1968), p. 29.

32. In his own lifetime, Maimonides's eschatology was interpreted in this way. He composed his essay "On the Resurrection of the Dead" to counter such views. Yet, his disciples could still insist that this dogma was "a necessary belief," not a "true belief" (*Guide* III, 32); that is, it is necessary in order to maintain the cohesion of the Jewish community.

33. Introduction to *Code, Yad Hahazakah.*

34. That Rabbi Isaac Luria (the "holy Ari") was the recipient of authoritative revelations, the Mithnagdim (opponents) as well as the Hasidim (pietists) agreed. The Gaon Elijah of Vilna (1720–1797) disputed the accuracy of some printed versions of Lurianic Kabbalah. Rav Sheneur Zalman of Liadi (1747–1812) maintained that "the Holy Ari" attained greater revelations than Moses. *Iggeret Hakodesh,* par. 19, in Vilna edition 1928, p. 254.

35. The Hasidim were not alone in believing that their leaders, the Zaddikim, were guided by the Holy Spirit *(Ruah hakodesh).* Similar experiences were attributed to the leader of the Mithnagdim, the Gaon Elijah of Vilna, by his disciples. See introduction of Rabbi Hayim of Volozhin (1749–1821) to Elijah's commentary on *Safra dizeniuta,* in "Shiveat Hameorot," (Vilna, 1913).

36. R. Mahler, in volume one of his *Dorot Ahronim* (Merhavia, Israel, 1952), assembled the relevant documents of the debates in France and Holland. The Orthodox *Parnassim* were, of course, opposed to any diminution of their power over the communal life of Jews. Some documents are discussed in Baruch Mevorach's *Napoleon Utekufata,* Jerusalem: Mossad Bialick, 1968.

37. G. E. Lessing, *The Evolution of the Human Race,* first published in German as, *Die Erziehung d. Menschengeschlechts,* 1780, par. 69.

38. Mendelssohn, *Jerusalem,* p. 356.

39. G. E. Lessing, *Theological Writings,* transl. H. Chadwick, ch. 1, p. 219.

40. *Ibid.,* ch. 3, p. 26.

41. Spinoza, *Gesammelte Schriften* III, p. 5.

42. A. Altmann, *Moses Mendelssohn,* pp. 698–759. Mendelssohn, *Morgenstunden* 1786, and *To Lessing's Friends.*

43. A. Altmann, *Moses Mendelssohn,* p. 200. B. Mevorach, Zion 30 (1965) pp. 158–70.

44. Christian Wilhelm Dohm, *Über die bürgerliche Verbesserung der Juden,* part 2, Berlin, 1783, p. 72, where the critiques and responses regarding Dohm's proposal are printed.

Comte de Mirabeau, *Sur Mendelssohn et sur la reforme politique des Juifs,* second ed., Leipzig 1853, p. 105.

45. Quoted in *Kayserling, Moses Mendelssohn—Sein Leben und seine Werke,* Appendix 57, Leipzig 1863.

46. On Hasidic messianism, see the chapter on Hasidism in this author's *The Evolution of Jewish Thought,* Abelard-Schuman, 1959; Arno Press, 1973. On the messianic philosophy of the Gaon Elijah of Vilna, see the voluminous work of Menahem M. Kasher, *Hatekufah Hagedolah* Jerusalem, 1969. On the interpretation of the Napoleonic Wars by the Zaddiks of Poland, see Martin Buber's novel, *For the Sake of heaven,* Philadelphia: J.P.S., 1946.

47. J. B. Agus, *Evolution,* pp. 348–54.

48. See the discussion of this passage in I. Heinemann, *Taamai Hamizvot Besifrut Yisroel,* vol. II. Jerusalem, 1956, pp. 16, 38.

49. The brochure of N. Z. H. Weisel, *Divrai Shalom Ve-emet,* 1782. Ezekiel Kaufman, *Gole Venaichar,* Tel Aviv, 1930, vol. II, p. 31; Mendelssohn, Gesam. Schriften, vol. VIII, p. 301; vol. III, p. 105.

50. Perez Smolenskin, *Maamorim,* Jerusalem, 1925, 4 vols., chiefly the essays *Am Olam* and *Et Lotaat.*

51. Raphael Mahler, *Divrai Yemai Yisroel-Dorot Ahronim,* Tel Aviv, 1956, vol. I, pp. 121–251.

52. In other books and articles, I described this belief as the "meta-myth," an essential component of mythological antisemitism. See also: *The Meaning of Jewish History,* vol. 2, ch. XVI; *Guideposts in Modern Judaism,* pp. 171–203; Arthur A. Cohen, *The Natural and the Supernatural Jew,* New York: Pantheon, 1962.

53. A. Cohen, *The Natural,* pp. 28, 29.

54. A. Altmann, *Moses Mendelssohn,* p. 502.

55. A. Altmann, *Moses Mendelssohn,* p. 509.

56. H. J. Schoeps, *The Jewish-Christian Argument,* New York: Holt, Rinehart and Winston, 1963.

57. H. J. Schoeps, *The Jewish-Christian Argument,* p. 129.

58. Eugen Rosenstock-Huessy, ed., *Judaism Despite Christianity,* University of Alabama Press, 1969, "Prologue-Epilogue," p. 75.

59. *Judaism Despite Christianity,* p. 70.

60. *Judaism Despite Christianity,* pp. 125 and 126.

61. *Judaism Despite Christianity,* p. 113.

62. *Judaism Despite Christianity,* p. 113.

63. *Judaism Despite Christianity,* p. 136.

64. Maimonides, *Guide of the Perplexed* III, 51.

65. Maimonides, *Guide of the Perplexed* III, 54.

66. Doubtless he was affected by the reactionary course of Catholicism culminating in 1864 in the acceptance at Vatican I of the *Syllabus of Errors,* which condemned every manifestation of liberalism.

67. Jakob Wassermann, *Mein Weg als Deutscher und Jude,* Berlin, 1921, p. 122.

68. *Judaism Despite Christianity,* p. 135.

69. Published in "Die Folke," 1819. See "Saul Ascher—First Theories of Progressive Judaism" by Ellen Littman, in Leo Baeck Institute *Yearbook V,* 1960, pp. 107–21.

70. F. Schleiermacher, *The Evolution of a Nationalist,* Austin and London: University of Texas Press, 1966.

PART FOUR

JACOB AGUS' IDEOLOGY OF AMERICAN JUDAISM: AMERICAN JEWS OR JEWISH AMERICANS?

SELECTIONS AND PREFATORY REMARKS
Milton R. Konvitz

RABBI AGUS was an admirer of the United States and an ardent advocate of Jewish participation in all facets of American life. He was, of course, not unaware of the challenge such participation posed to the maintenance and continuation of Jewish communal and individual life. Indeed, this challenge was a lifelong practical and ideological preoccupation for Agus.

The following selections, chosen to accompany Milton R. Konvitz' essay "Jacob Agus' Ideology of American Judaism: American Jews or Jewish Americans?" in *American Rabbi: The Life and Thought of Jacob B. Agus* (New York, 1996), are drawn from Jacob Agus' *The Jewish Quest* (New York, 1983), 1–10; *Dialogue and Tradition: The Challenge of Contemporary Judeo-Christian Thought* (New York, 1971), 569–88; and *Jewish Identity in an Age of Ideologies* (New York, 1978), 368–98.

13
WHO WE ARE

EVERY HISTORIC community establishes its specific character by reflecting on three aspects of its life—its self-image, its attitude to the universal values of culture and religion, its posture toward other groups and humanity generally. Naturally, these phases of culture interact and affect one another. But, as a rule it is easy enough to study them separately.

In the case of the Jewish people, each of the three orientations of collective consciousness is problematic.

The relationship of the Jewish people to God was affirmed to be unique by the Jews themselves and in the Christian world. Their metaphysical status was believed to be inherent in their ethnicity and destiny, and it was irrevocable. Naturally, the self-image of Jewish people and their attitude to their neighbors were determined in large part by this dogma of the Chosen People.

It is commonly asserted that in Jewish life, there is no distinction between nationality and religion. But Jewish thinkers could not be unaware of the dividing line between these two categories. The majority of the Jewish people lived in the Christian world, where this line of demarcation was carved out through centuries in bloody revolutions and civil wars. The movement of Jewish people from the periphery of western European life to its center depended upon and coincided with the progressive separation of church and state. In countries of the *ancien regime,* Jews could only be heretics and pariahs. Religious hostility overflowed often enough into the categories of nationality and race. In Spain, the theory of *limpieza* was evolved. It asserted that Jewish "blood" was corrupted by centuries of unbelief. This decay of religious bias into racist contempt was foreshadowed by the belief, which preachers read into the New Testament since the second century, that the Jewish people had been "rejected" by the Supreme Being, for having failed to recognize their Savior. Weaker and less dogmatic versions of this dogma persisted into the twentieth century in all the lands of Europe. It was widely believed that the Jew was separated from Christian society by a metaphysical barrier. In addition to the categories of race, nationality and religion, which distinguished other groups from one another, the Jew bore the stigmata of a special mystery, compounded of both a blessing and a curse, the grace of chosenness and the doom of rejection. The metaphysical gulf which set the Jews apart was encrusted in the course of time with many and diverse canards, which formed the mythology of Antisemitism.

A mirror-image of this complex of myths and fantasies has often bedeviled the self-consciousness of the Jewish people. The Jewish self-image was at times lifted out of the complexities of history and viewed as if Jews were a "people that dwells alone and is not counted among the nations" (Numbers 23:9). It does not merely cherish a specific body of beliefs and practices. It occupies a unique status, in relation to Providence, and in respect of all the nations of the world.

Collectivities are victims of vanity even more than individuals, and it is easier for the former to mask their pride in the adornment of idealism than it is for the latter. Once a tradition has taken root which appeals to the idealism of people as well as to their self-love, it becomes exceedingly difficult to disentangle the threads and to restore the original state of normalcy.

JEWISH IMAGE IN PAST AND PRESENT

In my book, *Jewish Identity in an Age of Ideologies,* I traced the diverse changes in the Jewish image and self-image that resulted from the movements of thought in the modern world.

So central was the Jewish heritage to the history of the western world that every change in the intellectual climate of Europe implied a subtle alteration in the image of the Jew, for better or for worse. Theology in the most general sense was long the "queen of the sciences", and a unique position in theology led to special consequences when in the last two centuries theologies evolved into ideologies. Every new vision of society influenced the character of the Jewish image and the nature of Jewish identity, whether it was a new understanding of nationality, or of social justice, or of the course of world history, or of the nature of evolution, or of the interpretation of Holy Scriptures; every upheaval in thought and society affected the concept of the Jewish people. Still, the more the Jewish image changed, the more it remained the same, in that it retained references to ancient stereotypes and the resonance of folk mythologies.

Is this situation likely to continue into the distant future? No one can answer this question with dogmatic certainty. The contemporary scene has been radically altered by the following sea-changes:

First, the vast majority of Jewish people now live in North America and in Israel. The American state is based on the principle of individual citizenship, with no special privileges being granted to any ethnic group. The ideology of American nationalism embraces all its citizens, regardless of race, color or creed. Naturally, the actual life of the American people does not always correspond perfectly with its ideal vision. There have always been some islands of exception, if not exclusion, in the American ideology—notably in the case of the American Indian, the Negro, the Mexican and others. But, the official ideology is the dominant force in American life, determining the main currents of its culture. Here is a nation that appreciates and celebrates the diverse ethnic components which generated it. So strong is its unity in law and culture that its pluralistic heritage can only reinforce its solidarity and its message to mankind.

The security of Israel is now included within the range of vital interests of America. While political alignments may be changed, the Israeli alliance with the United States appears to be firm and enduring. Even if America and Israel should go their separate ways in the unforeseen future, Israel is quite able to defend itself against its enemies. Furthermore, Israel's dependence upon American economic and military help serves to cement the relationship between American Jewry and Israel. American Jews feel that it is their duty to interpret Israel to America and America to Israel.

Second, the Christian world is engaged in a basic transformation of its view of the Jewish people. Since the Second World War there have appeared some fifty declarations on Jews and Judaism, which have reversed the traditional "teaching of contempt" of Judaism, and set a new policy of appreciation of the Jewish heritage. The effects of the new educational approach will be felt in the future, though history teaches us that occasional reverses may still be expected.

In a society so vast and diverse, we cannot expect to see sudden transformations. Traditions of evil as of goodness possess a momentum that is roughly proportionate to their age and ubiquity. But, on the highest levels there is now a fresh sensitivity to the horrors of Antisemitism which are latent in the history of western society. Hopefully, the memory of the Holocaust will not easily be put out of mind.

Third, in the lands of Central Europe, where Antisemitism was an endemic mass-religion, there are few or no Jews. In Poland, Rumania, Hungary and in the smaller contiguous states, the Holocaust left only stray remnants, abandoned cemeteries and mute monuments. That area, extending from the Baltic states to the shores of the Black Sea, was at one time the heartland of the Jews of the world, and the fertile source of mass-emigration. Out of it Jewish people, bearers of Yiddish culture and traditional loyalties, flowed for centuries westward and to the lands of the New World. It was also the home and center of economic Antisemitism, with the ancient heritage of hatred being buttressed by the desperate pressure of an impoverished peasantry bent on acquiring positions in the urban centers, where Jews had long been entrenched.

Fourth, the mythological component of Antisemitism was given some plausibility by the pre-Israel image of the Jew as an individual and the Jewish people as a collectivity. As individuals, Jews appeared to be uprooted, detached from the soil, shallow, skeptical and critical. In the eyes of the recently urbanized masses, barely a generation away from plows and pigs, Jews seemed to be foreign invaders, barring their way to progress. Jews were seen by the uprooted peasants as unnatural people, "city slickers", eking out a living by tricks and deceptions.

As a collectivity, Jews were seen as a ghostly phenomenon, a people landless and helpless, a "pariah"-people, cowardly and self-centered.

The emergence of the state of Israel served to cast these images into the dust-bin of the past. In Israel, the Jews proved themselves to be superb farmers and excellent soldiers. They have taken their place in the concert of nations, with the plow and with the sword. They are no longer a "wandering" people, homeless and helpless, but a people of flesh and blood, of passion and pride, altogether human.

THE EMERGENCE OF ANTI-ZIONISM

Strange are the ways of history. When old movements disintegrate, some of their momentum is taken over by new ideologies. Antisemitism, nurtured under the auspices of Christianity for centuries, erupted with volcanic force in the nineteenth century under the aegis of secular ideologies—chiefly romantic nationalism, utopian socialism, Germanic historicism and Nietzschean glorification of power.

In the last decades, the ideology of Anti-Zionism has begun to assume the momentum of Antisemitism, especially in the Muslim and Third World countries. This phenomenon may well preoccupy Jewish leaders in the future, for the Muslim world is rising like a giant who is slowly waking up and shaking off the cobwebs of sleep.

Anti-Zionism is far more than a rational expression of antagonism to this or that policy of the state of Israel, or even to its very existence. In certain countries, Anti-Zionism may be used as a "code word" for the old social disease of Antisemitism, but it is essentially a new phenomenon. The U.N. resolution equating Zionism and racism is a serious danger-signal, an attempt to launch a world-crusade. In the long run, the significant aspect of Anti-Zionism is the mythology in which it is enveloped.

Israel is viewed through a distorting lens and seen as a titanic force of global dimensions, sinister and even satanic. It is not examined in its true proportions as a small state struggling to survive in a cruel world, but it is viewed "through a glass darkly" as the tip of a mighty mystery, a monstrous "conspiracy" of the industrial democracies to capture and conquer the underdeveloped world. The myth of the "Protocols of the Elders of Zion" is taking new shape in the minds of millions.

When Jacobo Timmerman, editor of a daily in Buenos Aires, was kidnapped by right-wing terrorists and interrogated by army leaders he was asked three questions—"Are you a Jew?" "Are you a Zionist?" "Are you part of the Zionist Conspiracy?" He replied in the affirmative to each of the questions. In his view, his affirmative answer to the third question saved his life, for the Argentinian generals thought they could use him for a show-trial.

To us, the amazing phenomenon is the concern of Argentinian nationalists with a "Zionist conspiracy". How many lives does a myth have?—How deep and dark is the fantastic credulity of those who are suspicious of all intellectuals!

Anti-Zionism does have a "religious" basis, not only in Muslim but also in Christian countries. There, the impetus of popular prejudice and medieval myths is likely to persist even when the higher echelons of leadership have arrived at a more humane and progressive position. To be sure, even in Protestant countries, pro-Zionist sentiment was often inhibited, especially in liberal circles, but as a general rule, Zionism in England and America enjoyed widespread support.

In his careful study of "Vatican Diplomacy and the Jews during the Holocaust, 1939–1943" (New York, 1980), Father John F. Morley writes:

> "According to Maglione, Catholics all over the world looked to Palestine as a sacred land because it was the birthplace of Christianity. If, however, Palestine were to become predominantly Jewish, then Catholic piety would be offended and Catholics would be understandably anxious as to whether they could continue to peacefully enjoy their historic rights over the holy places". (p. 93)

This attitude was doubtless reinforced by the vague feeling that the reconstitution of the Jewish state would undo the belief that Jerusalem was destroyed in punishment for the crucifixion of Jesus.

However, with the passage of time, the state of Israel has been gaining in acceptance by nearly all Christian national organizations. The theological tradition of the Christian world contains the prophecies of the Hebrew Scriptures as well as the opinions of the Church Fathers. It is therefore natural for Christians to associate the Holy Land with the Jewish people. Also, in the face of an Islamic resurgence, Christians are likely to become more aware of their kinship with the Judaic heritage. Theological doctrines are not immune to changes induced by the great events of history.

Furthermore, Israel was born in response to basic human needs and by the freely expressed vote of an international body, the Assembly of the United Nations. It was therefore an all-human achievement, an attempt by the family of nations to provide some reparation for the horrendous crimes of the Holocaust. Christian nations shared in the burden of guilt for the crimes of Germany, because they participated in the millenial teaching of contempt for Jews. Hence, a special glow of idealism illuminated the image of the Jewish state. The sacrificial devotion of Jewish people all over the world was reinforced by the high regard of the western world. Nor was this attitude confined to an elite of moralists. The common people of the West were won over by the spectacle of a largely European people beating back the invasion of hordes of enemies, who were non-European and non-Christian. In the successive wars of 1948, 1956, 1967 and 1973, the decisive victories of Israel contrasted starkly with the global retreat of European nations from their colonial strongholds in Asia and Africa. While the British, French, Dutch and Portuguese withdrew from their colonies, the Jews drove home the lesson of Europe's supremacy in industry and science. By the same token, Israel became the mighty symbol and cutting edge of western imperialism, in the eyes of Arabs and Third World nations.

The negative image of Arabs in the western world was exacerbated by their military defeats, their seemingly hopeless impoverishment and their political ineptitude. Israelis had come to feel that if they must have enemies, they were fortunate that their enemies were Arabs—fanatical, incompetent, mostly illiterate and torn by parochial loyalties.

However, the war of '73 demonstrated that a radical change had taken place. The war coincided with the emergence of OPEC as an all-powerful factor in the economy of the West. Suddenly, the Arab case acquired immense international weight. The wheels of industry, it turned out, could grind to a halt at the pleasure of Arabs. It became equally clear that the Palestinian Arabs were no longer ignorant peasants, but that the children of the *fellahin,* herded in wretched camps which were set up after the wars of '48 and '67, had become college-trained executives and engineers. Aided by scholarships from the oil-rich countries, the young men and women from the refugee camps filled the campuses of American universities, as graduate students, specializing in oil technology and petrochemical studies. Many of the young Palestinians penetrated into crucial positions within some of the oil-states. They acquired powerful leverage on the international scene. Yet, their newly won affluence did not cool their nationalistic ardor, and their sense of having been wronged. On the contrary, they nurtured the anger and anguish of their people in the refugee camps and wherever they were dispersed. The growth of Arab nationalism could no longer be disregarded by the statesmen of the industrial democracies.

To be sure, a widely dispersed people, like the Arabs, may take several generations to attain the unifying mentality of a nation. Political intrigues and conflicting ambitions, along with rival sectarian suspicions, are likely to frustrate this goal, time and again. But, as in the case of nineteenth-century Italy and Germany, the national ideal becomes steadily more and more irresistible.

We must also take note of the fact that the moral image of Israel declined at the very time when the Arab case gained in credibility and power. The increasing nervousness of the Israeli government, the anxious haste to establish new settlements in the midst of Arab lands, the rough tactics used to suppress Arab demonstrations—all these factors helped to remove the aura of moral greatness from the cause of Israel. "The house of Israel" had become "like all the nations".

DILEMMA OF AMERICAN JEWISH LEADERSHIP

With the Jewish state besieged by enemies and perpetually in need of financial help and moral-political support, the leaders of American Jewry were impelled to center their collective efforts on aid to Israel. Even while the old rhetoric of Jewry as a religious community continued to be used, the substance of Jewish loyalty insensibly shifted from the pole of religion to that of nationality.

The needs of Israel fighting for its life were necessarily ranked ahead of any other concern.

Only on rare occasions do American Jewish leaders take an independent attitude, in keeping with their humane tradition of philanthropy. The Soviet Jews, who refuse to settle in Israel and elect to go to America and the West, continue at this writing to receive aid from American Jews. No one can tell how long the present situation will last—whether only a small trickle of emigration will be allowed, whether the Soviets will use their power to affect the situation one way or the other, whether American Jews will continue to put the individual rights of men and women above the manpower needs of Israel.

Jewish leadership in America today is in need of more subtlety and sophistication than ever before. It must not allow a temporary and partial coincidence of interests to distort its awareness of its enduring allies and antagonists. Traditionally, American Jews enjoyed the support of the liberals in politics and in religion. But in the case of Israel, the support of the liberals was always qualified. They could sympathize with Jewish needs and, when Israel was established, they could welcome the Jewish state as an ally of the democracies. But, this sympathy was counterbalanced and limited by the plight of the Palestinian refugees. As the moral claims of the Palestinians were pushed to the foreground by the commercial pressures of the oil-rich countries, a paradoxical situation developed. Liberals and Fundamentalists changed places vis-à-vis Israel.

The liberals, traditional friends of the Jews, began to temper their enthusiasm for the Jewish state, which they saw as a regressive force, that might become one day the flash-point of another war. The future must be based on states granting equal rights to all citizens, not on the presumed rights of nations and their collective historic rights. On the other hand, the religious Fundamentalists and political Conservatives, previously hostile to Jews as unbelievers, humanists and social progressives, now joined the advocates of an aggressive anti-Soviet posture, hailing Israel as a military outpost on the battlefront against Communism. The possibility of an all-out war does not faze them, since their apocalyptic view of history anticipates an Armageddon. So, the preachers of "Christian politics", "Christian Yellow Pages" and a "Christian America" are at this moment in favor of a "strong" Israel. At the same time, the liberal ministers of the mainline churches, whose staunch opposition to Antisemitism is unquestioned, became skeptical and even resentful of the "expansionist" claims of Israel.

This paradoxical reversal of roles may be only temporary. In any case, it must not be countered by stultifying slogans, such as "Zionism is Judaism", or "Anti-Zionism is Antisemitism".

Once an ideal has become a political reality, it cannot be protected by the immaculate banner of supernatural grace. The Ayatollah Khomeini has reminded us all of the sad truth that when religion bursts into the political arena, it becomes subject to the distortions of chauvinism, the limitations of earthly politics and the corruption of earthly instincts. No people has suffered more than the Jews from the unnatural union of politics and religion. Indeed, it has been the glory of historic Judaism to put in question the claims of sheer power, and to rank the law of God above all the laws of states and their rulers. The Jewish people emerged upon the stage of history, dedicated to the task of becoming a blessing "to all the families of the earth" (Genesis 12:2).

Of course, it is possible to criticize this or that policy of an Israeli government, without indicting either Judaism or the Jews of the world, and vice versa. This point need hardly be argued. But, we must acknowledge that in practice, a resolute policy of Anti-Zionism may, if sustained over a period of time, turn into the dripping venom of Antisemitism. Anti-Zionists may seek allies by reviving the old myths of a Jewish conspiracy; also, they may seek to put Jews in the industrial democracies on the defensive by awakening the slumbering demons of Antisemitism. Jewish leaders may also assist unwittingly in this tragic train of events by their uncritical support of an aggressive Israeli policy. For example, the claim that the West Bank belongs to Israel because "God gave it to us" invites the injection into world politics of ancient mythologies, by Muslims as well as by Christians. And the occasional efforts of Jewish leaders in the free countries to put the cause of Israel above all other considerations of the national interest cannot but awaken the resentment of the free nations. The reasoning of the widely respected U.S. Senator Charles McMathias in his article on the distortion of American policy by the pressure of ethnic groups is a case in point (*Foreign Affairs,* Spring 1982).

More than a century ago, Leo Pinsker attributed the international pathology of Antisemitism to the homelessness of the Jewish people. A landless people acquires a ghostly quality in the eyes of the populace. And people fear ghosts. With the emergence of Israel, this source of the Antisemitic mythology is now blocked. But, we may well see a new kind of Antisemitism based on the myth of a Zion-centered people that keeps apart from the nations while manipulating and distorting their policies. In question is not the old bugaboo of "dual loyalty" but of a singular, meta-historical loyalty to Israel, a mystique that transcends all national loyalties.

The formation of the Jewish state occurred under special circumstances, when hundreds of thousands of refugees crowded the camps of Europe. At that time, the need of a "haven of refuge" for Jews was clear and pressing. The discomfort and displacement of Palestinian Arabs seemed in human terms but a small price to pay for the solution of the Jewish tragedy. The years of "the ingathering of exiles" generated additional momentum and led to the evacuation of Jews from Arab and some European lands. The case of Soviet Jewry was more problematical. A large number of Russian Jews feel that in the Soviet world they are not allowed to become either "good Russians" or "good Jews". On the other hand, the masses of Russian Jewry are largely assimilated. After more than a decade of mass-emigration, the number of Jews in Russia is only slightly diminished. Also, most of the emigrants prefer to settle in the countries of the western world. It is freedom and the western style of living that they prize so highly, rather than the life and culture of Israel.

Once Zionism is perceived as no longer answering a great human need, it is questionable whether many nations would rank the nationalistic ideals of American Jews above the basic human rights of an indigenous population to dwell securely in the land in which they were born.

The task of Diaspora Jewry is to help Israel acquire fresh dimensions of moral and cultural greatness. With the aid of the Diaspora, Israel can attain new heights of achievement that will be meaningful to all men and women of good-will. In the field of interreligious understanding, Israel can become the natural center for basic studies and cultural events, celebrating the plural truths of the three great religions of the West. In the field of intercultural fraternity, the groundwork is already laid, since people from 50 different lands are living in Israel. In the field of scientific research and development, the greatest natural resource is the human brain and the resolve to apply it to the solution of human problems.

Hemmed in on all sides, the open frontier for Israel is the domain of intellectual and cultural greatness. If this horizon is explored, Israel may yet regain the adulation of the free world and demonstrate to the new nations of the world that it is through the high roads of culture that a nation attains its place in the sun.

In France and in Argentina, a new kind of Antisemitism is raising its head. If Israel does not gain peace, and does not regain its moral prestige, it is likely to become the source of a vile mythology in the lands of Islam primarily, but also in the countries of the West.

How shall we deal with this danger, especially as it is now barely "a cloud, the size of a man's hand" on the eastern horizon?

While we cannot plan the details of our strategy in advance, we can sharpen our intellectual perception of the choices confronting us at any point. We can learn to recognize our self-mythification, as it arose in history and provided the tar, which made the feathers of mythology cling to our image. We can note how the biblical claims of singularity and uniqueness were twisted into weapons which were turned against us. We can learn to repudiate the seductive fantasies of self-glorification and confront rationally and humanely the problems that trouble us. We can learn to build bridges of understanding with our Christian brothers, and, possibly also, our Muslim brothers.

14

ASSIMILATION, INTEGRATION, SEGREGATION: THE ROAD TO THE FUTURE

IN OUR FAST-MOVING world one must be inordinately clairvoyant or narrowly fanatical to risk any predictions concerning the future. The Jewish situation anywhere in the world is always sensitive to a variety of social pressures and to the shifting winds of the spiritual climate. There is scarcely a social phenomenon on the international scene that does not in some way affect the balance of forces determining the status and hopes of world Jewry. On any rational basis, it is possible for us to take account of presently visible factors only and to admit that all our conclusions are tentative, for if the past is any indication of the future, the even course of human events is likely to be interrupted by treacherous curves and hairpin turns.

If there is one prediction that we may hazard concerning the future of American Jewry, it is negative in character. We may assume with little fear of contradiction that the American Jewish community will not be monolithic, culturally or religiously, or even of relatively uniform texture. The free atmosphere of America makes it possible for any group of Jewish people, however small, to cultivate its own ideology and to build up institutions devoted to its perpetuation. Nor must we forget that ideologies are in the final analysis reflections of certain temperaments or character configurations, so that any way of thinking or living that is socially effective is probably embraced in response to certain psychic needs. The three major interpretations of the Jewish faith—Orthodoxy, Conservatism, and Reform—have endured long enough for us to recognize that they correspond in many instances to specific character types. It is not difficult to discover the springs of character and blocks of experience that make for a militant Jewish nationalism, on the one hand, or a hysterically precipitous assimilationism, on the other hand.

But while American society allows for the profusion of variety in marginal areas and fringe situations, it also favors the emergence and dominance of certain standard types. A massive mainstream flows mightily in the center, while many interesting eddies form along the uneven banks. All students of American society, from Tocqueville to Commager, concur in the recognition of a distinctively American character and of a widely pervasive pressure to conform to that type. Assuming a similar development in the case of the Jewish community, we can foresee the eventual dominance of certain Jewish types and attitudes. While all kinds of exotic combinations may continue to flourish on the sidelines, the standard Jewish personality of the future is even now being fashioned by the intangible realities of American society.

By the standard Jew we mean not the typical Jew, who represents the statistical average of all measurable qualities, but the personality pattern that the typical Jew seeks to approximate. The community, in all its institutions and in its multifarious dynamism, is nothing but the shadow of the standard Jew, reflecting the contours of his values and the play of loyalties within his personality.

In this essay, I propose to show, first, that the dominant Jewish personality of the future will identify himself more intimately with the American people than Jews have ever before succeeded in doing, second, that this development is likely to eventuate in the paradoxical situation where both the currents away from and toward Judaism will be immensely accelerated; third, that in the foreseeable future Jewish faith and culture will attain unprecedented heights of achievement even as the floodwaters of assimilation rise menacingly.

To appreciate the play of forces within the Jewish community, we have to accord due weight to its comparative youthfulness. While twenty-three Jews landed in New Amsterdam three hundred years ago, the vast majority of American Jews are sons and daughters of recent immigrants. With a total population of only a quarter million in 1880, when the mass migration of Russian Jews was begun, we may readily calculate that only 10 percent of our community can claim a residence of more than two generations. To be sure, the minority of early settlers did enjoy the hegemony of leadership down to the first half of the twentieth century by reason of its superior wealth and culture. But only the lingering remnants of this predominance are in evidence today, with the policies of the Jewish community reflecting ever more clearly the sentiments and convictions of the descendants of the East European immigrants. Here and there, especially in philanthropic circles, the impetus of the older type of leadership is still felt, but in the community as a whole, the prevailing spirit is that of a human mass that has but recently come into its own.

In every domain of activity within the Jewish community, traditions are still fluid and uncertain. In the sphere of religion, the Orthodox leaders are most painfully aware that their adherents have not yet fully absorbed the total impact of the American environment. Their greatest authorities are men who think and speak in Yiddish; their typical institutions are conceived in the ambition to slow down the ponderous processes of acculturation; their typical followers are still the men and women of the "old country" or their immediate descendants. The Conservative movement owes its very existence to the conviction that American Judaism is only now beginning to emerge; hence, its avid search for new patterns, its bold experimentalism, and its faith in the creative genius of the people. The Reform movement of today turns its back upon its own classical traditions in its eagerness to keep abreast of the surging currents in Jewish life.

In the community generally, there is hardly any activity that is not secretly questioned even by its most ardent supporters. The rising generation of community leaders is beginning to rethink first principles. Does the settlement-house kind of activity still make sense? Is a community center dedicated to the cultivation of "Jewish culture," apart from religion, either necessary or desirable in the ideal American community? What are the reasons for the investment of huge sums in "Jewish hospitals"? Would not the Jewish medical practitioner be better served if Jewish wealth were given in equally generous measure to the great general and university hospitals in every large city?

These and similar questions being raised ever more insistently in community forums throughout the nation are indicative of a soul-searching that is long overdue. In the past quarter century, the needs of Jews abroad were so overwhelming in scope and urgency that little attention and energy were left for the consideration of basic issues at home. Federations and welfare funds are scarcely one generation old, and they are still largely nonideological mechanical fund-raising devices, held in line by the pull of the purse strings, the deft manipulation of professional managers, and the avidity of the *nouveaux riche* for the approval of the older financial aristocracy. Any way you look at it, the American Jewish community is still young, and its future shape undetermined.

Two approaches are available to us as we seek to comprehend the inner dynamism of the emergent Jewish community. We may begin with a definition of the Jewish people and descend to an understanding of the situation of its American portion, arriving ultimately at a representation of the individuals making up the chain of Jewish communities. In this path, we shall be dealing with controversial abstractions, long before we come to grips with reality, and face the danger of losing our way in such endless disputes as those raging round the following questions: What are we — a race, a nation, a religion, a *"kith,"* a "unique" blend of many elements, a "freak of history," a "civilizational fossil"? And what is the legitimate goal of our group *vis-à-vis* the general community? Is it integration or assimilation? Or is it, perchance, a synthesis of cultural pluralism and global ethnicism?

The second approach is simpler by far and, in keeping with the inductive method of science, proceeds from the particular to the universal. We begin with the Jewish individual and then proceed to determine which loyalties and ideals, institutions and practices are likely to serve the growth of his personality, and which entanglements cannot but enchain him in a maze of contradictions and confusions. This approach is, moreover, in consonance with the emphasis on the worth of the individual, which was first projected into world affairs during the Renaissance, and which achieved its greatest triumphs here in the United States. If there is one quality of thought or sentiment that is "characteristically American," it is precisely this insistence on seeing all things from the standpoint of the individual. As Professor Ralph Perry put it in his brilliant study of the American mind:

"At the same time there has emerged from all this variety of impacts a characteristic American response — a selective response which tries all things but assimilates or rejects; a resultant of many causes, which itself acts as a cause.

"The latest misleading name for this selective response, this American bias, is 'collective individualism'! The term individualism signifies the irreducible reality, the genuine causal efficacy and the ultimate worth of the individual. . . . Collective individualism is the conscious philosophy, or fundamental belief, or unconscious presupposition, which credits such individuals, whether in competition or in concert, with a power to modify their environment and subject it to their ends; which endorses their claim to be masters and beneficiaries of social institutions; and which credits them with a hand in the making of history." [1]

We may expect, therefore, that the continuous pressure of American civilization will result in an increasing emphasis on the values of the Jewish individual. Indeed, this impact of the American vision happens to coincide in direction, if not in content, with the two most important movements in the history of modern Jewry—the emancipation and Herzlian Zionism. It was the chief ambition of the architects of Jewish emancipation to break down the isolation of the Jewish groups and to project the individual as the agent responsible both for the Jewish destiny and the Jewish faith. This ambition was perhaps best phrased in the famous slogan of Clermont-Tonnerre, "To the Jews as individuals, everything; to the Jews as a nation, nothing." Whereas during the Middle Ages the Jews constituted a community, dealing with the powers that were on a group basis, the emancipation aimed at the abolition of any lingering traces of a Jewish "nation within a nation" so that the individual could stand or fall on his own merits. The inner acceptance of this philosophy was embraced in the ideology of classical Reform.

Herzlian Zionism, too, was a rebellion against the "uniqueness" of the Jewish status, resulting from the presumed failure of the emancipation. Only in a land of their own would Jews be completely free to be simply individuals, picking and choosing out of their heritage, and out of European culture generally, whatsoever might appeal to them, without feeling themselves any longer dogged by the pursuing shadow of the collective fate. Furthermore, Herzl and several of his associates argued that if Zionism draws away from European lands those who desire to preserve their Jewish national identity the path of perfect assimilation will be made smoother for those who choose to stay in the Diaspora. Thus, the "uniqueness" of the Jewish collective identity will be dissipated. Some Jews will become members of a "nation like other nations"; the rest of Jewry will no longer feel restrained from becoming in good conscience nationals of the land of their birth, Jewish Germans,

Jewish Frenchmen, and so on. In either case they will be free men and women. It was Herzl's ardent ambition to liberate the Jewish individual in Palestine, as well as in the Diaspora, from the crushing shadow of a "unique" form of group existence. In his vision of the "Old–New Land," there was to be no unitary Jewish culture, not even one prevailing language, but a heterogenous mass of many different individuals using a variety of languages and representing diverse national cultures, each finding a hospitable haven for the fullest assertion of his individuality.

Ahad Ha'am, living in the midst of a community that had not yet tasted the sweetness of the dream of assimilation and had not felt the subsequent bitterness, could only note the negative aspects of Herzl's vision; hence, his scathing critique of Herzl's book. The Russian Jews of Ahad Ha'am's generation could hardly have been expected to appreciate the poignant pathos of Herzl's yearning for the consummation of the individual's freedom. There can be no doubt, however, that Herzl's, not Ahad Ha'am's, milieu and experience correspond more closely to the mental and social atmosphere of the American Jew.

Here, the emancipation is a far more potent reality than anywhere in Herzl's Europe. Here, even the occasional failures of the promise of emancipation can not negate the dream itself, for the emancipation is to us not a revolution but an axiom of American civilization. Thus, the impetus of Jewish life and American culture combine to put the Jewish individual in the forefront, rather than the status of the group. There does not exist one basic instrument for identification with the Jewish group, though the synagogue is rapidly becoming such a unit, especially in the smaller communities and in Jewish suburbia. Every synagogue is free to reflect the ideas and sentiments of its members. The individual is the focus of all values; affiliation with Judaism is entirely voluntary and undetermined both in degree and in kind.

Self-evident as this approach may seem, we must linger a little at this point in order to deal with the objection that the group and not the individual is primary in matters of culture. The implications of an individualistic approach are indeed revolutionary, and it may well be urged that by beginning with the individual, we do not take account of the "uniqueness" of the group, in all its mystical depth, and thereby do violence to its nature.

Let us concede then at the outset that all forms of culture are group phenomena. But let us also bear in mind that all advances in culture or religion were occasioned by individuals who successfully resisted the spell of group culture. For our purposes, we may define culture as the way people live, feel, and think, aspire and dream, and the way in which they articulate their inner life. In history, culture comes in plural and particularistic forms, as the cultures or subcultures of certain tribes, ethnic groups, nations, and races at different epochs in their development. Every individual is born and raised in a specific culture and even subculture, his personality being molded by the ideas and practices prevailing within the "closed society" of which he is part. But the growth of the individual and of the culture itself is achieved necessarily by resistance to the pressure of the "closed society," whether this advance consists in the promulgation of more universal values than those of the limited group, or whether it consists of the deepening of the inherent values of the "closed society." Invariably the exponents of each culture at its best constitute a small "creative minority" within it, to use a phrase of Toynbee's, or "the remnant that returns," to use an expression of Isaiah's. Only when a group is devoid of power to control its own destiny does it sometimes appear that the "creative minority" represents the entire group, since in that case the artistic and literary production of the elite constitute the only expressions of the life of the collective body. In brief, culture is of the group, but creativity in culture is of the individual.

Since we are concerned with the emergence of the standard American Jewish personality, we deal not with a static cultural situation but with the dynamic play of forces at the intersection of diverse cultures and ethnic loyalties. To appraise affairs fundamentally, we have to begin with rock-bottom reality, the mass of Jewish individuals seeking happiness and fulfillment. For us, the spiritual growth of the Jewish individual and his well-being constitute together the measure of all things. Everything else is superstructure that is all too often compounded of the debris of hollow clichés and outdated slogans. The individual is the one firm focus by reference to which all claims of a material or spiritual nature are to be judged. "The Sabbath is given over to you, not you to the Sabbath."[2]

To allow for the progressive emergence of the empirical individual is to envision the future Jewish community as consisting of Jewish Americans, not American Jews. Abstract and subtle as this distinction may appear to be, the fundamental issues of Jewish life hinge upon it.

Although it has become fashionable in our day to ignore the subtleties of classical logic, it is nevertheless true that people assume the genus and differentia of definitions in all their thinking and even in their everyday speech. Talk to any thoughtful Jew regarding the shape of the future, and back of his earnest soul-searching you will encounter the question, What am I essentially—a Jew or an American? He knows that both designations apply to him, but he desires to know whether in the domain of civil and public affairs he *is* the one or the other, automatically, as it were, apart from any volition or action on his part. Compliance with the law of the land is never in question among our people, but there is considerable confusion regarding the ultimate source out of which our loyalties, sentiments, and judgments spring into being. All American Zionists agree that our people owe "political loyalty" to America alone, but some of our people sometimes stress the adjective "political" as if it bore the connotations ephemeral and superficial. Still unresolved for many people is the feeling of fraternal unity, the sense of mine and thine, the awareness of one's identity. It is this core of identity, underlying all loyalties, that is basically in question whenever we discuss the shape of the future.

Generally, it is the realm of discourse that determines when any particular quality becomes substantive or adjectival. Thus, when the affairs of this world are in question, we speak of Methodist or Episcopalian or agnostic or fundamentalist Americans. If we move in the theological realm of dogmas, beliefs, and practices, then we may contrast American Protestants with British Protestants. The separation of Church and State became possible when religious differences were recognized to be matters of private conscience, relatively unimportant to the actual struggle of national or territorial groups for "a place in the sun." Thus, in the modern world, geographical and national bonds become substantive, with religious affiliations being recognized as adjectival in character. If the same situation is presumed to apply to Jews, then we may conclude that in all matters relating to the struggle of nations, we are on the way to becoming Jewish Americans.

Our point may be clarified by the following analogy. We may think of people as being subject to both horizontal loyalties, relating them to their fellow men, and vertical loyalties, relating them to universal human ideals. There is always tension and sometimes conflict between different horizontal loyalties, but none between horizontal and vertical loyalties. Of course, vertical ideals may lead indirectly to horizontal loyalties, but then they are subject to many qualifications, varying in accord with the intellectual climate prevailing in different parts of the world. Thus, Christians of one or another denomination, because of their loyalty to their faith, may establish a "mission" in a specific portion of the globe, acquiring, in a remote people, horizontal friendly interests that derive ultimately from a vertical, heaven-directed loyalty.

If now we allow for the increasing emphasis on individualism to run its course, we cannot see any reason for believing that the Jew will hold on to those horizontal loyalties that the rest of the American people have discarded. His vertical loyalties to Judaism will cause him to entertain horizontal loyalties to the bearers of Judaism wherever they may be, but such loyalties will be variable quantities, dependent upon many factors. There are probably three million Jews in Soviet Russia and in its satellites, men and women who are closer to us, in point of ethnic kinship and cultural background, than any other branch of world Jewry. But in terms of faith and political realities, the bonds between them and us are becoming ever more tenuous. Hence, looking into the future, we cannot but envisage the virtually complete severance of these bonds. On the other hand, the brown Jews of North Africa and the black Jews of Africa and Asia, much as they differ from us in race, are likely to be the objects of our enduring concern. If our hopes for the revival of Judaism in Israel are fulfilled, American Jews of the future will look to Israel as their spiritual center. If, on the other hand, the "Canaanite" mentality should gain ascendancy in the land of Israel, the bonds of loyalty between them and our children will become vestigial and minimal.

Basically, we assume that in the future American Jews will come to enjoy in their own mind and heart that status which the nineteenth-century Jews of Germany and France strove to achieve with might and main. It was a pathetic and stultifying experience for our people to imagine that they could become overnight Germans or Frenchmen "of the Mosaic faith." The term "German" or "French" included a profound strand of meaning which Jews could never make their own. They could become the best of all possible citizens, but they could not become part of those mystical biological entities that the European nations thought they were.

Between the state, as a political entity, and the nation, as a biological phenomenon, there flows unevenly the stream of cultural tradition, now swelling into a mighty tide, now ebbing into a shallow mud flat. But identifying themselves wholeheartedly with this cultural stream, the European Jews believed that they could ignore the bedrock of popular biology. However, the course of events in certain countries, though not in all the lands of Europe, proved them to be wrong. Modern nationalism became infected with the virus of biological romanticism ever more deeply, with catastrophic results for Jewish hopes on the European continent, save in England, France, the Low Countries, the Scandinavian countries, and Italy.

In contrast to the European situation, the term "American" does not contain any specific biological connotations, nor is it likely to acquire them in the foreseeable future. It is in the full light of history that the American people is emerging, and Jews have always been part of it. Hence, the ideal of Americanism cannot be so defined as to exclude Jewish Americans, and it is this ideal that carries potentially the greatest momentum. Of course, there is the term "Gentile," the last holdout of the underworld of prejudice, but it is so vacuous and all-inclusive a word as to be devoid of any serious possibilities for romantic aggrandizement. Only the imagination of a maniac could concoct out of the qualities of all nations on earth a unique Aryan essence that is presumably lacking among Jews. The "national origin" immigration laws were not ethnically exclusive in nature. Their aim was not the attainment of racial purity but rather the maintenance of racial balance. Although they were until recently discriminatory, these laws reflect the implicit recognition of the rights of all groups, albeit in the heavy-handed, rough-and-ready way of demagogues and of the untutored masses that follow them. Of decisive importance is the fact that the term "American" cannot serve the foul purposes of ethnic anti-Semitism.

Hence, it is altogether possible for the American Jew to achieve that fullness of integration with "the people of the land" that was denied to the Jews of Central Europe. Here the Jewish immigrant may well strive to become part not only of the "political" state that is America, but of that popular matrix of sentiments, ideals, memories and dreams, traditions, and even prejudices that constitute the American nation. If to be at home is not only to be in the possession of "rights" but also to be part of the people to whose service the political machinery of the state is dedicated, then the Jew can be here utterly at home, thinking of himself as an American of the Jewish faith, as "normal" in the civil sense of the term as any other citizen of the great country. This consummation, so ardently desired by the Jews of Western Europe for a century and a half, is here embraced in the cherished tradition of the country and in its basic social structure.

Ever since the brilliant essay of Ahad Ha'am on this theme was published, Jewish thinkers were familiar with the distinction between two kinds of assimilation—the healthy kind, in which a people digests and absorbs into itself whatever in the culture of the environment is suited to its nature, and the unhealthy kind, in which a people loses its own identity, dissolving completely within the "melting pot." This analysis is indeed extremely cogent in the consideration of certain cultural issues, but it is not relevant to the basic question of identification. Basically, the Jewish individual, not the group, is the subject of the integrating, or the assimilating, process. When he asks, "What should I know myself to be?" the healthy answer is the one that takes account of his particular position on the historical scene, his spiritual welfare, and his happiness. The historical position of the American Jew is the same as that of other descendants of immigrants; his spiritual welfare and his happiness both dictate a conception of Jewish loyalties that assigns them to the domain of vertical values where they supplement his American horizontal loyalties. For a century and a half, Jewish people in the Western world have been yearning and battling for "normality." This goal is now definitely on the horizon.

But so new is this possibility to the historical experience of our people that it appears to carry the overtones of treachery or desertion. Is there any moral backsliding in the notion of Jews considering themselves part of the American nation, with their Jewish loyalties falling in the adjectival category of faith and tradition? Let us hold up to analysis the varied meanings of the term "Jewish" in order that we might see exactly what is involved in the emergence of the Jewish American. Insofar as the term "Jewish" denotes our religious heritage, there is manifestly nothing narrowing or cramping in our conception, providing this heritage is taken seriously. In the mouth of marginal Jews this conception is tantamount to the avowal of total assimilation. What is at fault, however, is not their conception, but the virtual nonexistence in the Jewish consciousness of those people of any vertical loyalties. Loyalty to the Jews of Israel and other lands will depend upon the strength of the shared vertical Jewish loyalties both here and there. If then any objection is raised to this concept, it can only be on the ground of elements in our heritage that are neither national nor religious, but ethnic and quasi-metaphysical.

Indeed, there flows in the heritage of both Jews and Christians a current of thought and sentiment that would set the Jew apart from the rest of mankind by a mystical, metaphysical "iron curtain." On the Christian side of the curtain, this semiconscious penumbra accounts for the deeper layers of the miasma of anti-Semitism, out of which there issues the ghostly stereotype of the Jew as nonhuman, hence, a subhuman creature. These layers have been subjected to careful scrutiny in our own day. On the Jewish side, the notions deriving from the powerful undertow are difficult to identify. Yet, they are by no means unimportant in a study of the integration of the American Jew. Let us recall that the import of Napoleon's questions to the Assembly of the Elders was not whether Jews were willing to be "politically loyal" to the new state, but whether they were willing to consider Frenchmen as their "brothers." In his own rough dictatorial way, he sought to probe the scope and depth of the "ethnic exclusiveness" of Jewish people, which the reactionaries of his day did their best to exaggerate.

It would be idle to deny the occasional occurrence in Jewish writings of statements reflecting an isolationist ethnicism that is truly incompatible with the concept of an emergent American nation. But we maintain that Judaism also contains a stream of thought and feeling disavowing any such attitudes. In the tension between ethnicism and religion in Judaism, the healthy equilibrium was disturbed not infrequently by one tendency or the other. Because of the balance of contending forces within it, Judaism was able to assume in every age a form suitable to the noblest challenges of that age and its social realities. But such a synthesis cannot be achieved without a clear understanding of the elements that are rejected, as well as those that are embraced, in our interpretation of Judaism.

The mystical and extremely powerful feeling of "difference" between Jew and Gentile is an inescapable factor that cannot be ignored in any discussion of the future of the American Jewish community. The nature of this feeling on the part of Gentiles has been examined by psychologists and sociologists. There is unanimous agreement that this feeling is not due to any instinctive reaction against the Jewish "race." We must now inquire whether on the Jewish side this feeling is a psychosomatic reaction or an intuitive perception of the "peculiar" nature of our being, the fact that we are indeed "different."

At the outset, we must learn to distinguish between the sense of difference that is derived from vertical loyalties and the feelings of difference that are postulated on the horizontal plane. Vertical loyalties are altogether natural, healthy, and nonaggressive. In a sense, every culture and national tradition is a unique phenomenon, and there are several respects in which the vertical values of Judaism may be legitimately contrasted with the values of all other European groups, taken as a unit. On the vertical plane, there is no antagonism between the unique values of different groups. On the contrary, all cultured people feel enriched by whatever wealth may be produced by any national group. We Jews, victims though we were only recently of German hysteria and fury, nevertheless feel enriched by the music of a Beethoven, the philosophy of a Kant, the poetic maturity of a Goethe. On the other hand, any claims of difference on the horizontal plane cannot but result in hatred and arrogance, antagonism and aggression.

In normative Judaism, the claim of Israel to be an *Am Segulah* was always conceived in terms of vertical values. Thus, the *berakhah* over the Torah asserts that we are "chosen" because we are the bearers of Torah. The prophets were especially determined to elevate the Jewish sense of difference into the realm of spiritual loyalties. But if the psychology of Jewish people in all its facets is to be understood, we must bring up from the shadowy limbo the feelings of racial pride and arrogance that were associated at various times with the conception of a "treasured people." Slumbering in the collective subconscious of our people and recorded in a multitude of dusty tomes, this assertion of the superiority of the Jewish race would long ago have disappeared from the realm of practical affairs were it not for the new lease on life bestowed upon it by the Hitlerite madness. If Jewish people are attacked persistently as a "race," set apart by a mythical chasm from the rest of humanity, then it is natural for Jews to react in the same terms. We are still suffering from the aftereffects of the Hitlerite "shocks," which in many cases have brought the negative phases of ethnicism to dominance. In the psychoanalysis of an individual, forgotten memories have to be exposed to view if the patient is to be cured. Similarly, if we are to distinguish between healthy and sickly forms in which our "uniqueness" and "difference" are asserted, we must recall that the sickly forms always hovered on the fringe of normative Judaism, becoming predominant in the minds of Jewish people from time to time.

No widely held idea can be entertained by any group over a long period of time in absolute sameness and with perfect equilibrium among its varying facets and emphases. How then can we expect the notion of a "treasured people" to have been held at all times in the stillness of its prophetic perfection? Thus, Ezra's banishment of the Gentile wives and their children could not have been justified by the standards of a man like Rabbi Joshua ben Hananiah. We read in the Talmud that Rabbi Joshua insisted on the right of an Ammonite to marry a Jewess on the ground that "Sennacherib came and mixed up the nations."[3] The decrees concerning the "uncleanliness" of Gentiles and the interdiction of their oil, milk, and bread were similarly motivated by the excessive growth of ethnic zealotry.[4] Rabbi Eliezer's insistence that the "pious of the nations do not share in the World to Come" was certainly due to his nationalistic bias, as the contrary view of Rabbi Joshua ben Hananiah was a reflection of his consistent liberalism. Let us savor the taste of such passages as the following, without succumbing to the fascination of an all-reconciling and all-misunderstanding *pilpulistic* mentality: "For a holy people art thou to the Lord, Thy God . . . Hence we learn that *everyone* in Israel is accounted by the Holy One, Blessed be He, to be like all the nations of the world."[5]

"You are called 'man,' but the nations of the world are not called 'man.' "[6]

"All Israelites are sons of kings."[7]

"When the serpent cohabited with Eve, he threw corruption into her. Israel, having been at Sinai, its flow of corruption was stopped. The nations, not having stood at Sinai, their corruption did not cease."[8]

"When the Messiah comes, all people will be servants unto Israel."[9]

A highly esteemed author of a very popular pietistic work even dealt seriously with the question of why the nations have the same appearance as Jews, though the souls of the Israelites derive from the spirit of holiness, while the souls of the nations issue out of the spirit of uncleanliness.[10]

We need hardly explore this shadowy underworld of Judaism any further in order to realize that the seeming axioms of Jewish ethnic "uniqueness" were based upon ideas that our people today reject with the utmost vehemence. As the full depth of anti-Semitism cannot be understood apart from the myths of the ancient and medieval world, the pathos of racial "uniqueness" cannot be seen in its true nature apart from the acrimonious context in which it was conceived and nurtured. It is the same tradition that contains those noble teachings which have always counterbalanced the impact of glorified ethnicism.

Thus, many authors of the Talmud loved to imagine that some of the greatest rabbis were descended from Gentiles. One rabbi declared that a "Gentile who studies the Torah is like unto a high priest." [11] Another insisted that the special status of Jews as "sons" of the Lord is dependent upon their good conduct. One sage was so all-embracing in his breadth of view as to confer the name Jew on all who deny the validity of idolatry. [12] While the discriminations in Jewish Law against pagans are well-known, few are aware that the Talmud teaches the principle of universal philanthropy—"We are in duty bound to feed the poor of the nations together with the Jewish poor." [13] By the same token, the ambiguous attitude of Jewish Law toward Christians furnished inexhaustible material for renegades and hate merchants, but the views of a philosophic codifier like Rabbi Menahem Meiri, who specifically and systematically reinstated the category of monotheists in Jewish Law, did not become known until our own day. [14]

Indeed, our tradition is just as capable of furnishing aid and comfort to a humane liberalism as to a zealous ethnicism. Since the fury of ethnic zeal is sustained by the twin-headed Hydra of dogmatism and bitterness, we may look forward to the steady decline of the isolationist component of ethnicism within the pattern of contemporary Judaism. Thus, the aura of plausibility that clung to the dogma of racial "uniqueness" for so many decades is due to fade away along with the associated ideas and exotic phantasies of the twilight realm of Qabbalah.

The enduring interest of American Jewry in Jews of all lands, especially of Israel, is likely to accelerate this development, rather than to retard it. As time goes on, Israel will come to occupy in the consciousness of American Jews the same place as do the other lands in the hearts of the immigrants to these shores. Before the rise of the State of Israel, Jewish immigrants differed from all others in that there was no specific geographical focus for their sentiments. Jews were loyal to the world fellowship of Israel and its tradition, rather than to any specific country. Insofar as this universal fellowship is progressively being narrowed to one place on the map, Jewish people too will have a place "whence" in spirit they had come. Their national feelings will thus tend to follow the pattern of the steadily weakening national sentiments of other immigrant groups. The progressive preponderance of Oriental and African elements within the population of Israel might also serve as an additional demonstration that world Jewry is a fellowship of the spirit, not of blood or civilization.

Does the transformation of the genus "Jew living in America" to the genus "Jewish American" involve the progressive lessening of Jewish religious-cultural loyalties? The answer to this question is both Yes and No. On the one hand, the consciousness of "normality" will encourage those who have no feeling for the values of our tradition to drift into the anonymity of the general community. The Jewishly ignorant and the embittered, the eager opportunists and the dust-dry rationalists, the rootless intellectuals and the witless hangers-on will be likely to desert our ranks in a steady procession. On the other hand, the contrary tendency will also be intensified. Since the Jewish quality of one's being can no longer be regarded as an automatic category into which people fall with or without their will, it must necessarily find expression in positive acts of identification. Precisely because it fits into the American pattern of a unitary nation with multiple faiths, Jewish loyalty will derive accessions of strength from both the pervasive atmosphere of American culture and the momentum of Jewish tradition.

Political loyalties, social ties, and cultural-religious ideals constitute, respectively, the three dimensions of social life. If Jewishness is regarded as falling into the fundamental dimensions of our nature, like length and breadth, then it need not find expression in the cultural-religious dimension of height at all. Thus, in Israel, Jewish loyalty is preempted by all the ordinary tasks and concerns of citizenship and is not impelled to flow in religious channels, while, in the Diaspora, it tends even now to be felt in the dimension of height and asserted in humanitarian cultural and religious terms. This instructive contrast will become ever more apparent as Jews in America liberate themselves from the lingering social pressures that hemmed in the Jewish community of the past like an iron ring. Already, American Jews are beginning to act on an instinctive assumption of their status as Jewish Americans. The Central Conference of American Rabbis has adopted a program of proselytization among Gentiles, demonstrating by an action-symbol that Judaism is essentially a faith. Could it have launched this program earlier without provoking a storm of protests?

Already it is clear that Judaism in America, revolving around a typical modern congregation, is more likely to endure than Orthodoxy in

Israel. In spite of its virtual state monopoly, Orthodoxy in Israel is gradually withdrawing into a ghetto of its own making, becoming desiccated and fossilized. In contrast, Judaism in America is constantly challenged to prove its worth, hence, its vitality and vibrancy. Whatever is lost through the defection of Jews whose sole claim to the name is that of ethnic descent is likely to be more than made up by the enhanced determination of the three-dimensional Jews to respond affirmatively to the inescapable challenge of the American environment.

In sum, the complex strands of Jewish loyalty were always woven out of the rugged and earthy feelings of blood-kinship, as well as out of the fine and ethereal ideals of faith. The proportion and relative potency of these elements varied in accord with the liberalism and breadth of view of individual Jews and the fluctuation of fortune in our long history. During the past century, two causes combined to reduce the potency and relevance of faith—the growing secularization of life and the tightening of the vise of hatred directed against all Jews. Thus, the bonds of Jewish loyalty consisted, for many of our contemporaries, of the dark and mystical threads of "blood and soil," reinforced by the feelings of resentment against the outside world and enveloped in the fluffy clouds of nostalgic affection for ancient "ways of life." The resulting complex of emotions was unsatisfactory and, hence, dynamic in character, issuing in a longing for the "normalization" of feeling, either in the attainment of the fullness of emancipation or in the radical solution of the "in gathering of the exiles." The glowing promise of emancipation could not be realized in those lands where the national loyalty of Gentiles was conceived predominantly in ethnic and mystical terms. Standing at the threshold of the fourth century of Jewish life in America, we can foresee the progressive "normalization" of Jewish feeling; hence, the shrinking of the ethnic strands of loyalty, the forging of ever stronger bonds of fraternity with the American people, and the steady growth of the ideal and religious components of Judaism.

NOTES

1. Ralph Barton Perry, *Characteristically American,* New York, Knopf, 1949, pp. 36–37.
2. Mechilta, Yithro.
3. Berochot 28a.
4. Shabbat 17a and 153.

5. Ish Sholom, ed., *Sifra D'be Rab,* 97.

6. Yebamoth 61a.

7. Shabbat 128a.

8. Shabbat 146a.

9. Erubin 43b.

10. Isaiah Halevi Hurwitz, *Shnai Luhot Haberit,* p. 15.

11. Baba Kama 38a.

12. Megillah 13a.

13. Gittin 61a.

14. Beth Habehirah on Abodah Zara, by M. Meiri, ed., A. Schreiber, New York, 1944, pp. 46, 591. See Jacob Katz's *Exclusiveness and Tolerance,* New York, 1962, pp. 119–128.

15

JEWISH SELF-IMAGE IN THE POSTWAR WORLD

IN THEIR STRUGGLE for the fullness of emancipation, the Jews relied most heavily on the help of liberals and they redefined their identity in terms of individual freedom. The ideals and the temper of liberalism were ranged solidly on the side of Jewish people, as they struggled to overcome the effects of religious prejudices and ethnic zealotry. The conservative mood, apart from party platforms, resented any kind of change, and esteemed highly the worth of prejudice, as a helpful brake against the changing and disintegrating forces that operate in modern society.

In the case of Zionism, however, liberalism was ambivalent. The sympathies of liberals were with the Jews, but their ideals called for the solution of Jewish homelessness through the securing of the rights of individuals, wherever they happened to live. Already in the days of Herzl, the antisemites of Russia, Germany and France found it easier to sympathize with the cause of a Jewish homeland than the liberals, the old-time friends of Jewish people.

England was a special case, since its imperial interests coincided from time to time with its idealistic concern for the fate of Eastern European Jewry. The "Jewish homeland" was needed, it would be said, not for the solution of "the Jewish question" in England, but to provide for the stream of refugees from the East. Also, in England, the biblical tradition was strong and the Zionist ideal awakened echoes of ancient romantic visions. As J. L. Talmon put it:

"For one thing, no Jewish historian, whatever his evaluation of the various factors involved in the restoration of Jewish statehood, can ignore the fact that Zionism would never have had a chance for success if centuries of Christian teaching and worship, liturgy and legend had not conditioned the Western nations to respond almost instinctively to the words 'Zion' and 'Israel,' and thus to see in the Zionist ideal not a romantic chimera or an imperialistic design to wrest a country from its actual inhabitants, but the consummation of an eternal promise and hope." [1]

Anglo-American liberals were particularly sensitive to the charge of injuring the Palestinian Arabs, in the effort to render justice to the cause of world Jewry. After the establishment of the state of Israel, the cause of the Arab refugees clashed in the American conscience with that of the Jews in Israel.

A good illustration of this conflict is seen in the hesitant and equivocal posture of the *Christian Century Magazine* toward Zionism and Israel. While this central organ of the non-Fundamentalist Protestants was naturally sympathetic to the plight of Jewish refugees, it fought a persistent rear-guard action against the establishment of the Jewish state.

In his study, "American Protestantism and a Jewish State," Herzl Fishman concluded:

"A basic contradiction exists between the attitude of American Protestantism toward Jews as individuals and its attitude toward the Jewish people as a collective entity. Modern liberal Protestantism has consistently protested overt antisemitic acts against individual Jews and has labeled antisemitism a theological sin. But it has remained blind to the sharp contrast which exists between its theoretical objections to antisemitism and the practical injurious effects of its own subtle antisemitism on the destiny of the Jewish people as a collective body. Protestantism's liberal attitude toward Jews as individuals stands in sharp contrast to its persistently hostile attitude toward Jewish peoplehood." [2]

To be sure, Protestant liberals were joined in their critical attitude toward the Jewish State by such non-theological thinkers as Virginia Gildersleeve, Dorothy Thompson and the renowned philosopher, Ernest Wm. Hocking. On the other hand, Reinhold Niebuhr, a Christian "realist," was an ardent defender of the state of Israel.

We might perhaps discern the root of this ambivalence in the distinction between an ideological liberalism, that does not allow for the occurrence of exceptional situations, and an empirical liberalism, which recognizes the imperfection of all categorizations and takes account of the unique elements in every historical event.

So Jews were equally divided, with the ideological liberals holding on tenaciously to the concept of Jewish identity that was developed in nineteenth-century Western Europe, while the empirical realists recognized that an unprecedented situation called for a new response. The empiricists had to mediate between the ideological Jewish nationalists, for whom the center of Jewish life the world over was first the vision of Zion and later the state of Israel, and the ideological liberals; the compromise consisted in offering help to the poor immigrants in Israel and elsewhere, without identifying with them. While the ideologists at both ends of the Jewish spectrum affirmed their respective beliefs, the actual policy of Jewish leadership tended to reflect the views of the empiricists, since the logic of events was on their side.

It was the liberal concept of a society of individuals banding together to form a government that Jewish leaders accepted with alacrity ever since the American and French revolutions. But, the liberal society was never born in czarist Russia, where the majority of the Jews lived. As Jews from the Pale of Settlement moved westward toward Germany, France, England and America, they clung in the early generations to their identity, either in the form of Yiddish Socialist ethnicism, or Orthodoxy, or Hebraic Zionism. Had the tide of liberalism continued its vigorous flow, the ideals of Jewish "folkism," or of Zionism, or of "sacred ethnicism" would have remained the preoccupation of a few visionaries. But, the course of history was involuted, troubled by the "cultural lag" and by the ebb and flow of romantic nationalism. The liberation of the common man implied attention to popular prejudices. More people are moved by sentiment and passion than by logic and principles.

Within the Jewish community, the Holocaust, the subsequent long fight to bring the refugees to a safe haven, the battle to establish Israel and secure its existence, the series of crises and wars which followed— all these developments and challenges involved the cooperation of a generation of Jewish leaders in a vast effort of rescue and rehabilitation, which was totally unprecedented. It would have been strange indeed if such a tremendous undertaking had not generated feelings of fraternity and unity, so intense and pervasive as to surpass the visions and hopes of previous generations.

The liberals who approach the Jewish situation, armed with ready-made ideals of an open society, have to recognize the scars on the consciousness of today's generation of Jewish leaders, scars made by a series of cruel and unprecedented events. On the other hand, it is equally wrong for Jewish ideologists to create a theology of Jewish exceptionalism, based upon a concept of mystical "peoplehood," that they would not want to be adopted by other historic communities. The everlasting enemy of Jewish people is the champion of a "closed society," closed religiously by the ramparts of dogma and the acids of contempt for the outsider, or closed politically by reducing the state to the service of one historic nation, or closed bureaucratically by confining the privileges of citizenship to those who espouse the ideas of the ruling elite. In an open society, there will be at any one time some tension between ethnic subgroups, whose militant leaders clamor for more and more power and influence, and those who champion the national interest as a whole. It is not true, as a general rule, that what is good for any one such subgroup is good for the whole. On the other hand, the exponents of the national interest must recognize the evil consequences of the kind of patriotism that freezes minorities out of the national consensus. Such a rigid mentality would in time destroy all "creative minorities" within the nation. What is needed is a view of the national society that allows for a sympathetic understanding of the special needs of its component groups, and an implicit commitment on the part of all ethnic and historical communities to keep their respective concerns within the parameters of the national interest and the national ideal.

Basically, the Jews of America and of the free world generally remain ardently liberal. The vast majority describe their Jewish identity as being that of a religious community. They reject any tendency to secede from the general community and to form separate enclaves. Their Jewishness imposes upon them additional obligations, such as assistance to Jews who are in distress and to the state of Israel, which was set up for the purpose of rendering such assistance.

Their Jewishness is also a cluster of memories, a pattern of living and an indomitable hope, all interpreted in the light of a religious tradition. But their Jewishness does not separate them from other citizens, save in the dimension of religious faith and practice, and in the maintenance of a worldwide network of philanthropies, previously directed at diverse centers of distress and now focused on Israel.

J. L. Talmon, an Israeli historian, is somewhat unhappy with the tendency of liberals to interpret Jewish issues "in terms of tolerance or intolerance, in the context of the struggle between liberty and tyranny." While "Jewish nationalism and racist anti-semitism both attribute great significance to the Jewish phenomenon," the liberals view even the Holocaust "as an unfortunate, but only temporary, relapse into intolerance. The intentions of the liberals are good. But in one sense, their attitude is at best superficial, and at worst somewhat offensive to Judaism. The majesty attached to a unique fate is impaired and the awesome grandeur of an apocalyptic tragedy is wholly missed." [3]

Insofar as Talmon inveighs against the tendency of ideological liberals to gloss over the specific details of the Jewish situation, we go along with him. But, he also articulates a longing, however vague, for the aura of unique "majesty" to adorn Jewish self-consciousness. Is not this passion for national "grandeur" the very sin which perverted the national visions of the Fichtes and the Dostoevskys? Talmon speaks not of a Jewish mission but of a Jewish "fate," "to serve as a testimony, as a living witness, a touchstone, a whipping block and symbol—all in one." Again, we can go with him only part of the way. In a continent inflamed by the mystique of nationalism and race, the Jew served as "the outsider," the only concrete exemplar of the preponderant mass of humanity that is "non-Aryan."

But in a situation already bedeviled by an excess of mysticism, why deepen the mystery? As rational students, we cannot speak of an eternal or a unique fate. As circumstances change, the roles of nations are apt to change as well. From its very inception, Judaism opposed the notion of fate. Nations may choose tasks or missions, but fate is imposed from without by a blind force. We can do without such "grandeur." In order to survive as a creative religious community, the Jews of America need only to do their best in generally human terms, and the Jews of Israel need to win their neighbors over for coexistence in peace.

In neither case do we encounter an overwhelming need to strike the posture of "uniqueness." In history, all groups are actually different, therefore unique, but the essential goals of all people are alike and rational. To insist on fostering "uniqueness," as a presumed basis for survival, is to court the sickly fantasy of narcissism.

TOYNBEE AND HIS CHALLENGE

The English historian, Arnold J. Toynbee, virtually shocked the entire Jewish community by the challenge that he presented in his monumental work, "A Study of History." Completed at a time when Jewish people were undergoing both the anguish of the memories of the Holocaust and the exhilaration of Israel's triumphs, Toynbee's analysis touched a raw nerve in Jews. They were offended more by his comments on the nature and destiny of modern Israel than by his assessment of Diaspora Jewry. His views were resented all the more because he wrote as one who belonged to the traditional friends of Israel. Toynbee was a humanist, a liberal Christian, a cultivated intellectual and an avowed disciple of the great Hebrew prophets, particularly Deutero-Isaiah. Jews were accustomed to attacks from demagogues, chauvinists, purveyors of "mystiques" of one kind or another. But, to be the target of criticism at the hands of a superintellectual and a champion of humanism—this was a different matter altogether.[4]

In fact, Toynbee was by no means antagonistic either to Judaism or to Jewish people. Far from being an antisemite, he described the antisemitic heritage of the Christian world as one of its two great sins, the other being the institution of Negro slavery.[5] Furthermore, as an expert in the British Foreign Office, he was a dedicated anti-Nazi, having shared in the task of awakening the British public to the menace of Hitlerism.[6] All the more, then, Jews were shocked by Toynbee's critique, especially in respect of the following areas: his reference to Jewry as "a fossil of Syriac civilization," his persistent references to "Judaic zealotry" as the heritage of the Christian world, his denigration of Jewish nationalism in general and his critique of Israel in particular; his view of Jewish history as culminating in tragic failure in spite of remarkable spiritual achievements; and his gloomy estimate of the future of Israel. Each one of these critiques challenged the emergent self-image of Jewish intellectuals in the post-Holocaust, post-Israel's birth, post-Vatican II world. These barbs hurt precisely because they were partially true, though only partially so.

The term, "fossil," emerged out of Toynbee's classification of civilizations. In contrast to Spengler's description of cultures in terms of their respective "souls," symbolized by their diverse conceptions of space, Toynbee aimed to be empirical, down to earth, concerned with hard facts. A civilization was a "field of study"; that is, a geographical area, within which a measure of cultural unity prevailed, whether or not it was governed by one "universal state." In fact, the establishment of political unity was in his view a mark of regression or the beginning of the "breakdown" of a civilization, since further spontaneous growth was likely to be inhibited by the imperial Leviathan.

Toynbee's approach to world-history was motivated in large part by his revulsion against the great German historians, who prepared the way for the monstrous ideology of Nazism. The Hegelian tradition, which idealized the power-state as the incarnation of World-Reason, was implicit in the works of Ranke, Treitschke and Meinecke, let alone in the proto-Nazism of Spengler's "Prussianism."

In their so-called "world-historical" perspective, might is right, for "world-history is the world-court"; the war-making power of a state is the measure of its moral strength, and each historical epoch generates its own self-contained realm of values. It follows that such power-states cannot be judged in terms of a transnational, universal law. This adulation of the state was reinforced by the growth of romantic nationalism, which substituted the character of the "folk" and "the voice of blood" for the Hegelian World-Reason. The historical nation, as a biological entity, with all its dark mystery, was the heart and soul of the "nation-state." It is easy to see that such a "folkist" view made life intolerable for all ethnic minorities in Eastern Europe and, in the case of the Jews, it helped to bring on an antisemitic tide which seemed irresistible.

Toynbee was thoroughly disenchanted with European nationalism and the Teutonic worship of "blood and iron."[7] The two World Wars were seen by him as mighty civil wars; comparable to the Peloponnesian War, in which the confederation of Hellenic cities led by Athens battled against the alliance headed by Sparta. Nationalism was a social disease, the virulence of which was proportional to the extent the nation-state included elements of different nationalities. Hence, his projection of a transnational field of study, defined by external factors of similarity of language and mores.

In the case of the ancient Near East and the emergence of the Jewish people, he chose the entity which he entitled "Syriac Civilization," encompassing Babylonia, Syria, Canaan and later Judea. Within that ancient civilization Judaism functioned as the great Reform movement, transmuting the culture of its peoples in the light of the monotheistic ideas of the prophets, from Abraham to the great unknown prophet of the Exile.

Syriac civilization has been superseded in its homeland by Islamic civilization. It no longer plays a role in world-history. Only scattered remnants of it remain; the Nestorians in the Near East, the Parsees in India and the Jews in Europe.

But, though Toynbee made heroic efforts to overcome the Germanic tradition in the philosophy of history, he retained some of its impetus. He did not free himself altogether from the spell of biological categories. A society is, after all, not an organic entity, tempting as it might be to describe it in terms of birth and abortion, maturation and senescence, fossilization and death. In his effort to overcome the fascination of German historicism, he failed to go far enough, to judge by his own lights, and continued to substitute biological metaphors for sociological realities. A "fossil" is a biological term, borrowed from the theory of evolution. It refers to a creature which remains the same and no longer responds creatively to new challenges. This characterization opens the way for the nose of the camel of "Social Darwinism," with all its destructive potentialities. It reflects the romantic distinction between "old" and "new" nations. The latter are presumably entitled by the law of historical progress to sweep the former off the stage of history. Now, Toynbee distinctly disavows this conclusion, but it seems to be implicit in his categorization.[8]

In the self-image of Jewish people, the aura of antiquity is reverently extolled, but modern Jews also think of themselves as pioneers in every cultural endeavor. The Jewish people today, in Israel and in America, are far from being encased in a cocoon of ancient rites and dogmas. Apart from isolated enclaves here and there, they are in truth "old-new," engaged in transforming themselves as well as their environment. All great, civilized communities are "old-new," and the Jewish people are possibly "more so." By Toynbee's own definition, a growing civilization is one which presents ever fresh challenges to itself and then responds to them. Jewish people in modern times have kept abreast of every European ideological movement, reacting individually and communally to the changing winds of doctrine.

The average Jewish reader might not have resented Toynbee's characterization so much, if the latter had used a more felicitous phrase — such as, "the unchanged embodiment of ancient Hebraic culture." The term, "Syriac," appeared to many Jews as a deliberate obliteration of the Hebraic contribution to the treasure of human culture. Was not the character and destiny of the Jewish people determined largely by its deep sense of distinctiveness "from all the nations"? Why then have it coupled in one category with those ancient peoples that had no inner bonds with it and were related to it only by the external factors of geography, linguistics and chronology? Furthermore, at a time when Jews and Arabs were engaged in a mortal struggle, some readers felt that by subsuming Hebraic history under the Syrian rubric, Toynbee added insult to injury.[9]

But, the most telling objection to this phrase is the fact that it enshrines a "reductionist" view of Jewish life, that is all too prevalent. The tremendous variety and vigor of modern Jewish life is treated as if it were no more than the medieval ghetto-community; the latter is "reduced" to the ancient dispersion of the first century, and that community in turn is viewed as if it were the congregation of the returning exiles at the time of Ezra and Nehemiah. As Martin Wight points out, Toynbee at times identifies Judaism, not with the prophets, but with the pre-prophetic, so-called "Yahweh-religion," emphasizing "God's jealousy and Power."

In all these judgments, Toynbee reflected the ancient Christian view of Jewish history. Though he regarded himself consciously as a post-Christian, he was deeply steeped emotionally and imaginatively in the old Christian tradition, which continued to serve him as a source of myth and imagery. So, he wrote again and again of Jerusalem that "did not know the time of her visitation." While he did not believe that Jesus was the Messiah or "the Son of God," he utilized the saga of the New Testament as a treasury of metaphors, thereby contributing to the denigration of the Jewish people.

Every historian is tempted to write as if he were a judge of nations, rendering the verdict of history. With the benefit of hindsight, does it not appear fairly certain that Jews would have been happier if they had "accepted" Jesus as their Messiah and had then proceeded to convert the world? St. Paul himself was apparently convinced that the Gentiles would not have embraced Jesus as their Savior, if the Jewish Sanhedrin had recognized him as the Messiah. Furthermore, suppose the Jews of the first century saw the "handwriting on the wall" and recognized that their interests would best be served if they turned Christian, would they have become a great people if they silenced their doubts for the sake of worldly success? Obviously, they would have been untrue to the teaching of him who exclaimed, "What boots it for a man to win the world and lose his soul." As the Jewish people in Jesus' day and later saw it, the question at issue was one of "truth" and "falsehood," not of "survival," or "success," or "grandeur." And Toynbee himself, being a post-Christian, agreed that Jesus was not a "son of God," or the one in whom Israel's hope was indeed fulfilled.

Martin Wight pointed out that "Christianity did not 'break decisively with Judaism by recognizing and proclaiming that God is love.' "[10] The issue was "Messiahhood," not the character of God. Judaism affirmed that God is Love, but also Justice and Power. He is "our Father, our King," "Gracious and Merciful." According to an ancient Midrash, when the Lord set out to create mankind, He provided for the mingling of His two attributes of Justice and Love in the conduct of Providence; otherwise, the society of mankind would have fallen apart.[11]

Nor did Christianity emphasize only the quality of Love in its preaching: The early Christians accepted the gloomy perspective of the Apocalyptic preachers, like Ezra IV, who imagined that the vast majority of mankind would be cast into the everlasting fires of hell.[12] In contrast, the *Mishnah,* the authoritative edition of the Oral Law, declares, "The judgment of the wicked in hell is twelve months."[13] On the other hand, in the comments of the later teachers of the Talmud, eternal hell is reinstated.

Also, as is well known, the liberal Pharisees asserted that "the pious among the nations will share in the World to Come."[14] It is not necessary for Gentiles to become Jews in order to attain salvation. All they need to do is to abide by "the seven Noachian principles,"[15] which may be described as the universal laws of religion and ethics. They need not become part of any "Israel of the spirit," though they are welcome to join "Israel of the flesh"; they could continue to practice the "ways of their fathers," providing they imbued their traditional worship and social institutions with the love of God and the love of man.[16] Naturally, rabbis like Hillel believed that their Oral Law was the best "commentary" on the Golden Rule.[17] But then, there is all the difference in the world between the appreciative claim of a religionist, who maintains, "Your practice is good, mine is better" and the strident assertion of a fanatic, "Your ways lead to hell eternal; mine alone lead to salvation."

I do not maintain that all the Pharisees were liberal and tolerant and that all the early Christians were intolerant and obsessed with the fear of damnation. There was tension within both communities. Some Jewish teachers maintained that only Jews would be "saved."[18] In Christianity, the doctrine of *praeparatio evangelica* implied that seeds of divine truth were scattered in diverse pagan cultures, but they were fully contained in the Old Testament, albeit in a concealed, metaphorical form. In Judaism, the climax is still to come, in the messianic future. All cultures and faiths are in the stage of *praeparatio,* if they incorporate and cherish the Noachian principles; all are bidden to help prepare the way. So, after describing the glory of the Messiah, Micah states, "For all the nations will walk, each in the name of its god, and we shall walk in the name of the Lord, our God."[19] (Micah 4,5)

Why, then, did men of immense erudition and overflowing good will, like Toynbee, repeat the disparaging judgments of Judaism that have become virtually traditional in the Christian world down to our own day? In the first place, it is natural for non-specialists to ignore the great body of rabbinical literature that was in effect a continuing commentary on the Hebrew Bible. For a long time, only fragments of that literature were available to Christian scholars, and these fragments were frequently selected with guile and malice in order to prove the "depravity" of the rabbis.[20]

Consequently, modern Jews were viewed at times, as if they stepped bodily out of the pages of the Old Testament. And Israel's treatment of the Arabs is sometimes discussed against the background of the Deuteronomic injunction to annihilate the original inhabitants of Canaan.

As if there had been no growth and development from the earliest strata of Israel's tradition to the present! We recall that even masters of biblical criticism, like the radical New Testament scholar Bruno Bauer, described the Jewish people as "ahistorical," i.e., unchanged and unvaried by the ups and downs of history. Christian scholars of this type, be it noted, concurred with the Orthodox Jewish teachers who maintained a similar thesis, but one charged with inverse valence, namely, that in view of the absolute perfection of Torah there was no development and no change in Jewish teaching from Moses at Sinai to the Yeshivot of our day.

A persistent notion among Christian scholars, for which there is no Judaic parallel, is that the great prophets and saints in biblical Israel were "Christians" before Christ, whom Ezra and Nehemiah repudiated when they fashioned the basic patterns of Jewish life. A century of Jewish scholarship has uncovered the threads leading from the prophets to the Pharisees and to the rabbis of the Talmud. The rabbis regarded the prophets as interpreters of the Torah, not its opponents. On the Sabbath day, "the Law and the Prophets" were read in order to provide a dialectical basis for a fuller comprehension of the Divine Word.

In a deeper sense, the prophets at their best articulated the Divine Word, as it is perceived in a flash of mystical experience and then recollected and formulated in accord with the "inner light" of conscience and intelligence. In contrast to the ecstatic "prophetizers," the classical prophets appealed to the minds and hearts of their hearers. They sought to overcome the barriers of ethnic arrogance and ritualistic magic in order to present the "I-Thou" relation of man and God in its fullness. Therein lies their perennial charm and youthfulness.

It is precisely in this sense that the Pharisees continued the work of the prophets. They applied the canons of logic and ethics to the inherited tradition, transforming many an ancient law, which was in their view unjust.[21] They sought to translate the ideals of the Prophets— "the knowledge of the Lord," "the love of kindness," "deeds of justice," "walking humbly with the Lord"—into a daily pattern of living for all the people.

We may add that the great philosophers of Judaism, from Philo to Hermann Cohen and Martin Buber, continued to interpret the tradition in the spirit of the prophets. They sought to uncover the inner meaning of all the laws, in the assurance that clear thinking and ethical living constitute the Primary Intention of all the Commandments.[22]

With all the caveats, it cannot be denied that Toynbee's image of the "fossil" does reflect an important aspect of Jewish life, as it is seen from the standpoint of universal history. The scattered Jewish communities of the Diaspora form a different entity than the peoples around them. Toynbee recognized that what makes the Jews different is more than a creed.

Jews are a people, as well as an ecclesia, indeed a people that is darkly shadowed in the minds of their neighbors by a protean cloud of vague myths, hostile judgments and a disturbing sense of alienation. All these differentia were formed long ago in another culture. In the *milletal* system of the Turkish empire, the Jewish situation was not as peculiar as it might appear in the western world, but even there it bore the stigmata of inferiority and rejection. We recall that Leo Pinsker sought to capture the Jewish differentia in the image of a "ghostly" nation, arousing fear, suspicion and hate. Pinsker proposed what he called "Auto-emancipation," the acquisition of a territory, where Jews could settle and form a state of their own. In this way, they would acquire the blessing of "normalcy."

Short of that total transformation, the Jewish dispersion could be regarded either as a relic of the past, or as a precursor of the future. Toynbee accepts both alternatives. He regards Diaspora Jewry as a "fossil" of an ancient civilization. At the same time, he maintains that the Jews of the Diaspora could well serve as a vanguard of diaspora-communities scattered throughout the world. He cites the phrase, "civilization is deracination."[23]

"If we are right in looking upon the universal states that have already come and gone as having been the forerunners of a future world-state, the social structure for which the Jewish diaspora provides a model will have a practical, as well as an academic interest for the living generation of mankind and our successors . . .

"Now that the World is becoming one city, we may expect to see associations based on neighborhood come to be overshadowed by others based on spiritual affinity: that is to say, by diasporas in the broadest sense of the term in which this includes ubiquitous scattered minorities that are held together by religious and other ties of all kinds that are independent of locality."[24]

"In the Jewish model we see Man in the same chapter of his history clinging to some revelation, discovery, achievement, or way of life that he feels to be of supreme significance and value, and therefore exerting himself to preserve the separate identity of the 'Chosen People' that is the custodian of this pearl of great price. The 'Chosen People's' belief in its national mission gives it the spirit to maintain itself in diaspora after losing its national state . . ."[25]

It will be recalled that Simon Dubnow also regarded the model of the diaspora to be the "wave of the future." To Dubnow, Jews have reached long ago the highest level of national existence, that of "a spiritual nation," a level which other nationalities are likely to reach in the future. But whereas Dubnow was concerned with the maintenance of ethnic identity, Toynbee sees the great merit of the Jewish Diaspora in its potential to rise beyond ethnicity, as indeed Judaism has opened its gates before the first century to would-be converts and "spiritual converts," or "semi-converts." Toynbee calls upon the Jews to become more a "value-centered" community, than one obsessed with sheer survival. He would have Jews stress their ideals and values, their "mission," so to speak, rather that those exclusive preoccupations with ritualistic niceties and ethnic impediments which have made them a "peculiar people." Like Claude G. Montefiore, he urged that Jews include portions of the New Testament in their sacred literature, and reclaim as properly their own both Jesus and Paul—the former standing for the superiority of spirit to Law, the latter for the opening of gates wide to the Gentiles.

In these counsels, Toynbee arrived at the same position that so-called "classical Reform" attained at the turn of the century. He also reaffirmed the essentially liberal counsel to the Jews, given by the nineteenth-century historian, Theodor Mommsen. Liberal historians do not themselves resent the external particularities which separate the Jew from his neighbors, but in the light of history they fear the resurgence of popular antisemitism and the reappearance of demagogues ready and eager to fan the flames of hate and contempt for those who appear to be "outsiders." In the eyes of the populace, it is the appearance of alienism that counts, especially when those who so flaunt their separateness are also favored by an outsized share of the national pie. These liberal scholars, like the Reform ideologists, cannot be faulted for bringing us a message that some of us may not like.

Like the Jewish Reformers, Toynbee was basically optimistic. Though he chronicled the decline and fall of many civilizations, he believed that western civilization will arise from its present troubles, and overcoming the idolatry of the nation-state, proceed to build the great society of the future.

Like the Reformers, too, he was an impassioned foe of Jewish nationalism. But his anti-Zionist message was proclaimed at the very time when the hope of Zion had become the only viable solution for the hard-pressed Jews of Central and Eastern Europe. By the time the last four volumes of his "Study" appeared, the state of Israel had come into being and the anti-Zionist argument had lost its relevance and force within the Jewish community. Toynbee's critique of Zionism came up against the morally irresistible drive for the settlement of refugees in the Jewish Homeland and the need of guarding against a second Holocaust, this time in the Holy Land itself.

Toynbee's attitude toward the newly born state of Israel was motivated by a deep, subrational factor as well as by a number of meticulously reasoned considerations. It is not generally known that, as a young man working in the British Foreign Office, he had a hand in the issuance of the Balfour Declaration. During World War I, he concentrated on plans for the Near East. He argued in behalf of the breakup of the Turkish Empire into four successor-states; Turkey proper, Arabia, centered on Damascus, a national home for the Armenians, a national home for the Jews. He even asked Dr. Weizmann to read the part of his book dealing with the Jewish national home.[26] One of his articles in 1917 has been cited by a Zionist historian as "a major contribution to shaping and propagating the pro-Zionist policy in the War Cabinet."[27] At that time, the British were eager to secure the help of Russian and American Jewries for their cause and to forestall the plans of Germany to preempt the sympathies of the Zionists.

In his pro-Zionist argument, the young Toynbee acknowledged the validity of the claim of self-determination on the part of indigenous populations, but he claimed that the people of some areas in the Turkish Empire, particularly Palestine, were not yet ripe for freedom.

"There are some units, however, so raw in their growth or so deeply sunk in decay as to lack the attribute of sovereignty altogether—units which through want of population, wealth, spiritual energy, or all three together are unable to keep the spark of vitality aglow. Such dead units are the worst danger that threatens the peace of the world . . ."

There is no question but that the young Toynbee and his colleagues in the Foreign Office regarded the Arabs in Palestine as forming such a "dead unit":

"The people west of the Jordan are not Arabs, but only Arabic-speaking. The bulk of the population are *fellahin;* that is to say, agricultural workers owning land as a village community or working land for the Syrian *effendi* . . .

"These are Arabs in name who have nothing Arabic about them but their language—most of the peasants in Syria are such . . ."[28]

It is perhaps the early involvement of Toynbee in the undertaking of Great Britain to "facilitate" the building of a "Jewish homeland" in Palestine that accounts for the passion with which he later condemned that enterprise. In keeping with the tide of anticolonialism and anti-imperialism, Toynbee changed his position on all issues involving European predominance.[29] In his "Study," he inveighed against the *hubris* of western powers and bent over backward to render full recognition to non-Judaic religions and non-western cultures. He harped on the moral failure of all the religions deriving from Judaism—their exclusiveness, their intolerance, their inability to recognize that more than one pathway may lead to God. In contrast, he extolled the Hindu religions, which in his view, permitted and even favored the proliferation of divergent rites and creeds. So enamored did he become of the Hindu faiths that he virtually ignored the terrible "communal" battles between Hindus and Buddhists, which resulted in the elimination of Buddhism from the land in which it was born. There is today no dearth of religious fanaticism and intolerance on the Indian continent. And the effects of the Hindu religion on the liberation of the common man are certainly not comparable with those in the Judeo-Christian religious sphere. Consider the vile customs affecting widows, the aged and the untouchables, which still prevailed in India, at the time when the British assumed control. Certainly there is a strong, if subtle, connection between the ethical ardor of the Judeo-Christian tradition and its imputation of "jealousy" to the God of the universe, a "jealousy" which was then misdirected by dogmatists and fanatics. In the biblical view, God, who has taken the children of Israel out of the land of bondage, is also "jealous" of His people degenerating and regressing to lower, more primitive ways of living. For if God be the source of all ethical and spiritual ideals, then any unfaithfulness to Him must result in the decline and decay of the ideals He champions.

From our perspective today, it is certainly possible to separate ethical sinfulness from ritualistic transgressions. But, it took western mankind a long time to reach this stage. In history, the demonic and the divine are closely intertwined. So, the relative "tolerance" *vis a vis* different gods in India was associated with a horrible caste-system, the burning of widows and the degradation of the individual. By the same token, the social dynamism of Western Europe which generated the efflorescence of the Renaissance, the religious democracy of the Reformation, the liberalism of the English, American and French Revolutions, was the product of inner tensions within the Judeo-Christian tradition.

At this point, we take note of Toynbee's persistent description of the perversion of intolerance, or so-called "zealotry," as being Judaic in origin. He writes of "Judaic intolerance in the ethos of Christianity" or of "Judaically fanatical ferocity." [30] But, except for passages in his volume of "Reconsideration," he does not point out that the Christian belief that "God is love" is also derived from the same root. [31]

In sum, Toynbee's extreme anti–Zionist, anticolonialist, antiwestern *hubris* in religion and culture, are all inwardly related. [32] They reflect the passion of a penitent who bends over backward to beat his chest and say "mea culpa." But, one may question whether the ardor of penitence, good as it is for one's soul, is the right prescription for the channeling of the "pooled pride" of nations.

A good example of the issue before us is the allure of the notion of the chosen people. Toynbee regards the biblical notion of a people, set apart from the rest of mankind, as the source of the self-aggrandizement of Christian nations in the modern world. Ultimately, this narcissistic belief of the ancient Israelites took root in the minds of anti-Christian Germans, emerging as the Nazi madness of our own generation. Because he took this long view of the migration of an idea, he felt that his critics missed the point when they pointed to the usual "idealistic" interpretations of the chosen people concept in Judaism and Christianity: that "Israel of the Flesh" or "Israel of the Spirit" was chosen to serve and bless mankind, rather than to dominate and oppress it, or that "the concept of Israel's choice is one of humility, not of arrogance," or that Israel's destiny turned out to be one of suffering and dispersion, not of joy and triumph.

In a long note on this subject, he wrote, "I find this apologia unconvincing. I agree that the role of the 'Chosen People' has been 'everlastingly reclaimed' by the Jews, but I do not know of any evidence that it was 'reluctantly assumed' in the first instance. The Jews are not the only people who have been willing to offer up costly sacrifices on the altar of their collective self-centeredness. But self-centeredness remains the sin that it is, however high the price one may be willing to pay for the psychological satisfaction that one obtains from committing it."[33]

Toynbee expressed his agreement with my comment that the chosen people concept is bi-polar in character; collective self-centeredness in tension with collective self-dedication to the service of God and mankind. The former pole is known all too well, but the second is equally real in biblical and Jewish history. In the intertwining of the demonic and divine forces within this concept, the potentialities for great good and abysmal evil were certainly to be found. Nazism is an example of the demonic component of this notion, blended with the fury of a distraught and defeated people, which was maddened by the delusions and myths of racial mysticism and demoralized by the nihilistic theories of "Social Darwinism."

But we may ask, would not Nazism have emerged in any case, even if all references to the chosen people in Scriptures had been deleted? This is of course an unanswerable, iffy question. However, in all the writings about Hitler, we have yet to find a fascination for biblical themes. To be sure, the romantic nationalists, Fichte, Dostoevsky, Mazzini, Mickiewicz, did employ biblical imagery. And they did prepare the way for Hitler and his hordes.

On the other hand, it is impossible to remove ideas and beliefs from the records of history. We can reinterpret historical notions, stressing their idealistic components and calling attention to the dangers implicit in their demonic side. Can we question the powerful motivation for good of the chosen people idea, if it be regarded as an *example,* rather than as an *exception?* On this view, all peoples may at any one time be so situated as to be capable of rendering great blessings to mankind. And, as Kant reminded us, " 'Can' implies 'Ought.' " It is the collective duty of a talented or privileged people at any one time to render its service to other nations and "to become a blessing." Did not America after World War II act as a truly chosen people, in inaugurating the Marshall Plan and in offering aid to many impoverished and stricken nations? Is not the creation of the "Peace Corps" a similar expression of American generosity and its religious fervor? Sometimes, such a role is inescapable for a great people, in which case we can speak of its being "chosen" both by Providence and by its own voluntary commitment. Should we not encourage this concept of "chosenness" as an ideal for other nations as well—say, the oil-rich kingdoms and sheikdoms?

We agree with Toynbee that a demonic factor easily insinuates itself into a people's belief in its unique role. Therefore, whenever the notion arises, it should be subjected to merciless criticism, along prophetic lines. But we also maintain that the biblical notion contains a noble, divine aspect, for which there is a crying need in every generation, and more particularly in our rapidly shrinking world, which is divided between the prosperous and the poverty-stricken.

In Toynbee's criticism of Zionism and Israel, ethical and pragmatic elements were commingled. He was appalled by the flood of Palestinian refugees that resulted from the Arab-Israel civil war which followed the British evacuation in May 1948. In his judgment, a large number were expelled from Arab areas, while many refugees simply panicked. The net result of that catastrophe was the transfer of the status of refugees from hundreds of thousands of Jews of Europe to hundreds of thousands of Palestinian Arabs.

In his indignation, Toynbee went so far as to compare the fall of the Israelis from Grace to that of the Germans sinking into the moral abyss of Nazism. It was an unfortunate remark, which had only a modicum of justification in the context of his teaching that suffering ennobles and sanctifies. This biblical doctrine, Toynbee applied to the Jews of our day and expected them to behave like saints at the time when their very life was at stake. But the survivors of the Holocaust were driven by the fury of despair; they feared a repetition of their agony at the hands of the Arabs and they took no chances.

In his "Reconsiderations," Toynbee reasserted his condemnation of Zionism in general.

"On reconsideration, I do not find that I have changed my view of Zionism. I think that in the Zionist movement, Western Jews have assimilated Gentile Western civilization in the most unfortunate possible form."[34]

There is no doubt that the lot of the Arab refugees was tragic. But the blame was widely distributed. The United Nations did not undertake to carry out the Partition Plan which it voted. The neighboring Arab nations promptly invaded Palestine, threatening to complete the work of Hitler. In the conflict between an irresistible force and an immove-able wall, great heat will be generated, and very little light. Some Israeli writers agree that the conflict was tragic, in the dramatic sense—that is, it was a collision between two equally justified rights, not merely a conflict between right and wrong. The tragedy unfolded step by step, and none of the participants foresaw the end. Originally, the Zionist leaders were convinced that they would be heartily welcomed by the Arab people. They believed themselves to be bearing the gifts of west-ernization and prosperity to a long lost cousin-nation. The early rebel-lions of the Arabs in 1921 and 1929 were not taken seriously—they were the work of demagogues. And once Hitler came to power in Germany, the Jews had no choice. The "national homeland" was no longer a dreamlike vision; it was now the only practical possibility for large-scale Jewish immigration.

As for the Arabs, their successive defeats in 1949, 1956, 1967 and 1973 generated an incredible psychosis, the full measure of which is still unknown. Accustomed to think in long-range terms, Toynbee foresaw a progressive aggravation of the bitter mood of the Arabs. In private conversations and letters, he expressed the fear of an emerging Arab mass psychosis, directed against Israel in the first place and indirectly against all Jews. The madness of European antisemitism, with all its monstrous myths, he feared, would be duplicated in the Arab world, which was certain to grow in wealth, in population and in power. The hurt of an inferiority complex, rubbed raw by successive defeats, inflamed by whipped-up ethnic pride and sanctified by religious fantasies can result in a deadly brew. The longer the Arabs delayed taking their revenge against Israel, the more tragic would be the final struggle. And more than the life of Israel might be at stake, since in our shrinking globe an Arab-Israel war could easily set off a global Armageddon. While these fears seemed unduly pessimistic in the sixties, they appear more realistic in the seventies.

Toynbee was not alone in recognizing the terrible potential of a deepening Arab mass psychosis. J. L. Talmon wrote after the Six Day War:

> The anti-Israel obsession gave rise to a kind of systematic Manichean metaphysic, the focus of an entire philosophy of history, with the Jew as the devil incarnate from the days of patriarch Abraham himself till his assumption of the role of the lynchpin of an American-Imperialist-Zionist world-plot against the Arab world, the Socialist Commonwealth and all colonial peoples.
>
> By an unspeakably tragic irony the Zionism of Jewish exiles marching to the tune of "If I forget thee, O Jerusalem," not only created an Arab Zionism, propelled by a similar sense of exile and dream of a return to that very Jerusalem, but imparted the mad obsession with a world-wide Jewish conspiracy to the Islamic world, which however contemptuous of and unfriendly to Jews had in the past not known that essentially Christian neurotic preoccupation with Jewish deicide and the Protocols of Zion, from the dire results of which the Jews sought refuge in Palestine.[35]

Since those lines were written, the Yom Kippur War has been waged and the Arab oil-offensive launched, along with an intensified boycott of firms dealing with Israel. While the situation is at this writing more fluid and more promising, the fears of Toynbee and Talmon are still with us. Jerusalem is associated with the hope of moral perfection and ultimate peace in the minds of both Jews and Christians. But unless the course of events since the end of World War II is reversed, it is hard to believe that it has ceased to be the burning fuse of another catastrophe, of possibly global dimensions.

In sum, Toynbee's challenge to the self-image of Jewish people was deeply felt, but for the most part, bitterly resented. He projected the universal perspective, with which Jewish intellectuals have identified since the days of Moses Mendelssohn; he wrote as a liberal historian, subjecting all great events to the scrutiny of reason; he followed the empirical tradition of Anglo-American philosophy, testing every thesis, as he went along; he accepted the biblical world-view, though he tried to liberate himself from the parochial limitations of his time and place. For all these reasons Jewish intellectuals could not but feel ambivalent toward him. Just at the time when they had rediscovered their nationalism and had taken immense pride in the courageous saga of Israel's birth and growth, he, speaking for a cherished aspect of their own mentality, challenged their newly won self-image and their vision of the future of Jewry.

JEWISH NATIONALISTS AND THE LIBERALS

Do Jewish intellectuals feel now that their alliance with liberalism belongs to the past? There is no question but that some short-sighted nationalists whose sole concern is the promotion of Israel are inclined to discard the liberal orientation. They are more comfortable with the conservatives, who favor the Cold War, a return to a policy of strategic confrontation with the Soviet Union, an imperialist, hard-line posture toward the oil-countries, including the threat of their occupation, and a general reliance on force rather than on the building of an international order of law and justice. We have referred to the anger aroused by the editorial policy of the *Christian Century*. The publication of the Peace Plan by the Quakers in 1972 antagonized the Zionists quite as much as the comments of Toynbee. On the other hand, conservatives, by virtue of their regard for the uniqueness of every historic community, their allergy to general principles, their indifference to anticolonialist and anti-imperialist pleas, might be expected to react sympathetically to the cause of Israel and to the romantic-metaphysical ties of Diaspora Jews with Israel.

Such views, however, are not likely to prevail in the Jewish community. In the judgment of this writer, liberalism is part of the enduring self-image of Jewish people. It derives from both the dominant trend in Jewish philosophy and the invariant direction of Jewish life in the Diaspora.

The historical stream of Jewish thought consists of three confluent currents: the mystical, the folkist-romantic and the rationalistic-liberal. The mystical current has recently aroused a great deal of interest, especially as a subject of study and wonderment. The article on Kabbalah in the recently published *Encyclopedia Judaica* is more extensive by far than the one in the *Jewish Encyclopedia,* which was printed at the beginning of this century. The antics of the Hasidim, of the anti-Zionist variety (Satmar) and the pro-Zionist faction (Liubavich), have drawn the interest of the media. But apart from temporary fads and academic fashions, there is no reason to expect a mass-return to mysticism. While in his early years, Buber was virtually a mystic, in his later life, he moved toward an interpersonalistic philosophy. The vogue of Buber among intellectuals today does not result in any conversion to mysticism or Hasidism.

The folkist-romantic current, associated in the Middle Ages with the name of Halevi and greatly favored in the modern era by the preachers of Zionism, is not likely to achieve dominance. For this philosophy is so close to the world-view of the romantic precursors of Nazism as to scandalize those who take the trouble to study the history of ideas. A mystique of "the holy seed" has indeed been part of the total complex of Jewish thought. But it is a residue of ancient myths that Jews today cannot but disavow decisively. In the nineteenth century, racial mysticism was so innocent an idea that even a rationalist like Geiger could embrace it and make use of it in his endeavor to promote Jewish loyalty. An Eastern European philosopher like A'had Ha'am could similarly proclaim his belief that Jews are by nature "different" from all other nations in their perception of ethical issues. Today the massive horror of mystical-metaphysical racism is plain for all to see. No one who is at all aware of the momentum of ideas is likely to reclaim the poison of this mystique and reinfuse it into the body of Jewish thought.

By default then, if for no other reason, the dominant current of Jewish thought is the one of liberalism or rationalism. Associated in the Middle Ages with the name of Maimonides, it has stimulated waves of enlightenment, whenever circumstances permitted. In Israel, too, there is good reason to feel that the present gap between the self-enclosed Orthodox and the insular secularists will be bridged, once the political tensions are eased. As soon as Israelis can turn their energies from the harsh realities of war to the arts of peace, they will begin to fill the gap which now divides the intellectuals from the religionists with a neo-Maimonidean synthesis, more or less along the lines of the American liberal movements of Reform and Conservatism.

Insofar as Jewish experience in the past two centuries is concerned, there is no doubt whatever that the cause of Jewish freedom and dignity is one with that of liberalism. Recent studies of the politics of American Jews demonstrate that this association is well understood by the great majority of our people. Indeed it is as deeply rooted in the major works of Jewish thought as it is a reflection of contemporary realities.

However, the kind of liberalism which Jews are likely to embrace is one that is non-ideological and non-rigid. It is the liberalism of the Anglo-American world, which is empirical and down-to-earth. It includes a reverence for the domain of religious faith, which articulates in one way or another man's awareness of the transcendental character of his inner being. By the same token, it includes a deep respect for the diversities of collective experience which are enshrined in the hearts of different historical communities. It steers clear of both extremes—the obliteration of all traces of irrationality deriving from history and the glorification of such cultural residues as manifestations of the national soul. In sum, as liberalism balances the sanctity of the individual by the discipline of the state, so too it aims to bring into an unforced balance the individualities of subgroups and their parochial concerns with the national personality and its overall needs, all within the framework of universal ideals.

Such a balanced liberalism is dynamic, by its very nature, responding to the ebb and flow of innumerable factors. Jews are likely to be very sensitive to the changing moods of society, and with good reason. They can be easily hurt, if the swing of the national mood becomes extremist and irreversible. As J. L. Talmon put it:

> The tragic paradox of the Jews in modern times has been the fact that their existence and success have been dependent upon the triumph of the idea of oneness as represented by liberal democracy and socialism, while the very phenomenon of Jewry is an unparalleled demonstration of the enormous power of the element of uniqueness.[36]

Where "oneness" or national homogeneity is taken to be the essence of liberalism, the Jewish situation becomes indeed paradoxical. And it is not much help to tone down the more conspicuous features of Jewish distinctiveness. But genuine liberalism is freedom, as well as fraternity and equality. Its essence is not "oneness" or "fraternity," but rather a high regard for the individual; hence, also a decent respect for collective individualities. It does not aim at the homogenization of society, but at the maximization of freedom so that each of its components may attain its fullest realization. In a free society, there are likely to be any number of lumps in the soup. A Jewish community, open to all influences and not distorted either by a rigid fanaticism or by an insular nationalism, is not likely to be a misfit in a liberal society.

A CONCEPT OF JEWISH IDENTITY

What is the concept of Jewish identity that emerges from this study? Thoughtful Jews have reinterpreted their identity in response to the various ideological challenges of the modern world. The great ideological trends of the past two centuries are still part of our intellectual climate. We may expect that climate to be even more restless and dynamic in the future than it was in the past. How then shall we stake out the basic dimensions of Jewish identity?

Three geometric images of Jewish identity have come down to us from the past. One, the Herzlian view, which foresaw the concentration of those who wished to preserve their ethnic heritage in Israel and the assimilation of the rest. Two, the A'had Ha'amist view of the Jewish people as forming a circle, with Israel in the center and the various lands of the Diaspora on the periphery. Three, the view of Ravidowicz, suggesting that Israel and American Jewry form the two centers of an ellipse, with the rest of the Diaspora deriving inspiration from both.

Of the three images, that of an ellipse comes closest to the reality of the present day. It is also the least dogmatic of the three. The Herzlian view has long become obsolete, for most Jews repudiate assimilation as a possibility, let alone a goal. The A'had Ha'amist view is altogether too simplistic.

The components of Jewish life are so many, so dynamic and so diverse that "centrality" in one respect may be offset by "peripherality" in another. Certainly, in political terms, Israel is not the "center" or focus of Jewish loyalties, nor does it claim to be. In the future, an Arab-

Israeli type of personality, self-confident and proud of living in two cultures, may well emerge. Religiously, the lines of division in Judaism are not geographical, but ideological. To modern Jews, the "holiness" of the land of Israel is not literal, but metaphorical, reflecting the association of the land with historical memories and with the current pulsations of Jewish life. For a long time to come, Israel is likely to be the focus of concern and anxiety, as well as of compassion and pride for Jews the world over. So long as Israel is the finger of Jewry, caught in the door, to use Bialick's metaphor, it will be the chief worry of world Jewry.

Furthermore, it is dangerous, from a public relations standpoint, as well as frustrating from the vantage point of inner Jewish loyalties, to impose an abstract geometric pattern on a living, dynamic society, that is likely to face new and unpredictable challenges.

Instead of a fixed and frozen geometric image, we need a sociological category that permits and even encourages diversity and dynamic interaction with the several non-Jewish cultures of the Diaspora. Our self-image should allow for pluralism and growth.

Clearly, the one inference that we can draw with fair certainty from the above points and counterpoints is that no monolithic mold can possibly encompass the whole of the Jewish community. *We suggest the concept of a Jewish family of communities.* The great variety of responses to modern ideologies indicates that there is no specific and unvarying essence which is exclusively Jewish, other than descent from Jews and identification with the historic Jewish people. The Jewish religion is one of the unifying bonds, but theologically Judaism encompasses the entire spectrum from the naturalism of a Mordecai M. Kaplan, the "polydoxy" of Alvin Reines and the "paganism" of Rubinstein to the rock-ribbed ultra-Orthodoxy of the Hasidim, who are themselves divided into rival groups. The distance between the diverse theological positions within Judaism is fully as great as that which obtains within the Protestant world, and greater if we do not apply the Protestant label to the Unitarians-Universalists. To be sure, there are no clear demarcation lines between the several groupings, and the ideological gulfs are often bridged by sociological beams and ties. But, this is precisely what we mean by a family of communities.

The concept of a family suggests that Jewishness is both a matter of birth and of personal choice. One is born into a family, or he joins it by choice. While the unity of families is weakened as they expand, the family of Jewish communities is sustained by the momentum of a common history and by a conscious acceptance of the same faith. The Talmud describes the global fellowship of the Jewish people as a family of which God is the Father and the Congregation of Israel (Kenesset Yisroel) is the Mother.[37] The latter term refers to the biological-historical matrix of the Jewish people, the former to a personal relationship with the One God that a Jew is expected to acquire. It is pertinent to add that those who acknowledge only one parent are also members of the family.

Indeed, it has been the historic role of the Jewish people to explore the implications of a communal identity in which biological descent is sublimated into spiritual commitment. Identities fall into three categories—that of choice, as when a person chooses a profession or a religious fellowship or a political party; that of status, as when people are born into historical communities; that of covenant, in which personal choice and public status are blended together. Love is a matter of choice; marriage of covenant, children of birth. Jewish identity has always been of the covenantal variety. So, the prophet Hosea speaks of the betrothal of Israel to God, in all eternity, "through righteousness and justice, through steadfast love and compassion" (Hosea 2,21).

Variously as this covenant has been interpreted, it is essentially three-dimensional, containing a personal code of conduct, a cluster of communal obligations and a dedication to the service of God and mankind. In ancient and medieval times, the covenantal obligations were articulated in a rigid and monolithic set of precepts and beliefs. Today, the range of pluralism is vastly increased. And rightly so. In a living faith-community extending into many parts of the world, diverse challenges are bound to lead to a diversity of responses. Indeed, Jewish people since the days of Jeremiah have learned to combine a deep attachment to Judaism with a fervent devotion to the countries in which they lived. (Jeremiah 29,7)

Families grow out as they grow up. Through marriage, people come to belong to at least two families. So, Jewish people have learned to become part of the nations among whom they lived, without giving up the covenantal bonds which relate them to God and to the global fellowship of Israel. As members of a spiritual family, Jews need not fear that their heritage will be diluted and adulterated through the alliances they forge with members of other families. For a spiritual heritage is not impoverished but enriched by the influence of other cultures. An

American Jew will become more deeply Jewish, the more he absorbs the creative genius of the American nation, and vice versa.

A branch of the Jewish family is even now becoming a fresh and vigorous entity, the Israeli nation that is at once "new" and "old." If and when peace finally dawns in that part of the world, the Arabs in Israel will become part of that nation. At the same time, the divergence in character and outlook between the Israeli and the Jews of the Diaspora will become as obvious as the bonds of sentiment and mutual concern that will continue to bind them together. There is no telling today where the geopolitical currents of history will drag the state of Israel in the decades that lie ahead: toward a continued close association with America, toward neutral ground, toward the Soviet orbit or toward new configurations that are still beyond the horizon. A state follows the logic of national interest, whithersoever it leads. In the flux of history, communities with common memories may undergo new realignments of their own free will. The major portions of the Jewish people are like trains set on different tracks, moving off into the unknown horizon, with only a few people here and there jumping the tracks to join a different train. Consequently, we may indeed employ the slogan, "we are one," newly coined by the Jewish philanthropic agencies, providing we understand that we are also many and diverse. We are one, not as a creedal community and not as a political–cultural nation, but as a family of religious and national communities, a family of adults who are mature enough to go their separate ways and loyal enough to their common tradition to feel that they form "one fellowship." Hopefully, the various members of this family will continue to cherish not merely their common past but also their shared dedication to the building of the messianic kingdom, "when all nations will form one fellowship to serve God with a perfect heart."

Does this concept of Jewish identity imply an assimilationist or a nationalistic version of the future? In my view it implies the freedom for individuals to choose either direction and the likelihood that in several ways they will choose both. Mature adults sever the "silver cord" which keeps them enchained to the past and prevents them from submitting with hearts entire to new loves and fresh alliances with persons of other families. At the same time, healthy-minded adults find that they love their parents and families even more, when they fall in love and conclude a covenant with their loved ones. Some members of the Jewish family will choose to return to their ancestral home and throw in their lot with those who build the new Israeli nation. By the same token, many Israelis are even now moving in large numbers to America and Canada. But regardless of where they choose to live, they will belong to the Jewish family to the extent that they accept the one God as their Father and the Congregation of Israel as their Mother.

In both Israel and the lands of the Diaspora, Jews will choose to identify themselves in varying degrees with diverse aspects of the "sacred tradition." The entire spectrum of the Jewish religion, from an individualistic atheism or a nationalistic pantheism to the extremes of Orthodoxy, may now be encountered in both Israel and the Diaspora. To be sure, the proportions differ, the nuances of observance and the forms of organization are peculiar to the special circumstances of Israel and to the cultural climates of the various Diaspora lands. We may expect a continuous interaction among the several branches of the Jewish family, particularly in view of the explosion of the travel industry in recent years. At the same time, each community is likely to reflect the impact of its own peculiar cultural environment.

So, it appears likely that we shall be returning to the original conception of the Jewish people—a family of tribes, "the twelve tribes of Israel," all affirming loyalty to the One God. Each community will seek to achieve its own best synthesis of the common Jewish tradition and the prevailing culture. And the terms of that synthesis will be likely to reflect in each case the full panoply of possibilities.

In our perspective of the Jewish family of communities, dynamic change and development are to be expected. Our people will be constantly challenged to discriminate between that which is essential to Judaism and that which is merely accidental. The process of assimilation may assume benign as well as malignant forms. If people acquire from the general culture of their country its best elements and blend them with their historical tradition, they assimilate well. If they choose unwisely from among the elements of their own tradition and from the prevailing culture, preserving the dross and neglecting the pure metal in both cultures, they assimilate badly. In either case, they will be assimilating in some respects and preserving their heritage in other respects, for every living organism is constantly engaged in assimilating some element from the environment and rejecting others.

The problem that each Jewish community faces is to assimilate wisely the diverse influences that impinge upon it, and to grow in understanding, refinement and sympathy. In other words, the criteria of growth in each case are intrinsic to the life of that community, which includes the impetus from the past, the concerns of the present and the universal society of the future. And all the branches of the family share the same tradition, the same history, the same concerns and the same hopes.

APPENDIX: LETTER FROM ARNOLD J. TOYNBEE
TO JACOB B. AGUS

(From Union Theological Seminary, New York)

November 4, 1955

Dear Rabbi Agus:

I was very much touched by your most kind letter of November 1st and by the line you take in your article in the Fall issue of "Judaism".

So far, I have only had time to read the article very rapidly, but I greatly appreciate the generosity with which you point out the things in which you agree, as well as those in which you disagree, with my presentation of Judaism.

This kind of constructive criticism is, of course, not only a help but also a call to go on thinking. My mind is, I hope, still an open one, and as a matter of fact I am proposing to produce a series of studies in which I shall be reconsidering questions in my book which are obviously debatable either because of new knowledge or because of the discussion that has been aroused by what I have written.

I can see that Judaism will be one of these issues, and when I come to this, your article will be one of the things that I shall have at my elbow.

Meanwhile, may we keep in touch? I should be particularly interested, as you proceed, to learn something of your projected examination of the application of the various philosophies of history as they apply to the Jewish situation.

Thank you again.

Yours sincerely,
(signed) Arnold Toynbee

NOTES

1. J. L. Talmon, *The Unique and the Universal* (New York, 1965), p. 72.
2. Herzl Fishman, *American Protestantism and a Jewish State* (Detroit, 1973), p. 178.

3. J. L. Talmon, *The Unique and the Universal*, p. 121.

4. Jewish reactions to Toynbee were on the same large scale as those which followed the comments on the Jews of Bruno Bauer, Heinrich Treitschke and Adolf Harnack, only more so. It is indeed difficult to find a parallel to the storm of resentment and criticism aroused by Toynbee's work.

5. A. J. Toynbee, *A Study of History* (New York, 1954), vol. VIII, p. 272.

6. Joachim C. Fest, *Hitler* (New York, 1974), p. 506.

7. A. J. Toynbee, *Experiences* (New York, 1969), p. 136. "To believe that one's own tribe is God's Chosen People is the error of nationalism. Other peoples besides the Jews have fallen into it."

8. A. J. Toynbee, *A Study of History*, vol. XII, 1961, p. 419n.

9. Toynbee takes note of this criticism in his *Reconsiderations*, vol. XII, p. 412. In answer, he cites the massive archeological discoveries in Palestine, which place the biblical faith in its civilizational context. In his view, Christianity arose out of the suppressed Canaanite elements in the Jewish religion. See his critique of Albright, who rationalizes the presumed massacre of the Canaanites (*Ibid.*, p. 419) as representing the "right" of a "young" nation to remove an "old" and corrupt nation from the scene.

10. Martin Wight, in Annex to vol. VII, *A Study of History*, p. 738.

11. Genesis Rabba, 12, 15.

12. Matt. 18,8; Jude 1,7.

13. Shabbat 33a.

14. Rosh Hashono 17a.

15. Tosefta, Sanhedrin 13.

16. Hullin 13b.

17. Shabbat 30a.

18. Rosh Hashono 17a.

19. To be sure, this verse was not interpreted in an irenic way by the traditional commentators, Rashi and Mezudat David. But, Abraham Ibn Ezra and David Kimhi explain that it foretells that there will be no mass conversions to Judaism, prior to the coming of the Messiah. The modern, liberal interpretation is probably closer to the original intent of Micah, who accepted Isaiah's prophecy and added his own codicil.

20. The best known antisemitic collection of this type is that of Eisenmenger, which served as the basis of popular diatribes. But even the monumental *Kommentar zum Neuen Testament aus Talmud und Midrash* by Strack-Billerbeck, 4th edition, 1926, is, for all its vast erudition, saturated with contempt, in its interpretive passages.

21. For example, the *lex talionis* was changed to call for monetary compensation. Baba Kama 83b. Maimonides' *Guide* III, 41. Other examples are the case of the rebellious son, Deuteronomy 21, 18; Sanhedrin 71b; and the case of the heretical city, Deuteronomy 13,13; Sanhedrin 111a and 112b.

22. The continuity of the impetus of classical prophecy in the rabbinic Aggada, in medieval philosophy and mysticism, down to our own day is outlined in my essay, "The Prophet in Modern Hebrew Literature," which was first printed in *Hebrew Union College Annual* of 1957 (Cincinnati 1957), reprinted in my *Dialogue and Tradition* (New York, 1971). More extensively, this thesis underlies the entire argument in my book, *The Evolution of Jewish Thought* (New York, 1959).

23. *A Study of History,* XII, p. 214.

24. *Ibid.,* p. 216.

25. *Ibid.,* p. 217.

26. Oscar K. Rabinowitz, *Arnold Toynbee on Judaism and Zionism* (London, 1974), p. 221. Toynbee's books are *The Murderous Tyranny of the Turks,* preface by Viscount Bryce (London, 1917), and *Turkey: A Past and a Future* (New York, 1917).

27. L. Stein, *The Balfour Declaration* (New York, 1981), p. 322.

28. Rabinowitz, *Arnold Toynbee,* p. 232. "Syria and Palestine Handbook," No. 60. Toynbee, *Turkey: A Past and a Future,* (New York, 1927), p. 6.

29. A. J. Toynbee, *Experiences,* p. 266. "Israeli colonialism since the establishment of the state of Israel is one of the two blackest cases in the whole history of colonialism in the modern age; and its blackness is thrown into relief by its date . . . a crime that was also a moral anachronism."

30. Vol. VIII, p. 277.

31. *Reconsiderations,* vol. XII, p. 621, in which Toynbee takes note of Stecchini's criticism.

32. The relevance of anticolonialism to the plight of Israel is acknowledged by the Israeli historian, J. L. Talmon, in his book, *The Unique and the Universal* (New York, 1965), p. 266. "The Jews in Israel are in the ambiguous position of the last white settlers in Asia and Africa, after the European imperialists and colonizers had made their exit from the two continents."

33. Toynbee, *Study,* vol. XII, p. 624n.

34. J. L. Talmon, *The Unique and the Universal,* p. 123.

35. *Ibid.*

36. *Ibid 5b.*

37. Berochot 55b.

PART FIVE

THE CONCEPT OF GOD IN JACOB AGUS' THEOLOGY

SELECTION AND
PREFATORY REMARKS
William E. Kaufman

A KEEN STUDENT of theology, Rabbi Agus was sensitive to the criticisms raised against traditional notions of God. In response, he attempted to think through for himself the complex issues connected with this elemental metaphysical notion.

In chapter 4 of *Guideposts in Modern Judaism,* titled "The Idea of God," Agus offers his most elaborate treatment of his conception of God. Basing his reasoning on the principle of polarity enunciated by the American philosopher Morris R. Cohen, Agus argues that because life, mind, and purpose are the polar correlatives of space-time and the mechanical laws of nature, we can reasonably infer that the whole is mind as well as matter, purposiveness as well as mechanism, God as well as nature. He concludes that God is the Absolute Personality, the pole of Being standing in continual opposition and tension with the mechanical universe.

The following selection, chosen to accompany William E. Kaufman's essay "The Concept of God in the Theology of Jacob B. Agus" in *American Rabbi: The Life and Thought of Jacob B. Agus. (New York, 1996), Critical Studies* is from Jacob B. Agus' *Guideposts in Modern Judaism* (New York, 1954), 228–54.

16

THE IDEA OF GOD

THERE IS NOTHING that we do or think which does not in some way impinge upon the idea of God. For this idea is the most fundamental and all-embracing of concepts in the range of thought. How then shall we begin to explore the nature of God and arrive at any understanding of His essence? It is commonly believed that every argument must begin with definitions. Indeed, classical Greek philosophy followed this pattern. But in the case of God, we cannot define without begging the question. Was it not pointed out long ago that every definition constitutes a delimitation in some way or other, while God is the Infinite and the Undeterminable? Thus, if we should launch our search for God with a definition we should be compelled to follow Spinoza in assuming as our first axiom that which is the ultimate goal of our investigation.

We might begin by tracing the conceptions of God evolved by the great philosophers of history, and evaluating their adequacy in the light of modern knowledge and research. But if we begin in this fashion, would we ever end? Consider how multifarious are the ways in which God has appeared to man and how profitless the task of demolishing the images and concepts man has fashioned of Him! Such an undertaking appears imperative only if we accept Hegel's dogma that philosophy is nothing but the history of West European thought, being the record of the progressive unfolding of the universal mind through the social and literary molds of the most advanced nations of the world. In recent years, we have grown too humble to pose as the final incarnations of Absolute Reason. Furthermore, we do not go far in our study of the histories of philosophy before we realize that it is one's basic world-view which determines the manner in which he construes the intellectual evolution of mankind. In the beginning is the word of conviction; the whole world is then fashioned accordingly. If we probe deep enough, we find at the base of every metaphysical system either an intuition or a generalization.

We propose therefore to take as our starting point the most fundamental principles of thought, as these have been formulated in our time. Our conception will admittedly be dated, but for this very reason perhaps most meaningful in terms of our contemporary culture.

The highway to the heavenly heights of metaphysics is bifurcated at the very beginning into the short road of intuition and the long road of reasoned analysis. This crossroads is never left behind; it looms ahead so long as we persist in the quest of truth, for the short direct road of intuition continues to be ever available, as we proceed along the endless path of reason. Blessed moments of inspiration intersperse our lives, yielding glimpses of the holy and the ineffable. Such moments, however, are arrows shot into space, penetrating the infinite but not encompassing it. Overwhelming in their blinding intensity, they remain ambiguous in significance. They stimulate our imagination and enhance our vision, but in their fleeting vagueness they cannot serve as substitutes for logical thought. The temptation to construct the world of faith upon these evanescent flashes of insight, opposing an independent realm of the holy and the mysterious to the grey reality of mundane thought, is well-nigh irresistible to the religious thinker. Yet those who aim to "speak truth in their heart" dare not yield entirely. Glimpses of intuition have their place in the spiritual economy of life, but they cannot serve as substitutes for sustained reflection. The logic of life requires that we live before we know, that we treasure the flashes of faith before we complete the adventure of reasoned reflection, but this adventure remains our irrevocable task.

Predominantly, modern religious philosophy shies away from the rigid canons of logic. Perhaps it was Kant who set this pattern, when he declared that "pure reason" cannot pronounce judgment regarding metaphysical questions. In any case, the prevailing mood in the past two centuries has tended to relegate religion to the domain of feeling on the ground that the fields of reason and experience had been preempted by the triumphant, all-pervading spirit of science. Religion can only begin where reason ends, and many religious thinkers only too eagerly seek aid and comfort from the occasional perplexities of scientists and their confessions of failure.

This dichotomy of the human spirit may be helpful in allaying friction at college faculty meetings, but it is basically unhealthy and, at bottom, even dishonest. World culture can afford a "split personality" as little as the living individual, for it is emptied of all meaning if it does not seek perpetually to harmonize all fields of knowledge and to synthesize the insights deriving from every discipline of the human mind. By the same token, a faith which is founded on an esoteric experience of mystical unity or a romantic exaggeration of the normal feeling of wonder, bewilderment, and mystery belongs to the poetry of life, not to its substance.

Modern "existential" philosophies of religion are now available in a rich variety of shapes and forms, catering to many tastes; yet, they all have in common an overly elaborated and meticulously nurtured bill of protestations against the objective world and its canons of judgment, as if the best attitudes of our sober mentality constituted somehow a falling away from God. Those who center their faith on the presumed "sudden" incursion of the divine into the souls of men become inevitably, though unwittingly, prophets of doom and despair, since they insist upon the non-divine and even sinful character of man's rational aspirations for the good life, foreboding a monotonous succession of "crises" and catastrophes. Since the continuous application of reason to experience is the only highway of progress open to man, religion in modern times forfeited the sceptre of leadership when, in its most illustrious exponents, it hesitated to tread this highway and retired fearfully into the comforting shadows of subjective intuitions.

By its very nature, faith is an outgrowth of the inner life of man, but if it is not integrated with the total picture painted by science and experience, it cannot be aught else but ethereal poetry, clothed in the coarse garb of theological dark speech. Religion is at once insight and synthesis, the beginning of all wisdom and its final culmination. Hence we must not be content simply with the *feeling* of the Eternally Present, as He appears to the pious and the saintly. If we are to overcome the sense of inner desperation and unbalance which afflicts the consciousness of modern man, we must learn to recapture the ancient, classical synthesis between the personal God, apprehended in our religious experience, and the God of nature, envisaged as the ultimate goal of reasoned reflection. For, as the Kabbalists put it, God is One in the twin categories of dialectical "remoteness" and intuitive "closeness." In the words of the prophet Isaiah, "I am first and I am last."

Two mighty obstacles block the path of reason, in its quest for God, obstacles thrown up by two opposing schools of thought. On the one hand, proponents of what is generally called "scientism" tell us that the presently charted path of science is all in all, and that any attempt to go beyond the catalogued and classified body of proven knowledge is futile. The world is just as science paints it—a maddening whirl of atoms and electrons, particles and waves. True, the total body of all known facts is as a tiny, brightly lit boat floating upon the dark ocean of the unknown, but then science operates with the only possible method of expanding this luminous area of knowledge. Any attempt to venture beyond the sphere of scientific data is to commit the unpardonable sin of being unscientific.

On the other hand, we are told that reason and experience are inherently incapable of dealing with the quest of metaphysics. Our experience is of the finite, how dare we generalize from it concerning the infinite? And reason? Have not theologians delighted for centuries in dwelling lovingly upon its failures, in order that an inviolate limbo of unknowability might be secured for the varying dogmas of their respective faiths? As to the limitations of both reason and experience, it is not at all difficult to show the woeful inadequacy of our authenticated knowledge for the quest of metaphysics. Have not the most important facts concerning the soul of man been brought to light only in recent years? It is only a generation since the tractability of human nature to mechanical conditioning was discovered, and two generations since we learned of the vast, slumbering depths of the human psyche, dwelling in the recesses of the unconscious.

Let us, then, state at the outset, in answer to both of these objections, that our quest is not for the type of clear and certain knowledge that we have in mathematics or physics. We seek to obtain proximate knowledge of the realm that supervenes knowledge, grounds for faith, the direction of the curves leading from the known to the unknown. Our purpose is to batter down the high wall between religious faith and scientific knowledge, exploring the intervening cross-currents and charting the paths between them.

Accordingly, we reply to those who erect science into a self-sufficient philosophy of life that they err in two directions. In the first place, they fail to realize that we cannot and dare not leave the "unknown" alone, for it comprises the essence of our being, the very ground of our existence, and the meaning of all our strivings. The quest for God and for our own innermost self is one and the same, for if the riddle of selfhood is solved, all is given. The self which thinks and wills, yearns and despairs—what is it? No category of knowledge yet devised embraces it, much less explains it. Depth-psychology may explore its limitations, abnormal psychology may trace its occasional deviations, but in its essence, it remains as mysterious as ever it was in the days of Plato and Aristotle. And this mystery, wrapped in an enigma, is our own being. What sort of wisdom is it then that would ignore the most important object of our quest—to wit, our own selves?

As to the outside physical universe, only the naive can imagine that the atoms and electrons of present-day science constitute the ultimate stuff of existence. Have we not learned in our own day that matter is nothing but "congealed" energy? Einstein's formula for the conversion of matter into energy has become common knowledge in our atomic age. But, is its impact understood? One of the inferences to be drawn from it is certainly to the effect that the world is not simply an aggregation of so many whirling particles, traveling at various speeds. If we define energy as the force that moves matter and matter as congealed energy, what is it that we end up with, but a vicious circle? We will return to this problem in a moment.

At present, we merely wish to indicate the limitations of scientism. They may be listed as follows: firstly, the failure to recognize the tragic earnestness of the metaphysical quest; secondly, the failure to realize the logical insufficiency of the concepts of physics for the understanding of the essential "stuff" of the universe, since what metaphysics seeks to do is to explain the fundamental concepts of physics, as physics does to chemistry, chemistry to biology, and biology to psychology; thirdly, the inability to see that the very nature of the metaphysical quest implies a different method than that employed by science, its objective being the double "unknown" of science—that of the self and that of the whole of the universe.

Now, of course, neither the self nor the whole of the universe can be an object of knowledge in the strict sense of the term, for we cannot stand outside them. Yet we are aware of the self as a unity and we know that the whole is not simply a verbal generalization, since science indicates that the universe is governed by identical laws of cause and effect. The chains of necessity which rule the helium and hydrogen atoms on earth hold in thrall the same atoms as they generate the terrific heat of the sun. Here, on earth, we get messages from elements identical with ours in remote universes, millions of light-years from us. The whole, then, is one.

The method of science is to proceed from the study of the parts to that of the whole. It is a good method, and it works. Suppose, however, it were possible to go from the whole of the universe to the parts as the self does in fact operate in our own being, and in the process, obtaining guidance for life? Such a procedure would be non-scientific, but not unscientific, since it would supplement the data obtained by the usual methods of science.

So much for scientism. As to the protagonists of the ineluctableness of the "unknown," we can only reply that there must be a point-by-point correspondence between ultimate reality and the concepts to which the path of reason ultimately leads. We are told that knowledge is a function of two factors—of our own mental powers and of the influences that impinge upon our mind and senses from the great "unknown." Accepting this analysis, we see that if the elements of our mental powers are kept constant, by the rigor of logic, then the data in our minds must be related to the "unknown," in a point-by-point correspondence. This argument of the modern "realists" appears incontrovertible, insofar as it refutes the lovers of the Dark Unknown, but the manner in which it is to be applied remains in question.

The path of reason, then, consists in the formulation of the most fundamental laws of existence, as they derive from our total knowledge, and in extending these laws to the whole of the universe. At this point, however, we must confront the titanic figure of Kant and all the schools of philosophy which follow from his basic premise. Is reason to be identified with the ordered summation of our knowledge, or is it to be considered in its "purity," as a self-governing, independently existing entity, becoming ever "purer" as all the data of the senses are abstracted from it? Kant's insistence on the absolute "purity" of logic presented philosophy with an artificial dichotomy, which plagued it for more than a century and a half. First, the world of experience was artificially divided into the mind and the "given" data; then, of course, the twain could never meet again. Without entering into a detailed analysis of the

Kantian root-principle and its modern offshoots, we take as our starting point the realistic principle that reason is what reason does—that is, reason is the manner whereby knowledge is ordered in our minds. We refuse to break up the irreducible and to draw a line between "pure" logic and sense-data, for the two are inextricably intertwined and any such line is bound to be arbitrary. Content as we are to obtain proximate knowledge of that which corresponds to ultimate reality, the Kantian critique of reason, drawing an impassable line between the sensible and the realm of metaphysics, does not arise to invalidate our effort.

Let us, then, proceed to discover the most fundamental principles of "reason in operation," reason as it is applied to the understanding of reality, and then note how they may be applied to the twin "unknowns" of our quest—the self and the whole.

A study of the logic implied in the methods of science yields two basic generalizations—the principle of causality and the principle of polarity. The first principle has been employed explicitly in philosophy since the days of Aristotle, while the nature of the second principle has been either completely misunderstood, or else variously misinterpreted. Yet this second principle of reason is just as important a clue to the inner structure of reality as the first. The principle of polarity has been variously anticipated and formulated in the history of thought. In our own day, it was best expounded by Morris R. Cohen in his monumental work, *Reason and Nature* (Glencoe, Ill., 1931), and in a number of smaller works on the logic of science.

This principle, as formulated by Cohen, states that "opposites, such as immediacy and mediation, unity and plurality, the fixed and the flux, substance and function, ideal and real, actual and possible . . ." all enter into the pattern of our understanding (p. 165). Knowledge is so constituted that concepts which are in polar opposition to each other enter into every concrete situation. If only one polar concept is insisted upon as the one true principle, knowledge is reduced to absurdity. "Like the north (positive) and south (negative) poles of a magnet, all [polar concepts] involve each other when applied to a significant entity" *(ibid.).*

Only a student of the history of philosophy is able to appreciate the manifold applications of this principle for the understanding of the ancient controversies between the nominalists and the realists, the mechanists and the vitalists, the idealists and the empiricists. Note, for instance, its application to the question whether reason is only a generalization of sense-data or whether these data are themselves ordered and categorized by reason? Manifestly, both alternatives are absurd, when taken singly. "The principle of polarity warns us that while the rational and sensory elements of our intellect are inseparable, they are distinct. We may grant that in every case of actual, analytic reasoning, some sensory element, no matter how faint, is present, and yet we must insist on the relative independence of the rational element" (p. 196). "The efforts of the human intellect may be viewed as a tension between two poles—one to do justice to the fulness of the concrete case before us, the other to grasp an underlying abstract universal principle that controls much more than the case before us. . . . None of our works shows forces in perfectly stable equilibrium . . . But, in pure science as in personal religion and poetry, intense concentration on one phase rather than justice to many is the dominant trait" (p. 368).

Thus, scientists generally are prone to rule out the possibility of an integrating, purposive principle, operating within a living organism, such a principle being the polar opposite of the mechanistic principle which proceeds from the part to the whole. In this attitude, mechanistic scientists are guilty of ignoring the principle of polarity. "The vice of mechanism in practice is at bottom similar to that of vitalism—it will not open its imagination to the possibility of physically determining factors, quite other than those already known" (p. 282).

The principle of polarity is not an axiom but a generalization, describing the fundamental character of man's sustained attempt to understand himself and the universe. It is the most fundamental generalization available to us, in that it indicates not only the process of understanding but its goal as well. The goal of our intellectual efforts is polar in character—namely, to see every event as a particularization of a system of universal principles. This polarity is reflected in the principle of sufficient reason, which is the fundamental principle of all scientific research. In Cohen's formulation, this principle reads as follows: "Everything is connected in definite ways with definite things, so that its full nature is not revealed except by its position and relations within a system" (p. 150).

The "system" which embraces all events is manifestly the totality of all existence. But this totality is the great "unknown." All events derive from it, all data of knowledge lead to it; yet, the whole remains "unknown."

Can the whole, in its infinite mystery, be understood in terms of the principle of polarity which prevails within it? Cohen refused to draw this inference, on the ground of the "whole" not being "an object of knowledge." However, once we grant that it is not knowledge in the technical sense, that we seek but grounds for faith, such an application becomes logically incontrovertible. And who would be so bold as to scorn the converging rays of knowledge, leading from the finite to the infinite, in the idle quest for full and clear comprehension, for the total embracing of the Deity within the canons of our understanding? Furthermore, the "whole," in a qualitative sense, is given to us in our consciousness of our own personality, as will be made clear in the sequel. The human personality is a chunk of reality and it is understandable only in terms of the polar concepts of purposiveness and mechanism. May it not be then that God and the mechanical universe imply each other, even as the one and the many, space and time, the point and the field? But we are anticipating our argument. Let us return to the task of discovering the fundamental operating concepts in the universe.

When we envisage the whole of existence, in all its mysterious immensity and grandeur, what are the alternative concepts before us? What is the real difference between the naturalists and the theists? Manifestly, the former maintain that the whole is merely a numerical summation of all that exists, with the laws that regulate the finite parts of the visible universe prevailing throughout its invisible and non-reachable positions. The other alternative consists in the attribution to the whole of the qualities of selfhood, consciousness, and purposiveness.

For our present purpose, we may leave out of consideration all transcendental conceptions of the Deity, since they do not assume that creation points to the Creator in any sense save that of logical contradiction or of historical failure. In the transcendental view, the examination of the world about us cannot possibly of itself lead to the idea of God. It is when we realize our "nothingness" and humbly admit our failure, that the Wholly Other is revealed to us. Transcendentalism, by its very definition, cannot favor the endeavor to understand the ultimate nature of being through the instrumentality of reason. Hence the choice before us is the whole as a mechanical summation of parts *versus* the whole as being a self in which particulars may be related to the totality of being in the categories of purposiveness and consciousness.

The naturalist alternative is simply an extension into the infinite of our experience with the physical universe. The theistic position regards our experience with living selves as providing the clue for the understanding of the whole. In living organisms, events occur in accord with the mechanistic laws of physics and chemistry; yet the organism as a whole affects somehow the operation of its tiniest parts, directing all changes toward the goal of preserving the self.

Naturalists may well grant the presence of a vital principle in living organisms and yet insist that there is no reason to generalize from that principle and to regard it as the clue for the understanding of the whole. The very complexity of physical conditions needed for the operation of this principle would militate against its ubiquity—unless it be considered a numinous principle, inhering in a realm that is outside our space-time world. Such a conception, we must point out again, belongs to the philosophy of transcendentalism, which cannot possibly be inferred from the events of the sensible universe. Thus, the very attempt of the vitalists to draw a fundamental line of demarcation between physical and biological phenomena is in fundamental opposition to the theistic endeavor to conceive of the physical universe as an organism, endowed with mind and purpose.

If, on the other hand, life, mind and purpose are seen to be the polar correlatives of space-time and the mechanical laws of motion, then we should be enabled to infer on the strength of the principle of polarity that the whole is mind as well as matter; purposiveness, orderliness, and will, as well as mechanism, chaos, and law; life as well as death; God as well as nature. The search for God by way of logical analysis implies the inner coherence of all our experience, with the meanest and lowest data of knowledge forming part of a process that transpires between two infinitely remote poles—that of mechanism and matter, on the one hand, and that of spirit and God, on the other hand. The growth of our knowledge is likely to fill in the many lacunae in this process, extending it ever farther into the receding limbo of the two infinites. But we may well ask whether the outlines of this process are not already visible. Faith in the fundamental reality of our moral and spiritual values is still needed to fill in the picture of the whole. The bare outlines, however, emerge out of our present knowledge of the universe. We can hardly begin to understand the world in which we live or our own selves without postulating the divine pole of reality.

The universe in which we live is hopelessly mysterious, in its outer reaches as in the unimaginable complexity of its minutest particles. Of the vastness of the infinite void we cannot ever expect to receive more than occasional glimpses. But the world that is open to our senses, how do we understand it? The merest acquaintance with the facts of science awakens us to the realization that the qualities which are apprehended by our senses are not really present in the world as it truly is. In the real world, there are no tastes, colors, and sounds, only a hectic chaos of whirling particles and trembling waves. At one time, it was believed that atoms and molecules constituted the irreducible bricks of the universe. The world was a vast assemblage of these tiny particles, travelling through space like myriads of billiard balls, and all the complexities of its phenomena were nothing but reflections of the motions and gyrations of these simple particles.

At present, even the general public is aware that matters are not quite so simple. In the first place, there does not seem to be any limit to the divisibility of matter, with the most recently discovered particles being possibly subject to further breakdowns. We confront now the possibility that empty space may merely be an abstraction, representing a pole of existence, which is only reached asymptotically. In the second place, we now know that matter and energy are at bottom somehow one. In modern physics, it was realized long ago that electrons sometimes behaved as if they were not particles of matter, but multi-dimensional waves of energy. The emergence of the quantum theory, insisting that energy comes in spurts, like particles, and the Einstein relativity theory, erasing the absolute line of distinction between space and matter, made the old vision of the universe as a mass of moving particles completely out of date. Finally, the rapid progress of atomic science in the last decade demonstrated in world-shaking experiments the possibility of converting matter into energy. We know now that matter in all its forms is but a coagulation, as it were, of energy, which is the basic reality in the world about us—the energy of radiation, gravitation, nuclear attraction, electromagnetism, and heat. But with the exception of heat, none of these forms of energy can be understood in the mechanistic terms of whirling particles.

What then is energy? The term has meaning for us in that it is derived from a number of situations in which it is always associated with matter. In physics, energy is defined and measured in terms of the capacity to set matter into motion. But if matter is itself a form of energy, how shall we think of energy?

For a long time, science clung to the notion that the waves of light and electromagnetism were undulations in a quasi-material substance called ether, for motion could be understood only as the motion of something, and the conception of light as waves could be taken to make sense only if there were really something in which the waves could take place. Then the theory of an ether was given up, and the waves of energy were left waving while yet there was nothing to wave. Finally, the relativity theory gave the *coup de grace* to the conception of space as the vast inert container of moving particles, proving that there was no absolute boundary between space and matter, since space was itself quasi-material, "bending" and "contracting" round masses of matter. Thus, the mechanistic theory of the universe is now as dead as a door-nail.

More and more, we are driven to the realization that the physical universe must be viewed in terms of the "field" and "point" polar relationship. The "field" is the pattern of infinite relations to which every "point" in space is subject. As in every polar relationship, each pole represents a direction of being, rather than a definite state or quality. Neither the "point" nor the "field" exist as such, but every existent is a combination of both in varying degrees. The final, irreducible element of existence is as the trembling of a chord, withdrawing into a definite point in space, yet issuing out of itself, in response to the "field" in which it is found. Things are not spatial entities alone, but "events," in Whitehead's terminology, units of space–time, reflecting the tension and the rhythm of the polar relationship.

How profoundly revolutionary is this point-field polar concept! We are accustomed to think of true reality as motionless, massive stability, but now the realization dawns upon us that in reality things are tensions and rhythms. Nothing exists that is wholly self-enclosed, but things are real insofar as they partake of the two opposites—particularity reaching down to a point in space, and responsiveness to the total field of relations. Behold this paradox: if it were possible to take a still shot of the universe at any one point in time, eliminating all incipient relations, the universe would be absolute nothingness! For it is in the tension between the two poles of existence that events endure.

Yet difficult as is the point-field polar concept for the layman, modern mathematics long ago constructed the logical framework for its understanding. It was through the logic inherent in mathematical formulae that Einstein's theories were developed. The groundwork was laid in the seventeenth century by Descartes' theory of analytic geometry, which solved complicated problems of curvature by translating them into a field of relations, based on two coordinates. The essential congruence of this theory with fundamental reality is demonstrated in the circumstance that by means of it the actual curves of motion in the physical universe could be calculated. Related to the field-concept is the theory of the differential, dy/dx, which expresses in mathematical language the asymptotic character of incipient motion or change. A differential is defined as the ratio of two rates of change when the amount of change approximates zero. With this paradoxical method of "approaching zero," modern mathematics was able to unlock and plot all forms of change, opening up new vast fields of calculation, while the earlier concepts of pre-modern algebra and geometry could only describe an abstract, static world. The differential, as contrasted with the conception of a static point, and the integral, as contrasted with the elementary notion of a class of objects or group of points, reflect together the polar concepts of this dynamic universe, the restless quality of its being, matter and energy "approaching" the two poles of being in itself and in relation respectively, without quite reaching either pole. In the mechanistic view of the universe, the process of explanation consists in the equating of each effect as the arithmetical summation of the forces that impinge upon it, as in Newton's laws of motion. But the question remains unanswered as to the manner in which influence proceeds from part to part—the influence of gravitation, for instance, or the force of nuclear attraction. In the organismic view, each part is explained by the whole, but the differentiation into parts remains unexplained. The principle of polarity offers us a synthesis of both mechanism and organism.

The essence of the polar relationship is seen in the circumstance that when the attempt is made to apprehend either pole as an existent, the result is incomprehensible absurdity. Thus, the attempt to envisage matter is led, through the channels of analysis, to energy, while the corresponding attempt to conceive of energy leads to the description of it as a quality of matter. This paradox is carried over into the ultimate units of the universe whatever they may be. As we have noted, reality in its ultimate shape cannot but bear a point-to-point correspondence with the fundamental character of the phenomena that science describes to us.

We thus arrive at the conception of a universe, in which all parts exist in a state of tension—tension between the tendency to particularization and responsiveness to the total system of which it is a part. If human terms could be used to express this two-way quality of every existent, we could speak of the tension between the poles of self-assertion and self-surrender. In the history of thought, quasi-human expressions were indeed employed to characterize that which must remain inexpressible, since all forms of expression derive from the phenomenal world while fundamental reality reposes behind the veil of phenomena. Suffice it for us at this stage to note the polar character of existence, the tension between point and field which constitutes the ineluctable mold of reality.

We have said that the fundamental character of all existents is given in the tension between "point" and "field." The meaning of the polar quality of "point" is clear enough, but what do we mean by the term "field"? Is not the limit of the field of force in which every existent is found rather vague and indefinite? To be sure, in the inanimate universe, there is no definite limit to the field of relations of each point. Fields of force are superimposed upon each other in concentric circles, declining in relevance and shading off into the infinite. While we can envision the end result of the tendency toward absolute rest in an absolute point, we do not see the "field," as a terminal goal, but as the first link in a chain. If the second law of thermodynamics, which foresees the ultimate running down of the energy in the universe and the achievement of a perfectly stable equilibrium, were to be fully realized, we should require only a "general theory of space" to describe the unvarying stillness of sameness and death.

However, there appears to be a contrary tendency in the universe, running counter to the law of entropy—a tendency for "fields" to assert themselves as particularizations or "points" over against their environment. A field of force is a way of reacting to change at any one moment of time. But when the field is itself individualized to the point of maintaining a unitary pattern of action, in spite of continuous change, we have in fact an achievement of individuality—that is, the establishment of a permanent pattern of energy relations. Thus, when radiation suffusing space condenses into an atom, establishing a powerful and complex field of force in a tiny area of space, we recognize in the process the emergence of an individuated field. The emergence of a living cell, constituting a unitary pattern of action, in spite of continuous change, is another great milestone on the ladder of the individuation of fields of force. Jan Smuts' emphasis on "wholes" in nature, imposing their patterns upon their constituent parts, so that these parts function in a manner that is measurably different from the way they function when they are separated, is of interest in demonstrating additional links in this chain of individuation. Every step consists in the achievement of a pattern representing a measure of freedom from the sway of the outside environment. Atoms, cells, multicellular plants, animal cells, animals, mankind: all these stages of creation represent a continuous ascent upon the infinite ladder of individuation and freedom.

The manner whereby energy condenses into matter or atoms coalesce into cells, as well as all the other steps in the vertical ascent of creation, is properly the subject for scientific research and investigation. Suffice it to note that the universe can only be understood in terms of a polar relationship, between point and field—a relationship which is steadily compounded, the "fields" becoming "points" as against other "fields," the whole picture presenting a continuous state of tension, not only along the horizontal plane of space-time, but also on the vertical plane of individuation and freedom.

In this scale of being, the human personality presents the highest, observable field of individuation. Speaking objectively, the human personality represents the greatest measure of freedom attained in the scale of creation: the capacity to reflect on the experiences stored in memory, to envision alternative procedures, to reason and to evaluate, to imagine and to create are but so many expressions of the field-building capacity or the power of freedom that is stored in the human personality. In turn, freedom must be understood not as a break in the chain of cause and effect, or as the injection of a "non-materialistic" factor in the economy of nature, but as the causation and self-maintenance of a "field" or an individualized pattern of action as against the rest of existence.

If now we have learned to recognize an infinite tendency in the rising scale of being, proceeding from the electromagnetic field of force that is space to the human personality, we must next inquire whether we can logically escape the assumption of an Infinite Personality, representing the ultimate pole of being, on the vertical coordinate of freedom. We have seen that the understanding of the universe requires the application of two polar principles that are set over against each other, and we have learned that the same polarity of field and point, whole and part, freedom and mechanism, pervades the whole range of creation. In the human personality, freedom attains its highest manifestation, but it is still far from perfect. Applying the principle of polarity, we conclude that an Absolute Personality representing the highest measure of the field-building capacity, constitutes a pole of being, standing in continual opposition to and tension with the mechanistic universe. God and the physical universe are the two polar concepts of thought, and since logical thought is in correspondence with reality, we are justified in concluding that the space-time continuum, as it exists in itself, and the Deity, as the projection into the infinite of the field-making capacity, are the two poles of being.

We have spoken of freedom in the human personality as the power of field-building and field-maintaining. This equation is not apparent at first glance. However, bearing in mind the point-field relationship as the most fundamental generalization of reality, we recall that the emergence of life was a leap unto a higher level of the relationship that obtains throughout existence. In a living cell, each part is manifestly in a functioning relation to the whole, with the result that the field or pattern of force is maintained, while the parts continue to change. In the emergence of consciousness, we see another level of this field-building capacity, the data of the senses being set in relation to each other, with the sensations of the present moment viewed against the experience of the past. So immediate is the field of consciousness, in the simplest experience, as for example, in the apprehension of color or sound, that we are not aware of the operation by which the mind relates the new experience to the accumulated data in it, identifying the new sensation as a definite color or a meaningful sound. Yet we know that colors and sounds are meaningful to us only because they are so related to the ever-growing field of memory. The process of relating each datum to the apperceptive mass of consciousness is incomprehensible on any mechanical basis. Several decades ago, in the heyday of materialism, much was made of Pavlov's conditioned reflex experiments on a dog whose brain had been severed from the spine. The extreme care that had to be taken in order to establish a selective reaction of the dog's saliva to the sound of the bell amounted in fact to the establishment of an artificial field of relations in the dog's nervous system by the experimenter. In a similar manner, it is possible for the hypnotist to affect and distort the consciousness of the person subjected to his influence. But in consciousness, many sensations are automatically related to the field of experience, each falling into its own groove. And precisely this selective capacity is the distinctive quality of consciousness. While in nature, fields of force operate in only one pattern, in the field of consciousness, many different possibilities are viewed in relation to each sensation, until an identity is established. Treating of the different manner in which events are arranged in nature and in consciousness, William James wrote of the "hard" order that prevails in nature as contrasted with the "soft" order of arrangements that is characteristic of consciousness. He was right in calling attention to the flexibility of consciousness, but wrong in his choice of terms. For the distinction is not one of "hardness" and "softness," but of the unitary field of force versus the capacity in consciousness of setting many events in relation to each other and thereby establishing new fields. As life implies the power of the self-maintenance of a field, consciousness implies the capacity of setting data into relation with each other, thereby setting up new fields. Neither life nor mind is explained by these powers, but the progressive advance in terms of the point-field polar relationship is nevertheless apparent.

This polarity is manifested especially in the operation of logical thought. Aristotle it was who first reflected on the nature of logic and formulated the principles of what came to be known as deductive logic. There is the major premise affirming a proposition concerning a class of objects, as when it is said, "All men are two-legged." There is the minor premise, declaring of one individual that he belongs to the above class, such as the statement, "Socrates is a man." Inevitably, the conclusion follows, "Socrates is two-legged." In this syllogistic process, we have first the vision of a class or a field, followed by the recognition of an individual, leading to the inclusion of that individual within the class. In other words, the process of logical reasoning consists in the setting up of a field of relations between an infinite group of objects, or a class, and an individual object.

Francis Bacon is generally credited with the popularization of the inductive process of reasoning, which advances from a series of particulars to the formulation of a general law, instead of proceeding in the reverse way from the general to the particular. In inductive logic, too, a number of particular facts are classed together and used for the formulation of a law, which describes a field-point relationship. This type of reasoning first lifts a number of particular events out of one field of relations, then recognizes them as forming a new field, in which each event is related to a class or field of consequences. Bacon was interested not so much in the formulation of known facts as in the discovery of new truths. Hence, not logic, but the creative thinking process was his main concern. Now in the process of thinking, observations of particular events form the starting point, but when the universal law leaps out of the multitude of particulars, the achievement is again made possible only by the setting up of a field or class which embraces all the particulars. Thus, whether you begin at the one end or the other, reasoning consists in the setting up of fields of relations and in studying the identities thus discovered.

Hermann Cohen, who founded the new-Kantian school of "critical" philosophy, sought to discover the manner in which "pure" thought operates—that is, thought which is abstracted from any data that are provided by the senses. The net result of his investigation was the suggestion already referred to, that the differential, dy/dx, and the corresponding mathematical process of integration, constitute the *twin* poles of thought. Here, too, we see the projection of point-field relationships, or the capacity to build fields of relationship, as the essential distinction of the thinking process.

Logical thinking is the most perfect form of the field-building capacity that is available to us. Exemplified in the building up of the hypothetical constructs of mathematics, human logic is manifestly not a body of knowledge and procedures, complete in itself, but a continuously expanding circle, certain to transcend all its presently visible boundaries in both scope and refinement. Did Euclid in all his brilliance foresee the possibility of a non-Euclidean geometry of space? Did Newton, in all the exactitude of his calculations, sense the possibility of a "curvature" of space? Even so, we may be certain that the "general field-theory" of Einstein will one day be further refined through the emergence of new concepts—that is, new vistas of fields. Mathematical thought, which is logic in action, is an endless quest for the comprehension of the possibilities of the field-building capacity, and its end is not in sight. It is an advance toward the Deity, the Eternally Present, the Field-Builder of the universe in which we live.

We know that logical thinking is not the only form of activity of the human mind. There is the vast extent of "pre-logical" thought, characteristic of the mind of primitive man, to which Lévy-Bruhl pointed, and there are also the profound depths of the unconscious that Freud and his associates have begun to plumb. While we cannot at this point enter into an analysis of these insights, we invite the reader to examine for himself whether all these forms of thinking are not due to the formation in the mind of incomplete fields. In the unconscious, as well as in primitive thought, we have associations formed on the basis of similarities that we, in our clearest moments of reflection, consider "irrelevant" because they do not take the whole of the relevant fields into consideration. By the same token, it will appear upon analysis, that the cures effected by psychiatry are achieved by opening up the vista of a larger field. The impulse that was side-tracked and allowed to fester in a blind-alley is brought into the total pattern of values and ideals of the human personality, so that a rational "adjustment" is achieved. In Otto Rank's writings, particularly, it is made clear that it is the self, as a field-making entity, that is cured through its own assertion and through the encouragement of the analyst.

The process of achieving logical clarity is endless in both extent and subtlety, and if humility succeeds in dissuading us from stopping at any one point, the rational process leads on to the Pole of Being that is God. But the way of reason is not the only road to Deity. Is not our experience of beauty the recognition of the rightness of a pattern of events that enters into our ken? As reason differs from imagination in that the fields built up by the latter are arbitrary while those of the former are "right" and "true," so the beautiful differs from the ugly in that its fields are automatically "approved" by us. There is an element of universality and personal disinterestedness in the awareness of beauty. Things *are* beautiful; they are not made thus by the vagaries of our taste. The fields of relationship, in color or in sound, that constitute beauty and harmony are manifestations of God's fields. In cognizing them, we join in approving His handiwork, even as it said: "And the Lord saw all that He had made, and behold, it was very good."

If the aesthetic appearance is the silent symbol of the relationships projected by Deity, our moral faculties bring home to us the imperative quality of the Divine Field. For the essence of morality is expressed in the double command: to integrate our own self to the fullest, so as to accord every element of our being its rightful place within our personality, and to place our own self within the larger wholes of the family, the state, and the emergent society of mankind. The nature of the first command has been frequently neglected in European thought, owing partly to the formalistic methods of philosophy and partly to the pervasiveness of the neo-platonic contempt for the flesh that has entered into the mainstream of our thinking. Yet it is basic, as modern depth-psychology has demonstrated. The social implications of the progressive awareness of ever larger wholes in society are obvious.

Thus, God as the field-building pole of being is approached through the highways of reason, aesthetics, and ethics. We think of Him as the Self of the Universe, related to our self, in its field-building capacity, as our self is related to the material world. Yet these ways of cognizing are only formal, belonging more to philosophy than to religion. Basic as these avenues are, they constitute only the substructure of religion. For it is in attachment to God and His will that religion is born, and once this attachment is discovered, a new level of aspirations and feelings is opened up for the human personality.

It is in prayer that religion is born. In the beginning is the self's immediate reverence before the Master of the universe, its abasement before the Majesty of its source. It is not the believer in God who prays, but it is the worshipper who believes. The polarity of being has its correspondence and reflection in the life of the soul, which moves rhythmically from aggressive self-assertion in the world of reality to passive self-surrender to the Maker of this world.

PART SIX

JACOB B. AGUS ON THE MEANING OF JEWISH HISTORY AND EXPERIENCE

SELECTIONS AND
PREFATORY REMARKS
Neil Gillman

THE ISSUE OF JEWISH identity, involving the perennial questions of what it means to be a Jew, especially in our time (i.e., after the Holocaust), the rebirth of the State of Israel, and the remarkable growth of American Jewry, was one that continually occupied Rabbi Agus. In his various writings on Jewish history, theology, and American Jewry, this concern was never far from the center of the discussion.

The following selections, chosen to accompany Neil Gillman's essay "Jacob B. Agus on the Meaning of Jewish History and Experience" in *American Rabbi: The Life and Thought of Jacob B. Agus* (New York, 1996), are from Jacob Agus' *The Evolution of Jewish Thought* (New York, 1959), 396–420; and *Dialogue and Tradition* (New York, 1971), 450–500.

17

EPILOGUE TO THE EVOLUTION OF JEWISH THOUGHT

THE EMANCIPATION of the Jews of western Europe, proceeding apace from the first decade of the nineteenth century, brought the individual Jew to the fore, liberating him from the pressure of enforced communal loyalties. In the course of time the bonds of communal loyalty were weakened; the congregation, a voluntary association of free individuals, came to take the place of the overall community which one entered by birth and left by death or an act of conversion. As a result all the cleavages in Jewish life were widened and deepened.

In the nineteenth century the meaning of the term "Jewish thought" became both wider and narrower than in all previous centuries. It was now wider since the resonant voices outside the pale of the community would not be ignored. Is it justifiable to leave out of our discussion, for example, such men as Heine, Börne and Bergson, whose inspiration derived at least in part from Jewish sources as well as from Jewish experience?

On the other hand, "Jewish thought" came to embrace a necessarily narrower compass than in the past, for the Jew as man is now part of the European community, and the Jew *qua* Jew is such only by virtue of his theology and his "misfortune," the burden of anti-Semitism.

Each of the currents comprising the variegated stream of Jewish thought is intensified and deepened by the massive challenge of modernists. Rationalistic Judaism has eventuated in the modern movements of Reform and Conservatism, with the latter group adding a strong dose of nationalist romanticism and a dash of mysticism to its rationalistic approach. Orthodox Judaism in the eastern countries has become more isolationist than in previous centuries, barricading itself against the incursion of secular learning and the solvent effects of the rationalistic spirit. In eastern Europe the dark cobwebs of Qabbalistic mysticism remained undisturbed well into the twentieth century, while in western Europe Orthodoxy embraced an uneasy alliance with modern culture, seeking support from the anti-intellectualist trends of modern thought and continuing the traditional current of romanticism, in both its ethnic and affective forms.

But the divergent trends do not separate into independent denominations or even independent schools of thought; they continue to affect, influence and mold one another. We encounter in Judaism the phenomenon which sociologists call the "cultural lag"—namely, the fact that only the upper layer of any society changes culturally with the times, while the medium layer changes more slowly and a large portion of society continues its slumber virtually undisturbed. Accordingly, no matter how far the advanced elements of Jewry developed in their quest for a new synthesis of Judaism and the modern spirit, a remnant of the old mentality persisted in every generation. Consequently, in Orthodox ranks today all shades of the premodern spectrum of beliefs can still be found, and individual thinkers, beginning their intellectual adventure in the Orthodox community, are compelled to find their own way to a tenable philosophy of life out of the darkly shadowed, tortuous paths of medievalism.

Secularism is distinctly a new phenomenon in "Jewish thought." Created in the first place by the impact of rationalism, it assumed a Jewish garb under the influence of ethnic romanticism. While the secularists in the first half of the nineteenth century generally accepted the "entrance ticket to European culture," converting to Christianity, those of the latter half of the past century remained as a rule officially within the Jewish community. In the last decades of the century they provided the leadership and impetus of the Zionist movement.

Nothing demonstrates the complex interaction of opposing intellectual forces in Jewish life so much as the emergence of Zionism. In the first place, it was made possible by the influence of rationalism, which undermined the old faith in the eventual coming of the Messiah. On the other hand, its reassertion of Jewish ethnicism drew inspiration and vitality from the romantic current in Judaism, which described the people of Israel as a uniquely endowed nation, set apart by divine decree or by the fatalities of history from all the families of the earth. At the same time, the mystical trend in Orthodox Judaism rediscovered in Zionism a quasi-magical device for hastening the steps of the Messiah. While rationalistic Zionists sought to build a homeland for the Jew as a means of overcoming the Jewish "abnormality" of status in the lands of the Diaspora, and of encouraging the "normal" processes of assimilation in the Diaspora, romantic Zionists sought to employ a Jewish homeland as a means of preserving the "abnormal" status of a "unique" people, countering the trends of assimilation. As this is written, this issue is still unresolved.

Now that the State of Israel is a reality, the exponents of rationalistic Judaism look upon it as a creative center of Jewish faith and culture, not as a means of liquidating the Jewish communities in the Diaspora. Accordingly, they encourage the moral stature of the state rather than its military might, just as they favor the promotion of the spiritual values of Judaism in every country where Jews are found. And they see no good purpose served in the world-wide effort to encourage emigration to Israel, undercutting the psychological rootedness of the Jewish Diaspora so as to bring about its degeneration and disappearance. On the other hand, those who draw their inspiration from the romantic current of Judaism see the Jew as "unique" and "different," forever arrayed against the "nations," with no hope of peace for him, except in his own land, where the strength of his arms will protect him from his enemies. Thus do the issues of today reflect the impetus of the divergent currents of yesterday.

As we turn back for a synoptic view of the different currents within the stream of Judaism we note first the fallacy of all monolithic renderings of this tradition. Friends and foes loved to write of Judaism as if it had a single view of life, providing one answer to all-important questions. Not only psychopathic anti-Semites, painting Judaism in the darkest hues, but even philosophical interpreters of culture, too, construed the Jew as one psychological type and Judaism as a monochromatic picture on the unfolding scroll of human history. Hence, the potent fantasies concerning the characteristics of the "Semitic mind."

Renan saw the Jewish spirit as one of surpassing but monotonous brightness, like the glare of sunlight in the desert, oblivious of the variety of shade and color in nature, seeing the upper surface of things with harsh clarity, but ignoring the reality of depths and shadows. A whole school of historians goes back to Fichte and Schleiermacher for inspiration. In their view, the Jewish faith is the reflection of the peculiarity of Jewish genius, which consists of a calculating cleverness and business shrewdness; incapable of profundity, inventiveness or the appreciation of the romantic nature of man. Wellhausen conceived the difference between prophecy and mysticism in terms of this concept. Mysticism is an expression of the piety of the Aryan soul, in which man surrenders all of himself in the fullness of love. The Semite, according to this school, is capable only of receiving and taking, not of loving and giving. Accordingly, the Bible envisions the prophet as filling himself up with the divine spirit.

Even in socialist circles this mischievous conception of a peculiar Jewish mind was given fresh currency and the semblance of authority by Karl Marx, who maintained that the god of the Jew was the dollar bill and his worship a form of bargaining and haggling.

To counter this nonsense, many Jewish writers set up opposing fantasies of their own, extolling the Jewish "genius" and soothing the wounded vanity of their people. For example, Abraham Geiger, with all his liberalism and sober rationality, wrote of the existence of a Jewish "genius" for religion, shared by no other people; Samuel David Luzzatto asserted that pity was the unique quality of the Jewish soul; and Ahad Haam maintained that the rational quest for the dominion of absolute justice was the underlying impetus of the Jewish mind.

Need poison be countered by anti-poison drugs, or can mankind be educated to dispense with the drug of collective egotism and learn to take life as it is, without the sinister solace of artificial concoctions? After all, counterpoisons are also drugs. We believe that the best defense against the barbs of bigotry is the serenity of objective thought, not the fevered passion of superheated ethnic zealotry.

We have seen a wide variety of theological positions in the long and winding pathways of Jewish thought. How broad is the panorama thus unfolded! How rich is the spectrum of colors ranging from the twilight moods of mysticism to the stark clarity of rationalism, from the lofty heights of universalist idealism to the dark depths of collective "sacred egoism"!

We find exponents of both alternatives in the discussion of such central issues as the following:

(1) THE TRANSCENDENCE OF GOD VERSUS HIS IMMANENCE

Rationalists like Maimonides asserted that God was remote from earthly concerns and far beyond the grasp of human faculties. His Providence does not extend to the masses of people, "the poor and the broken in spirit," but only to the well-proportioned and well-disposed, those reflective and saintly souls whose lines have fallen in pleasant places, and who undertake the arduous philosophical disciplines leading to the comprehension of His difference from the material world. All Biblical miracles were predetermined in advance of creation, built into the inflexible system of iron necessity that governs the universe. The only pathway to God is that of reason, and this pathway is impersonal, consisting in the elimination from our mind of human interests and the actual stuff of experience.

On the other hand, the doctrine of divine immanence is well represented in the stream of Jewish thought. In the ethnic romanticism of Halevi, God is portrayed as being in direct communication with the people of Israel, when they are gathered in the land of Israel. A divine effulgence was visible, at least to the sages and to the prophets, and a divine voice could be heard at critical moments. In Qabbalah, man's power to affect the divine pattern of *sefiroth* was deemed to be so direct and immediate as to be virtually automatic, the Deity acting toward man, "like a shadow." The material world was only the lowest garment of the substance of reality. And man's soul is not entirely enclosed in his body, being rooted in the realm of *sefiroth*.

In naïve or unreflective Judaism, both concepts of the Deity could be found side by side. Consequently, the Talmud and a huge mass of popular pietistic literature employ rationalistic and mystical concepts, almost interchangeably, for their "religious value," if we may coin a new phrase, without any awareness of their mutual incompatibility.

(2) HUMAN DIGNITY VERSUS HUMAN SINFULNESS

Does a person best reflect the "image of God" within him when he is made aware of his dignity or of his sinfulness? This question points to a psychological cleavage that cuts deep. On the one hand, there is the "active" piety of those who consider man to be "a partner of the Lord" in the establishment of His kingdom on earth. God is best served by the fullest assertion of man's faculties and gifts. Man is bidden to use his faculty of rational judgment, in the determination of right and wrong, and in the amelioration of existing evils. When men assert their perceptive powers in the domains of thought and action, they give concrete expression to the divine element in their nature. For man and God are united in rationality, love of goodness and gentleness, and in reverence for law. In general man is the agent of the divine *nisus* for perfection.

This way of thinking is reflected not only in the rationalistic school but also in the sober mood of the Talmudic sages. The concept of a covenant between man and God in which both parties to the agreement undertake to abide by certain actions is a perfect expression of "active" piety. God does not compel man to accept any law, but man does what is right out of loyalty to his own higher nature, which is Godlike. And this concept underlies the reasoning of *Halachah,* Jewish law. If the children of Israel had not voluntarily undertaken to observe the law, they would not have been obliged to abide by it, for in the domain of reason and ethics all rational and moral beings are equal.

But while the mood of "active piety" is well represented in Judaism, the opposite mood of total surrender to the divine will is also rather frequently encountered. This attitude is permeated with a deep awareness of human failure. Man's greatest achievements are but vanity and naught. It is in sin that we are born. "And if thou dost act righteously, what does thou give unto Him?"

"What are we, what is our life, what our kindness, our righteousness, our salvation, our power, our heroism? And the superiority of man over the beast is naught, for all is vanity." [1]

In this mood we feel that God's only demand is man's self-abasement. Not by being "like unto God," but by total surrender, by "a broken heart," by the practice of humility so thoroughgoing as to approach self-negation, does God take delight in us. By active striving we achieve nothing, for God neither desires our good right arm nor can we exert any of our faculties to good effect without falling victim to the perverting and ensnaring forces of pride and sin.

Several historians of religion take the contrast between the active and the passive moods of piety to be the fundamental distinction between Judaism and Christianity. But actually many variations of passive piety are found not only in the romantic and mystical currents of Jewish thought, but also in the pietistic literature *(Mussar)* of popular Judaism.

The opposition of several leading Orthodox rabbis to the introduction of an organ in the synagogue was motivated by the belief that beauty and dignity minister to man's sense of self-importance, discouraging the penitential mood of sinfulness. "A sinner must not bedeck himself with beauty, a sinner must not take on the garments of pride."[2]

As a rule, the doctrine of "original sin" is not central in Judaism, but at various times it has been strongly affirmed. In the Talmud we find the dogmatic assertion that all who did not stand at Sinai suffer from the "corruption of the serpent."[3] In Qabbalah the souls of all non-Jews are presumed to be "rooted" in the domain of the "shells."

In Halevi's philosophy, even converts cannot expect to achieve equality with born Jews following the advent of the Messiah nor to become recipients of the "gift of prophecy." The capacity for the "divine quality" is denied by Halevi to non-Jewish mankind as a whole, which is doomed to grope in the darkness. Also, the proposition that it is possible for man, unaided by revelation, to live a life of goodness and attain a share in the world to come is both affirmed and denied in Jewish tradition.[4]

(3) IS THE CONTENT OF RELIGION SOME THINGS TO BE DONE OR SOMETHING TO BECOME?

This question probes deep into the nature of piety. When religion consists of a number of rites to perform and commandments to execute, we have a pattern of piety that is external to man's true being. It may be dogmatically asserted that the rites in question exert a quasi-magical effect on the soul and in the cosmos, "purifying" man's inner nature and providing "food for the upper worlds." But in the actual performance of the rites there is no inherent sequence of effects upon the psyche of the worshiper. In this pattern of piety the supreme value of the ritual is asserted, and the value of any universal ethical and esthetic virtues is questioned.

Such a completely externalized religion may be softened by the additional requirement of "duties of the heart," supplementing those of physical performance. But, characteristically, these obligations of the mind and heart are not conceived of as mandatory and essential to the rite itself.

This nonspiritual concept of piety is certainly encountered within the sacred literature of the Jewish faith. It is virtually assumed in the stream of *Halachic* (legalistic) nonphilosophic Judaism. It is justified somewhat hesitantly in the romantic current of Jewish thought. In Qabbalah we find elaborate rationalizations for the belief in the cosmic effects of the performance of the *mizvoth*.

But the opposing concept of the nature of piety is also well represented in Judaism. In the rationalistic school, the *mizvoth* are conceived of as instruments of piety embodying universal, ethical and esthetic values. The *mizvoth* were intended to train men and women in the acquisition of good habits, noble ideas and lofty sentiments. The context of religion is not the execution of certain commands, but the fulfillment of the divine potential in human nature. God is not a king, intent upon the enforcement of His orders, but our Father, concerned with helping us to attain the fullness of our stature. Religion is not a burden on our backs, but an aspiration in our souls to grow into our ideal likeness. Understood in this way, the virtue and truth of other religions may be honestly acknowledged without giving up the belief in one's own religion. Faith becomes not the guardianship of "eternal verities," but the quest for the truths of eternity, a search for wider horizons for the life of the soul, a courageous ascent and an endless task.

(4) IS MAN COMPLETELY FREE TO WORK OUT HIS OWN SALVATION, OR IS HIS FUTURE PREDETERMINED?

The predominant emphasis in Judaism is unquestionably on the side of man's freedom. The Torah affirms that man is free to choose between good and evil, the blessing and the curse, life and death. In the Talmud, we are told that everything in a person's life is fixed in advance save his righteousness. "All is in the power of heaven, save the fear of heaven."[5] Rabbi Akiba set the stage for a philosophical riddle that occupied all the masters of Jewish philosophy when he asserted, "All is foreseen, but the choice is given."[6] The power of repentance is infinite in scope; even the greatest sinners can, if they will, transform their lives and attain the greatest heights of piety.[7]

On the other hand, Crescas, who has been called "the most Jewish of all the philosophers," declares that even a person's piety is predetermined and human freedom is only an illusion. In Qabbalah, non-Jewish humanity, drawing its sustenance from the "shells," can hardly be expected to do anything that is genuinely good. Those who become converts to Judaism, so the legend goes, possess souls which were present at Sinai when the covenant was concluded. A verse from Proverbs (14:34) is an oft-quoted maxim: "Even the kindness of the nations is sinful."

The advent of the Messiah, who will usher in the Kingdom of God, is both fixed in the mind of God and also dependent on Jewish repentance. If Jewish merit and penitence do not succeed in hastening the arrival of the Messiah, then he will come in the previously appointed time.[8]

In the rationalistic current of Jewish thought, it is assumed that man's reason is free and untrammeled and that man can attain the good life by the exercise of his native endowments of intelligence and conscience. Both assumptions are contested in the romantic and mystical schools of Jewish thought. Reason is declared to be the shameless servant of the will, and the will in turn is "rooted" by birth and early upbringing either in the spheres of holiness among loyal Jews or in the unclean dominion of the "other side," among the rest of mankind. Halevi introduces the argument in his famous book by telling of an angel that appeared to King Bulan and warned him, "Thy thoughts are acceptable but thy deeds are not." Acceptable deeds, for Halevi, are spelled out in the codes of the Jewish faith. Non-Jewish humanity is for the ethnic romantics, by and large, precluded from salvation.

For the rationalists, divine grace is not needed as the condition for man's goodness, since this favor is granted to man at birth and by education in the shape of the twin lights in his soul, conscience and intelligence. For the romantics and mystics, divine grace and the "merit of the fathers" is of the essence. For man's soul is virtually besieged by the malicious forces of Satan. And those which are not "rooted" in the divine pleroma are almost inevitably steeped in sin.

(5) IS THE DIVINE WILL INHERENT IN THE NORMAL AND
NATURAL PROCESSES OF HISTORY, OR IS IT
"TRANSHISTORICAL," BREAKING INTO THE FLUX OF
HISTORICAL EVENTS WITH PREDETERMINED RESULTS?

This question seems labored and casuistic; yet, it points to the real issue between those who believe that human progress is a gradual result of the strains and stresses of social forces and those who envision the high points of peace and prosperity as being attained by unpredictable incursions of God's grace. When the question is asked, "Does Judaism believe in human progress?" the answer cannot be given in the simple syllables of "yes" or "no."

The vision of the Messianic era was born in Judaism, a many-splendored vision of hope and beauty incarnate. But this vision represented not the upward path but the ultimate goal, the situation at "the end of days." Nor did that vision stand alone, unassociated with other eschatological hopes and fantasies. After a period lasting from forty years to four hundred years, according to different traditions, it was believed that the human personality would become metamorphosed and life in all its aspects would be completely transformed, ushering in the wondrous era of "the world to come." [9] Perfection in body and soul would then be the unfailing rule—but the human body would then be transformed into a new, heavenly substance, no longer a thing of flesh and blood.

Is the goal reached through the processes of history? A rationalist like Maimonides believed that the Messianic era would be attained by the normal processes of history, for God had prearranged all human events and, through the prophets, had made known His will. Even Maimonides did not see any progress toward this goal in the events of his day, looking for confirmation of his faith to the verses of Scripture and the traditions of his family. In his letter to the Yemenites he tentatively expressed the hope that the Messiah would appear in his own generation.

Nevertheless, we can find in Maimonides the seeds of a philosophy of historical progress. For he affirmed the Resurrection and the fantasies of the "world to come" not as true ideas, but only as beliefs necessary for the maintenance of the community. And in both Christianity and Islam he saw the divine impulse at work, preparing the ground for the ultimate triumph of the "true faith."

Nahmanides and his school did not envision the fulfillment of the Messianic dream in any progressive manner. The belief in the Messiah was a dogmatic assertion, of the same type as the Resurrection, and as little given to progressive realization. The authors of the apocalyptic *Midrashim,* one and all, envisioned a series of catastrophes, taxing human endurance and culminating in disasters from which only a few survivors will escape. The help of the Lord will come suddenly.[10] Human repentance can hasten the coming of the Messiah, but repentance was conceived by the romantics and the mystics in purely dogmatic terms.

In general, the pietists of Judaism did not see any progressive improvement in the behavior of their contemporaries—either Jews or Gentiles. It is of the essence of Orthodoxy to idealize the past, not the future. "If the people of early times were like angels, we are like men, and if they were men we are donkeys." [11] Even the wicked men of the past like Balaam and Nebuchadnezzar were conceived to be great in their own way, so that miracles could be performed for their reproof or enlightenment.

A doctrine of the cumulative merit of redemption was contained in Qabbalah, especially as taught in the Lurianic school. But the accumulation of merit was believed to be taking place in the occult essence of the universe, not in the unfolding of the visible events of history.

(6) IS FAITH AN EXTENSION AND ANTICIPATION OF THE LIGHTS OF CONSCIENCE AND INTELLIGENCE, OR IS IT THE ACCEPTANCE OF TRADITIONAL DOGMAS OUTSIDE THE DICTATES OF REASON AND ETHICS?

This question might be phrased in many different ways. Indeed, it underlies almost every issue in theology. The Scholastics distinguished between faith as "trust in God" and faith as "assent" to a proposition. For the believers of the first category, faith is a blend of love, trust and intuition; hence, they will interpret the documents of revelation in accord with the precepts of reason. They will eschew literalism in practice and dogmatism in theory, interpreting the legendry of their faith as parables and the rites of their religion as action-symbols of faith. If, however, faith is conceived not as an insight of the soul but as its submission to an external fiat, reason will not be allowed a decisive role as the source of truth, and moral principles too will be subverted to serve the worldly interests of the "chosen people," who are pledged to maintain the one and only true faith. The mentality of fundamentalism, deriving from an insistence on the literal truth of the documents of revelation, is inescapably zealous and exclusive. Fundamentalists may accommodate themselves to the pressures and needs of modern society, but they cannot in truth acknowledge the rightness of the values upon which it is founded.

Was Judaism, then, pro-rational or anti-rational? Was it a religion of dogmas, affirmed on the testimony of tradition, or was it a religion of faith in the inspired guidance of prophets and saints, sages and philosophers?

Here again the answer depends on the particular school of thought within Judaism. The rationalists maintained that revelation and reason concurred fully in their essential import; that revelation provided instruction in those areas where the testimony of reason was indecisive and uncertain; that the documents of revelation needed to be interpreted in the light of reason; that the purpose of revelation was to fortify man's intellectual moral adventure, assuring him of the ultimate success of his efforts, for man's highest values are rooted in eternity.

The romantics and mystics, on the other hand, labored hard and continuously to assert the contrary claim. God takes delight in confounding man's pride of reason. This is why Abraham was tested by the command to sacrifice Isaac. Would Abraham follow the rationalists and refuse the demand of God on the ground of its unreasonableness, or would he slaughter his son in obedience to God and in defiance of reason?

The battle between the rationalists and their opponents can be traced in Judaism to the Biblical period, the contest between the true prophets and the numerous contemporary "prophetizers." The prophets identified the insights of a keen conscience with the will of God, whereas the "prophetizers" sought to find God in an emotional frenzy that extinguished the light of consciousness. And this battle is by no means over. For the human situation renews for us perennially the choice between placing our faith in the testimony of a revered tradition or in that of our heart and mind.

There is an active, open-eyed, open-minded and open-hearted type of piety, arising out of the projection of man's highest values against the cosmic curtain of eternity. Opposed to this piety of the harmonious personality there is the religion of those who are predominantly moved by fear—fear of the dark depths of their own souls. Psychologically speaking, they need a faith of closed horizons, shutting the doors tight against the longing of the soul; hemming it in by the barriers of dogma and by a rigid regimen of conduct that is presumed to be unalterable. The affirmation of a dogma is for them an action-symbol, setting limits to the restless dynamism of heart and mind which they deeply distrust.

Proponents of both alternatives and of some mediating positions as well will find in the treasures of Judaism ample support for their views.

(7) IS JUDAISM A UNIVERSAL RELIGION, EMPLOYING A NATION
AS ITS HISTORICAL VEHICLE, OR IS IT THE "WAY OF LIFE"
OF THE JEWISH PEOPLE, THE EXPRESSION OF THE CULTURE
AND SANCTA OF THE JEWISH PEOPLE?

This question is couched in modern terms, reflecting distinctions which are meaningful only in a society where religion and politics are separated. Nevertheless, in our survey of the development of Jewish thought we have dealt continuously with the wider implications of this distinction. On several different occasions we distinguished between Judaism as a structure of universal ideals and sentiments, rites and symbols, and Judaism as sublimated ethnicism, refined by a high ethical tradition and associated with a great religious tradition.

In the current of rationalistic Judaism, the motives of ethnicism dwindle into relative insignificance. Maimonides' interpretation of the Jewish faith does not assume a wide gulf between Jews and the rest of mankind. The *mizvoth* of the Torah are only educational devices. Judaism is an excellent school. But some men will go through the best schools, learning very little, and others, studying in mediocre institutions or even self-taught, will find their way to the presence of the Almighty. Even the Messianic era was conceived by Maimonides not primarily as an epoch of national triumph but as an era of universal good will, when all men will accept the "true faith," surrender the follies of national ambition and devote themselves to philosophical meditations.

"The sages and the prophets longed for the days of the Messiah, not in order that they might govern the whole world, lording it over the pagans and being exalted by all nations; nor that they might eat, drink and rejoice, but in order that they might enjoy the leisure to engage in the study of Torah and wisdom, free from interference and oppression, attaining thus to life eternal." [12]

Albo spoke of the general category of a "Divine Torah," allowing the possibility of several divine faiths, each suited to the varied circumstances of people living in different portions of the globe. To be sure, in his Epistle to the Yemenites, Maimonides hews close to the line of ethnic zealotry, forced as he was to appeal to the sentiments and mentality of simple-minded people, "of women and children." Similarly, we encounter concessions to popular prejudice in all the writings of rationalistic Judaism. But essentially and in principle, philosophical Judaism was universalistic and free from the zealotries of ethnicism. In this respect the current of philosophical Judaism continued, widened and deepened the sparkling mountain streams of prophecy. For the great prophets, too, defined religion by means of universal and ethical standards; combatted the ethnic pride and prejudice of their contemporaries; conceived of the "congregation of Israel" in the ideal terms of the loyal remnant and looked forward to the conversion of all mankind.

To be sure, in the books of prophecy we occasionally encounter verses reflecting ethnic pride and prejudice. The prophets were children of their time as well as geniuses of faith. Ethnic zealotry was after all part of their environment. Their genius was manifested, however, not when they yielded to the sentiments of the people, but when they confronted their contemporaries with new ideas and sought to redirect national zeal into spiritual channels.

On the other hand, there is no lack of support for the ethnic conception in the central ideas of nonphilosophical Judaism, in the romantic and in the mystical currents of thought. The Talmud operates consistently on the supposition of a wide and deep chasm, yawning between Jewry and "the nations."

The sages of the Talmud differed on such issues as whether Jews are called "children of God" regardless of the quality of their piety and the ethics of their conduct; whether the "pious of the nations" do or do not have a share in the "world to come"; whether the term "man" in the Torah refers to Israelites only or to all men; whether the severe laws in the Pentateuch regarding the neighboring nations of Palestine were to be applied in the centuries following the destruction of the Temple; whether or not proselytes should be sought out and welcomed; whether or not the dietary laws should be made progressively more stringent, so as to interpose a more forbidding barrier between Jews and Gentiles. The liberal position was never lacking in Judaism, but at times it was overwhelmed and overruled.

In romantic and mystical Judaism, the Jewish people is elevated to the rank of a "superhumanity" which alone is capable of communing with God. The term "the God of Israel" is interpreted literally to suggest an intimate, organic and exclusive relationship, as if God could be revealed to mankind only by the agency of the people of Israel. As we noted before, the Qabbalists taught that only the souls of Jews were derived from the Supreme Being. Gentiles were even forbidden to study the

Torah, according to the authorities belonging to this school, for the Torah was the private possession of the one people that God loves and protects by His Providence. Even the lofty concept of the Messianic era was frequently perverted in popular literature and distorted by the proponents of this view so as to express the bitter frustration of a persecuted people rather than the noble vision of inspired prophets. The Messiah was to avenge the wrongs perpetrated against Jewish people and compensate them for their years of suffering, restoring to Jews their rightful position as "sons of Kings." This caricature of the Messianic vision, however, was rarely allowed to stand unchallenged, uncorrected and untransformed by the refining genius of philosophical piety.

(8) IN VIEW OF THE MANIFOLD TENSIONS AND POLARITIES IN JEWISH THOUGHT CAN WE SPEAK OF THE "MAINSTREAM" OF JUDAISM?

Subjectively, it is certainly quite natural and almost inevitable for contemporary writers to identify their own interpretation of Judaism as the "mainstream." Throughout our discussion, we have not failed to make clear our own alignment with the rationalistic school, which is sometimes also designated as the current of philosophical Judaism. We believe that God reveals Himself primarily through the twin lights of conscience and intelligence and that the written documents of revelation need to be interpreted in the light of the living Word of revelation. We believe that this recognition of the primacy of the living Word is the central insight of Judaism, a faith that was hammered out of teachings of prophets and sages. While the "prophetizers" of the Bible and of Canaanite culture were presumably passive vessels in the grip of their "frenzy," the Hebrew prophets identified the "still, small voice" of a sacred, sensitive conscience with the voice of the Lord.

At the same time, we must not forget that Judaism is far larger than any school of thought. Objectively, we cannot ignore nor make light of the other currents of Judaism. Nonphilosophical Judaism, with its rigid, legalistic mentality, was at all times a potent reality. The vast, darkly shadowed halls of Qabbalah constitute part of the Jewish tradition, and the self-exalting works of the Romantic school, rhapsodizing on the "unique" glories of the Jewish soul, are among the treasured possessions of the faith. We may, if we choose, consider the philosophical interpretation as the "mainstream," or the "essence," or as being "normative"; but then we need to acknowledge frankly that we follow our own personal preference.

In the modern period there have appeared a plethora of popular books, all purporting to describe the "essence" of Judaism. As a rule the author's private interpretation of what is "true" or "authentic" is given as the "essence," and all that does not fit into his category is dismissed as relatively unimportant, unauthentic or marginal. Sometimes, too, the old casuistic skills of our Talmud-trained ancestors are made use of to prove that contradictions do not annoy the "unique" genius of the Jewish mentality, which thinks in terms of "both-and," not "either-or" categories. As we have noted, opposing points of view were due to the clash of diverse currents of thought within the tradition, not to a unique faculty or a peculiar logic. Such efforts at romantic self-aggrandizement would be laughable if they were not tragic reminders of the essential similarity of human nature the world over. It is precisely the defenders of the "uniqueness" of German genius, Polish genius, Russian genius, etc., who glory in a similar discovery of the "transnational" domain, where the categories of the intellect are inapplicable, and dreams of ethnic superiority can be indulged to the heart's content.

Actually, Judaism as a great religious tradition reflects diverse approaches and insights which are organized in different patterns to suit the varying mentalities which compose a world-wide community. In his massive work, *A Study of History,* Prof. Arnold J. Toynbee attempts to prove that the great religions reflect the different psychical structures of mankind, with each religious tradition corresponding to one psychological type. As a matter of fact, all variations of character are found in every people, and a great tradition growing over a long period of time will naturally reflect the insights and needs of every important category of human personality.

However, this reasonable approach to the mysteries of faith was countered by equally powerful trends toward dogmatism. Thus, the self-righteous dogmatist, who bans and burns the books of his opponents, is not an unfamiliar figure in the history of Jewish thought.

For a variety of historical reasons, conflicting positions were tolerated within the confines of Judaism. The awesome greatness of God was felt so powerfully that the sages were disposed to recognize the legitimacy of different approaches. The heart of so great a mystery cannot be reached by any single pathway. For the proponents of a nondogmatic faith, it appears reasonable enough to project shafts of light into the cosmic mystery from many different angles, without being able to see how they fall into a consistent and logical pattern. The prophetic-rationalistic school of Jewish thought naturally favored this attempt to see God and His works from a great diversity of standpoints. Fortunately, the cause of tolerance was aided by the circumstances that the law can more easily take account of actions than of thoughts, and Jewish piety was molded in the patterns of legalism. So the actions of the Jew were regulated with the utmost zeal and precision, while his thoughts were allowed a relative measure of freedom.

Finally, the most decisive factor in the creation of a wide domain of tolerance within the tradition of Jewish theology was the absence of an all-powerful central authority. It is in the conflict of cultures and in the mutual confrontation of diverse points of view that philosophy comes to life and flourishes. In the Biblical period, prophets vied against priests and against kings. By the Second Commonwealth, there was only a narrow area where Sadducees and Pharisees could agree. Besides the official academies, there was always the free proliferation of private schools, and their traditions achieved recognition in the course of time. The Babylonian Gaonate dominated the Jewish scene only for a few centuries, and their authority was challenged by the Qaraites. When the power of the Geonim was broken, Jewish intellectuals needed to take into account only the guidance of their own conscience, the opinion of their colleagues and the broad areas of agreement among the people generally.

Consequently, a rich and many-sided tradition came into being which reflected the full spectrum of colors resulting from the focusing of Divine light upon the various psychic planes of the prism of human genius.

In view of the diversity of trends within the stream of Jewish thought, wherein does the unity of the Jewish tradition consist? We find the unifying principle in the text, the context and the emphasis of all schools in Judaism. The unity of a river consists of the bedrock and banks of the channels through which it flows, the intermingling of the tributaries in the course of its flow and the impetus of direction shared by its waters. In Judaism, the unity of source is the chain of sacred literature, the unity of bedrock is the social structure of Jewish life and the unity of impetus is the quest for the realization of the Godlike qualities of the human personality. The text is the series of sacred documents, the Pentateuch, Bible and Talmud, and all the varied books of the classical tradition. All interpreters of Judaism, as far as their ideas may range, return for inspiration and guidance to the same sacred books. There exists also the unifying code of conduct regulating worship, home ritual and everyday life.

As the stream flows, some of its waters are evaporated by wind and sun; and fresh rivulets bring new waters from the countryside; stagnant pools form here and there in the low marshlands as well as rushing eddies in narrow defiles; yet the stream is one, the unpracticed eye noticing scarcely any distinction among its waters, while the experienced sailor can sail up the stream, from the channels in the delta to its sources in the mountains of antiquity.

The context is the total life of the Jewish community. It is impossible to separate the evolution of ideas in Judaism from the social and economic forces in Jewish history. The unity of Jewish communal life, fashioned by many historic forces, provided a forum for the airing of opposing views and the conciliation of conflicting opinions.

The nature of the communal bedrock for the flow of Jewish thought changed in the course of time from the confederacy of twelve tribes to a unified nation and from the political unity of a nation to the social unity of a religious community. The effective meaning of the category of a religious community did not remain static. At all times, Jewishness involved awareness of a very real communal setup. The bedrock and channels were there, painfully real, even if observers differed concerning its nature and proper designation.

In addition, certain emphases belong to the tradition as a whole, characterizing its every facet in greater or lesser degree. The emphases on God's unity, on the rationality and goodness of His Will, on the freedom of the human personality, on the ethical vocation of man and his destiny as a "partner of the Lord"—all these emphases, different though their significance may be in the different currents of Jewish thought, belong to the spiritual impetus of Judaism as a whole.

These emphases are of special significance in the consideration of the place of Judaism within the larger context of the Judeo-Christian tradition. As against the Christian challenge concerning the divine nature of

Jesus, all branches of Judaism upheld the rationalistic-ethical position. We have had occasion to mention Nahmanides' contention that the "mind of a Jew" will never consent to the proposition that God became man, being born out of the womb of a woman, or that God needed to sacrifice "His son," in order to atone for the sins of mankind and compensate for the corruption of "original sin." Nahmanides belonged to the mystical current of Judaism; nevertheless, as against Christian dogma, he too employed the weapons of reason and the objective validity of ethical principles.

This contrast runs through every domain of religious expression. The rational and moral nature of God precludes His devising a method of salvation which is based on the acceptance of dogma and the surrender of the faculty of moral judgment.

Men must be judged by their "works," not by their faith. The good God could not have predetermined any individual or group of individuals for perdition. God requires from us, not the feelings of trust and total surrender, but our co-operation in the building of His Kingdom. God is love, but love is not the sheer feeling of benevolence; it is sustained devotion to the construction of the ideal society in this world. If religion be conceived as a field of tension between the pole of active, rational and moral piety, devoted to the "daytime" spirit of optimistic and constructive idealism, and the pole of passive, emotional piety, esthetic and reflective, devoted to the "nighttime" spirit of love, peace and goodwill, then Judaism, in all its diversity, will be found closer to the first pole. While the love of God in Islam is chiefly surrender to His Will, and love in Christianity is primarily an act of self-giving, love in Judaism is devotion to "the fashioning of the world into a Kingdom of God."

So the hero-image of Judaism is primarily the prophet, fighting for truth and justice, and secondarily the sage, studying and outlining the ideal patterns of the good life; the hero-image of Christianity is the mystic, whose soul has sounded the depths of the mystery of existence, and secondarily the saint who suffers in love for the sake of humanity.

The challenge of Judaism tends to make the Christian world more prophetic, more communal minded, more rational and ethical, more concerned with the "works" of love. The Christian challenge to Judaism tends to break down the self-exalting impetus of ethnicism and to caution against the externalization of religion and its hardening into a series of lifeless rituals. The rationalistic school in Judaism has always been responsive to the variety of intellectual and esthetic challenges posed to it by its daughter religion.

We cannot conclude our review of the currents of thought in historic Judaism without taking account of the question that has come to loom so large throughout the modern period: What is the significance of the Jewish tradition for western civilization and humanity as a whole?

It was the current of philosophical Judaism that placed the greatest emphasis on the concept of the Jew as the custodian of eternal truths for the sake of all mankind. But we found ourselves dealing with radically different versions of these truths. What happens to the concept of treasuring eternal truths if the exponents of Judaism differ so radically on the understanding of these truths?

We do not and cannot claim to know all about God nor all about man's need for salvation. As Jews, we do not strike the pose of all-knowing prophets, but rather "sons of prophets," determined seekers of truth. The Jews are heirs of a hundred generations of deeply earnest men and women who sought God by the feeble lights in their possession. They denied themselves many things for the sake of their faith, forswearing the luxuries of life and even life itself when the test came, but they never denied the God of their heart. The history of the Jewish faith is the magnificent tale of an endless quest by a world-wide community, a community of people remaining true to its search in spite of many temptations and refusing to compromise with its conscience.

The Jews became an eternal people because they set for themselves an endless task, a task that may never be consummated but that will be brought ever closer to realization. This task is all-embracing, presenting a challenge in every aspect of life. Because Judaism asserts the doctrine of God's unity, the task of comprehending His work in nature and in history is a never-ending challenge to human thought. God's unity cannot be comprehended within finite time, for the task of synthesizing all categories of wisdom expands as our knowledge grows. By insisting that human nature contains the "image of God," Judaism released a powerful, revolutionary force making for freedom and justice. This too is an impetus driving toward wide and then wider horizons, for the meaning of freedom and justice is unfolded only through the diverse processes of history. Because the Jewish religion is based on the doctrine of a covenant with God, the intellectual-ethical domain becomes the common ground of man and God. But the implications of this covenant at a particular time or in the vision of the future are worked out anew by every generation.

Abstract truths susceptible of verbal formulation belong to the universal society of scholars and thinkers. They can in no way be staked out as a private domain by any people or any community. A religious tradition represents the application of truth to the total life of a community, and this application of accumulated insights to the problems of life requires the agency of institutions, the charm of rites and the momentum of the love and loyalty of generations. But the task of applying eternal truths to temporary situations is never finally accomplished. Here is where the experience and wisdom of one tradition poses a challenge to and serves as a corrective for another tradition.

It is important to bear in mind the distinction between eternal truths and their embodiment in institutions. Abstract truths are best conveyed through books and through instruction within the academic world. The applied truths of religion, affecting as they do the whole of life, are transmitted through the institutions and practices of a living, historical community. Eternal truths are invigorated with the sinews of life by the impetus and scope of a vital tradition, but religious traditions may hinder as well as help the continuing application of truth to the ever-changing stream of life. A tradition may hallow a temporary application and erect it as a barrier against the free interaction of thought and life. The very greatness of a tradition, recording the successful confrontation of great problems with eternal truths in ages past may cause its adherents to become unduly worshipful of instruments and institutions, unduly arrogant toward other faiths and psychologically unable to meet fresh situations with creative vigor. The wholeheartedness and finality of a religious tradition preserves the spirited momentum of the past, but it tends to hallow the static solution rather than the ever-dynamic method. Hence, the mutual confrontation of two or more traditions is always helpful for the maintenance of their power of self-criticism and self-renewal.

The significance of the Jewish tradition within the larger context of western civilization consists precisely of the challenge it presents to other religious traditions. The historic stream of Judaism flows beside other streams, reflecting the same great tensions and problems within a different context and containing different solutions. It is because of the sameness of eternal truth and the difference of historic experience that

Judaism confronts the other great religions with a creative and continuing challenge.

Jewish apologists felt themselves constrained in the past to insist on the "uniqueness" of Judaism. They thought that Judaism could be esteemed as being of surpassing worth only if it were known as different from all other faiths in a deep and essential sense. Judaism, they felt, could be protected from the criticism that is freely directed at other traditions only if it were shown to be "unique." But the claim of uniqueness is itself far from being unique. Romantic writers of every nation and religious tradition love this word, for it seems to mark out a charmed circle, free from the revolving sword of reason. Actually, Judaism is unique in the same sense that other faiths are unique—as a compound, not as a chemical element. We have shown the variety of responses within it to the challenges of the hour. Each school of thought responded in the idiom used by the corresponding schools in other traditions. The history of Jewish thought, in all its multifarious expression, is of universal significance because it is the account of responses to perennial universal problems. Dealing with the great polar tensions of one religion, it reflects the dynamic forces in all religious cultures.

These polar tensions are threefold in character, corresponding to the three dimensions of every faith: its ideological structure and its search for truth; its institutional character, consisting of its rites and forms of worship; its sociological structure, outlining the duties of the individual to the other members of the "in" group, and the relation of the "in" group to the rest of mankind. These three dimensions correspond to a classification of Judaism attributed to Simon the Just— *Torah* (learning), *Avodah* (worship) and *Gemiluth Hassadim* (social obligations and acts of loving kindness).

The first polar tension is between the belief in one true faith and the assertion that all faiths are equally good and true for their worshipers. This tension may also be described in terms of the contrast between the subjective approach, which sanctions all that is one's own, and the objective point of view, which rises above all possessive prejudices.

Both the dogmatists and the relativists, the intellectual isolationists and the champions of impartiality, find it easy to define their positions and to stake out their claims. But neither the cause of truth nor the spiritual welfare of humanity is served by them, for the spirit of man is expressed in both subjective feeling and objective thought. The authentic response of the human soul to this polarity is to find a dynamic balance of the two moods, resulting in a mediating position between the two extremes.

Within the Jewish tradition, we find several ways in which this tension was resolved. While the solutions of the past may not be entirely adequate for the problems of the present, they should not be ignored in searching for new solutions.

The second polar tension of religious tradition is that between the inner and outer expressions of the faith, between the emphasis on "the service of the heart" and the sacramental concept of ritual acts. Religions are inevitably articulated in institutions, myths and rites; else they are still-born abstractions. But the moment they are expressed in external actions, the danger arises of the external performance becoming a hallowed end in itself instead of being only an aid to piety. Hence, the dilemma: no religion without rituals; yet how often do the ritual acts stifle the inner life of the faith!

In some Christian circles, this polar tension is described as the contrast between Pharisaic Judaism and early Christianity. This hoary accusation is a delusion based upon the caricature of the ancient Pharisees and of Judaism. Actually, in Jewish tradition, we encountered several different ways of meeting this perennial problem of organized religion.

The third polar tension is perhaps the most important in our modern world. We find it the more difficult to visualize because we are ourselves caught up in its coils. It is the tension centering round the concept of a "chosen people." Is it the intention of this concept that the people ought to be dedicated to the ideals of God, or does it mean that the life of the people is supremely important because the ideals of God are attached to it? The two alternatives do not appear to be mutually exclusive. Yet there is a real choice between the two attitudes in every concrete situation. In the one case the community acts as a "prophet-people," gauging its policies by means of universal, ethical principles and sacrificing its own temporal welfare for the sake of its ideals. In the other case the welfare of the nation itself is ranked as the supreme value and embraced with the wholeheartedness and totality of devotion that is characteristic of genuine piety. In effect the second alternative turns nationalism itself into a zealous religion and all universal ideals are accorded only secondary significance. The posture of a "prophet-people" is still assumed, but the ideals of prophecy are no longer the goal of the nation's existence and the measuring rod of its actions, only so much guise and disguise.

The problem of a "chosen people" is not peculiar to Judaism, since every religious tradition of necessity accords supreme significance to the collective existence of its devotees. This tension is inseparable too from the impetus of nationalism, which in modern times has achieved, more than once, the devotions due religion. However, in Jewish tradition, the polar tension in the concept of the "chosen people" has had an unusually long and many-sided development. No one can expect to contribute to the resolution of this perennial problem without taking account of the variety of ways in which this problem was viewed in the long record of Jewish experience.

In sum, the significance of the Jewish tradition transcends the limits of the Jewish community.

The Jew does not claim to be the sole custodian of eternal truths, but he does set for himself the endless task of applying eternal truths to the changing problems of life. The Jewish people are heirs of a long tradition of truthful search. Within this tradition, we find different approaches to the solution of those perennial problems of a living faith, which every generation encounters afresh.

NOTES

1. *Daily Prayer Book.*

2. The contrast between the active and passive moods of piety is well drawn by Josiah Royce in his *The Spirit of Modern Philosophy* (Boston 1897). Among recent theologians, James Parkes construes the difference between Judaism and Christianity in terms of this contrast. The opinions of Orthodox authorities concerning the organ are collected in the booklet *Aile Divrai Habrith.*

3. *Sabbath,* 146 a.

4. Tosefta, *Sanhedrin,* 13. See *Masekheth Gerim,* Chap. 1, where a prospective convert to Judaism is at first discouraged, but if he persists he is told, "The world was created only for the sake of Israel, who alone are called 'sons of the All-Present' and alone are beloved of Him. All the discouraging words we spoke to you were for the purpose of increasing your reward."

5. *Berokhoth,* 33 b.

6. *Aboth* 3; 15.

7. *Aboda Zara,* 10 b.

8. *Sanhedrin,* 68 a.

9. *Ibid.,* 99a.
10. Yehuda Ibn Shemuel, *Midreshai Geulah* (Jerusalem, 1954).
11. *Sabbath,* 112 b.
12. Maimonides' Code, *Hilchoth Melochim.*

18

THE CONCEPT OF ISRAEL

ISRAEL IS AT ONCE the name of a people, a state, a religious community, and an ethereal ideal. A certain ambiguity characterized the term "Israel" from the very beginning. Jacob's name was changed to Israel in order to indicate his elevation to a high cosmic status. He was on a par with angels, "for thou hast struggled with God and men, and hast prevailed."[1] Philo interprets Israel to mean "he who sees God," that is, the man of Divine visions.[2] Certain it is that from the moment of its historic genesis, the people of Israel considered itself to be "covenanted" unto the Lord. A covenant is more than a love affair, no matter how impassioned, since it cannot conceivably be terminated at the whim of either partner. It is rather like a marriage, as marriage was originally intended to be; exclusive, enduring, indeed eternal.[3] Accordingly, the people of Israel are also called "sons of the living God," or the "firstborn son," or the treasure-people.[4]

It is not possible, in any case, to speak of the historic community of Israel without taking note of its special relation to the God who was different from all other gods, a Being unique and alone *(Ehad)*. A people that is lifted out of the mass of struggling humanity by the One God, set apart from all other nations and given a unique cosmic status, cannot but deem itself radically different. When the elders suggest to the prophet Ezekiel that it might be wise for "the house of Israel to become like all the nations," he storms at them, "It shall not be."[5] The very thought is absurd. The children of Israel are not at liberty to mold their own destiny. They are committed. They "belong" to God, who will rule over them as their "King," with "wrath outpoured," whether they will it or not.

This feeling of *radical difference* from the Gentiles became a powerful historical force. It affected the policy of the last kings of Israel. So Hezekiah resisted Sennacherib, pinning his faith on the One God, for whose sake he inaugurated a reformation. Josiah carried forward that spiritual revolution and centralized all sacrificial worship in the Holy Temple of Jerusalem. Though he died on the battlefield, his reform was not undone.[6] In time, the feeling of being radically different penetrated into the depths of the national psyche. Jeremiah phrases in Aramaic the message that the exiles were to bring to Babylonia: "So shall ye say unto them, 'The gods that did not make heaven and earth will pass away from the face of the earth.' "[7]

In this formula, Jeremiah articulated the uniqueness of the One God of Israel. He is not merely one, but He stands above and beyond the whole of creation as its master. He transcends the battles between the diverse gods and the empires that worship them. But this God, who is alone, is not simply the God of the universe that all can find and worship in their own way. He, too, is committed, covenanted, bound by His spoken word. He is wedded to Israel, as it were; He had sworn an oath to the patriarchs; He had spoken to all the Israelites at Sinai; He had revealed to them His Torah. Thus was the import of Israel's message given a more personal tone and a cutting edge: "It is *our* God, the God of Israel, who is the One God of the universe."

It is this double message that demonstrates the two-sidedness of the concept of Israel. The self-image of the historical community reached up to the universal realm of metaphysical entities. It "corresponded" to a heavenly reality.[8] But this self-image also contained a written history of a living people, its poignant memories, its agonizing anxieties, its bread-and-butter needs, its flesh-and-blood desires and hopes.

The two-sided character of the Jewish self-image and its resultant sense of radical difference from all other nations evoked a corresponding reaction among the non-Jewish population. How could they help but react with an extra measure of hostility to a people that considered itself especially set apart from all others, separated by a distinction that ranks far and beyond the usual differences that separate all human groups? If they acknowledged the unique status of Israel and its message in an affirmative way, they became either converts, semiconverts, or sympathetic hangers-on.[9] If they reacted against either the cogency of the message or the claim of Israel's election, they came to regard the Jews as "the most odious race of mankind." Here was a people that insulted and assaulted their gods and arrogated to itself an exalted cosmic rank. In many cases, admiration and scorn were combined in a puzzling complex of hate. Thus, classical anti–Semitism emerged as one of the responses of the pagan world to the twin challenges of Israel and its monotheism. In their turn, the Jewish people felt the loneliness of their situation to be a direct consequence of their covenanted status.[10] If God had chosen to make them different, their destiny in history must also be different. When the nations are uplifted, they are degraded; when the others are defeated in the End of Days, then Israel's turn will come.

In periods of bitter rivalry and persecution, the notion of being chosen as *against* the rest of humanity tends to take the place of the feeling of being chosen *for the sake of humanity*. The eschatological vision becomes zealot, narrow, and exclusive, a vindication of Israel rather than the triumph of its teaching.[11] Thus, the actual situation of Jewish people at any one time helped to shape the outlines of their collective self-image. Their earthly misery and their cosmic power, their martyrdom in the present and their Messianic glory in the future lent vitality and vividness to one or another aspect of the traditional concept of Israel.

One trinity of ideas remained unbroken throughout the long history of the Jewish people down to the emergence of our secular age: the presumed unity of the conceptions of Israel, Torah, and God. Israel was covenanted to the Lord, and Torah was the bond that united them— the contract which stipulated the terms and conditions of a union that could be cruelly stretched, but never entirely severed. It is in the Zohar that this unity is formulated in the most incisive way: "Israel, the Torah and the Holy One, blessed be He, are one."[12]

The Qabbalistic author assumed that each of the three entities in this triad was a cosmic current that extended all the way from this lowly earth to the highest heaven. The glory of God fills the world, but in His essence the Lord is infinite, transcending all humanly conceivable categories. The designation "the Holy One, blessed be He" corresponds to the aspect of the Divine Being that is directly concerned with the administration of earthly affairs.[13] In a similar way, the Torah is in this earthly life a body of laws, principles, and narratives; but up in the heavens it is an ethereal essence, "written in black fire or white fire," and consisting of an articulation of the Names of the Lord.[14] So, too, the people of Israel "correspond" to a heavenly essence that merges at its source into the effulgence of the Divine Being.[15]

This mystical concept of Israel illustrates the extent to which the collective self-image of the Jews was an integral part of the prevailing theology. Its contours varied in accord with one's philosophic approach. Accordingly, we may best describe the concept by filling in the details in the several self-images as they appear at the rationalistic pole of thought and at the mystical pole. It will then be possible to indicate the degree to which one or another concept predominated in the minds of the legalistic authorities, who steered generally a middle course between the two extremes.

Already in the Talmud and Midrashim the mystical character of Israel is suggested. "The image of Jacob is carved into the throne of Glory,"[16] we are assured, and, when the patriarch enjoyed his famous dream, the angels went up and down on the heavenly ladder, comparing the upper image with the lower one.[17] The Throne of Glory symbolizes the aspects of Divine power that relate to the administration of mundane affairs. We are told that this Throne of Glory "hovered over the deep" before the creation of the cosmos.[18] The souls of the righteous are kept there after death until the Messianic redemption, the resurrection, and the World to Come.[19] Another passage tells us that "the Patriarchs— they are the Divine Chariot"[20]—that is, they are part of the mediating channel of Divine grace. Abraham, in particular, had a continuing function in heaven. His prayers and those of the other patriarchs keep the scales of mercy weighted against those of justice.[21] Also, he stands at the gates of hell in order to prevent those who are circumcised from being thrown into its yawning abyss.[22]

The close mystical association between Israel and the Divine Being is adumbrated in the concept of the *Shechinah,* the Divine Presence. In one sense, the *Shechinah* is found where love, compassion, and devotion abide.[23] In yet another sense, "ten persons who steadily engage in the study of Torah, the *Shechinah* rests with them . . . even five . . . even three . . . even one . . ."[24] In a more potent, more openly manifest way, the *Shechinah* was found in certain synagogues in Babylonia.[25] But in a special and more immediate sense, it dwelt in the Holy Temple, and it departed thence prior to the destruction of its abode, although, according to some authorities, "the *Shechinah* did not move away from the western wall."[26]

The Holy Temple "corresponded" to the sanctuary in one of the heavens, and the Archangel Michael offered "lambs of fire" on the heavenly altar, matching the sacrifices of the high priest. Now that the Holy Temple is in ruins, Michael continues to sacrifice on his altar the souls of the saints.[27]

The sanctuary in the wilderness and later the two Temples were visible habitations of the Divine Presence, but even when these were destroyed, the *Shechinah* did not depart from Israel. "Wherever the Israelites were exiled, there the *Shechinah* too went into exile."[28]

Indeed, Moses was assured that the *Shechinah* will be associated with Israel, and Israel only. "Said Rabbi Johanan in the name of Rabbi Yosé: Three things did Moses ask of the Holy One, blessed be He, and He granted them to him—that the *Shechinah* shall abide in Israel . . . that it shall not abide on the 'worshipers of stars,' and that he might know the ways of Providence. . . ."[29]

Explaining the superiority of the pure-blooded Israelite in regard to the capacity to intuit the Divine Presence, the philosopher Halevi writes: "The *Shechinah* which is visible to our eyes is presently lacking, for it is revealed only to the prophet or to the people generally only in the selected place, and this is the meaning of our prayer for the return of the Lord to Zion, 'and may our eyes behold when Thou returnest unto Zion.'

"But the hidden, spiritual *Shechinah* dwells with every born Israelite, who is also a believer in the true faith, whose deeds are pure, whose heart is true, whose soul is attuned to the God of Israel."[30]

This association was so commonly accepted that to be converted was described as "entering under the wings of the *Shechinah*."[31] In the course of the discussion concerning the non-Jewish identity of Job, some rabbis in the Talmud argue that he could not have lived after the death of Moses: "After Moses died, did the *Shechinah* abide on worshipers of stars [that is, non-Jews]?"[32]

The bond between Israel and the *Shechinah* was so close that every worshiper was "to feel as if the *Shechinah* were opposite him."[33] So deep was this awareness that some rabbis considered it sinful to walk erect, or with head uncovered: "It pushes the legs of the *Shechinah*."[34] This mystical consciousness of the Divine Presence heightened the tone of Jewish piety: "He who commits a sin in secret, it is as if he pushed the legs of the *Shechinah*."[35] The Divine Presence was a comforting reality to the downhearted: "The *Shechinah* rests on the heads of the sick";[36] "When a person is troubled, how does the *Shechinah* speak— 'my head hurts, my arm hurts.' If the Holy One, blessed be He, is so pained by the blood of the wicked, how much the more so by the spilled blood of the righteous?"[37]

In their prayers, Jews were admonished to think of the "exile of the *Shechinah*" or of the "anguish of the *Shechinah*," rather than of their own troubles.

After detailing the mystical effects of evil deeds in closing the channels of mercy, an Orthodox pietist of the nineteenth century describes the function of prayer: "Though the law of the Talmud permits a person to bring to mind his own troubles when he prays, the core of his intention must not be the petition to assuage his own sorrows, since it is through suffering that his sins are purged. . . . But the essence of his intention must be the need on high, for there might be an involvement of his Name, if the honor of Israel is involved. . . . But even if there be no desecration of the Name, the Divine Presence feels his pain, and if the worshiper forgets his own pain in his intense concentration on the anguish of the Lord, then indeed his sins are forgiven. . . ."[38]

The ideal "congregation of Israel" *(Keneset Yisroel)* is often treated in Talmud and the Midrashim as an interlocutor with the Deity. It presents the case of the empirical people to the Lord and the demands of the Lord to the people. Anyone who partakes of the pleasures of life, without a prior offer of thanks *(berocho)*, "it is as if he robbed the Holy One and *Keneset Yisroel*."[39] The benedictions were formulated and instituted by the rabbis, acting in the Name of God. So *Keneset Yisroel* is the heavenly counterpart of the sacred tradition.

"Said *Keneset Yisroel* to the Holy One, blessed be He—acknowledge this as my favor to Thee, that I made Thee known to the mighty in the world [that is, in the discussion, to the Jewish people]."[40]

Here, too, the ideal congregation is regarded as distinguished from the actual, living people of Israel. Referring to the symbolism of the Song of Songs, which portrays the Lord and Israel as a lover and his bride, a Talmudic sage says, "I am a wall, that is *Keneset Yisroel*, 'and my breasts are like towers,' these are the synagogues and houses of study."[41]

Naturally, even in the first centuries of our era some Jewish people frequented the circuses and theaters of their cities more than the synagogues. Yet, the ideal congregation is imagined to speak as follows: " 'I did not sit among players.'[42] Said *Keneset Yisroel,* 'Master of the Universe,' I have never gone to theaters and circuses of the nations of the world, and played with them."[43]

To the mystics, the revealed Torah was only an earthly shadow of the heavenly entity.[44] Since the written and oral laws refer almost exclusively to the people of Israel, an intimate association had to be assumed between the Divine Being and the ideal congregation of Israel. I have already referred to the unity of the triad—God, Torah, and Israel.[45] At times, Torah is left out, and a dual unity is asserted: "The Holy One, blessed be He, and *Keneset Yisroel* are called one."[46] The image of a lighted candle is often used: "Israel is the wick, Torah is the oil, the Divine Presence is the flame."[47]

The pre-existence of the heavenly Torah was a widespread assumption in the literature of the Midrash. From this belief it followed almost inevitably that the congregation of Israel, its acceptance of the earthly Torah, its destiny, and its eventual redemption through the Messiah, were also previsioned. "If the Holy One, blessed be He, had not foreseen that after twenty-six generations the people of Israel will accept the Torah, he would not have written in it—Command the children of Israel.' "[48]

The Torah was the goal of creation, since it represented the *will* of God, while all creation was merely the *work* of God. Hence, the Midrash asserts that the Torah furnished the design for all creation, and the "Holy One, blessed be He, looked in the Torah as He created the world."[49]

It follows that Israel, the people of Torah, occupies a central role in the administration of this world, not merely in the World to Come. On its account, the sun shines, the rains come down to bless the soil, and the golden harvest ripens at summer's end. By the same token, however, the failure of the empirical people to abide by the precepts of the Law causes the order of nature to be disturbed, with dire consequences for all mankind. If the nations had only known of this relationship, "they would have appointed two policemen for every Jew," to make certain that he observed the entire Law.[50] All earthly gains are due to the merits of Israel; "even boats that travel from Gaul to Spain are blessed only for the sake of Israel."[51] On the other hand, the catastrophes of nature and history are also due to Israel.[52] While the constellations of the stars and the ministering angels usually and largely control the affairs of "the nations of the world," the people of Israel are lifted above this natural order and governed directly by God. "There is no *mazal* [determination of stars] for Israel."[53] They are "beloved more than the ministering angels."[54]

Even while they glorified the congregation of Israel as an ethereal "City of God," the mystics allowed that not all living Jews were equally exalted. The Talmud asserts that "all Israelites have a share in the World to Come" and "will not see the face of hell."[55] Yet, the Zohar, which concentrates and magnifies the mystical streams in the ancient tradition, declares, "Not all Israelites are alike, for some of them are princes, deriving from the Holy Kingdom [*Shechinah*], and some of them are slaves, deriving from the side of the slave [Satan]."[56] Also, "Israel is called man and beasts; if they merit, they are man, fashioned after the one above; if they do not merit, they are called beasts."[57]

The notion that the people of Israel contain a vital core of saints who are closely associated with the Divine administration of the world is rooted in Talmudic literature, though it was left for the Hasidic movement of the eighteenth century to provide concrete institutionalization of this belief.

We read in the Talmud that "the Holy One, blessed be He, decrees, but the Saint repudiates it"; also that "the Saint decrees and the Holy One, blessed be He, abides by this decision." These saints suffer for the sins of their people, and their anguish is accepted as a sacrifice of atonement for their contemporaries. Since the order of the world depends upon these saints, "no Saint perishes until a Saint of equal stature is created."[58] While the world may exist even for the sake of one saint, it was widely believed that "there are never fewer than thirty-six saints who confront the *Shechinah* every day."[59]

The Qabbalists deepened the gulf between the pneumatic saints and the ordinary scholars.[60] The power of the saints is felt even after their death, when their souls enter into hell in order to redeem the wicked who were attached to them in some way.[61]

The Hasidic movement created many saint-centered societies on the supposition that each saint was an embodiment of the redeemed world. In him, the evil desire and the impulses of material nature had been transmuted into forces of holiness. Even the occasional sin of the saint is due to a holy impulse. "The Holy One, blessed be He, in his Mercy impels the Saint to sin, so that he might fall from his high level and descend to that of the public; then, later, when the Saint raises himself to his holy height, he uplifts the people along with himself." [62]

The emphasis on the ideal of sainthood did not lead, in the Hasidic movement, to the weakening of the ethnic element in Jewish piety. The saint was never thought of in isolation, but as the living center of "all Israel." His prayer is focused on the "exile of the *Shechinah*," and in behalf of all Israel.

In the mystical stream of thought, the Jewish people were a unique metaphysical creation; hence, they were biologically different from the rest of mankind. We read in the Talmud: "Why are the worshipers of stars unclean? Because they did not stand at Mount Sinai. Because when the serpent cohabited with Eve, he threw uncleanliness into her. The Israelites had their uncleanliness removed at Sinai. The worshipers of stars, not having been at Sinai, their uncleanliness was not removed." [63]

We have here a version of original sin, which is purely racistic, assuming that Jews are free by birth from the corruption which is the lot of humanity. Yet, this racist emphasis was contradicted by the law which admits Gentile converts into the holy community. The Talmud assumes that, in the case of converts, "though they were not present at Sinai, their *mazal* was there." [64] This means that they were included in the Holy Community, but in a category of their own ("under the wings of the *Shechinah*," as against "over the wings of the *Shechinah*"). [65]

The romantic philosopher Halevi assumes that even in the Messianic era, the descendants of converts will be distinguished from those of pure Israelitic lineage in this, that only the latter will be endowed with the gift of prophecy: "Whoever clings to this way, will participate along with his descendants in our nearness to God. But the convert will not have equal standing with the Israelite by birth, since only the Israelites by descent are suited for prophecy. . . ." [66]

In the Talmud, the gift of prophecy is further restricted, even in the future, only to those whose line of descent is completely unblemished: "The Lord causes His *Shechinah* to rest only on the pedigreed families in Israel." [67]

The racist dogma permeates the mystical stream in Judaism down to the present day. Halevi stands close to the center between the mystical and rationalistic currents, for he admitted the worth of the other monotheistic faiths: "We deny to no man the reward for his good deeds, no matter which creed he belongs to. But we see the perfect good which comes to the people that are close to Him, in their lifetime. . . ."

"But our destiny it is to cleave to the divine quality in prophecy and in states of mind that are close to it. . . ."[68]

The belief in the dogma of Jewish centrality and supremacy in the Divine scheme of creation became more deeply rooted in the popular mind in the late Middle Ages as a result of the decline of rationalism and the growing influence of Qabbalah. In fact, the medieval era continued for the Jewish masses of Central Europe down to the twentieth century. We find the most extravagant formulations of the holy character of Israel in the last few centuries. Israel should properly be the "portion of the Lord," because "the Perfect One should have the perfect."[69] A sixteenth-century pietist wonders why the physical appearance of Jews is so much like that of non-Jews, seeing that their souls are drawn from radically different heavenly realms. The founder of the Liubavich dynasty of Hasidim asserts that of the two souls of every Israelite, one is a Divine portion of the Lord Himself, and the other derives from the shell of *nogah* (radiance), which is both good and bad, while the souls of the other nations are formed "out of the unclean shells, which have no good at all."[70]

A nineteenth-century Hasidic author wrote: "Every nation has a certain holy spark, even as it possesses vicious qualities, since 'Thou givest life to them all,' and this is the purpose of the Jewish exile, to absorb these sparks. . . .

"As the root of *Keneset Yisroel* is the love of the Israelites for God, so the root of all the nations is their love for the pleasures of this world. . . ."[71]

So deeply rooted is this dogma in the tradition that even some of the modernist reformers of the nineteenth century could not resist its impact. Thus, Geiger, the architect of Reform Judaism, spoke of a Jewish "genius" for religion.

The mystical temper predominated in Jewish life only in the darkest periods of political oppression and cultural stagnation. Whenever the warm winds of enlightenment mellowed the hostility of the Jews' neighbors, the Jewish spirit regained an equilibrium between the insular mentality of self-glorifying myths and the open horizons of theistic humanism. In such open cultures as those of the Hellenistic era, of the Moslem Renaissance, of Christian Humanism, and of the Age of Enlightenment, the rationalistic threads in the web of tradition came to light.

Contrary to a widespread impression, the Talmud contains significant components of a moral-rational approach to the understanding of the Jewish character and destiny. A broad definition of what it means to be a Jew is offered on a purely intellectual plane: "Everyone who denies idolatry is called a Jew." [72]

"Said Rabbi Elazar, The Holy One, blessed be He, exiled Israel among the nations for the sole purpose of adding converts to their number. So, it is said 'and I shall sow it in the ground.' [73] Doesn't a person sow one measure only in order to harvest many more?" [74]

According to this view, the dispersal of Israel was not due to an outburst of Divine wrath, but, on the contrary, to His concern for the redemption of mankind. The "chosenness" of Israel was, therefore, to be interpreted not as an exclusive privilege, setting Israel apart from the nations, but as a task, to bring hosts of men and women to the service of the Lord. Israel is the "firstborn," but not the only child. In the Torah, the "firstborn" cannot lay claim to the whole inheritance, but only to a portion double that of his brothers. Israel's vocation is to be an *example,* not an *exception,* to the other nations. It is not set apart, but set ahead, and ordered to work for and with other peoples.

Elaborating on Israel's task to "witness" unto the nations, the Midrash applies the law in regard to those who withhold testimony from judges: "If he does not tell, he shall bear his sin—if you will not explain my Divinity to the nations of the world, I shall punish you. . . ." [75] This missionary task was imposed upon Israel from the very beginning: "The Holy One, blessed be He, gave the Torah to Israel in order that they might bestow its merit upon all the nations." [76]

Naturally, the people of Israel are not alone in this task. The wise and the pious, wherever they may be, are allies of Israel. They are "priests," so to speak, individually, as the people of Israel were designed to be a "people of priests": "The Holy One, blessed be He, will grant to the pious among the nations a share in the life of the World to Come . . . because they are priests to the Holy One, blessed be He. . . ." [77]

The duty to "bring people under the wings of the *Shechinah*" is treated as a supreme *mizvah.* Said the leading sage of third-century Palestine, Rabbi Johanan: "Why was Abraham our father punished and his children were enslaved in Egypt for two hundred and ten years? Because he separated people from entering under the wings of the *Shechinah.* As it is said, the king of Sodom said to Abraham: 'Give me the souls, while you take the property' (and Abraham returned the captives, without converting them)."[78]

For this reason, it was mandatory for masters to convert their slaves; they, in turn, were then obliged to observe the practices that were obligatory on Israelite women. Upon liberation, these slaves would become full-fledged Israelites, qualifying to be counted in the prayer-quorum of the synagogue.

The interpretation of a Biblical verse offered the great Rabbi Johanan ben Zakkai an opportunity to illustrate and to condemn the chauvinism of his disciples.[79] In Proverbs 14:34 (usually rendered, "Righteousness exalteth a nation, but sin is a reproach to any people"), the Hebrew original puts the last two words in the plural—"the nations"—and it seems to draw the line between the one people—Israel—and all other nations. The zealous disciples vied with one another in finding an interpretation that would exalt Israel and scorn the Gentiles, namely, "even the charitable deeds of the nations are imputed to them as a sin, because of the impurity of their motives or their arrogance."[80] Then the aged master points out the true meaning of the verse: "As the sin-offering would bring forgiveness to Israel, so does charity bring forgiveness to the nations of the world."[81] This interpretation is the one favored by Abraham Ibn Ezra in his commentary.[82]

We may assume that this discussion took place after the burning of the Temple, when the Israelites, too, could count only on deeds of charity, along with prayer and repentance, for the expiation of their sins. Jew and Greek became one in their need for forgiveness. When the same rabbi was apprised of the burning of the Temple, he said, "We have a nobler means of atonement—righteousness and charity."[83]

The tension between the moral-rational and the romantic-mystical interpretations of the difference between Israel and the nations can be recognized in the many debates in the Talmud in regard to such issues as to whether Torah should be taught to slaves or not;[84] whether those who accepted Judaism and were baptized, but did not undergo circumcision, were to be considered full-fledged members of the community,[85] whether the laws of the Torah, barring intermarriage with the neighboring nations, were to apply to their descendants at all times, or possibly even be extended to all Gentiles, as Ezra and Nehemiah inferred, or whether those laws were no longer valid because "Sennacherib came and mixed up the nations."[86]

There was also the theological question of "exclusive salvation," that is, whether the Gentile who accepts the "Seven Principles of Noah," and is classified as a *ger toshav*, must do so in the presence of three learned Israelites and on the basis of a dogmatic acceptance of the Torah of Moses.[87] Finally, we encounter the well-known dispute as to whether or not "the pious of the nations have a share in the World to Come."[88]

The lines of demarcation are frequently blurred, particularly since dialecticians always endeavor to impose systematic consistency upon ancient controversies. The same Midrashic work might contain views that are in diametric opposition to one another. In an honored Midrash we encounter a dramatic affirmation of the equality of all men in the sight of God: "I call heaven and earth to witness that a Gentile or an Israelite, a man or a woman, a slave or a servant-girl—the Holy Spirit rests upon him only according to his deeds. . . .[89]

"Is it conceivable that the Lord will discriminate between a Gentile and a Jew, between a man and a woman, between a slave and a servant-girl? No, whatever *mizvah* one does necessarily brings its reward, for it is said, 'and Thy righteousness is like the mighty mountains.' "[90]

But we also find in the same Midrash the assumption that, in point of fact, only Israelites are "God's children," and they alone are due to share in the glories of the World to Come: "Though everything is His, and all are His creatures, He does not delight in all, but only in the seed of Abraham. . . .[91]

"Once, as I was going from place to place, I met an old man. Said he to me, 'Will the nations of the world exist in the days of the Messiah?' I said to him, 'All the nations of the world that tortured Israel and oppressed Israel will come and behold its joy, then return to dust and not ever be revived. But all the nations and peoples that did not oppress or torment the Israelites will become the peasants and vineyard-keepers for the Israelites. . . .' But this is only the days of the Messiah, not the World to Come. . . ."[92]

We need add only that the zealous author discriminated among Israelites as well. He praised the Lord for choosing the sages and their disciples "to the end of all the generations," assigning to the "sinners in Israel" the dubious distinction of being destined to be burned within the "Great Synagogue and the Great Academy of the Future."[93]

While the Aggadic material of the Talmud varies greatly, containing even crude insertions by vulgar hands, the Halachic material is more organized and consistent. In Talmudic law, Ezra's insistence on the "Holy Seed" is definitely repudiated. Converts are warmly welcomed after due warning of the hardships they may expect to encounter: "When a person comes to be converted, we say to him, 'Why do you wish to convert? Don't you know that Israel is at this time driven, distressed and troubled?' If he says, 'I know, and I am not worthy to join them,' he is immediately accepted. He is then told the roots of the faith—the unity of God and the prohibition of idolatry, elaborating on the meaning of these principles. Then, he should be told of the *mizvoth*, the light and the awesome ones. . . .

"And he should be told that by means of those *mizvoth* he will merit the life of the World to Come, and that there is no complete Saint, except for the wise who know and observe these *mizvoth*. He should be addressed as follows:

"Be it known to you that the World to Come is kept only for the saints, and they are Israel. The circumstance that in this world Israel is troubled is really a favor to them, for they cannot receive an excess of favors in this world, like the worshipers of stars, lest they become arrogant and err, losing the reward of the World to Come. But, the Lord does not punish them too severely, that they might not disappear. For all the nations will perish, but they will endure."[94]

In the eyes of the Law it was a *mizvah* to induce a person to accept the Jewish faith. "Whoever brings one person under the wings of the *Shechinah*, it is accounted to him as if he had fashioned and brought a person into the world."[95] To be sure, some of the converts reverted to their pagan ways, causing all Israel to be guilty of sin in accordance with the principle that "all Israelites are responsible for one another."[96] Some of the rabbis protested for this reason against "those who accept converts."[97] Still, the legal authorities considered that all the nations will be converted in the time to come.[98] Once converted, a person has the same privileges as those who were born Jewish, except that he may not be a judge or a king over Israel.[99] He is expected to think of Abraham, Isaac, and Jacob as his ancestors, for "Abraham has been called 'the father of a multitude of nations.' "[100]

Hellenistic Judaism, to judge from the writings of Philo, was conspicuously liberal in its interpretation of the concept of Israel as the vanguard of humanity. Although Philo speaks of the Jewish people as "sons of God," he maintains that all who have knowledge of the universal Father are "children of God." [101] The people of Israel represent symbolically "those who have a vision of God." [102] Prophecy (in the highest or dogmatic sense), resulting in laws, was reserved for the Israelites of the Biblical period, but the message of the Scriptures is universal. Indeed, Philo indentifies Plato's "philosophic frenzy" with one of the phases of prophecy. "For what the disciples of the most approved philosophy gain from its teaching, the Jews gain from their law and customs, that is, to know the highest and the most ancient cause of all things." [103] Out of Abraham "there issued a whole people, and it is of all nations the most beloved by God, for, as it seems to me, to them priesthood and prophecy were given for the benefit of the entire human race." [104]

Philo describes proselytes as being related to Jews "by kinships of greater dignity and sanctity than those of blood." [105] Praising the proselyte "who comes to God of his own accord," he adds, "in order that all men who behold this example may be corrected by it, learning that God receives gladly virtue which grows out of ignoble birth, utterly disregarding its original roots." [106]

The semiproselytes, or the "spiritual proselytes" (to use Wolfson's term), are included in the Mosaic polity of the "sons of God." They are the philosophers and the righteous men who share the monotheistic philosophy of life. Thus Philo speaks of "the blameless life of pious men who follow nature and her ordinances" and of "all who practice wisdom either in Grecian or Barbarian lands and live a blameless and irreproachable life" as belonging to the ideal community.

The Torah itself was, to Philo, not a mystical entity and a supreme source of values, but an educational instrument conveying the saving truths that God had built into human nature. The Sabbath is a covenant between God and mankind, not merely between God and Israel. It is a call for men to share in the Divine activity of contemplation. In his listing of ten festivals, Philo leaves out Hanukkah and Purim, possibly because he regarded them as national observances. He listed "every day" if it is lived as a holy day. In Philo's judgment, Passover was not so much a festival of national freedom as a perennial call on all men to "pass over" from a life of passion to the life of yearning for God. Similarly, Sukkot was not a symbol of Divine concern for the Israelites, but rather a symbol of the equality of all men and of the duty of cultivating the virtue of gratitude.

For Philo, therefore, the empirical community of Israel was still the most beloved community, but ideally its boundaries shaded into a twi-

light zone, embracing those who in various degrees dedicated themselves to the love of God. Philo, too, looked forward to a Messianic era
when Israel would triumph, but then all other nations would merge
with it: "I think that each nation would abandon its peculiar ways and,
throwing overboard their ancestral customs, turn to honoring our laws
alone, for when the brightness is accompanied by national prosperity, it
will darken the light of others as the risen sun darkens the stars." [107]

The rationalistic and mystical streams in Judaism diverged more decisively in the Middle Ages than they did in the Talmudic and early
Gaonic periods. For a century the Jewish world was torn by a long
and bitter controversy between the followers of Maimonides and the
antirationalists. Both schools included in their category of Israelites the
"righteous proselytes," that is, those who were fully converted to Judaism. However, regarding those who worshiped the one God in purity
of thought and in ethical action, the romanticists and the legalists
hesitated to make use even of the category of *ger toshav* ("semiproselytes") of the Talmud. [108] As was earlier noted, some maintained that the
ger toshav is one who accepts only the "seven *mizvoth* of the sons of
Noah" on the basis of Mosaic revelation and by way of a formal
declaration in the presence of three learned men. Others added that this
category applied only "at the time when the Jubilee institution was in
effect." [109] In this school, even the "pious of the nations" were merely
peripheral to the only bearers of salvation, the empirical people of
Israel.

On the other hand, the rationalistic school in nonlegalistic works
projected the concept of a spiritual elite, who, apart from any rites and
ceremonies, advance ever closer to the Divine Being through the service of mind and heart. For them, the empirical people of Israel were
significant only insofar as they were likely to produce a greater number
of such philosophical saints. [110] The "Torah-society" was designed and
ordered to stimulate the emergence of men and women who love God
and ceaselessly meditate on the wonders of His creation. But it is not
the *mizvoth* in themselves that generate holiness or "nearness of God,"
but their presumed effect upon the moral character of the individual
and the peaceful order of society. This effect is by no means certain or
even likely in the case of the majority of the people. Saintly philosophers may arise among all nations, and only a few Jews may qualify for
the honor. The living people of Israel were, therefore, in Maimonides'
view, by no means coeval with the spiritual elite, those who approach

most closely to the Divine Being. It was a good school, indeed the best possible school, designed by the Lord Himself. But even in the best schools some students will be no wiser on their graduation than on their initiation. And students of poor schools have been known to excel. Salvation or fulfillment is an individual achievement.

Isaac Arame, whose work *Akedat Yizhak* was long a popular source book for preachers, manages to combine the view of individual judgment, on the one hand, and the collective salvation of Israel, on the other. He maintains that "one is truly designated as *Yisroel* [an Israelite] only if he is a saint *[Zaddik]*," for an Israelite and a saint are synonymous in respect of their tasks. " 'All Israelites' [that are assumed to have a share in the World to Come] means those who fulfill the obligations imposed upon an Israelite." The Torah, according to Arame, is so designed as to lead all its devotees to salvation. Writing in the last decade of the fifteenth century, Arame saw hope only for "the remnant" of the nations that will accept the Torah: "For He scattered and subordinated Israel among them, in order that they [that is, the nations] should be encouraged to learn to know the Israelites, their customs and the ways of their Torah, so that they will desire and accept it [the Torah]. In this way, Israel will cause a remnant of the nations to be saved, that they might call on the Name of God. But they see and do not take it to heart . . . interpreting the verses of Scriptures as they desire. . . ."[111]

Maimonides maintained that only "true ideas" lead to God, but those ideas are accessible to the human mind and are readily deducible from first principles. They comprise the doctrines of God's unity and incorporeality, the first two of the Ten Commandments. All the other *mizvoth* are principles of training for the individual and of a properly ordered society. He summarizes his view of the various categories of religious people in a famous passage: "I will begin the subject of this chapter with a simile. A king is in his palace, and all his subjects are partly in the country and partly abroad. Of the former, some have their backs turned toward the king's palace, and their faces in another direction; and some are desirous and zealous to go to the palace, seeking 'to inquire in his temple,' and to minister before him, but have not yet seen even the face of the wall of the house.

"Of those that desire to go to the palace, some reach it, and go roundabout in search of the entrance gate; others have passed through the gate, and walk about in the antechamber; and others have succeeded in entering into the inner part of the palace and being in the same room with the king in the royal palace. But even the latter do not immediately on entering the palace see the king or speak to him; for after having entered the inner part of the palace, another effort is required before they can stand before the king—at a distance or close by—hear his words, or speak to him.

"I will now explain the simile which I have made. The people who are abroad are all those that have no religion, neither one based on speculation nor one received by tradition. . . .

"Those who are in the country, but have their backs turned toward the king's palace, are those who possess religion, belief and thought, but happen to hold false doctrines. . . . Because of these doctrines they recede more and more from the royal palace, the more they seem to proceed. . . .

"Those who desire to arrive at the palace, and to enter it, but have never yet seen it, are the mass of religious people, the multitude that observe the Divine commandments, but are ignorant.

"Those who arrive at the palace, but go roundabout it, are those who devote themselves exclusively to the study of the practical law; they believe traditionally in true principles of faith, and learn the practical worship of God, but are not trained in philosophical treatment of the principles of the Law, and do not endeavor to establish the truth of their faith by proof.

"Those who undertake to investigate the principles of religion have come into the antechamber; and there is no doubt that these, too, can be divided into different grades.

"But those who have succeeded in finding a proof for everything that can be proved, who have a true knowledge of God, insofar as a true knowledge can be obtained, and are near the truth, wherever an approach to truth is possible, they have reached the goal, and are in the palace in which the king lives."[112]

In Maimonides' gradation, the philosophers of the nations who seek God are far ahead of the masses of the empirical people of Israel, coming nearer to God than the zealous Talmudists who only go around and around the palace of the king. A commentator expressed the views of many shocked pietists when he wrote, "Many of the wise rabbis said that this chapter was not written by the master [Moses Maimonides]. And if he wrote it, it should be hidden or, better, burned. For how could he say that those who contemplate the laws of nature are on a higher level than those who busy themselves with the duties of religion?"[113] Maimonides did not list the belief in the Chosen People among his principles of faith. He welcomed genuine converts most warmly, writing in a famous letter to a convert: "You may say, 'our God and God of our fathers,' for Abraham is your father. Since you have entered under the wings of the *Shechinah,* there is no difference between us and you. . . . Let not your pedigree be light in your eyes. . . . If we trace our descent to Abraham, Isaac, and Jacob, you trace it to Him who spoke and the world came into being."[114]

However, in his popular and legal works, Maimonides employs the imagery and rhetoric of the people, in the belief that the maintenance of the Torah-society requires that certain popular opinions be stated by the philosophers as if they were true. (In his letter to the Jews of Yemen, he asserts that those who leave the fold are not descended from ancestors who stood at Sinai.) These "necessary truths," as he calls them,[115] help to bridge the gap between the philosophers and the populace, creating an enduring, vital community in which the few guard the many from gross errors, and the many help the few to attain human fulfillment.

Divine Providence, in the judgment of Maimonides, was not focused on the people of Israel except insofar as the Messianic age was predetermined, but normally the degree of Divine guidance depended on the extent of attachment to the Divine Being by single individuals. However, to placate his opponents, Maimonides reintroduced the belief in the resurrection and in the World to Come as predestined events at the end of history.

The radical intellectualism of Maimonides was repudiated by many of his successors. Arame postulates a special miraculous form of Divine Providence that is distinctive for Israel as a people. In turn, there are several levels of Divine Providence in Israel, depending upon degrees of piety.[116] Some felt that "nearness to God" was more a matter of love or of faith or of Divine grace than of sustained reflection. But the axiom that the way to holiness is infinite and that it is reached by inward meditation and self-scrutiny was accepted by many popular preachers and pietists.

The axiom that the pathway to God runs through the intentions of the heart and the further realization that this pathway is infinite could, in theory at least, blur the distinction between the "people of Torah" and those without the Covenant. It is this emphasis on inwardness that, in the Hasidic movement, served to elevate the dignity of the unlearned masses. The application of the same principle to non-Jews was already foreshadowed by Rabbi Judah the Prince, editor of the Mishnah, who upon being told of a Gentile who offered his life for God wept and cried out, "Indeed, it is possible for a person to acquire his world in one hour." Albo added the principle that the Lord may well give different Torahs to various peoples. "Even when the Torah of Moses was valid for the Israelites, there was the Torah of the sons of Noah for all the other nations. There is no doubt that people would attain through it their fulfillment as human beings, since it was Divine, though it was not of the same degree of attainment as the Israelites could obtain through the Torah. . . . So we see that it is possible to have two Divine Torahs at one time, but for different peoples." [117] Since the "chosenness" of Israel was effected by the Torah, which specifies the terms of the Covenant, it could no longer be regarded as an exceptional phenomenon. To be sure, in Albo's view, the merit of the Mosaic Torah consisted in the fact that "human perfection could be attained by means of even one of the *mizvoth*. . . ." [118]

All through the Middle Ages the intimate association between ethnic feeling and religious loyalty in the concept of Israel was not questioned. The rationalists might recognize the relative holiness of other faiths, but only for non-Jewish groups. They might interpret the purpose of Israel's existence in terms of the education and ultimate redemption of all mankind. "For indeed the earth belongs to me, and the pious of the nations are precious to me, without a doubt. 'But, ye shall be unto me a kingdom of priests.' In this respect, you will be my treasure — you will be a kingdom of priests to instruct and to guide the entire human race, that they might all call on the Name of God and serve Him together, shoulder to shoulder, as Israel will be so transformed in the future." [119]

Even the mystics thought of Israel as the vanguard of the redeemed portion of humanity in that it is the Jewish function to gather the "Holy sparks" that have become imprisoned by the "shells of uncleanliness" throughout the world. These holy sparks must be rescued before the appearance of the Redeemer. The Messianic redemption of Israel would justify the Divine intention in the creation of man; through Israel's triumph, the human race would come into its own and attain fulfillment.

For Christian theologians as for Jewish thinkers, the ethnic separateness of the Jewish people was axiomatic. The place of the Jew in the medieval world was determined by the fact that he was of the "stock of Abraham." Socially, too, the Jews were nearly a self-governing enclave. They were outside the feudal system, not as individuals, but as a corporate body. Taxes were nearly always levied upon the community as a whole, and it was up to the Jewish authorities to distribute them. In the Spanish communities, Jewish authorities had the right to impose severe corporal punishments. In the German and Slavic areas, similar, though unofficial, means of discipline were frequently available. Furthermore, the semi-autonomous Jewish communities had in common the same basic laws and religious literature. The local variations, considerable as they might be—especially those between the monogamous society of Ashkenazic Jewry and the polygamous society of Sephardic and Oriental Jewry—did not prevent the Rabbinic authorities from moving freely throughout the Diaspora and speaking in the name of a common sacred tradition.

Those in Moslem or Christian lands who left the Jewish faith might still be considered members of the Jewish community in the first generation on the ground that they were irrevocably committed by the oath that their souls took at Sinai. "Once Israel was chosen to be God's people, no Israelite can become a member of another nation. They belong to God's people, even against their will and even if they leave the fold of their religion. Therefore, said the prophet, 'When thou passest through the waters, I will be with thee.' This is an allusion to the angry waters of baptism through which pass all those who accept their religion [Christianity]." [120]

The travail of the Marrano families in both Christian and Moslem lands is well known, but in the course of time they disappeared from the Jewish community. Even the Frankist Jews who joined the Catholic Church *en masse* in 1759, with the intention of retaining their own collective identity, did not leave more than a nostalgic memory in the first half of the nineteenth century, when Adam Mickiewicz, the poet laureate of Poland, was their most illustrious descendant.

It was through the changes in their religious convictions as well as outside pressure that some Jews left the fold. Their rationalist views might lead them to feel that the various monotheistic religions are so many social expressions of one philosophy, so that a change from Judaism to Catholicism is not very different from the change of one language to another. In their view, those differences that were left were not worth the cost of lifelong martyrdom.

On the other hand, Jewish pietists might be led by the impetus of the mystical tradition to feel that the Christian faith was the logical development of Biblical Judaism. Abner of Burgos, Spain, who was converted in 1321, was a famous and ardent convert, and he addressed many books and pamphlets to his former co-religionists, calling upon them to emulate his example. His arguments were directed chiefly against the rationalists.

"Abner began with a critique of the rationalist interpretation of Judaism, cultivated by the Jewish intellectuals who were his friends— and for this he found ample support in Qabbalistic doctrine—and moved ultimately to a position of complete identification with the Christian ideology."[121] The majority, however, retained a balanced faith, rejecting the extremes of both rationalism and mysticism.

The modern period opened with the dawn of the Age of Reason. The intelligentsia began to glory in the balancing of religious tradition by rational and moral enlightenment. At the same time, the feudal age with its corporate bodies began to evolve into the modern State, which consists of individual citizens.

The new ideals and circumstances confronted the Jewish people with the task of reorienting their own self-image to suit the new categories of social thought. Spinoza met this challenge by calling for the complete dissolution of the Jewish community. Reducing the core of Jewish faith to a few principles that could be applied in diverse historical religions, Spinoza maintained that the vast body of Jewish law applied only to a self-governing community, living in its own land. He did not rule out the possibility of the emergence of a Jewish state in Palestine, but, insofar as the Diaspora was concerned, he declared that only the essential principles of faith in Judaism were valid. As to the people of Israel, they were no more "chosen" than any other nation that accepts its lot with gratitude and seeks to make the most of its heritage for the benefit of mankind. ". . . We have shown that the divine law, which renders man truly blessed, and teaches him the true life, is universal to all men . . . ingrained in the human mind."[122]

Although Spinoza lived as a lonely Titan on the border of the Jewish community, his philosophy exerted enormous influence on the Jewish intellectuals who remained within the community. Yet his contention that the State had the right to regulate all the actions of its citizens, as distinct from thoughts and feelings, ran counter to the emerging liberal philosophy of government.

For a century Jewish statesmen in the West allied themselves with the dominant ideology of liberalism. Religion and State must be separated; the State should abolish the corporations and estates of feudalism and base itself on a free and equal citizenry; all institutions, including those of religion, should be subjected to the scrutiny of reason. The concept of Israel, argued Moses Mendelssohn, should not be taken as an example of the ideal unity of religion and civil government. For ancient Israel was a unique creation, intended for the meta-historical, especially chosen people of the Biblical period, and reserved also for the meta-historical period of the Messianic era in the future. In historical times, the laws of reason, common to all men, must govern human society. Religion, consisting of the free interaction of the Divine mind and the human heart, cannot be subject to the coercion of the State. Also, in historical times, the Jews were simply a religious community, with the hope for a return to Zion being merely a transworldly, pious dogma, affirming an action on the part of God, not on the part of the empirical community. "This state existed only once in the world. Call it the Mosaic society by its proper name. It has already disappeared from the earth. Only God knows in which people and at which time we shall again see a similar situation."[123]

Mendelssohn agreed with Spinoza that the Torah was a revealed law of action intended for a specific community, but he maintained that the Jews of his day were still individually obligated to abide by the Torah insofar as a personal observance of ritual laws was concerned. Mendelssohn also agreed that the ideas necessary for salvation were placed by God in the hearts and minds of all peoples, that they are in no sense, therefore, a monopoly of Israel. The loyalty of Jews to their Law is due to the impetus of the past. They were born into the Torah-community, but the salvation of mankind does not depend upon them. All men are judged by God as individuals, and as individuals the Jews should enter the State. The concept of Israel, for Moses Mendelssohn, was dual in nature: total separateness and a metaphysical dimension in the distant past and in the mythical future, but social integration, in all ways except religion, in this mundane realm.

Mendelssohn's concept of Israel was a logical development of the rationalist stream in Jewish thought; it implied a complete repudiation of the romantic-mystical currents that removed the empirical community of Israel as well as the ancient and eschatological ones from the common course of human events. His viewpoint was certainly shared by the upper circles of Jewry in Western Europe, but in the long belt of Jewish mass-settlements, extending from the Baltic to the Black Sea, the influence of Qabbalah was reinforced by the rise of Hasidism. The wall between East and West, established by the division of Poland and the policy of the Czarist Empire, was supplemented by a cultural-religious schism between the rationalist philosophy of Western Jewry and the mystical isolationalism of Eastern Jewry. Although this wall was constantly breached by the flow of immigrants from East to West and by the return of young men from the universities of the West, it nevertheless remained an obdurate social factor down to our own generation.

In the West, the exponents of Judaism were aware that the ancient Covenant of Israel with the Lord needed to be complemented by a second covenant between Israel and the nations. The new covenant would be far more than a business transaction, but, like the ancient one, it would involve a total reorientation of heart and mind. Unlike the various agreements of the Middle Ages, the new society called for the attainment of "fraternity" with the host-nations. No longer was the Jewish status to be that of an alien enclave, tolerated by the sovereign under certain conditions; the Jews were to become members of one unit—the Nation-State—which, on the surface, was a legal-rational entity and, below the surface, an idealized fellowship which reached down to the dark bedrock sentiments of a blood-brotherhood. So it was that the Grand Sanhedrin of Paris was asked whether the Jews would regard Frenchmen as their brothers.

Because the rationalists had already subscribed to a concept of Israel that included the fellowship of the right-thinking, it was but a small step for them to identify the fellowship of the right-thinking with the society of the enlightened in the eighteenth century, with German *Kultur* in the nineteenth, with the French homeland of liberalism, and with the architects of a free society in England and America. Although they could not join a blood-brotherhood without physical assimilation, they could become part of the new cultural fellowship as well as its political expression, excepting only religion.[124] "The Freedom of the Jews," noted a French-Jewish author, "has put an end to our exile."[125]

This trend of thought within Western Judaism was reinforced by the rising tide of liberalism in Europe that aimed to separate the Church from the State, that is, the fellowship of culture and politics from the traditional institutions of religion. The liberal world was based upon the association of individuals, sharing cultural values as well as political loyalties. The Jewish individual could become part of this new fellowship, since his specifically Jewish loyalties were restricted to the transworldly realm, the mythical past, and the eschatological future.

But the liberals within Judaism, as well as similarly minded men and women in the Catholic and Protestant worlds, were pulled back by the residual, romantic-mystical forces in their respective traditions. The European nations of nineteenth-century Europe were Janus-faced, now turned toward the liberal vision of an open society, now facing back to the older plan of a closed society associated with one or another religious tradition, and going back through the mists of prehistoric time to the primitive, yet potent, feelings of blood-brotherhood. The religious romanticists, who called for a Catholic France, a Protestant Germany, a Greek Orthodox Russia, were allied psychologically with the ethnic romanticists, who idealized the Slavic or the Russian soul, the Teutonic character or the Gallic spirit.[126] Both kinds of collective romanticism were engaged in fighting the same, all-pervasive enemy, the rational spirit in philosophy, the egalitarian spirit in politics, the progressive *élan* in culture and in social legislation. Soon enough the emancipated Jew became the symbol of the hated age of liberalism to the romantic lovers of the good old days. To the protosocialists and economic romanticists the Jew symbolized the rising industrial era, with all its vulgarity and corruption, causing the coarse and uncultured *nouveau riche* to usurp the leadership of the wellborn and the well-bred.[127] To the ethnic romanticists, the ideal age antedated the historic era, when an alien Christianity and a citified culture were imposed upon the guileless noble savages, whose innate culture was too inward and too refined to be noticed by the earliest chroniclers with their monkish minds. To the religious romanticists, the emancipated Jew was also the symbol of the passing of an idealized age, the great Middle Ages, when religion dominated the private as well as the public life of the country, separating the faithful flock from the goats who would not so believe, and putting the latter in their proper places.

In each of these three phases of romanticism, a distorted image of the Jew was constructed around a grain of truth. Jews were predominantly an urban people, participating actively in the creation, first, of a commercial and, later, of an industrial society. They were long the one and only tolerated religious minority. Their ethnic roots went deeper into the past and farther into distant lands than did those of their neighbors. Moreover—and on this point the three kinds of romanticism concurred again, though, on the whole, they were mutually contradictory—the Jew was a child of mystery, doomed by a dark destiny to dwell apart from, and in opposition to, the rest of humanity.

Thus, the "meta-myth" of modern anti-Semitism was born—the mythological notion of the Jew as being metaphysically set apart from the rest of mankind. Between the Jew and the rest of the nations of Europe the gulf was cosmic, eternal, and unbridgeable. This myth, deriving from both Jewish and Christian dogmatism, was now set up in three dimensions: religious romanticism, ethnic culture, and the economic sphere.

In Europe of the post-Enlightenment age, religion was rooted in "feeling" rather than in supernatural revelation. Thus the dogmatic image of the Jew was transposed into the language of "feeling"; his "Semitic" nature could not possibly appreciate the noble sentiments of Christianity. In this view, the Jewish nonacceptance of the Christian faith was transposed from theology to biology. In the realm of politics the same myth implied that the Jew could enter only into superficial alliances with the host-nations, since, in moments of national crisis, the Jew would listen to the voice of his blood. He belongs to a unique species of mankind, a mystical category that is *sui generis,* an international nation.

In the dimension of economic life this myth projected two images that reflected the same animus, although they were mutually contradictory. In the literature of proletarian rebellion and antibourgeois propaganda, the Jews took on, collectively, the lineaments of Shylock, that caricature of the heartless capitalist.[128] In the reactionary literature of those who struggled against the exploding age of industry, the Jew was the economic radical, the new Messianic enthusiast, who had no roots in or love for the ancient virtues of aristocracy.

The one meta-myth combined the feelings of traditional religion, the "pooled pride" of ethnicism, the resentments of the military aristocracy, and the militant malice of the new proletarian radicals. It is easy to see that these diverse elements could be given a spurious façade of unity through the meta-myth of anti-Semitism, though this development did not appear until the rise of the Nazi movement.

Echoes of the meta-myth abounded in the Jewish world, since writers in the Western as well as the Eastern world were exposed to the same influences that produced the romantic reaction to the liberal revolution. Samson Raphael Hirsch reasserted the claims of Orthodoxy along the romantic-mystical lines of Judah Halevi. His vision of a *Yisroel-Mensch* imposed the luminosity of humanism upon the image of a unique ethnic group segregated supernaturally from the Gentile world. Even Geiger, the rationalist, taught that the Jews were endowed with an ethnic genius for religion. Krochmal wove a new pattern of Jewish history around the ancient dogma that, while the Gentiles worshiped certain angels, the people of Israel were alone dedicated to the One God. Ahad Ha'am asserted that in the domain of ethics the Jewish national soul was at work. And it was unique, incomparable, unlike that of all other nations.[129]

Even the Jewish writers who left the fold shared in some of the manifestations of the myth that was torn from its Judeo-Christian context. Disraeli viewed the Jews as not merely another ethnic group but a Messianic race, bearing the seeds of universal salvation.[130] To Marx, the Jew was the capitalist par excellence, the class enemy that had to be overcome. Moses Hess, the one-time socialist, projected the vision of a Jewish utopia in Jerusalem reborn. Even to Léon Blum, the Jew was uniquely disposed to bring into realization the glorious utopia of socialism.[131]

Jewish secularism, however, did not appear as a worldwide movement until the year 1897 when the World Zionist Organization came into being in Basel and the nucleus of the Jewish socialist movement was formed in Vilna. From that time to the present, the variety of Jewish self-images did not change drastically. The revolutionary events of the past two generations—the transfer of the center of gravity of the Diaspora from the Old World to the New, the replacement of czarist oppression by communist repression, the annihilation of Central European Jewry, the rise of Israel, and the virtual liquidation of the Diaspora in Moslem lands—all these developments have been fitted into the following spectrum of shades and nuances, marking the contemporary concept of Israel.

Going from right to left, we have, first, the ultra-Orthodox group, which is small in numbers but intense, even feverish, in devotion. Theirs is an airtight world that rejects the underlying categories of the secular age and employs the ancient axioms of the romantic-mystical school of medieval Judaism. They regard the State of Israel not as a Messianic-eschatological event, but as simply another framework within which the people of Torah may live or not, as they choose.[132] While they agree that it is a *mizvah* to live in the Holy Land, they insist on viewing this *mizvah* within the perspective of the ancient commentaries as if there were no State and no ingathering. Indeed, in their view, the Jewishness of the secularists and the socialists who control the government of Israel is so woefully attenuated as to border on the meaningless. The Torah—and the Torah alone—is the sole yardstick of belonging to the "people of God." The Messianic-eschatological State is one in which the Torah is the constitution, the Holy Temple is brought down from heaven or built up, the Sanhedrin is reconstituted with the help of the Holy Spirit, and the Messiah is revealed. All else belongs to the historical world, where the loyal remnant of the meta-historical people must make do, waiting for the coming of the Promised One.

The moderate Orthodox (*Mizrahi*, or Religious National Party, or the modern Orthodox in the Diaspora) assume that the concept of Israel is bipolar, national, and secular as well as religious and fundamentalist. They participate in the government of Israel, recognizing the Jewishness of all ethnic Jews who have not broken away from the fold officially and flagrantly. They regard the State of Israel as the "beginning of the growth of our redemption." They look upon the present situation as the twilight between the night of exile and the day of Messianic redemption, the borderland between history and meta-history. They have not given up the hope for the fullness of redemption, but they feel that its course must not be plotted in advance.[133] Hence, it is the duty of all Jews to work for the upbuilding of the land, the ingathering of the exiles, and the sovereignty of Torah within the limits of a modern state. They waver between the teaching that it is a meritorious deed for a Jew to settle in Israel and the doctrine that it is the bounden duty of a Jew to live in the land of Israel. This indecision is due only in part to practical considerations; essentially, it is a reflection of the feelings of tension between the compulsions of our temporal existence and the claims of the meta-historical realm that is even now taking shape. Were not the excesses of twentieth-century anti-Semitism, culminating in the Nazi "final solution," precisely the "pains of the Messiah" that the ancient tradition foretold? Was not the flight of the Arabs from Israel in

1948 a miracle that made possible the ingathering of the exiles? Do we not live in a world where the light of redemption and the night of exile are commingled? If so, how is one to tell whether any issue is to be seen in the sober perspective of everyday existence or in the wondrous mirror of the days of the Messiah? For the present, there is no answer to this question.

The ideology of the national-religious movement in Israel was expressed most profoundly by the great Orthodox mystic Rabbi Abraham Isaac Kuk. While he esteemed all forms of nationalism to be fragmentary and partial expressions of the holy dimension, he considered Jewish nationalism to be clearly and fully Divine, the "foundation and essence of Judaism." [134] "Torah and Zion are two sanctities that supplement and imply each other." [135]

The Divine quality of the "congregation of Israel" is not due to any achievements of the empirical people, but to the free act of God. [136] But the living people can bring its Divine endowment to fruition only when it is healthy, physically as well as spiritually. "The wisdom of holiness shines only in the land of Israel. Whatever is envisaged in the Diaspora is nothing but the corollaries of the understanding and its branches. . . . In the land of Israel, the spiritual fountain of the inwardness of holiness, which is the light of the life of the soul of the congregation of Israel, flows spontaneously." [137]

In the mind of Kuk, the yearning to live in the land of Israel is itself proof of the activity of the Holy Spirit that functions primarily only in the Holy Land. "The Holy Spirit received in Palestine continues to function, even if the recipient should by chance go to the Diaspora, either through an error or for some compelling reason. . . . The more difficult it is to bear the atmosphere of the Diaspora, the more one feels the spirit of uncleanliness of the unclean soil, the more true it is that the soul has inwardly assimilated the holiness of the land of Israel and that the grace of the Lord did not desert it. . . ." [138]

Yet, Kuk believed that the redemption of Israel would bring salvation to all mankind, since there was an inner correspondence between the spirit of Israel and that of humanity. "Original Jewish creativity, in thought and in the practical achievements of life, is not possible for Israel, save in the land of Israel . . . and this is a great boon for Israel and the world. . . . Judaism of the Holy Land is salvation itself." [139]

This last statement is a neo-Qabbalist doctrine, equating the "secrets of Torah" with the course of redemption.

In Israel there is no organized religious ideology apart from the Orthodox and the ultra-Orthodox. The secularists fall into two categories—
the romanticists who continue to use the traditional categories of
thought, albeit with new meaning (for example, substituting "the Rock
of Israel" for "the God of Israel"), and the humanists or leftist socialists
who seek to build a state that will in no way differ from other progressive countries. The romanticists intend to retain the bond between the
Synagogue and the government of Israel because they consider the
Jewish religion to be the matrix of Jewish culture and inseparable from
the life of Jews. For them, too, a Jew who converts to another faith
cannot be designated as a Jew. They do not necessarily believe in a God
who chooses, but they do affirm with impassioned zeal that the Jews
are the Chosen People, somehow separated from all the nations, set
apart and charged with a Messianic vocation. They sound the tocsin for
the ingathering of the exiles, specifically for the immigration of American Jews, partly because they feel so insecure and partly because they
can see no future life for Jews in the Diaspora. Thinking in nationalistic
terms, they consider the Hebrew language to be the key to the tradition, and the mark of assimilation to be the nonuse of Hebrew.

Yet nationalism does not exhaust their concept of Israel, since their
national awareness is forged in the crucible of the meta-myth. By itself,
the national ethos does not inspire a process of global concentration;
the Irish do not leave the "fleshpots" of America; the Italians are not
deserting the sidewalks of New York; and even the French Canadians
with all their bitterness against the English and the Protestants show no
signs of emigrating *en masse* to *la patrie*. It is nationalism plus the protean
cloud of myth and mystery that extends to the heavens, appearing as a
"pillar of flame" by day and a "pillar of smoke" by night. The Jew feels,
in the light of his history, that his is a special glory; but he also feels that
he is dogged by a massive satanic hate which can never be overcome.
Even after Israel has been established, the Jew is still not among the
nations, but unique, as against them all. Certain it is that if the gates of
Russia were opened, many thousands would flock to Israel and to the
West in order to be able to affirm their unity with the millennial stream
of Jewish history—this in spite of the fact that the present generation of
Russian Jews received hardly any religious or even Hebraic instruction.

Romantic secularist nationalism is a real factor in the life of Jewish
people today, even if it seems irrational to liberals and humanists. It
enshrines the feelings of identity that were nourished by the religious

tradition, though it negates the central faith of the heritage. It is a reaction to, or the Jewish counterpart of, the meta-myth in the Christian world. It is the equal and opposite reaction to the nationalist frenzy in the twentieth century. Finally, it reflects the awareness of Jewish history that throws a vast shadow on our age. Three thousand years cast a strange spell, like a heaven-piercing pyramid so massive that it seems to be part of the inner structure of the universe.

Romantic nationalism in Israel is balanced by the ideals of humanism and socialism that European Jewry embraced so heartily. It is these ideals that impel the government of Israel to undertake a program of foreign aid that is far out of proportion to its size and resources. More than fifty new and underdeveloped nations are being assisted by technicians and scientists sent out of this small state of barely 2,565,000 people. Scholarships by the hundreds are made available to students from Asian and African nations. The Histadrut (Organization of Workers) maintains a year-round institute for the training of African industrial managers and secretaries of cooperatives. Toward the Arabs in Israel, the Histadrut directs a number of projects with the purpose of developing the skills of these people and of furthering their integration into the economy of the land.

The lamentable rift between Israel and the Arabs was not due to the absence of a humanist approach in the ideology of Zionism. On the contrary, the vision of Zion (rebuilt in the writings of Herzl, Ahad Ha'am, Lilienblum, and Borohov) included the native Arabs of Palestine in the idyllic picture of a noncompetitive, nonexploitative, nonaggressive utopia. The "exiles" would go back to awaken the East, as returning natives armed with the technical skills of the West. They would embrace the Arabs as long-lost "brothers," descendants of Abraham, laying the foundation for a joint renaissance of the two kindred nations.

That the Arab phase of the Zionist ideology went so tragically awry was due to a number of factors. The returning Jews were actually Europeans, in the cultural sense, and "Semites" only in their own dreams and in the eyes of anti-Semites. The rhythm of their life was centuries away from that of the Arab masses, while the Arab leaders could gain standing in the eyes of the mandatory government only as nationalist agitators and revolutionaries. A generation later, to sit for a few months in an English jail was a prerequisite for any would-be savior of his country. Again, the contending ideals of romantic nationalism and liberal humanism did not move on the same plane. The former

429
The Concept of Israel

aimed at making the life of Israel possible, while the latter detailed that which the life of Israel would make possible. As Herbert Spencer pointed out long ago: in a crisis, the necessities of life will always prevail over its ideals. The rebuilding of Israel was effected by way of an uninterrupted series of crises.

The renowned religious thinker Martin Buber traced the mystical dimension of the Zionist idea from the dim beginnings of Biblical history to the present day. A modernist and an antitraditionalist in the field of ritual, Buber was essentially a mystic, though with reservations. He did not aspire to achieve unity with God or to overcome "selfhood," but he was perpetually aware of a Divine Presence, a Divine call that may address us in diverse ways. While his mystical or existentialist philosophy is shared by few people, his interpretation of the Zionist ideal is resonant with the undertones and overtones of Jewish history: he spoke of Zionism as an age-old religious and popular reality, adapted to the universal form of the national movements of the nineteenth century. This reality was the holy matrimony of a "holy" people with a "holy" land, the local point of which was the name of Zion.

"In other respects the people of Israel may be regarded as one of the many peoples on earth, and the land of Israel as one land among other lands, but in their mutual relationships and in their common task they are unique and incomparable. And, in spite of all the names and historical events that have come down to us, what has come to pass, what is coming and shall come to pass between them, is and remains a mystery. From generation to generation, the Jewish people have never ceased to meditate on this mystery."[140]

Buber regarded this "mystery" as an objective phenomenon, by no means comparable to the similar illusions of other nations. In the case of Israel, the "mystery" was embraced in authentic faith. It was given by the Divine Commander: "The essential point is that Israel heard the will of the Lord of the world at the beginning of its expedition to Canaan and conquered the land in the perfect and well-founded faith that it was accomplishing His Will . . . at all times there have been peoples who have given divine labels to their passions and interpreted the acts of violence born of their own greed for possessions, power, and destruction as commanded by these divinities . . . but, so far as we are able to judge from the record, no other people has ever heard and accepted the command from heaven as did the people of Israel. So long as it sincerely carried out the command, it was in the right and is in the right insofar as it still carries it out. Its unique relationship to its land must be seen in this light. Only in the realm of perfect faith is it the land of this people. . . . Where a command and a faith are present, in certain historical situations, conquest need not be robbery." [141]

Coming down to modern Zionism, Buber showed how the "love of Zion" steered the quest of Jewish leaders for a haven of refuge toward Palestine, regardless of rational and pragmatic considerations that pointed to other territories. Such westernized intellectuals as Pinsker and Herzl wavered, but the instinct of the masses was sure and firm. Ahad Ha'am, rationalist though he was, recognized the mystical dimension of the land of Israel and projected the ideal of a cultural center. Yet Ahad Ha'am did not go far enough when he wrote of the "power of the historical feeling that unites the people and the land." For Buber, the bond between the people and the land was not merely subjective feeling. "The decisive question is the objective reality which is mirrored in the historical feeling." He asked, "Is it merely a historical reality, transient like all merely historical things, capable of being annulled by new historical facts like all merely historical things? Or is what has befallen this people in its encounter with this land, and this land in its encounter with this people, the token and expression of a suprahistorical relationship?" [142]

For Buber, there was no question that a "suprahistorical" reality is incarnate in the Zionist enterprise. He quoted approvingly from the writings of A. D. Gordon, the revered *Halutz* and mystic. " 'It seems as if the whole nature of the plenitude from on high that is poured from all worlds into the soul of man, but especially into the soul of the Jew, is entirely different from what it is in the lands of the Diaspora.' "

Gordon was a mystical poet, but not religious in a formal sense. He apotheosized the spirit of the land of Israel because of its intimate union with the people of Israel. "David's harp can only regain its power here in the land of Israel." And the land speaks, as it were, to the people. "It is not we, it is our land that speaks to the people. We have merely to express and intimate the words spoken by the land, and we say to you, to the whole people: 'The land is waiting for you.' " [143]

Buber's ascription of a mystical dimension to the people Israel and to its bond with the land of Israel is based upon two sources: the romantic folkism of his youth and the testimony of the Hebrew Bible. Though he had disavowed the mystical racism of his early writings, he had continued to glorify the primitive sense of direct communion with God, nature, and folk.

All who are able to see through the web of romantic illusions must recognize that if we posit sanctified "feeling" as our guide, there is no way for mankind to keep from repeating the bloody errors of the past. The elimination of the context of rational culture from the quest of reality puts all ethical considerations on a secondary plane. To reassert Biblical nationalism as unique, because the Israelite conquest was kept within the framework of a divine command, is to open the floodgates to similar feelings and similar consequences.[144]

Buber did not believe in the literal revelation of the Divine will in the Hebrew Bible. It is the light of meaning that a person experiences when he studies the Scriptures that is Divine. Like Spinoza, Buber regarded the entire Law as invalid, but unlike the great rationalist, he looked to the feelings of devotion for guidance, and he esteemed the "mystery" of Israel as a "spiritual reality" that is objective and normative.

The mystical concept of Israel, in all its variations from the Qabbalists to Buber, contains several dynamic tendencies that might lead to the self-transcendence of the individual and the nation. First, the emphasis on inwardness in the service of God.[145] In comparison with the supreme significance of the intention of the individual, the boundaries between the various systems of serving the Lord lose some of their dogmatic rigidity. If the whistle of a shepherd boy could open the heavens, why not the Gregorian chant or the cry of the *muezzin?* There is an undercurrent of antinomianism in any upsurge of mysticism. Second, the projection of an infinite dimension in the cultivation of religious feeling reduces the finite variations among diverse sects to insignificance. Third, the awareness of an ever-present mystery militates against the need of dogmatists to direct the events of history by their own power and do God's work for Him, as it were. The overtones of skepticism toward the affairs of this world introduce a healthy detachment from the plausible panacea of the moment.

As we move from the romantic-mystical side of the spectrum to the rational and humanistic views, the concept of Israel tends to break along the line between religion and nationalism.

The nationalists, like Dubnow and Ahad Ha'am, regard the Jewish religion as one of the historical expressions of national culture. While there are no radical breaks in history, the creative energies of the people may be expected to seek new expressions in keeping with the spirit of the times. Both Dubnow and Ahad Ha'am were convinced that the age of religion had ended. The Jewish people, who had formerly lived within the protective walls of the "inner ghetto" of law and myth, must now rearrange their life in order to be a "cultural," or a "spiritual," people. Ahad Ha'am saw the future Jewish world-community as one organic body, with its heart in Israel and its scattered limbs in the Diaspora. He maintained that this "center and periphery" arrangement would sustain the Jewish sense of being radically different (the meta-myth in our analysis), and would halt the "normal" processes of assimilation.

Dubnow portrayed the entire panorama of Jewish history as of a "spiritual nation," a people that learned long ago to confine the drives of nationalism to the domain of culture and self-government. He fought for the principles of autonomy in behalf of all minority nationalities. In the interim between the two world wars, Dubnow's philosophy became the basis of the minority clauses of the Versailles Treaty as well as of the organization of the Jewish communities in Eastern Europe. Long before the holocaust, the currents of life had ebbed away from the secularist communities and all their agencies. The community organizations of the large Polish cities were torn between the two irreconcilables—the Bundists and the Orthodox. In the Soviet Union, the Yiddish organizations lacked popular support, with most Jewish parents preferring Russian schools and cultural fare. It was not the Yiddish language that appealed to them in the first instance, but the ideals and sentiments of the literature—ideals that the communists did their best to undermine. The impassioned will to live as a Jew falters and fades away in the atmosphere of secularism.

In America, the philosophies of Ahad Ha'am and Dubnow were brought up to date and revised in the Reconstructionist movement, founded by Professor Mordecai M. Kaplan. Religion is not a temporary dispensable "garment" of the enduring genius of the people, but it is the crown and glory of every civilization. Religion is the "firstfruits" of the evolving civilization of the Jewish people.[146] It should change in accord with the changing patterns of the life of the people, reflecting their collective hopes and ideals. Organizationally, Israel should be constituted as a world-community centered in the Holy Land, where its civilization is dominant, and extending into the Diaspora, where Jews will live in "two civilizations." Liberal in religion, Reconstructionism is romantic in its concept of the "organic community." But, unlike Ahad Ha'am, Kaplan disavows the "chosenness" and the uniqueness of the Jewish people. The meta-historical phase of the concept of Israel belongs to a supernaturalist world-view that should give way to a naturalist philosophy of religion and to a concept of Israel that reintegrates it into the evolving society of mankind.

At the extreme end of the nationalist spectrum, the attempt was made to remove the ethnic plane entirely from the concept of Israel. The Jewish community was simply a religious community—nothing more. This view emerged with some hesitation, even in the ranks of the classical Reformers. Abraham Geiger still postulated a Jewish racial genius in the domain of religion. At the turn of the century, classical Reform was radically opposed to the Zionist view of Israel as a nation. The Jews ought to take on the national character and the specific culture of the nations among whom they live, retaining only their own distinctive faith. Their mission to humanity consists in the promotion of "ethical monotheism."

Perhaps the most profound thinker among the ideologists of this school was Hermann Cohen, who thought of Israel as the vanguard of humanity. Its religion consists of the glorification and sanctification of pure ethics. Its collective purpose is to help establish the "Kingdom of Heaven," the perfect society of universal justice for all mankind. Its destiny is to be the "suffering servant" of humanity, since all chauvinists and zealots, sensing in the Jew the harbinger of the time to come, vent their fury upon him.[147]

Cohen combated the Zionist ideal not on the ground of its impracticality or its utopianism, but because it was a deliberate attempt to reject the noble role of martyrdom. "They do want to be happy," he complained of the Zionists.

Cohen's disciple, Franz Rosenzweig, veered sharply from rationalism to existentialism. He believed in the revealed religion of Judaism, not in a "religion of reason," and he thought of the people of Israel as a community formed by Divine will and lifted out of the course of history—a meta-historical people. But Rosenzweig's view was remarkable in that, for him, the Christian community was engaged in fulfilling Israel's mission. The people Israel was like the sun; the Christian community was the effulgence of Divine rays permeating the nations with the spirit of monotheism. The boundary line between Judaism and

Christianity was not along the plane of intellectual thought, since the Divine Being could be caught only figuratively or symbolically within the meshes of human reason. Existence is prior to thought in the life of the community, as in the experience of the individual. Our role is determined by our place within the unfolding charade of world history. Specific functions were assigned by Providence to each community: the cultures of India, Greece, and China to prepare the ground; the people of Israel to preserve the heavenly fire; the Christian community to convert the pagan world. Both communities are the agencies of Divine redemption, since "salvation is from the Jews."

Rosenzweig based his conception upon the assertions of both Halevi and Maimonides that Christianity and Islam are "preparations" for the coming of the Messiah and the ultimate triumph of Judaism. Yet his view is a distinct advance, for they operated within the context of a literalist faith. Hence, the deviations from the "pure" faith were grave sins. At the same time, Rosenzweig moved within the thought-world of modern Judaism, where diverse religions are so many pathways to the one goal. For him, the being of God was the ultimate truth, and deviations were only distractions that were unavoidable in any case.

Rosenzweig saw the course of revelation in the actual processes of history, inverting Hegel's dictum, "The rational is the real." For him, "The actual is the way to Truth." Thus anti-Semitism, embodying Christian resentment of the metaphysical character of the Jews, was, in the view of Rosenzweig, part of the Divine revelation, as was the defiant stubbornness of the Jew, his indomitable pride in possessing the fullness of truth, believing himself to be standing at the goal toward which others only stumble and fumble—a self-assurance that exasperates and offends.[148]

Rosenzweig felt that Judaism was both "more and less" than nationality and also "more and less" than a religious denomination. It was unique, meta-historical in the present because of its meta-historical roots in the past and the persistent incursions of Divine grace within the stream of history. He conceived of the Zionist enterprise as being in the same relation to Judaism as socialism is to Christianity. Both social movements operate on the basis of opposing ideologies, but historically they fulfill the real purpose of religion: the establishment of a just society here on earth.[149]

The position of classical Reform is still maintained by some ideologists, but it is now largely defunct, chiefly because the course of events has rendered it academic. The Jews of the Western countries could not shed their nationality in one century when the Eastern Jews were so obviously reasserting their ethnic character and their determination to reconstitute themselves as a nation. The triumph of racist anti-Semitism in Germany made all theories worthless. For a while, at least, the vision of one humanity had turned into a cruel mirage.

Yet, in spite of his temporary successes and his slaughter of six million Jews, Hitler failed. His downfall served to clear the air and to usher in an era rich, in hope and boundless in promise. The apostles of hate have retreated into the shadows, and concerted efforts are made in many parts of the world to overcome the dragon's teeth of bigotry still embedded in the soil of contemporary culture.

No concept can be understood apart from the historical context in which it is placed. In the past generation, the Nazis provided an object lesson of the powerful momentum of ancient hatreds. At the same time, the rapid realignments in the postwar world, projecting the vision of a Europe united, demonstrated the range of freedom in human affairs. It is not written in the stars that France and Germany must forever fight against each other. Nor is it written that the Jews must be forever homeless wanderers. The rise of Israel through the voluntary effort of individuals in the course of two generations is perhaps the greatest demonstration of the range of freedom in the history of mankind. Its foundations were laid by individuals from many parts of the world, and they received their inspiration from books; they labored for several decades to realize a vision that appeared to be hopeless, but which was, for them, the quintessence of spiritual rebirth—a blend of hope, faith, and love.

If we should now proceed to project the concept of Israel into the future, we must take note of the following considerations.

First, the continuity of trends in Jewish history. As a community that is constituted by reverence for a sacred literature, we cannot ever dismiss any of the major movements of antiquity. We may expect that there will always be fringe-groups, and by no means only in isolated communities, that will cherish ancient myths and legends, however antiquated they may seem to those who are in the mainstream. We do not have an authoritative body to define the faith for all Jews. We may regret many passages in the Talmud, and we might want to edit some of its discussion. But as a collection of notes and a record of ancient disputes, it belongs to the past. To the Conservative and Reform, it is a literary monument of the past to be studied with ardor and devotion, but not as a guide for our times. Still, there will always be some pietists who will insulate their minds from all contemporary winds of doctrine and force their living souls into the frozen molds of ancient times.

For this reason, the entire spectrum of opinions from the past looms as a perpetual pageant of potentialities for the future.

Second, the gradational character of the concept of Israel. Whether Israel is defined primarily in ethnic or in religious terms, allowance must be made for those who will associate themselves with it partially or marginally. In the domain of religion, we run the gamut from ultra-Orthodoxy to total skepticism, stopping short only at the lines of express atheism. In the domain of ethnic loyalty, we have the Canaanites of Israel at one end and the Councilites of America at the other. Ethnic assimilation can be as gradational and near-total as an asymptotic line.

Third, the interaction of the concept and the complexities of life. The equilibrium of tensions within the Jewish community is naturally responsive to the changing forces in the general society. Every flare-up of anti-Semitism is likely to frustrate the liberals and to strengthen the isolationists. Every intellectual movement in philosophy, as in statecraft, will challenge either the religious or the ethnic phase of the concept of Israel and evoke a corresponding response. The self-image of the Jew is too intimately enmeshed in the texture of life to be kept pure and inviolate, "unspotted of the wold."

Fourth, the diversity of views within Israel. The diversity is too great to permit any kind of meaningful, communal unity. Jews will agree that anti-Semitism is evil and that a united effort to combat it is possible. They will also respond to campaigns for refugees and for the relief of whatever branch of Jewry is sorely threatened at the moment. But short of the necessity to combat the physical threat of annihilation, Jews are unlikely to act in concert or even to share a vision of the future. On the other hand, a persistent threat, maintained for a long time, might well call into being an association of organizations representing world Jewry, a quasi-community that might continue to exist for years, by the impetus of sheer momentum, after the emergency has passed.

Fifth, several tendencies that might eventuate in the expansion of the scope of the "invisible Synagogue" and the identification of Israel with the moral-spiritual vanguard of humanity. The strong component of rationalism within Judaism focuses attention on the moral-spiritual core of faith, the "religion of reason"; in this view, the diverse faiths of our time incorporate this core in varying degrees.

The rites and ceremonies of the different denominations are only so many varying instruments. It is not the instruments, but the manner in which they are used that matters.

The mystical trend also favors the view of a greater Israel, insofar as it deprecates the criteria of ritualistic conformity, and it points to the infinite dimension of religious intention and enthusiasm. The "inter-subjectivity" of the realm of feeling corresponds to the objective standards of the rationalistic philosophers.

On the ethnic plane, the secular version of Messianism implies an active commitment to the task of building the "Kingdom of Heaven" here on earth. This goal may well go hand in hand with the warning that emerges out of so many pages in our tradition — the warning against the varied seductions of pseudo-Messianism. Jewish Messianists are cautioned by their history against the assumption that any project or plan or person represents the final hope of mankind. The Messiah is up in heaven; he is a vision, a goal, a hope; in historic times, he is not here and now.

The secularized version of Jewish Messianism was embodied in the past century in three movements, each promising redemption for the Jew and claiming to be the final form of Judaism in the End of Days.

The first ideal which appeared in this light was that of individualistic liberalism. All men were to be torn out of their historic context and left to float in splendid isolation within the ethereal realm of absolute law. The Jews in France and Western Europe were indeed emancipated by the upsurge of liberalism. As we have seen, to many of our nineteenth-century philosophers, the "religion of reason" was indeed the soul and substance of Judaism.

The second ideal to acquire the deep pathos and ringing resonance of Messianism was the vision of socialism. It was represented as a contemporary "scientific" version of the prophetic quest of righteousness, of the "Kingdom of Heaven" on earth. At the same time, it would liberate the Jews from the historic hates of anti-Semitism which — so it was proven again and again — derived from the "inner contradictions" of capitalist society.

The third ideal which appeared to be the light of the Messiah was that of Zionism. The Jew would be redeemed from the crushing burdens of hate, and his faith would be revitalized in the land of its birth.

We can now say without fear of contradiction that these three secular versions of Messianism represented different colors in the ideal spectrum, but that none of them constituted the final revelation. Each movement achieved fulfillment in the modern world, but each also eventuated in certain frustrations of its own.

Here, then, we have concrete illustrations of the dangers of pseudo-Messianism.

Two major events are likely to intensify the attraction of the movements at the two ends of the spectrum. First, the rise and rapid growth of the State of Israel is likely to dramatize and reinvigorate the ethnic base of Israel. Second, the growth of the ecumenical movement is likely to strengthen the humanist trend in the concept of Israel, transforming it into the vision of the invisible fellowship of all who seek the Lord with heart and soul. This development is likely to gather additional momentum if Moslem intellectuals should fall into line. We may expect some deep and sustained soul-searching among Jews, and this will result in according full recognition to the latent universalism within the Jewish faith.

Will the universalist trend be opposed by the resurgent national loyalties centered on the young and fragile state? The State of Israel is dominated by secularists, though the Synagogue is not separated from the government. To the preponderant majority of Israeli, the concept of Israel is largely that of a nationality united by sentiments of affection and concern with the nuclear center in Israel—largely, but not entirely. The bond between nationality and religion has been hammered out by the forces of history. The nonreligious have approved of the law prohibiting the raising of pigs, or disqualifying the "Jewishness" of a Brother Daniel.

The secularists may embrace their religious heritage in one of two ways. They may esteem the Jewish faith to be an asset and instrument of the national ethos, in which case they will stress the doctrines and customs that confer a mystical aura upon the national being. Consciously or not, they would seek to revive and glorify the meta-myth. On the other hand, they may spurn the manipulative and cynical approach toward the Jewish religion and, in their earnest search for spiritual roots, discover and make their own the prophetic core of Judaism, the eternal quest of the soul for truth and holiness. In that case, they would strengthen the unifying thread between their historic past, their vision of the future, and their bold social experiments that are designed to follow the narrow pathway between Messianism and pseudo-Messianism.

In sum, the "chosenness" of Israel remains a tantalizing challenge to Jewish people, whether they be secularist or religious. The dogma derives not only from the many-sided tradition that we have analyzed, but from two sources that are perennially replenished: the wonder of Jewish history and the personal experience of the Divine.

Within the complex course of history, the role of the Jew has been particularly conspicuous. His past appears to be unique as the agent of monotheism, as the target of hate, as an object of mystery, as a pioneer, and as a pariah. Many secularist Jews will find in the experiences of their own day subjective confirmations of the meta-myth, which they are likely to articulate in the literary-cultural terms of their day. Strange as it may sound, the secularist mentality has had no difficulty in accepting the status of "chosenness," while rejecting belief in a God who chooses. The resources of the mythological imagination are endless. It would be easy to cite abundant evidence from contemporary "mystics of Jewish history," who reassert the metaphysical uniqueness of Israel, though in all other respects they are realists and pragmatists.

At the same time, "chosenness" is a phase of the individual's experience of grace. As we move in thought and feeling away from the outward appearance of things and yearn for the "nearness of God," we do get on occasion that flash of illumination which is the basic quantum of religion. It is at once a feeling of surrender and of assurance. As we yield in trust, we feel the upwelling of the Divine within us. We are accepted, we are loved, we are anointed, we are commissioned—these are various ways in which our grateful reception of Divine favor is expressed. This sense of possession that accompanies all religious experience is so close to the notion of "chosenness" as to merge with it. To be sure, religious experience also leaves us with the feeling of privation—we know that we do not know—hence, its inexhaustible dynamism.

Thus, personal religious experience, in the case of Jews, is likely to seek confirmation in the rhetoric of the Jewish tradition and in the collective experience of the Jewish people. In turn, the ancient doctrine in all its variations acquires the fresh resonance of contemporary experience from the mystical fervor of deeply religious people.

Rooted in the sacred tradition, in history, and in religious experience, the "chosenness" of Israel, however, it is interpreted, will long continue to intrigue the imagination of Jews and non-Jews alike.

NOTES

1. Genesis 32:28.
2. *De Congressu Eruditorum Causa,* 10.
3. The school of Shammai maintained that divorce was permissible only in the event of the woman's adultery. Their attitude was similar to that of Jesus (Sanhedrin 90a).
4. Hosea 2:1. Exodus 4:22, 19:5.
5. Ezekiel 20:32.
6. II Kings 19:15–31, 23:25–27.
7. Jeremiah 10:11.
8. The notion of "correspondence," which was developed extensively in Qabbalah and in the medieval commentaries, was probably contained in the Torah. The vessels of the Sanctuary were modeled after heavenly patterns (Exodus 25:9). In the higher reaches of pagan thought, the same assumption was axiomatic—the ritual on earth affected a corresponding reality in the invisible world.

Abraham Ibn Ezra (Exodus 25:40, *Commentary*) lays down a general principle: "We know that His Glory fills the world; still, there are places where His Power is more manifest than in others, either because the recipient is more adapted, or because of the higher Power supervening above a certain area. Therefore, the place of the Holy Temple was chosen. And if the Lord put wisdom in your heart, you will understand the Ark, the Cover, the Cherubim that spread out their wings. . . . These are the Glory of the Lord."

9. Isaiah 56:3. Esther 9:27. Zechariah 2:15. Daniel 11:34.
10. Thus the Hellenizers are described as eager "to conclude a *covenant* with the nations around us." The Covenant of Israel with God interposed an obstacle to their fraternity with their neighbors (I Maccabees 1:11).
11. On the other hand, in times of peace, the concept of Israel was expanded generously to include "those who seek the Lord," or "those who fear the Lord" (Psalms 34:11, 69:33, 118:4, 135:20).
12. This much-quoted passage occurs in various forms. A more careful formulation is this: "Three series of levels are bound together: the Holy One, blessed be He, Torah, and Israel" (*Zohar,* Vayikro, 73; also *Zohar,* Vayikro, 93).
13. *Zohar,* Beshalah, II, 64b. Rabbi Shimeon asks how the generation of the desert could doubt if the Lord was among them, seeing that the clouds of Glory were around them. He answers that they sought to know the relation between "the Ancient One, the Hidden of Hidden," and the "Miniature Face *(Zeir Anpin)* that is called YHVH."

14. "The Commandments of the Torah are all limbs and fragments that add up to one mystery. . . . He who removes even one of the Commandments, it is as if he diminished the image of the faith . . . for they all add up to the pattern of Man. . . . For this reason, Israel is called one people . . ." (*Zohar*, Teruma, 162b). Nahmanides in the introduction to his commentary on the Pentateuch: "We have a true tradition that the entire Torah consists of the Names of the Holy One, blessed be He . . . that the Torah written with black fire on white fire was to be so construed. . . ."

15. "And when the Holy One, blessed be He, decided to destroy His House below and the Holy Land below, He first removed the Holy Land above (*Shechinah*) and lowered it from the level where it drew from the Holy heavens (*Tiferet*), and only then did He destroy the earth below" (*Zohar* II, 175a). This action was in keeping with the general principle, "The Lord does not cause a nation to fall, before He casts down its prince above" (Shemot, Rabba 21a).

16. Hullin 91b. Bereshit Rabba 82.

17. Rashi, in Hullin 91b: the image of Jacob was that of the man in the Divine Chariot.

18. Rashi, Genesis 1:2.

19. Shabbat 152b.

20. Bereshit Rabba 47.

21. Baba Mezia 85b.

22. Bereshit Rabba 51.

23. Sotah 17a.

24. Aboth 3:7.

25. Megillah 29a. The commentary of the *Mahavsha* distinguishes between the *Shechinah,* as such, and *giluy shechinah,* the revelation of the Divine Presence.

26. Rosh Hashona 31a. Shemot Rabba 2:2.

27. Menahot 110a. In time to come, the altar that is above will descend to earth (*Midrash Aseret Hadibrot,* 1).

28. Megillah, 29a.

29. Berochot 7a.

30. Halevi, *The Kusari,* V, 23.

31. Shabbat 31a. Sanhedrin 96a.

32. Baba Bathra 15b.

33. Baba Bathra 9.

34. Berochot 43a. Kiddushin 31a.

35. Hagigah 16a.

36. Shabbat 12b.

37. Hagigah 15b.

38. R. Hayim Volozhin, *Nefesh Hahayim,* II, 11.

39. Berochot 35b.

40. Menahot 53a.

41. Pesahim 87a.

42. Jeremiah 15:17.

43. Lamentations, Rabba.

44. "Woe is to the wicked who say that the Torah is only the narrative, for they look at the garment only. . . . The narratives are the garment of Torah . . ." (*Zohar,* Bamidbar 152).

45. *Zohar,* Vayikra 73.

46. *Zohar,* Vayikra 93.

47. *Tikkunai Zohar,* 21.

48. Bereshit Rabba 1.

49. *Ibid.*

50. Tanhuma, Behukotai 2.

51. Yebamot 63a.

52. *Ibid.*

53. Shabbat 156a.

54. Hullin 91a.

55. Sanhedrin 90a.

56. *Zohar,* Bamidbar 244.

57. *Zohar,* Bamidbar 147.

58. Yomah 38b.

59. Sukkah 45b.

60. Raya Mehemna, Deuteronomy, Tetse.

61. *Tikkunai Zohar,* 32, p. 72b. R. Margolis, *Shaarai Zohar,* Jerusalem, 1956. Berochot 15b.

62. R. Elimelech, *No'am Elimelech,* Vayehi.

63. Shabbat 146a.

64. *Ibid.*

65. See R. Margolis, *Shaarai Zohar,* in reference to Yebamot 49a and Shabbat 146a.

66. Halevi, *The Kusari,* I, 115.

67. Kiddushin 70b.

68. Halevi, *The Kusari,* I, 109.

69. *Kitvai Maharal MiPrag,* I, 127.

70. *Tanya,* ch. 1, 2.

71. R. Zadok HaKohen, *Zidkat HaZadik,* 256, 257.

72. Megillah 13a.

73. Hosea 2:23.

74. Pesahim 87a.

75. Vayikra Rabba 6:8.

76. Tanhuma, Deuteronomy 52.

77. Yalkut, II Kings 296.

78. Nedarim 32a.

79. Proverbs 14, 34.

80. Yebamot 48b.

81. Baba Bathra 10b.

82. See note by W. Bacher, *Agadotha Tanaim Veamoraim* (Berlin, 1922) I, 26.

83. J. Berochot 2:1, *Standard Prayer Book for Rosh Hashono and Yom Kippur:* "Repentance, prayer, and charity avert the severe decree." Also, Berochot 17a and 26a.

84. Yoma 87a.

85. Yebamot 57a.

86. Yadaim 4, 4.

87. Abodah Zara 64b.

88. Tosefto, Sanhedrin 13.

89. Ish Sholom, ed., *Tana dibai Eliyahu,* ch. 45.

90. *Ibid.,* ch. 135.

91. Seder Eliyahu Raba, 2.

92. *Ibid.,* p. 121.

93. *Ibid.,* p. 14.

94. *Shulhan Aruch,* Yore Dea, 268.

95. Horayot 13a.

96. Shebuot 39a.

97. Yebamot 109b.

98. Abodah Zara 3b.

99. Yebamot 102a.

100. J. Bikkurim 1:4.

101. *De Confusione Linguarum,* M. I. 426. Genesis 17:5.

102. *De Congressu Eruditionis Gratia.*

103. *De Virtutibus.*

104. *De Abrahamo,* M., 1, 15.

105. Wolfson, *Philo* (Cambridge, Mass., 1948) II, p. 401, Note 25.

106. Praem 26, 152.

107. *Moses* II, 7, 44. Wolfson, in Note 100 of *Philo* (II, p. 417), equates the opinion of Philo with that of the Talmud, citing as reference Abodah Zara 24a. But the term *gerim gerurim* connotes contempt and a lower status than that of righteous proselytes, let alone Israelites. That term is still compatible with another reference in the Talmud that in the Messianic age all Gentiles will become "slaves of Israel." Airubin 43b.

Rashi explains the term *gerim gerurim* (dragged converts) as meaning that "they will convert of their own accord, but we shall not receive them, because their motivation is the triumph of Israel." This interpretation is in accord with the oft-quoted principle: "We do not receive converts in the days of the

Messiah. So too, converts were not accepted in the days of Kings David and Solomon." See Yebamot 24a. In the Talmudic text, the implication is that the Lord will delight in humiliating them. See Abodah Zara 3b.

108. See Tossafot on Abodah Zara 2a.

109. Maimonides, *Yad,* Hilchot Issurai Bia 14:7.

110. The distinction between Maimonides' legalistic and philosophic works has been the subject of heated debates. Philosophy deals with principles, not laws. In the long night of exile and dispersion, the medieval rabbis felt powerless to amend the law and to bring it into conformity with their principles. See Maimonides, *Yad,* Hilchot Issurai Bia 14:7.

111. I. Arame, *Akedat Yizhak,* 60.

112. Maimonides, *Guide,* III, 51.

113. Shem Tov ben Joseph, ad hoc.

114. Teshuvot HaRambam.

115. Maimonides, III, 28 and 36.

116. *Akedat Yizhak,* Gates 15, 31, 38, 56.

117. J. Albo, *Sefer HaIkkarim,* I, 25.

118. *Ibid.,* 23.

119. Seforno, *Commentary on the Pentateuch.* Exodus 19:6.

120. I. Abravanel, *Mashmia Yeshuah,* Saloniki, 1526, Amsterdam, 1644.

121. I. Baer, *A History of the Jews in Spain,* Philadelphia, Jewish Publication Society, 1961, p. 335, Note, p. 446.

122. *Tractatus Theologica Politicus,* R. H. M. Elwes, transl., London, 1909, ch. 5.

123. *Jerusalem,* Part II.

124. Rabbi Ishmael of Modena (1723–1811), a leading Halachic authority, wrote as follows in answer to Napoleon's inquiry about "fraternity": "Though the term brotherhood implies natural kinship, there is a unity of faith between the Frenchmen, or the other peoples of Europe, and the Jews. Since these nations serve the One God, each in their own way, they are now accounted in the eyes of the children of Israel as brothers, for we are obligated to deal with them in fraternity and love, in friendship and peace, and the Holy Torah commands us to help their needy." See J. B. Agus, *The Meaning of Jewish History* (New York, 1963), II, 330.

125. Agus, II, 338.

126. About Fichte's opposition to Jewish emancipation and his concept of the eternal struggle between the people of *Vernunft* and the people of *Verand,* see Agus, *op. cit.,* pp. 333–342.

127. Toussenel, a notorious socialist, in *Jews, the Kings of the Epoch* (Paris, 1900) wrote: "Like the masses of the people, I apply the odious name of Jew to all the people who lived by the manipulation of money, to all the exploiting parasites who live by the sweat of others."

128. The pre-Marxist socialists of France were generally anti-Semitic. So were Fourier, Toussenel, and Leroux. Even Karl Marx, in his youthful articles on the question of Jewish emancipation, maintained that the real problem was emancipation from Jewry. He identified Jewry with the capitalists. It is only in the latter two decades of the nineteenth century that the socialists of Europe realized that anti-Semitism, as the "socialism of fools," was a tool of the reactionary forces. See Agus, *op. cit.,* pp. 334–344.

129. "But every true Jew, be he orthodox or liberal, feels in the depths of his being that there is something in the spirit of our people—though we do not know what it is—which has prevented us from following the rest of the world along the beaten path, has led to our producing this Judaism of ours, and has kept us and our Judaism 'in a corner' to this day, because we cannot abandon the distinctive outlook on which Judaism is based. Let those who still have this feeling remain within the fold; let those who have lost it go elsewhere. There is no room for compromise."

This excerpt from Ahad Ha'am's reply to Montefiore reveals the pathetic contradiction between his "sovereignty of reason" in matters of faith and his surrender to what may be called the "sovereignty of feeling" in urging the authority of a sense of radical difference. See Leon Simon, *Ahad Ha'am* (Philadelphia, 1912), p. 127.

130. See B. Disraeli, *Coningsby* (London, 1928), "The Jews, independently of the capital qualities for citizenship which they possess, are a race essentially monarchical, deeply religious and essentially Tories. The fact is, you cannot crush a pure race of Caucasian organization."

131. See Louise Elliott Dalby, *Léon Blum, The Evolution of a Socialist,* New York, 1963. Blum is quoted as believing that the Jew would take an active part in the building of a socialist state because of the "national law of their race." For Blum, the Jewish religion was only a tissue of ceremonies, but the real faith of the Jew was justice. "If Christ preached charity, Jehovah wanted justice," or "it is not an oversight of Providence that Marx and Lassalle were Jews." Blum felt that the "essence of Jewish thought is, perhaps, the gift for ideal reconstruction of the world."

132. By the term "ultra-Orthodox," I refer here to the members of the *Agudat Yisroel,* not to the still more zealous pietists such as the Grand Rabbi of Satmar (Rabbi Joel Taitelbaum). This group holds that it is a sin to participate in the government of Israel to the extent of voting in the elections to the *Keneset.* Their main reason is the statement in the Talmud that the Israelites took an oath not to come out from exile by collective effort and "not to force the End" (see Kethubot 111a).

Referring to the decimation of world Jewry in our day, this rabbi writes: "Now in our generation it is not necessary to go searching for hidden reasons, since the sin which brought this catastrophe upon us is clearly stated in the words of our Sages who, in turn, learned it from the Holy Writ—not to end the exile by a united effort and not to force the End, 'lest I make your flesh free for all like that of the deer and the antelope' " (*Vayoel Moshe*, Brooklyn, 1959, p. 5).

And he thinks of redemption as occurring through repentance and the works of piety: "For the Holy Temple above is constructed through the labors of the saints and their good deeds. And when it is completed, our righteous Messiah will come, but the wicked cause the destruction of that which the saints build up" (*ibid.*, p. 11).

The first task of the Messiah, who will bring back the *Urim Vethumim*, is to compel Israel to return to the ways of Torah (*ibid.*, p. 134). The first group of those resurrected from the dead will precede the Messiah or accompany Him when He is revealed (*ibid.*, p. 135).

133. The Maharal of Prague, favorite author of Chief Rabbi A. I. Kuk: "It is impossible for redemption, that is, an exalted form of existence, to come all at once." See *Kol Kitvai Maharal*, II, p. 347.

134. Agus, *Banner of Jerusalem* (New York, 1946) p. 61.

135. A. J. Kuk, *Azkarah*, II, p. 364.

136. *Shabbat Haaretz*, Introduction, sec. ed., p. 7.

137. Kuk, *Orot Hakodesh*, pp. 133, 134.

138. Agus, *op. cit.*, p. 215.

139. *Loc. cit.*

140. Martin Buber, *Israel and Palestine*, London, 1952, Introduction.

141. *Ibid.*, p. 49.

142. *Ibid.*, p. 147.

143. *Ibid.*, pp. 160–161.

144. Sidney and Beatrice Rome, eds., *Philosophic Interrogations*, New York, 1964. Buber replies to my question on pp. 77, 78.

145. The elaboration of the infinite pathway of the "duties of the heart" was the meeting ground of the philosophical and Qabbalist schools, as well as the preoccupation of the popular preachers. See Bahya Ibn Pakuda, *Duties of the Heart*, Introduction.

146. Mordecai M. Kaplan, *Judaism as a Civilization*, New York, Macmillan, 1935.

147. Agus, *Modern Philosophies of Judaism*, New York, Behrman, 1941.

148. Rosenzweig, *Stern der Erlösung* (Frankfurt, 1930), p. 670.

149. *Ibid.*, p. 580.

PART SEVEN

JACOB B. AGUS AND THE CONSERVATIVE MOVEMENT

SELECTIONS AND
PREFATORY REMARKS
Mordecai Waxman

FOR FOUR DECADES Rabbi Agus was an active presence within the Conservative movement. In addition to his work on the movement's Committee on Jewish Law and Standards, he served, among other positions, as chairman of the Conservative Rabbinical Assembly's Continuing Conference on Conservative Ideology and as a member of the editorial board of the journal *Conservative Judaism* (as well as being a frequent contributor to that journal). Almost no significant aspect of the movement between 1946 and 1986 escaped his attention or failed to elicit his response.

The following selections, chosen to accompany Mordecai Waxman's essay "Jacob B. Agus and the Conservative Movement" in *American Rabbi: The Life and Thought of Jacob B. Agus* (New York, 1996), consist of Jacob B. Agus' "Reevaluation of the Responsum on the Sabbath" and "Birth Control: A Dissent," both drawn from the files of the Rabbinical Assembly, and essays from Agus' *Guideposts in Modern Judaism* (New York, 1954), 307–19; and *The Jewish Quest* (New York, 1971), 195–202.

19

REEVALUATION OF THE "RESPONSUM ON THE SABBATH"

AN EVALUATION of the actual consequences of any one decision by the Law Committee is exceedingly difficult.

Its positive impact in the direction of a reacceptance of a Sabbath synagogue attendance program has been counteracted by several factors. The responsum was designed to be part of a national, massive Sabbath Revitalization Effort. The revitalization campaign could be launched and sustained only by the central agencies of the Conservative movement. No single rabbi could possibly command the staff and the resources for any such enterprise. Our central agencies ignored this effort altogether, with the result that the Sabbath Revitalization Effort remained merely an intra–Rabbinical Assembly project.

In a logically organized movement, the ideological decisions of the rabbinate become the policy of the lay organization, and the various executives of the central agencies regard it as their duty to put into effect the proposals of the rabbinic authorities. No such situation obtained in the past decade within the Conservative organization. In the opinion of those who do control our central institutions, the "Responsum on the Sabbath" in particular and the Sabbath Revitalization Effort in general were ill advised and even harmful. The national publications did not publicize it. Printed only in the RA Proceedings, it was exceedingly difficult for anyone to obtain a copy of it. The United Synagogue could find neither time nor money for this project. When the extent of publicity accompanying other projects in our national organization is remembered, we realize that the indifference of our central agencies to this project was indeed monumental.

I write of the frustration of this effort not in anger but in explanation. Not for a moment do I question either the integrity or the devotion to Judaism of any one of the executives of our national organization. For the most part, they were sincerely convinced of the downright perniciousness of the Sabbath proposal. They succeeded in preventing a vote from being taken on the floor of the Rabbinical Assembly convention so as to nullify the *takkanah* character of the responsum and to prevent any united action. A sincere difference of opinion was involved, and the façade of organizational unity only served to hide it.

Apart from any revitalization efforts, did the Sabbath responsum help to sharpen our position and to clarify our stand in behalf of a genuine, forthright, and viable faith? From my experience in Baltimore and from my visits in other cities, it is clear to me that the effects of the responsum were altogether wholesome. The Orthodox rabbis, who either ridiculed or criticized this proposal ten years ago, had to mollify their opposition with various degrees of equivocation. In my travels throughout the country I find that our people are proud of the rejection of dissimulation that the responsum signaled. A definitive answer to this question could only emerge out of a study in depth of our movement. *An initial step in this direction would be the preparation of a questionnaire to be circulated among our colleagues and to a representative group of laymen.*

It is certain that the movement of the population toward the suburbs was accelerated during the past decade; that the concept of a small, neighborhood synagogue rendering adequate service to a small membership is now more impractical than a decade ago; that many of our colleagues ride to the synagogue on the Sabbath and that they do so now without any reflection on their spiritual probity or stature.

Several years ago, a very prominent leader in our movement wrote to me expressing the fear that the Sabbath responsum had the effect of widening the rift between the Conservative and Orthodox communities. Were it not for that responsum, he opined, the Conservative organizations would have come in time to embrace the entire "traditional" community.

I question both the premises and the conclusion of this argument. If we are to have an "ecumenical" movement for unity, it should be directed as much to our Reform brethren as to our Orthodox colleagues. To me, the only kind of religious unity that is salutary is the one that derives from the recognition of the distinction between the ethical–spiritual core of faith and the ritualistic–historical expressions of it. Hence it is only in the growth of the liberal spirit that we can eventually attain the goal of creative unity.

Unity is neither desirable nor attainable by way of squeezing all of Jewish life back into "the four ells of *halachah*," as it took form in the *Shulhan Arukh;* nor is it either desirable or attainable by way of fostering a rank anarchy of individual interpretations behind a facade of official loyalty to the *halachah;* nor is it either desirable or attainable by way of negotiations between "spiritual statesmen on the summit" on a *quod pro quid* basis.

Genuine unity is of the spirit, not of external forms. If we in the Conservative movement achieve some success in affecting and elevating the lives of our people, our Orthodox and Reform brethren will be inspired to do likewise.

In actual practice, the Sabbath responsum, is now being tacitly accepted even by Orthodox congregations. I know of one exceedingly prominent congregation that plans to "sell" its parking lot every Friday afternoon to a Gentile. The laymen of the congregation privately ridicule the position of their rabbi. I know of another one where the directors persuaded the rabbi to restate the Sabbath responsum in a "kosher" way, by putting its decision in the form of a biblical quotation.

If there is any one practice that officially separates the Conservative congregations from the Orthodox, it is that of mixed pews. I was involved in several litigations of this issue. Yet I know of no effort to abolish this practice for the sake of an illusory goal of unity.

The so-called new *ketubah* evoked far more opposition among the Orthodox than the Sabbath responsum. It also antagonized the Reform. The Sabbath responsum, by contrast, cannot be strongly opposed either on the intellectual level or in terms of the realities of our day. Ideologically, few Orthodox spokesmen either can or will dispute the right of a community to create *takkanoth*. Practically, it is hardly possible for them to oppose it openly.

Here is an area where forthright decisions are certain to meet with increasing acceptance.

I refer to the Sabbath responsum as a *takkanah,* not a *hetair.* The latter is an individual interpretation; the former is a communal enactment. The acceptance of the responsum by the majority of the Law Committee may be taken as positive action of the Rabbinical Assembly, since this is the only form of endorsement available in our organization. Presumably, the committee could be disavowed and dissolved by the convention if its decisions did not correspond to the sentiments of our colleagues. In turn, rabbis may be presumed to retain the confidence of their respective congregations. A *takkanah* is validated by the express acceptance of the people of any one community.

It would have been far better for the movement if the Sabbath responsum had been directly endorsed by the Rabbinical Assembly and then freely accepted by the United Synagogue and its affiliates. We should then have had truly autonomous legislation, bearing potent ethical-spiritual influence. But even without these formal expressions of assent, the character of the responsum is still that of *takkanah,* not that of a *hetair.* Some of our colleagues are apparently of the opinion that the *takkanah* principle should be invoked only on rare occasions and that we should be guided, in the case of the Sabbath, by the principle of free interpretation. They are apparently of the opinion that *takkanah* legislation opens up vast new horizons and is thus dangerous for us to contemplate. In their eagerness to keep the rate of change slow and deliberate, they prefer to rely on the art of stretching the Law by the subtleties of interpretation.

Actually, the sole difference between a *takkanah* and an interpretation is that the former is a communal enactment and the latter is a private opinion. It is clear that a conscious policy of limitless commentary, allowing free interpretation by individual rabbis, borders on anarchy. On the other hand, a communal enactment is likely to restrain arbitrary and extremist policies and to frame new enactments in the spirit of the tradition as a whole and of previous precedents.

The line between free interpretation and *takkanah* legislation should be drawn in keeping with the distinction between *general* rules and *individual* applications. For example, an individual rabbi should answer a *sheilah* of the type "Is this bottle of wine kosher?" But no individual rabbi should undertake to deal with a question of the type "Shall the practice of designating wine as nonkosher *(setam yainom)* be declared no longer valid in our day?" When general rules are involved, we cannot invoke the principle of freedom of interpretation without destroying the fabric of norms and standards that have been built up through centuries of travail.

Traditionally, wide latitude was allowed in matters of doctrine, *aggadah,* but only a minimal measure of freedom in the domain of *halachah.* The only alternative to the controlled standardization of *takkanoth* is the prolification of anarchy.

Some say, "But we established the system of family pews by the process of interpretation." In this case, the "interpreting" was evidently done by individual rabbis and congregations acting spontaneously, without guidance by any rabbinic body. As recently as thirteen years ago, a most revered professor of the seminary wrote to a congregation in Baltimore in behalf of the Law Committee, asserting that mixed pews were a violation of the Law. Continued development in this direction would make us Janus-faced, with a stance of official orthodoxy masking a state of spiritual bankruptcy and widespread anarchy. If the reconstituted Committee on Jewish Laws and Standards is to be frightened away from *takkanoth,* the trend toward total anarchy will continue unchecked, and the Conservative movement will disintegrate.

The distinction between general rules and individual interpretations determines the meaning and scope of a *takkanah.* I take it that the Committee on Jewish Laws and Standards should deal with individual cases as well as general rules. No one can question the *right* of the committee to issue a series of interpretations and applications of the Sabbath responsum, though one may differ in regard to the *wisdom* of any one recommendation. If any one such interpretation is widely questioned, a procedure for discussion, debate, and decision should be devised.

1. In regard to attendance at bar mitzvah services, that is, whether or not a person should ride to a synagogue where the bar mitzvah service of a friend is held: this question involves a *general* rule, for it is a regular, frequent, even a standardized practice. I fail to see any reason why it should be exempted from the general *takkanah,* permitting riding to the synagogue. The fact of a social obligation being involved is merely another *mitzvah* that is performed, in addition to the act of worship. If, except at rare instances, the Talmud permits interruption of prayer for the greeting of a friend, should we now disdain social courtesies as things unholy? When people come to a synagogue, they take part in a *mitzvah gedolah* without reference to their motivations—such as, did they come to hear the rabbi, or criticize the cantor, or cavil at the *gabbai,* or get the latest gossip, or make an impression on some people?

If the intentions of the original committee are relevant to this discussion, I can state that I do not recall the discussion of any such exemption. For myself, I consider such an interpretation extremely unwise and harmful.

2. As to riding for the purpose of visiting the sick, this question was not included in the original *takkanah*. It constitutes a domain for new decisions. My own recommendation is as follows:

As a general rule, *bikkur holim* should not be considered as sufficient motivation for riding on the Sabbath.

However, cases may arise, as, for instance, a rabbi's visit prior to a very serious operation. This mitzvah may acquire extreme urgency. Then, if a *sheilah* is presented to the rabbi, he should feel free to advise his congregant to ride for this purpose. The governing consideration should be *letzorech,* as it is on *Yom Tov.*

3. Regarding the attendance of a rabbi at a *berith milah:* this is also a regular and frequent occurrence, requiring explicit action by the committee.

As I see it, a rabbi is not essential to the performance of *berith milah.* A *mohel,* as we know, is allowed to ride on the Sabbath, even in accordance with Orthodox law. But since a rabbi is not essential to the ceremony, in normal circumstances, he should not ride.

However, occasions sometimes arise when the rabbi's participation is essential. Thus, if the circumcision is performed by a Jewish doctor, it is essential that the rabbi participate in the mitzvah directly. In that case, he should feel free to ride.

4. Several questions arising from the Sabbath responsum, and previously debated:

Should a rabbi feel free to choose his residence without regard to the possibility of walking to the synagogue? As I recall, we felt that a rabbi—indeed, all men—should seek to live in relative proximity to the synagogue. He should try to live within walking distance, riding only when, as, and if necessary.

Should a rabbi make it a practice to visit the sick in the hospital on the Sabbath? Not on a regular basis, but only if it is a special case of extreme urgency.

Should a person drive to the golf course on the Sabbath? By no means. (This question happened to arise.)

Should a synagogue provide a bus for the transportation of children to attend services on the Sabbath? This question involves a matter of *general* policy. The rabbis taught us that rabbinic enactments should not be done furtively but openly, as in the case of *pikuah nefesh dohe Shabbat.* Hence a Conservative synagogue should not hesitate to provide transportation for children on the Sabbath so that they might attend services.

Should Jewish organizations be allowed to hold business meetings on the Sabbath? We have made strong representations on this point to all national organizations. We were not able to obtain the cooperation of the Reform Ritual Committee in regard to this issue. Professor Israel Bettan was at that time chairman of this committee. But we did obtain assurances from nearly all Jewish organizations that Sabbath programs would be designed to reflect the sanctity of the day. Here is an example of greater stringency than previous *halachah* and Jewish practice.

Should Jewish community centers be open on the Sabbath? This question is exceedingly complex. It is only tangentially related to our "Responsum on the Sabbath." It should be studied separately and on the basis of reports from rabbis in the field.

Lastly, I wish to commend the committee on its undertaking to reevaluate the Sabbath responsum. The procedure of *takkanah* legislation contains its own means of rectification. Every new *takkanah* is in the nature of an experiment.

Let us not be discouraged by the need of articulating our decisions in even greater detail and taking account of newer problems. Such is our heritage. Our entire sacred tradition is the compendium of *takkanoth* in previous generations. The living traditions that we shall leave to the future will consist in effect of the *takkanoth* we institute in our lifetime. No greater privilege is given to any man than the opportunity of refining the faith, expanding the vistas, and elevating the culture of future generations of his people.

20

BIRTH CONTROL: A DISSENT

I DISSENT from the line of reasoning pursued in this responsum. It is forced, contrived, inconclusive, and beside the point. It does not deal, on the personal plane, with the rightness of sex in marriage as an expression of love, and on the global front, it does not take account of birth control as an ideal.

1. From the standpoint of Jewish law, as it was developed in keeping with the literal interpretation of verses and with due regard for Qabbalistic and proto-Qabbalistic notions, birth control is prohibited in normal circumstances, the chief reason being precisely the implied "interference" with divine action. This is the biblical sin of Anan. All *pilpul*-istic quibbles are irrelevant, since they do not touch the moral issue at the core of the problem.

2. As a Conservative body of rabbis, we do not accept the Law as such, turning and twisting it toward a predetermined goal, but we proceed to the heart of the matter by examining the principles involved in this situation:

(a) Do we believe that the sexual act is in itself sinful, becoming admissible and even holy only when it is used for procreation? There are certainly many trends in Judaism affirming the unclean nature of marital love, but we today do not accept them. We find ourselves in accord with the many passages which assert that marital love is an expression and fortification of a holy union. Marriage is a sacred bond of love, quite apart from the raising of children.

"It is not good that the man should be alone; I will make a help meet for him" (Genesis 2:18).[1] We affirm that husband and wife should seek the fulfillment of sexual intimacy as an attestation of their love, after taking due contraceptive precautions, without the slightest trace of fear or guilt in their hearts. "Man and woman, if they merit it, the Divine Presence is with them."

(b) Do we believe that certain children are "destined" to be issued from certain unions, so that contraception prevents them from being born? Again, there are passages reflecting such ideas, but they belong to the infancy of our tradition. Whatever is God's will is not given to us to frustrate. It is by heeding the call of holiness in our hearts that we most nearly approach the will of God, and love is the chief ingredient of holiness. If married love, with contraceptive methods used, is good and holy, it is in accord with the divine will.

(c) Do we believe that the quantity of human life is more important than its quality? It is possible to make out a good case in Jewish tradition in favor of quality as against quantity. In dealing with the poverty-stricken and overpopulated areas of the globe, this is precisely the issue. *A positive effort in the direction of planned parenthood* is needed throughout the world. Such an undertaking requires more than a tacit acknowledgment that it is permitted only if parents can convince themselves of the existence of danger to themselves or to the children. We need a frank and healthy affirmation of the rightness of marital companionship and love, regardless of the duty of raising a family.

Jacob Agus, 1960
Not official CJLS (not voted on)

NOTE

1. In the original responsum by Rabbi Agus, this verse is quoted in Hebrew.

21

LAW IN CONSERVATIVE JUDAISM

NEED FOR A READJUSTMENT OF JEWISH LAW

THE CONCEPTION of revelation, outlined in the first part of this essay, has many points of contact with the opinions and judgments of diverse philosophic luminaries in the past. However, we do not lay claim on its behalf for the designation, orthodox. The subjective acceptance of the Law, as the way of serving God, we maintain to be the fundamental quality in the Jewish pattern of piety. But, we also allow room for the objective analysis and consideration of various aspects of the Law, in terms of the universal values of piety and in the light of the actual results and effects of certain Halachic precepts in the circumstances of the modern world. We regard the two attitudes not as antithetical forces, but as complementary phases of the life of the spirit. Before the organic structure of Jewish life was shattered by the Romans, both attitudes found expression in the teaching and legislation of the Rabbis. Thru the vicissitudes of exilic life, the subjective attitude came to prevail more and more, as the wounded soul of our people sought to strengthen the barricades against the hostile world. It is now our task to demonstrate how the two attitudes may be harmonized in the daily life of the modern observant Jew.

In the daily practice of Judaism, the subjective attitude must prevail very largely. In the routine of life, a faith cannot be lived and doubted at the same time. The essential characteristic of Jewish piety consists in the acceptance of and implicit obedience to the Divine Will, concretized into Divine Law. Objective considerations are normally left to the corps of intellectual leaders—prophets, scribes, Sages and Rabbis. The Synhedrin of the past carried out the function of objectively assaying the operations and achievements of the various phases of Jewish Law, instituting the necessary "takkanot," in accord with their findings.

The problem we face today, making the emergence of a Conservative movement logically inevitable, arises out of the circumstances that the historical instruments of objective self-criticism and adjustment have broken down. The breakdown of a living authority in Jewish religion did not occur all at once, the Synhedrin having been followed successively by the "vineyard of Yavneh," the assembly at Ussha, the school of R. Judah the Prince, the academies of Babylonia, the "Geonim," the occasional assemblies thru the Middle Ages, down to the present when there exists virtually no authority at all. Concomitantly with this breakdown of the social instruments for religious leadership, there took place a similar degenerative process in the inner structure of "Halachah." The guiding principles of "Halachah" have become so constituted, thru the continuous preponderance of the subjective attitude, as to lead automatically to an irreversible process in legislation. Whatever may have been desirable at any one time, became fixed for all time thru such legalistic methods as the following: the "derivation" of the principle from the interpretation of a verse, the principle that no court can annul the "takkanot" of a previous court, unless it be greater than the first in wisdom and in numbers, and the concomitant principle—a typical product of subjective piety, that in the succession of generations, scholarship and piety are steadily decaying.

Thus, if Judaism is to become again a living faith, significant in terms of modern ideas and values and relevant to the psychological needs of today, an instrument must be forged whereby both poles of the life of the spirit may be harmonized and concretized in the life of our people.

WHY THE LAW COMMITTEE IS INSUFFICIENT

In our attitude toward "Halachah," three logical positions are possible. We may accept it as one organic body, with all its practical precepts, its legal principles and its structure of authority, as embodied in the Orthodox rabbinate. Or, we may accept it, in part, and reject it in part, using as the principle of selection, ideas derived from our basic philosophy of life. Or, we may reject "Halachah" altogether as an unnecessary encumbrance for modern life.

The first position is Orthodox. Let no one fool himself into believing that by juggling the principles of the "Shulchan Aruch" thru the minds of the Law Committee of the Rabbinical Assembly, any other result can be obtained than that which is reflected in the current Responsa literature of the Orthodox rabbis. We need a law making body, not a law interpreting committee. So long as the basic materials for decision are identical, no other results are possible. In our current historiography, it is customary to describe some of the great Halachists as "m'kilim," responsive to the needs of their day, and to tar others with the brush of "machmirim," strict adherents of the letter of the law. Accordingly, it was felt that if the Conservative "Halachah" committee were to assume the consistent attitude of "l'hokail" a vital movement would emerge in the course of time, combining "Halachah" with life. Actually, this conception is based upon an extreme exaggeration of the era of freedom in Jewish law. If one takes up the Orthodox position in respect of "Halachah," his sphere of choice is reduced to the very minimum. In spite of the so-called "diffusion of authority" in the Jewish law, an "Halachah"-true Jew has a straight and narrow path to follow. His authorities are the "g'dolai Yisroel" of every age. For him, a "gadol b'yisroel" is defined not only in terms of surpassing Talmudic erudition, but also by reference to the standards of piety, which are themselves defined in terms of "Halachah." We deal here with a closed circle of authority, which may have its own schools of interpretation and emphasis, its own unsolved problems and moot points, but which is nonetheless contained within well-defined borders. One may argue ad infinitum on the relative importance of "minhag" and "Halachah," but one cannot, by any such "pilpul," alter the fact that whatever the proper balance between these two sources of authority be, that circumstance is reflected in the actual practice of the "Halachah"-true world—those who abide by the decisions of the "g'dolai Yisroel." A "minhag" is a valid source of authority only when it is a "minhag Vatikim." (Custom of the proven pious.) One hears frequently these days of Reform rabbis describing the practices of their members and the ceremonies of their temples as falling under the category of "minhag America," as if that designation implied automatic halachic endorsement. In reality, "Halachah" is not only a set of principles, precepts and precedents, but a "way" of making decisions, entailing a set of authorities in the past and in the present. If we think of the Talmud, "Shulchan Aruch" and the Responsa literature as the sole collective source material of halachic authority, then we must accord those who mold themselves exclusively in the pattern of these books the prerogative of expressing the voice of "Halachah."

THE WAY OF TAKKANOT

Manifestly, then, the Conservative movement cannot be described as falling within the limits of "Halachah"-true Judaism. On the other hand, it does not reject "Halachah" in the slightest in theory and it does not accept "Halachah" very largely in practice. What, then, is our principle of selection?—Obviously, this principle of selection must be justified in terms of our basic philosophy of religion; at the same time, it must be fitted formally into the structure of "Halachah."

Reform Judaism started out by revoking the principle of legislation from Judaism, step by step. It began by chafing under the strain of "chumroth" (severities) imposed by the latter day rabbis; then it proceeded to abolish the enactments of the "Geonim" and "Rishonim" (early authorities), following up this step with the revocation of the authority of the Talmud and then finally negating Biblical law as well. Some Conservative thinkers in our day seem to favor the same course of action. They think nothing of opposing the Orthodox authorities of their own day or of the immediate past, but they still presume to invoke the authority of the "Rishonim," failing to see that by restricting steadily the realm of rabbinic legislation to the ever more distant past they launch themselves onto the slippery incline of Karaitic thinking, which is utterly retrogressive and futile. If we follow the principle that the rabbis of our own days are incompetents and that the rabbis of the past were all-knowing, we undermine the very basis for development and growth in religion, even while we presume to speak in the name of religious progress. Obviously, the past cannot of its own momentum effectively progress in the contemporary world. Again, if we deny Divine sanction to the "Rishonim" and grant it to the masters of the Talmud, or if we deny it to the "Amoraim" and "Tannaim," reserving it for the prophets, we should be operating with a mechanical principle of selection, for which there is no basis in our philosophy of Judaism. The Karaites did believe in the literal revelation of the Torah and they further assumed that the rabbis of the Talmud corrupted the Mosaic tradition. We do not hold to either of these views. Furthermore, for us

Divine revelation is expressed as much thru the conscience of Israel, the "sons of the prophets," as thru the vision of the prophets themselves. From our viewpoint, then, the present is more determinative than the past, and the immediate past more authoritative than the remote past.

It seems to me that the only proper course for Conservative Judaism consists not in the progressive diminution of the sphere of legislation, but, on the contrary, in its steady expansion. We must learn to utilize the principle of "takkanot" in charting the path of our movement. This principle is fully in accord with our dynamic conception of revelation. It renders Jewish law flexible and timely, affording a legal channel of expression for the living "conscience of catholic Israel." In Jewish law, the sphere of "takkanot" is virtually limitless. According to Maimonides, the enactments of the rabbinical courts, which derive their binding power from the principle of "lo Tosur" (Thou shalt not depart from the decision of the Court), have the force of a Torah-itic commandment. While in theory, "takkanot" cannot permanently supersede the laws of the Torah or the rabbinic enactments of the past, they can do so temporarily, "I'sha'a," if the enactment is justified by local and contemporary conditions. Here, then, is an instrument, which is capable of doing exactly that which Conservative Judaism maintains needs to be done. Let us see how this instrument may and should function in our movement.

PROPOSAL FOR A "JEWISH ACADEMY"

"Takkanot" can be made in Jewish law, by the elected representatives of the communities together with their rabbinic authorities. Thus, they must have two sanctions—the one deriving from the most sensitive conscience and the most creative scholarship of the age, the other deriving from the democratic principle of "the consent of the governed." Accordingly, we must form an assembly capable of discussing intelligently and thoroughly all aspects of Jewish life, whence concrete suggestions for "takkanot" should emerge from time to time. Also, we must provide for periodic convocations of laymen and rabbis, representative of the entire movement, who shall be empowered to accept or reject the proposed "takkanot." To exercise the first function, we propose the establishment of a Jewish Academy, consisting of selected rabbis, scholars and laymen, who would discuss thoroughly and regularly all phases of Jewish doctrine and practice. The second function must naturally be left to a joint special session of the United Synagogue and the Rabbinical Assembly.

The term "Jewish Academy" is chosen in order to suggest the resemblance to the French Academy and to eschew the notion of claiming the authority of the ancient Synhedrin. Like the French Academy, it should consist of the greatest men in our movement, those who have achieved distinction in the fields of scholarship, rabbinic leadership, Jewish education and social welfare. Like the Academy, too, appointments should be made for life or for long terms—such appointments constituting the highest marks of recognition in our movement. This academy should meet at regular intervals to discuss institutions of Jewish life, principles and dogmas of the faith, the latest developments in various fields of study bearing upon the philosophy of religion and ways and means of dealing with specific problems. Its first task shall be to lead and guide our movement in a nationwide, "tshuvah" effort, calculated to reestablish a minimum of observance among the members of our congregations. Its members should be made available for periodic consultation with congregational groups, so as to stimulate and arouse a deep loyalty to Judaism.

In short, the Academy would become the central guiding agency for Conservative Judaism, the upper house for legislation in our movement.

This suggestion is so obvious and natural that one need not argue in favor of it so much as in refutation of the criticisms that might be directed at it. Let us therefore proceed to analyze the possible objections to this plan.

Firstly, it will be said that the "takkanot" will have to be so far reaching in the beginning that the established structure of "Halachah" will be incapable of withstanding the impact of sudden change. The residual loyalty to Jewish law in the hearts of our people will in consequence not be channeled thru the new "takkanot," but will be totally shattered. The distance between theory and practice in Conservative ranks is presently so vast, that any attempt to bring the law down to life, cannot but begin with a tremendous antinomian effort, that will of its own momentum undermine the respect which Jewish law still evokes among our people. The first acts of the projected Jewish Academy will have to be directed against some sections of "Halachah," it may be said. Therefore, the negative character of the Academy would be fixed in the public mind, thereby accelerating the present stream of defections from Jewish law.

The answer to this objection is that the initial "takkanot" need not at all be negative. The processes of life, of their own impetus, combine to render certain phases of the Law obsolete. Our task is very largely of a positive character—to strengthen and protect those phases of Judaism, which are most significant from our viewpoint. By doing little or nothing to encourage the regular attendance of women in "mikvoth," and by doing all in our power to stimulate attendance in synagogues, we shall be directing the course of Jewish life. There is no need for "takkanot" to sanction non-observance, but there is great need for "takkanot" to raise the level of observance. Certainly, our first endeavors should be directed toward the achievement of a minimum of observance among our people—so that membership in a synagogue shall not be purely a financial transaction. The term "conservative," must be made to stand for a positive commitment to Judaism, not only for minor changes in public worship.

The next series of "takkanot" shall deal with the correction of certain abuses in Jewish life, as in the matter of desertion and the refusal of the husband to grant a divorce.

Whatever changes need be made in the order of the services, cannot be described as negative in character, since their purpose will be the improvement of the spiritual quality of worship and the attraction of greater numbers of people to the synagogue.

Secondly, it will be argued that a group of associated synagogues, such as the United Synagogue, cannot be considered legally a Kahal, for the purpose of making "takkanot." "Takkanot" involving the Jewish religion cannot be made by different communities or even by the Jewries of entire countries, but they presuppose the ingathering of Israel in the Holy Land and the re-establishment of a Synhedrin in Jerusalem. The "takkanot" that were made by diverse communities in the past were minor in character and cannot be compared with the radical departure that is likely to be represented by a series of "takkanot," expressive of the Conservative ideology. The principle of "catholic Israel" militates against any break with other sections of the Jewish people.

This argument would be irrefutable, if there had existed presently that degree of universality of observance which the "Shulchan Aruch" postulates. The fact is, however, that the masses of our people have already broken away from the ancient moorings of Jewish Law and that the Reform movement which rejected nearly the whole of ritual law is still considered part and parcel of the Jewish community. Accordingly, our task is not one of breaking down fences, but, on the contrary, of erecting dams against the eroding floodwaters of desertion from the standards of the synagogue.

An association of synagogues in our time may be likened to an association of communities in the past, especially in reference to matters affecting congregational life, since uniformity of observance among Jewish people today is out of the question. To wait for the agreement of the entire Jewish people would be tantamount in practice to the utter bankruptcy of our religious leadership—a shamefaced confession to the taunt of Longfellow that the Jew walks backwards with his eyes glued to the dead letters of the book held in his hands. Nor would such a course of action be justified in theory, since now there is neither an identity of basic convictions between us, the Reformed, the indifferent and the Orthodox, nor an institution like the Synhedrin of old, thru which differences of opinion can be reconciled and adjudicated.

As to the actual scope of community "takkanot," we know that from the objective psychological viewpoint, as distinguished from the subjective one of strict legalism, there is ample precedent for virtually all that needs to be done. The "takkanot" of Rabbenu Gershom were certainly most far reaching in sociological terms, though they were meant for and were accepted by only the Ashkenazic Jews. But, even if it be granted that there is not enough precedent for what might have to be thus legislated, are not our time and circumstances so strikingly new as to justify the creation of new precedents?

Another possible objection to the plan herein outlined is that there exists presently no agreement in Conservative ranks, concerning basic and vital issues; that, in consequence, any attempt to legislate thru "takkanot" would lead to the widening of existing splits; that the group which would rally round the plan would be too small to command any respect and achieve any permanent results.

As a matter of practical judgment, this objection must certainly be weighed with great care. Doubtless, we dare not attempt to make up with one fell blow for a century of arrested progress. Caution and extreme deliberation will be needed, but it is impossible to evade the inherent logic of the situation. Whatever the relative strength of the various groups in Conservative Judaism may happen to be at this moment, the following considerations remain true: that the basic divisions in Judaism are in respect of "Halachah"; that the middle position between the full acceptance of the Orthodox and the complete repudiation of Reform can be theoretically grounded either on the Karaitic principle, repudiating the authority of the rabbis, or on the "lo tossur" principle, the magna carta of rabbinic legislation. Since the Karaitic principle, in spite of its initial coincidence with the trend of popular feeling, and the apathy of our leadership is intellectually sterile and practically a weak-kneed Reform movement, lacking boldness and consistency, it follows that the Conservative movement can only follow the pathway of "takkanot," or else disappear from the scene, as a movement.

The question raised by this objection, therefore, is a very fundamental one—to wit, is there room on the American scene for a Conservative movement, as distinguished from a Conservative way-station? To phrase the question is to answer it. There is not only room, but crying need, for a Conservative movement. If there were no such steadily emerging movement, it would have had to be created. For our time calls for a bold constructive approach, which neither Reform nor Orthodoxy can give—the former thriving on the growing decay of tradition, the latter reduced to a desperate holding action.

Actually, I am convinced that, if the pathway of "takkanot" is chosen by the Conservative movement, its following will grow from year to year, thru the accession of the liberal graduates of "yeshivoth" and the younger Reform rabbis, who are even now dimly groping toward the Conservative position. There is no firmness either to the right of us or to the left of us. Voices clamoring for a living authority and a "new Halachah" can be heard on all sides. Yet, only the Conservative movement is strategically so situated as to be capable of forging a firm instrument of leadership.

What if our "takkanot" are repudiated by the Orthodox and spurned by the Reform elements? Shall we not then be contributing to a widening of the existing splits in American Jewish life?—In answer, let us reflect that the present course of inaction is not at all conducive to unity or uniformity, save that of the cemetery. A bold course of action would serve to galvanize our own movement and imbue it with enthusiasm and conviction. It would enable our own men to preach, to teach and to guide with utter sincerity, feeling themselves part of a movement, that really knows whither it is going. It would help to overcome the mood of frustration and cynicism, which vitiates the effectiveness of so many of our men, releasing thereby untapped springs of creative energy. If it be true that our movement today lacks enough men of outstanding spiritual calibre, is not that lack itself to be attributed to the lassitude and confusion of our leadership? Why, not having lacked genius and character in the past, should we assume that we shall lack it in the future? If, then, many of the earnest souls in the Orthodox and Reform camps should choose to join our group, well and good. If their reaction will be largely one of repudiation, they cannot fail to emulate our example of courageous action and to proceed to mend their own fences in their own way. The net result in either case cannot but be beneficial.

22

A THEOLOGICAL FOUNDATION
FOR THE HALACHAH

A PHILOSOPHY of Halachah is an integral portion of one's world-view in general. At least, it is so in my case. I beg the reader's indulgence for the outline form of exposition, which necessarily raises more questions than it answers.

GOD

I believe in God as the Ultimate Reality of the Cosmos, the unifying and harmonizing Principle of existence. The philosophic school which most nearly reflects my views is that of *panentheism,* where the cosmos is viewed as being *in* God. I consider that this school represents the "perennial philosophy" at which Aristotle and Maimonides aimed; Bergson reconciled it with the data of evolution; Alexander and Whitehead described it as "organismic"; and Hartshorne defended it in contemporary thought. The cosmos contains a crescendo of "wholes," structured clusters of energy which function as if they were unitary beings. In the course of evolution, ever more elaborate organisms have evolved, with mankind representing the emergence of free personalities, capable of sensing the divine principle of organismic unity and harmony. The "image of God" in man is the fleeting, finite and fragmentary realization of the Divine creative thrust. For all its transitoriness, man's awareness of God is certain, intuitive and a source of self-renewal.

We may speak of God as Person, in both affirmative and negative senses. In its affirmative meaning, personhood means unity in space and time, imposing one Law upon the whole of creation, embracing the past in memory and the future in intention and in affirmation. In its negative sense, personality is self-defined by that which it excludes. So, in the case of God, while all events are His work, through the operation of the laws of nature, not all events, taken in isolation, reveal His will. In a work of art there is a framework, material content which may be infinitely varied, and the intention of the artist that may be clearly manifested or only dimly apprehended by unconscious intuition.

Personality is the highest exemplar of holistic unity that we encounter in our human experience. Personality points to God, without delimiting Him. He is "the Soul of souls" *(neshamah lineshamah)*. We dare not attribute the merely human qualities of speech and temperament to Him, except in a metaphoric sense. Rabbi Simlai's restriction of divine revelation at Sinai to the first two of the Ten Commandments is an apt description of divine-human encounters.[1] God opens ever new horizons by His self-revelation in our hearts and minds. He is revealed in man's ascent from slavery to freedom and in the progressive rejection of idolatry, be it gross or subtle.[2] Every revelation of God's Will in the human soul can turn idolatrous when it is taken to be the last word of the living God. Every step toward freedom that mankind takes is divine in inspiration and orientation, but it is just a finite step, no more, on an infinite road.

REVELATION

God reveals Himself to us in many different ways. His Will is manifested at the several cutting edges of the human spirit—in the infinite outreach of man's quest for understanding, in the imperative call to overcome the ills of society, in the inspiring moments of holiness. Plato's triad, the True, the Good and the Beautiful, was an inspired but time-conditioned formulation. Truth is an elusive goal and the awareness of limitation accompanies man's intellectual quest. Ethical imperatives are divine, but every step of social progress uncovers new tasks. The glory of beauty is most liable to perversion through the seduction of pleasure. True beauty includes the dimension of the sublime or the holy—hence, an intimation of infinity.

In each aspect, the awareness of negation, knowing that we do not know, is integral to the experience of revelation. As in the nineteenth Psalm, day speaks unto day and night unto night but "there is no speech, there are no words." Indeed, viewed in the perspective of the history of religions, the faith of the biblical authors stresses the negational dimension of the faith-event more than the affirmative one. The Hebrew Scriptures "de-sacralized" not only nature, but also history, setting strict categories for the manifestations of the divine will.

Several modern Jewish thinkers, succumbing to the influence of German philosophy, contrasted the pagan sanctification of nature with the Jewish sacralization of history. It is true that God is revealed most clearly in the expanding domains of the human spirit, but the course of human events is not identical with the advance of ethical sensitivity and moral vision. God is revealed *in* history, not *through* it. Judaism rejects the arrogant triumphalism of the historicists, whose slogan is "world history is the world court." The God of Israel appears in history as the champion of slaves, intent on reversing the course of history. And for two millennia, and against all odds, the Jewish people cherished the hope of rebirth. Only certain events in history manifest the divine will; others are consequences of the darker side of human freedom. As the *Mekhilta* on the crossing of the Red Sea points out, God appears at times as a leader on the battlefield, at other times as a sage teaching in a *yeshiva*.[3] As to which is which, in every instance the conscience of great and holy men must judge.

In addition to this general revelation, which is fleeting and unstructured, Judaism affirms the special revelation, which is embodied in its literature and its patterns of living. In the Hebrew Scriptures, the sacred tradition is mediated through the minds of three kinds of holy men— the priests, the sages and the prophets. "For Torah shall not perish from the priest, nor counsel from the wise, nor the word from the prophet" (Jer. 18, 18). (This is why we use the acrostic *Tanakh*—Torah, prophets, writings.) Different aspects of wisdom and piety are likely to be conveyed by each category of teacher. Because of the tensions resulting from these different approaches, the biblical faith was dynamic and many-sided. While archaic elements remained, countervailing influences were set in motion.

To consider matters of Halachah apart from their historic settings and deeper meanings is to follow in the wake of the ancient priests exclusively. The Talmud recognized that sheer legalism was a disease of religion. "Whoever says, 'I care only for Torah' will lack even Torah" (*Yebamot* 109b).

The "Sages of Israel," as the Pharisaic scholars called themselves, tried to preserve the ethical thrust of the prophets and the wisdom of the sages as well as the ritual of the priests. In the opening Mishnah of *Avot*, they even excluded the priests from the chain of transmission. The Aggadah contains, in gnomic form, maxims reflecting the philosophies of the ancient world, along with the impassioned ethical fervor of the prophets. Philo, the first philosophical exponent of Judaism, was a Greek-speaking Aggadist, incorporating into the tradition the so-called "beauty of Japheth."

Scholars have discerned two diverse approaches in the Palestinian schools of Rabbis Akiva and Ishmael—the former inclining toward literalism, the latter toward a reasoned interpretation. The literalist school produced also the *Shiur Komah* (descriptions of the Divine Glory) type of mystical literature which formed the foundation of Kabbalah, while the rationalistic school kept the gates open to the contemporary winds of philosophic speculation. Medieval Jewish philosophy, climaxed in Maimonides' *Guide*, was the most massive attempt to synthesize the three currents of tradition—that of priest, sage and prophet.

Maimonides effected this synthesis in three crucial ways—by viewing the tradition in the light of the history of religions and describing rituals as protests against ancient idolatries; by postulating Secondary Intention on the part of God as the source of the entire sacrificial system in the Holy Temple; and by introducing the distinction between "true doctrines" and "necessary doctrines." The former are true in themselves, the latter are affirmed by the sages in order to retain the cohesion of the community.

While lesser philosophers, both before him and after him, were content to separate and insulate the two domains of reason and religion, Maimonides insisted that worship must be whole-souled. Only if Judaism promotes philosophical piety does it have the right to demand self-sacrifice and even martyrdom. We learn from Maimonides that not all *halachot* are born equal. We have to study their origin in history, their justification in philosophy, their pragmatic consequences, their merit in terms of the primary intention of faith.

To be a Jew is to share in the priestly, prophetic and philosophical tradition of the living community of Israel *(K'lal Yisroel),* with the inevitable development of diverse schools of interpretation!

HALACHAH

Conservative Judaism is one such school. It seeks to be true to the *whole* of our sacred tradition, to its inner philosophy as well as to its outer expression. As Conservative Jews we accept the Halachah as a starting point, not as a blueprint. It is one of the given components of our tradition, not all of it. Torn from its context in life and thought, Halachah is meaningless.[4] Every particular command should be open for evaluation in terms of the totality of the evolving sacred tradition.

For the purpose of clarification, some negations are in order:

We are not literalists—that is, we do not assert that the Torah was dictated to Moses, word for word, and that the Oral Law was transmitted verbally to him and to his successors. Therefore, the inner logic of a great deal of Halachah is, for us, not in itself persuasive. Nor is a custom in itself hallowed in our eyes solely because it has been practiced by many or even most of our people. For example, *shlogen kapores.* We have outgrown folkist romanticism. Nor do I and many of my colleagues follow the German super-conservative school of Savigny which idolized the institutions created by history as sacred, "positive-historical." We know all too well how many anti-Jewish horrors were sanctioned by that attitude.

We see the Jewish global community as centered in its religious life around sages—more exactly, priests, prophets and teachers of wisdom. In contemporary life, those categories do not coincide with any particular organized group. The rabbinate, in its totality, does not today exhaust the category of the ancient *hakhamim.* There are academic philosophers, individual scholars, educators and social workers, journalists and authors, who, in diverse ways, contribute to the making of the Jewish mentality. Associations of synagogues come closest, perhaps, to the representation of *Kenesset Yisroel,* the religious fellowship of Israel. With the progressive contraction of the domain of religious life to the precincts of the Synagogue, the norms and standards adopted by congregations will be decisive in molding the Halachah of the future.

TAKKANOT

The Talmud speaks of those who violate an ordinance of the sacred tradition as rebellious children, disobeying their Father, who is God, and their Mother, the Congregation of Israel. Every ordinance is a product of both parents. We recognize the work of God in the living people, molded as it is by its historical institutions and guided by its spiritual leaders.

Therefore, in our view, the tradition develops by way of new *takkanot,* new *aggadot* and new *minhagim. Takkanot* are ordinances of conduct initiated by the spiritual elite; *aggadot* are new ideas that arise either out of Judaism or out of universal culture; *minhagim* are customs initiated by the people and concurred in by the *elite.* No strict lines of demarcation can be drawn between these several instruments of halachic development. Scholars used to draw absolute distinctions between the imposition of dogmas upon the free mind, which is intolerable, and the imposition of ordinances of conduct upon a free people, which is acceptable. The distinction is only partially valid, for there is no conduct that causes mighty changes in society, which does not imply certain ideas, and there are no ideas of consequence which do not affect the lives of people.

Takkanot, aggadot and *minhagim* aim to affect all concerned Jews, but they are usually initiated by individual congregations *(takkanot hakehillot).*

K'LAL YISROEL

The Conservative movement focused attention on the concept of *K'lal Yisroel.* I accept Dr. Gordis' interpretation of the term as the consensus of the concerned. In a free society, agreement will be gradational. In regard to essentials there will be a consensus, while there will be ample room for variations in ideology and practice.

A new factor of uncertain character is likely to modify the impact of *K'lal Yisroel*—namely, the government of Israel. Its relation to matters of personal status is well-known. Orthodox pressure in regard to Sabbath observance is also a factor. But, social issues are even more significant, if we think of Halachah in its ethical dimensions. We have to take account of questions in the realm of political science that our predecessors could comfortably ignore. What is the ideal relation of the Jewish religion, its Aggadah and its Halachah, to the Jewish state? Is the citizen of such a state ipso facto a member of the Jewish people? Should such a state be structured in keeping with the laws of Torah, or the principles of Torah, or the concepts of liberal democracy, the *hokhmah* of our time? Will the equality of the *ger*, affirmed thirty-six times in the Torah, apply to all the non-Jews in a Jewish state? Is a Jewish state conceivable that is not democratic? Shall Israel follow the model of western democracies, separating religion from government, or the model of an "Islamic state," à la Ayatollah Khomeini?

Manifestly, the character of Halachah in Judaism will be powerfully affected by the extent of its involvement with the government of Israel. Laws of religion and of government are different in essence. To make governmental privileges dependent on the practice of religious rituals and on the *kashrut* of those who administer them is a horrendous requirement in a western society. We cannot tell how Israel will develop in the future. So much depends upon whether a large Arab minority, consisting of the residents of the West Bank and Gaza as well as Israel proper, is embraced within the boundaries of the state. With a non-Jewish minority of nearly 40%, a new constitution may evolve, definitely separating religion from government. Also, spiritual forces emerging from grass-roots Israeli life may well lead to an acceptance of religious pluralism.

Halachah as religious law can be perverted into secular law, but, ideally, the two domains must be kept apart. For secular law takes no account of intention or relegates it to the background, while, in religion, the demands of spirit and piety are all important. In any case, the import and orientation of the *K'lal Yisroel* ideal is certain to be affected by developments in Israel, which cannot now be foreseen.

The negative implication of *K'lal Yisroel* is the refusal to read out of Jewish life those who differ from the majority in their interpretation of Judaism. A blurring of the lines of ideology within the Jewish community is the inevitable consequence of such a policy. There may not even be complete consistency within the Conservative movement, because of the need to reconcile the imperatives of progress with reverence for unity.

A case in point is the enfranchisement of women within congregational life. The first step was to institute *Bat Mizvah* observances as part of the Sabbath services. The next step was to grant *aliyot* and other honors to women, and to count them as part of a *minyan*. Once these steps have been accepted by the overwhelming majority of Conservative congregations, others, such as the ordination of women, might well be in order.

The gradational pace of change is itself part of the Conservative approach. In our endeavor to be faithful to the whole of our tradition, we need to shun the broad decisiveness of the ideologues.

If the rise of Israel is bound to affect the course of Halachah by changing the objective circumstances of Jewish life in Israel and by adding a fresh and triumphant note to our *aggadot,* the ecumenical movement is also likely to introduce new patterns of Jewish-Christian-Moslem relations. Like the State of Israel, the interfaith movement, involving Judaism, was a delayed reaction to the Holocaust.

It is important to recognize that the Halachah in regard to non-Jews was frozen in the form that it assumed at Yavneh at the end of the first century. Some general principles were enunciated—such as the Noachide laws, in all their ambiguities, the recognition that not all Gentiles are worshippers of "strange gods," etc. But, the relevance and application of these laws to Christians and, later, to Moslems, was left undetermined and was vitiated by the demands of apologetics. The times were not suitable for a positive evaluation.

In our day, the interfaith movement has already resulted in the breaking down of barriers in the field of learning and teaching. The old prohibition of "teaching Torah to Gentiles" is no longer taken seriously. In the field of *gemilut ḥasadim* there is bound to be increasing cooperation. Joint religious services to celebrate great national events are becoming the norm, rather than the exception, in American public life. What shall be the governing principles of such interfaith activities?

Other issues in this field have already moved to the forefront of our agenda. Can we continue to close our eyes to intermarriages and refuse to participate in their sacralization? Can we refuse to acknowledge the Jewishness *in potentia* of the child of a Jewish father and a Christian mother?

Must we regard intermarriage always as a loss, instead of as a potential gain? If the living faith of liberal Christians is close to our "sacred tradition," where is the line to be drawn? Has the time come to revive the category of *yirai hashem,* the Fearers of the Lord, insofar as Christian spouses of Jews are concerned? What are the parameters of the obligation to welcome strangers into our religious fellowship in our day?

These and similar questions are bound to open up new areas for the different philosophies of Jewish law.

SUMMATION

In sum, Halachah is intimately related to the contemporary forms of wisdom and the unfolding vistas of personal and social ethics. Hence, our critical understanding of Bible and Talmud enters into our interpretation of the dynamics of Jewish law, as well as our philosophical conception of the nature of the divine thrust in history. Halachah must be responsive to the best ideals of every age. To be sure, "whatever *needs* not to be changed, needs *not* to be changed." Advances should be made with due regard to contemporary sensibilities, to the lessons of history and to the visions of the future. In our age, the emergence of the State of Israel and of the interfaith movement present fresh challenges to the making of Jewish law.

NOTES

1. B. T. *Makkot* 23b. In the name of R. Yishmoel, *Horayot* 8a.

2. Philo interprets "the image of God" in man to be the capacity for freedom.

3. Additional references in Ephraim E. Urbach's *Hazal* (Jerusalem, 1969), p. 29, note 1.

4. In this sense, the Midrash speaks of Torah as "the decayed fruit of the wisdom that is above" (*Genesis Rabbah* 17, 5, 44, 17).

PART EIGHT
JEWISH LAW AS STANDARDS

SELECTION AND PREFATORY
REMARKS
Elliot N. Dorff

GIVEN HIS TRADITIONAL talmudic training and extensive talmudic erudition, aligned with his sense that the halakah (Jewish law)
required some modification to be meaningful in our time, it is not
surprising that Rabbi Agus was an active participant in the discussion
over the development of a distinctively Conservative philosophy of
Jewish law. He officially joined the Conservative Rabbinical Assembly
in 1946 and was a member of its Committee on Jewish Law and
Standards from 1948 to 1986.

The following selection, chosen to accompany Elliot N. Dorff's essay
"Jewish Law as Standards" in *American Rabbi: The Life and Thought of
Jacob B. Agus* (New York, 1996), is drawn from Jacob B. Agus' *Guide-
posts in Modern Judaism* (New York, 1954), 85–137.

23

THE CONSERVATIVE
MOVEMENT

In point of organization and the official crystallization of ideology, the Conservative group is the most recent alignment on the American scene. While the Jewish Theological Seminary, the focal point of the movement, was first organized in 1887, largely as a protest against the adoption of the Pittsburgh Platform, the institution virtually ceased to function following the death of its founder and first president, Sabato Morais. Later, as the massive tide of immigration from Central and Eastern Europe brought into being a large, inchoate Jewish population that was not yet integrated into the pattern of American culture, the social gulf between the Reform and Orthodox communities became wide and all but impassable. In order to assist the East-European Jews to achieve their own synthesis of tradition and modernism, a group of public-spirited citizens, headed by Jacob H. Schiff, invited in the year 1902 Prof. Solomon Schechter from England to reorganize the Seminary and to build around it an association of traditional synagogues. In fifty years, the movement has come to embrace some 450 rabbis and 500 synagogues, as well as an impressive number of central institutions.

In Western Europe, the Conservative or moderately Reform interpretation of Judaism had achieved predominance by the end of the nineteenth century. Outside of England, the leading congregations and communities of Germany, Austria and France were Conservative, with the Leipsig and Augsburg synods of 1869 and 1870, respectively, striving consciously for the attainment of "the golden mean."[1] The Seminary in Breslau, under the leadership of Zechariah Frankel, provided the greatest number of rabbis for the synagogues of the German "culture-sphere," which included the cities of Hungary and the Scandinavian countries.

However, the graduates of this Conservative school did not band together, upon their arrival in the United States, to foster their philosophy and program on a national scale. For many years modern traditionalist rabbis like Jastrow, Szold and Kohut attempted to find a common working basis with the determined leaders of American Reform. Only slowly and reluctantly were the ways of the Conservative and Reform wings of American Jewry parted, with the consequent emergence of the United Synagogue and the Rabbinical Assembly as the organs of a new party. Motivated by a deep attachment to the total community of Israel, the Conservative group was therefore projected upon the American scene as a distinct movement virtually against the will of its founders and leaders, who sought to heal the wounds of sectarianism and to serve the entire body of Israel. It was the hope and conviction of Prof. Schechter that the United Synagogue would become the central rallying point of American Jewry, lending to the Orthodox masses the polish of "culture" and bringing the errant Reformers back to the community, in "unison and peace." At the founding convention of the United Synagogue, he declared:

"Indeed, what we intend to accomplish is not to create a new party, but to consolidate an old one, which has always existed in this country, but was never conscious of its own strength, nor perhaps realized the need of organization. I refer to the large number of Jews who, thoroughly American in habits of life and modes of thinking and, in many cases, imbued with the best culture of the day, have always maintained conservative principles and remained aloof from the Reform movement which swept over the country. They are sometimes stigmatized as the Neo-Orthodox. This is not correct. Their Orthodoxy is not new. . . . A better knowledge of Jewish history would have taught them that culture combined with religion was the rule with the Jew. . . . The 'new' Orthodoxy represents therefore very little that is new. It was the normal state of the Jew in Spain. . . ."[2]

In his loving estimate of Jewish tradition, Dr. Schechter assumed that the momentum of the fundamentalist trend was in his day completely spent and that a liberal interpretation of Judaism could confidently expect to inherit the mantle of Orthodoxy. All that the Orthodox masses lacked was "culture," and, in their progressive adoption of American ways and patterns of thought, they could be expected to retain "reverence for the Bible as the word of God" and "love for the institutions and memories of the past." Conscious that he represented the healthy mainstream of tradition, Dr. Schechter rejected even the designation "neo-Orthodoxy" as being too suggestive of innovations.

However, the logic of events brought the Conservative movement into being as an identifiable group consciously formulating its own standards of piety, and rendered hollow and meaningless any residual endeavor to pretend otherwise. Today, Conservative synagogues are easily recognized by one or more of the following practices:

With rare exceptions, the women's gallery is abolished and families worship together. Worshippers wear the "tallith" at their morning prayers and "t'fillin" at the daily weekday services. The congregations sponsor an intensive program of Hebrew education and employ either the Orthodox prayerbook or the one of the United Synagogue. The main changes in the United Synagogue Prayer-Book consist in the elimination of a petition for the renewal of the sacrificial system. The prayers of the Mussaph services are retained but the tense is changed so that it becomes a recitation of what our ancestors did in the past. The translation of "m'hayeh hamaisim," is so phrased as to suggest God's creative power, not to teach the dogma of the resuscitation of the dead.

Prayers in English are included in the services. Many synagogues employ the organ to aid the cantor and choir, but the cantillation is in the musical tradition of the synagogue. Worshippers sit with covered heads. With the exception of one synagogue, two days of every festival are observed, and all synagogues celebrate the two days of Rosh Hashono. All boys are prepared for the Bar Mitzvah ceremony; the Bas Mitzvah ceremony for girls is rapidly becoming a standard procedure, while the ceremony of Confirmation is also included in the total educational program. The dietary laws are observed in all public functions of the synagogue. The approved pattern of Sabbath observance for Conservative laymen includes permission to ride to the synagogue on the Sabbath, emphasizes the practices making for the hallowing of the day and distinguishes clearly between avoidable and unavoidable types of work. As of the present, Conservative rabbis do not perform marriages for divorcees without a Jewish bill of divorcement ("get"); by a decision of the Committee on Jewish Laws and Standards a descendant of a priestly family (Kohen) is permitted to marry a divorcee or a convert.

TRENDS WITHIN THE MOVEMENT

In the past decade, thoughtful observers were frequently more impressed with the divisions inside the Conservative movement than with the overall character and ideology of the United Synagogue. It was commonly assumed that the "right wing" of Conservatism shaded off into liberal Orthodoxy, that the "left wing" represented a blend of Reform with nationalism and that the "center" consisted of the steadily diminishing company of the hesitating and the unconvinced. Actually, the past generation has witnessed the steady rise of the "center" group within the movement, leading to the evolution of a vigorous and scholarly interpretation of Judaism that bids fair to set the dominant pattern for the future.

Occupying the middle position between Orthodoxy and Reform, Conservatism may be understood either as a critique of the former or as a protest against the latter trend. Historically, the Conservative movement has arisen both in America and in Europe by way of secession from the camp of radical Reform. But, the congregations which constitute at present the United Synagogue had come into the Conservative camp from the ranks of Orthodoxy. The full implications of the movement have not yet been revealed. However, it is already clear that it contains vital ideas which lend it coherence, relate it to the noblest trends of thought in the past and open it to the influence of the best minds of the present. While these ideas are not stressed in equal degree by all Conservative rabbis, they do constitute a consensus of basic convictions that is more significant than the variety of emphases among the marginal adherents of the movement.

REPUDIATION OF THE LITERALISTIC CONCEPTION OF REVELATION

Along with Reform, the Conservative movement does not teach that every word in the Torah and every statement of the Oral Law were literally pronounced by the Deity. The naive picture of revelation as consisting of the "Lord dictating and Moses transcribing" is taken to be no more than a symbolic representation of the process of Divine inspiration, that is itself beyond the power of human comprehension. "The Torah speaks in the language of men," as the rabbis put it, and, as our understanding deepens, we must learn to disentangle the human, the conditioned and the temporary elements from the Divine, the absolute and eternal truths. We cannot ever draw the line with either certainty or finality, but we must envisage this line as best we can, in our endeavors to meet the challenge of changing circumstances. To the Conservatives, then, the Torah *contains* the Word of God, especially when it is understood by way of a total self-identification with the historic experience of Israel, but the detailed precepts, phrases and words of the Holy Scriptures are not all, in their bare literalness, the word of God.

On the other hand, the Conservative view differs from the Reform position, as stated in the Pittsburgh Platform, which considered only the moral law as "binding." Jewish tradition, in its entirety, including the Halachah, or the system of precepts and laws, is a steadily unfolding body of revelation which is never wholly free from the manifold limitations of the human mind nor at any time entirely bare of the Divine spark of inspiration. The legalism of the rabbis was not a corruption of prophetic idealism but an inspired, collective endeavor to translate it into the realities of life.

The source of Divine teaching is our sacred tradition in its *entirety,* including the ideas of our philosophical literature and even those of deviationist trends. The greatness of Jewish tradition consists precisely in its richness, variety and hospitality to differing views, permitting various doctrines and practices to recede into the background, as other principles and laws move into the center of attention. Reverence for tradition in its totality, precludes both the revolutionary mood and the piety of naive literalism and legalism, encouraging both the process of continuous reevaluation of the past in the light of the present and the judgment of the present in the light of the past.

There is, of course, ample precedent for this insistence that the Word of God is not simply the written letter of the Torah, but that it consists in the synthesis of the letter with the living spirit of interpretation, which issues out of the best scientific and philosophic knowledge of every age. Masters of the "Mishnah," like Rabbi Joshua ben Hananyah, derived this principle from the verse, "it is not in heaven," and, in the Middle Ages, philosophical Judaism took this principle for granted all through its triumphant advance. Yet, the implications of a non-literal doctrine of revelation are more significant in our day because of the development of the scientific method in the study of history, especially the rise of biblical criticism.

For several decades, the Conservative movement shied away from the scientific study of the Holy Scriptures, principally because the science of "higher criticism," as it was developed in Germany by scholars who were keenly conscious of their "Aryan" supremacy, was largely vitiated by a kind of "higher antisemitism," as Schechter aptly phrased it. Nevertheless, it was Profesor Schechter's first ambition, upon his arrival in the United States, to promote the scientific study of Scriptures by Jewish scholars, utilizing the rich treasures of our own commentaries as well as the discoveries and views of modern research and archeology.[3] Rooted deeply in the soil of tradition, Conservative scholars have brought to the study of Scriptures a kind of sympathetic understanding of the genius of the Bible that was sadly lacking in previous years. The massive labors of Y'heskel Kaufman, which served to demonstrate the fundamental errors of radical criticism and the essential monotheism of the Jewish faith, in its earliest beginnings, are appreciated and taken up in the Conservative outlook. Thus, for example, Rabbi Solomon Goldman, in his introduction to the Bible, takes account of the massive achievements of modern research; reviews the general field of biblical criticism and the particular question of the authorship of the Book of Genesis; arrives at the conclusion that "the critics have overreached themselves," that "the religion of the Patriarchs was monotheistic," and that Moses was probably the author, editor and compiler of the documents that constitute the first book of the Bible.[4]

The authority of Holy Scriptures for our day is twofold in origin — the truth of its central philosophy of monotheism and the interpretation that it enshrines of the enduring bent of mind of the Jewish people. Monotheism is not so much a series of intellectual propositions, as the nineteenth-century Reformers thought, but a fundamental attitude of the soul, which is validated by human experience generally. For us as Jews, monotheism is, in addition, the soul of our historic heritage and the substance of our collective experience. It is through our complete identification with the life of our people, in the tragic travail of the past as in the living aspirations of the present, that we come to experience the vibrant reality of the monotheistic way of life. Judaism is not only philosophy; it is also a complex of psychic attitudes, a structure of loyalties and sentiments and a pattern of living.

In the Conservative view, the historic unity of God (metaphysical ideas), Torah (the detailed precepts governing the life of the individual) and Israel (the consciousness of ethnic unity and oneness of destiny), has been disturbed by the Reformers in their overemphasis on philosophical abstractions and by the Orthodox in their exclusive concentration on the precepts of the Torah. The impetus of Conservative thought is definitely in the direction of the re-creation of the original tri-partite unity, recognizing in the living people of Israel the synthesizing agent between the testimony of revealed tradition and the growing light of contemporary thought.

In its refusal to cut Judaism to a preconceived pattern of what a "religion" should be like and in its determination not to regard Judaism as a "finished," unchanging set of dogmas and deeds, Conservatism sees "the word of God" as a living stream of tradition and aspiration, rather than as a fixed pattern, or formula, or book, or collection of books.

Conservative scholarship finds ample support for this view in the historical analysis of the evolution of Judaism. As a foremost historian of our time put it:

"Neo-Orthodoxy, equally with Reform, is a deviation from historical Judaism. No less than Reform, it abandoned Judaism's self-rejuvenating historical dynamism. . . . It is Conservative Judaism which seems to show the greatest similarities with the method and substance of teaching of the popular leaders during the declining Second Commonwealth, inasmuch as clinging to the traditional mode of life, it nevertheless allows for the adaptation of basic theological concepts to the changing social and environmental needs."[5]

THE "POSITIVE-HISTORICAL" VIEWPOINT

It was in the name of the "positive-historical" approach to the problems of Jewish theology that Zechariah Frankel, founder of the Conservative movement, seceded from the Frankfort Conference of Reform Rabbis in the year 1845. The issue in question was whether the use of Hebrew in the service was only "advisable," as the Conference contended, or whether it was absolutely essential.[6] Trivial as this issue might appear to us today, it reflected the fundamental divergence that was to eventuate into the Conservative protest against the unhistorical rationalism of Reform. On any rational basis, worshippers should pray in the language they know best, and the law of the Mishnah concurs in this proposition. But, in prayer, the individual must learn to merge his identity with that of the collective body of Israel, and the Hebrew language is the effective medium whereby the individual Jew is made to feel the unity, continuity and distinctiveness of Israel as the people of revelation. Insistence upon Hebrew as "essential" for Jewish worship was, therefore, in effect tantamount to the negation of the basic Reform principle, that religion was strictly a relationship between the individual and God.

Essentially, the awkward phrase, "positive-historical," implies, in the first place, an attitude of humility toward the great achievements of the past. In every age, it is well for man to remember that his ideals and judgments, self-evident as they may appear to him, might only be partial facets of the infinite mystery of reality, the inadequacy of which will be as obvious to future generations as are the certainties and absolutes of past generations to us. It is good to embrace "the spirit of the age" in wholehearted devotion, but our enthusiasm must be tempered by the realization that the "weltanschauung" of our generation, as of all preceding epochs, is after all only a limited and partial view of that which can never wholly be known. Indeed, this fundamental humility is one of the essential functions of religion, in that it provides a perpetual counterbalance to the pride of reason and the inevitable acquisition of blind spots that accompanies the reception of every new vista.

In the nineteenth century, the feeling was widespread that humanity was standing on the final plateau of history, so that all the relative insights of the past were ready to be gathered up in the blaze of the final self-revelation of the Absolute Mind. We have seen how this conviction operated within the Reform movement in the uncritical adoration of "the spirit of the age." Frankel's insistence on "the positive-historical" approach was in effect a call to see the present in the light of the past and to recognize the limitations of our most cherished convictions. In the same spirit, Schechter declared that Judaism would never have survived if Jewish people had been ready to accept any apparent contemporary fad or trend as the final "verdict of history," as Geiger did when he wrote:

"History has given her judgment (against the Hebrew language) even though this judgment is not yet carried out, and all lamentations against this condition of things are useless. No protest is justified against the forces of history."[7]

In the second place, the term "positive-historical" implies an attitude of reverence toward the *processes* whereby changes are effected in the religious life of a people. Frankel, Zunz and Schechter were fundamentally historians. They were not averse to any change in the pattern of worship or the regimen of prescribed rituals, provided that change was brought about organically, naturally, smoothly, as a development of cumulative historical forces, not as an artificial fiat of a few men. As a living tradition, Judaism can and must continue to grow in accord with its inner genius, but it must not be tailored to suit abstract geometric patterns, which may be theoretically more systematic and rational.

Continuing this line of reasoning, the Conservatives generally favor that interpretation of the Law which allows the living authorities of each age ample scope to enact such amendments as are needed for the "strengthening of the faith" ("hizuk hadath"). The chief target of their criticism of Orthodoxy is its tendency to reduce the authority of contemporary rabbis and courts to the vanishing point, so that the domain of law and life are hopelessly separated. As Prof. Schechter first phrased this criticism in a review of Weiss' study of the evolution of the Jewish tradition:

"What Weiss really objects to is a *weak* authority—I mean that phonograph-like authority which is always busy in reproducing the voice of others without an opinion of its own, without originality, without initiative and discretion. The real authorities are those who, drawing their inspiration from the past, also understand how to reconcile us with the present and to prepare us for the future."[8]

In brief, then, the Conservatives favored the vitalization of tradition by strengthening the authority of contemporary rabbis rather than the abandonment of tradition in favor of a rationally reconstructed faith.

In part at least, this debate reflected the issue between the European liberals and conservatives in the general field of public law. Are laws made in accordance with an abstract system of ethics, or must they be allowed to develop in keeping with their own inherent impetus? The liberals of European politics argued in behalf of systematic legislation based upon the implications of "the rights of man," while the conservatives maintained that freedom must be allowed to broaden slowly, "from precedent to precedent." Applying the conservative argument to the problems of Judaism, Frankel and later Schechter maintained that the law must issue out of the life of the people, reflecting their sentiments and channeling their aspirations. While the Reformers conceived of religion largely as a set of abstract truths and consequently assigned to the religious leaders of every age the task of formulating and crystalliz-ing the ideology and program of Judaism, the Conservatives regarded faith as a complex structure of sentiments, loyalties and ideals, shared by all the people and therefore to be molded by the people.[9]

In this "positive-historical" view, Judaism is continuously being mod-ified by the changing habits of the people and by the process of inter-pretation of Jewish law, which, too, is not meant to be abstract and self-contained, but pragmatic and life-centered. Conservative scholars like Prof. Louis Ginsburg, Louis Finkelstein, Hayim Chernowitz and Saul Lieberman demonstrated in a massive series of researches how the Law reflected the changing needs and aspirations of the people in the varying strata of its gradual formation. Thus, the Conservatives accept the entire structure of Jewish law as valid for our time, save insofar as it was modified by the practice of the people, insisting, however, that the Law arose as a human response to a Divine call and that it continue to be developed in such a manner as to respond to the deepest spiritual needs of our time.

As to the application of this principle, the Conservative movement has been slow and fumbling. Only in recent years has the attempt been made to systematize, clarify and apply in practice the implications of the Conservative interpretation of Jewish law.

THE NATIONALISTIC MOTIF

Even before the rise of modern Zionism, the Conservative movement was motivated by a deep love for the living people of Israel, in all its peculiarities, foibles and loyalties. While the Reformers sought to elimi-nate all traces of nationalism from the prayer-book, the Conservatives insisted on the indispensability of Hebrew and on the need of retaining the ideal of rebuilding the historic homeland. As Mannheimer, the leader of Austrian Conservatism, put it: "I am one of those who do not rationalize the Messianic belief; I believe in and defend the national interpretation of this dogma and hope for a national restoration. . . ."[10]

In the Conservative view, the very existence and life of the Jewish people was a supreme religious ideal, for they could not envisage the

Jewish faith as being separated even in theory from the people that projected it upon the stage of history. Bitterly repudiating the anti-nationalism of the Reformers, Schechter wrote that they (especially Geiger) "saw in Israel a religious corporation, a sort of non-celibate monks, whose *raison d'être* was not in themselves, but outside of them. . . .

"We would have been spared all the terrible persecutions if we could ever have agreed to eliminate from it the national features and become a mere religious sect."[11]

"It was just those things which distinguished us from our surroundings and separated us from the nations, such as devotion to the Pentateuch, the keeping of the Sabbath, the observance of the covenant of Abraham, and the loyalty to the dietary laws, to which we clung for thousands of years with all our life and for which we brought numberless sacrifices. Is this now the time, when the thought of nationalism is universally accepted, to destroy it as far as Israel is concerned?"[12]

If the inspiration of Reform was the bold rationalism of a Maimonides, the guiding light of Conservatism was Halevi, who taught that Judaism was the living tradition of a Divinely chosen and uniquely endowed people. Taken collectively, Jewry was a people of prophets, and anything that redounded to the benefit of the physical wellbeing of the people strengthened the foundation of the true faith. This organic unity of the particular people with the universal faith was articulated in the accents of contemporary thought by men like Samuel David Luzzato, who saw the Jewish spirit as being arrayed against the secular spirit of Hellenism or "Atticism," as he put it, in all epochs and in every phase of culture, and Nahman Krochmal, who interpreted the entire sweep of Jewish history in terms of the unbreakable bond between the people Israel and the Absolute Idea of God.

Of particular importance in later years were the ideas of Ahad Ha'am, who saw the genesis of every ideal in the "will to live" of the people and in the progressive unfolding of its national soul. It was the unique bent of the Jewish mind to seek to order all phases of life in accord with "absolute justice." This "Torah of the heart" is the genuine dynamic and enduring impetus of Judaism; all else is temporary, peripheral and expendable. Thus, it is possible to identify oneself with Jewish life for the sake of spiritual self-fulfillment, even if one does not accept the idea of God and does not observe any phase of the ceremonial pattern of the Jewish faith. In an age when intellectuals hesitated to express belief in

God, Ahad Ha'am's ideas functioned as powerful centripetal forces for the Jewish community, directing attention to the cultural and spiritual content of the Jewish faith and stimulating a broad loyalty to the total complex of Jewish values. And it was within the hospitable compass of the Conservative movement that the seeds of Ahad Ha'amism found their most fertile soil.

THE MOTIF OF ANTI-SECTARIANISM

Allied to the national ideal is the resolve to build bridges of understanding between the varied and contradictory interpretations of the Jewish faith, so as to retain the vision of the all-embracing unity of a common tradition. Thus, secular Zionism was so enthusiastically welcomed by Conservative Jews as to erase the lines of demarcation between them, though, of course, it represented only one phase of the tradition. To the believer in the motto, "nothing that is Jewish is alien to me," every creative expression of Jewish life, one-sided and unbalanced as it may be, is still part of the total organic complex that is Judaism. In particular, the Conservative group was cast in the role of the mediator and interpreted between the Orthodox and Reform conceptions of Judaism. Rabbi Moshe Sofer and Rabbi Malbim were the implacable opponents of Geiger, Holdheim and Zunz, but to the Conservatives, both sets of leaders belonged to the one tradition that they sought to make meaningful for their day and age. While the Reformers concentrated their loving attention upon the *essence* of Judaism, the Conservatives sought to take account of the *totality* of the tradition, with the understanding that varying phases of the tradition might leap into the focus of significance at different times, while other phases temporarily move into the background. Thus Prof. Schechter wrote:

"In other words, is it not time that the new theology should consist in the best that all the men of Israel, including Geiger, gave us, but should modify and qualify his views, dating from a rationalistic age, by the loyalty to the law of Rabbi Akiba Eger and Rabbi Mordecai Baneth, by the deep insight into Jewish history of a Zunz and a Krochmal, by the mysticism of a Baal Shem and some of his best followers, and by the love of Israel's nationality and its perpetuation of Herzl or Ahad Ha'am?" [13]

In this quotation, the argument is pointed against the Reformers, but it was directed with equal logic against the Orthodox, who reduced all of Jewish life to Torah, condensed all of Torah into the "four ells of Halachah," and all of the historically varying trends within Halachah into the rigid molds of the "Shulhan Aruch." In opposition to the steadily narrowing spiral of the "faithful" by Orthodox standards, the Conservatives stress the fullness of the historic tradition, which included reverence for all that is genuinely Jewish and all that the cumulative knowledge of the age acknowledges to be true. The precepts of the Halachah were not to be viewed in isolation, but against the historic background from which they emerged and in the light of the total tradition which they expressed. A century of Jewish scholarship has demonstrated the responsiveness of the law and its official interpretation to the exigencies of life and the requirements of the contemporary spiritual climate. Thus, the validity of Halachah is reaffirmed, but only as one of the factors of the rich and varied tradition of Israel.

And within the tradition, the source of authority is shifted from the written word to the living people, in all its confusion, variety and uncertainty. What is lost in definition and clearness is gained in vitality, relevance and comprehensiveness.

"Since then the interpretation of Scripture or the Secondary Meaning is mainly a product of changing historical influences, it follows that the center of authority is actually removed from the Bible and placed in some *living body* which, by reason of its being in touch with the ideal aspirations and the religious needs of the age, is best able to determine the nature of the Secondary Meaning. This living body, however, is not represented by any section of the nation, or any corporate priesthood, or Rabbihood, but by the collective conscience of Catholic Israel as embodied in the Universal Synagogue."[14]

THE "HIGH SYNAGOGUE" MOTIF

An enduring emphasis in Conservatism is the high estimate of the importance of rituals and time-honored symbols in religious life. While Geiger maintained that, with the advance of culture, symbols become unnecessary, the Conservative movement in Europe and America insisted that religion was a total involvement of the soul and that its symbols and rites are directed to the vast reaches of the unconscious and the irrational. The massive researches into the psychology of religious consciousness that were conducted under the inspiration of William James, McDougall and the Freudians confirmed the truth of the ancient insights, that symbols of action are of incalculable value in the economy of spiritual life. After a century and a half of unidirectional rationalism, the modern world was reminded that the human personality was rational on the surface only and that symbols of word and deed frequently reached the depths that concepts could only point to. This realization was included in the ideology of American Conservatism, which was taking shape even as students of religion turned their attention from logic and metaphysics to depth-psychology and social anthropology.[15]

Thus, in Conservatism, the prevailing tendency is not to abolish ceremonial practices, but as far as possible, to revitalize them and even to create new ritualistic channels for the articulation of religious feeling. Worship with covered heads and in "tallith" and "t'fillin," the Dietary laws and the distinctive rites of each festival are cherished. The Consecration ceremony for children entering the Hebrew School and the Bas Mitzvah observance, as well as the practice of blessing children on the Sabbath nearest their birthdays, are instances of the search for new vehicles of religious expression. The emphasis on the principle of creativity is particularly strong in the Reconstructionist version of the Conservative philosophy, which will be discussed presently.

THE FACTOR OF NEO-MYSTICISM

A renewed appreciation of the mystical element of religious experience is a potent factor in the formation of the Conservative ideology. While in the early days of Reform, the doctrines of Kabbalah and the institution of Hassidism were derided as monstrous aberrations, the twentieth century saw the rise of a neo-Hassidic movement which glorified the romantic and mystical trends in Jewish tradition. The works of Martin Buber, I. L. Peretz and Sh. Horodetzky exhibited the genuine beauty of mystical piety and its deep roots in the indigenous culture of the East-European Jews.

Thus, Prof. Schechter pleaded for the infusion of the mystical piety of the Baal Shem Tov into the life of the modern Jew.[16] Repeatedly he exposed the dry and narrow approach of the rationalistic Reformers.

"Rationalism could well appreciate all the virtues of manliness, but it could never value properly those qualities of obedience, submissiveness, meekness and self-denial which constitute a holy life."[17]

The impact of mysticism is partially antinomian, since attention is directed away from legalistic correctness and toward the travail of the spirit. To mystics the observance of any law is not as important as the spirit in which it is observed. For this reason, the Lithuanian "mithnagdim," in their zealous passion for the Law, feared and fought the mass-movement of Hassidism. But, the enduring pressure of mysticism is in the direction of a progressive intensification of loyalty to ancient practices and even in behalf of the proliferation of new customs and practices. It is in conformity to the established rituals and ceremonies that the mystical personality finds refuge from the blinding radiance of ecstatic piety, a powerful bond with the religion of the masses and a persistent protest against the pride of reason. While both rationalism and mysticism seek the spirit behind the Law, the former expects the ceremony to speak to the worshipper whereas the latter expects the worshipper to speak through the ceremony. Thus, at the various Reform conferences, the rituals which are not connected "directly and naturally" with some worthy spiritual purpose were declared to be no longer valid. In contrast, the Conservative movement follows the guiding principle of Franz Rosenzweig, who, in a famous letter to a group of disciples, declared that it is not the objective character of the ceremony that is decisive, but the question whether or not we today can still bring ourselves to say through the rite or symbol, "Praised art Thou, O Lord, our God."[18]

"Practice precedes theory for us," he wrote, "whereas, with the Reform movement, the contrary was true."[19] In the beginning is the act of commitment to the Jewish faith and destiny—an act which is more volitional than rational, and for which virtually any rite may serve if it is part of the divinely designed synthesis of Torah and Israel. "Your Hassid too did not begin with Kavanah (intention). That will come one day, of course. But, to desire to begin with it, as people tell us we must, is entirely un-Jewish."

To Rosenzweig, God is the creative principle of love, subsisting behind the universe. Flashes of His love interpenetrate the cosmic process from time to time, setting into motion the current of redemption which will one day sweep mankind up to the blessed peaks of the Kingdom of God. It is of the nature of love to be selective. Hence, the recipients of the Divine ray of love inevitably feel themselves to be "chosen." The Jewish people was thus "chosen" by God, in a concrete and historical fashion, insofar as its collective consciousness is illuminated by this central religious experience of its prophets and saints. The individual Jew shares in this transforming experience if he surrenders his individual identity to the collective consciousness of his people, willing, feeling and thinking of himself only as a cell in the organism of the nation. Since Israel is fashioned as a community by the Torah, especially the Divine Law, obedience to the Law is an automatic articulation of the sense of belonging to the Jewish community. Only those who belong can enjoy the feeling of being the object of Divine love and of being part of the "chosen" people.

Thus, while Rosenzweig placed the living people in the focus of attention, rather than the letter of the Law, he insisted that the worshipper must make every effort to address God through the approved channels of Halachah, discarding only the rites which have lost altogether the power to stir the religious consciousness. "I should not dare to declare any law as human, because it has not yet been permitted to me to say through it in proper fashion, 'praised art Thou.' " At the same time, he declared, "Judaism is not Law. It creates Law, but is not it, it is to be a Jew." [20]

It is through the symbols of action that the worshipper comes to feel, not as a disembodied "man in general," but as an integral part of the living body of Israel, that was made eternal by the Word of God. "People understand differently when they understand in doing. Every day in the year, Bileam's speaking ass may be a legend to me; on the Sabbath Balaak, when it speaks to me out of the uplifted Torah, it is not." [21]

While Martin Buber is wary of all organized forms of religious expression, especially of all rituals, the impact of his philosophy is felt in a growing reverence for the mystical trends in Jewish thought, especially Hassidism. The early writings of Buber dealt with the nature of the inherent genius of Jewish thought. As the leading exponent of "spiritual Zionism" in Western Europe, Buber sought to define the character of the Jewish elan, which he envisaged as a subterranean stream of consciousness, finding expression at various epochs in the emergence of mighty cultural and religious movements. The creative impulse of the Jewish people, he maintained, was not to be sought in the ideas and norms of Judaism, that are assembled in the Talmud, but in the unconscious drives that come to the surface in folk-piety, on the one hand, and in the prophetic-mystical experience of saints, on the other hand. The national "soul" of Israel is like a restless, surging stream, and the dogmas and rituals of official Judaism are the rocks and boulders thrown off by the raging waters.

Buber agreed with Ahad Ha'am in maintaining the thesis that the underlying genius of the Jewish national soul, the "Torah of the heart," must be distinguished from the dogmatic structure of the Jewish faith. But, while "Ahad Ha'am" regarded the pure doctrines of absolutist ethics as constituting the enduring substance of the Jewish way of life, Buber insisted that the "inner Torah" was no rational ideology of any kind, but an intuitive grasp of the nature of man's relation to the Supreme Being. The Jew of history, especially as he appears in the Holy Scriptures, interpreted the travail of human destiny in terms which derived from this intuitive vision. However, the vision itself cannot ever be fully concretized in man-made schemes. Hence, the successive rise and fall of mystical movements in Jewish life, each endeavoring to renew and recapture the dynamic substance of faith, which consists in a direct confrontation of the human soul with the Living God.

Buber's contribution to the contemporary ferment of ideas consists of three fundamental ideas, which he has elaborated in a great number of books:

(a) The national soul of Israel is the fundamental reality in the spiritual life of all Jews. The artist and the writer become creative, only when they permit the unconscious spirit within them to operate freely. And the unconscious spirit of the individual is at bottom merely an expression of the Great Unconscious spirit of the nation. Hence, it is as a son of one's people, and only as such, that any individual can address himself meaningfully to humanity.

"Now, the folk is to him (the individual) a community of people who were, are and will be a community of dead, living and those yet unborn, who together constitute a unity; and this is his "I" which is but a necessary link eternally determined to occupy a definite place in this great chain. What all the people in this great chain have created and will create, that he feels to be the work of his own inner life; what they have experienced and will experience, that he perceives to be his own inner fate." [22]

The individual Jew is so constituted that he is inevitably sensitive to all contradictions and imperfections of society. Hence, he is always in search of the "Kingdom of God." But, the meaning of his restless striving cannot become clear for him unless he learns to understand himself as a Jew, "for only the one truly bound to his people can answer with his whole being." [23]

To discover his own true being, the Jew must learn to embrace in mind and heart the entire history of his people.

"All religious creation, all genuine personal religion is a discovery and a taking up of an ancient treasure, a development and a liberation of the grown subterranean religion." [24]

(b) In the Hassidic movement of eighteenth century Poland, Buber finds a modern expression of this "subterranean" religion. While Buber does not accept the dogmatic substructure of Hassidic piety, he calls attention to the pattern of living which arose spontaneously among the untutored, poverty-stricken masses of southern Poland, reflecting the Jewish yearning for God's sovereignty.

In his numerous works on the subject of Hassidism, he stresses especially the following points:

(1) The hassid is perpetually ready for the appearance of God's redemptive power. Hence, his childlike naivete and his eagerness to believe the miracles of the saints. Hence, too, the awakening of the myth-building faculty among the masses. As Plato discovered long ago, it is only through myths that the paradoxical nature of reality may be grasped.

(2) The hassid is taught to worship God in rapture and ardor, and the "tzaddik" attains high levels of ecstasy in his worship. Thus, God is found by the dark and mysterious paths of feeling, not on the prosaic highway of reason.

(3) The hassid achieves unity in his own personality. He is not engaged in an endless struggle against his own lower nature. But, body and soul are joined together in joyous adoration of God.

(4) The hassid is not other-worldly. He is taught to concentrate his efforts upon the achievement of the good life here on earth, especially by way of "deeds of loving kindness." Nor is he expected to confine himself to the well-trodden pathways of ritual piety. The hassid was bidden to discover fresh ways of expressing his religious feeling.

(5) The hassidic community, in which the "tzaddik" forms the living center, is an illustration of the warm fellow-feeling of a society based upon a common religious experience. It is through the confrontation by his soul of the Supreme Being that man attains a generosity of spirit which makes possible his wholehearted entrance into the intimacies of a genuine, organic community.

(c) Man confronts God as a "person" and enters into a dialogue with Him. In saying "Thou" to God, man discovers his own "I," as a responsible self, a partner of the Lord in the creation of the good society. Buber has described the "I-Thou" dialogue-relationship in so thorough and brilliant a manner that no student of modern thought can afford to ignore it.

Following are the essential points in his presentation:

(1) The "I-Thou" relation is basically different from the attitude that we assume toward things, which he designates as the "I-it" relation. In dealing with things, we live in a world where we ourselves constitute the center. But, in facing a person, we enter a new dimension of existence, where the relation subsisting between the persons involved becomes itself the fiery core of reality.

"If I face a human being as my *Thou,* and say the primary word *I-Thou* to him, he is not a thing among things, and does not consist of things. . . . But, with no neighbor, and whole in himself, he is *Thou* and fills the heavens. This does not mean that nothing exists except himself. But, all else lives in his light." [25]

(2) Though we address human persons as "Thou," we feel that our perception of their personality extends beyond the appearance that confronts us. There is the radiance of infinity about the "Thou" relation, so that we glimpse the Supreme Personality looming behind those who evoke the word "Thou" from us, in all its depth and pathos. "In each *Thou,* we address the eternal Thou." [26]

(3) The "I-Thou" relation is wholly quality, not quantity, entirely in the present, not in the space-time world. Thus, it comes as an augury of a domain of existence that is different from the space-time world which we are inclined to regard as the whole of being. It is the key to reality.

(4) Love is the apex of the "I-Thou" relation.

"Love is the responsibility of an 'I' for a 'Thou.' In this lies the likeness—impossible in any feeling whatsoever—of all who love, from the smallest to the greatest and from the blessedly protected man, whose life is rounded in that of a loved being, to him who is all his life nailed to the cross of the world, and who ventures to bring himself to the dreadful point—to love *all men.*" [27]

(5) It is through our readiness to love all men and all things and to address them in word and deed as "Thou," that we find God

in the world. For God is the eternal Thou. "Men do not find God if they stay in the world. They do not find Him if they leave the world. He who goes out with his whole being to meet his *Thou* and carries it to all being that is in the world, finds Him who cannot be sought.

"If you explore the life of things and of conditioned being you come to the unfathomable, if you deny the life of things and of conditioned being you stand before nothingness, if you hallow this life you meet the living God."[28]

(6) Buber repudiates the goals of so many mystics—that of union with the Divine Being or that of absorption into the Divine Abyss. To him, the ecstatic apex of the "Thou" relation is still a relation between two beings, and there is no loss of personality. At this point, Buber parts company—and very distinctly—with the vast majority of mystics in Christianity and in the Hindu world.

(7) The dialogue-relation implies a mutual need on the part of both man and God.

"You know always in your heart that you need God more than everything; but do you not know too that God needs you—in the fullness of His eternity, needs you?"[29]

(8) The "I-Thou" relation is double faceted—addressed to man, it points to God; addressed to God, it points to man.

"Meeting with God does not come to man in order that he may concern himself with God, but in order that he may confirm that there is meaning in the world."[30]

In sum, Buber's philosophy is a lengthy homily on the meaning of human and Divine love. The full import of his message is only now beginning to be felt in America.

Prof. Abraham J. Heschel is the exponent of neo-mysticism on the American scene. A member of the faculty of the Jewish Theological Seminary, he is a scholarly and brilliant defender of a non-dogmatic type of Hassidism. Holiness is, to him, a dimension of existence, of which all men are aware, in gradations varying from the sense of wonder and bafflement of the average person to the overwhelming, lightning-like tremors of the saint in the blessed moments of ecstasy. Hence, piety is not a subjective attitude, but a "response" to the Divine call.

"What gives rise to faith is not a sentiment, a state of mind, an aspiration, but an everlasting fact in the universe, something which is prior to and independent of human knowledge—*the holy dimension* of all existence." [31]

God needs man even as man needs God, and in obedience to the Divine Law, man joins in the fulfillment of the Divine Will. "The pagan gods had selfish needs, while the God of Israel is only in need of man's integrity." [32]

But, "man's integrity" includes his endless yearnings for the good life, yearnings which interpenetrate every aspect of life. Hence, the Law, guiding our life, must be regarded as an organic unity, not as a collection of precepts.

"What constitutes the Jewish form of living is not so much the performance of single good deeds, the taking of a step now and then, as the pursuit of a way, being on the way; not so much the acts of fulfilling as the state of being committed to the task, of belonging to an order in which single deeds, aggregates of religious feeling, sporadic sentiments, moral episodes become parts of a complete pattern." [33]

In illustration of this central purpose of building the dimension of holiness into life, Prof. Heschel describes the institution of the Sabbath as "a palace in time with a Kingdom for all." [34] Glancing away from any considerations regarding the origin of the Sabbath or the need of modifying some of its laws, the author devotes himself to the task of explicating the mood of the Sabbath as being the focus of time touched by eternity, spent in mystical wonder and contemplation in contrast to the space-oriented mood of work and civilization. As the approach of the mystic stands in polar opposition to the scientific and pragmatic attitude, so does the spirit of the Sabbath when time is lived with intimations of eternity, differ from the secular and mundane spirit. It follows that one may not enter the Holy of Holies of Judaism with the boots and tools that are generated by the "spirit of the age." Only from within is reform possible, issuing out of the organic growth of the spirit in the domain of holiness.

Thus, mysticism as a living experience, a communicable mood and a popular attitude functions as a potent brake upon the process of ritualistic reformation and modernization.

THE CONTRIBUTION OF RATIONALISM

The predominant position of Halachah or law in the Jewish pattern of piety was cited by Christian theologians in both ancient and modern times as proof of the "inferiority" of Judaism. Is not the "inwardness" of feeling far superior to the concern of the Pharisee with the exactitude of ritual performance and the casuistries of the Law? By the same token, Jewish scholars are wont to point to the rationality and sober balance of a faith that is firmly raftered by the pillars and joints of a God-given law. Doubtless, the most closely reasoned exposition of the virtue of reverence for law is contained in the massive volumes of Hermann Cohen, the greatest philosopher that German Jewry has produced.

Continuing along Kant's pathway of "critical idealism," Cohen declared the quality of lawfulness to be the ultimate goal of all "pure" directions of the spirit. In the labors of pure reason for the comprehension of the nature of Being, we must not expect to stop at any point and say, "that much is given to us from without as our ineluctable starting-point." As we probe deeper and deeper into the nature of the universe, we find that every material substance inevitably dissolves into a mathematical formula, and the elements of this formula may in turn be analyzed and further resolved into more ultimate elements. Hasn't this process been revealed in the evolution of modern science during the past century, as molecules gave way to atoms, atoms to electrons and protons, while these in turn are even now steadily being decomposed into mesons, waves, curvatures of space, foci of electromagnetic waves and what not? This process is necessarily endless for the human mind can rest only in the stable groove of a formula describing the laws of change.

Even so, in the domains of ethics and esthetics, the productions of the human spirit take on more and more the quality of lawfulness as they attain progressive refinement through the ages. "Pure" ethics is not a matter of "feeling" kind or charitable, but of acting in accord with an inwardly acknowledged law of action. Cohen envisaged the course of history as leading to a progressive unfolding and expansion of "culture-consciousness," which consists in its turn of the three basic quests of the human personality for truth, for rightness and for beauty. Each one of these quests is fulfilled in the discovery of immutable laws governing the fundamental areas of being.

In Cohen's system, religion constitutes at once the source, the apex and the unifying factor of the unfolding "culture-consciousness." The culture of our age is not the creation of saints, scientists and artists, but their collective discovery. All true discoverers share in common the capacity to overcome selfish concerns and private prejudices so as to apprehend reality as a whole and see it truly. Thus, it is the self-transcending impulse of religion that impels the builders of culture in all domains, though, in their pursuit of a partial goal, they sometimes forget to take account of the fundamental craving for truth which is the stirring of God within their soul.

The God-idea rises out of the hunger for purity, which takes these forms—the assurance of the thinker that reason corresponds to reality and is not merely a human delusion, the faith of the ethical personality that its laws of human action are true to the fundamental nature of things and the intuition of the artist that beauty of all types is a reflection of the inner harmony of the universe. Inner truthfulness is the ultimate premise and validation of our emergent "culture-consciousness," and this quality of truthfulness is the source of the quest for beauty, righteousness and truth. Thus, religion, like the God-idea, is twofold in nature. It is a quest for the laws of true being and faith in their validity.

It follows that the virtue of reverence for law should be fundamental in our religious consciousness. Indeed, in Judaism, the believer is trained to be law-abiding, and hence perpetually hungry for the "purity" of conscience and the "purity" of the understanding. Cohen did not believe in a sudden, one-time revelation of the Law at Sinai, but he regarded the central insight of Judaism that piety must be molded through the forms of law as being of decisive importance. It is through mind and conscience that God is revealed in our "culture-consciousness," while the Law of Judaism is intended to fortify our reverence for the basic laws of being. The pious man does not seek to attain mystical oneness with God, but he aspires to make his personal existence count for the attainment of the Divine goals of perfection. To be concerned with the fate of one's soul in this life or in the hereafter is to succumb to the spell of the pagan mentality. Judaism, or the "religion of reason," trains its devotees to labor, not for personal salvation, but for the building of the ideal society. The Jew asks, not "how do I find salvation for my soul?" but "what is my vocation?" or better still, "how can I best serve the goals implied in the eternal laws of thought, ethics and esthetics?" Piety, then, consists in the inner acceptance of the laws of being as the basis of a code of personal behavior.

Manifestly, Cohen's elaborately developed philosophy served to fortify the Conservative position, especially its insistence on the need of retaining the legal molds of Jewish piety and legislating new standards whenever necessary, in order to cultivate the sense of reverence for the Law.

THE EMERGENCE OF EXISTENTIALISM

The genius of Franz Rosenzweig is felt as a living influence in the intellectual circles that incline toward the impassioned decisiveness of existentialism. Starting out with the insistence that man cannot relate himself to God by the sheer process of objective thought, Rosenzweig declared that the human individual, in his inward being, continuously rebels against the abstractions of philosophy that deny the worth of individual existence. At the same time, our soul is unhappy when left alone in isolation from the universe. It finds the meaning of its life and destiny in the message of love that is directed to it from Him who dwells behind the veil of existence. Thereafter, the soul seeks to unfold the infinite implications of the assurance of Divine love that has come to it. True philosophy, then, begins with an act which is prior to thought, an act which transpires in the space-time world, between two ultimate beings, the individual and God, who endure in the realm of eternity.

In Rosenzweig's view, the Jewish people as a whole owes its unique character and destiny to such an act of Divine Love—an act of revelation, which the collective consciousness of the Jewish people has translated into a host of sacred books and a Law. It is through the Law that the Jewish people have been lifted out of the stream of history and removed from the ceaseless battle of nations for the goods of this world. The Law became for Israel a substitute for land, language, culture and government. Yet, Judaism is more than Law, consisting in that deposit of Divine energy that had been placed by God in the historic memory of the Jewish people.

The bold sweep of Rosenzweig's thought may be captured in a few sentences, but the full import can only be gained from a close study of his writings. Behind the veil of phenomena in the visible universe, Rosenzweig recognizes three ultimate elements—the world as it is in itself, subsisting behind all appearances; the human soul in its deepest reality, apart from the ideas, notions and sentiments floating on the surface of consciousness; God, as He is in Himself, apart from all ideas and arguments concerning Him. Each one of these elements can only be pointed to, but not grasped in thought. Yet, there are contacts between these ultimate elements. The contact between God and men is revelation, the contact between God and the world is creation, the contact between man and the world is redemption.

How do we know that such contacts do indeed take place? The emergence of ever higher forms of life in the cosmic surge of evolution is one answer, demonstrating the continuance of Divine creation. And this argument has been elaborated in such philosophies as those of Henri Bergson and S. H. Alexander. Rosenzweig is interested more in the testimony of the human soul and in the evidence provided by the history of mankind. Out of the travail of his own soul, he had learned that currents of Divine love come to us in blessed moments, like healing rays from the sun, transforming our nature and stamping it with the seal of eternity. These sudden bursts of love from above he describes as acts of revelation, and the experience of Divine revelation he accounts to be the source of piety, and the final foundation of true philosophy.

"Whoever has not yet been reached by the voice of revelation has no right to accept the thought of creation as if it were a scientific hypothesis."

All philosophers, who derived their inspiration from Aristotle, shied away from attributing love to God. Does not love imply needing someone else for self-fulfillment, whereas God is self-sufficient and perfect? Rosenzweig finds in love the one key to the ultimate processes of being. "Love is like language itself, sensual-suprasensual." Love, he points out, comes in two phases—the love of the lover and the beloved. God's love or revelation is the love of the lover, a "momentary self-transformation," shifting from eternity into time, from the absolute stillness of His Being into contact with a particular person or people.

Love is essentially a give and take proposition. Hence, it is experienced in the flow of speech and the rapture of song, while it eludes forever the static mesh of mathematical logic. God's healing Grace, and the receptive humble human soul meet on the fleeting borderline of time and eternity, in an event so utterly unique as to be indescribable. A dialogue between two people in love, who find in each other the fulfillment of their life, furnishes the closest analogy to the event of revelation.

"Does God take the first step, or does man? Is it possible for man to take it? This is a real question. . . . The whole matter continues in the form of an unending dialogue. . . ."[35]

While the love of the lover is arbitrary and momentary, the awakened love of the human soul is as that of the beloved, expressed in a yearning to disseminate love to one's fellowmen and in a humble waiting or solitary prayer for the repetition of the miracle of revelation and the final consummation of its promise. As the wordless glow of the blessed moment yields to the coolness and clarity of speech, God's parting message is phrased as a command to live in love. "Thou shalt love the Lord, Thy God," and "thou shalt love thy neighbor as thyself." Also, the human soul touched by the Divine ray of revelation knows itself to be "chosen" as an instrument of redemption—"I have called thee by thy name; you are mine."

The Holy Scriptures and the sacred literature of Judaism are divinely revealed in the sense that the creative elan which projected them into existence was the genuine reflection of Divine love. This fact may be seen in the congruence of the Bible with this philosophy of love and in the historical effect of the Bible. For human history is the actual record of the process of redemption.

"The Bible is not the most beautiful book in the world, not the deepest, the truest, the wisest, the most fascinating and whatever other superlatives there may be—at least no one can be convinced of these advantages who is not already prejudiced in its favor. But the Bible is the most important book. This one can prove, and even the most enraged Bible-hater has to admit this at least for the past, and through his inveterate hatred, he admits it also for the present. For here there is no question of personal taste or of disposition of the soul or of spiritual direction, but only a question of the hitherto transpired events of world history." [36]

Naturally, Rosenzweig does not accept the doctrine of literal revelation, since the content of revelation is simply the Divine mystery of love. Thus, he wrote to an exponent of neo-Orthodoxy:

"Our difference from Orthodoxy consists in the circumstance that we cannot draw any conclusions concerning the literary process of the composition of the Bible and the philological value of the traditional text out of our belief in the sacredness and the peculiar value of Torah. If Wellhausen and all his theories were indeed right, and if the Samaritans really possessed a better text, that would not touch our belief in the slightest." [37]

Rosenzweig's reverence for history led him to esteem every facet of Jewish life and to stigmatize as "little Jews" the Zionists who reduced Judaism to ethnicism and the Orthodox who froze it into the neat package of what they called Torah. He saw the focal center of Jewish loyalty in the inner acknowledgment of being part of the Jewish people. The sense of blood-unity cannot but lead to the feeling of oneness with the fateful destiny of the Jewish people, and the living community in turn is but the expression in history of the "chosenness" of the Jewish people, by an act of Divine love. Dramatized in the Holy Scriptures in the majestic imagery of the Covenant at Sinai, the "chosenness" of Israel makes of its ethnic base and its spiritual message an unbreakable entity, so that any identification with Jewish life, be it ever so tenuous in the beginning, cannot but lead to the full acceptance of Judaism in the richness of its totality—unless this process is artifically blocked by false concepts of the nature of Jewish life.

The richly suggestive quality of Rosenzweig's thought can hardly be conveyed in any summary. Hegelian to the core, he was empirical in approach, thoroughly undogmatic and self-critical, gentle and saintly— a *homo religiosus* in every fiber of his being. In the past decade, the vogue of Rosenzweig has been growing steadily among American intellectuals. Yet, the German idiom of his thought sets a definite limit to his influence.

Recently Will Herberg assayed to expound the philosophy of existentialism in the dramatic and popular manner of an American journalist. The unhappy dependence of philosophy upon temperament is demonstrated in the transformation of the gentle piety of the Frankfurt saint into the ebullient buoyancy of the "leap of faith" by the impulsive and impetuous Herberg.

In "Judaism and the Modern Man," Will Herberg asserts first the utter meaninglessness and frustration of life when a man takes himself to be the "measure of all things." The individual cannot find meaning in his own existence, and, in his despair, he looks to a collective entity for the sustenance of his spirit. Thus, the proletariat, the nation or the racial blood-stream becomes the false surrogate for God.

Since then man cannot live without faith in something, the only true alternative before us is the idolatry of our self, individual or collective, or the worship of God. A "leap of faith" is called for, whereby the self emerges out of the imaginary shell which encloses it and finds itself to be suspended from a Divine thread. But, so paradoxical is the nature of faith, that, when once acquired, it appears to have been inescapable.

"We must dare the leap if the gulf is ever to be crossed; but once the decision of faith has been made, it is seen that the leap was possible only because the gulf had already been bridged for us from the other side." [38]

In other words, faith is at once a human, subjective act and a Divine objective fact. Thus, God is not the passive and hidden Ground of Being, but an active Spirit that is somehow akin to our deepest self.

"The ascription of personality to God is thus an affirmation of the fact that in the encounter of faith God meets us as person to person." [39]

It is the Grace of God that makes human rightness possible, not only in the act of faith but in all the spheres of human life.

"The weakness and evil in man operate out of the freedom of his own nature; his capacity for good, though grounded in his nature, needs the Grace of God for its realization." [40]

In this sense, Herberg accepts the reality of "original sin," balancing it by the belief in man's "original perfection" that is due to the unfailing availability of Divine Grace. Human life is perpetually in danger of relapsing from God and into the frustration of sin. Hence, the drama of salvation.

"The salvation we crave is salvation from the fears, the futilities, the frustrations of existence. . . .

"Estranged from God, we are torn out of the very texture of being and left a mere fragment, cut off from the only real source of security available to us. Is it any wonder that thus isolated from what is real within and without, our existence loses its foundation and we are compelled to live out our lives in restless frustration, forever trembling at the brink of chaos and dissolution?" [41]

Up to this point, Herberg developed the general ideology of existentialism, which sees the entire panorama of life from the viewpoint of man facing God in the moment of decision. Proceeding to the analysis of Jewish life and destiny, the author insists on the "uniqueness" of the phenomenon of the Jew, resulting from the covenant between God and Israel that had been effected by an enduring "existential" relationship.

Steering a middle course between fundamentalism and modernism, Herberg accepts the Holy Bible as Divine Revelation, insofar as it tells of the perennial encounter between God and man. Yet, more, Scripture tells of "the self-disclosure of God in his dealings with the world." Revelation is an event in history, Divine in substance but human in expression. As the medieval, rationalistic expounders of the Bible found the philosophy of Aristotle in the words of Scripture, so Herberg insists that Scripture is true, but only as interpreted in existential fashion.

"The views of Abraham on the nature of things and even on the 'nature' of the divine were presumably far more 'primitive' than those of Isaiah so many centuries later, but their faith was the same, for they stood in the same crisis of confrontation with God, shared the same ultimate covenantal commitment, and recognized the same Lord and His absolute claim." [42]

Are all works reflecting the same faith equally revealed? Herberg hedges away from this conclusion, declaring that "revelation" at Sinai was for Jews "einmalig," once and for all, "not in the sense of course that God thereafter no longer reveals Himself in his contact with men but in the sense that all other 'visitations' of God, both before and after, yield their meaning only when seen with the eyes of faith from the perspective of this central event." [43]

The circularity of this argument is manifest. Scriptures are read with "the eyes of faith," as faith is contemporaneously understood, and then it becomes the standard of judgment of all other revelation. From a modernist viewpoint, there is no harm in this continuous interaction, Scripture being accepted by collective consent and convention as the text and context of organized religion. But, Herberg takes pains to deny "general" revelation as being a "possibility in fact." He insists that "though God is everywhere to be discerned in his person, activity and works, the mind of sinful man is incapable of finding him through his own unaided powers." [44] If then we cannot trust our modern world-view to be the adequate basis for the separation of the true core of "revelation" from the human and relative myths with which it is encrusted, how can we look to Scripture for guidance? For the Orthodox, the word of God is clearly spelled out in literal truth, and for the liberals, who trust the insight and values of humanity, there is a solid enough base for the interpretation of "revelation," distinguishing between the life-giving, eternal grain and the tasteless chaff. But, to accept Scriptures in "essence" only while denying the validity of our human power to discriminate between the shadow and the substance of faith is to maintain a logically indefensible position. "Existentially," of course, the solid basis is the psychological experience of faith, as a felt, immediate awareness of Divine love, containing its own illumination and validation.

The same paradoxical notion is entertained by the author in regard to the concept of Israel. While he does not accept the fundamentalist interpretation of the doctrine of the "chosen people," he insists that "the history of Israel" constitutes a mode of self-revelation of God. It is through the life of Israel, in all its particularity, that God reveals His message to mankind.

"If God is a Living God, operative in and through the particularities of history, then it no longer seems so strange that he should effect His purposes through particular groups of people or even that he should 'create' particular groups for his special purposes."[45]

Herberg maintains, then, that "salvation is of the Jews," in conscious defiance of the entire sweep of modernity and the broad tolerance of liberalism. The very being of Israel is a mysterious anomaly, which can not be understood in the mundane terms of sociology. We are a "unique" people, unclassifiable with other groups and incomprehensible by ordinary human standards.

"It is a *supernatural* community, called into being by God to serve his eternal purposes in history. It is a community created by God's special act of covenant, first with Abraham, whom he 'called' out of the heathen world, and then supremely, with Israel corporately at Sinai."[46]

This "super-historical" community is charged with the mission of bringing "salvation" to the world. The Jew lives his life "authentically" when he responds affirmatively to the demands and duties that are implied in "Jewish covenant-existence." It is through the laws of the Torah that the Jew takes his "authentic" place in the cosmic scheme of things. But, Torah for the existentialist does not mean simply the rigid precepts of the "Shulhan Aruch." Since it is upon the personal experience of faith that his piety is founded, the author insists on the need of taking account of the human and historical elements in the ritual of Judaism. As a blend of the historical and the "super-historical," the Torah must not be frozen into a rigid set of unvarying laws. "It is the historical belief and practice of the community of Israel—Kelal Yisroel—that provides us with the contents of 'halakah.'"[47]

In sum, Jewish existentialism begins with that double phased experience, which is an act of Grace on the part of God and a "leap of faith" on the part of man at one and the same time. In the light of this total commitment of the soul, the biblical-rabbinic faith emerges as a satisfying exposition of the meaning of human life and the Divine Imperative. The people of Israel emerged through a similar collective "existential" experience, and its entire being is forever caught in the tension between the historical and the "super-historical." The "authentic" response of the individual to the Divine call is to live the life of holiness, and for the Jew, this authentic response implies the wholehearted acceptance of the Law, insofar as it is a living reality to the conscience of "Catholic Israel."

THE "RECONSTRUCTIONIST" MOVEMENT

The "left" wing of the Conservative movement consists of the disciples and followers of Prof. Mordecai M. Kaplan, for many years the leading member of the faculty of the Jewish Theological Seminary. For seventeen years now, this intra-Conservative group has been loosely organized in a Reconstructionist fellowship, which has its headquarters in the Society for the Advancement of Judaism. "The Reconstructionist," a brilliantly edited and exceedingly stimulating bi-weekly, is the official organ of this group. In addition, a number of pamphlets and books have been published by The Reconstructionist Society in furtherance of its views.

In some of its projects, The Reconstructionist Fellowship transcends the lines of denominational differences, especially in its advocacy of varied programs for the Jewish community as a whole. Also, some Reform rabbis have joined the fellowship, which remains however predominantly Conservative in orientation and practice.

In general, the Reconstructionist trend might be described as pragmatic in philosophy, liberal in theology and nationalistic in emphasis. The awkward name chosen by the group reflects the central plank of its platform—to reconstruct the chaotic conglomeration that is contemporaneous American Jewry after the pattern of the "organic community." In place of the crazy-quilt jumble of organizations, the Reconstructionists contend, there should be formed in each city an all-inclusive communal organization that would provide for every legitimate need and ideal of its members. The rise of the Welfare Funds and Community Councils is a welcome development in this direction, but, even if this process is consummated in every city, the result will still fall short of the goal of an "organic community." For, while these communal agencies undertake to provide for the philanthropic and recreational needs of the people, they rarely assume full responsibility for the task of Jewish education and they do not ever undertake to minister to the religious needs of the community. In the "organic community," the synagogue and school should occupy the "nuclear" position, since religion constitutes the main expression of Jewish group life.

In effect, then, the Reconstructionists advocate that American Jewry give up the congregational form of organization, which is indigenous on the American scene, and return instead to the "Kehillah" pattern of Central and Eastern Europe. As to the difficulty of reconciling conflicting interpretations of Judaism, Dr. Kaplan maintains that the Jewish community might well follow the example of any modern nation, which fosters the principle of "unity in diversity." The "organic community" should not find it an insuperable task to work out an equitable arrangement whereby all interpretations of Judaism would be treated with equal consideration and its constituent members would attend the synagogues of their choice.

In addition to its religious and educational functions, the community-organization would provide through designated committees for Zionist work, public-relations, philanthropic and recreational activities, so that there would be no need for any independent or supplementary organization. Also, those activities which are now neglected, such as new creations in art and music, would be assiduously cultivated by the "organic community," which would envision Jewish life as a whole and lovingly care for its every phase and expression. The separate "organic communities" would be organized into a national community and ultimately into a world-community that would take its place beside the great national states of the world.

"World Jewry should unite as a people, and apply to the United Nations for recognition of its claim to peoplehood."[48]

This plan for the reorganization of American Jewish life is not suggested simply on the ground of neatness of structure or efficiency in operation. For Dr. Kaplan, the "organic community" is an expression in organizational terms of the essential character of the Jewish people. If the pattern of organization does not correspond to the dynamic forces that are operative in any group, then the group disintegrates in frustration and despair. For organizational structure is to the living ideology of a group, as the body is to the soul. In every phase of its organized life, American Jewry should express its character as an ethnic-cultural group, its enduring "peoplehood," so as to articulate and keep alive the "we" feeling of the individual Jew. By his membership in the "organic community," the individual expresses his sense of belonging to the Jewish people, and it is this sense of sharing in the life and destiny of a people that is the matrix of all its cultural creations and values.

In the Reconstructionist ideology, the Conservative emphasis on the living people in the triad of people, God and Torah is carried to its outermost limit. Judaism is defined as the evolving religious civilization of the Jewish people. In his magnum opus, "Judaism as a Civilization," Dr. Kaplan omitted the adjective, "religious," which The Reconstructionist Fellowship now uses invariably. Even so, the factor of faith is conceived as only one of the elements of Jewish civilization, though historically the dominant one. It is conceivable that religion in the future might be expressed through forms of cooperative living that have nothing in common with the rites and even the ideas of traditional Judaism. Also, it is quite possible that the creative genius of the people will be unfolded in cultural directions other than those of faith and ethics—such as art, for example. The high esteem for creative expression, among the Reconstructionists, leads them to accord to the domain of art a supreme rank among the shining constellations of the Jewish spirit. Writes Dr. Kaplan in his latest major work, "We can be sure of a Jewish future only when Jewish art is so developed as to reconcile the Jew to his lot in life."[49] As if the art of the ancient Greeks, superb as it undoubtedly was, availed to maintain the Greek people, once they exchanged the gods of Olympus for the Savior from Nazareth!

The Reconstructionists do not minimize the role of religion in the "religious civilization" that is Judaism, especially for Diaspora Jewry, but they maintain that religion itself derives its vital power from the "we"-feeling of the people. The Jewish religion lost its hold upon the masses of our people, when the sense of ethnic loyalty was weakened by outside attractions and inner disorganization. The substitution in America of fragmentary congregational and denominational loyalties for the massive loyalty to the Jewish community as a whole served to weaken the purely religious sentiments of our people.

"It is significant that in past ages, when Jews led an autonomous communal life, this particular complaint that the individual could not experience God in the worship of the synagogue was unheard of."[50]

This assertion is manifestly belied by the sad decline of the Jewish faith in the communities of Poland and Germany that were organized on a Kehillah-basis. Yet, it derives necessarily from the Reconstructionist conception of religion as the sublimation of group-feeling.

On this view, religion springs out of the life of the people, its social function being to hallow and to fortify the institutions, things, events and memories that the people require for their collective existence.

Hence, a religion is woefully weakened when it is abstracted into a system of salvation and separated from the ethnic aspirations and concerns of the people among whom it has arisen. Dr. Kaplan asserts this claim in spite of the magnificent historical triumph of the Christian faith, maintaining that "national creeds" will in time replace the unitary Christian faith, which has arisen through the impetus of "religious imperialism."[51] Like the titans of mythology, a religion is powerful only when it retains contact with the soil of national life, in all its varied and earthy ambitions.

"The Jewish people has demonstrated the validity of the principle, which has been repeatedly verified by the experience of mankind, that a folk religion retains its relevance and vitality so long as it confines itself to those who have evolved it."[52]

It follows that the Jewish religion can only be regenerated if it is put back into the total complex of Jewish life, the individual congregation yielding to the all-inclusive community as the basic unit of identification, and the rites of religion surrendering their claim to the exclusive loyalty of the Jew in favor of all other forms of cultural expression.

"Paradoxical as it may sound, the spiritual regeneration of the Jewish people demands that religion cease to be its sole preoccupation."[53]

The will to live as a Jew is the fundamental source and motivation of Jewish existence, but, to be deserving of our highest loyalty, the life we seek must be conceived in the loftiest spiritual terms. Hence, the emphasis on the creation of new values and the construction of social instruments to serve the high ends of prophetic idealism. "All this effort at reconstruction and reinterpretation must come entirely from the urge of an inward creative life."[54]

The supernaturalist motivations of the traditional Jewish faith should be replaced by a this-worldly interpretation of salvation—i.e., the individual fulfills his highest potentialities through the disciplines of the spirit in general and the Jewish way of life in particular. In turn, the Jewish people justifies its existence and survival, by transforming itself into an instrument for the elicitation of the greatest spiritual potential from the Jewish individual.

As to the idea of God, the Reconstructionists are hopelessly pragmatic. The conception of God as the ideal Personality they reject, preferring to think of Him as a "process that makes for salvation."

"It is paradoxical," they maintain, "for a person not to be associated with a physical body," thus dismissing out of hand the long philosophical tradition dating from Plato and Philo and represented in modern philosophy by Lotze in Germany and Bowne in America. The term, "process," reflects the view of modern physics that all existents are not static things, but events in time, or processes. As to how this particular process operates either in nature or in human nature, they are unwilling to speculate provided this "belief in God" results in a commitment to live life on a high spiritual plane. In the words of Kaplan, "when we believe in God, we believe that reality—the world of inner and outer being, the world of society and of nature—is so constituted as to enable man to achieve salvation."[55] Or in still simpler, pragmatic terms, "God is what the world means to the man who believes in the possibility of maximum life and strives for it."[56]

Defined thus generally as an implication of man's striving for the life abundant, the choice between religious faith and atheism is seen to depend more on the glandular makeup of a person than on intellectual arguments. Atheism, on this view, is either a semantic error or a complex of the sickly and the frustrated. The intellectual assent to abstract truths that is implied in faith is reduced to the barest minimum. After the fashion of the behaviorists, who did not believe that mental processes were truly causative factors in the determination of human conduct, Dr. Kaplan writes, "The belief in God is not logically inferred from the will to live. It is the psychic manifestation of the will to live."[57] By the same token, the practice of worship is described as an implication of the same "will to live."

"The need for communing with that Power is part of our very will to live as human beings."[58]

With this concept of God and religion, it follows that rituals and ceremonies cannot be accepted as literally revealed precepts, nor as expressions of fundamental truths, but as socially evolved aids to the good life, or, more technically as "religious folkways." We cannot speak of "law" in Jewish religion, the Reconstructionists declare, since we have no sanctions for the enforcement of legal directives. Also, the Jewish community as a whole could legislate only in regard to those elements that are common to all the interpretations and trends that are current in Jewish life. Thus, it can formulate the rules that are to govern the relationship of committees and societies to the central community organization, and it can also deal with the domain of "public law," such as marriage and divorce. In the sphere of rituals, each denominational trend may formulate its own guiding principles and standards, imputing no guilt to those who prefer other "folkways" for self-expression.

"The vocabulary of 'law,' 'sin,' 'pardon' is ideologically and pragmatically unjustified as applied to ritual."

Rites and ceremonies are forms of collective art, which spring ideally from the life of the people.

"But, the moment we get away from the legalistic approach, we treat Jewish observances as religious folkways designed to ensure the enhancement of the value of Jewish life, the affirmative injunctions assume the more important role."[59]

In keeping with this emphasis on the enrichment of Jewish practice through creative expression, the Reconstructionists published a Passover Haggadah, which added hymns and readings concerning the ideal of freedom and the personality of Moses, while deleting passages which they considered unworthy, such as the enumeration of the plagues, the prayer for the punishment of Israel's enemies and the references to Israel as the "chosen people." In their view, the doctrine of the "chosen people" is an unworthy indulgence in self-glorification, no matter how fancifully it is reinterpreted. In this spirit, they edited and published a Prayer-Book, which was accepted for use, however, only in two synagogues.

ISSUES AND PRACTICE IN THE CONSERVATIVE MOVEMENT

The ideology of Reconstructionism functions as one of the trends within the Conservative movement—fairly influential in some directions, but falling short of predominance. The movement, for the most part, insists on a personal conception of the Deity, the unique historical position of Israel as the people of revelation, the recognition of the totality of the tradition as the source of authority rather than the folkways or practices of the people and the belief in the continued validity of Jewish Law or Halachah, when it is interpreted as part of a dynamic, life-oriented tradition.

For many years, the Law Committee of the Rabbinical Assembly functioned in strict compliance with the letter and spirit of the "Shulhan Aruch." Even the practice of mixed seating in the synagogue was not approved but only condoned in the spirit of the historian Zunz, who remarked that the spirit of peace and harmony in a community is more important than the harmony or disharmony of organ-music. Thus, in practice, Conservative congregations deviated from Orthodoxy while, in theory, the Law was declared to be unchanged. At the Convention held in Chicago in 1948, a resolution to the effect of binding the movement to strict compliance with the "Shulhan Aruch" was proposed and defeated. The Law Committee was then reorganized so as to reflect all trends within the movement. At its first meeting, it assumed the designation, Committee on Jewish Law and Standards, in order to indicate that its scope is the application of the totality of the tradition to Jewish life, not merely the interpretation of the letter of the Law. Nor was the Committee to be confined to the task of writing responses to specific inquiries. Wherever new standards were to be set up, the Committee was to propose and to formulate resolutions for the movement.

To the majority of its members, the process of legislating standards of ritual observance is a direct implication of the character of Jewish piety. In Judaism, man's response to the Divine challenge takes the form of a self-imposed "law" of action. While all men might concede the value of prayer and study, the religious Jew imposes upon himself the regular disciplines of prayer three times daily and the mitzvoth of Torah-study at fixed times. This response of the individual is guided and molded by the collective "laws" of the people, so that the resolve of each Jew is reinforced and conditioned by the acceptance and the observance of the entire group.

The fruitfulness of this approach was demonstrated in the analysis of the problem of Sabbath observance. The Committee did not substitute for the Sabbath-halachah a general principle, such as the obligation to hallow the day by positive actions only, nor did it proceed to interpret the Law in blithe disregard of existing conditions. Firstly, it set the problem in a positive setting by launching a campaign for the Revitalization of the Sabbath, calling upon all congregants to pledge the acceptance of certain minimal standards of Sabbath-observance—to refrain from doing work on the Sabbath which is avoidable and which is not in keeping with the spirit of the day, and to hallow the Sabbath-day by positive practices, such as Kiddush and candle lighting, attendance at services, etc. These general rules were spelled out in detail in the course of the campaign, which is even now in progress.

Secondly, the Committee affirmed the applicability of the principle of "takkanah"-legislation to our time and place. Jewish Law can be made and modified today in the same manner as it was made and modified in the past. Accordingly, the Committee called upon the Rabbinical Assembly to permit the practice of riding to the synagogue on the Sabbath, as a new "takkanah" designed to "strengthen the faith," a "takkanah" made necessary by the peculiar circumstances of American life. When it is difficult or impossible to walk, the Committee declared it to be a "mitzvah" to make use of motor transportation for the sake of attending public worship. This decision was approved by the majority-report of the Committee and accepted by the Rabbinical Assembly. The minority-report arrived at virtually the same conclusion.

Whether one "mitzvah" or another is to take precedence in the event of a conflict between their requirements is the kind of question that can only be weighed in the balance of contemporary needs and consequences. Which decision is likely to result in a more vital and meaningful faith for American Jews? In the light of this question only one answer was possible. Nor was it difficult for the Committee to cite specific precedents for the rule that a "great mitzvah" (mitzvah g'dolah) may set aside normal prohibitions (especially as an "horaath sha-ah," a decision limited to a specific time and place). And regular attendance at Sabbath services is in the circumstances of American life today, a "great mitzvah," essential for the vitality of our faith.

Thirdly, the Committee declared the use of electrical gadgets on the Sabbath to be permitted, if the use to which they are put is in consonance with the holiness of the day. Manifestly, electricity could not have been prohibited by Talmudic legislation, even as it could not have been specifically permitted. Therefore, the Committee proceeded to evaluate its use from the standpoint of its relation to contemporary needs, making use in its Responsum of technical distinctions in the Talmud for the purpose of overcoming technical difficulties.

At times, the Committee is stricter in the maintenance of religious standards than the bare letter of the Law. Thus, it makes use of its influence to dissuade Jewish organizations from holding business-meetings on the Sabbath, though traditionally Jewish problems were discussed on holy days in medieval times, care being taken in those days to avoid infringement of the ritualistic laws. It is recognized that in modern circumstances not a shred would be left of the traditional pattern of holiness if Jewish organizations were allowed to hold business-meetings on the Sabbath. Also, the Committee is even now combatting the suggestion to permit Gentile players on the Sabbath to play dance music for the entertainment of dinner-guests at a Bar Mitzvah celebration in the vestry-hall of the synagogue. Ample precedent for this practice could be cited, from a strictly legalistic viewpoint, especially since the movement sanctions the employment of the organ at the services. Also, the Hassidim would dance on the Sabbath. But, in the opinion of the Committee, the consequences of this practice in the circumstances of American life would be deleterious to the dignity of the synagogue and the holiness of the Sabbath. Accordingly, the Committee called upon all Conservative synagogues to discountenance any such practice.

In the domain of Jewish Law, the main issue confronting the movement at this writing is the so-called "Agunah" question, which really includes a number of problems relating to marriage and divorce. Suppose the husband refuses to give a "get" or "halitzah," what recourse is left to the woman? What if a Kohen desires to marry a divorcee or a converted woman? What to do in the event of desertion when the woman obtains a divorce from the civil court and the whereabouts of the husband is unknown? What to do with the many cases that are classified by the government first as "missing in action" and later declared to be dead, without the testimony of living witness that is required by Jewish Law?

Already, in 1937, the late Rabbi J. L. Epstein proposed an elaborate plan involving the principle of conditioned marriage and making it possible for the woman to write her own "get," under the direction of a rabbinic court, in certain cases. Owing to the frantic protests of the Orthodox rabbis, this plan was never put into effect. The present plan of the Committee is all-embracing in scope and radical in approach. The principle of "takkanah"-legislation would be so employed as to solve the above-mentioned problem without removing the rabbi, and the Jewish faith he symbolizes, from the realm of divorce and remarriage. The details of this plan are even now under discussion, but there is virtual agreement within the movement that Jewish law must be preserved through a dynamic process of interpretation and continuous legislation, reflecting the realities of our day.

NOTES

1. David Phillipson, *The Reform Movement,* (reprint: New York, 1968) p. 305.

2. *American Jewish Yearbook* (Philadelphia, 1916) p. 62.

3. *Ibid,* p. 58.

4. S. Goldman, *In the Beginning* (New York, 1949), p. 101.

5. Prof. Salo Baron as quoted by Robert Gordis in *Conservative Judaism* (New York, 1956).

6. Phillipson, *The Reform Movement,* p. 190.

7. See Schechter's essay on "Abraham Geiger" *Studies in Judaism,* 3rd ser. (Philadelphia, 1924), 47–83 and Geiger in *Jüdische Zeitschrift,* vol. 7 (1869), p. 7.

8. Schechter, *Studies in Judaism* (New York, 1905), vol. I, p. 212.

9. *See* debate on Frankel's resignation in "Protokolle," Frankfurt Conference.

10. Phillipson, *The Reform Movement,* p. 87.

11. Schechter, *Studies in Judaism,* vol. III, p. 69.

12. *Ibid,* p. 78.

13. Schechter, essay on "Abraham Geiger" in *Studies in Judaism* (Philadelphia, 1924), vol. III.

14. Schechter, Introduction to *Studies in Judaism,* vol. I.

15. See Eric Fromm, *The Forgotten Language* (New York, 1951).

16. Schecter, Introduction to *Studies in Judaism,* Vol. I.

17. *Ibid.,* p. 72.

18. Franz Rosenzweig, *Briefe* (Berlin, 1935), p. 543.

19. *Ibid,* p. 356.

20. Agus, *Modern Philosophies of Judaism* (New York, 1941), pp. 206, 207.

21. *Ibid.*

22. *Reden über das Judentum* (Berlin, 1932), First Lecture.

23. *Heruth* (Berlin, 1919), p. 8.

24. *Ibid,* p. 10.

25. Martin Buber, *I and Thou,* trans. R. Gregor-Smith (Edinburgh, 1937), p. 8.

26. *Ibid,* p. 6.

27. *Ibid,* p. 15.

28. *Ibid,* p. 79.

29. *Ibid,* p. 82.

30. *Ibid,* p. 115.

31. A. J. Heschel, *Man Is Not Alone* (New York, 1951), p. 237.

32. *Ibid,* p. 245.

33. *Ibid,* p. 270.

34. A. J. Heschel, *The Sabbath* (New York, 1955).

35. Nahum Glatzer, *Franz Rosenzweig* (New York, 1961), p. 286.

36. F. Rosenzweig, *Kleine Schriften* (Berlin, 1937), p. 178.

37. Rosenzweig, *Briefe,* p. 581.

38. Will Herberg, *Judaism and Modern Man* (New York, 1951), p. 39.

39. *Ibid,* p. 60.

40. *Ibid*, p. 76.
41. *Ibid*, pp. 116, 117.
42. *Ibid*, p. 248.
43. *Ibid*, p. 251.
44. *Ibid*, p. 255.
45. *Ibid*, p. 264.
46. *Ibid*, p. 271.
47. *Ibid*, p. 299.
48. M. Kaplan, *The Future of the American Jew* (New York, 1948), p. 80.
49. *Ibid*, p. 118.
50. M. Kaplan, *Meaning of God in Modern Jewish Religion* (New York, 1962), p. 246.
51. M. Kaplan, *Judaism as a Civilization* (New York, 1934), p. 340.
52. *Ibid*, p. 343.
53. *Ibid*, p. 345.
54. M. Kaplan, *The Meaning of Reconstructionism* (New York, 1960), p. 25.
55. Kaplan, *Meaning of God in Jewish Religion*, p. 26.
56. *Ibid*, p. 328.
57. Kaplan, *Future of the American Jew*, p. 172.
58. *Ibid*, p. 184.
59. *Ibid.*, p. 424.

PART NINE

JACOB B. AGUS
AS PULPIT RABBI

SELECTIONS AND PREFATORY
REMARKS
Mark Loeb

RABBI AGUS made his career as a communal rabbi first in Chicago, then in Dayton, Ohio, and then for more than thirty years in Baltimore at Congregation Beth El. The role of communal rabbi was one that he took very seriously and from which he gained great personal satisfaction.

The following selections, chosen to accompany Mark Loeb's essay "Jacob B. Agus as Pulpit Rabbi" in *American Rabbi: The Life and Thought of Jacob B. Agus* (New York, 1996), are from Jacob B. Agus' *The Meaning of Jewish History* (New York, 1963), 1:11–31; and *The Jewish Quest* (New York, 1983), 62–76.

24

RELIGION AND NATIONALISM

ANYONE WHO SETS out to study the history of the Jew concludes very soon that at all times the factors of both nationalism and religion were involved in the makeup of the Jewish community. Whether the unity of descent or the unity of faith was more dominant at any period is frequently a matter of judgment and controversy. But that both factors were involved in the structure of the Jewish mentality, the historian can hardly doubt. The point that students of the subject, however, are most prone to overlook is not the potency of either one of these factors but the paradoxical character of both of them, in human nature generally, and particularly in the historic consciousness of the Jew.

Manifestly, religion and nationalism cannot ever be separated completely. *Those who have to fight for their religious beliefs, or to suffer for them, come to think of themselves as a people.* Adolf Harnack points out that the Christians in the Roman Empire of the third century called themselves a "third race," *tertium genus.*[1] Many of the sectarian movements in the Christian world reflected ethnic rivalries. Pure nationalism, without any tincture of religious faith, is a characteristically modern phenomenon. Our secular, democratic society is the result of developments in Western Europe, where people recoiled in disgust from the horrors of a previous all too tight union between "organized" religion and government. It is the Church and State as organizations that the modern West seeks to keep apart. But the Church is only a temporal, inadequate instrument of religion, and the State as a political institution reflects only partially the complex dynamism of a living people. The two vital ideals subsisting behind their respective organizational facades cannot but be mutually related. For the human mind is one, and the goal of both ideals is the good life. Both ideals concern themselves with the character and destiny of a certain community; both appeal to the desire of individuals to merge their personal identity with that of a large entity, which stands above the vicissitudes of time; both are products of an inner tension and polarity.

To study the forces operative in Jewish history, we need to take account of the tensions within both of these ideals. As we shall see, both ideals are in themselves bi-polar. In addition, both nationalism and religion serve as organizing instruments, confirming society's structure which is vertical, rather than horizontal. The ideas and ideals of an elite or a dominant group become the cement of a pyramid, with the people at the base repeating the same formulae and slogans, as if they were myths and rites, without necessarily understanding them.

In the writing of Jewish history, we need to guard against a pervasive theological bias, since the character and destiny of the people of Israel form part of the Jewish, Christian, and Moslem faiths. Western liberals, cognizant of the long battle of progressive men and women against the oppression of the Church, are likely to introduce an anti-religious bias into the interpretation of Jewish history. All too often the resultant histories are inverted theologies or ideologies.

We do not expect the reader to credit us with supreme objectivity, but we can minimize the degree of distortion by revealing the weights and measures that we intend to employ. The reader will then be able to check the cogency of our discussion, step by step.

Our concept of religion is devoid of fixed dogmas. Religion is to us an ongoing quest, not a finished possession. We do not assume a certain number of true ideas or a body of revealed truths. As we see it, man's confrontation with the mystery of existence is the living core of faith. But this central event grows in meaning and scope with the expansion of man's knowledge and the refinement of his feelings.

Essentially, religion is a wave-like movement, a polar tension between the abiding Reality without and the ultimate self within. Since man is unable either to envisage the cosmos as a whole or to contemplate his own self, he is compelled to follow one or both of the following procedures. Either he understands the world in terms of images of the self—ghosts, demons, angels, gods. Or he understands his own being in terms of the events of the outside world—stones, winds, material particles. Most commonly, the two alternatives interact and modify one another.

As the consciousness of religion deepens, these two orientations become philosophic alternatives. It is possible to see the entire universe in terms derived from the self contemplating itself. The entire universe is then interpreted either as the work of an Infinite Self, or as the reflection of that Infinite Being. The Cosmos is, then, a "macroanthropos." On the other hand, man may see his own being in terms of what he conceives to be the components of the external world, so many atoms and electrons obeying universal and inexorable laws. Man is then a "microcosmos."

These subjective and objective views have many ramifications, since they are essentially ways of thinking and feeling. In the objective orientation, man reduces the role of feeling to a minimum, though he cannot eliminate it altogether. He strives to reason; that is, to let his mind reflect the principles and the order that exist in reality. Rationality is a readiness to observe, to learn; ideas are employed as a kind of shorthand with which to describe experience. In this mood, man is able to see himself from the outside, as it were; hence, to criticize and to analyze the ideas in his own mind and in the group to which he belongs.

In his subjective orientation, man retreats from the world in the endeavor to be true to his own self. Rationality and criticism are then reduced to a minimum, while feeling, as fear, as generalized anxiety, or as a specific concern, as love or as hope, is steadily deepened and intensified. Since man cannot put his finger on the core of his own being, he tries to find his self either in an ideal "self-image," or in the collective self of a historic group, or in the image of an envisioned Supreme Being. Usually, these three alternatives are followed at the same time. In this mood, man delights to surrender to God, insisting that the ordered world of rationality is somehow in a "fallen" state. Generally also, subjective pietists extol all that is associated with their group, its past, its metaphysical character, and its ultimate destiny.

Most people are familiar with these two basic approaches as mutually exclusive alternatives. In our generation, the Existentialists preempt the subjective way of thinking, in keeping with Kierkegaard's slogan, "subjectivity is truth." On the other hand, the champions of objectivity in philosophy generally describe themselves as Positivists, though few would follow Auguste Comte, founder of French Positivism, in adopting the entire panoply of organized religion in behalf of their worldview. As is well known, Comte sought to organize a ritual, build a priesthood, ordain sacraments, and write a catechism, embodying the principles of his positivistic philosophy.

In our view, religion is the life of the soul; *i.e.,* it is man's effort to orient himself to Reality. Hence, it necessarily contains both orientations of heart and mind. It follows that religion is a dynamic phenomenon; its life is the yearning of man to reach for firm anchorage; it is expressed in the hunger for truth, the longing for the sublime, the passion for righteousness, the outreaching for permanence and genuine worth. As a vital phenomenon, religion is never complete, never at rest, never finished. Progress in any one direction provides the challenge for adjustment and growth in all other phases of human life. Man seeks for the fullness of his life, by means of this rhythm, which brings all his powers into focus.

What is it then that we take to be the marks of growth in a living faith?

First, a living faith is one which is repeatedly and deeply *internalized; i.e.,* it is a powerful subjective reality. Its practices and its dogmas are not merely external rituals and uninspiring formulae, but they bite deep into the souls of their worshipers. What is subjective cannot be fully susceptible of expression; it can only be characterized as a unique realm of experience, radically different from the faith of others. Internalization is essentially the standard of faith that the Existentialists offer. In Jewish thought, it was Bahya who gave the classic formulation to the thought that the dimension of inwardness is infinite in depth.[2] The "commandments of the heart," reverence and love of God, trust in Him and utter devotion to His cause in the world, are indeed susceptible of numberless gradations. In the last two centuries of Jewish life, the Hasidic movement concentrated its mighty genius on this aspect of the faith, bringing fresh life and vitality to the Jewish religion.

Internalization is not easily captured in the official formulations of a faith. The extent to which it occurs at any one time and in the hearts of any people is always uncertain, for nothing happens more frequently in religion than the substitution of formulae for feelings. It is not possible to draw exact comparisons among different faiths, at least within those of the Judeo-Christian tradition, in respect to the intensity of religious feelings they arouse. In every tradition, there will be found those for whom their faith is an empty formula or rite, and some for whom it is a powerful, inspiring reality. Even the persistent hammering away of some sects about the virtues of humility and genuine piety can itself degenerate into a pious posture. Such is the paradox of human nature that the ideal of humility is itself at times the slogan of the narrow-hearted, arrogant dogmatists. For to embrace an ideal is to take pride in it and to assume the inferiority of all who do not see the light. All whose faith is basically subjective assume that "others" are religious only in external forms. The usual Christian image of the Pharisee, and by implication, of the Jew is that his faith is only an empty shell, a matter of "dos" and donts," of laws and actions, not principles and feelings. Schleiermacher, in his classic discussion of "religious feeling," disparages the faith of the French, the Russians, and the English as well as the faith of the Jews. Each of these groups has returned the compliment at one time or another.

Students of religion are not apt to overlook the significance of emotional intensity in the life of religion, but they are quite likely to ignore the importance of the swing of the spiritual pendulum toward the pole of objectivity. The quest of rationality and objective truth is often regarded as a denial of faith or as a flight from God. The usual policy of scholars is to restrict the meaning of faith to the subjective moods of piety, when the soul retreats from the glare of the day to seek the calm of Divine communion in the comforting shadows of a revered tradition. But this very policy of confining religion to one phase of the soul's activity leads inevitably to the dissolution of the bonds of meaning and relevance between faith and life. A one-sided religion is a meaningless one, for meaning *is* relatedness, the absence of a gulf; the undammed stream of thought in a rhythmic current flowing from the universal to particulars and then back again. To erect barriers within the soul is to invite frustration and futility.

Actually, the quest of religion is for the maximum of relatedness with the ultimate ground of reality. We could define religion as the quest for unity with God; but as a matter of psychological fact, God is not always envisioned as present at the goal, and unity with Him is unattainable. We speak then of a ground of reality and of a maximum of relatedness. Two ways present themselves to us, both together leading to this goal though separately they lead in opposite directions. In the one, we attain relatedness by *looking at* the universe; in the other, by letting our minds drift away from surface facts in order to *feel part of* its inner substance.

And we know that we are *part of* reality, while we *look at* any portion of it.

If we could know all about ourselves we would know the heart of the universe; yet, if we cannot know ourselves we can *be ourselves,* and to be *part of* reality is also somehow to know it.

In the objective as in the subjective orientation of the mind, we find ourselves at first submitting to an outer reality and then asserting that reality within us. Both self-surrender and self-assertion mark the posture of the soul as it seeks the maximum of relatedness, either by way of reason or by way of feeling. In the fervor of faith, man begins by surrendering to God. Tired of pushing elbows against the crowd, man acclaims God as the kindly shepherd, all-loving and all-knowing. Man sees himself as a lamb, willing to be led wheresoever the Shepherd wills. Yet, somehow, nearly every psalm that begins with the trustful mood of total surrender ends on a note of triumphant participation in the Divine Being. He accepts us as a part of Himself, and we accept Him as part of ourselves. As we yield in trust, we rise in strength. Thus, the twenty-third psalm, which sounds the note of total resignation in its opening lines, goes on to speak of being led in righteous paths "for His Name's sake," of "being anointed" for a high sacred purpose, and it ends with the confident assertion of being part of the Divine household, dwelling "in the house of the Lord forever."

In most psalms, the submissive and the assertive aspects of the soul are placed side by side, without any particular sequence. Now the psalmist sings of the Lord as his strength, his light, his invincible protector; now he submits to Divine guidance in perfect trust. Erich Fromm points out that healthy love is of a double nature, containing both submissiveness and assertion.[3] In faith as in love, self-surrender and self-realization are blended, as the bright flame and its dark underside. When we love, we are held in love.

"How shall we love the Divine Presence?" asks a sixteenth-century mystic. His answer: "To the point of finding it impossible to separate from it."[4]

It is this paradoxical unity of submission and assertion that we find also in the objective orientation. The quest of "clear and adequate ideas" is a heroic undertaking. The thinker subordinates all that is dear to him to the austere judgment of implacable reason. He can hide nothing that is precious from the cutting knife of reason; he cannot ask for favors; he can expect no personal consideration. Submission to the rational process in all its ruthless impartiality is by no means easy. Yet those who like Spinoza follow this pathway of utter submission find that they are realizing their inmost selves in joy. For the light of reason, like the love of God, is within us as surely as it is beyond us. It was not the understandable bias of a philosopher but an indubitable truth of human nature that led Aristotle to assert that rationality is the essence of humanity. This truth is evident, however, only at certain times. Spinoza writes of an intuitive kind of reasoning, in which thought proceeds automatically.[5] A point is reached when we no longer think our thoughts, but the process of thought, like a mighty stream carries us along. Who has not experienced this dual unity of rational contemplation? In thought as in faith and love, we win our self as we lose our self.

The rational quest is thus as much a part of religion as the pietistic-mystical yearning for the "nearness of God." A rabbinic legend tells of an angel in heaven that in the daytime carries the word *Emeth*, truth, on its forehead and at night carries the word *Emunah*, faith. Both day and night form part of the cycle of the soul. The essential unity of man's need for love and his quest of truth is reflected in the prayer of Socrates, "Beloved Pan, and all ye other gods who haunt this place, give me beauty in the inward soul, and may the outward and the inward man be at one."[6]

In his search for truth, man puts all that is subjective to the test. He criticizes the things that are so precious because they are "his own," his own cultural tradition, his own religious heritage, his own people, his own convictions and prejudices. In the faculty of pure reason, he rises above himself as the empirical man of a specific time and place. Long and arduous is the path of self-criticism. Many are the idols to be demolished, many are the defenses to be shattered, many are the disguises of the naked soul, and agonizing beyond comparison is the task of penetrating them. But the rational quest for self-knowledge is as endless as that for knowledge of the world. And it is man's destiny to be forever caught in the oscillation of the spirit from subjective faith to objective reason, from the nighttime quest for faith and peace to the daytime quest for clarity and action. The man of reason cannot and ought not escape his involvements in life. He needs to feel his unity within an ongoing tradition, to join with others in celebrating the mystery of life and its great values. He needs to use the "language" of faith, which consists of symbols and myths and rites, articulating the unspeakable wonders of life. He will interpret and transform the creed and the ritual of his community, but he remains part of it, for reason is but one of the facets of man's spirit. Religion is to reason as the mind is to the senses, not as the senses are to one another.

Our second criterion in the study of religions, then, is the extent to which they incorporate the objective, rational factor. More specifically, we need to inquire whether the quest for wisdom is recognized as a Divine commandment, whether the domain of objective thinking is uncircum-scribed, whether the rites and dogmas of the tradition are subjected consistently to the rigorous examination of reason.

Finally, as our third criterion, we shall ask whether the extension of the objective approach is translated into a universal, non-parochial ethic.

An ethical philosophy of life is the creation of both subjective piety and objective thinking. Neither the feelings of empathy nor the critical acumen of logic can by themselves generate a truly ethical approach to the problems of life. For ethics is more than a complex of gentle feelings like piety, love, sympathy, courage, and loyalty. These feelings are as native to humanity as their opposites—cruelty, ruthlessness, callousness, and brutality. The instinctive equipment of man includes both sets of feelings. The predominance of either set of feelings in any phase of life depends on the structure of ideas in a given culture more than on any other factor. So soon as the curtain opens on the drama of human history, we encounter the gentle feelings of humanity, but they are limited in application to narrow circles—the family, the clan, the tribe, the social caste, the city, or the nation. And every forward step in the extension of the boundaries of ethical obligation and responsibility is achieved by means of rational criticism, which pushes forward the boundary stones set up by tradition. Every wall dividing the "in" group from the "out" group, with one set of morals for the former and another for the latter, is breached by the thrust of the soul toward greater objectivity. Romantic faith, on the other hand, cautions against the removal of any fences; it tends to draw the veil of sanctification over all that is traditional and characteristic of the "in" group.

By the same token, rational thought in itself cannot generate an ethical faith. From the summit of rationality, philosophers like Plato and Aristotle can devise ideal constitutions, which make for efficiency and justice. But the philosophers cannot plan the reactions of the individuals composing their utopian state. Constitutions may be set up, laws may be laid down, compliance may be efficiently assured. But the quality of ethics is found not in law and administration as such, but in the motives and attitudes of the men and women in the state. Thus, the Greek philosophers already assigned to religion the task of educating the people for life in the ideal state.

The domain of ethics is the product of a dynamic synthesis of reflection and feeling. The ardor and zeal of generosity and self-denial derive from subjective faith, while reason imposes the universality of principle upon these protean feelings. In the search for objective knowledge, man eliminates himself altogether from the equation; in the sphere of ethics, a man inquires how he can best utilize the powers of his self for the overarching community. Hence, both a deep concern for self and personal destiny as well as the awareness of a series of concentric circles of society are the poles of the ethical ideal.

Hermann Cohen suggested that the ethical ideal could be employed as the sole index of maturity in the study of religions. From the vantage point of our analysis, we can agree that the ethical ideal depends upon the equilibrium between the two orientations of the soul and their intensities. Hence, it is an excellent index of maturity. But the ethics of any faith or culture is itself a dynamic, restless quality, bi-directional, multi-faceted, susceptible of a thousand subterfuges.

In the analysis of an ethical ideal, we must be prepared to recognize the diverse compromises between subjective bias and objective reflection. Beyond the level of the legendary and the primitive, no religion arises on the horizon of mankind which does not teach some form of love of neighbor. And the command of the Torah, "love thy neighbor as thyself," is a sublime synthesis of subjective feeling and the objective view of a community of neighbors. But the growth and maturation of faith will be manifested in the manner whereby limitations of the meaning of the term "neighbor" are progressively overcome. Limitations of clan and caste, of tribe and nationality, of sectarian orthodoxy and deviation, of collective prejudice and stereotype are more frequently obstacles to ethical progress than flaws in the formulation of ethical principles.

In sum, we have arrived at three criteria of the growth of religion: the intensity and depth of internalization of rites and dogmas, the consistency and extent of objective criticism embraced in the tradition, and the balance between the subjective and objective factors as it is demonstrated in the ethical standards of the community.

We need to indicate at this time why these criteria are more useful than those employed by other historians and philosophers. Without undertaking to survey all the philosophies in world literature we shall easily recognize the alternative criteria of growth as: first, dogmatic standards; second, either universality of concept alone or intensity of religious experience alone; third, philosophical ideas; fourth, orientations toward the future rather than the past.[7]

Dogmas of any kind we disavow as being of subjective and symbolic worth exclusively. Our analysis of faith ignores altogether the notion of preternatural revelation, because we assume that God reveals Himself to us in all ways. It would be arbitrary and arrogant to set aside only selected books, or certain experiences of certain people as being the sole content of revelation. We can see things only from the human point of view. Poets and mythologists may write from the standpoint of God. And the language of poetry and the symbols of mythology are indispensable to prayer. But they are useless to the sober task of exposition. On the other hand, Olympian impartiality and boundless universalism is a relatively easy stance for those whose inner life is pale and thin. Witness the Sophists of Greece. They could speak of humanity in general with great ease, because loyalties, private or universal, mattered very little in their lives. Philosophical ideas are by their very nature common to the thinking fraternities of any one age or culture. They are easily transferable to different contexts. Thus, the Medieval philosophies of Christianity, Islam, and Judaism employed the same ideas in diverse configurations. In a similar way, the religions of the Hellenistic-Roman period operated with the same discrete concepts.

For this reason, we did not set monotheism against polytheism as a criterion of progress. In the so-called great ages of faith, every monotheistic creed was in actual practice a skein of tensions between the ideals of monotheism and the multiple expressions of pagan polytheism. While the belief in One God is a great advance over the belief in many gods, from the ethical as well as from the logical point of view, the decisive inquiry is what kind of monotheism? Leaps toward monotheism were not rare in the ancient world.

Toynbee's criterion of progress—the change of the admired and imitated individual from the past to the contemporary scene—is from our point of view an external, one-sided standard. He would regard as a sign of progress every act of "breaking the cake of custom." This is formally true, insofar as progress is outwardly visible. But custom-keeping and custom-breaking can both be acts of religious inspiration as well as deeds of desecration. It is the inner attitude of man that counts. In his subjective orientation, man turns to archaic forms and ancient heroes for inspiration. All religious revivals take the form of "returning" to an ancient, long-neglected truth. All practical movements are formally oriented toward the future. But no person is free from either of these orientations. Rationalistic-ethical religious reformers may be led to select ancient heroes as symbols of the transformation that they advocate, interpreting the revolution of the ancients in their own way. It is the content of religious teaching that matters, not its symbolic guise.

The most important reason for the usefulness of this analysis is the fact that it takes account of the paradoxical character of all religions. Religion is not simply a static complex of rites, myths, sacred institutions, and sacraments. Such a description can only capture a fleeting aspect of the living reality which is multi-faceted and ambivalent. As a dynamic field of tension, Judaism is likely to be articulated at any one time in radically different ways, by those who represent its objective-rationalistic genius and by those who reflect its subjective-romantic impetus. Generally speaking, the intellectual leaders are apt to cling to the pole of humanism and rationality, while the masses are certain to center their ardor on the emotional and the esthetic, the dogmatic and the mythical, the superstitious, and the ethnic phases of the tradition. But, this probable polarization is complicated by the well-known fact that any popular cause will never lack educated and eloquent spokesmen. There will always be a kind of elite, who devote themselves to the fortification of the popular faith, either because they have not outgrown the mentality of the people or because it normally pays to tell the people what they want to hear. Honest intellectuals are often misled by the spurious rationality of "common consent." Therefore, we cannot be content with the distinction between "popular" and "official" aspects of a faith.

Also, as we noted, faith, like a tree, should grow in depth as well as in height. Often indeed, the advance of the human spirit in one direction results temporarily at least in the shrinking of other aspects of the faith. Have not rationalistic ages been notoriously insensitive to the deeper nuances of faith?

All ideals, tragically enough, cast a shadow even as they throw a beam of light into the Unknown. Like a flashlight suddenly directed at one point, the brightness of illumination thus generated makes the darkness at its edges all the more impenetrable. Since religion constitutes the totality of idealism, this paradox affects its structure far more powerfully than it does other aspects of human culture. Hence, the importance of this threefold criterion.

In all our discussion of the nature of religion, we have not designated any ideas as being absolutes. We did not assume a concept of God, so true and perfect as to serve as a standard by which lesser conceptions are to be judged. Neither did we assume that certain revealed truths were from time to time injected into the course of history. Nor did we assert that the bi-polar orientation of the human spirit was bound to result in a steady and necessary pace of progress. Do we then propose a relativistic view of history? Is our perspective totally devoid of secure landmarks and guidelines that are rooted in the nature of things? By no means. We must distinguish between the idea of perfection and a perfect idea. In history, we recognize the aspiration to attain perfection as the noblest endeavor of man. The philosopher seeks the perfection of truth, the statesman the perfection of public ardor, the priest the perfection of man's accord with the Ultimate, the prophet the perfection of the individual's striving for ethical action. But this outreaching of the human spirit must not be identified with the fullness of possession. "Ye shall be holy, for I the Lord am holy"[8]—while God *is* holy, man can only *become* holy. We cannot assume that we stand today at the final goal-post of human history, judging the faltering efforts and tragic travail of man from the peak of perfection. It is precisely this prideful dogma that we have to guard against, for it is the proximate cause of stagnation and sterility. We hear this note in the last gasp of Roman paganism, an edict of the Emperor Diocletian; "For it is the height of criminality to reexamine doctrines once and for all settled and fixed by the ancients."[9]

Do we then deny the reality of absolute truths? No. But we deny the human possession of these absolutes; at least, we do not affirm such absolutes as the axioms of our inquiry. Truth grows out of the clash and juxtaposition of data, whereby the correctness of tentative judgments is tested. When we set ourselves the task of judging the nature of the *whole* of being, we cannot maintain the absolute truth of any verdict, since all the relevant facts are not available. The Absolute is there, but any formulation of it is bound to bear the marks of time and the stigmata of partiality. As to Divine revelation, we intend to set things down from the human point of view. All new insights, all successful breakthroughs either in the perception of truth or in the apprehension of moral and esthetic values can be described as data of revelation. Such a description is motivated by subjective needs, the language of feeling, the dialectic of imagination, or the logic of social necessities. In private prayer and in public worship, we naturally employ the symbolic language of man's inner life. But, apart from poetry and prayer, we can only describe things from the human point of view, as insights, in which truth and folly are inevitably mixed, not as Divinely revealed truths.

The needs of our human situation require that we speak and act *as if* our highest ideals had independent existence. Rooted in the Cosmos, they compel our attention and demand the surrender of our self. This logic of the human imagination was recognized by John Dewey as a basic fact. The human imagination at its best is not arbitrary and loose. It too is subject to certain inherent necessities and regularities. This is the secret of good art. And the greatest Art of all is religion, the art of the good life. In order that the diverse goals and purposes of life be integrated and endowed with meaning, we need to project an all-embracing ideal into the Universe and then submit to judgment in the light of this Supreme Ideal. We have to live in the present as if the ultimate goal of man's search were known. At the same time, we must not confuse the psychology of subjectivity and of a creative imagination with the logic of objectivity and the nature of the Absolute.

On this view, progress is never certain. Nor can the religious climate of any one age be easily assayed. Our three criteria of progress are likely to afford us contradictory testimony regarding the piety of any generation. The differences among individuals within the same polarized religious tradition are, from our standpoint, far more significant than the identity of external symbols and dogmas. Frequently, the so-called advance of man's mind is only the record of development of a small elite, while behind the charade of changing intellectual fashions popular religion remains virtually the same. In any case, we cannot offer a clear dissection of periods and phases. Somewhat after the fashion of market-analysts, we shall strive to take account of the "depth" of facts and feelings as well as of their statistical frequency.

Nationalism, like religion, is in any one age a patchwork of compromise between the two orientations of the soul. Objectively we reason in terms of the human family as a whole. But this concept is fleeting and abstract. Man's imagination is hard put to endow the concept of man in general with a solid anchorage and the feel of reality. Perhaps mankind will not really attain a "clear and adequate idea" of itself, until "the little men from Mars" lay siege to our planet.

Tragically enough, it is only by slow and painful stages that the group-consciousness of people is broadened. Primitive man is governed by clans. It takes a measure of intellectual tradition to create a tribe, which is an association of clans. Through a similar development, an association of tribes comes into being, cherishing a common past and common religious objects of worship as well as a common language and possibly a common government. An association of tribes may evolve into a nation through the acceptance of an inner judicial and administrative system. The emergence of a United States of Europe presages the concept of a "family of nations."

At each stage in their ascent from the clan to the great society of the future, people have to resolve the tension between the subjective mood which sanctifies the existing barriers and a modicum of increasing objectivity. Clinging to all that is "his own"—clan or tribal custom— primitive man tends to resist any objective criticism of tribal mores or any widening of tribal boundaries. As far as historic memory goes, men always treated those who were akin to them with consideration and rough justice. But they were very slow in recognizing the rights of "foreigners." Differences in sex and in social class were at one time considered sufficient to exclude a person from the inner circle of kinship. Thus, the patricians and the plebeians of early Rome were for many centuries not allowed to intermarry. And the status of women in ancient Rome was so low as to be only one notch above that of the slave. Exclusion of "strangers" from all rights in the country was general throughout the ancient world. Even philosophers like Plato and Aristotle maintained that only Hellenes were designed by nature to be free, while "barbarians" were intended by nature for menial work and slavery. So wise, liberty-loving, and tolerant a statesman as Pericles sponsored an Athenian law that prohibited an Athenian citizen from marrying a Greek woman from another city.

The subjectivity of tribalism is overcome only in part by the dawning of objective intelligence, for the bias of ethnicism is more resistant to reason than the dogmas of faith. In large part, tribal allegiance is overcome in sentiment and in imagination by the building up of a more potent and more radiant aura around the larger culture-sphere of the nation. Thus, during the nineteenth century, the vision of Germany became far more radiant than that of any of its component states, and during the twentieth century, the concept of a Teutonic race displaced for many the idea of the State. Similarly, Italy as a whole could appeal to more powerful, romantic loyalties than either Tuscany, or Venice, or Sardinia. The larger unit was endowed with an "image" so resplendent that all parochial and provincial loyalties were put in the shade.

The national "image" contains a blend of many objective values along with the subjective picture of the nation. It is maintained that the nation in question is a superior breed of humanity, more devoted than other breeds to liberty or to order, to democracy or to aristocracy, to religion or to science, to rationalism or to romanticism. Whichever of the two pairs of values is chosen by the prophets of nationalism at any one time depends on the ideal that happens then to be fashionable. And the various economic or social groups comprising the nation add the tincture of their particular, political faiths to the national "self-image."

It is important to realize that the boundaries of nations, in ancient as in modern times, were the result of accidental causes. No one today takes seriously the nationalist ambitions of the Scottish or the Welsh, of the Basques or the Burgundians, of the Prussians or the Swabians, of the Pisans or the Florentines. Yet these groups were at one time "nations"; they would still be "nations" today, had only a few purely political or military events taken a different turn.

We think of the Hellenes as a "nation." The language, faith, and culture of the Hellenes were indeed great and distinctive. In addition, they had some religious institutions in common. The association of twelve tribes in the Delphic amphictyony was the closest the Greeks came to the achievement of unity before Philip of Macedonia.

Nevertheless, the Athenians considered themselves a "nation," and they set out to establish an Athenian Empire with other Greek cities as their colonies. This ambition was not only due to a political ideal, namely, their infatuation with the concept of a *Polis,* a self-governing city, but also to their belief that they were a "treasure-people," "the educators of Hellas." They were not willing to accord to other Greek cities the privileges of freedom which they demanded for themselves.

544

Their Athenian "idealism" was so strong that they coldly condemned the entire male populations of conquered Hellenic cities to slaughter, and sold the women into slavery.

The "self-image" of a nation is partly the product of its political history and partly the product of a cultural tradition, and it depends as much upon the capacity to forget as upon the capacity to remember. The structure of the nationalist imagination requires the myth of an original, ancestral family out of which the nation emerged, as a complex organism grows out of a simple nucleus. This myth of common descent becomes in turn the focus of popular feeling and its so-called ideology. Blood and soil tend to shunt culture and ideals into the background. Biological nationalism is thus inherent in the nature of the movement, by reason of the romance and mystery, myth and magic that envelops all that is subjective. Once it becomes frankly biological, nationalism is launched on the slippery road toward the myths and idols of racism. Then the "purity" of the nation's blood is extolled with dogmatic zeal and jealously guarded.

But as we have seen the genius of nationalism contains a potent dose of objective idealism. Without the aid of this universal concept, the "self-image" of the nation would not have become strong enough to overcome the centrifugal forces of tribe and province. The inclusion of universal ideals is also compelled by the need to placate man's rational faculties. Within the domain of nationalism, accordingly, a perpetual tug of war ensues between objective ideals and sheer, blood-based ethnicism. This inner tension is articulated at various times, in the conflict between those who give primacy to the ideals of the nation and those who stress the supreme worth of the nation's life.

When people have grown civilized enough to be ashamed of sheer instincts, but not yet critical enough to view themselves objectively, they are quite likely to use universal ideals as the guise and disguise of their instincts. The initial step of Adam and Eve on their way to civilization was to cover their nakedness with a fig-leaf. Thus, once an ethnic group has acquired an idealized vision of the collective "self-image," its nationalism is far more potent than natural, unsophisticated ethnicism.

For such is the peculiar logic of human nature. Collective dedication to an ideal leads to collective self-glorification and the glorified self-image becomes the excuse for inflicting massive crimes upon the "un-glorified" section of humanity. Thus, did the "liberty-loving" Athenians of the Golden Age set out to deprive other Greek cities of their freedom. Similarly, the Israelites, newly consecrated as "a people of priests and a holy nation" proceeded with gusto to exterminate the Canaanites. The illustrations for this theme in our own day could fill a library.

The ambiguous loyalties of nationalism stand astride man's progress toward a universal society. They are like a tunnel through which mankind must needs pass on its way toward a brighter horizon. Seen from the side of tribalized and feudalized societies, nationalism is a mighty movement of liberation and progress. It enables a backward population to overcome the stunting yokes of petty, parochial loyalties, which stand in the way of a united effort to mobilize its constructive energies. It provides the energy to batter down feudal privileges and to launch a nation on the road to economic progress. Only nationalism, whipped to a frenzy, can provide the enthusiasm and energy needed for the forced marches of the Asian and African "nations" toward a tolerable standard of living.

Neither in Russia nor in China could Communism muster the vast energies it needed without arousing the slumbering loyalties of a resurgent nationalism. Thus even so rigid and inflexible an ideology as Communism was compelled to make common cause with nationalism, though in theory the Communist faith is strictly internationalistic.

In addition to its role as a liberating force in the backward areas of the globe, nationalism fulfills a cultural and humanizing function in the countries of the West. It erects walls which help the individual to feel at home in the vast and open space of a friendless world. It sets up a style of life and a heroic standard and it persuades the individual to submit to the charm and spell of the national virtues. For most people, the vision of humanity is still a vague abstraction, while the nation provides a concrete and vital image, which relates them to society. People can feel as leaves on the tree of life of the nation, but it taxes their imagination too much to see themselves as leaves on the tree of humanity. The domain of human culture is for the present a confluence of diverse and distinct streams of tradition, not a homogeneous ocean in which the salts of different cultures are dissolved. The national ideal is therefore still of vital importance in the total economy of man's spiritual life, though the vision of an Atlantic Community or of a Western "family of nations" is already on the horizon.

At the same time, nationalism is the largest single barrier in the path of an emergent universal society. It distorts the judgment of people quite as much as the dogmatism of a fundamentalist faith, and it leads inevitably to injustice and war. It will be overcome in the future by the very process that brought nationalism into being—namely the movement of the soul toward ever wider dimensions of objectivity and ever deeper layers of subjectivity. The perfection and well-being of the individual transcends the ideal of nationalism on the coordinate of subjectivity, while the emergence of the vision of a universal society transcends the parochial boundaries of nationalism on the coordinate of objectivity. Thus, nationalism, like religion, can be transcended and advanced by the same rhythm of spiritual alternation.

Idolatry in religion is the resistance of the soul to the dynamism of a living faith. When the mind refuses to proceed from the recognition of many gods to belief in One God, we have polytheistic idolatry. When an image that reflected a novel insight at one time is worshiped as the final vision of the Supreme Being, we have iconolatry. When a ritual act (not a dogmatic belief) is asserted to be the ultimate Will of God, we have an idolatry of action (orthopraxis as against orthodoxy). Whenever any system of thought is set up as the final summation of truth, we have the peculiar idolatry of ideologists and academicians. In each case, the footprints of man's progress are cherished rather than the direction of his advance.

The inability of a people to transcend their own national loyalties is the inherent idolatry of nationalism. The same resistance of the spirit is at fault in both politics and religion. When a people insists on sticking to the level of "know nothingism," or worse, using objective ideals for the purpose of sanctifying the collective egotism of the nation, we have the typical sin of idolatry in its nationalistic garb.

Progress in nationalism as in religion can be gauged by the same standards—the continuity of tension between subjective loyalties and objective ideals, the progressive deepening of the vision of the ideal individual, and the ideal society of mankind, the refusal of the people to idolize themselves and their readiness to submit their collective aims to objective scrutiny.

In certain circumstances, nationalism and religion tend to coalesce. Emile Durkheim, the French sociologist, overstated the degree of the relationship when he maintained that religion generally was simply the projection onto the metaphysical screen of the national group-consciousness. But it cannot be denied that in primitive societies, the distinction becomes nebulous; even the so-called higher religions which address their message to all, nurture on occasion the feelings of nationalism, and derive strength from the ethnic consciousness of their people.

When a particular national group of a certain faith is involved in a struggle against enemies of another faith, as well as of a different nationalism, then the two ideals tend to merge. Thus, the Poles in their national struggles against the Protestant Germans and the Greek Orthodox Russians sought comfort and sustenance in their Catholic faith. Similarly, the Irish Catholics could not be open-minded concerning the arguments of the English Episcopalians and Presbyterians. Many of the sectarian divisions in Europe reflected ethnic rivalries. Thus, the Czechs flocked to the banner of John Huss and a number of the German princes rushed to the standard of Martin Luther. In earlier centuries, the Goths accepted the Aryan form of Christianity. The native Egyptians and the Armenians embraced a Monophysite version of Christianity and the Persians, overwhelmed by the Arab Moslem invaders, sought shelter under the aegis of the heretical Shiia sect.

To all the nations of Europe, the Christian faith came from an extra-national source. Still, some of the European nations acquired their national consciousness and their faith at one and the same time. The Poles, the Russians, and the Hungarians remembered very little, if anything, from their pre-Christian days. And the Christian Spanish nation was forged in the fires of a continuous Catholic crusade against the Iberian Moors.

When the loyalty of religion is reinforced by ethnic bonds, we may expect redoubled tension between objective idealism and subjective self-glorification in both domains of the human spirit. The idealistic phases of nationalism are likely to be unfolded and illuminated, since religion focuses attention on the individual and on objective human ideals. On the other hand, the saintly aura of religion might bathe the raw impulses of nationalism in a mysterious glow and raise them beyond the reach of rational criticism. Similarly, the bonds of ethnic loyalty are likely to furnish a powerful cementing force to the ritualistic phases of religion, since ethnicism is essentially romantic, subjective, and conservative. On the other hand, concern with the actual problems of a living people is likely to prevent a religion from becoming totally other-wordly, mystical, and rigidly dogmatic. Nationalism tends to direct the fervor of religious devotion into the channels of the actual historic community. It checks the flight of the mystic, restrains the fancy of the poet, assuages the ardor of the ascetic, and recalls the fanatical dogmatist to the realities of life.

In Judaism, the unity of ethnic awareness and religious loyalty is fundamental and of a peculiar intimacy. Accordingly, we may expect to find the usual tensions of ethnicism and faith magnified and intensified, with the surge of idealism reaching occasionally peculiar heights even as from time to time the pathos of sacred egotism may sink to the lowest depths. As we turn our attention to the formative period of the Jewish mentality, we find the heights of objective thought and universal sympathy conjoined with intensified feelings of ethnic pride and religious exclusiveness. Instead of the usual monolithic picture, depicting either nobility of soul or meanness of spirit, we find both extremes of the universal tensions of the human spirit. In Jewish experience, we see exemplified the basic tensions of humanity—only more so.

NOTES

1. Adolf Harnack, *The Expansion of Christianity* (Boston, 1957), vol. 1, "Excursus on the Third Race."
2. Bahya Ibn Pakuda, *Duties of the Heart* (Jerusalem, 1970), Introduction.
3. Erich Fromm, *The Art of Loving,* New York, 1959.
4. Elijah de Vidash, *Reshith Hochmo,* Shaar Ahavah, Chapter 4.
5. B. Spinoza, *Ethics,* Book V.
6. Plato, *Phaedrus,* 279C.
7. Harnack, the historian of the early Church, attributed the decline of Christianity to its encounter with Greek philosophy, resulting in the substitution of dogmas for living experience. R. Sohn considered institutionalism to be the cause of decline. Adolf Harnack, *Outlines of the History of Dogma* (Boston, 1957).
8. Leviticus 11:44.
9. Naphtali Lewis and Meyer Reinhold (eds.), *Roman Civilization* (New York, 1955), vol. II, p. 585.

25

THE COVENANT CONCEPT—
PARTICULARISTIC,
PLURALISTIC, OR FUTURISTIC?

IN A DRAFT STATEMENT by a group of rabbis attending an interfaith seminar, the following sentence occurred: "It must be emphasized
that the traditional Jew cannot conceive of God entering into a covenant with another special group of humans".

Since the statement was tentative, the authors asking that it "*not* be
reproduced or printed", we do not here identify the source. But the
harsh exclusiveness of this sentence is so painfully clear that it may well
serve as an introduction to our theme.

Naturally, the term "the traditional Jew", can be taken in the sense
of the average person, the man in the street. We can hardly expect to
encounter theological sophistication at streetcorners. Still, the purpose
of all theology is to affect the thought and feeling of the common man.
In that sense, this assertion may not be fallacious. But if tradition be
taken in its fullness, then this remark is as untrue as it is naive. What is
the meaning of the covenant in traditional Judaism?—Is it as simplistic
and exclusive as the quoted statement implies? Or does it allow for a
pluralistic conception with the possibility being projected of several
covenants valid simultaneously, or does the very nature of a covenant
with the Transcendent God exclude the presumption of knowing God's
Will, in its fullness?—If so, other covenants with other peoples cannot
be ruled out.

Our analysis will deal with the covenant concept in Judaism, but the
implications of our study are manifestly ecumenical. In each of the three

549

monotheistic faiths—Judaism, Christianity, Islam—the same dilemmas and problems, even if not the same solutions, will be found.

We begin with the covenant concept, as it appears in the Hebrew Scriptures. The biblical authors were searching for an apt metaphor of man's encounter with God. They thought of God as Creator of "heaven and earth"; they experienced God's "nearness" to their hearts and souls;[1] they were certain of His sustaining power—"underneath are the everlasting arms";[2] they despised the superstitions and abominations of the pagans, and by way of contrast knew themselves to be uniquely favored, exalted, chosen, loved; they yearned for a concrete practice or symbol that would serve as a perpetual reminder of the fleeting moments of exultant faith. While they were aware of the human impossibility of grasping the fullness of the Divine Will, they, humanly enough, sought to imprison the Infinite within the bounds of the finite. The concept of a universal emperor governing his far flung empire indirectly, through intermediaries, and covenanting with one people as objects of his special concern seemed to fit these experiences.

In essence, the golden moments of revelation occur in the lives of all people. Deep crises and existential contradictions are followed by the reassertion of the familiar landmarks of the spirit. This rebound from anomie and despair is at times synthetic rather than a return to the status quo ante. Surges of reassurance in the value and truth of a transmitted tradition, serve to integrate newly perceived spiritual ideals with the practices of the past. An illumination suggestive of infinite horizons supervenes upon an intoxicating enthusiasm for a particular tradition, bounded by fixed dogmas and ethnocentric myths.

The prophetic experience of revelation is the general faith-event in our life, molded by an impassioned ethical concern and articulated poetically.[3] Faith is an event, a process, a pulsation, as are all things in an organismic universe. In this event, the Whole becomes an overwhelming reality to a person, in thought as truth, in feeling as love, in the resolve so to act as to repeat the experience. Love generates the yearning for more love and the determination to make oneself and society fit "dwelling places for the *Shechinah*".

The faith-event contains several polarities—God is transcendent, yet He is somehow "near to those who call upon Him in truth". He is the One God of all mankind, but He chooses certain persons, peoples, moments, to express His Will. He demands loyalty and faithfulness to all that is humane and ethical, but also loyalty and faithfulness to Himself.[4] He favors that which all good men everywhere feel is good and right, but He also demands specific sanctifying rituals, which are peculiar to His service—"be ye holy, for I am holy".[5] Above all, His Will is both clear and elusive—clear enough to be known by every person, in his "solitariness", or in his moments of "ultimate concern", but also He is so elusive that only when people are given a "new heart and new spirit" can they truly serve Him.[6]

In sum, in the moments of revelation, we experience three dimensions of feelings—each with its own Yea and Nay. *Reassurance*—the Transcendent God is "near" to the pious, as Protector and Redeemer; but also far, with all our insights being feeble stabs in the dark—"the Lord is in His holy temple, let the whole world be silent before Him".[7] *Reorientation* to specific ideals and goals, along with an awareness of His concern for all men and the elusiveness of His Will. *Rededication* to the quest of His nearness, in the future, since in the present the bounds of finitude cannot encompass the Infinite. The negative awareness, that we can neither comprehend nor impose limits on either His Being or His Will or His Purpose, is as integral to the experience of revelation as the affirmative grasp of some commands or symbols, which were associated with holiness at a particular time and place.

Indeed, the knowledge that we do *not* know God's Will is as essential to the Divine encounter in monotheism as the same affirmation in the philosophy of Socrates. The first two of the ten commandments "were spoken by the Power itself", we are told in the Talmud.[8] The other eight were pronounced by Moses. In other words, the Divine encounter itself contains only a *Yea*—God is here as Revealer and as Redeemer, and a *Nay*—no words and no figures can represent Him fully. So, when Moses asked "to see His Glory", he was told that only fleeting memories of His having passed, metaphorically, "His back" could be apprehended.[9]

Biblical religion, we must remember, was unique, not in its affirmation of a revelation or a covenant, for these were common convictions in the pagan world. The uniqueness of the biblical faith lay in its negation—the One God towers above and beyond any representation or any revelation. In dedicating the Holy Temple as "the dwelling place" of God, King Solomon stated, "The Lord has chosen to dwell in darkness".[10]

n view of the twofold cutting edge of revelation, we may well inquire vhether the covenant concept can serve as an adequate metaphor for he experience of revelation. Manifestly, the concept itself varied greatly ven in the earliest periods of the Hebrew Scriptures. There was the :ontract between equals, two friends, or man and wife. More typical of he ancient world was the contract between a godlike King and his ʳassals. The famed biblical scholar, Harry Orlinsky, maintains that the ᵒrmer experience was paradigmatic to the biblical authors.

"In the view of the biblical writers, God and Israel had entered ᵥoluntarily into a contract as equal partners to serve and further the interests of one another exclusively".[11]

While he allows that the biblical authors assumed the existence of a concurrent covenant with humanity, he does not provide for the sense of infinite horizons in any genuine religious experience. In a note, he disputes the validity of "the vassal type of covenant of ancient peoples".[12]

In our view, his interpretation fits some passages of the Bible. But, it is altogether inadequate for the understanding of the spectrum of meanings in the biblical covenant concept. The tensions and paradoxes within the concept ranged from the seemingly arbitrary Divine choice of and covenant with Abraham to the absence of a Divine commitment in the Faithful Agreement of Ezra and Nehemiah.[13] Abraham's call is described as a kind of exodus, the beginning of the destiny of Israel. And it is stated in terms of universality—"and all the nations of the earth will be blessed through you".[14] The dimension of "not yet" is echoed in the prediction of 400 years of slavery and torment for the children of Israel. The one note of "equality" is detectable in Abraham's bold outcry—"can it be that the judge of the entire earth will not do justice?"[15] But, even then Abraham acts as a spokesman for humanity, who is also a humble petitioner, not an equal partner.

The covenant of Ezra and Nehemiah is concluded not between God and men but between the leading men of Jerusalem themselves. There is no reference in the introductory prayer of Ezra and Nehemiah to the covenant of Moses either at Sinai or in the prairies of Moab. At Sinai God gave commands, true *Torot,* good *mizvot.*[16] God commands and the Jew obeys. Nehemiah's only reference to a covenant is to the one concluded with Abraham, "the father of a multitude of nations".

As we survey the various references to a covenant in the Hebrew Sciptures, we find that this notion is open-ended in several ways; it is counterbalanced by several other covenants—the covenant with mankind, represented by Adam and Eve, also by Noah and his descendants; with Abraham as the father of all who convert. Indeed the call for a renewal of the covenant in the future is integral to the awareness of a covenant in the past.

Moses himself felt the need of renewing the covenant in the prairies of Moab; so did Joshua,[17] Jehoioda,[18] and King Josiah.[19] Special covenants were drawn up in order to achieve national reforms—to free the Hebrew slaves in Jerusalem[20] and to expel the foreign women.[21] In addition, special covenants were made with the children of Levi, of Aaron and of David.

The prophets were uncomfortable with the notion of setting conditions for and limitations upon God's Will. God's relations with Israel were due to His goodness, His love, His compassion. The first Isaiah does not mention the word, covenant. His call for Israel's loyalty draws upon the natural feelings of gratitude for special favors. Isaiah was keenly conscious of the transcendent majesty of the Lord—the "mysterium trememdum" of holiness. "High as are the heavens above the earth, so high are My thoughts to your thoughts".[22] Hosea accuses the people of transgressing the covenant, "like Adam", referring possibly to generally human sins.[23] Amos speaks of Israel's singularity in "being known" to God, but he also affirms that "they (Israelites) are like the children of the Ethiopians unto me".[24]

In the later prophets, the notion of a covenant is referred to the future and its very meaning is spiritualized. Hosea describes the future covenant when war will be no more and Israel will be betrothed in steadfast love, in compassion and in faithfulness.[25] Jeremiah speaks of "putting the Torah in the hearts of the people" as a new covenant. Ezekiel predicts "a covenant of peace, an eternal covenant".[26] Deutero-Isaiah foretells in one of the "Servant" chapters a new creation of the people whereby they will be transformed "into a covenanted people, a light to the nations".[27] Malachi's "angel of the covenant" also belongs to the future and is apparently concerned with the purification of the ritual.[28]

Manifestly, many of the biblical authors were keenly aware of the dangers inherent in the notion of the covenant—the narcissistic feeling of superiority; the legalistic tendency to reduce a living faith to so many fragmented practices;[29] the confining of the transcendent and eternal God within the narrow limits of a time-conditioned body of specifications. In sum, the covenant concept may easily be corrupted to the point of shutting out the openness of the faith-event, its dynamism, its infinite outreach. To counter the formalism inherent in the covenant concept, the Bible frequently adds the words, *hesed,* steadfast love, or *shalom,* peace, to the word, *berit,* covenant.

The tensions within the covenant concept became more marked during the Hellenistic period. It suffices to note that Philo hardly refers to any covenant. In his life of Abraham, he writes of the divine commands written in nature as well as in the Torah.[30] Abraham's migrations are symbolic of "the search for the true God". Abraham was "himself a law and an unwritten statute".[31] He stresses the humanistic purpose of the choice of Israel—"the nation dearest of all to God, which as I hold, received the gift of priesthood and prophecy on behalf of all mankind".[32]

As the latest edition of the Theological Dictionary of the New Testament summarizes the evolution of the covenant idea in the Septuagint and Philo,

"The divine will self-revealed in history and establishing religion—this is the religious concept of the *diathiki* in the LXX and it represents a significant development of the Hebrew term even while preserving its essential content".

"Even in Philo the firmly developed religious concept shines through the enveloping imagery. The term is obviously a formula for the gracious will of God disclosed in history".[33]

Paul's development of covenant theology by contrasting the covenant of Abraham with that of Moses and the covenant of spirit with that of the letter set the stage for a bitter polemic with the Jewish Sages.[34] Matthew's formulation of Jesus' saying at the Last Supper brought Paul's interpretation into the central life of the Church.[35]

The third century rabbis countered by asserting that "Abraham our father observed all the commandments of the Torah, even to the mixing of cooked food"[36] (a rabbinically-instituted ordinance, whereby one was permitted to prepare food on a holiday for the Sabbath). Both religions were dominated frequently by the champions of an exclusionist theology.

However, even in the ancient world, non-exclusionist voices were heard from time to time. The tannaitic sages affirmed the validity of the *Seven Laws of Noah,* that is, of the universal revelation of ethics and faith.[37] They also declared that true prophets arose among the Gentiles.[38] A prophet, as the rabbis taught, was a messenger sent to a particular people. In other words, more than one valid body of revealed laws is possible. We recall that while the Stoics believed in the universal dissemination of "seeds of reason", the rabbis regarded Wisdom itself as deriving from the Supreme Being.[39] Indeed, for the rabbis, Wisdom was a concomitant of Torah, inseparable from the Torah itself, the gift of revelation. "If there is no wisdom, there is no piety; if there is no piety, there is no wisdom".[40] In this spirit Rabban Gamliel defended Peter and the apostles, offering a pragmatic counsel—"Refrain from these men and let them alone, for if this counsel or this work be of men, it will come to naught, but if it be of God, ye cannot overthrow it; lest haply ye be found to fight even against God".[41] The head of the Pharisaic school allowed that there might be other versions of revelation than those entrusted to his care. Similarly, at the trial of Paul, when Gentile Christians were already a dominant factor, the Pharisees declared, "We find no evil in this man; but if a spirit or an angel hath spoken to him, let us not fight against God".[42]

These liberal opinions were echoed in *The Ethics of the Fathers,* where an Alexandrine Sage declares that "an ecclesia for the sake of heaven is certain to endure".[43] We can hardly doubt that he referred to the Christian church—it endures because it is inspired by the love of God. Another second century Sage asserted that a Gentile who sincerely engages in the study of Torah—either of the universal teachings of Noah or the Law of Judaism—is like the High Priest, who enters the Holy of Holies.[44]

Such voices, however, were rare in the troubled centuries of the ancient world. The predominant atmosphere of the Talmud was zealously exclusive. The Gentiles, taken as a whole, were presumed to have violated the Noachide laws.[45] They were therefore utterly condemned. Satan's corruption had marred their judgment; their only chance is to convert to Judaism when the Messiah comes; in that case they will enter the dubious category of "unwilling converts" *(gerim gerurim).*[46] The Israelites, too, would not have accepted the Torah, if they had been free to follow their own inclinations. But the Lord lifted up the mountain-range of Sinai and held it over their heads, threatening to bury them if they did not consent to abide by the Torah. It was only in the time of

Mordecai and Esther, a millenium or so after Moses, that the Israelites proved themselves to be willing martyrs for the sake of Torah.[47]

Did the biblical authors believe that God could not or would not conclude a Torah-like covenant with other peoples?—There appears to be no warrant for any such belief. Isaiah looked forward to a triumvirate of the chosen:

"In that day Israel will be the third with Egypt and Assyria, a blessing in the midst of the earth, whom the Lord of hosts has blessed, saying 'Blessed be Egypt my people, and Assyria the work of my hands, and Israel my heritage' ".[48] The notion that all genuine worship is addressed to the One God is implied by Malachi.

"For from the rising of the sun to its setting my name is great among the nations, and in every place incense is offered to my name, and a pure offering; for my name is great among the nations, says the Lord of hosts".[49]

Zephaniah compares the diverse rituals of the various nations to a babel of languages, which will be turned into "pure speech", the worship of the One God.[50]

As to the Sages of the Talmud, we noted their ambivalence. We encounter references to an oath that God took not to *transfer* His covenant to other nations.[51] His faithfulness precluded any revocation of His relationship to Israel, as Paul argued in Romans 9–11, but it did not prevent Him from adding new persons to His people or contrariwise reducing His people to the barest minimum. No one questioned that the Messianic Age would witness the conversion of all nations to the true faith of Israel.[52] And the "light of the Messiah" might appear slowly and by degrees, like the dawn.[53] So, in the eschaton, all mankind will be included in God's plan of redemption.

To be sure, the Sages assert that the Lord consented to Moses' request not to allow His *Shechinah* to rest on nations other than Israel, but then this tradition reflects the opinion of the exclusionists, who were opposed by the moderates and the rationalists.[54]

Exclusive voices predominated, we may assume, in times of bitter polemic and persecution. "Lest you will say that another Moses will bring us another Torah from heaven . . . (we are assured) that no part of it was left in heaven".[55] Here, then, the negational phase of revelation, the humble acknowledgment of finitude is totally ignored. As a rule, the Sages were reluctant to set up categorical distinctions between the several non-Jewish faiths, exempting some, like the Christians and the

Zoroastrians, from the general category of idolatry. They spoke of the Noachide principles in general, and in specific cases, a Sage could testify, "I know this or that Gentile is not an idol-worshipper".[56] They also observed that "the Gentiles outside the borders of the land of Israel are not idolators, but they are simply following the customs of their fathers".[57]

In respect of non-Jews, then, only God can tell whether they worshipped Him in truth.

If an entire nation embraced the Jewish faith, then they would feel that they were part of greater Israel. So in the letter of Joseph, the Khazar King, we read that he believed the descent of his people was from Japhet, Noah's son, and Togarmo, but that he trusted "the Lord, God of Israel will hasten our redemption, gather our exiles and our scattered ones. . . ."[58] By joining the faith of Israel he and the Khazar nation became part of the larger people of Israel, sharing in its promise of earthly redemption.

Saadia calls the chapter in his book, dealing with the Sinaitic revelation, "Command and Admonition". All rational laws are obligatory for all men. But "in respect of non-rational laws . . . the Creator added them for us by way of command and admonition in order to multiply our reward and our prosperity on their account".[59]

In his view, the covenant with Abraham, the father of all converts to monotheism, continues to be valid, even after the Torah of Moses was accepted by the Israelites.[60]

In his philosophic work, *The Guide of the Perplexed,* Maimonides does not even refer to the verse which tells of Moses concluding the covenant by the sprinkling of blood on the altar and the people.[61] In his interpretation, the authority of the Torah rests on its truth, as attested by the supreme prophetic genius of Moses, not on any contract, duly drawn up, signed and scaled. The very term, *berit,* covenant, hardly occurs in the *Guide of the Perplexed.*

To be sure, in his ninth principle of faith, Maimonides speaks of the belief that the Torah will never be "exchanged" *(muhalefet)* and that there will never be "a different Torah" *(Torah aheret)* deriving from the Creator.[62] Maimonides did not intend to rule out change and adjustment within the life of Torah, as some commentators imagined, but to assert that in its essence the Torah contains philosophic truth, and truth is immutable. Doubtless, he sought to reinforce Jewish resistance to the belligerent assertions of both Christians and Moslems that their revelations abolished the Torah of Moses. On the other hand, he recognized that the two daughter-faiths of Judaism served to prepare humanity for the Messianic Age by disseminating the ideas of monotheism and the scriptural ethic.[63] The philosopher-poet Judah Halevi suggested the metaphor of a tree with a broad stem and three branches. The fruit produced by the three branches will ultimately contain the same seeds, those planted by Abraham.[64]

The fourteenth century philosopher, Joseph Albo, who was called upon to represent Judaism in the famous disputation at Tortosa in 1413–1414 asserted "that it is possible for two divine Torot to be true simultaneously for two different communities".[65]

Albo argues that the Lord is a physician who may well prescribe different medicines to the same person at different times and to different people at the same time.[66]

But while the medieval rationalists allowed for plural covenants, the mystics and romantics thought otherwise. The oft quoted maxim, "the Holy One, blessed be He, the Torah and Israel are one", which the authors of the above mentioned draft take as their fundamental maxim, occurs in the Zohar and it reflects the mystical current of Judaism.[67]

Indeed, the mystical ideology taught that Jews were biologically distinguished from the rest of mankind, their souls being rooted in the highest realm of holiness. A very popular mystic wondered at the fact that Gentiles don't look so very different from Jews, though the souls of the latter derive their sustenance from the Divine Pleroma, while the souls of the former are rooted in the "other side", the demonic realm.[68] Here, then, was a Jewish counterpart to the Spanish infatuation with *limpieza,* limiting posts of responsibility to pure-blooded descendants of "old Christians", on the ground the Jewish souls were corrupted by centuries of disbelief in Christian dogmas. Characteristic of the opposition between the ethnocentric-mystical interpretation of the covenant and the humanist-rationalist view is the contrast in the two interpretations of the "priestly" function of Israel—offered by Rashi and Seforno respectively. Rashi interprets "priests" as meaning princes, that is, the Israelites will become the governors of all other nations; Seforno asserts "this is the import of a 'Kingdom of priests,' to teach and to explain to all men the task of serving God together . . . ."[69]

In the past two centuries, the rationalist-humanistic concept of revelation prevailed in Jewish thought of the western world.

Moses Mendelssohn, the champion of Enlightenment, wrote that the mark of a false religion is precisely its claim to exclusiveness.[70] Even the unbending defender of uncompromising Orthodoxy, Samson Raphael Hirsch, conceived of Jewish destiny in universal terms.

"Their (the Israelites) speedy removal from the Land (of Israel) brought about their spiritual and moral salvation. . . . The State and Temple went to ruin, but the people . . . went out to assume the burdens of their great mission in the Dispersion".

Hermann Cohen brought this rationalist-humanistic trend to its climax, as is evident from the following quotations:

"Man, not the people and not Moses; man, as rational being, is the correlate of the God of revelation".[71]

"The Covenant is the instrument of faithfulness. Therefore, God concludes a covenant with Noah, with Abraham and with Israel".[72]

"God does not love Israel more or differently than His love for men in general. . . . In Israel, God loves Israel only as a model, a symbol of mankind, a mark of distinction within it, for only monotheism is able to establish the unity of the human race".[73]

In his magisterial work, *Jewish Theology,* Kaufmann Kohler, longtime President of the Hebrew Union College, considers the Jewish "trinity" to be not the unity of God, Israel and Torah, but God, Man and the Kingdom of God. He retained his humanistic vision, though he subscribed to some racistic ideas. Reflecting the preoccupation with race in the early decades of the twentieth century, he wrote, "In fact, the soul of the Jewish people reveals a peculiar mingling of characteristics, a union of contrasts which make it especially fit for its providential mission in history".[74]

Martin Buber, as is well known, is unclassifiable. At one time, a folkist, a mystic, an interpreter of *Hassidism,* he moved steadily toward a position "on the boundary", between romanticism and rationalism. In his description of the faith-event in Judaism as a personal "believing in", contrasted with a propositional "believing that", which he attributed to Christianity, he focused attention on the openness of revelation, its transcendence of all knowing. He rejected the legalistic phase of Judaism in order to keep himself open to fresh experiences. He was aware of the danger of reducing religion to a contract, duly signed and delivered. His admiration for *Hassidism* was due to his "idealization" of their movement, especially in its early phases. He identified with their presumed endeavor to transcend the boundaries of the Law.

Franz Rosenzweig, in keeping with his Hegelian orientation, interpreted the covenant between God and Israel as a living tradition, rather than as a book or a series of books. The Divine Will is dynamic, consisting of thrusts of redeeming vitality. Revelation is a continuing phenomenon, with bursts of God's love eliciting new expressions of Israel's love. Rosenzweig regarded the Christian community as a providential instrument for the realization of the covenant with Israel. In his famous metaphor, the function of Christianity is to convert the world; that of Israel to be faithful to its ideal self. Like the sun, which is unthinkable without its rays, the covenant is inconceivable without both Israel and the Church.

Mordecai M. Kaplan devoted his life to the formulation of a synthesis between Jewish nationalism and humanism. He called for the rejection of the dogma of the "Chosen People", in the sense of a people set apart and insulated from the life of humanity. To him, the notion of a special covenant with Israel was abhorrent. All nations are called upon to apply to their own life the prophetic teaching of "ethical nationhood."

We conclude from all the above that the proposition we quoted at the beginning of this essay reflects only one of the several strands composing the Jewish tradition. It articulates the judgment of the fundamentalists, romantics and mystics, certainly not the view of the prophetic-philosophical school, from Abraham to Rosenzweig and from Maimonides to Mordecai Kaplan. I need hardly add that I identify with the philosophical trend in Jewish thought, in the interpretation of the covenant concept. I take the paradigm of the covenant to be Abraham's rebellion against the practice of sacrificing children rather than "his passing between the pieces" of slaughtered animals. The former was then a revolutionary ideal, the latter was already an archaic way of formalizing a contract. The "Faithful Agreement" of Ezra and Nehemiah is to me a demonstration of the way the Jewish tradition took form—through a series of self-assumed ordinances, or *takkanot*. All that we do to express our love of God articulates the voice of God within us. So, the rabbis spoke of ordinances that they themselves formulated as "commandments" of the Lord. There were also survivals from the dim past, such as the system of sacrificial offerings. Such archaic practices should be consciously confined to the past, while their inner spirit is cherished as part of the sacred tradition. In this self-renewing and self-critical spirit, the covenant concept remains valid even in our day.

I offer the following propositions as both a personal confession of faith and as a contemporary expression of the prophetic-philosophical school of thought:

1. A covenant establishes a living tradition, whereby the piety of past generations is preserved as the heritage of succeeding generations. It is through the Jewish tradition that I grew up to feel the majesty and the message of God. But it is also the same tradition that encouraged me to study and to appreciate the open horizons of philosophy and the ardor of other faiths. The emphasis on God's transcendence in Judaism kept me from surrendering to the notion that God's Will, in its fullness, is reflected within my tradition exclusively.

2. A lifetime is needed to sense the import of a great historical faith and relate it to contemporary experience. Therefore, we cannot but live within the confines of one tradition. But, divine revelation in all its dimensions is universal and all-human. Hence, we must learn to maintain a vital tension between our subjective feelings, rites and symbols and the objective world, as it is presented to our minds and hearts by the emergent world-wide culture of which we are part.

3. God is the source of all great and ennobling ideals. Our experience of holiness blends harmoniously all ideals and values, even as the mind synthesizes the impressions of the senses. So, revelation is an extension and harmonization of human values, not a rejection of them. If aught is not humanizing, it is not divine. The thrusts of revelation are not those which shatter the structures of human wisdom, but those which extend and enhance the slow and stumbling efforts of mankind. Just as the God we worship is revealed in the marvels of cosmic creation and the daily wonders of life and spirit, rather than in the so called "miracles" which impress the gullible, so the Word of God is revealed primarily in the common experience and tested wisdom of mankind, secondarily in particular cultures.

4. Particular revelations are vehicles of spiritual power, but their specific content is metaphorical. Our finite minds can reflect the Infinite Mind only "through a glass, darkly", by the utilization of fragments of human experience. Not all metaphors are born equal. They can function as rungs on Jacob's ladder, but also as slippery steps toward the pit of self-righteous illusions. The metaphors of ritual and dogma, in my faith, as in other religious communities, are always more than action-symbols or figures of speech. They are freighted with the memories of the past and

charged with the covenanted loyalty of a living community. As such, they are invaluable, providing we bear in mind their metaphorical character.

5. I repudiate the notion that God "contracted" His Will within the stated precepts of the Jewish tradition, in the same manner as He "contracted" His Infinite Being in order to create this finite universe. This Kabbalistic notion of *tsimtsum* (contraction) cannot be understood literally. In "contracting" Himself, it is He who does the contracting, at every point. There cannot be aught which escapes His Power, "The whole earth is full of His Glory". The description of His self-limitation in allowing room for human freedom is intended to suggest the existence of two levels of reality—as seen by man and as seen by God *(mitsidenu* and *mitsido)*. "Self-contraction" is meaningful only in a metaphorical sense, as "when a father reduces his mind to the level of a small child" when he tells a childish fable or plays childish games. The father's mind remains incomprehensible to the child, while the world of the child is make-believe to the father.

The doctrine of God's "self-contraction", or "withdrawal", or "eclipse", seems plausible when it is applied to the reality of human freedom. If humans are truly free, God must have limited His own Power. But, I contend that it is precisely in the free mind of man that God is most manifest. There are situations in life, where the Presence of God is hidden from our sight, and there are window-like areas, which are transparent to His radiance. In all cases, we can only speak of God's "absence" as a subjective feeling, not as an objective reality. God is everywhere, and He is manifest wherever the "things of God" are realized.

6. When we speak of "the Chosen People" in Judaism, I take the phrase to refer to the ideal Israel, the covenanted people, as in Isaiah's formulation, "to be a covenanted people, a light to the nations". We of Israel are called upon to act as an *example* to other individuals and nations, not as an *exception*. More is expected from those to whom more was given in history, through no merit of their own. At any one time, a particular person or people may have a treasure of spiritual gifts to share with others. But, no individual or people is permanently and in all ways separated from or uplifted above the rest of mankind.

I consider that the Golden Rule applies to communities as well as to individuals—no community should claim exclusive rights or privileges or a unique cosmic status. We should learn to "understand in love" other faiths as we expect others to understand us in love.

NOTES

1. Deuteronomy 30, 14. Isaiah 50, 8. Psalms 34, 19. Psalms 145, 19. Psalms 73, 28.

2. Deuteronomy 33, 27.

3. J. B. Agus, *The Prophet in Modern Hebrew Literature,* in the Goldenson Lectures, 1955–1966, Hebrew Union College Press, Cincinnati, Ohio.

4. Micah 6, 8.

5. Leviticus 19, 2.

6. Ezekiel 36, 26; 11, 19; 18, 31.

7. Habakkuk 2, 20.

8. B. T. Makkot 23b.

9. Exodus 33, 12–23; 34, 1–8.

10. 1 Kings 8, 12.

11. H. Orlinsky, *The Situational Ethics of Violence,* in *Violence and Defense in the Jewish Experience,* J.P.S. Philadelphia, 1977, p. 58.

12. Ibid., note 1, p. 45.

13. Nehemiah 10, 1.

14. Genesis 12, 3.

15. Genesis 18, 25.

16. Nehemiah 9, 13.

17. Joshua 24, 25.

18. 2 Kings 11, 17.

19. 2 Kings 23, 2, 3.

20. Jeremiah 24, 8.

21. Ezra 10, 3.

22. Isaiah 55, 9.

23. Hosea 6, 17.

24. Amos 3, 2; 9, 7.

25. Hosea 2, 20–22.

26. Ezekiel 34, 25. Jeremiah 31, 31.

27. Isaiah 42, 6; 49, 8.

28. Malachi 3, 1.

29. Isaiah 28, 10, 13.

30. Philo. *De Abrabamo,* XIII, 60. Ed. Loeb Classics.

31. Ibid., XLV, 275.

32. Ibid., XIX, 98.

33. *Theological Dictionary of the New Testament,* ed. Gernstel Kittel, Grand Rapids, 1964, Vol. II, pp 127, 128.

34. Galatians 3; 2 Corinthians 3, 6.

35. Matt. 26, 28.

36. B. T. Yoma 28b.
37. B. T. Sanhedrin 56a. Hullin 92a.
38. B. T. Baba Bathra 15b.
39. B. T. Berochot 55a.
40. Abot 3, 14.
41. Acts 5, 38, 39.
42. Acts 23, 9.
43. Abot 4, 11. It is believed *Hasandlor* means the Alexandrian.
44. B. T. Baba Kama 38a.
45. Hullin 92a. Baba Kama 38a.
46. B. T. Avoda Zara 3b.
47. B. T. Sabbat 88a.
48. Isaiah 19, 24.
49. Malachi 1, 11.
50. Zephaniah 3, 9.
51. B. T. Gittin 57b.
52. In Maimonides' formulation of this belief, it is not clear whether "the true faith" of the future will be Judaism or universal religion. *Hilchot Melochim,* XII.
53. Shohar Tov, Tehillim 18. Jerusalem Berochot I, 1.
54. B. T. Baba Bathra 15b.
55. Deuteronomy Rabba 8, 6.
56. B. T. Avoda Zara 65a.
57. B. T. Hullin 13b.
58. Letter of Joseph, King of Khazaria, in introduction to Halevi's *Kuzari.*
59. Saadia, Emunot Vedeot, III, 1.
60. Ibid., III, 7.
61. Exodus 24, 8.
62. Maimonides' introduction to the eleventh chapter of Sanhedrin, in his commentary to the *Mishnah.*
63. Maimonides' Code, *Hilchot Melochim,* S, 12, in the uncensored edition of Constantinople.
64. Judah Halevi, *The Kuzari,* IV, 23.
65. Joseph Albo, *The Book of Principles,* translated by I. Husik, published by J.P.S. Philadelphia, I, 25.
66. Ibid., II, ch. 13–23. See the comments in ch. 10 of Louis Jacobs' *Principles of the Jewish Faith* pp. 302–319, Basic Books, N.Y. 1964.
67. Zohar, Emor, III, 93b.
68. R. Isaiah Hurwitz, *Shenai Lubot Haberit,* Introduction.
69. Exodus, 19, 6.
70. M. Mendelssohn, *Jerusalem,* part two.

71. H. Cohen, *Religion of Reason,* translated from the German by R. Hallo, p. 79.

72. Ibid., p. 441.

73. Ibid., p. 149.

74. K. Kohler, *Jewish Theology,* New York 1968 edition, p. 327.

BIBLIOGRAPHY OF THE WORKS
OF JACOB B. AGUS

BOOKS

Modern Philosophies of Judaism: A Study of Recent Jewish Philosophies of Religion. New York: Behrman's Jewish Book House, 1941.

Message of Judaism. Dayton, Ohio: Beth Abraham United Synagogue Center, Ohio, 1945.

Banner of Jerusalem. New York: Bloch Publishing Company, 1946. Reissued under the title *High Priest of Rebirth: The Life, Times and Thought of Abraham Isaac Kuk.* New York: Bloch Publishing Company, 1972.

The Goldenson Lecture: The Prophet in Modern Hebrew Literature. Cincinnati: Hebrew Union College Press, 1957.

Guideposts in Modern Judaism. New York: Bloch Publishing Company, 1954.

The Evolution of Jewish Thought: From Biblical Times to the Opening of the Modern Era, New York: Abelard-Schuman, 1959. Published in French and Spanish translations. Reissued by New York's Arno Press, 1973.

The Meaning of Jewish History. 2 vols. New York: Abelard-Schuman, 1963.

The Vision and the Way: an Interpretation of Jewish ethics. New York: Frederick Ungar, 1966.

Dialogue and Tradition: The Challenges of Contemporary Judeo-Christian Thought. New York: Abelard-Schuman, 1971.

Jewish Identity in an Age of Ideologies. New York: Frederick Ungar, 1978.

The Jewish Quest: essays on basic concepts of Jewish theology. New York: Ktav Publishing House, Inc., 1983.

566

ARTICLES

"The Offensive for Judaism." *Jewish Outlook* (February 1938): 7–8; (March 1938): 6–8.

"Reply to Critics." *Jewish Outlook* (September 1938): 11–12.

"Thinkers Who Came Home." *Jewish Outlook* (November 1939): 8–11.

"Democracy in Jewish Life." *Reconstructionist* 7, 10 (June 1941): 18–19.

"The Character of Jewish Piety." *Reconstructionist* 8, 5 (April 1942): 14–18.

"Nusach ha Chaim ha Yehudi be-Amerika u-ve-Eretz Yisrael." *Mezuda* 7 (1945): 17–30.

"Orthodox Zionism." *New Palestine* 35, 17 (June 1945): 225–27.

"The Status of American Israel—A Conservative View." *Conservative Judaism* 2, 2 (February 1946): 1–14.

"La-Heker Hegayon Ha-Kabbalah." *Sefer Hashanah li-Yehuday America* 8–9 (1946): 254–79.

"Torah M'Sinai—A Conservative View." *Conservative Judaism* 3, 2 (February 1947): 23–42.

"Ish Hamistorin." *Talpiot* (Nisan 1948): 20–30.

"A Rabbi Speaks His Mind." *Congress Weekly* 14, 13 (March 1947): 5–8.

"Goals for Jewish Living." *Menorah Journal* 36, 1 (winter 1948): 1–25.

"Law in Conservative Judaism." *Conservative Judaism* 5, 1 (October 1949): 26–40.

"Ends and Means of Jewish Life in America." *Menorah Journal* 37, 1 (winter 1949): 10–36.

"Laws as Standards." *Conservative Judaism* 6, 4 (May 1950): 8–26.

"Obsolescence in Jewish Ritual Law." *Conservative Judaism* 7, 4 (June 1951): 9–19.

"Ancient Sanhedrin or Sanhedrin-Academy." *Judaism* 1, 1 (January 1952): 52–63.

"The Idea of God." *Judaism* 1, 3 (July 1952): 203–17.

"Assimilation, Integration, Segregation—The Road to the Future." *Judaism* 3, 4 (April 1954): 498–510.

"Mitzvot—Yes; Averot—No." *Reconstructionist* 21, 6 (April 1955): 9–14.

"Toynbee and Judaism." *Judaism* 4, 4 (fall 1955): 319–32.

"Can Judaism without Walls Endure?" *National Jewish Monthly* (March 1956): 14–56.

"Towards a Philosophy of Jewish History." *Judaism* 5, 2 (spring 1956): 99–107.

"An Answer to Rabbi Blumenthal." *Conservative Judaism* 11, 2 (spring 1956): 18–27.

"Nationalistic Philosophies of Jewish History," *Judaism* 5, 3 (summer 1956): 256–71.

"Mixed Pews in Jewish Tradition." *Conservative Judaism* 11, 1 (fall 1956): 32–41.

"Rebuttal of Presentation of Rabbi Lapidus and the Statements of Rabbis Silver and Soloveitchik." *Conservative Judaism* 11, 1 (fall 1956): 53–58.

"Synthesis in Current Philosophies of Jewish History." *Judaism* 6, 1 (winter 1957): 56–69.

"Polarity in Jewish History." *Judaism* 6, 2 (spring 1957): 160–70.

"The Meaning of the Mitzvot: An Analysis of Heinemann's *Ta-amei Ha-mitzvot Besiphrut Yisrael*." *Conservative Judaism* 11, 4 (summer 1957): 24–34.

"Standards and the Ideal." *Reconstructionist* 24, 4 (April 1958): 18–23.

"The Nature and Task of Liberal Judaism." *Judaism* 7, 4 (fall 1958): 291–301.

"Claude Montefiore and Liberal Judaism." *Conservative Judaism* 13, 2 (winter 1959): 1–21.

"Tradition and Change." *Conservative Judaism* 13, 2 (winter 1959): 46–54.

"Survival: Faith and Culture *versus* Blood and Politics." *Menorah Journal* 48, 1–2 (autumn–winter 1960): 1–8.

"Toward a Philosophy of Hope." *Judaism* 9, 2 (spring 1960): 99–111.

"An Analysis of Milton Steinberg's *Anatomy of Faith,* ed. Arthur Cohen." *Conservative Judaism* 14, 4 (summer 1960): 1–4.

"Towards a Philosophy of Hope." *Judaism* 9, 4 (fall 1960): 351–65.

"Toward a Conservative Philosophy of Jewish Education." *Synagogue School* 19, 3 (March–April 1961): 5–15.

"Toynbee's Epistle to the Jews." *Commentary* 3, 32 (September 1961): 239–42.

"Freedom and the Judeo-Christian Tradition." *Jewish Heritage* (summer 1962): 5–11.

"Jewish Philosophy and World Tensions." *Midstream* 8, 3 (September 1962): 67–82.

"Mass Crime and the Judeo-Christian Tradition." *Minnesota Review* 3, 2 (winter 1963): 205–19.

"Chances for American Survival: The Staying Power of Religion." *Jewish Heritage* 6, 3 (winter 1963/64): 21–24.

"Hacia una filosofia Judía." *Maj'shavot* 3, 1 (March 1964): 5–14.

"Filosofías nacionalistas de la historia Judía." *Maj'shavot* 3, 2 (July 1964): 5–23.

"It's the Mythology of the Jewish and Christian Traditions That Hinders Fruitful Communication between the Two." *National Jewish Monthly* 79 (September 1964): 20–24; 79 (October 1964): 14–18.

"God and the Catastrophe." *Conservative Judaism* 18, 4 (summer 1964): 13–21.

"A Jewish View of the Problem of War Prevention Today." *Torch* (winter 1965): 10–13.

"Case for Dialogue." *National Jewish Monthly* 81, 1 (September 1966): 26–32.

"A favor del diálogo." *Maj'shavot* 6, 3 (November 1967): 57–67.

"Myth, Faith, and Reality in Jewish Life." In Max Kreutzberger, ed., *Studies of the Leo Baeck Institute* (New York, 1967), 179–264.

"Context and Challenge: A Response to Rylaarsdam." *Bulletin* 48, 2 (spring 1968): 35–44.

"Religious Ethics in the Contemporary Scene." In *The Future of Ethics and Moral Theology.* Chicago: Argus Communications Co., 1968.

"Israel and the Jewish Christian Dialogue." *Journal of Ecumenical Studies* 6, 1 (winter 1969): 18–36.

"Jerusalem in America." In Elwyn A. Smith, ed., *The Religion of the Republic.* Philadelphia: Fortress Press, 1971, 94–115.

"Revelation as Quest: A Contribution to Ecumenical Thought." *Journal of Ecumenical Studies* 9, 3 (summer 1972): 521–43.

"Jewish Self-Definition—Classicism and Romanticism: Our Basic Alternative." *Central Conference of American Rabbis* 19 (autumn 1972): 3–15.

"The Homecoming of the Talmud." *United Synagogue Review Quarterly* 26 (spring 1973): 4–5.

"Judaism and the New Testament." *Journal of Ecumenical Studies* 13, 4 (fall 1976): 596–613.

"Perspectives for the Study of the Book of Acts." In Arthur Chiel, ed., *Perspectives on Jews and Judaism.* New York: The Rabbinical Assembly, 1978, 7–17.

"The Dialogue—Exceptionalism as Metamyth." *Central Conference of American Rabbis* 21 (autumn 1979): 3–15.

"Continuing Creativity in Maimonides' Philosophy." In A. Katsh and L. Nemoy, eds., *Essays on the Occasion of the Seventieth Anniversary of the Dropsie University, 1909–1979.* Philadelphia: Dropsie College, 1979, 11–31.

"Neo-Maimonism." *Conservative Thought Today.* New York: The Rabbinical Assembly, 1980, 9–20.

"Six Jewish Thoughts." *Journal of Ecumenical Studies* 17, 1 (winter 1980): 110–11.

"A Theological Foundation for the Halakhah." *Judaism* 29, 1 (winter 1980): 57–63.

"The 'Yes' and the 'No' of Revelation." In L. E. Frizzel, ed., *God and His Temple.* South Orange, N.J.: Dept. of Judeo-Christian Studies, Seton Hall University, 1980, 215–30.

"God in Kaplan's Philosophy." *Judaism* 30, 1 (winter 1981): 30–35.

"The Religion of Ethical Nationhood." *Conservative Judaism* 34, 4 (March–April 1981): 28–33.

"The Covenant Concept—Particularistic, Pluralistic, or Futuristic." *Journal of Ecumenical Studies* 18, 2 (spring 1981): 217–30.

"Foreword to Pinchas Lapide and Jurgen Moltmann, *Jewish Monotheism and Christian Trinitarian Doctrine.* Translated by Leonard Swidler. Philadelphia: Fortress Press, 1981, 17–24.

"The Future of Jewish Messianism." In Michael D. Ryan, ed., *Human Responses to the Holocaust.* Texts and Studies, vol. 9. New York: E. Mellen Press, 1981, 225–38.

"A Jewish View of the World Community." In A. Finkel and L. Frizzel, eds., *Standing before God.* New York: Ktav, 1981, 339–74.

"The Mitzvah of Keruv." *Conservative Judaism* 35, 4 (summer 1982): 33–38.

"The Messianic Ideal and the Apocalyptic Vision." *Judaism* 32, 2 (spring 1983): 205–14.

"Choosing Life." *Present Tense* 10, 2 (winter 1983): 64.

"Between Faith and Skepticism." In Jacob J. Petuchowski, ed., *When Jews and Christians Meet,* Albany: Suny Press, 1988, 3–7.

BROCHURES

Jewish Ethics and Labor Israel. New York: American Histadrut Cultural Exchange Institute, 1965.

Syllabus for the Study of the Sabbath. Baltimore: The Week End Jewish Layman's Institute and Beth El Congregation, 1980.

BOOK REVIEWS

"Sepher Al Torah Hasod Shelanu: Major Trends in Jewish Mysticism—The Hilda Stich Stroock Lectures, Gershom Scholem." *Hadoar* 23, 37 (August 18, 1944): 719–20.

Kaplan, Mordecai M., *The Future of the American Jew. Jewish Quarterly Review* 39, 2 (October 1948): 181–204.

Cohon, Beryl D., *Judaism in Theory and Practice. Jewish Social Studies* 12, 4 (October 1950): 397–99.

Baeck, Leo, *The Essence of Judaism. Jewish Social Studies* 12, 4 (October 1950): 413–14.

Maybaum, Ignaz, *The Jewish Mission. Jewish Social Studies* 14, 2 (April 1952): 186–88.

Halevy, Jehuda, *Kuzari: The Book of Proof and Argument. Jewish Social Studies* 14, 3 (July 1952): 253.

Kegley, Charles W., and Brettel, Robert, eds., *The Theology of Paul Tillich. Judaism* 3, 1 (winter 1954): 80–89.

Glatzer, Nahum N., *Franz Rosenzweig: His Life and Thought. Jewish Social Studies* 16, 3 (July 1954): 273.

Glenn, Menahen G., *Israel Salanter. Reconstructionist* 20, 10 (July 1954): 26–27.

Kohn, Eugene, *Religion and Humanity. Jewish Quarterly Review* 45, 3 (January 1955): 245–49.

"History and Zeitgeist: Dinur, Ben Zion, *B'Mifneh Hadoroth.*" *Midstream* 1, 1 (August 1955): 100–103.

Lieberman, Chaim, *The Christianity of Sholem Asch. Judaism* 4, 2 (spring 1955): 186–88.

Patterson, Charles H., *The Philosophy of the Old Testament. Jewish Social Studies* 17, 4 (October 1955): 330–31.

Epstein, Isidore, *The Faith of Judaism. Jewish Quarterly Review* 46, 3 (January 1956): 278–89.

Lebowitz, J., *Torah U-mitzvot Bizman Ha-zeh. Conservative Judaism* 10, 4 (summer 1956): 47–50.

"Is Toynbee an Anti-Semite? Samuel, Maurice, *The Professor and the Fossil.*" *National Jewish Monthly* (November 1956): 32–35.

Waxman, Mordecai (ed.), *Tradition and Change. Conservative Judaism* 13, 2 (winter 1959): 47–54.

Blau, Joseph L., Philip Friedman, Arthur Hertzberg, and Isaac Mendelsohn, eds., *Essays on Jewish Life and Thought. Jewish Social Studies* 22, 3 (July 1960): 186–91.

Gargan, Edward T., *Intent of Toynbee's History. Conservative Judaism* 17 (fall–winter 1962–1963): 48–60.

"Reconsiderations. *Study of History,* v. 12." *Conservative Judaism* 17 (fall–winter 1962–1963): 48–60.

"Between Two Traditions: Gordis, Robert, *The Root and the Branch.*" *Midstream* 10, 1 (March 1964): 109–11.

Glatzer, Nahum N., ed., *Faith and Knowledge: The Jew in the Medieval World. Jewish Social Studies* 27, 2 (April 1965): 122.

Jacobs, Louis, *Principles of the Jewish Faith. Religious Education* 60, 3 (May–June 1965): 248–50.

Kohn, Hans, *Living in a World Revolution, My Encounters with History. Jewish Social Studies* 27, 3 (July 1965): 207–8.

Efros, Israel I., *Ancient Jewish Philosophy. Jewish Social Studies* 27, 4 (October 1965): 250–51.

Gordis, Robert, *Judaism in a Christian World. Congress Bi-Weekly* 34, 6 (March 20 1966): 15–16.

Heschel, Abraham Joshua, *The Insecurities of Freedom. Jewish Social Studies* 29, 2 (April 1967): 120–22.

Bea, Augustin, Cardinal, *The Church and the Jewish People. Jewish Social Studies* 29, 2 (April 1967): 120–22.

Neusner, Jacob, *A Life of Rabban Yohanan ben Zakkai* and *A History of the Jews in Babylonia. Judaism* 17, 1 (winter 1968): 108–13.

Macdonald, Duncan Black, *The Hebrew Philosophical Genius. Jewish Social Studies* 30, 3 (July 1968): 182–83.

Gilbert, Arthur, *Vatican Council and the Jews. Congress Bi-Weekly* 36, 2 (January 1969): 19–21.

Kohler, Kaufmann, *Jewish Theology Systematically and Historically Considered. Jewish Social Studies* 31, 4 (October 1969): 349–52.

Rosenzweig, Franz, *The Star of Redemption,* trans. William H. Hallo, *Reconstructionist* 38, 2 (March 1972): 24–29.

Schweitzer, Frederick M., *A History of the Jews since the First Century A.D. Jewish Social Studies* 34, 3 (July 1972): 267–70.

"Bringing Clarity into the Mystical: Scholem, Gershom, *The Messianic Idea in Judaism and Other Essays on Jewish Spirituality.*" *Judaism* 21, 3 (summer 1972): 376–83.

"A Review Essay: *The Encyclopedia Judaica.*" *Conservative Judaism* 26, 4 (summer 1972): 46–57.

"A Review Essay: Finkelstein, Louis, *Pharisaism in the Making.*" *Conservative Judaism* 28, 3 (spring 1974): 60–65.

"Types of Redemption: Contribution to the Theme of the Study Conference Held at Jerusalem, 14–19 July, 1968." *Jewish Quarterly Review* 65, 1 (July 1974): 52–53.

Scholem, Gershom, *Kabbalah. Jewish Quarterly Review* 66, 4 (April 1976): 242–44.

Buber, Martin, *Briefwechsel aus sieben Jahrzenten. Jewish Quarterly Review* 67, 1 (July 1976): 59–62.

"Charting the Map of Jewish Theology: Jacobs, Louis, *A Jewish Theology.*" *Jewish Quarterly Review* 67, 2–3 (October 1976–January 1977): 168–71.

"Schaeder's *Martin Buber:* Schaeder, Grete, *The Hebrew Humanism of Martin Buber.*" *Jewish Quarterly Review* 67, 4 (April 1977): 237–41.

Halkin, Hillel, *Letters to an American Jewish Friend. Judaism* 27, 1 (winter 1978): 120–26.

"Kaufmann's *Religion in Four Dimensions:* Kaufmann, Walter, *Religions in Four Dimensions—Existential, Aesthetic, Historical, Comparative.*" *Jewish Quarterly Review* 69, 1 (July 1978): 55–57.

Weinstein, Joshua, *Buber and Humanistic Education. Jewish Quarterly Review* 69, 4 (April 1979): 245–47.

Gordis, Robert, *Understanding Conservative Judaism;* Martin Bernhard ed., *Movements and Issues in American Judaism;* Jerry V. Diller, ed., *Ancient Roots and Modern Meanings;* Norman B. Mirsky, *Unorthodox Judaism.*" *Judaism* 29, 2 (spring 1980): 248–55.

Kaplan, Mordecai M., *The Religion of Ethical Nationhood. Conservative Judaism* 34, 4 (March–April 1981): 28–33.

"Diamond's *Philosophy and Religion:* Diamond, Malcolm L., *Contemporary Philosophy and Religious Thought.*" *Jewish Quarterly Review* 72, 1 (July 1981): 53–56.

Alexander Altmann Festschrift: S. Stein and R. Loewe eds., *Studies in Jewish Religious and Intellectual History. Jewish Quarterly Review* 72, 2 (October 1981): 132–39.

Thoma, Clemens, *A Christian Theology of Judaism. Jewish Quarterly Review* 72, 4 (April 1982): 312–16.

Goodman, Lenn Evan, *Monotheism. Judaism* 32, 3 (summer 1983): 367–68.

Siegele-Wenschkewitz, Leonore, *Neutestamentliche Wissenschaft vor der Judenfrage. Journal of Ecumenical Studies* 20, 4 (fall 1983): 696–97.

Mendelssohn, Moses, *Jerusalem. Jewish Quarterly Review* 75, 2 (October 1984): 192–94.

A. R. C. Leaney, *The Jewish and Christian Worlds. Journal of Ecumenical Studies* 23, 2 (spring 1986): 318.

LETTERS AND REPLIES TO LETTERS

"The Rabbinical Assembly and Jewish Law." Open letter to the editors. *Reconstructionist* 19, 6 (May 1953): 26–28.

Response to letter from Bernard Heller. *Conservative Judaism* 15, 3 (spring 1961): 40–41.

Letter to the Editor. *Conservative Judaism* 15, 3 (spring 1961): 42–44.

Response to letter from Werner Steinberg. *Conservative Judaism* 27, 3 (spring 1973): 84–85.

"The Jackson Amendment." *Present Tense* 2, 1 (autumn 1974): 2.

"Old Testament." Response to I. Franck, on Spinoza's onslaught on Judaism. *Reconstructionist* 44 (fall 1979): 27.

SYMPOSIA

"The Jewish View of Man and the New Democratic Order." *Proceedings of Seventh Annual Convention of the Rabbinical Council of America* (June–July 1942): 20–29.

"The Meaning of Galut in America Today." *Midstream* 9, 1 (March 1963): 5–9.

"The Quest for Jewish Values: Questions for Thinking Jews." *Jewish Heritage* (spring 1965): 21–34; (summer 1965): 28–43.

"The State of Jewish Belief." *Commentary* 42, 2 (August 1966): 73–76.

"The Holocaust: Summation of the Colloquium." Paper delivered at Dropsie University, Philadelphia, 1973, 50–52.

"The Congregational Rabbi and the Conservative Movement: Ten Questions." *Conservative Judaism* 29, 2 (winter 1975): 9–10.